NEW REVISED EDITION

Louis Rukeyser's Business Almanac

LOUIS RUKEYSER
Editor-in-Chief

JOHN COONEY
Managing Editor

GEORGE WINSLOW
Chief Researcher

SIMON & SCHUSTER

New York   London   Toronto   Sydney   Tokyo   Singapore

Simon and Schuster
Simon & Schuster Building
Rockefeller Center
1230 Avenue of the Americas
New York, New York 10020

SIMON AND SCHUSTER and colophon are registered trademarks
of Simon & Schuster Inc.

Designed by Irving Perkins Assoc.
Manufactured in the United States of America

1 3 5 7 9 10 8 6 4 2

Library of Congress Cataloging-in-Publication data
Louis Rukeyser's business almanac / Louis Rukeyser, editor-in-chief;
John Cooney, managing editor; George Winslow, chief researcher. —
New rev. ed.
p.   cm.
Includes index.
1. United States—Economic conditions—1981– 2. Industry and
state—United States. 3. United States—Industries. 4. Finance—
United States. I. Rukeyser, Louis. II. Cooney, John.
III. Winslow, George.
HC106.8.L67   1991
330.973'0928—dc20   91-30290   CIP
ISBN 0-671-70728-0

CONTENTS

LIST OF TABLES

PREFACE

When I first started doing a great deal of public speaking, about a quarter century ago, I asked my father, who had done more than his share in his day, if he had any tips to give me. "Yes," he replied. "Keep in mind that when a speaker has finished his presentation, decent people, polite people will generally try to say something nice to him about the speech he has just made. Accept those words graciously, but ignore them; they don't mean a thing. If they really like you, they'll have you back."

As usual, the old man was on target. And in that spirit, it's particularly gratifying to be writing the Preface to the second edition of this book, not only because it's good to be invited back (to paraphrase the wit and wisdom of Sally Field, "We think you really, really like us") but because so much has happened since the last edition that if we didn't give you a comprehensive, revised update now, the book wouldn't be nearly as useful—and maybe you wouldn't really, really like us so much anymore.

The three years since the first edition have produced as much economic drama as we normally expect in three decades. In Europe, Karl Marx is well and truly dead. The Cold War has ended, largely because of the collapse of one of the alleged superpowers: the Soviet Union (an increasingly hollow name) has more than enough to contend with within its own troubled borders. Its erstwhile satellites race to mouth the slogans of capitalism and someday may even learn how to practice it. East and West increasingly blur, and sometimes, as in Germany, totally disappear. Meanwhile, European economic and political unity marches toward a new chapter starting in 1992, while the United States (once such an eager sponsor of such unity) frets about what it will actually mean to America's interests.

At home, the first impulse of the nineties has been to repudiate the eighties. The S&L crisis, a debacle whose price tag seems to rise geometrically with each recounting, would be serious enough by itself, even if doubts had not been cast by now on the stability of virtually every other major financial industry, from the banks to the insurance companies. Junk bonds often turned out, apparently to a number of people's surprise, to be exactly what they were called; their chief sponsor, Drexel Burnham, disappeared, and its resident genius, Michael Milken, was sent to the slammer.

But just when all seemed downhill, the country's spirits were lifted by triumph in the Persian Gulf, an antidote to the belief that we were hapless incompetents on the international scene. And even as America underwent a painful recession, after the longest period without one in the nation's peacetime history, some independent thinkers began to wonder if recent years had, in fact, been as unremittingly evil as media legend now contends. They sought, in place of easy prejudices, hard facts. And that's where—for thinkers of all opinions—we come in.

With the possible exceptions of sex and baseball, no subject in America is the object of so much uninformed bombast as the state of business and the economy. And why not? As Talcott Williams, first director of the Columbia University Graduate School of Journalism, remarked in 1913, "All men have opinions; few men think." It's plainly a more reliable source of emotional release, not to mention much more fun, to vent one's spleen against enemies real or imagined than to engage in the painful process of confronting reality. Wallowing in prejudice and paranoia can be a marvelous substitute for mastering facts, provided only that you view life as your personal psychiatrist's couch. If, on the other hand, you are actually concerned with learning something and/or getting ahead, you may want to try a different tack. And that's where this book comes in.

The most astounding thing about this tome is that it wasn't done long ago. Anyone who, like myself, has gone looking for some specific piece of information on the economic scene and then spent hours tracking down a source that properly should have been right at hand will appreciate the value of having a single volume covering so much of interest and importance about American business. For this, all manner of credit is due to the Herculean efforts of Managing Editor John Cooney and Chief Researcher George Winslow, who by now are surely capable of putting themselves to sleep by reciting employment statistics and trade trends, and therefore will have no further need in this lifetime for the conventional counting of sheep. What they have produced, boiling away the nonessential and shaping the fascinating, has already been of immense use to me, as I hope it will be to you.

Change is the theme of this book, as it is the theme of life. Understanding the relationship between the past and the present is a prerequisite for mastering the future. Tomorrow's winners are unlikely to be those people who say, like the character in the old joke, "My mind's made up; don't confuse me with facts." The successes of the last decade of the twentieth century are far more likely to be built on the words of Francis Bacon, who declared in 1597, "Knowledge is power." The prolific English essayist, philosopher, and statesman, a tremendously busy man even if he didn't write Shakespeare's plays, delivered his insight centuries before the information explosions from computers, opinion polls, and magazines specifically designed for red-haired carpenter-skiers. But it is still the way to bring home the bacon today.

Our concern here is to go beyond the mere reporting of numbers and to give you a sense of what they may mean to you. Hence, for example, we tell you the facts on the aging of America and then report both the favorable and unfavorable implications of this phenomenon. (My own bias, incidentally, is unreservedly in favor of continued aging. The alternative, as I understand it, is worse.) This kind of knowledge is essential to an understanding of the future prospects in this country of everything from selling pizzas to funding Social Security. And in addition to their obvious utility on the job and in financial matters, such data can make terrific family dinner-table conversation. We learn, for instance, that the median age of the population today is roughly twice what it was in 1820, when the average American was less than 17 years old. Don't despair, though; he probably thought his parents were squares, too.

None of us, of course, is truly average. Did you drink your assigned 24 gallons of beer last year? And if you did, how did you possibly find room for your 596 pounds of dairy products as well? (One possible answer, we learn, is that 62 percent of Americans are overweight. Those 8 million bagels we eat every day probably don't help.) I haven't got around to measuring yet, so I can't tell you whether I personally am producing the typical citizen's allotted 3.43 daily pounds of garbage, but if you count all the Wall Street reports I have to read each week, I suspect that is a distinct underestimate in my case. Garbage in, garbage out.

While we're being personal, I suspect that each of us will at least subconsciously be superimposing his or her own job history on the account of the changing patterns of employment in America. In less than a century, the majority of American workers have gone from overalls to blue collars to pinstripes. Women now account for two out of three net new workers, changing the lives and the minds of every American. Columbia's Talcott Williams, were he commenting today, three quarters of a century later, would undoubtedly be pressured to substitute "persons" for "men" in his memorable quote about thinking (though, in truth, many women may find the original version more telling). We report both the passing problems and the ultimate hope of moving toward a society that uses the full economic and human potential of all its citizens.

Some of the findings are unexpectedly happy. The right to bellyache about the boss is part of the Constitution, and one of the most frequently exercised portions thereof, but we find that an overwhelming majority of major lottery winners decide to keep on punching the same old time clock. Could it be that most Americans are less miserable than some of our weepier literature suggests?

I am reminded of a couple of visits I made to Iowa State University in the 1970s, at a time when farmland prices were soaring as unrestrainedly as they later tumbled. After my second speech in Ames, while chatting with some members of the faculty, I said: "Look, I've never claimed to be an expert on agricultural economics, but I can add. I know the average price of Iowa farmland today; I know the average size of an Iowa farm, and I have some idea of the capital costs involved in farming. Put all those numbers together, and the clear conclusion is that the average Iowa farmer today is a paper millionaire. Now, I know all the counterarguments: he doesn't live like a millionaire, he doesn't have the cash flow of a millionaire. But assuming that the paper calculations are right, why don't more Iowa farmers sell out and move to Scottsdale?"

The reply was illuminating. "Well, some do," I was told, "but you have to remember that the average farmer likes to farm. We like to tell the story around here of the Iowa farmer who hit the lottery for two million dollars. A reporter asked him, 'Henry, what are you going to do with all that money?' And Henry answered, 'I guess I'll just keep on farming till it's gone.' "

So it is with many of us: we just plain like what we're doing. But like Henry himself, who at times in the eighties may have regretted his earlier resistance to change, we are likely to wind up wealthier and wiser if we improve our information and understanding. This book tries to help both with the broad issues of American business and with the practical details, from investing and personal finance to the worlds of culture and entertainment, that may enable you to plow your personal plot with deeper delight and more fertile profit in the years ahead. Please look on this book as a collaboration that very much includes you: if an error has crept in, or if there's something not here that you'd like to see in a future edition, please do let us know. It's your almanac, too, and here's hoping that all your business turns out to be just great.

Louis Rukeyser

HOW TO USE THIS BOOK

Why a business almanac?

The answer is simple. Until now, there hasn't been one around and there should be. Over the years we could have saved an awful lot of time looking up the potpourri of business and economic information we have compiled here. What makes the almanac unique is that it tells us as much about ourselves as about our corporate society. How we earn our money. How we spend our money. Who woos our money. Who steals our money. Who has most of the money. Who doesn't.

The list goes on. Who, for instance, are the richest men and women in America? The highest-paid executives? Which are the biggest companies in the nation? Which are the most secretive? What's the background of this T. Boone Pickens character? And what kind of a businessman is Ralph Lauren?

Just what is the International Monetary Fund? Who were the robber barons and what did they do? Who are the biggest crooks around today? How about arms dealers? What have been the biggest-grossing movies, books, record albums, videotapes?

You'll find the answers to these questions and hundreds more right here, organized in such a way that they can be found individually or read in conjunction with related facts and information—the big picture as well as the fascinating details of our economic history and our everyday business life.

Although, of course, we couldn't put *everything* in these pages, we've tried to make the almanac comprehensive. And we hope it is a compendium that entertains as well as informs. Thus, there is plenty for everyone: little-known facts for the trivia buffs, basic information for those who are unfamiliar with business, and a lot of useful information for everyone, no matter what his or her level of business or financial sophistication.

The gamut of information runs from small businesses to big businesses, from advertising to unions, from ingenious inventors and entrepreneurs to the corporate heavy hitters. We sought out the successes and the screwups, the visionaries and the scallywags. And the book is thoroughly indexed. You can easily turn to sections for information that interests you the most and the facts you need the most, all compiled from the most authoritative and up-to-date sources.

Here's how the book is put together:

We lead off with "The Economy: An Overview." The U.S. economy is in a state of transition with a lot of factors working on it for good and ill. If you number among the folks who find it baffling, don't despair. Throughout the rest of the book you'll find the facts and figures, the trends and statistics that will bring it all into focus.

Part I deals with "People in Business." That's us, the people who work (and, unfortunately, those of us who aren't working if we want to be) and what we're like—the jobs we hold, the money we make, and what the work world holds if we are men, women, minorities, and union members.

Part II is called "The Haves." Just what is money and who are the folks who have most of it? Here are the old family money and the nouveau billionaires, how they got it and how they keep it—or lose it.

Part III concerns "The Heavy Hand." This section is about the government's role in our economy—how it works and how it got the way it is. We also look at the power brokers who shape the laws that govern corporate America: the lobbyists, the regulators, and the taxmen.

Part IV deals with "The Business of Business." It discusses the businesses that are expanding and those that are contracting—our booming services and our eroding manufacturing. Here are also the small businesses that come and go, providing so much of our economic vitality.

Part V is about "The Money Game"—the markets for stocks and bonds, futures and mutual funds. There's an explanation of each of those markets and how they have been acting in the 1980s. Here, too, you can find out about insurance and pensions, Social Security and real estate.

Part VI details the nation's "Widget Makers." Here's a breakdown of scores of businesses and industries and what's going on in them. We've included descriptions of how each industry is doing as well as profiles of many important people and companies, tables that show trends, and the trivia, which often reveals more about an industry than any table possibly can.

Finally, we give a rundown of "The Heavy Hitters: America's Biggest Companies." Here are financial profiles of the leading utilities as well as industrial, transportation, retailing, and financial companies, the money they've made, and their return to investors.

Overall, the book is a look at business in America, what we have created and how it shapes our lives. Here are the facts and figures, stories behind successes and flops, and a wealth of business lore that hasn't been compiled in any other book.

We hope you enjoy it. Perhaps more than that, we hope you find it useful.

The Economy: An Overview

THE ECONOMY

The U.S. economy has slogged into an era that can be called the Great Time of Doubt. After breathlessly extolling the wonders of an economically strong America during the booming 1960s, economists wrung their hands and beat their breasts in the 1970s and 1980s as they saw signs of fiscal doom everywhere. Now the economic soothsayers are hedging their bets.

The Cassandras of yore had reason to be teary—actually, a lot of reasons. In the 1970s, inflation and double-digit interest rates were growing faster than a 13-year-old boy. The ranks of the jobless were swelling at a terrible pace. Debt was weighing down both consumers and business like Mafia-style cement shoes. And trade was showing a nagging deficit, which would have been fine if the nag hadn't turned into a scold in the 1980s and the early 1990s.

Surely even our politicians could see something was wrong. Surely they wanted to do something about it. Well, they did. At least they said they did. But being politicians, they were better at promising than delivering panaceas for our economic ills. The one lesson our presidents consistently teach us is that their economic elixirs are never all they're cracked up to be. Often they just muck things up even more. Maybe we should be grateful their cures aren't fatal.

Not so strangely, though, they all find economists who tout whatever is the muddled presidential economic message of the moment as the right one. After all, why should a president hear what he doesn't want to hear? Wouldn't it be refreshing for a president or presidential candidate to answer the question, "What's going to happen with the economy?" with "Who knows?" Because nobody really does.

That's especially true because the Great Time of Doubt persisted until 1991. From one month to the next, the economy baffled just about everybody. Sometimes it seemed as if we were headed into a recession. Other times it seemed as if we were poised for an expansion. After the stock market crash of October 1987, a recession appeared almost inevitable. Then it didn't. Then it did. Then it came.

So what have we got here? The answer is an economy still reeling from the harsh monetary and fiscal policies of the decade. Such policies loaded more than $1 trillion onto the federal debt while bashing inflation down from double-digit levels to 4.6% in 1990. For its part, the dollar was like an erratic cruise missile—soaring in the early to mid-1980s and then nose-diving and then jiggling.

The economy has been shaken by the phenomenon described by the 1980s buzzword *disinflation,* the process of bringing inflation down. The Federal Reserve Board's vigorous monetary policy from 1979 to 1982 actually ended double-digit inflation, but there's always a price to be paid for anything good. The fallout included having product prices tumble for certain key sectors of the economy: farming, manufacturing, and oil production.

And the policy also helped bring on our horrendous trade problems. It's not too hard to figure out how. Where did the nation turn to finance big budget deficits and spur expansion when the Fed got stringent about money? Overseas, of course. A swollen river of foreign capital roared into the U.S. That sent the dollar heading toward the moon. As a result, imports got cheap. Thus, the trade deficit headed toward the moon too.

So what do you do when the dollar goes up like a helium balloon that a child accidentally let go of? Try to grab the string and pull it back down. In 1985, Treasury Secretary James Baker began trying to pull the dollar down. Meanwhile, the trade deficit ballooned to $171.2 billion in 1987, and in 1990 the size of the deficit gasped in and out, contracting a little, expanding a little to finally end up at $108.7 billion. The lesson: dollars that go up easily don't necessarily come down easily. And when they come down, they can come down too far.

And in the midst of all this, there have been those mixed economic signals—some good, some bad.

First the good news. Unemployment, inflation, and interest rates fell well below what they were. Even after the market meltdown in October 1987, the stock market returned to one of its best rolls ever. So wealth, at least in terms of portfolios, was greater than ever, which helped the economy for quite a while.

Statistics and generalities, of course, mask how individuals are making out. Most pharmaceutical executives should be pleased with the way business boomed, but there are a lot of long faces in the steel mills. And thanks to improved benefits, today's new retirees, for the most part, are better off than people who retired 30 years ago, but today's college graduates probably have a tougher time getting the kinds of jobs they want than did graduates 20 years ago. They are all experiencing the mix of good and bad in the economy.

As for the bad, there's plenty of it. The most spectacular came in October 1987 when the market made everybody uneasy by going into those wild gyrations that saw it plunge 508 points in just one day, October 19, the worst point drop on record, which jammed temporarily one of the best run-ups on record. More than $500 billion in asset value was erased overnight, bringing total losses for a two-month period to more than $1 trillion. And that made *caution* the new buzzword, which, of course, has a negative connotation for the economy.

But stock prices are a less than perfect indicator of what's ahead for business. Stock market declines signaled the eight post-World War II recessions, but stocks fell by more than 10% on no fewer than 20 other occasions during this period. In other words, to modernize an observation made years ago by economist Paul Samuelson, the stock market has now predicted 28 of the last eight recessions.

So a Wall Street debacle doesn't necessarily mean that the economy has to fall through the floor, or that troubling market movements are echoes of the crash of 1929. But worried shareholders often think twice or thrice about what they will buy, and that worry can squeeze the economy. Few economists saw a rerun of the Great Depression but they all went scrambling back to their drawing boards to revise downward their figures on how the economy would fare.

What the 1987 market skid did was simply point out some of the horrors that were mounting for years, especially the bleak U.S. trade and deficit figures. Budget deficits have been around an awe-inspiring $200 billion in recent years ($220.4 billion in 1990, a mere $100 billion higher than the Bush administration forecast in January 1990). The Reagan administration got the dubious achievement award for attaining what once would have seemed ludicrous: the U.S. has the distinction, for the first time since the First World War, of owing foreigners more than they owe us. And the lower dollar hasn't dramatically improved the trade picture, though U.S. exports have been growing lately—a heartening change after years in which American manufacturing almost became something people talked about in the past tense, as the productivity gains of American workers continued to disappoint.

Through it all, the administration has said—over and over—that a boom is just around the corner; well, maybe the next corner. Just be patient. Meanwhile, the ranks of the administration's cheerleaders thinned quite a bit and the Cassandras revved up for a good blast of gloom and doom.

No wonder. Along came the savings and loan nightmare (see page 223), which threw a monkey wrench into any effort to get a grip on the economy. And Saddam Hussein's invasion of Kuwait, with its accompanying military bills for the U.S. and the resultant surge in the price of oil, heated up an already accelerated rate of inflation.

As if to provide a sorry attempt at comic relief from these horrors, President Bush and the Congress created a spectacle as they publicly trashed one another while trying to work out a budget agreement. In the end, the nation watched the President's lips as he raised taxes and ate crow. Neither side, of course, was willing to put any significant sacred cows on the chopping block while fiddling with the budget.

If you look at the record, the law of averages was on the side of the Cassandras. The latest economic expansion is traceable to late 1982. The fact that it lasted with a few fits and starts until 1990 was remarkable if only because the five previous peacetime growth periods lasted only an average of 33 months. By that measure, simply avoiding a recession as long as we did was a big deal.

So with nothing fitting previous patterns, who can blame economists (artists or scientists or whatever they claim to be) if they aren't too sure which prediction to hang themselves by today? After all, nobody has ever before witnessed such behavior in the modern economic world.

Even though the forces at work on the economy and the economy itself are different from what we have ever experienced, there are some ways to get a better idea of what kind of shape the economy is in in the 1990s. That means stepping back a bit and seeing what the economy did previously.

We can start with that ingenious barometer known as the misery index, the creation of Arthur Okun, chairman of President Johnson's Council of Economic Advisers. Arriving at the index is so simple, you don't even have to say, "Economic mumbo jumbo." Just add the annual inflation rate to the unemployment rate. Presto! You now know whether the mood of the nation is upbeat or downbeat.

Okun contended that when the combination hit 9%, the nation toppled into unhappiness. If it hit 20% or higher, the nation was miserable. In 1990, with a jobless rate of 5.5% and inflation having gone up 4.6%, we were an uneasy 10.1%.

Although the misery index sounds too simple to be accurate, Okun may have had something here. In 1976, when Jimmy Carter was president, unemployment stood at 7.6% and inflation had gone up to 5.8%, for an unhappy 13.4%; the year Carter was voted out of office, the index reached a miserable 20.6%. In prosperous and presumably happy, if not ecstatic, 1966, unemployment was a low 3.7% while inflation grew 2.9% for a benign 6.6%. And people who get nostalgic for the Eisenhower era may have their memories influenced by a 4% unemployment rate coupled with an annual inflation rate increase of only 1.5% for a seemingly serene 5.5% in 1956.

OUR CHANGED ECONOMY

Economies are always in a state of flux, but until we actually examine our own it's frequently hard to see just how dramatic the change can be. The change affects everything from how much we earn to the jobs we hold, the balance of political power domestically, and our foreign relations. Sometimes it's startling to note.

The once-mighty steel companies and their politically powerful unions, for instance, are mere troubled shadows of their former glorious selves. The industry was devastated by a combination of management's not investing in badly needed plants and equipment, unreasonable labor demands, ham-handed government regulatory and tax policies, and cheaper imports. And the combination of woes reflects, to a large degree, what has been happening to the manufacturing sector of our economy.

The biggest structural change in the economy has been the switch over to a service economy from a goods-producing economy. Service-producing businesses such as real estate, insurance, finance, retailing, and health care accounted for 77% of jobs by 1991, up from 46% in 1955. Meanwhile, our goods producers, the manufacturing, construction, and mining sectors, accounted for only 24.5% of all civilian nonagricultural jobs, down from 41% in 1955. (The drop in farm jobs as a percentage of civilian employment has been even more dramatic. Today, only 2.9% of jobs are held by farm workers, down from 21% in 1940.)

There's no reason to believe the service economy won't keep gaining ground. A Conference Board study, for instance, concludes that just about all U.S. job growth through the rest of the century will be in the service area. The report sees the biggest job jumps in the goods-distribution chain, such as in retailing and wholesaling; in people-tending industries such as health care; and, because we are a nation of slobs producing nearly 150 million tons of garbage a year, in "cleaner-upper" jobs, because "a litter-prone society requires plenty of manpower to handle its mess."

There has been change in income as well. Employee compensation, including wages, salaries, and benefits, has climbed steadily over the past 30 years to about 75% of total income from about 67%. Interest income climbed to more than 10% in the 1980s and 1990 from less than 2% in the 1950s. But the share of income from corporate profits has dwindled to about 8% in the 1980s from 14% in the 1950s. And rental income is now less than 1%, down from 4% of all income 30 years ago.

But while wages have climbed, productivity hasn't kept pace. Lagging productivity has become one of the nation's biggest problems. A factory worker who gets $1 an hour more has to produce $1 worth of goods more just for his output to remain the same. In the 1980s, average hourly wages rose 3.9% a year, but output rose by one-third that amount. Just how bad things have gotten was revealed in a Labor Department study of average yearly productivity gains from 1973 to 1984 for eight industrial nations: U.S. performance was the worst: Belgium, 6.2%; Japan, 5.9%; France, 6.4%; the Netherlands, 4.6%; Italy, 3.8%; West Germany, 3.4%; Great Britain, 2.3%; the U.S., 2.1%.

Part of the productivity problem comes from the shift to a service economy. It's usually a lot harder to show productivity gains in service jobs. As more and more jobs wind up in that category, the problem becomes greater. But another factor is the failure of U.S. companies, compared to those in other countries, to plow money back into plants and equipment that will prod productivity. The wreckage of the once-mighty U.S. steel industry is a constant reminder of that.

Some aspects of the economy don't change all that much. Consumer spending, for instance, is about two-thirds of the gross national product (GNP), about the same as it has been for the past 30 years. Business spending on capital equipment, however, fluctuates somewhat: 12% or more of the GNP in recent years; 9% in the 1960s; 11% in the 1950s. Likewise, defense spending is now around 7% of the GNP, up from 5% in the late 1970s but down from 14% in the 1950s.

One big and worrisome change in the economy is the increase in federal, consumer, and corporate debt in the mid- and late 1980s, which topped $10 trillion and should continue to rise rapidly if whopping federal deficits continue. For a peacetime economy, former Federal Reserve Board chairman Paul A. Volcker said, the buildup may reflect a "fragility in the financial system." Such debt represents about 40% of the GNP, up from 25% in 1980.

Of course, that 40% is well below the 60% in the mid-1950s, but that big number reflected a debt hangover from the heavy borrowing to finance the Second World War, when federal debt actually exceeded the GNP. Now Congress and the White House have tentatively nicked the federal budget, but realistically, the Gramm-Rudman law to obliterate the deficit may as well never have been passed for all it's paid attention to. The reason, naturally, is that it's too politically perilous to make the needed spending cuts. (Optimists hoped that the stock market's gyrations would finally force Congress and the administration to toe the line of fiscal responsibility.) The problem with not squeezing the budget hard during an economic expansion is that, when a recession comes, the choice will be between foregoing the usual response of deficit spending—or letting the red ink flow totally out of control.

In addition, consumer debt ($3.4 trillion in 1989) is growing faster than incomes. Installment debt, for instance, is about 17% of personal income, up from 12% in the 1970s and almost twice what it was in the 1950s. Corporate debt is more troubling because of its ramifications. And corporate liquid assets (cash and anything that can readily be turned into cash) are only about 7.5% of the GNP, or half what they were in the 1950s. The big problem with corporate debt is that it often stymies new investment, as spare cash is used to pay off interest on borrowed money. (Since 1982, corporations added $1.1 trillion in debt.)

Such debt only serves to point out another problem—the number of companies going out of business. The rate has mushroomed during the decade. In 1990, the failure rate hit 75 per 10,000 companies, up from 35 in 1976. That represented $64 billion in liabilities, up from $3 billion in 1976. (The highest failure rate ever was in the Depression year 1932 when the rate was 154 per 10,000.)

But if you think that's something, look at our trade debt today. In 1976, the U.S. had a $4.2 billion trade surplus. The past few years have each suffered from $100 billion-plus trade deficits. The decline of the dollar began to help a little, but then became a major problem when it sank too low. The effects are often slow in coming, and import prices haven't risen as much as expected. Besides, a growing segment of our economy is dependent upon imports for businesses and jobs, and these can only be hurt by tumbling dollars and jingoistic tariffs.

The White House and segments of Congress repeatedly tried badgering countries that have big trade surpluses with the U.S.—West Germany, Taiwan, and Japan, especially Japan—to expand their economies as a way of helping to bring down the U.S. trade deficit. But how can Japan and West Germany cure America's bleak trade picture? The most they could possibly lop off the U.S. deficit is $15 billion or so. While that's more than a drop in the deficit bucket, it still isn't much more than a ladle's worth.

It doesn't appear that inflation will come roaring back. Creeping back is more like it. The more we pay for imports, the more inflation we get. Monetary policy remains a question mark. Congress keeps spending. And what happens if oil prices get higher as a result of the Middle East mess?

In the interim, the U.S. has become a debtor nation, something that at one time would have been considered preposterous. Until mid-1985, the value of U.S. assets in other nations exceeded that of U.S. assets held by foreigners, a situation that had held true since 1914. Then the balance tipped the other way. Now we're on the downside, and the prospects for what that means aren't so hot. We've wound up in a damned-if-we-do-damned-if-we-don't bind. If the situation continues, increased payments to foreigners on their U.S. investments will lower the standard of living for Americans. Yet, if such investments were withdrawn from the U.S., the result could be a credit-market squeeze that would drive up interest rates and set the stage for another recession.

But what all this obscures to some degree is the fundamental issue of the marked decline in U.S. competitiveness. Although there were signs of a manufacturing rebound in recent years, the sickness of American manufacturing alone more than accounts for the entire decline of U.S. trade. While it's great that the service industry has come on strong, we still need manufacturing if we want our economy to become truly vigorous. That means we have to compete with foreigners, not simply raise trade barriers against them. To compete, we need unions that deal responsibly with management, including recognizing the need for increased automation if any manufacturing jobs are to survive in America. We also need management that puts badly needed money into automation, even when that means postponing short-term profitability for the sake of long-term gains. Unfortunately, what we need and what we get are often two different animals.

If that sounds a tad cynical, it's just that the past is all too often an indicator of the future, at least where politicians are concerned. The market scare of 1987 didn't scare them enough to keep plugging away at our problems. What will it take?

On a more upbeat note, you'll be able to judge from the following pages that things have been worse. Until the stock market panic of October 1987, we hadn't had a panic in this country for quite a while (see page 8). And we sidestepped a recession for a good long time, the longest peacetime period since they started keeping records in the last century (see page 8). Our GNP is up (see Table I-1 below). Corporate profits rose steadily each year between 1982 and 1989 (see Table I-2), but then so did our trade deficit (see Table 3).

So what does that mean to the future? We wish we could tell you but we can't.

The Reaganomics that was to cure our ailing economy turned out to be a lot less startling—and coherent—than either its proponents or its detractors once claimed. Bushonomics is so incomprehensible even Bush's policymakers can't articulate it. Who is going to come up with a realistic program that includes tough calls on trimming the federal budget while avoiding recklessly reinflating the economy? That isn't too much to hope for. Is it?

DEPRESSIONS AND RECESSIONS

Depressions and recessions are economic bad news. When the economy retracts, there's a long-term decline in output, income, trade, and the number of people working. Depending on how long it goes on and how deep it is, we call one of these nasties a recession or a depression. Between 1920 and now, there have been more than a dozen of them.

Fortunately, just about all of them lasted only about a year. Only one lasted long enough and was deep enough to be a depression, but that was the Great Depression, the 43-month contraction between 1929 and 1933. By 1933, unemployment was about 25% compared to 6% to 9% for the six recessions between 1948 and 1975. Depressions hurt a great deal. Families suffer because of reduced income and prices, profits, interest rates, capital investment, income and buying power, and other parts of the economy are hard hit.

PANICS

Financial panics are more than forgetting to mail a check to the mortgage company. They are economic nightmares and they used to be almost a way of life in the U.S. Between 1790 and 1907, there were 21 panics—that's one every five or six years.

What happened? There were runs on banks, a lot of defaults on loans, big companies going belly-up, and stock prices going through the floor. (By comparison, the stock market panic on October 19, 1987, when stocks fell 508 points, doesn't look so bad.)

They usually came about when there was some horrific failure that shook people's belief in the economy. That's what happened in 1857 when the Ohio Life Insurance Company of Cincinnati failed. Another panic came about in 1873 when a lot of big companies failed. When the Reading Railroad and the National Cordage Company failed within months of each other in 1893, that sparked a stock-market panic.

After a panic in 1907, Congress passed the Aldrich-Vreeland Act (1908) to initiate bank reforms and to provide for the issuance of emergency bank currency. Ultimately, an investigation into the panic resulted in the establishment of the Federal Reserve System in 1913.

There weren't any more panics until the stock-market crash of 1929 and the subsequent host of bank failures—more than 9,000 between 1929 and 1933. In 1933, President Roosevelt temporarily shut down the nation's banks and created an insurance mechanism, the Federal Deposit Insurance Corporation, to avert panics. The FDIC eased depositors' anxieties because it meant that if a bank failed, depositors wouldn't necessarily lose money. Thus, it headed off the widespread withdrawals and reduction in bank credit that had taken place in the past.

Table I-1 Trends in Federal Debt
(dollar amounts in billions)

| | Debt held by the public[1] | | Debt held by the public as a percent of: | | Net interest as a percent of total outlays |
	Current dollars	Constant 1982 dollars[2]	GNP	Credit market debt[3]	
1950	219.0	921.0	82.1	55.3	11.4
1955	226.6	839.0	58.6	43.3	7.6
1960	236.8	761.3	46.7	33.7	8.5
1965	260.8	772.4	38.8	27.0	8.1
1970	283.2	682.7	28.6	20.7	7.9
1975	394.7	686.2	25.9	18.4	7.5
1980	709.3	837.0	26.6	18.7	10.6
1981	784.8	841.9	26.3	18.8	12.0
1982	919.2	919.2	29.3	20.2	13.6
1983	1,131.0	1,085.1	34.0	22.4	13.8
1984	1,300.0	1,201.5	35.3	22.7	15.7
1985	1,499.4	1,344.4	37.9	23.2	16.2
1986	1,736.2	1,516.2	41.5	23.6	16.1
1987	1,888.1	1,599.6	42.7	23.1	16.0
1988	2,050.3	1,685.8	42.9	23.1	16.2
1989	2,190.3	1,728.2	42.7	22.8	16.5
1990	2,410.4	1,828.6	44.6	23.4	16.2
1991 estimate	2,717.6	1,974.7	48.4		15.3
1992 estimate	2,995.4	2,090.9	50.0		15.7
1993 estimate	3,200.0	2,153.9	49.8		16.1
1994 estimate	3,261.9	2,119.3	47.4		16.6
1995 estimate	3,267.3	2,051.1	44.5		15.8
1996 estimate	3,250.7	1,973.4	41.6		14.6

[1]Debt in current dollars deflated by the GNP deflator for the fiscal year with FY 1982 = 100.

[2]Source: Federal Reserve Board flow-of-funds accounts. Total credit market debt owed by domestic nonfinancial sectors, modified to be consistent with budget concepts for the measurement of Federal debt. Projections not available.

[3]Interest on debt held by the public is estimated as the interest on the public debt less the "interest received by trust funds" (subfunction 901 less subfunctions 902 and 903). It does not include the comparatively small amount of interest on agency debt or the offsets for other interest received by Government accounts.

Table I-2　Gross National Product, 1929–1990

(billions of dollars, except as noted; quarterly data at seasonally adjusted annual rates)

Year or quarter	Gross national product	Personal consumption expenditures Total	Durable goods	Non-durable goods	Services	Gross private domestic investment Total	Fixed investment Total	Nonresidential Total	Struc-tures	Producers' durable equip-ment	Resi-dential	Change in busi-ness inven-tories
1929	103.9	77.3	9.2	37.7	30.4	16.7	14.9	11.0	5.5	5.5	4.0	1.7
1933	56.0	45.8	3.5	22.3	20.1	1.6	3.1	2.5	1.1	1.4	.6	−1.6
1939	91.3	67.0	6.7	35.1	25.2	9.5	9.1	6.1	2.2	3.9	3.0	.4
1940	100.4	71.0	7.8	37.0	26.2	13.4	11.2	7.7	2.6	5.2	3.5	2.2
1941	125.5	80.8	9.7	42.9	28.3	18.3	13.8	9.7	3.3	6.4	4.1	4.5
1942	159.0	88.6	6.9	50.8	31.0	10.3	8.5	6.3	2.2	4.1	2.2	1.8
1943	192.7	99.5	6.5	58.6	34.3	6.2	6.9	5.4	1.8	3.7	1.4	−.6
1944	211.4	108.2	6.7	64.3	37.2	7.7	8.7	7.4	2.4	5.0	1.4	−1.0
1945	213.4	119.6	8.0	71.9	39.7	11.3	12.3	10.6	3.3	7.3	1.7	−1.0
1946	212.4	143.9	15.8	82.7	45.4	31.5	25.1	17.3	7.4	9.9	7.8	6.4
1947	235.2	161.9	20.4	90.9	50.6	35.0	35.5	23.5	8.1	15.3	12.1	−.5
1948	261.6	174.9	22.9	96.6	55.5	47.1	42.4	26.8	9.5	17.3	15.6	4.7
1949	260.4	178.3	25.0	94.9	58.4	36.5	39.5	24.9	9.2	15.7	14.6	−3.1
1950	288.3	192.1	30.8	98.2	63.2	55.1	48.3	27.8	10.0	17.8	20.5	6.8
1951	333.4	208.1	29.9	109.2	69.0	60.5	50.2	31.8	11.9	19.9	18.4	10.2
1952	351.6	219.1	29.3	114.7	75.1	53.5	50.5	31.9	12.2	19.7	18.6	3.1
1953	371.6	232.6	32.7	117.8	82.1	54.9	54.5	35.1	13.6	21.5	19.4	.4
1954	372.5	239.8	32.1	119.7	88.0	54.1	55.7	34.7	13.9	20.8	21.1	−1.6
1955	405.9	257.9	38.9	124.7	94.3	69.7	64.0	39.0	15.2	23.9	25.0	5.7
1956	428.2	270.6	38.2	130.8	101.6	72.7	68.0	44.5	18.2	26.3	23.5	4.6
1957	451.0	285.3	39.7	137.1	108.5	71.1	69.7	47.5	18.9	28.6	22.2	1.4
1958	456.8	294.6	37.2	141.7	115.7	63.6	65.1	42.4	17.5	24.9	22.7	−1.5
1959	495.8	316.3	42.8	148.5	125.0	80.2	74.4	46.3	18.0	28.3	28.1	5.8
1960	515.3	330.7	43.5	153.2	134.0	78.2	75.1	48.8	19.2	29.7	26.3	3.1
1961	533.8	341.1	41.9	157.4	141.8	77.1	74.7	48.3	19.4	28.9	26.4	2.4
1962	574.6	361.9	47.0	163.8	151.1	87.6	81.5	52.5	20.5	32.1	29.0	6.1
1963	606.9	381.7	51.8	169.4	160.6	93.1	87.3	55.2	20.8	34.4	32.1	5.8
1964	649.8	409.3	56.8	179.7	172.8	99.6	94.2	61.4	22.7	38.7	32.8	5.4
1965	705.1	440.7	63.5	191.9	185.4	116.2	106.2	73.1	27.4	45.8	33.1	9.9
1966	772.0	477.3	68.5	208.5	200.3	128.6	114.4	83.5	30.5	53.0	30.9	14.2
1967	816.4	503.6	70.6	216.9	216.0	125.7	115.4	84.4	30.7	53.7	31.1	10.3
1968	892.7	552.5	81.0	235.0	236.4	137.0	129.1	91.4	32.9	58.5	37.7	7.9
1969	963.9	597.9	86.2	252.2	259.4	153.2	143.4	102.3	37.1	65.2	41.2	9.8
1970	1,015.5	640.0	85.7	270.3	284.0	148.8	145.7	105.2	39.2	66.1	40.5	3.1
1971	1,102.7	691.6	97.6	283.3	310.7	172.5	164.7	109.6	40.9	68.7	55.1	7.8
1972	1,212.8	757.6	111.2	305.1	341.3	202.0	191.5	123.0	44.5	78.5	68.6	10.5
1973	1,359.3	837.2	124.7	339.6	373.0	238.8	219.2	145.9	51.4	94.5	73.3	19.6
1974	1,472.8	916.5	123.8	380.9	411.9	240.8	225.4	160.6	57.0	103.6	64.8	15.4
1975	1,598.4	1,012.8	135.4	416.2	461.2	219.6	225.2	162.9	56.3	106.6	62.3	−5.6
1976	1,782.8	1,129.3	161.5	452.0	515.9	277.7	261.7	180.0	60.1	119.9	81.7	16.0
1977	1,990.5	1,257.2	184.5	490.4	582.3	344.1	322.8	214.2	66.7	147.4	108.6	21.3
1978	2,249.7	1,403.5	205.6	541.8	656.1	416.8	388.2	259.0	81.0	178.0	129.2	28.6
1979	2,508.2	1,566.8	219.0	613.2	734.6	454.8	441.9	302.8	99.5	203.3	139.1	13.0
1980	2,732.0	1,732.6	219.3	681.4	831.9	437.0	445.3	322.8	113.9	208.9	122.5	−8.3
1981	3,052.6	1,915.1	239.9	740.6	934.7	515.5	491.5	369.2	138.5	230.7	122.3	24.0
1982	3,166.0	2,050.7	252.7	771.0	1,027.0	447.3	471.8	366.7	143.3	223.4	105.1	−24.5
1983	3,405.7	2,234.5	289.1	816.7	1,128.7	502.3	509.4	356.9	124.0	232.8	152.5	−7.1
1984	3,772.2	2,430.5	335.5	867.3	1,227.6	664.8	597.1	416.0	141.1	274.9	181.1	67.7
1985	4,014.9	2,629.0	372.2	911.2	1,345.6	643.1	631.8	442.9	153.2	289.7	188.8	11.3
1986	4,231.6	2,797.4	406.0	942.0	1,449.5	659.4	652.5	435.2	139.0	296.2	217.3	6.9
1987	4,515.6	3,009.4	423.4	1,001.3	1,584.7	699.5	671.2	444.9	133.7	311.2	226.3	28.3
1988	4,873.7	3,238.2	457.5	1,060.0	1,720.7	747.1	720.8	488.4	139.9	348.4	232.5	26.2
1989	5,200.8	3,450.1	474.6	1,130.0	1,845.5	771.2	742.9	511.9	146.2	365.7	231.0	28.3
1990ᴾ	5,463.0	3,658.1	481.6	1,194.2	1,982.3	745.0	747.2	524.3	147.2	377.2	222.9	−2.2
1982:IV	3,212.5	2,117.0	263.8	786.6	1,066.5	409.6	469.5	354.9	137.6	217.3	114.7	−59.9
1983:IV	3,545.8	2,315.8	310.0	837.9	1,167.9	579.8	548.8	383.9	127.4	256.5	164.9	31.0
1984:IV	3,851.8	2,493.4	346.7	879.6	1,267.1	661.8	616.8	435.0	146.6	288.4	181.8	45.0
1985:IV	4,107.9	2,700.4	373.2	932.7	1,394.5	654.1	646.8	451.3	155.9	295.5	195.5	7.2
1986:IV	4,297.3	2,868.5	422.0	952.1	1,494.4	648.8	660.9	435.8	133.7	302.2	225.1	−12.2
1987:IV	4,647.6	3,079.1	427.4	1,019.9	1,631.8	741.4	685.7	457.5	137.2	320.4	228.1	55.7
1988:I	4,735.8	3,147.7	448.9	1,029.8	1,668.9	729.2	700.8	473.1	135.5	337.6	227.7	28.3
II	4,831.4	3,204.3	453.7	1,049.1	1,701.5	746.0	723.8	491.3	140.8	350.5	232.6	22.2
III	4,917.9	3,268.2	454.2	1,073.2	1,740.7	765.6	727.4	493.8	142.2	351.6	233.6	38.2
IV	5,009.8	3,332.6	473.1	1,088.0	1,771.5	747.5	731.3	495.3	141.2	354.0	236.0	16.2
1989:I	5,101.3	3,371.7	466.4	1,106.7	1,798.6	769.7	743.1	506.5	146.5	360.0	236.6	26.6
II	5,174.0	3,425.9	473.6	1,127.1	1,825.1	776.7	744.0	511.4	144.2	367.2	232.7	32.7
III	5,238.6	3,484.3	487.1	1,137.3	1,859.8	775.8	746.9	518.1	147.0	371.0	228.9	28.9
IV	5,289.3	3,518.5	471.2	1,148.8	1,898.5	762.7	737.7	511.8	147.1	364.7	225.9	25.0
1990:I	5,375.4	3,588.1	492.1	1,174.7	1,921.3	747.2	758.9	523.1	148.8	374.3	235.9	−11.8
II	5,443.3	3,622.7	478.4	1,179.0	1,965.3	759.0	745.6	516.5	147.2	369.3	229.1	13.4
III	5,514.6	3,693.4	482.3	1,205.0	2,006.2	759.7	750.7	532.8	149.8	383.0	217.9	9.0
IVᴾ	5,518.9	3,728.1	473.5	1,218.3	2,036.3	714.0	733.6	525.0	142.8	382.2	208.6	−19.5

Table I-2 Gross National Product, 1929–1990 (continued)
(billions of dollars, except as noted; quarterly data at seasonally adjusted annual rates)

| Year or quarter | Net exports of goods and services | | | Government purchases of goods and services | | | | | Final sales | Gross domestic purchases[1] | Percent change from preceding period | | |
	Net exports	Exports	Imports	Total	Federal Total	National defense	Non-defense	State and local			Gross national product	Final sales	Gross domestic purchases[1]
1929	1.1	7.1	5.9	8.9	1.5			7.4	102.2	102.8			
1933	.4	2.4	2.1	8.3	2.2			6.1	57.6	55.7	-4.2	-5.5	-4.2
1939	1.2	4.6	3.4	13.6	5.2	1.3	3.9	8.3	90.9	90.1	7.0	5.4	7.3
1940	1.8	5.4	3.7	14.2	6.1	2.3	3.9	8.1	98.3	98.7	10.0	8.1	9.5
1941	1.5	6.1	4.7	25.0	17.0	13.8	3.2	8.0	121.0	124.1	25.0	23.2	25.7
1942	.2	5.0	4.8	52.0	49.4	49.4	2.6	7.8	157.2	158.8	26.6	29.9	28.0
1943	-1.9	4.6	6.5	88.9	81.4	79.8	1.6	7.5	193.4	194.6	21.2	23.0	22.6
1944	-1.7	5.5	7.2	97.1	89.4	87.5	2.0	7.6	212.3	213.0	9.7	9.8	9.5
1945	-.5	7.4	7.9	83.0	74.8	73.7	1.1	8.2	214.4	213.9	.9	1.0	.4
1946	7.8	15.2	7.3	29.1	19.2	16.4	2.8	9.9	206.0	204.5	-.5	-3.9	-4.4
1947	11.9	20.3	8.3	26.4	13.6	10.0	3.6	12.8	235.7	223.3	10.8	14.4	9.2
1948	7.0	17.5	10.6	32.6	17.3	11.3	6.0	15.3	256.9	254.7	11.2	9.0	14.0
1949	6.5	16.4	9.8	39.0	21.1	13.9	7.2	18.0	263.4	253.8	-.5	2.5	-.3
1950	2.2	14.5	12.3	38.8	19.1	14.3	4.7	19.8	281.4	286.0	10.7	6.8	12.7
1951	4.5	19.8	15.3	60.4	38.6	33.8	4.8	21.8	323.2	329.0	15.7	14.8	15.0
1952	3.2	19.2	16.0	75.8	52.7	46.2	6.5	23.1	348.6	348.4	5.5	7.9	5.9
1953	1.3	18.1	16.8	82.8	57.9	49.0	8.9	24.8	371.1	370.3	5.7	6.5	6.3
1954	2.6	18.8	16.3	76.0	48.4	41.6	6.8	27.7	374.1	370.0	.2	.8	-.1
1955	3.0	21.1	18.1	75.3	44.9	39.0	6.0	30.3	400.2	402.9	9.0	7.0	8.9
1956	5.3	25.2	19.9	79.7	46.4	40.7	5.7	33.3	423.6	422.9	5.5	5.8	5.0
1957	7.3	28.2	20.9	87.3	50.5	44.6	5.9	36.9	449.6	443.7	5.3	6.1	4.9
1958	3.3	24.4	21.1	95.4	54.5	46.3	8.3	40.8	458.3	453.5	1.3	1.9	2.2
1959	1.5	25.0	23.5	97.9	54.6	46.4	8.2	43.3	490.0	494.3	8.5	6.9	9.0
1960	5.9	29.9	24.0	100.6	54.4	45.3	9.2	46.1	512.3	509.4	3.9	4.6	3.1
1961	7.2	31.1	23.9	108.4	58.2	47.9	10.2	50.2	531.4	526.6	3.6	3.7	3.4
1962	6.9	33.1	26.2	118.2	64.6	52.1	12.6	53.5	568.5	567.7	7.6	7.0	7.8
1963	8.2	35.7	27.5	123.8	65.7	51.5	14.2	58.1	601.1	598.7	5.6	5.7	5.5
1964	10.9	40.5	29.6	130.0	66.4	50.4	16.0	63.5	644.4	638.9	7.1	7.2	6.7
1965	9.7	42.9	33.2	138.6	68.7	51.0	17.7	69.9	695.2	695.4	8.5	7.9	8.8
1966	7.5	46.6	39.1	158.6	80.4	62.0	18.3	78.2	757.8	764.5	9.5	9.0	9.9
1967	7.4	49.5	42.1	179.7	92.7	73.4	19.3	87.0	806.1	809.0	5.8	6.4	5.8
1968	5.5	54.8	49.3	197.7	100.1	79.1	21.0	97.6	884.8	887.2	9.3	9.8	9.7
1969	5.6	60.4	54.7	207.3	100.0	78.9	21.1	107.2	954.1	958.3	8.0	7.8	8.0
1970	8.5	68.9	60.5	218.2	98.8	76.8	22.0	119.4	1,012.3	1,007.0	5.4	6.1	5.1
1971	6.3	72.4	66.1	232.4	99.8	74.1	25.8	132.5	1,094.9	1,096.4	8.6	8.2	8.9
1972	3.2	81.4	78.2	250.0	105.8	77.4	28.4	144.2	1,202.3	1,209.6	10.0	9.8	10.3
1973	16.8	114.1	97.3	266.5	106.4	77.5	28.9	160.1	1,339.7	1,342.5	12.1	11.4	11.0
1974	16.3	151.5	135.2	299.1	116.2	82.6	33.6	182.9	1,457.4	1,456.5	8.3	8.8	8.5
1975	31.1	161.3	130.3	335.0	129.2	89.6	39.6	205.9	1,604.1	1,567.4	8.5	10.1	7.6
1976	18.8	177.7	158.9	356.9	136.3	93.4	42.9	220.6	1,766.8	1,764.0	11.5	10.1	12.5
1977	1.9	191.6	189.7	387.3	151.1	100.9	50.3	236.2	1,969.2	1,988.6	11.7	11.5	12.7
1978	4.1	227.5	223.4	425.2	161.8	108.9	52.9	263.4	2,221.0	2,245.6	13.0	12.8	12.9
1979	18.8	291.2	272.5	467.8	178.0	121.9	56.1	289.9	2,495.2	2,489.4	11.5	12.3	10.9
1980	32.1	351.0	318.9	530.3	208.1	142.7	65.4	322.2	2,740.3	2,699.8	8.9	9.8	8.5
1981	33.9	382.8	348.9	588.1	242.2	167.5	74.8	345.9	3,028.6	3,018.7	11.7	10.5	11.8
1982	26.3	361.9	335.6	641.7	272.7	193.8	78.9	369.0	3,190.5	3,139.7	3.7	5.3	4.0
1983	-6.1	352.5	358.7	675.0	283.5	214.4	69.1	391.5	3,412.8	3,411.8	7.6	7.0	8.7
1984	-58.9	383.5	442.4	735.9	310.5	234.3	76.2	425.3	3,704.5	3,831.1	10.8	8.5	12.3
1985	-78.0	370.9	448.9	820.8	355.2	259.1	96.0	465.6	4,003.6	4,092.8	6.4	8.1	6.8
1986	-97.4	396.5	493.8	872.2	366.5	277.8	88.7	505.7	4,224.8	4,329.0	5.4	5.5	5.8
1987	-114.7	449.6	564.3	921.4	381.3	294.6	86.7	540.2	4,487.3	4,630.3	6.7	6.2	7.0
1988	-74.1	552.0	626.1	962.5	380.3	297.2	83.1	582.3	4,847.5	4,947.8	7.9	8.0	6.9
1989	-46.1	626.2	672.3	1,025.6	400.0	301.1	98.9	625.6	5,172.5	5,246.9	6.7	6.7	6.0
1990ᵖ	-38.0	670.4	708.4	1,098.0	424.2	314.0	110.2	673.8	5,465.3	5,501.1	5.0	5.7	4.8
1982:IV	14.1	335.9	321.9	671.8	293.2	205.4	87.7	378.7	3,272.4	3,198.5	4.2	11.0	4.3
1983:IV	-25.8	364.7	390.5	676.1	276.1	221.5	54.6	400.0	3,514.8	3,571.6	12.4	7.8	13.1
1984:IV	-67.9	385.7	453.6	764.5	326.0	244.1	81.9	438.5	3,806.8	3,919.7	4.7	7.0	5.5
1985:IV	-103.2	369.2	472.4	856.7	376.6	268.6	108.0	480.1	4,100.7	4,211.2	6.2	5.5	8.3
1986:IV	-108.9	402.4	511.3	888.9	368.8	280.7	88.1	520.1	4,309.4	4,406.2	4.2	4.7	4.9
1987:IV	-115.0	485.8	600.7	942.0	388.2	296.0	92.2	553.9	4,591.9	4,762.6	8.7	4.5	8.1
1988:I	-82.0	525.7	607.8	940.9	374.8	296.6	78.3	566.1	4,707.4	4,817.8	7.8	10.4	4.7
II	-74.3	540.4	614.7	955.4	377.7	297.1	80.6	577.7	4,809.2	4,905.7	8.3	8.9	7.5
III	-69.6	558.7	628.3	953.8	367.4	295.5	71.9	586.4	4,879.7	4,987.5	7.4	6.0	6.8
IV	-70.3	583.1	653.5	1,000.0	401.1	299.6	101.6	598.9	4,993.6	5,080.1	7.7	9.7	7.6
1989:I	-48.5	609.7	658.2	1,008.5	398.3	298.2	100.1	610.2	5,074.7	5,149.8	7.5	6.7	5.6
II	-51.3	628.8	680.0	1,022.7	402.5	300.6	101.9	620.2	5,141.3	5,225.3	5.8	5.4	6.0
III	-49.3	623.7	673.0	1,027.8	399.2	306.3	93.0	628.6	5,209.7	5,287.9	5.1	5.4	4.9
IV	-35.3	642.8	678.1	1,043.3	399.9	299.2	100.7	643.4	5,264.3	5,324.6	3.9	4.3	2.8
1990:I	-30.0	661.3	691.3	1,070.1	410.6	307.2	103.4	659.6	5,387.2	5,405.3	6.7	9.7	6.2
II	-24.9	659.7	684.6	1,086.4	421.9	309.6	112.3	664.6	5,429.9	5,468.2	5.1	3.2	4.7
III	-41.3	672.7	714.1	1,102.8	425.8	312.6	113.2	677.0	5,505.6	5,555.9	5.3	5.7	6.6
IVᵖ	-55.9	687.7	743.7	1,132.7	438.5	326.5	112.0	694.2	5,538.4	5,574.8	.3	2.4	1.4

[1]Gross national product (GNP) less exports of goods and services plus imports of goods and services.
Source: Department of Commerce, Bureau of Economic Analysis.

Table I-3 Corporate Profits by Industry, 1929–1990
(billions of dollars; quarterly data at seasonally adjusted annual rates)

Corporate profits with inventory valuation adjustment and without capital consumption adjustment

Year or quarter	Total	Domestic industries Total	Financial[1] Total	Financial[1] Federal Reserve banks	Financial[1] Other	Nonfinancial Total	Nonfinancial Manufacturing	Nonfinancial Transportation and public utilities	Nonfinancial Wholesale and retail trade	Nonfinancial Other	Rest of the world
1929	10.5	10.2	1.3	0.0	1.3	8.9	5.2	1.8	1.0	0.9	0.2
1933	-1.2	-1.2	.3	.0	.3	-1.5	-.4	.0	-.5	-.7	.0
1939	6.5	6.1	.8	.0	.8	5.3	3.3	1.0	.7	.3	.3
1940	9.8	9.6	1.0	.0	.9	8.6	5.5	1.3	1.2	.6	.3
1941	15.4	15.0	1.1	.0	1.0	14.0	9.5	2.0	1.4	1.1	.4
1942	20.5	20.1	1.2	.0	1.2	18.9	11.8	3.4	2.2	1.5	.4
1943	24.5	24.1	1.3	.0	1.3	22.8	13.8	4.4	3.0	1.6	.4
1944	24.0	23.5	1.6	.1	1.6	21.9	13.2	3.9	3.2	1.6	.4
1945	19.3	18.9	1.7	.1	1.6	17.3	9.7	2.7	3.3	1.5	.3
1946	19.6	18.9	2.1	.1	2.0	16.8	9.0	1.8	3.8	2.1	.7
1947	25.9	24.9	1.7	.1	1.6	23.2	13.6	2.2	4.6	2.9	1.0
1948	33.4	32.2	2.6	.2	2.3	29.6	17.6	3.0	5.5	3.6	1.3
1949	31.1	29.9	3.1	.2	2.9	26.8	16.2	3.0	4.5	3.1	1.1
1950	37.9	36.7	3.1	.2	3.0	33.5	20.9	4.0	5.0	3.6	1.3
1951	43.3	41.5	3.6	.3	3.3	37.9	24.6	4.6	5.0	3.7	1.7
1952	40.6	38.7	4.0	.4	3.7	34.7	21.7	4.9	4.8	3.3	1.9
1953	40.2	38.4	4.5	.4	4.1	33.9	22.0	5.0	3.8	3.1	1.8
1954	38.4	36.4	4.6	.3	4.3	31.8	19.9	4.7	3.8	3.4	2.0
1955	47.5	45.1	4.8	.3	4.5	40.3	26.0	5.6	5.0	3.6	2.4
1956	46.9	44.1	5.0	.5	4.5	39.1	24.7	5.9	4.5	4.1	2.8
1957	46.6	43.5	5.2	.6	4.6	38.3	24.0	5.8	4.4	4.0	3.1
1958	41.6	39.1	5.7	.6	5.1	33.5	19.4	5.9	4.6	3.6	2.5
1959	52.3	49.6	6.8	.7	6.0	42.9	26.4	7.0	5.9	3.6	2.7
1960	49.8	46.7	7.2	1.0	6.2	39.5	23.6	7.4	4.9	3.6	3.1
1961	50.1	46.8	7.0	.8	6.3	39.8	23.3	7.8	5.0	3.7	3.3
1962	55.2	51.5	7.3	.9	6.4	44.2	26.0	8.4	5.8	3.9	3.7
1963	59.8	55.8	6.8	1.0	5.8	49.0	29.3	9.3	5.9	4.4	4.0
1964	66.2	61.8	6.9	1.1	5.8	54.9	32.3	10.0	7.5	5.1	4.4
1965	76.2	71.5	7.5	1.4	6.2	64.0	39.3	11.0	8.1	5.6	4.6
1966	81.2	76.7	8.5	1.7	6.8	68.2	41.9	11.8	8.2	6.3	4.4
1967	78.6	73.9	9.0	2.0	7.0	64.9	38.6	10.7	9.1	6.5	4.7
1968	85.4	79.9	10.4	2.5	7.9	69.5	41.4	10.8	10.4	6.9	5.5
1969	81.4	74.8	11.2	3.1	8.1	63.7	36.7	10.3	10.5	6.1	6.5
1970	69.5	62.6	12.2	3.6	8.6	50.4	26.7	8.2	9.6	5.9	6.9
1971	82.7	75.1	14.1	3.3	10.7	61.0	34.3	8.5	11.7	6.5	7.6
1972	94.9	85.5	15.4	3.4	12.0	70.2	40.8	9.0	13.4	6.9	9.3
1973	107.1	92.6	15.8	4.5	11.2	76.8	46.2	8.5	13.9	8.2	14.5
1974	99.4	82.4	14.7	5.7	8.9	67.8	39.8	6.7	12.9	8.3	17.0
1975	123.9	109.5	11.2	5.7	5.5	98.3	53.6	10.3	22.2	12.2	14.4
1976	155.3	139.3	15.9	6.0	9.9	123.4	70.9	14.8	23.0	14.7	16.0
1977	183.8	165.5	21.6	6.2	15.4	143.9	80.6	17.9	27.5	17.8	18.3
1978	208.2	186.0	29.1	7.7	21.4	156.8	88.7	20.9	27.3	20.0	22.2
1979	214.1	180.4	27.8	9.6	18.2	152.6	87.5	15.2	28.7	21.1	33.7
1980	194.0	159.6	21.0	11.9	9.0	138.6	77.1	17.6	21.6	22.4	34.4
1981	202.3	173.8	16.5	14.5	1.9	157.3	88.5	19.5	32.5	16.8	28.5
1982	159.2	131.2	11.8	15.4	-3.6	119.4	58.0	19.3	34.6	7.5	28.0
1983	196.7	166.6	18.1	14.8	3.3	148.5	70.1	28.5	38.9	10.9	30.2
1984	234.2	203.3	13.0	16.7	-3.7	190.3	88.8	38.5	51.2	11.8	30.9
1985	222.6	191.4	22.8	16.8	6.1	168.6	79.7	33.0	44.1	11.8	31.2
1986	228.3	195.2	32.0	16.0	16.0	163.2	59.5	36.3	44.1	23.4	33.1
1987	255.9	218.4	20.7	16.2	4.4	197.8	86.7	40.6	37.9	32.6	37.5
1988	289.8	246.5	22.4	18.1	4.3	224.1	106.5	44.1	37.1	36.4	43.3
1989	286.1	235.2	15.4	20.7	-5.2	219.8	96.1	43.6	38.7	41.4	50.9
1990p	292.1	238.1	18.6	21.9	-3.3	219.6	91.8	42.0	40.3	45.5	54.0
1982:IV	150.7	121.6	18.7	14.8	3.9	102.9	46.8	16.3	33.6	6.2	29.1
1983:IV	223.4	190.7	15.5	15.4	.1	175.2	88.6	31.3	43.1	12.2	32.7
1984:IV	224.6	193.9	13.6	17.4	-3.8	180.3	79.8	38.1	51.8	10.5	30.6
1985:IV	228.4	193.6	26.0	16.3	9.7	167.6	83.8	30.6	38.5	14.6	34.8
1986:IV	226.1	193.4	28.6	15.6	12.9	164.8	64.8	35.3	41.0	23.8	32.6
1987:IV	268.6	226.2	19.8	16.6	3.2	206.4	98.2	40.8	37.8	29.6	42.4
1988:I	278.0	235.7	19.2	17.4	1.8	216.4	103.2	40.1	38.2	35.0	42.4
1988:II	285.3	244.9	21.1	17.3	3.8	223.8	106.8	44.2	35.0	37.8	40.4
1988:III	287.1	243.5	25.0	18.2	6.8	218.5	103.3	45.1	33.0	37.0	43.7
1988:IV	308.7	261.9	24.1	19.3	4.8	237.8	112.6	47.2	42.3	35.7	46.8
1989:I	292.1	241.5	24.0	20.2	3.8	217.4	102.0	45.0	33.7	36.8	50.6
1989:II	291.5	244.9	21.6	21.1	.5	223.4	98.9	46.2	40.7	37.6	46.6
1989:III	285.3	236.0	9.2	20.5	-11.3	226.9	99.9	42.9	41.4	42.7	49.3
1989:IV	275.3	218.4	6.9	20.8	-13.9	211.5	83.7	40.2	41.9	45.7	56.9
1990:I	285.5	232.6	16.1	20.8	-4.7	216.5	90.1	41.5	39.2	45.7	52.9
1990:II	298.8	249.9	18.2	21.1	-2.9	231.7	100.8	41.9	44.4	44.6	48.9
1990:III	298.7	241.1	21.7	22.6	-.8	219.3	91.2	42.8	39.5	45.9	57.6

[1]Consists of the following industries: Banking; credit agencies other than banks; security and commodity brokers, dealers, and services; insurance carriers; regulated investment companies; small business investment companies; and real estate investment trusts.

Note.—The industry classification is on a company basis and is based on the 1972 Standard Industrial Classification (SIC) beginning 1948, and on the 1942 SIC prior to 1948.

Source: Department of Commerce, Bureau of Economic Analysis.

THE GLOBAL ECONOMY

Remember all the head-spinning talk of the "European Economic Miracle" that was to be formalized in 1992 with the creation of an all-powerful economic bloc? Western Europe was going to be the world's hottest market; 320 million free-spending consumers were champing at the bit to buy everything from limos to laptops. Throughout the 1990s, the European economic hodgepodge would be transformed into a sleek, fast-paced marketplace brimming over with fantastic opportunities. Well, sluggish growth, inflation, and surging oil prices have taken much of the luster off the forecasts.

That's not to say the European juggernaut was wishful thinking. Just that the troubling reality of the economic indicators has tempered the heady expectations. Inflation is rising, capital spending is slowing, exports are tumbling, and growth is falling.

Germany's reunification certainly bolstered the European GNP in 1990 so it expanded by about 2.4%. That, however, would be Europe's slowest growth since the mid-1980s. Indeed, analysts have stopped looking to Europe to prop up the sluggish world economy as an economic slowdown swamps the U.S. and Japan faces economic stresses of its own. And if oil prices soar again, economists predicted that Europe's growth could skitter down to 1%.

Even before Saddam Hussein was inspired to rouse the world to raise arms against him, however, European profits were being whittled away by the cheap dollar and a slowdown in exports to the troubled U.S. Sagging consumer confidence softened spending and a lot of Europeans started putting more of what they earned into savings. Meanwhile, faced with overcapacity in many industries (electronics and automotive being especially hard hit), European companies trimmed investment plans.

All this took its toll on the plans that called for galloping toward unity in 1992. The move to establish a single trading bank and currency, for instance, were delayed. No one doubts that Europe is intent on creating that 320 million consumer market that will be the economic rival of the U.S. and Japan. Just when it will happen is another matter.

In the European Market's favor is that major European companies will tap their pools of equity investment to finance restructuring, to beef up research and development, and to invest vast sums to improve the continent's infrastructure and drag the dismal East European economies into the tail end of the twentieth century.

The real wild card in Europe is the emergence of the former Soviet satellite nations. What will become of these former Eastern-bloc colonies?

At best, the oil-price shocks arising from Iraq's invasion of Kuwait represented a grave setback to Eastern Europe. One of the few compensations for having been under Moscow's thumb was cheap, subsidized oil, but that benefit was being phased out. David Roche, of Morgan Stanley, estimated that by mid-1991 some 80% of Eastern Europe's oil supplies would come from real money, at market prices. He called it "a matter of major concern."

Nor is it hard to figure out why. A price level of $25 or more a barrel would take all of Bulgaria's export earnings, 75% of Czechoslovakia's, and more than 50% of East Germany's and nearly a third of Poland's. The archaic plants of Eastern companies are twice as wasteful of energy as their Western neighbors'. Effective conservation will take billions of dollars and a great deal of time.

The darkest scenario is that this new handicap could contribute to economic collapse and political disintegration, leading to European-style images of Saddam Hussein. The *Financial Times* of London conjured up the possibility of this new threat: "anti-capitalist, anti-communist, anti-Western nationalism, with politicians who came to power on a policy of cooperation with the West being seen as failures and being swept aside by mini-Saddams who want to reassert the national values, even reconquer lost national territories."

Even short of such geopolitical cataclysms, the underlying truth is that Eastern Europe remains perilously far from the economic dreams that motivated its push for freedom. The Congressional Joint Economic Committee made public in 1990 a Central Intelligence Agency report that said the new democracies could be rocked by unrest if their citizens were unwilling to accept hardship for years to come. The report warned bluntly that these economies were likely to worsen, producing recessions, higher unemployment, and enduring consumer shortages.

Despite such concerns, U.S. and other Western companies have pumped hundreds of millions of dollars into Eastern European joint ventures ranging from automobile production to telecommunications. Thus, one can expect some of their corporate voices to be added to cries for more American governmental aid to Eastern Europe. In the long run, though, what is truly required is a faster-paced economic liberation on the part of those Eastern governments—and a more realistic popular sense of the inevitable pain en route to genuine prosperity.

In Japan, too, things aren't quite what they used to be. After a heady decade of having incredibly cheap money at their disposal, the Japanese in 1990 found the era at an end. Just from 1986 to 1989, the Japanese nonchalantly underwrote a staggering $162.4 billion in overseas investment for such massive takeovers as the $3.4 billion Sony buyout of Columbia Pictures Entertainment Inc. But then the Tokyo stock market went into a tailspin. By October of 1990, the market had plummeted by a sickening 41%, erasing about $1.8 trillion in value. (That's about 75% of Japan's GNP.) Interest rates soared and, ever-anxious to attract money, corporations began offering sweeter deals on bond issues.

But though the stock market sank and interest rates climbed 2.6% to 8% in 1990, business spending in Japan climbed in 1990 and the economy grew by a very healthy 6%, the strongest rate since just prior to the oil crisis of 1973.

One of the strengths of Japan was that many of the major companies were so cash strong that they didn't have to utilize the troubled capital markets. They still had on tap the $190 billion in equity that was raised in 1989. Matsushita Electric Industrial Co., for instance, had a $24.6 billion cash reserve in 1990, while Toyota's was $15.9 billion. Thus, a terrible crimp in corporate capital spending plans could be avoided for quite some time. (In

1989, Japan spent $549 billion on plants and equipment, the first time a country outspent the U.S. [$513 billion] since the Second World War.)

Also working in Japan's favor in this time of doubt is that its own consumer market has been greatly expanded in recent years and the Japanese presence in markets throughout the Pacific Rim has expanded as well. Unless a severe global recession develops, the Japanese appear well prepared to weather downturns in the U.S. or elsewhere.

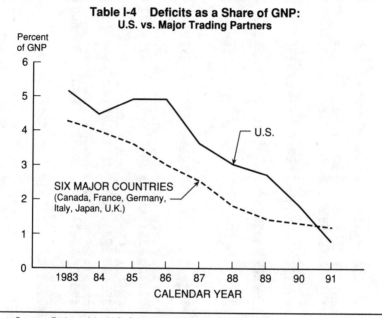

Table I-4   Deficits as a Share of GNP:
U.S. vs. Major Trading Partners

Source: Budget of the U.S. Government, fiscal year 1991.

Table I-5   U.S. International Transactions, 1946–1990

(millions of dollars; quarterly data seasonally adjusted, except as noted. Credits (+), debits (–))

Year or quarter	Merchandise[1,2] Exports	Imports	Net	Services Net military transactions[3,4]	Net travel and transportation receipts	Other services, net[6]	Investment income[5] Receipts on U.S. assets abroad	Payments on foreign assets in U.S.[3]	Net	Balance on goods, services, and income[4]	Unilateral transfers, net[4]	Balance on current account
1946	11,764	−5,067	6,697	−493	733	310	772	−212	560	7,807	−2,922	4,885
1947	16,097	−5,973	10,124	−455	946	145	1,102	−245	857	11,617	−2,625	8,992
1948	13,265	−7,557	5,708	−799	374	175	1,921	−437	1,484	6,942	−4,525	2,417
1949	12,213	−6,874	5,339	−621	230	208	1,831	−476	1,355	6,511	−5,638	873
1950	10,203	−9,081	1,122	−576	−120	242	2,068	−559	1,509	2,177	−4,017	−1,840
1951	14,243	−11,176	3,067	−1,270	298	254	2,633	−583	2,050	4,399	−3,515	884
1952	13,449	−10,838	2,611	−2,054	83	309	2,751	−555	2,196	3,145	−2,531	614
1953	12,412	−10,975	1,437	−2,423	−238	307	2,736	−624	2,112	1,195	−2,481	−1,286
1954	12,929	−10,353	2,576	−2,460	−269	305	2,929	−582	2,347	2,499	−2,280	219
1955	14,424	−11,527	2,897	−2,701	−297	299	3,406	−676	2,730	2,928	−2,498	430
1956	17,556	−12,803	4,753	−2,788	−361	447	3,837	−735	3,102	5,153	−2,423	2,730
1957	19,562	−13,291	6,271	−2,841	−189	482	4,180	−796	3,384	7,107	−2,345	4,762
1958	16,414	−12,952	3,462	−3,135	−633	486	3,790	−825	2,965	3,145	−2,361	784
1959	16,458	−15,310	1,148	−2,805	−821	573	4,132	−1,061	3,071	1,166	−2,448	−1,282
1960	19,650	−14,758	4,892	−1,057	−964	639	4,616	−1,238	3,379	6,886	−4,062	2,824
1961	20,108	−14,537	5,571	−1,131	−978	732	4,999	−1,245	3,755	7,949	−4,127	3,822
1962	20,781	−16,260	4,521	−912	−1,152	912	5,618	−1,324	4,294	7,664	−4,277	3,387
1963	22,272	−17,048	5,224	−742	−1,309	1,036	6,157	−1,560	4,596	8,806	−4,392	4,414
1964	25,501	−18,700	6,801	−794	−1,146	1,161	6,824	−1,783	5,041	11,063	−4,240	6,823
1965	26,461	−21,510	4,951	−487	−1,280	1,480	7,437	−2,088	5,350	10,014	−4,583	5,431
1966	29,310	−25,493	3,817	−1,043	−1,331	1,497	7,528	−2,481	5,047	7,987	−4,955	3,031
1967	30,666	−26,866	3,800	−1,187	−1,750	1,742	8,021	−2,747	5,274	7,878	−5,294	2,583
1968	33,626	−32,991	635	−596	−1,548	1,759	9,367	−3,378	5,990	6,240	−5,629	611
1969	36,414	−35,807	607	−718	−1,763	1,964	10,913	−4,869	6,044	6,135	−5,735	399
1970	42,469	−39,866	2,603	−641	−2,038	2,330	11,748	−5,515	6,233	8,486	−6,156	2,331
1971	43,319	−45,579	−2,260	653	−2,345	2,649	12,707	−5,435	7,272	5,969	−7,402	−1,433
1972	49,381	−55,797	−6,416	1,072	−3,063	2,965	14,765	−6,572	8,192	2,749	−8,544	−5,795
1973	71,410	−70,499	911	740	−3,158	3,406	21,808	−9,655	12,153	14,053	−6,913	7,140
1974	98,306	−103,811	−5,505	165	−3,184	4,231	27,587	−12,084	15,503	11,210	[6]−9,249	1,962
1975	107,088	−98,185	8,903	1,461	−2,812	4,854	25,351	−12,564	12,787	25,191	−7,075	18,116
1976	114,745	−124,228	−9,483	931	−2,558	5,027	29,286	−13,311	15,975	9,894	−5,686	4,207
1977	120,816	−151,907	−31,091	1,731	−3,565	5,680	32,178	−14,217	17,961	−9,285	−5,226	−14,511
1978	142,054	−176,001	−33,947	857	−3,573	6,879	41,824	−21,680	20,144	−9,639	−5,788	−15,427
1979	184,473	−212,009	−27,536	−1,313	−2,935	7,251	63,096	−32,961	30,136	5,603	−6,593	−991
1980	224,269	−249,750	−25,481	−1,822	−997	8,912	71,388	−42,532	28,856	9,467	−8,349	1,119
1981	237,085	−265,063	−27,978	−844	144	12,552	84,975	−53,626	31,349	15,223	−8,331	6,892
1982	211,198	−247,642	−36,444	112	−992	12,981	85,346	−57,097	28,250	3,907	−9,775	−5,868
1983	201,820	−268,900	−67,080	−163	−4,227	13,859	81,972	−54,549	27,423	−30,188	−9,956	−40,143
1984	219,900	−332,422	−112,522	−2,147	−9,153	14,042	92,935	−69,542	23,394	−86,385	−12,621	−99,006
1985	215,935	−338,083	−122,148	−4,096	−10,788	14,008	82,282	−66,115	16,166	−106,859	−15,473	−122,332
1986	223,367	−368,425	−145,058	−4,907	−8,939	18,551	80,982	−70,013	10,969	−129,384	−16,009	−145,393
1987	250,266	−409,766	−159,500	−3,530	−8,298	18,262	90,536	−85,210	5,326	−147,739	−14,575	−162,314
1988	320,337	−447,323	−126,986	−5,452	−4,060	21,032	110,048	−108,438	1,610	−113,857	−15,005	−128,862
1989	360,465	−475,329	−114,864	−6,320	659	26,123	127,536	−128,448	−913	−95,314	−14,720	−110,034
1988:												
I	76,497	−109,988	−33,491	−1,075	−1,776	4,736	26,980	−24,580	2,400	−29,206	−3,476	−32,682
II	79,392	−110,494	−31,102	−1,139	−1,062	5,079	26,739	−26,330	409	−27,815	−3,060	−30,875
III	80,511	−111,290	−30,779	−1,144	−624	5,391	27,942	−28,083	−141	−27,297	−3,461	−30,758
IV	83,937	−115,551	−31,614	−2,094	−599	5,829	28,386	−29,445	−1,059	−29,537	−5,008	−34,545
1989:												
I	88,267	−116,360	−28,093	−1,763	−57	5,899	30,872	−30,407	465	−23,549	−3,555	−27,104
II	91,111	−119,333	−28,222	−1,667	39	6,164	31,932	−33,889	−1,957	−25,643	−3,006	−28,649
III	89,349	−119,152	−29,803	−1,114	−192	7,031	32,102	−32,085	17	−24,061	−3,530	−27,591
IV	91,738	−120,484	−28,746	−1,776	870	7,030	32,629	−32,068	561	−22,061	−4,631	−26,692
1990:												
I	96,262	−122,545	−26,283	−1,287	1,075	6,217	31,541	−29,546	1,995	−18,283	−3,385	−21,668
II	96,758	−119,860	−23,102	−1,382	479	6,885	33,082	−31,681	−999	−18,119	−4,366	−22,485
III[p]	96,159	−125,911	−29,752	−1,648	350	7,115	33,082	−30,627	2,455	−21,480	−4,105	−25,585

[1]Excludes military.
[2]Adjusted from Census data for differences in valuation, coverage, and timing.
[3]Quarterly data are not seasonally adjusted.
[4]Beginning 1960, includes transfers of goods and services under U.S. military grant programs.
[5]Fees and royalties from U.S. direct investments abroad or from foreign direct investments in the United States are excluded from investment income and included in other services, net.

Table I-5   U.S. International Transactions, 1946–1990 (continued)
(millions of dollars; quarterly data seasonally adjusted, except as noted)

Year or quarter	U.S. assets abroad, net [increase/capital outflow (−)]				Foreign assets in the U.S., net [increase/capital inflow (+)][3]			Allocations of special drawing rights (SDRs)	Statistical discrepancy	
	Total	U.S. official reserve assets[3,7]	Other U.S. Government assets	U.S. private assets	Total	Foreign official assets	Other foreign assets		Total (sum of the items with sign reversed)	Of which: Seasonal adjustment discrepancy
1946		−623								
1947		−3,315								
1948		−1,736								
1949		−266								
1950		1,758								
1951		−33								
1952		−415								
1953		1,256								
1954		480								
1955		182								
1956		−869								
1957		−1,165								
1958		2,292								
1959		1,035								
1960	−4,099	2,145	−1,100	−5,144	2,294	1,473	821		−1,019	
1961	−5,538	607	−910	−5,235	2,705	765	1,939		−989	
1962	−4,174	1,535	−1,085	−4,623	1,911	1,270	641		−1,124	
1963	−7,270	378	−1,662	−5,986	3,217	1,986	1,231		−360	
1964	−9,560	171	−1,680	−8,050	3,643	1,660	1,983		−907	
1965	−5,716	1,225	−1,605	−5,336	742	134	607		−457	
1966	−7,321	570	−1,543	−6,347	3,661	−672	4,333		629	
1967	−9,757	53	−2,423	−7,386	7,379	3,451	3,928		−205	
1968	−10,977	−870	−2,274	−7,833	9,928	−774	10,703		438	
1969	−11,585	−1,179	−2,200	−8,206	12,702	−1,301	14,002		−1,516	
1970	−9,337	2,481	−1,589	−10,229	6,359	6,908	−550	867	−219	
1971	−12,475	2,349	−1,884	−12,940	22,970	26,879	−3,909	717	−9,779	
1972	−14,497	−4	−1,568	−12,925	21,461	10,475	10,986	710	−1,879	
1973	−22,874	158	−2,644	−20,388	18,388	6,026	12,362		−2,654	
1974	−34,745	−1,467	[6]366	−33,643	34,241	10,546	23,696		−1,458	
1975	−39,703	−849	−3,474	−35,380	15,670	7,027	8,643		5,917	
1976	−51,269	−2,558	−4,214	−44,498	36,518	17,693	18,826		10,544	
1977	−34,785	−375	−3,693	−30,717	51,319	36,816	14,503		−2,023	
1978	−61,130	732	−4,660	−57,202	64,036	33,678	30,358		12,521	
1979	−64,331	−1,133	−3,746	−59,453	38,752	−13,665	52,416	1,139	25,431	
1980	−86,118	−8,155	−5,162	−72,802	58,112	15,497	42,615	1,152	25,736	
1981	−110,951	−5,175	−5,097	−100,679	83,032	4,960	78,072	1,093	19,934	
1982	−124,490	−4,965	−6,131	−113,394	93,746	3,593	90,154		36,612	
1983	−56,100	−1,196	−5,006	−49,898	84,869	5,845	79,023		11,374	
1984	−31,070	−3,131	−5,489	−22,451	102,621	3,140	99,481		27,456	
1985	−27,721	−3,858	−2,821	−21,043	130,012	−1,083	131,096		20,041	
1986	−92,030	312	−2,022	−90,321	221,599	35,588	186,011		15,824	
1987	−62,946	9,149	997	−73,091	218,470	45,210	173,260		6,790	
1988	−84,176	−3,912	2,969	−83,232	221,442	39,515	181,927		−8,404	
1989	−127,061	−25,293	1,185	−102,953	214,652	8,823	205,829		22,443	
1988: I	4,569	1,502	−1,594	4,661	26,079	24,840	1,239		2,034	2,970
II	−19,856	39	−847	−19,048	65,270	5,970	59,300		−14,539	−2,995
III	−42,383	−7,380	1,957	−36,960	49,797	−2,015	51,812		23,344	−4,630
IV	−26,508	1,925	3,452	−31,885	80,295	10,720	69,575		−19,242	4,656
1989: I	−32,859	−4,000	962	−29,821	68,402	7,797	60,605		−8,439	3,093
II	−1,381	−12,095	−303	11,017	2,794	−4,961	7,755		27,236	−1,697
III	−44,076	−5,996	574	−38,654	74,136	13,003	61,133		−2,469	−4,953
IV	−48,745	−3,202	−47	−45,496	69,320	−7,016	76,336		6,117	3,560
1990: I	32,877	−3,177	−659	36,713	−32,988	−8,203	−24,786		21,780	2,804
II	−31,721	371	−808	−31,284	25,496	5,541	19,954		28,711	−988
III[p]	−26,451	1,739	−379	−27,811	52,471	13,642	38,829		−435	−5,303

[6]Includes extraordinary U.S. Government transactions with India.
[7]Consists of gold, special drawing rights, foreign currencies, and the U.S. reserve position in the International Monetary Fund (IMF).
Note.—See *Survey of Current Business*, June 1990, for discussion of redefinitions and other adjustments to data, as well as relationship of data shown here with data in the national income and product accounts.
Source: Department of Commerce, Bureau of Economic Analysis.

Table I-6   The World Economy

Figures in italics are for years other than those specified.

		Population (millions) mid-1988	Area (thousands of square kilometers)	GNP per capita Dollars 1988	GNP per capita Average annual growth rate (percent) 1965–88	Average annual rate of inflation (percent) 1965–80	Average annual rate of inflation (percent) 1980–88	Life expectancy at birth (years) 1988	Adult illiteracy (percent) Female 1985	Adult illiteracy (percent) Total 1985
	Low-income economies	2,884.0	36,997	320	3.1	8.8	8.9	60	58	44
	China and India	1,904.0	12,849	340	4.0	2.8	5.8	63	56	42
	Other low-income	980.0	24,149	280	1.5	18.2	13.8	54	62	51
1	Mozambique	14.9	802	100	—	—	33.6	48	78	62
2	Ethiopia	47.4	1,222	120	-0.1	3.4	2.1	47	—	*38*
3	Chad	5.4	1,284	160	-2.0	6.2	3.2	46	89	75
4	Tanzania	24.7	945	160	-0.5	9.9	25.7	53	—	—
5	Bangladesh	108.9	144	170	0.4	14.9	11.1	51	78	67
6	Malawi	8.0	118	170	1.1	7.2	12.6	47	69	59
7	Somalia	5.9	638	170	0.5	10.3	38.4	47	94	88
8	Zaire	33.4	2,345	170	-2.1	24.5	56.1	52	55	39
9	Bhutan	1.4	47	180	—	—	8.9	48	—	—
10	Lao PDR	3.9	237	180	—	—	—	49	24	16
11	Nepal	18.0	141	180	—	7.8	8.7	51	88	74
12	Madagascar	10.9	587	190	-1.8	7.7	17.3	50	38	33
13	Burkina Faso	8.5	274	210	1.2	6.5	3.2	47	94	87
14	Mali	8.0	1,240	230	1.6	9.3	3.7	47	89	83
15	Burundi	5.1	28	240	3.0	6.4	4.0	49	74	66
16	Uganda	16.2	236	280	-3.1	21.2	100.7	48	55	43
17	Nigeria	110.1	924	290	0.9	13.7	11.6	51	69	58
18	Zambia	7.6	753	290	-2.1	6.4	33.5	53	33	24
19	Niger	7.3	1,267	300	-2.3	7.5	3.6	45	91	86
20	Rwanda	6.7	26	320	1.5	12.5	4.1	49	67	53
21	China	1,088.4	9,561	330	5.4	0.1	4.9	70	45	31
22	India	815.6	3,288	340	1.8	7.5	7.4	58	71	57
23	Pakistan	106.3	796	350	2.5	10.3	6.5	55	81	70
24	Kenya	22.4	580	370	1.9	7.3	9.6	59	51	41
25	Togo	3.4	57	370	0.0	6.9	6.1	53	72	59
26	Central African Rep.	2.9	623	380	-0.5	8.5	6.7	50	71	60
27	Haiti	6.3	28	380	0.4	7.3	7.9	55	65	62
28	Benin	4.4	113	390	0.1	7.5	8.0	51	84	74
29	Ghana	14.0	239	400	-1.6	22.8	46.1	54	57	47
30	Lesotho	1.7	30	420	5.2	8.0	12.2	56	16	26
31	Sri Lanka	16.6	66	420	3.0	9.4	11.0	71	17	13
32	Guinea	5.4	246	430	—	—	—	43	83	72
33	Yemen, PDR	2.4	333	430	—	—	4.5	51	75	59
34	Indonesia	174.8	1,905	440	4.3	34.2	8.5	61	35	26
35	Mauritania	1.9	1,026	480	-0.4	7.7	9.4	46	—	—
36	Sudan	23.8	2,506	480	0.0	11.5	33.5	50	—	—
37	Afghanistan	—	652	—	—	4.9	—	—	—	—
38	Myanmar	40.0	677	—	—	—	—	60	—	—
39	Kampuchea, Dem.	—	181	—	—	—	—	—	—	—
40	Liberia	2.4	111	—	—	6.3	—	50	77	65
41	Sierra Leone	3.9	72	—	—	7.8	—	42	79	71
42	Viet Nam	64.2	330	—	—	—	—	66	—	—
	Middle-income economies	1,068.0	37,352	1,930	2.3	20.4	66.7	66	31	26
	Lower-middle-income	741.7	24,451	1,380	2.6	21.7	80.8	65	32	27
43	Bolivia	6.9	1,099	570	-0.6	15.7	482.8	53	35	26
44	Philippines	59.9	300	630	1.6	11.7	15.6	64	15	14
45	Yemen Arab Rep.	8.5	195	640	—	—	11.6	47	97	86
46	Senegal	7.0	197	650	-0.8	6.5	8.1	48	81	72
47	Zimbabwe	9.3	391	650	1.0	5.8	12.1	63	33	26
48	Egypt, Arab Rep.	50.2	1,001	660	3.6	7.3	10.6	63	70	56
49	Dominican Rep.	6.9	49	720	2.7	6.8	16.8	66	23	23
50	Côte d'Ivoire	11.2	322	770	0.9	9.5	3.8	53	69	57
51	Papua New Guinea	3.7	463	810	0.5	8.1	4.7	54	65	55
52	Morocco	24.0	447	830	2.3	6.0	7.7	61	78	67
53	Honduras	4.8	112	860	0.6	5.6	4.7	64	42	41
54	Guatemala	8.7	109	900	1.0	7.1	13.3	62	53	45
55	Congo, People's Rep.	2.1	342	910	3.5	6.7	0.8	53	45	37
56	El Salvador	5.0	21	940	-0.5	7.0	16.8	63	31	28
57	Thailand	54.5	513	1,000	4.0	6.3	3.1	65	12	9
58	Botswana	1.2	582	1,010	8.6	8.1	10.0	67	31	29
59	Cameroon	11.2	475	1,010	3.7	8.9	7.0	56	55	44
60	Jamaica	2.4	11	1,070	-1.5	12.8	18.7	73	—	—
61	Ecuador	10.1	284	1,120	3.1	10.9	31.2	66	20	18
62	Colombia	31.7	1,139	1,180	2.4	17.4	24.1	68	13	12
63	Paraguay	4.0	407	1,180	3.1	9.4	22.1	67	15	12
64	Tunisia	7.8	164	1,230	3.4	6.7	7.7	66	59	46
65	Turkey	53.8	779	1,280	2.6	20.7	39.3	64	38	26
66	Peru	20.7	1,285	1,300	0.1	20.5	119.1	62	22	15
67	Jordan	3.9	89	1,500	—	—	2.2	66	37	25

18

Table I-6 World Economy (continued)

		Population (millions) mid-1988	Area (thousands of square kilometers)	GNP per capita Dollars 1988	GNP per capita Average annual growth rate (percent) 1965–88	Average annual rate of inflation (percent) 1965–80	Average annual rate of inflation (percent) 1980–88	Life expectancy at birth (years) 1988	Adult illiteracy (percent) Female 1985	Adult illiteracy (percent) Total 1985
68	Chile	12.8	757	1,510	0.1	129.9	20.8	72	—	6
69	Syrian Arab Rep.	11.6	185	1,680	2.9	8.3	12.9	65	57	40
70	Costa Rica	2.7	51	1,690	1.4	11.3	26.9	75	7	6
71	Mexico	83.7	1,958	1,760	2.3	13.0	73.8	69	12	10
72	Mauritius	1.1	2	1,800	2.9	11.8	7.8	67	23	17
73	Poland	37.9	313	1,860	—	—	30.5	72	—	—
74	Malaysia	16.9	330	1,940	4.0	4.9	1.3	70	34	27
75	Panama	2.3	77	2,120	2.2	5.4	3.3	72	12	12
76	Brazil	144.4	8,512	2,160	3.6	31.5	188.7	65	24	22
77	Angola	9.4	1,247			—	—	45	—	59
78	Lebanon	—	10	—	—	9.3	—	—	—	—
79	Nicaragua	3.6	130	—	−2.5	8.9	86.6	64	—	—
	Upper-middle-income	326.3	12,901	3,240	2.3	18.9	45.0	68	31	24
80	South Africa	34.0	1,221	2,290	0.8	10.1	13.9	61	—	—
81	Algeria	23.8	2,382	2,360	2.7	10.5	4.4	64	63	50
82	Hungary	10.6	93	2,460	5.1	2.6	6.4	70	*	*
83	Uruguay	3.1	177	2,470	1.3	57.8	57.0	72	4	5
84	Argentina	31.5	2,767	2,520	0.0	78.2	290.5	71	5	5
85	Yugoslavia	23.6	256	2,520	3.4	15.3	66.9	72	14	9
86	Gabon	1.1	268	2,970	0.9	12.7	0.9	53	47	38
87	Venezuela	18.8	912	3,250	−0.9	10.4	13.0	70	15	13
88	Trinidad and Tobago	1.2	5	3,350	0.9	14.0	5.3	71	5	4
89	Korea, Rep. of	42.0	99	3,600	6.8	18.7	5.0	70	—	—
90	Portugal	10.3	92	3,650	3.1	11.7	20.1	74	20	16
91	Greece	10.0	132	4,800	2.9	10.5	18.9	77	12	8
92	Oman	1.4	212	5,000	6.4	19.9	−6.5	64	—	—
93	Libya	4.2	1,760	5,420	−2.7	15.4	0.1	61	50	33
94	Iran, Islamic Rep.	48.6	1,648	—	—	15.6	—	63	61	49
95	Iraq	17.6	438	—	—	—	—	64	13	11
96	Romania	23.0	238	—	—	—	—	70	*	*
	Low- and middle-income	3,952.0	74,349	750	2.7	16.5	46.8	62	51	40
	Sub-Saharan Africa	463.9	22,240	330	0.2	12.5	15.5	51	65	52
	East Asia	1,538.0	14,017	540	5.2	8.7	5.6	66	41	29
	South Asia	1,106.8	5,158	320	1.8	8.3	7.5	57	72	59
	Europe, M. East, & N. Africa	395.6	11,420	2,000	2.4	13.2	25.8	64	53	41
	Latin America & Caribbean	413.6	20,293	1,840	1.9	29.4	117.4	67	19	17
	Severely indebted	495.5	20,057	1,730	2.0	28.3	107.9	66	23	20
	High-income economies	784.2	33,739	17,080	2.3	7.9	4.9	76	—	—
	OECD members	751.1	31,057	17,470	2.3	7.7	4.7	76	—	—
	Other	33.1	2,682	8,380	3.1	15.9	10.8	71	—	—
97	Saudi Arabia	14.0	2,150	6,200	3.8	17.2	−4.2	64	—	—
98	Spain	39.0	505	7,740	2.3	12.3	10.1	77	8	6
99	Ireland	3.5	70	7,750	2.0	12.0	8.0	74	—	—
100	Israel	4.4	21	8,650	2.7	25.2	136.6	76	7	5
101	Singapore	2.6	1	9,070	7.2	4.9	1.2	74	21	14
102	Hong Kong	5.7	1	9,220ᵇ	6.3	8.1	6.7	77	19	12
103	New Zealand	3.3	269	10,000	0.8	10.2	11.4	75	*	*
104	Australia	16.5	7,687	12,340	1.7	9.3	7.8	76	*	*
105	United Kingdom	57.1	245	12,810	1.8	11.1	5.7	75	*	*
106	Italy	57.4	301	13,330	3.0	11.4	11.0	77	4	*
107	Kuwait	2.0	18	13,400	−4.3	16.4	−3.9	73	37	30
108	Belgium	9.9	31	14,490	2.5	6.7	4.8	75	*	*
109	Netherlands	14.8	37	14,520	1.9	7.5	2.0	77	*	*
110	Austria	7.6	84	15,470	2.9	6.0	4.0	75	*	*
111	United Arab Emirates	1.5	84	15,770	—	—	0.1	71	—	—
112	France	55.9	552	16,090	2.5	8.4	7.1	76	*	*
113	Canada	26.0	9,976	16,960	2.7	7.1	4.6	77	*	*
114	Denmark	5.1	43	18,450	1.8	9.3	6.3	75	*	*
115	Germany, Fed. Rep.	61.3	249	18,480	2.5	5.2	2.8	75	*	*
116	Finland	5.0	338	18,590	3.2	10.5	7.1	75	*	*
117	Sweden	8.4	450	19,300	1.8	8.0	7.5	77	*	*
118	United States	246.3	9,373	19,840	1.6	6.5	4.0	76	*	*
119	Norway	4.2	324	19,990	3.5	7.7	5.6	77	*	*
120	Japan	122.6	378	21,020	4.3	7.7	1.3	78	*	*
121	Switzerland	6.6	41	27,500	1.5	5.3	3.8	77	*	*
	Total reporting economies	4,736.2	108,088	3,470	1.5	9.8	14.1	64	50	39
	Oil exporters	593.3	17,292	1,500	2.0	15.1	21.4	61	43	35
	Nonreporting nonmembers	364.5	25,399	—	—	—	—	70	—	—

*According to Unesco, illiteracy is less than 5%.

19

Table I-6 World Economy (continued)

Average annual growth rate (percent)

	GDP		Agriculture		Industry		(Manufacturing)		Services, etc.	
	1965–80	1980–88	1965–80	1980–88	1965–80	1980–88	1965–80	1980–88	1965–80	1980–88
Low-income economies	5.4	6.4	2.6	4.4	8.8	8.7	8.2	9.7	6.0	6.0
China and India	5.3	8.7	2.7	5.4	8.2	11.4	8.0	10.5	6.3	8.6
Other low-income	5.5	2.0	2.3	2.3	10.0	1.7	9.1	5.9	5.7	3.4
1 Mozambique	—	-2.8	—	-0.8	—	-7.1	—	—	—	-3.1
2 Ethiopia	2.7	1.4	1.2	-1.1	3.5	3.5	5.1	3.7	5.2	3.6
3 Chad	0.1	3.9	-0.3	2.6	-0.6	7.7	—	—	0.2	4.2
4 Tanzania	3.7	2.0	1.6	4.0	4.2	-2.0	5.6	-2.5	6.7	1.0
5 Bangladesh	2.4	3.7	1.5	2.1	3.8	4.9	6.8	2.4	3.4	5.2
6 Malawi	5.6	2.6	4.1	2.7	6.3	3.0	—	—	6.7	2.4
7 Somalia	3.4	3.2	—	3.9	—	2.3	—	-0.1	—	1.2
8 Zaire	1.4	1.9	—	3.2	—	2.5	—	1.7	—	0.3
9 Bhutan	—	—	—	—	—	—	—	—	—	—
10 Lao PDR	—	—	—	—	—	—	—	—	—	—
11 Nepal	1.9	4.7	1.1	4.4	—	—	—	—	—	—
12 Madagascar	1.8	0.6	—	2.2	—	-1.0	—	—	—	-0.1
13 Burkina Faso	—	5.5	—	6.4	—	3.7	—	—	—	5.5
14 Mali	3.9	3.2	2.8	0.3	1.8	8.1	—	—	7.6	5.8
15 Burundi	5.6	4.3	6.7	3.1	17.4	5.8	6.0	6.1	1.4	6.3
16 Uganda	0.8	1.4	1.2	0.3	-4.1	6.4	-3.7	2.3	1.1	3.4
17 Nigeria	6.9	-1.1	1.7	1.0	13.1	-3.2	14.6	-2.9	7.6	-0.4
18 Zambia	1.9	0.7	2.2	4.1	2.1	0.3	5.3	2.5	1.5	0.0
19 Niger	0.3	-1.2	-3.4	2.8	11.4	-4.3	—	—	3.4	-8.0
20 Rwanda	4.9	2.1	—	0.3	—	3.6	—	3.4	—	3.4
21 China	6.4	10.3	2.8	6.8	10.0	12.4	9.5	11.0	10.3	11.3
22 India	3.6	5.2	2.5	2.3	4.2	7.6	4.5	8.3	4.4	6.1
23 Pakistan	5.1	6.5	3.3	4.3	6.4	7.2	5.7	8.1	5.9	7.4
24 Kenya	6.4	4.2	4.9	3.3	9.8	2.8	10.5	4.6	6.4	5.5
25 Togo	4.5	0.5	1.9	4.2	6.8	0.0	—	-0.5	5.4	-1.7
26 Central African Rep.	2.6	2.1	2.1	2.6	5.3	2.0	—	0.2	2.0	1.7
27 Haiti	2.9	-0.2	—	—	—	—	—	—	—	—
28 Benin	2.1	2.4	—	4.2	—	5.8	—	7.4	—	-1.0
29 Ghana	1.4	2.1	1.6	0.5	1.4	1.9	2.5	3.1	1.1	4.9
30 Lesotho	5.7	2.9	—	1.8	—	1.6	—	12.4	—	4.1
31 Sri Lanka	4.0	4.3	2.7	2.7	4.7	4.4	3.2	6.2	4.6	5.3
32 Guinea	—	—	—	—	—	—	—	—	—	—
33 Yemen, PDR	—	—	—	—	—	—	—	—	—	—
34 Indonesia	8.0	5.1	4.3	3.1	11.9	5.1	12.0	13.1	7.3	6.4
35 Mauritania	2.0	1.6	-2.0	1.5	2.2	4.9	—	—	6.5	-0.5
36 Sudan	3.8	2.5	2.9	2.7	3.1	3.6	—	5.0	4.9	2.0
37 Afghanistan	2.9	—	—	—	—	—	—	—	—	—
38 Myanmar	—	—	—	—	—	—	—	—	—	—
39 Kampuchea, Dem.	—	—	—	—	—	—	—	—	—	—
40 Liberia	3.3	-1.3	5.5	1.2	2.2	-6.0	10.0	-5.0	2.4	-0.8
41 Sierra Leone	2.8	0.2	3.9	2.2	-0.8	-4.9	0.7	-2.0	4.3	0.7
42 Viet Nam	—	—	—	—	—	—	—	—	—	—
Middle-income economies	6.1	2.9	3.2	2.7	5.9	3.2	8.2	3.8	7.2	3.1
Lower-middle-income	6.5	2.6	3.3	2.8	7.8	2.5	7.9	2.4	7.0	2.6
43 Bolivia	4.5	-1.6	3.8	2.1	3.9	-5.7	5.9	-5.6	5.4	-0.2
44 Philippines	5.9	0.1	4.6	1.8	8.0	-1.8	7.5	-0.3	5.2	0.7
45 Yemen Arab Rep.	—	6.5	—	2.9	—	11.5	—	12.8	—	6.2
46 Senegal	2.0	3.3	1.3	3.2	4.8	3.8	3.5	3.4	1.3	3.2
47 Zimbabwe	5.0	2.7	2.4	2.5	—	1.7	—	2.1	—	3.4
48 Egypt, Arab Rep.	6.8	5.7	2.7	2.6	6.9	5.1	—	5.6	9.4	7.3
49 Dominican Rep.	7.9	2.2	6.3	0.8	10.9	2.5	8.9	1.0	7.3	2.5
50 Côte d'Ivoire	6.8	2.2	3.3	1.6	10.4	-2.4	9.1	8.2	8.6	4.2
51 Papua New Guinea	4.1	3.2	3.2	2.7	—	5.6	—	1.0	—	2.0
52 Morocco	5.6	4.2	2.4	6.6	6.1	2.8	—	4.2	6.8	4.2
53 Honduras	5.0	1.7	2.0	1.1	6.8	0.8	7.5	1.9	6.2	2.4
54 Guatemala	5.9	-0.2	—	—	—	—	—	—	—	—
55 Congo, People's Rep.	6.3	4.0	3.1	2.0	9.9	5.1	—	7.1	4.7	3.5
56 El Salvador	4.3	0.0	3.6	-1.4	5.3	0.4	4.6	0.3	4.3	0.7
57 Thailand	7.2	6.0	4.6	3.7	9.5	6.6	11.2	6.8	7.6	6.8
58 Botswana	14.2	11.4	9.7	-5.9	24.0	15.1	13.5	5.0	11.5	10.3
59 Cameroon	5.1	5.4	4.2	2.4	7.8	7.8	7.0	6.2	4.8	5.5
60 Jamaica	1.3	0.6	0.5	0.9	-0.1	0.0	0.4	1.6	2.7	0.9
61 Ecuador	8.7	2.0	3.4	4.3	13.7	2.2	11.5	0.6	7.6	1.1
62 Colombia	5.8	3.4	4.5	2.4	5.7	5.1	6.4	2.9	6.4	2.7
63 Paraguay	6.9	1.7	4.9	2.7	9.1	0.1	7.0	1.3	7.5	2.0
64 Tunisia	6.6	3.4	5.5	2.4	7.4	2.4	9.9	6.0	6.5	4.4
65 Turkey	6.3	5.3	3.2	3.6	7.2	6.7	7.5	7.9	7.6	5.1
66 Peru	3.9	1.1	1.0	3.6	4.4	0.4	3.8	1.6	4.3	1.2
67 Jordan	—	4.2	—	6.0	—	3.6	—	3.4	—	4.4

20

Table I-6 World Economy (continued)

Average annual growth rate (percent)

	GDP		Agriculture		Industry		(Manufacturing)		Services, etc.	
	1965–80	1980–88	1965–80	1980–88	1965–80	1980–88	1965–80	1980–88	1965–80	1980–88
68 Chile	1.9	1.9	1.6	3.8	0.8	2.2	0.6	2.0	2.7	1.3
69 Syrian Arab Rep.	8.7	0.5	4.8	0.5	11.8	1.4	—	—	9.0	0.2
70 Costa Rica	6.2	2.4	4.2	2.5	8.7	2.3	—	—	6.0	2.5
71 Mexico	6.5	0.5	3.2	1.2	7.6	−0.1	7.4	0.2	6.6	0.7
72 Mauritius	5.2	5.7	—	4.0	—	9.0	—	11.4	—	4.6
73 Poland	—	—	—	—	—	—	—	—	—	—
74 Malaysia	7.3	4.6	—	3.7	—	6.1	—	7.3	—	3.6
75 Panama	5.5	2.6	2.4	2.5	5.9	−0.8	4.7	0.7	6.0	3.5
76 Brazil	8.8	2.9	3.8	3.5	10.1	2.6	9.8	2.2	9.5	3.1
77 Angola	—	—	—	—	—	—	—	—	—	—
78 Lebanon	−1.2	—	—	—	—	—	—	—	—	—
79 Nicaragua	2.6	−0.3	3.3	−0.2	4.2	0.4	5.2	0.6	1.4	−0.9
Upper-middle-income	5.6	3.3	3.2	2.5	4.7	3.7	—	—	7.5	3.7
80 South Africa	3.8	1.3	—	1.7	—	0.2	—	0.2	—	2.6
81 Algeria	6.8	3.5	5.7	5.6	7.1	3.8	9.5	6.1	6.7	2.7
82 Hungary	5.6	1.6	2.7	2.4	6.4	1.0	—	—	6.2	1.9
83 Uruguay	2.4	−0.4	1.0	0.3	3.1	−1.8	—	−0.5	2.3	0.2
84 Argentina	3.5	−0.2	1.4	1.4	3.3	−0.8	2.7	−0.2	4.0	−0.2
85 Yugoslavia	6.0	1.4	3.1	1.2	7.8	1.3	—	—	5.5	1.4
86 Gabon	9.5	−0.2	—	—	—	—	—	—	—	—
87 Venezuela	3.7	0.9	3.9	3.8	1.5	−0.1	5.8	3.3	6.3	1.4
88 Trinidad and Tobago	5.1	−6.1	0.0	4.5	5.0	−8.6	2.6	−9.5	5.8	−3.4
89 Korea, Rep. of	9.6	9.9	3.0	3.7	16.4	12.6	18.7	13.5	9.6	8.9
90 Portugal	5.3	0.8	—	−0.9	—	1.0	—	—	—	1.3
91 Greece	5.6	1.4	2.3	−0.1	7.1	0.4	8.4	0.0	6.2	2.5
92 Oman	13.0	12.7	—	9.4	—	15.1	—	37.9	—	12.2
93 Libya	4.2	—	10.7	—	1.2	—	13.7	—	15.5	—
94 Iran, Islamic Rep.	6.2	—	4.5	—	2.4	—	10.0	—	13.6	—
95 Iraq—	—	—	—	—	—	—	—	—	—	—
96 Romania	—	—	—	—	—	—	—	—	—	—
Low- and middle-income	5.8	4.3	2.8	3.7	6.8	5.3	8.2	5.9	6.9	3.9
Sub-Saharan Africa	4.8	0.8	1.3	1.8	9.4	−0.8	8.7	0.2	5.0	1.4
East Asia	7.2	8.5	3.2	5.7	10.8	10.3	10.6	10.2	8.6	8.0
South Asia	3.7	5.1	2.5	2.5	4.4	7.3	4.6	7.9	4.5	6.1
Europe, M. East, & N. Africa	6.1	—	3.5	—	4.9	—	—	—	8.6	—
Latin America & Caribbean	6.0	1.5	3.3	2.5	6.0	1.1	7.0	1.3	6.6	1.6
Severely indebted	6.0	1.5	3.2	2.7	6.2	1.0	7.1	1.3	6.6	1.6
High-income economies	3.7	2.8	0.8	2.3	3.2	1.9	3.6	3.2	3.7	3.0
OECD members	3.6	2.9	0.8	2.2	3.1	2.2	3.6	3.2	3.7	3.0
Other	8.0	−1.3	—	12.7	—	−7.0	—	6.0	—	4.6
97 Saudi Arabia	11.3	−3.3	4.1	15.2	11.6	−6.0	8.1	7.9	10.5	2.6
98 Spain	4.6	2.5	2.6	0.9	5.1	0.4	5.9	0.4	4.1	2.1
99 Ireland	5.0	1.7	—	2.2	—	1.7	—	—	—	0.6
100 Israel	6.8	3.2	—	—	—	—	—	—	—	—
101 Singapore	10.1	5.7	2.8	−5.1	11.9	4.5	13.2	4.8	9.4	6.6
102 Hong Kong	8.6	7.3	—	—	—	—	—	—	—	—
103 New Zealand	2.4	2.2	—	3.3	—	4.2	—	3.5	—	2.0
104 Australia	4.0	3.3	2.7	4.4	3.0	2.2	1.3	1.1	5.7	3.7
105 United Kingdom	2.4	2.8	−1.6	3.4	−0.5	1.9	−1.2	1.5	2.2	2.5
106 Italy	4.3	2.2	0.8	1.0	4.0	1.1	5.1	1.9	4.1	2.7
107 Kuwait	1.2	−1.1	—	23.6	—	−2.3	—	1.4	—	−0.9
108 Belgium	3.8	1.4	0.4	2.5	4.4	1.1	4.6	2.3	3.7	1.2
109 Netherlands	3.8	1.6	4.7	4.1	4.0	0.8	4.8	—	4.4	1.6
110 Austria	4.1	1.7	2.1	0.7	4.3	1.1	4.5	1.6	4.2	1.9
111 United Arab Emirates	—	−4.5	—	9.3	—	−8.7	—	2.7	—	3.7
112 France	4.0	1.8	1.0	2.3	4.3	0.1	5.2	−0.4	4.6	2.4
113 Canada	5.1	3.3	0.8	2.7	3.5	3.0	3.9	3.6	6.9	3.2
114 Denmark	2.7	2.2	0.9	3.3	1.9	3.4	3.2	2.4	3.2	2.0
115 Germany, Fed. Rep.	3.3	1.8	1.4	1.9	2.8	0.4	3.3	1.0	3.7	2.1
116 Finland	4.0	2.8	0.0	−1.1	4.2	2.7	4.9	3.0	4.8	3.3
117 Sweden	2.9	1.7	−0.2	1.8	2.3	2.9	2.4	2.9	3.4	0.8
118 United States	2.7	3.3	1.0	3.2	1.7	2.9	2.5	3.9	3.4	3.3
119 Norway	4.4	3.8	−0.4	1.3	5.7	4.7	2.6	1.8	4.1	3.4
120 Japan	6.5	3.9	0.8	0.8	8.5	4.9	9.4	6.7	5.2	3.1
121 Switzerland	2.0	1.9	—	—	—	—	—	—	—	—
Total reporting economies	4.1	3.1	2.0	3.2	3.9	2.5	4.3	3.8	4.2	3.2
Oil exporters	6.4	1.0	3.1	2.7	6.3	−0.1	7.7	3.7	7.6	2.4
Nonreporting nonmembers	—	—	—	—	—	—	—	—	—	—

21

Table I-6 World Economy (continued)

	GDP (millions of dollars)		Agriculture		Industry		(Manufacturing)		Services, etc.	
					Distribution of gross domestic product (percent)					
	1965	1988	1965	1988	1965	1988	1965	1988	1965	1988
Low-income economies	161,340	886,620	44	33	28	36	21	—	28	32
China and India	117,730	610,250	44	32	32	40	24	—	24	28
Other low-income	42,660	273,080	45	33	17	27	9	—	38	40
1 Mozambique	—	1,100	—	62	—	20	—	—	—	18
2 Ethiopia	1,180	4,950	58	42	14	17	7	12	28	40
3 Chad	290	920	42	47	15	18	12	15	43	35
4 Tanzania	790	2,740	46	66	14	7	8	4	40	27
5 Bangladesh	4,380	19,320	53	46	11	14	5	7	36	40
6 Malawi	220	1,080	50	37	13	18	—	—	37	44
7 Somalia	220	970	71	65	6	9	3	5	24	25
8 Zaire	3,140	6,470	21	31	26	34	16	7	53	35
9 Bhutan	—	300	—	44	—	28	—	6	—	28
10 Lao PDR	—	500	—	59	—	20	—	7	—	21
11 Nepal	730	2,860	65	56	11	17	3	6	23	27
12 Madagascar	670	1,880	31	41	16	16	11	—	53	43
13 Burkina Faso	260	1,750	53	39	20	23	—	13	27	38
14 Mali	260	1,940	65	49	9	12	5	5	25	39
15 Burundi	150	960	—	56	—	15	—	10	—	29
16 Uganda	1,100	3,950	52	72	13	7	8	6	35	20
17 Nigeria	5,850	29,370	54	34	13	36	6	18	33	29
18 Zambia	1,060	4,000	14	14	54	43	6	25	32	43
19 Niger	670	2,400	68	36	3	23	2	9	29	41
20 Rwanda	150	2,310	75	38	7	22	2	15	18	40
21 China	67,200	372,320	44	32	39	46	31	33	17	21
22 India	50,530	237,930	44	32	22	30	16	19	34	38
23 Pakistan	5,450	34,050	40	26	20	24	14	17	40	49
24 Kenya	920	7,380	35	31	18	20	11	12	47	49
25 Togo	190	1,360	45	34	21	21	10	8	34	45
26 Central African Rep.	140	1,080	46	44	16	12	4	8	38	44
27 Haiti	350	2,500	—	31	—	38	—	15	—	31
28 Benin	220	1,710	59	40	8	13	—	6	33	47
29 Ghana	2,050	5,230	44	49	19	16	10	10	38	34
30 Lesotho	50	330	65	21	5	28	1	13	30	52
31 Sri Lanka	1,770	6,400	28	26	21	27	17	15	51	47
32 Guinea	—	2,540	—	30	—	32	—	5	—	38
33 Yemen, PDR	—	840	—	16	—	23	—	—	—	61
34 Indonesia	3,840	83,220	56	24	13	36	8	19	31	40
35 Mauritania	160	900	32	38	36	21	4	—	32	41
36 Sudan	1,330	11,240	54	33	9	15	4	8	37	52
37 Afghanistan	600	—	—	—	—	—	—	—	—	—
38 Myanmar	—	—	—	—	—	—	—	—	—	—
39 Kampuchea, Dem.	—	—	—	—	—	—	—	—	—	—
40 Liberia	270	990	27	37	40	28	3	5	34	35
41 Sierra Leone	320	1,270	34	46	28	12	6	3	38	42
42 Viet Nam	—	—	—	—	—	—	—	—	—	—
Middle-income economies	199,900	2,200,750	20	12	33	40	19	24	46	50
Lower-middle-income	111,840	1,061,910	22	14	28	38	19	25	50	50
43 Bolivia	710	4,310	23	24	31	27	15	17	46	49
44 Philippines	6,010	39,210	26	23	28	34	20	25	46	44
45 Yemen Arab Rep.	—	5,910	—	23	—	26	—	12	—	50
46 Senegal	810	4,980	25	22	18	29	14	19	56	49
47 Zimbabwe	960	5,650	18	11	35	43	20	31	47	46
48 Egypt, Arab Rep.	4,550	34,330	29	21	27	25	—	14	45	54
49 Dominican Rep.	890	4,630	23	23	22	34	16	16	55	43
50 Côte d'Ivoire	760	7,650	47	36	19	25	11	16	33	39
51 Papua New Guinea	340	3,520	42	34	18	31	—	9	41	36
52 Morocco	2,950	21,990	23	17	28	34	16	18	49	49
53 Honduras	460	3,860	40	25	19	21	12	13	41	54
54 Guatemala	1,330	8,100	—	—	—	—	—	—	—	—
55 Congo, People's Rep.	200	2,150	19	15	19	30	—	8	62	54
56 El Salvador	800	5,470	29	14	22	22	18	18	49	65
57 Thailand	4,390	57,950	32	17	23	35	14	24	45	48
58 Botswana	50	1,940	34	3	19	55	12	5	47	42
59 Cameroon	810	12,900	33	26	20	30	10	13	47	44
60 Jamaica	970	3,220	10	6	37	42	17	21	53	52
61 Ecuador	1,150	10,320	27	15	22	36	18	21	50	49
62 Colombia	5,910	39,070	27	19	27	34	19	20	47	47
63 Paraguay	440	6,040	37	30	19	25	16	17	45	46
64 Tunisia	880	8,750	22	14	24	32	9	16	54	54
65 Turkey	7,660	64,360	34	17	25	36	16	26	41	46
66 Peru	5,020	25,670	18	12	30	36	17	24	53	51
67 Jordan	—	3,900	—	10	—	25	—	12	—	65

Table I-6 World Economy (continued)

	GDP (millions of dollars)		Distribution of gross domestic product (percent)							
			Agriculture		Industry		(Manufacturing)		Services, etc.	
	1965	1988	1965	1988	1965	1988	1965	1988	1965	1988
68 Chile	5,940	22,080	9	—	40	—	24	—	52	—
69 Syrian Arab Rep.	1,470	14,950	29	38	22	16	—	—	49	46
70 Costa Rica	590	4,650	24	18	23	28	—	—	53	54
71 Mexico	21,640	176,700	14	9	27	35	20	26	59	56
72 Mauritius	190	1,600	16	13	23	33	14	25	61	54
73 Poland	—	—	—	—	—	—	—	—	—	—
74 Malaysia	3,130	34,680	28	—	25	—	9	—	47	—
75 Panama	660	5,490	18	9	19	18	12	8	63	73
76 Brazil	19,450	323,610	19	9	33	43	26	29	48	49
77 Angola	—	—	—	—	—	—	—	—	—	—
78 Lebanon	1,150	—	12	—	21	—	—	—	67	—
79 Nicaragua	570	3,200	25	21	24	34	18	24	51	46
Upper-middle-income	88,200	1,138,840	18	—	39	—	—	—	42	—
80 South Africa	10,540	78,970	10	6	42	45	23	25	48	49
81 Algeria	3,170	51,900	15	13	34	43	11	12	51	44
82 Hungary	—	28,000	—	14	—	37	—	—	—	49
83 Uruguay	930	6,680	15	11	32	29	—	24	53	60
84 Argentina	16,500	79,440	17	13	42	44	33	31	42	44
85 Yugoslavia	11,190	61,710	23	14	42	49	—	—	35	37
86 Gabon	230	3,320	26	11	34	51	—	—	40	38
87 Venezuela	9,820	63,750	6	6	40	36	—	22	55	58
88 Trinidad and Tobago	690	4,400	8	5	48	31	—	9	44	64
89 Korea, Rep. of	3,000	171,310	38	11	25	43	18	32	37	46
90 Portugal	3,740	41,700	—	9	—	37	—	—	—	54
91 Greece	5,270	40,900	24	16	26	29	16	18	49	56
92 Oman	60	8,150	61	3	23	43	0	6	16	54
93 Libya	1,500	—	5	—	63	—	3	—	33	—
94 Iran, Islamic Rep.	6,170	—	26	—	36	—	12	—	38	—
95 Iraq	2,430	—	18	—	46	—	8	—	36	—
96 Romania	—	—	—	—	—	—	—	—	—	—
Low- and middle-income	363,680	3,060,950	31	18	31	39	20	—	38	44
Sub-Saharan Africa	27,490	149,550	43	34	18	27	9	—	39	39
East Asia	92,420	893,410	41	22	35	43	27	—	24	36
South Asia	64,510	312,070	44	33	21	27	15	17	35	39
Europe, M. East, & N. Africa	69,200	—	24	—	34	—	—	—	40	—
Latin America & Caribbean	95,330	808,340	16	10	33	39	23	27	51	52
Severely indebted	105,150	897,390	17	10	34	39	23	27	50	52
High-income economies	1,391,700	13,867,530	5	—	41	—	30	—	55	—
OECD members	1,373,380	13,603,060	5	—	41	—	30	—	55	—
Other	11,020	234,370	6	—	54	—	11	—	41	—
97 Saudi Arabia	2,300	72,620	8	8	60	43	9	8	31	50
98 Spain	23,750	340,320	15	6	36	37	—	27	49	57
99 Ireland	2,340	27,820	—	10	—	38	—	—	—	52
100 Israel	3,590	44,960	—	—	—	—	—	—	—	—
101 Singapore	970	23,880	3	0	24	38	15	30	74	61
102 Hong Kong	2,150	44,830	2	0	40	29	24	22	58	70
103 New Zealand	5,410	39,800	—	10	—	33	—	23	—	57
104 Australia	22,920	245,950	9	4	39	34	26	18	51	61
105 United Kingdom	89,100	702,370	3	2	46	42	34	27	51	56
106 Italy	72,150	828,850	10	4	37	40	25	27	53	56
107 Kuwait	2,100	19,970	0	1	70	51	3	10	29	48
108 Belgium	16,840	153,810	5	2	42	34	31	24	53	64
109 Netherlands	19,640	228,280	—	5	—	37	—	24	—	58
110 Austria	9,480	127,200	9	4	46	45	33	32	45	51
111 United Arab Emirates	—	23,850	—	2	—	55	—	9	—	44
112 France	99,660	949,440	8	4	38	37	27	27	54	59
113 Canada	46,730	435,860	6	4	41	40	26	23	53	56
114 Denmark	8,940	90,530	9	5	36	37	23	25	55	58
115 Germany, Fed. Rep.	114,790	1,201,820	4	2	53	51	40	44	43	47
116 Finland	7,540	91,690	16	7	37	43	23	29	47	50
117 Sweden	19,880	159,880	6	4	40	43	28	30	53	54
118 United States	700,970	4,847,310	3	2	38	33	28	22	59	65
119 Norway	7,080	91,050	8	4	33	45	21	21	59	51
120 Japan	91,110	2,843,710	9	3	43	41	32	29	48	57
121 Switzerland	13,920	184,830	—	—	—	—	—	—	—	—
Total reporting economies	1,755,990	17,018,400	10	—	39	—	28	—	52	—
Oil exporters	77,910	921,070	19	12	32	35	14	16	48	51
Nonreporting nonmembers	—	—	—	—	—	—	—	—	—	—

Source: World Bank

23

PART I

People in Business

Chapter One

THE AVERAGE AMERICAN

Although few people would like to admit that they are "just average," finding the elusive average American is a big business. Statisticians, demographers, and marketing researchers track the lives and times of Americans from cradle to grave, collecting statistics about their jobs, their eating habits, their vacations, and even what goes on in their bedrooms. The everyman and everywoman who emerge from these data might be nobody in particular—no one, after all, has 1.8 children and has sex with 4.5 men during a lifetime. But that hardly matters. About $5 billion is spent every year collecting statistics on American life—how we spend our money, where we live, and what we want—simply because these facts are worth tens of billions of dollars to corporate planners marketing new products or government officials planning economic policy.

POPULATION

There are 252.5 million Americans in 1991, just waiting to be surveyed. That represents a dramatic increase from the beginning of this century, when there were 76 million Americans, or from 1790, when there were a mere 3.9 million Americans.

When the first census was taken in 1790, America was a nation of rural pioneers—95% of the population lived in rural areas or in towns with fewer than 2,500 people. It wasn't until 1920 that over half the population lived in towns with more than 2,500 people, but since then America has become a country of city slickers. Today, over three quarters (77%) of the population live in urban areas.

And despite the country's well-deserved reputation for pioneering the hinterlands, living near the beach remains popular. About 53% of all Americans live within 50 miles of the ocean.

POPULATION FORECASTS

Even if there are more Americans than ever before, parents are having fewer Americans, average or otherwise. Only half of the 65.8 million families in the 1990s have a child under 18, and the average American woman has only produced 1.8 kids during her lifetime, down from 3.7 children in the late 1950s—the height of the baby boom. A birth rate of 2.1 is necessary to sustain zero population growth if the country has no immigration.

As a result, the population of the United States increased only 10.3% between 1980 and the 1990 census, the second-smallest increase in American history. (The smallest came during the Great Depression.) In contrast, during the baby-boom decade of the 1950s the population rose 18.5%, and throughout the first half of the 19th century the population exploded at a rate of more than 30% a decade—faster than some third-world countries are growing today.

This means that if the average woman decides to produce 1.8 children during her life and the average American lives to be 81.2 years old, as government forecasters believe they will, then there will be nearly 268 million Americans in the year 2000. At that time, the country will be 13.3% black, 9.4% Hispanic, 3.6% other, and 74.2% white non-Hispanic. (The percentages add to over 100 because people of Spanish origin may be of any race— black, white, or Asian.) Some time in the year 2025 the population should top the 300 million mark.

By the year 2080 the face of America will have changed dramatically. The number of white non-Hispanics will fall from 192 million in 1990 to only 176 million in 2080, while the number of Hispanics will increase from 19.9 million to 59.6 million. The number of black Americans will grow from 31.4 million in 1990 to 55.7 million in 2080 while the number of members of other races will increase from 7.5 million to 23.4 million. In 2080, only about 56% of the country will be white non-Hispanic. About one fifth of the population will be Hispanic, followed by almost 18% black, and about 7.5% will be other races, including Asian.

THE AGING OF AMERICA

The average American is getting along in years. In 1820 the median age of the population was only 16.7, and by 1940 only 4.1% of the population was over 65. Today, however, 12.6% of the population is over 65 and the median age is 33, up from 27.9 in 1970. In the year 2000, when the baby-boom generation hits middle age, the government estimates that 35.9% of the population will be over 45 and 13.0% will be over 65. And in 2080, 73.1 million Americans, 23.5% of the population, will be over 65 and nearly half the population (47.3%) will be over 45. The number of people over 85 will hit 18.2 million in 2080, 5.9% of the population. Today only about 1.3% of the population is over 85.

But an older population isn't necessarily bad for business. If you think of the elderly as doddering old folks living on meager pensions, then you're at least 15 years out of date. Americans over 50 consume $800 billion worth of goods and services each year. They control one third of the country's net worth, even though they account for only one sixth of the population, and hold about 40% of all financial assets. The poverty rate of Americans over 65 has declined from 33% in 1959 to 12.2% today. The over-65 set has the largest disposable income of any age group, and as their numbers grow, the markets catering to those over 50 will boom.

The aging of America will also be good for those growing up and entering the job market in the last years of the 20th century. With fewer younger workers to provide goods and services for an aging population, economists expect wages and salaries to rise. Unlike many members of the baby-boom generation, who had to fight for scarce jobs and accept lower standards of living than their parents, the members of the baby-bust generation will have more career opportunities and disposable income.

The bad news is the cost of caring for an older America. With fewer and fewer workers bearing the tax burden of supporting social programs for the elderly, Social Security and pension funds are headed toward financial trouble. And as medical science manages to keep people alive longer and longer, the cost of health care will skyrocket. One study estimates that, in order to house the baby-boom generation during their last years, a 100-bed nursing home will have to open *every day, 365 days a year,* between now and the year 2000.

INCOME

The economic slowdown of the 1970s and early 1980s hit the average American squarely in the pocketbook. With adjustment for inflation, the median income of the average household actually declined between 1969 and 1983, falling from $31,534 in 1970 to $30,111 in 1982. White families saw their income slide from an average of $32,713 in 1970 to only $31,614 in 1982, while black families saw their paychecks dwindle from an average of $20,067 in 1970 to only $17,473 in 1982. Since then, however, an economic rebound has improved incomes. The American family now has a median income of $34,213, with whites earning $35,975, blacks $20,209, and Hispanics $21,769. Less encouraging are statistics on net worth (the value of a family's assets minus its debts). According to a 1991 Census Department study, American households had a median net worth of $35,752 in 1988, down from $37,012 in 1984. The net worth of the typical white household, $43,280, was more than 10 times that of the average black household, $4,170, and the typical married white couple was worth $62,390, much more than the average black couple, $17,640. As mentioned above, older Americans were wealthier than any other age group. Families headed by someone aged 55 to 64 had a median net worth of $83,750, while those aged 35 to 44 were worth $40,264. About 26.2% of all Americans were worth less than $5,000 and 56.9% were worth under $50,000.

But when it comes to income, not everyone's hurting. About 2% of all families, or about 1.3 million families, have a net worth of $1 million or more according to a recent study by the Federal Reserve. In terms of constant 1982 dollars, the number of people making more than $41,456 a year increased by 112% between 1969 and 1983. Today 25.7% of all families earn more than $50,000 a year, up from 17.4% in 1970.

As the rich have been getting richer, the poor have been getting poorer— or, at least, officially more numerous. By the government's count, only 11.4% of the population lived in poverty in 1978 but 13.1% do today. The most drastic increase in poverty has been among whites, not minorities. In 1973, 15.1 million whites lived in poverty (8.4%); by 1983 there were 24 million whites, about 12.1%, below the poverty line. But over time Americans have made progress in the war against poverty. In 1960, 22.2% of the population lived in poverty. And in the last few years the poverty rate has dropped again, to 13.1% (31.9 million people) in 1988. That year 20.8 million whites (10.1% of all whites) and 9.4 million blacks (31.6%) lived in poverty. About 5.4 million Hispanics (9.4%), who may be of any race, had incomes below the poverty line, which was $12,092 for a family of four in 1988.

PERSONAL CONSUMPTION

Out of each year's income, the average American spends $3,664 a year for food, $7,569 on housing, $4,600 on transportation, $1,135 on health, and $289 on booze. Over the course of the year, the average American eats some 93.7 pounds of fresh fruit, 89.8 pounds of fresh vegetables, 115 pounds of red meat, 596 pounds of dairy products, and 61.7 pounds of sugar. He or she drinks 24.1 gallons of beer, 2.4 gallons of wine, 44.8 gallons of soft drinks, 11.2 gallons of juice, 26.5 gallons of coffee, and 25.6 gallons of milk. Not surprisingly, about 62% of Americans are overweight.

Personal consumption also adds up to a lot of garbage. Americans produce 148.1 million tons of garbage a year. That is about 3.43 pounds of garbage every day of the year for every man, woman, and child, up from 2.5 pounds in 1960. At that rate, the average American would produce over 90,000 pounds of garbage during his or her life.

THE FAMILY

There are now about 92.8 million households and about 65.8 million families in the U.S., but the American family is no longer the happy, close-knit unit portrayed in *Father Knows Best,* with the pipe-smoking suburban commuter as the chief wage earner and a contented housewife who works, without pay, to raise her three children. Rising divorce rates, working mothers, fewer children, and a changing economy have all changed the way many families live. Since the family is the basic consumer unit, these changes are sending shock waves through the economy.

Rising divorce rates have changed the composition of many American families. Women who were married in the late 1970s were twice as likely to see their marriages break up as those who were married between 1960 and 1964. About half of all marriages involve someone who was previously married, up from 31% in 1970.

Broken marriages mean that more and more children are growing up in

Table 1-1 Income in America

Characteristic	All races[1] Aggregate money income (bil. dol.)	Mean income (dol.)	White Aggregate money income (bil. dol.)	Mean income (dol.)	Black Aggregate money income (bil. dol.)	Mean income (dol.)	Hispanic[2] Aggregate money income (bil. dol.)	Mean income (dol.)
Total	2,927.2	32,144	2,630.7	33,526	211.3	20,743	140.5	24,666
Age of householder:								
15–24 years old	102.0	19,504	90.7	20,630	8.5	12,573	10.4	18,601
25–34 years old	621.6	30,200	554.2	31,913	50.0	19,277	40.8	23,493
35–44 years old	763.8	39,529	676.0	41,154	60.4	26,647	39.2	28,737
45–54 years old	597.0	43,796	532.5	45,997	43.6	27,689	25.3	30,631
55–64 years old	447.3	34,818	410.7	36,445	26.7	20,174	16.8	24,474
65 years old and over	395.6	20,333	366.7	21,029	22.2	12,622	8.1	15,332
Region:								
Northeast	660.9	34,535	604.2	35,641	40.6	22,937	25.2	22,238
Midwest	691.9	30,886	640.4	31,945	40.7	20,171	9.4	24,470
South	929.2	29,928	808.5	32,130	108.1	19,735	43.4	23,347
West	645.3	34,918	577.6	35,424	21.9	23,776	62.6	26,936
Size of household:								
One person	380.1	17,363	340.6	18,048	32.6	12,355	11.4	13,547
Two persons	951.5	32,482	883.2	33,793	50.5	19,860	28.2	22,421
Three persons	608.0	37,615	543.0	39,645	45.2	23,754	29.5	25,663
Four persons	599.6	42,394	536.8	44,326	43.3	26,923	35.5	29,951
Five persons	251.8	41,413	219.5	43,687	21.1	26,588	18.8	27,841
Six persons	84.8	38,981	69.3	41,197	10.0	27,597	9.0	27,861
Seven persons or more	51.4	38,971	38.3	43,241	8.6	25,269	8.1	30,858
Education attainment of householder:								
Elementary school:								
Less than 8 years	102.5	15,579	81.2	16,431	17.5	12,494	25.1	16,279
8 years	90.2	17,509	80.0	17,816	8.8	15,143	6.8	17,603
High school:								
1–3 years	238.5	21,182	206.1	22,759	28.3	14,112	18.1	19,860
4 years	952.9	29,069	860.9	30,065	75.2	21,139	41.0	26,443
College:								
1–3 years	540.6	34,677	482.8	35,646	40.6	26,078	22.7	31,367
4 years or more	1,002.5	50,879	919.7	51,669	40.9	37,700	26.7	46,163
Occupation of longest job of householder:								
Total[3]	2,481.9	38,017	2,233.5	39,219	173.5	26,637	123.5	29,094
Managerial and professional specialty	966.9	52,465	892.2	53,036	41.4	40,714	30.0	46,845
Technical, sales, and administrative support	596.8	37,456	536.0	38,564	40.5	26,303	25.9	30,408
Service workers	163.2	23,039	128.4	24,542	28.9	18,188	14.0	22,086
Farming, forestry, and fishing	53.6	24,707	50.6	25,228	1.9	14,902	5.7	19,878
Precision production, crafts, and repair	378.6	35,130	350.6	35,429	21.1	30,532	20.9	27,876
Operators, fabricators, and laborers	320.4	29,664	273.6	30,343	39.5	25,681	26.8	24,956

[1]Includes other races not shown separately.
[2]Hispanic persons may be of any race.
[3]Includes in Armed Forces, not shown separately.
Source: U.S. Bureau of the Census, *Current Population Reports,* series P-60, No. 162.

single-parent homes. Only 7% of all married couples live in poverty, while over 45% of all households headed by a single mother are impoverished. Because single-parent homes headed by women usually are poorer, 20% of all kids under the age of 15 were living in poverty in 1986. While the median income for a married couple with children is $36,389, the income for a single-parent family headed by a woman is only $15,346.

Another revolution going on in the American family is the massive migration of women from unpaid household work into the labor market. Over half of all women are now in the labor force, and unlike women of earlier generations, many of these women have young children. Half of all mothers with children under the age of 1 year are in the labor force and over 29 million children under the age of 15 have working mothers. Nearly 18.2 million women have children under the age of 18. Yet only 2% of all employers run their own day-care centers and only 3.1% helped their employees pay for child-care expenses. As a result, the average working mother spends about $45 a week on child care.

Families are also more willing to postpone having children. To prevent

Table 1-2 Spending in America—Average Income and Expenditures

This chart shows what the average urban household spends on various kinds of products every year. It also breaks expenditures down for various kinds of consumers by age, region, and income. What is called a consumer unit here could be a single person, a family, or a group of unrelated people.

Characteristic	Income before taxes	Total expenditures	Food, total	Food at home Total	Cereal and bakery products	Meats, poultry, fish, and eggs	Dairy products	Fruits and vegetables	Food away from home	Alcoholic beverages
All consumer units	27,326	24,414	3,664	2,099	299	572	274	356	1,565	289
Age of reference person:										
Under 25 years old	12,621	14,368	2,204	1,046	141	245	150	170	1,158	310
25–34 years old	27,835	24,177	3,567	1,989	283	522	271	310	1,578	353
35–44 years old	36,240	31,473	4,638	2,538	370	684	334	413	2,100	359
45–54 years old	36,941	31,708	4,625	2,627	362	764	337	437	1,999	336
55–64 years old	31,038	25,707	3,887	2,310	312	668	291	404	1,577	257
65–74 years old	18,598	18,888	2,971	1,897	281	509	239	362	1,074	164
75 years old and over	12,912	12,230	2,104	1,496	232	393	192	311	609	74
Region of residence:										
Northeast	27,494	25,079	3,921	2,206	327	649	289	387	1,715	342
Midwest	25,772	23,021	3,458	1,975	284	536	260	317	1,483	251
South	26,479	23,292	3,443	1,957	271	539	248	324	1,486	244
West	30,373	27,309	4,019	2,379	333	592	322	424	1,640	356
Size of consumer unit:										
One person	15,006	14,693	1,988	981	139	239	130	188	1,007	261
Two persons	28,990	24,761	3,585	1,996	275	551	249	358	1,589	305
Three persons	33,055	28,549	4,209	2,456	342	685	319	389	1,753	294
Four persons	38,282	32,753	5,053	3,066	455	837	411	486	1,987	305
Five persons	35,141	31,976	5,624	3,401	491	962	458	546	2,223	328
Six persons or more	29,458	31,016	5,605	3,687	545	1,028	517	604	1,918	212
Single consumers:										
No earner	8,757	10,250	1,571	1,048	158	257	141	215	524	78
One earner	18,795	17,417	2,234	943	129	228	124	173	1,292	367
Consumer units of two or more persons:										
No earner	14,249	15,423	2,992	2,115	310	603	260	390	877	147
One earner	26,597	24,447	3,934	2,408	345	661	321	408	1,526	259
Two earners	37,710	31,202	4,389	2,468	347	679	321	398	1,921	341
Three or more	45,217	38,378	6,050	3,405	488	955	450	551	2,644	378
Husband and wife consumer units:										
Total husband and wife consumer units	36,114	30,659	4,580	2,666	380	732	348	443	1,914	297
Husband and wife only	32,307	26,541	3,757	2,081	286	572	256	377	1,676	286
Husband and wife with children:										
Oldest child under 6	35,505	29,414	3,815	2,435	333	639	336	379	1,379	248
Oldest child 6 to 17	37,263	32,899	5,206	3,033	464	803	414	466	2,173	299
Oldest child 18 or over	45,238	37,966	5,994	3,440	485	1,000	451	567	2,554	374
One parent, at least one child under 18 years.	14,737	16,521	2,933	1,869	265	551	247	295	1,064	171
Single person and other	17,237	16,590	2,401	1,281	181	336	167	232	1,120	293
Occupation of reference person:										
Self-employed workers	32,372	30,291	4,477	2,345	330	620	304	416	2,132	388
Wage and salary earners:										
Managers and professionals	44,232	34,782	4,524	2,289	326	608	306	387	2,234	392
Technical, sales, and clerical workers	29,607	26,343	3,824	2,067	287	569	268	334	1,757	361
Service workers	18,551	18,726	3,082	1,794	253	506	235	290	1,288	235
Construction workers and mechanics	30,549	26,568	3,913	2,261	323	626	307	338	1,652	332
Operators, fabricators, and laborers	24,796	22,144	3,678	2,289	329	616	300	371	1,389	265
Retired	15,383	15,905	2,761	1,807	268	488	226	353	954	160
Income before taxes:										
Complete reporters of income	27,326	24,776	3,753	2,143	306	586	279	358	1,610	303
Quintiles of income:										
Lowest 20 percent	4,611	10,355	1,916	1,321	190	364	173	241	595	122
Second 20 percent	11,954	15,686	2,772	1,830	270	506	236	316	942	189
Third 20 percent	20,943	21,708	3,575	2,061	300	555	274	338	1,514	325
Fourth 20 percent	33,276	29,603	4,332	2,441	347	668	314	393	1,891	340
Highest 20 percent	65,750	46,470	6,164	3,060	426	836	395	503	3,104	539
Incomplete reporting of income	NA	22,668	3,321	1,923	268	517	258	344	1,398	233

Total	Housing Shelter	Fuel, utilities, and public services	Household operations and furnishings	House-keeping supplies	Apparel and services	Transportation Vehicle purchases	Gasoline and motor oil	All other transportation	Health care	Pensions and Social Security	Other expenditures	Personal taxes
7,569	4,154	1,671	1,403	341	1,446	2,022	888	1,690	1,135	1,881	3,831	2,455
4,307	2,700	813	645	149	887	1,688	609	1,112	338	775	2,137	928
8,099	4,803	1,500	1,484	312	1,442	2,019	894	1,630	766	2,037	3,371	2,513
9,835	5,517	1,975	1,952	391	2,006	2,698	1,108	2,137	1,085	2,710	4,899	3,574
8,985	4,827	2,068	1,650	440	1,943	2,760	1,180	2,281	1,255	2,913	5,429	3,877
7,290	3,573	1,901	1,422	394	1,392	2,168	976	1,854	1,383	2,256	4,244	2,901
5,965	2,918	1,597	1,099	352	1,035	1,269	667	1,338	1,688	610	3,179	961
4,521	2,306	1,323	657	235	545	422	332	639	1,596	139	1,856	632
8,101	4,590	1,753	1,406	352	1,707	1,907	786	1,766	1,051	1,796	3,701	1,964
6,833	3,488	1,682	1,332	331	1,309	2,051	868	1,578	1,099	1,760	3,813	2,275
7,014	3,665	1,735	1,278	337	1,378	2,106	937	1,550	1,204	1,794	3,624	2,519
8,850	5,338	1,467	1,695	350	1,456	1,967	939	1,981	1,152	2,261	4,328	3,022
5,039	3,080	1,036	738	186	884	1,011	467	1,042	695	941	2,363	1,429
7,551	4,108	1,695	1,387	361	1,401	1,950	897	1,774	1,423	1,926	3,948	2,665
8,653	4,626	1,968	1,693	365	1,619	2,719	1,068	2,014	1,221	2,384	4,368	2,906
10,065	5,288	2,114	2,168	495	1,985	3,008	1,218	2,158	1,198	2,761	5,004	3,761
9,493	5,000	2,209	1,845	439	1,945	2,584	1,261	2,115	1,283	2,470	4,871	2,523
8,949	4,651	2,274	1,537	486	2,291	2,337	1,260	1,908	1,268	1,939	5,245	1,768
4,184	2,271	1,093	641	178	532	500	259	572	993	11	1,550	351
5,568	3,581	1,000	796	190	1,095	1,328	596	1,334	511	1,517	2,867	2,083
5,197	2,430	1,520	882	366	894	747	574	946	1,578	39	2,311	488
7,931	4,217	1,842	1,477	395	1,479	1,769	870	1,590	1,287	1,607	3,719	2,176
9,558	5,296	1,936	1,935	391	1,795	2,783	1,143	2,185	1,222	2,943	4,842	3,714
9,929	5,093	2,412	1,936	488	2,319	4,122	1,588	2,820	1,368	3,437	6,369	4,005
9,189	4,867	2,024	1,870	428	1,754	2,679	1,152	2,137	1,455	2,552	4,864	3,340
8,006	4,277	1,792	1,546	390	1,407	2,103	962	1,923	1,611	2,133	4,352	3,059
10,389	5,689	1,811	2,486	402	1,681	2,749	981	1,858	1,138	2,637	3,920	3,407
10,165	5,474	2,142	2,096	452	2,040	2,717	1,220	2,049	1,273	2,785	5,143	3,376
9,370	4,544	2,414	1,914	498	2,132	4,142	1,606	3,039	1,536	3,280	6,492	4,461
5,808	3,309	1,384	875	240	1,132	1,400	530	912	492	843	2,298	984
5,507	3,264	1,209	808	226	1,037	1,176	566	1,169	775	1,081	2,585	1,474
9,116	4,864	2,118	1,737	397	1,560	2,047	1,024	1,964	1,658	2,368	5,688	2,254
10,835	6,272	1,916	2,243	404	2,256	2,823	1,064	2,461	1,223	3,467	5,739	4,741
8,010	4,570	1,653	1,441	347	1,688	2,404	951	1,878	999	2,286	3,941	3,081
5,937	3,281	1,410	921	325	1,160	1,777	745	1,218	657	1,343	2,570	1,383
7,624	4,092	1,749	1,452	331	1,353	2,763	1,206	1,854	983	2,308	4,232	2,980
6,426	3,420	1,596	1,124	286	1,123	2,152	1,065	1,624	835	1,833	3,144	2,173
5,237	2,502	1,470	927	338	836	958	557	1,099	1,583	234	2,481	692
7,491	4,074	1,646	1,404	368	1,455	2,016	881	1,690	1,135	2,121	3,929	2,455
3,823	2,106	1,078	453	187	548	614	372	565	734	130	1,530	118
5,108	2,759	1,358	708	283	938	1,216	641	1,060	1,061	569	2,132	530
6,485	3,480	1,595	1,043	367	1,211	1,801	891	1,456	1,146	1,486	3,332	1,443
8,519	4,566	1,858	1,662	433	1,839	2,699	1,120	2,105	1,211	2,857	4,580	2,903
13,506	7,450	2,337	3,148	572	2,738	3,747	1,382	3,261	1,523	5,555	8,056	7,273
8,138	4,653	1,826	1,426	234	1,430	2,055	930	1,720	1,140	388	3,312	NA

Source: U.S. Bureau of Labor Statistics, *Consumer Expenditure Survey: Integrated Survey Data, 1984–87,* Bulletin 2333.

any surprises, 36.7% of American women use some form of contraceptive, the most popular method being the pill, followed by the condom. And when birth control fails, women increasingly turn to abortions. There are now 422 abortions for every 1,000 live births. Thanks to birth control and declining fertility rates, immigrants will play an even more important role in the economy of the future. The Hudson Institute estimates that immigrants will fill 21% of all the new jobs created between now and the year 2000.

There is a reason why many women are using contraceptives: half of all married women have sex at least one year before they are married. Only 30% of all married women were virgins in the month they were married; nearly 73.3% of all single women between 20 and 24 have had sex.

Even though it's been said that Americans are becoming a country of family planners, government studies show that many Americans still arrive unexpectedly. Exactly 28% of all children are "mistimed" according to one study and another 9.6% are "unwanted." About 24.5% of all children are

Table 1-3   U.S. Population and Projections

(In thousands, except as indicated. Includes Armed Forces abroad.)

Year	Total	Under 5	5–13	14–17	18–24	25–34	35–44	45–64	65 and over	85 and over
Total:										
1985	238,631	18,453	29,654	14,731	28,739	41,786	32,004	44,652	28,608	2,696
1990	249,657	19,198	32,189	12,950	25,794	43,529	37,847	46,453	31,697	3,313
2000	267,955	17,626	34,382	15,381	24,601	36,415	43,743	60,886	34,921	4,926
2080	310,762	17,202	31,650	14,316	25,296	37,237	36,222	73,748	73,090	18,227
Spanish origin:										
1985	17,286	1,999	2,997	1,282	2,349	3,254	2,129	2,391	885	67
1990	19,887	2,282	3,472	1,353	2,386	3,629	2,788	2,851	1,126	95
2000	25,225	2,496	4,382	1,825	2,766	3,804	3,803	4,430	1,719	168
2080	59,571	3,436	6,311	2,868	5,114	7,510	7,735	14,427	12,170	2,616
White non-Hispanic:										
1985	186,791	12,930	21,390	10,940	21,603	32,253	25,611	37,024	25,039	2,414
1990	192,040	13,243	22,705	9,266	18,919	32,874	29,664	37,836	25,531	2,928
2000	196,918	11,496	23,235	10,595	17,200	26,011	32,783	48,097	29,502	4,286
2080	175,996	9,430	17,430	7,866	13,863	20,473	21,020	41,415	44,526	11,841
Black:										
1985	29,074	3,057	4,448	2,149	4,136	5,212	3,404	4,339	2,329	189
1990	31,412	3,215	5,098	1,944	3,798	5,880	4,295	4,624	2,579	257
2000	35,753	3,079	5,776	2,545	3,773	5,316	5,811	6,479	2,975	412
2080	55,698	3,181	5,842	2,652	4,676	6,773	6,981	13,337	12,255	2,834
Other races:										
1985	6,444	583	982	431	784	1,254	980	1,025	403	29
1990	7,456	593	1,112	461	826	1,381	1,261	1,298	522	38
2000	9,548	704	1,250	525	1,022	1,509	1,577	2,142	818	69
2080	23,439	1,385	2,514	1,120	1,982	2,982	3,003	5,522	4,931	1,101

Percent distribution

All races	Total	Under 5	5–13	14–17	18–24	25–34	35–44	45–64	65+	85+
1985	100	7.7	12.4	6.2	12.0	17.5	13.4	18.7	12.0	1.1
1990	100	7.7	12.9	5.2	10.3	17.4	15.2	18.6	12.7	1.3
2000	100	6.6	12.8	5.7	9.2	13.6	16.3	22.7	13.0	1.8
2080	100	5.5	10.2	4.6	8.1	12.0	12.3	23.7	23.5	5.9

	All races*	Spanish origin	White non-Hispanic	Black	Other
1985	100	7.2	78.3	12.2	2.7
1990	100	8.0	76.9	12.6	3.0
2000	100	9.4	74.2	13.3	3.6
2080	100	19.2	56.6	17.9	7.5

*Subtotals do not add to 100% because people of Spanish origin may be of any race.
Source: U.S. Bureau of the Census, *Current Population Reports,* series P-25, No. 995.

now born to unmarried women: 16.7% of all white children, 10.1% of all Asian children, 29.5% of all Hispanic children, and 62.2% of all black children are born out of wedlock.

However, many of those who are having kids are waiting until they're older and more financially secure. In 1970 only 19% of all women had their first child after the age of 25; by the 1980s 36% were having kids for the first time after 25.

All of these trends have changed the face of the average home. The birth of fewer children and an aging population have shrunk the size of the average American household. Today there are only 2.62 people in the average household, down from 3.33 in 1960. Almost one quarter of all households (24.0%) were made up of a single person, up from 9.1% in 1950. In contrast, only 27.0% consisted of a married couple with children under the age of 18, down from 45.1% in 1950. Married couples with no children under 18 living with them make up 29.9% of all households, while unrelated people living together comprise 28.5%.

Yet despite all the strains that have been pulling many families apart, most Americans are still staying close to home. When asked how far they live from their parents, 71% of all adults said they lived within 100 miles, and 44% lived within 10 miles, according to a survey by Ethan Allen, Inc.

Chapter Two
AMERICA AT WORK

HIGHLIGHTS AND TRENDS

• In 1870, approximately half of all American workers (53%) could be found down on the farm. But by 1920 more Americans (11.2 million) were employed in manufacturing than agriculture (10.8 million). And over the last forty years the labor force has changed its appearance once again, exchanging its blue collars for white and pink collars. Today over three quarters of all nonagricultural workers are employed in service-producing industries.

• And the trend toward service jobs will continue, with 92% of all the 18.1 million new job openings between 1988 and 2000 being created in service-producing industries.

• Major changes will hit the labor force during the rest of the century. As population growth slows, the labor force is expected to grow at a slower rate than it did during the 1970s. But it will still increase by 1.2% a year, faster than the population, which will grow about 0.8% a year through 2000.

• Minorities, immigrants, and women will make up more and more of the labor force. Women will account for 62% of the increase in the labor force between now and 2000, while immigrants will account for about 21% of the growth in the labor force and blacks 16.7%, Hispanics 27%, and Asians 10%.

GETTING A JOB

There's good news and bad news at the employment office in the 1990s. The good news is demographic. In contrast to the 1970s and early and mid-1980s, when the baby-boom generation hit the labor market, producing keen competition for scarce jobs, the employment outlook for the 1990s is much brighter. Between now and 2000, the labor force is expected to grow about 1.2% a year, faster than the population, which will grow only about half as fast, 0.7% a year.

That means better pay and lower unemployment for many workers, trends that will put money in the bank for many younger workers. If the baby-boom generation continues to produce smaller families, fewer younger workers will be entering the labor force. With less competition for jobs, the sons and daughters of the baby boomers will be able to command better salaries, face less competition for career advancement, and see shorter lines at the unemployment office.

The bad news is that some of the new jobs won't pay as well as many jobs—like unionized blue-collar jobs—that once made up the backbone of the labor force. Service industries will produce 16.7 million new jobs, virtually all of the 18.1 million jobs created between now and 2000, and the 20 occupations showing the largest job growth are all service jobs. For example, there will be more new jobs created between now and 2000 for salespersons (730,000) than any other occupation. Yet, sales workers earn only $258 a week, compared to the average paycheck of $415. Seven of the ten largest job-producing occupations—salesworkers, waiters, janitors, clerks, nurse's aides, receptionists, and secretaries—all pay less than the average wage.

But don't buy the argument that the economy is only producing low-paying jobs. A field where employees earn $569 a week, registered nursing, will produce 613,000 new jobs. And about 479,000 new jobs will be created for general managers and top executives and 382,000 for truck drivers, both high-paying occupations.

But the availability of fewer younger workers will be hard on some industries. By 2080 only 8.1% of the population will be between the ages of 18 and 24, down from 9.2% in the year 2000 and 13.1% in 1982. That will cut the number of people in college, will decrease the amount of money spent for education, and will probably cut the number of jobs available. Employers who are already having a hard time filling low-paying service jobs behind the cash register or the restaurant counter will undoubtedly be forced to up the ante. But the hardest-hit employer could be the Armed Forces. Since the Pentagon is still the largest employer of young people, the business of war is likely to get increasingly expensive and high-tech.

THE JOBS OF THE FUTURE

Overall, employment is expected to grow 15.3% to 136.2 million by 2000, according to Labor Department projections. The service economy will create more jobs than any other part of the economy (16.7 million) as service-industry employment grows 20.9% or about 1.6% a year to 96.4 million in the year 2000. About 760,000 construction jobs will be created as the number of construction workers grows 14.8% to 5.9 million at the start of the 21st century. The entrepreneurial spirit of the 1980s will continue through the rest of the century as the number of self-employed nonfarmworkers increases by 1.2 million (13.8%) to 9.9 million.

But mining, manufacturing, and agriculture will not fare so well. The number of manufacturing jobs will drop 1.6% from 19.4 million in 1988 to 19.1 million in 2000, with 216,000 jobs lost in the durable goods sector of manufacturing and 100,000 lost in nondurable goods. Mining will see employment drop 2.2% to 705,000, and woes in the farm belt will cut the number of agricultural jobs by 134,000 to only 3.1 million, a 4.1% plunge. As a result, the number of people employed in agriculture, mining, and manufacturing will be way below their 1979 levels of 3.4 million, 958,000, and 21.0 million respectively.

Between 1988 and 2000, Labor Department forecasters believe that government employment will grow by 1.6 million to 19 million. Since problems with the federal deficit are expected to keep the number of federal employees virtually constant, almost all that growth will occur at the state and local levels.

WORKING IN AMERICA

An economic rebound has improved civilian employment, bringing the number of Americans with jobs up to 118.5 million in January of 1991, up from 108.9 million in 1985 and 100.9 million in 1980. And the job market continues to reflect the long-term growth of the service economy. Between 1946 and 1990, as many Americans exchanged a blue collar for a white or pink collar, service-producing industries grew from 58.6% to 77.1% of nonagricultural employment.

Yet during the same period, employment in goods-producing industries—construction, mining, and manufacturing—declined from 41.4% to only 22.9%. Agricultural employment also declined, falling to only 3.2 million—down from 8.3 million in 1946. Manufacturing now accounts for only 17.4% of all civilian nonagricultural jobs, down from 35.3% in 1946 and 27.3% in 1970.

Government employment in an age of fiscal austerity has grown from 16.2 million in 1980 to 18.3 million in 1990. In contrast, about 18.8 million jobs were created in the private nonagricultural sector during that period. (See Part III, "The Heavy Hand," for a discussion of government, and also see the chapters "Services," "Manufacturing," and "Agriculture.")

These employment trends are likely to continue into the 21st century. By the year 2000, manufacturing, mining, and construction will account for 21.0% of nonagricultural jobs, down from 29.5% in 1976. Meanwhile, services will account for nearly four fifths of all jobs (79%), up from 70.5% in 1976. Manufacturing will employ only 15.6% of all nonagricultural workers, down from 24.0% in 1970, and government's share of the job market will drop from 18.8% to 15.6%. Even so, the U.S. will enter the 21st century with only about 100,000 more factory workers than government bureaucrats.

Women workers are one of the fastest-growing sectors of the economy, up 24.7% between 1980 and 1990. About 58% of all women were in the labor force—either looking for work or employed—in 1990, up from 33.9% in 1950 and 51.5% in 1980. In contrast, the percentage of men working or looking for a job is actually declining. The labor-force participation rate for men dropped from 86.7% in 1950 to 76% in 1990. (See the chapter "Working Women.")

Not everyone has been helped by the economic recovery of the past five years. But unemployment has declined from a postwar high of 10.6% at the end of 1982 to 5.4% in 1990 before a recession increased unemployment to over 6% in early 1991.

Unemployment rates for minorities have remained disturbingly high: 11.3% for blacks in 1990 (down from 18.9% in 1982) and 8.0% for Hispanics (down from 15.3% in 1982).

In 1990, nonagricultural workers put in 206 billion hours at work every week, up from 182 billion in 1985. But over the long term the average American has been putting in less and less hours at his or her job. In 1990, the average nonsupervisory production worker worked about 34.8 hours per week, about five hours less than the average working week in 1947.

This trend toward a shorter and shorter workweek can be traced to the rise of retail and service industries, areas of the economy with larger numbers of part-time workers. In 1990, about 20.3 million Americans worked part-time. About 5.1 million of those workers said they worked part-time because there wasn't enough work at their job or they couldn't find full-time work. But most (15.2 million) said they wanted to work part-time.

By the 21st century these demographic trends will play a major role in reshaping the labor force. An older America will mean an older labor force, with the median age of the American worker rising to 38.9 years. That's up

---

LOTTERY WINNERS

People grouse about their jobs, but how many people would up and quit if they came into a windfall? Not many if you judge by lottery winners. Within a year of hitting the jackpot, only 24% of state lottery winners stopped working, and that included 13% who were of an age to retire. Only 9% of those who won between $500,000 and $1,000,000 dropped out of the rat race.

---

from 34.7 years in 1979 but still slightly less than 1962, when the typical age was 40.5 years. The proportion of young workers aged 16 to 24 will also drop from 18.5% in 1988 to only 15.9% in 2000.

Women will continue to enter the labor force in record numbers. They will account for about 62% of the labor force growth through the end of the century and by the year 2000 will account for nearly half of the labor force (47.3%), up from 38.5% in 1972 and 42.1% in 1979.

The American workplace in the 21st century will also have more minorities than ever before. By the year 2000, Hispanics will account for 10.1% of the labor force, up from 5% in 1979 and 7.4% in 1988. Asians will hold 4.0% of all jobs, up from 2.3% in 1979 and 3.0% in 1988. The proportion of blacks will grow more slowly, hitting 11.7% in 2000, up from 10.2% in 1979 and 10.9% in 1988.

Table 2-1 Working in America

These charts show the working-age population, the labor force, employment, unemployment, and the labor-force participation rate. Remember that the labor force includes people who are working and those who are looking for work. Employment includes part-time workers. The labor-force participation rate shows the percentage of working-age people who are employed or looking for work. The increasing labor-force participation rate for women shows, for example, that more and more women are employed or looking for work.

Year or month	Civilian noninstitutional population	Resident Armed Forces	Labor force including resident Armed Forces	Employment including resident Armed Forces	Civilian labor force Total	Employment Total	Employment Agricultural	Employment Nonagricultural	Unemployment	Unemployment rate All workers	Unemployment rate Civilian workers	Civilian labor force participation rate	Civilian employment/population ratio
					Thousands of persons 14 years of age and over						**Percent**		
1929					49,180	47,630	10,450	37,180	1,550		3.2		
1933					51,590	38,760	10,090	28,670	12,830		24.9		
1939					55,230	45,750	9,610	36,140	9,480		17.2		
1940	99,840				55,640	47,520	9,540	37,980	8,120		14.6	55.7	47.6
1941	99,900				55,910	50,350	9,100	41,250	5,560		9.9	-56.0	50.4
1942	98,640				56,410	53,750	9,250	44,500	2,660		4.7	57.2	54.5
1943	94,640				55,540	54,470	9,080	45,390	1,070		1.9	58.7	57.6
1944	93,220				54,630	53,960	8,950	45,010	670		1.2	58.6	57.9
1945	94,090				53,860	52,820	8,580	44,240	1,040		1.9	57.2	56.1
1946	103,070				57,520	55,250	8,320	46,930	2,270		3.9	55.8	53.6
1947	106,018				60,168	57,812	8,256	49,557	2,356		3.9	56.8	54.5
					Thousands of persons 16 years of age and over								
1947	101,827				59,350	57,038	7,890	49,148	2,311		3.9	58.3	56.0
1948	103,068				60,621	58,343	7,629	50,714	2,276		3.8	58.8	56.6
1949	103,994				61,286	57,651	7,658	49,993	3,637		5.9	58.9	55.4
1950	104,995	1,169	63,377	60,087	62,208	58,918	7,160	51,758	3,288	5.2	5.3	59.2	56.1
1951	104,621	2,143	64,160	62,104	62,017	59,961	6,726	53,235	2,055	3.2	3.3	59.2	57.3
1952	105,231	2,386	64,524	62,636	62,138	60,250	6,500	53,749	1,883	2.9	3.0	59.0	57.3
1953	107,056	2,231	65,246	63,410	63,015	61,179	6,260	54,919	1,834	2.8	2.9	58.9	57.1
1954	108,321	2,142	65,785	62,251	63,643	60,109	6,205	53,904	3,532	5.4	5.5	58.8	55.5
1955	109,683	2,064	67,087	64,234	65,023	62,170	6,450	55,722	2,852	4.3	4.4	59.3	56.7
1956	110,954	1,965	68,517	65,764	66,552	63,799	6,283	57,514	2,750	4.0	4.1	60.0	57.5
1957	112,265	1,948	68,877	66,019	66,929	64,071	5,947	58,123	2,859	4.2	4.3	59.6	57.1
1958	113,727	1,847	69,486	64,883	67,639	63,036	5,586	57,450	4,602	6.6	6.8	59.5	55.4
1959	115,329	1,788	70,157	66,418	68,369	64,630	5,565	59,065	3,740	5.3	5.5	59.3	56.0
1960	117,245	1,861	71,489	67,639	69,628	65,778	5,458	60,318	3,852	5.4	5.5	59.4	56.1
1961	118,771	1,900	72,359	67,646	70,459	65,746	5,200	60,546	4,714	6.5	6.7	59.3	55.4
1962	120,153	2,061	72,675	68,763	70,614	66,702	4,944	61,759	3,911	5.4	5.5	58.8	55.5
1963	122,416	2,006	73,839	69,768	71,833	67,762	4,687	63,076	4,070	5.5	5.7	58.7	55.4
1964	124,485	2,018	75,109	71,323	73,091	69,305	4,523	64,782	3,786	5.0	5.2	58.7	55.7
1965	126,513	1,946	76,401	73,034	74,455	71,088	4,361	66,726	3,366	4.4	4.5	58.9	56.2
1966	128,058	2,122	77,892	75,017	75,770	72,895	3,979	68,915	2,875	3.7	3.8	59.2	56.9
1967	129,874	2,218	79,565	76,590	77,347	74,372	3,844	70,527	2,975	3.7	3.8	59.6	57.3
1968	132,028	2,253	80,990	78,173	78,737	75,920	3,817	72,103	2,817	3.5	3.6	59.6	57.5
1969	134,335	2,238	82,972	80,140	80,734	77,902	3,606	74,296	2,832	3.4	3.5	60.1	58.0
1970	137,085	2,118	84,889	80,796	82,771	78,678	3,463	75,215	4,093	4.8	4.9	60.4	57.4
1971	140,216	1,973	86,355	81,340	84,382	79,367	3,394	75,972	5,016	5.8	5.9	60.2	56.6
1972	144,126	1,813	88,847	83,966	87,034	82,153	3,484	78,669	4,882	5.5	5.6	60.4	57.0
1973	147,096	1,774	91,203	86,838	89,429	85,064	3,470	81,594	4,365	4.8	4.9	60.8	57.8
1974	150,120	1,721	93,670	88,515	91,949	86,794	3,515	83,279	5,156	5.5	5.6	61.3	57.8
1975	153,153	1,678	95,453	87,524	93,775	85,846	3,408	82,438	7,929	8.3	8.5	61.2	56.1
1976	156,150	1,668	97,826	90,420	96,158	88,752	3,331	85,421	7,406	7.6	7.7	61.6	56.8
1977	159,033	1,656	100,665	93,673	99,009	92,017	3,283	88,734	6,991	6.9	7.1	62.3	57.9
1978	161,910	1,631	103,882	97,679	102,251	96,048	3,387	92,661	6,202	6.0	6.1	63.2	59.3
1979	164,863	1,597	106,559	100,421	104,962	98,824	3,347	95,477	6,137	5.8	5.8	63.7	59.9
1980	167,745	1,604	108,544	100,907	106,940	99,303	3,364	95,938	7,637	7.0	7.1	63.8	59.2
1981	170,130	1,645	110,315	102,042	108,670	100,397	3,368	97,030	8,273	7.5	7.6	63.9	59.0
1982	172,271	1,668	111,872	101,194	110,204	99,526	3,401	96,125	10,678	9.5	9.7	64.0	57.8
1983	174,215	1,676	113,226	102,510	111,550	100,834	3,383	97,450	10,717	9.5	9.6	64.0	57.9
1984	176,383	1,697	115,241	106,702	113,544	105,005	3,321	101,685	8,539	7.4	7.5	64.4	59.5
1985	178,206	1,706	117,167	108,856	115,461	107,150	3,179	103,971	8,312	7.1	7.2	64.8	60.1
1986	180,587	1,706	119,540	111,303	117,834	109,597	3,163	106,434	8,237	6.9	7.0	65.3	60.7
1987	182,753	1,737	121,602	114,177	119,865	112,440	3,208	109,232	7,425	6.1	6.2	65.6	61.5
1988	184,613	1,709	123,378	116,677	121,669	114,968	3,169	111,800	6,701	5.4	5.5	65.9	62.3
1989	186,393	1,688	125,557	119,030	123,869	117,342	3,199	114,142	6,528	5.2	5.3	66.5	63.0
1990	188,049	1,637	126,424	119,550	124,787	117,914	3,186	114,728	6,874	5.4	5.5	66.4	62.7

Table 2-1 Working in America (continued)

Year or month	Total	Civilian Total	Males	Females	Both sexes 16–19 years	White	Black and other	Black	Total	Civilian Total	Males	Females	Both sexes 16–19 years	White	Black and other	Black
		Labor force participation rate								Employment/population ratio						
1948		58.8	86.6	32.7	52.5					56.6	83.5	31.3	47.7			
1949		58.9	86.4	33.1	52.2					55.4	81.3	31.2	45.2			
1950	59.7	59.2	86.4	33.9	51.8				56.6	56.1	82.0	32.0	45.5			
1951	60.1	59.2	86.3	34.6	52.2				58.2	57.3	84.0	33.1	47.9			
1952	60.0	59.0	86.3	34.7	51.3				58.2	57.3	83.9	33.4	46.9			
1953	59.7	58.9	86.0	34.4	50.2				58.0	57.1	83.6	33.3	46.4			
1954	59.6	58.8	85.5	34.6	48.3	58.2	64.0		56.4	55.5	81.0	32.5	42.3	55.2	58.0	
1955	60.0	59.3	85.4	35.7	48.9	58.7	64.2		57.5	56.7	81.8	34.0	43.5	56.5	58.7	
1956	60.7	60.0	85.5	36.9	50.9	59.4	64.9		58.2	57.5	82.3	35.1	45.3	57.3	59.5	
1957	60.3	59.6	84.8	36.9	49.6	59.1	64.4		57.8	57.1	81.3	35.1	43.9	56.8	59.3	
1958	60.1	59.5	84.2	37.1	47.4	58.9	64.8		56.1	55.4	78.5	34.5	39.9	55.3	56.7	
1959	59.9	59.3	83.7	37.1	46.7	58.7	64.3		56.7	56.0	79.3	35.0	39.9	55.9	57.5	
1960	60.0	59.4	83.3	37.7	47.5	58.8	64.5		56.8	56.1	78.9	35.5	40.5	55.9	57.9	
1961	60.0	59.3	82.9	38.1	46.9	58.8	64.1		56.1	55.4	77.6	35.4	39.1	55.3	56.2	
1962	59.5	58.8	82.0	37.9	46.1	58.3	63.2		56.3	55.5	77.7	35.6	39.4	55.4	56.3	
1963	59.3	58.7	81.4	38.3	45.2	58.2	63.0		56.1	55.4	77.1	35.8	37.4	55.3	56.2	
1964	59.4	58.7	81.0	38.7	44.5	58.2	63.1		56.4	55.7	77.3	36.3	37.3	55.5	57.0	
1965	59.5	58.9	80.7	39.3	45.7	58.4	62.9		56.9	56.2	77.5	37.1	38.9	56.0	57.8	
1966	59.8	59.2	80.4	40.3	48.2	58.7	63.0		57.6	56.9	77.9	38.3	42.1	56.8	58.4	
1967	60.2	59.6	80.4	41.1	48.4	59.2	62.8		58.0	57.3	78.0	39.0	42.2	57.2	58.2	
1968	60.3	59.6	80.1	41.6	48.3	59.3	62.2		58.2	57.5	77.8	39.6	42.2	57.4	58.0	
1969	60.8	60.1	79.8	42.7	49.4	59.9	62.1		58.7	58.0	77.6	40.7	43.4	58.0	58.1	
1970	61.0	60.4	79.7	43.3	49.9	60.2	61.8		58.0	57.4	76.2	40.8	42.3	57.5	56.8	
1971	60.7	60.2	79.1	43.4	49.7	60.1	60.9		57.2	56.6	74.9	40.4	41.3	56.8	54.9	
1972	60.9	60.4	78.9	43.9	51.9	60.4	60.2	59.9	57.5	57.0	75.0	41.0	43.5	57.4	54.1	53.7
1973	61.3	60.8	78.8	44.7	53.7	60.8	60.5	60.2	58.3	57.8	75.5	42.0	45.9	58.2	55.0	54.5
1974	61.7	61.3	78.7	45.7	54.8	61.4	60.3	59.8	58.3	57.8	74.9	42.6	46.0	58.3	54.3	53.5
1975	61.6	61.2	77.9	46.3	54.0	61.5	59.6	58.8	56.5	56.1	71.7	42.0	43.3	56.7	51.4	50.1
1976	62.0	61.6	77.5	47.3	54.5	61.8	59.8	59.0	57.3	56.8	72.0	43.2	44.2	57.5	52.0	50.8
1977	62.6	62.3	77.7	48.4	56.0	62.5	60.4	59.8	58.3	57.9	72.8	44.5	46.1	58.6	52.5	51.4
1978	63.5	63.2	77.9	50.0	57.8	63.3	62.2	61.5	59.7	59.3	73.8	46.4	48.3	60.0	54.7	53.6
1979	64.0	63.7	77.8	50.9	57.9	63.9	62.2	61.4	60.3	59.9	73.8	47.5	48.5	60.6	55.2	53.8
1980	64.1	63.8	77.4	51.5	56.7	64.1	61.7	61.0	59.6	59.2	72.0	47.7	46.6	60.0	53.6	52.3
1981	64.2	63.9	77.0	52.1	55.4	64.3	61.3	60.8	59.4	59.0	71.3	48.0	44.6	60.0	52.6	51.3
1982	64.3	64.0	76.6	52.6	54.1	64.3	61.6	61.0	58.2	57.8	69.0	47.7	41.5	58.8	50.9	49.4
1983	64.4	64.0	76.4	52.9	53.5	64.3	62.1	61.5	58.3	57.9	68.8	48.0	41.5	58.9	51.0	49.5
1984	64.7	64.4	76.4	53.6	53.9	64.6	62.6	62.2	59.9	59.5	70.7	49.5	43.7	60.5	53.6	52.3
1985	65.1	64.8	76.3	54.5	54.5	65.0	63.3	62.9	60.5	60.1	70.9	50.4	44.4	61.0	54.7	53.4
1986	65.6	65.3	76.3	55.3	54.7	65.5	63.7	63.3	61.1	60.7	71.0	51.4	44.6	61.5	55.4	54.1
1987	65.9	65.6	76.2	56.0	54.7	65.8	64.3	63.8	61.9	61.5	71.5	52.5	45.5	62.3	56.8	55.6
1988	66.2	65.9	76.2	56.6	55.3	66.2	64.0	63.8	62.6	62.3	72.0	53.4	46.8	63.1	57.4	56.3
1989	66.8	66.5	76.4	57.4	55.9	66.7	64.7	64.2	63.3	63.0	72.5	54.3	47.5	63.8	58.2	56.9
1990	66.6	66.4	76.1	57.5	53.7	66.8	63.7	63.3	63.0	62.7	71.9	54.3	45.4	63.6	57.3	56.2

Source: Department of Labor, Bureau of Labor Statistics.

Table 2-2   The Work and Earnings of America

This chart shows the number of workers in various nonagricultural industries from 1960 to 1990. The next part of the chart shows average weekly earnings from 1964 to 1990.

Year and month	Total	Total private	Goods-producing Total	Mining	Construction	Manufacturing	Total	Transportation and public utilities	Wholesale trade	Retail trade	Finance, insurance, and real estate	Services	Federal	State	Local
1960	54,189	45,836	20,434	712	2,926	16,796	33,755	4,004	3,153	8,238	2,628	7,378	2,270	1,536	4,547
1961	53,999	45,404	19,857	672	2,859	16,326	34,142	3,903	3,142	8,195	2,688	7,619	2,279	1,607	4,708
1962	55,549	46,660	20,451	650	2,948	16,853	35,098	3,906	3,207	8,359	2,754	7,982	2,340	1,668	4,881
1963	56,653	47,429	20,640	635	3,010	16,995	36,013	3,903	3,258	8,520	2,830	8,277	2,358	1,747	5,121
1964	58,283	48,686	21,005	634	3,097	17,274	37,278	3,951	3,347	8,812	2,911	8,660	2,348	1,856	5,392
1965	60,765	50,689	21,926	632	3,232	18,062	38,839	4,036	3,477	9,239	2,977	9,036	2,378	1,996	5,700
1966	63,901	53,116	23,158	627	3,317	19,214	40,743	4,158	3,608	9,637	3,058	9,498	2,564	2,141	6,080
1967	65,803	54,413	23,308	613	3,248	19,447	42,495	4,268	3,700	9,906	3,185	10,045	2,719	2,302	6,371
1968	67,897	56,058	23,737	606	3,350	19,781	44,160	4,318	3,791	10,308	3,337	10,567	2,737	2,442	6,660
1969	70,384	58,189	24,361	619	3,575	20,167	46,023	4,442	3,919	10,785	3,512	11,169	2,758	2,533	6,904
1970	70,880	58,325	23,578	623	3,588	19,367	47,302	4,515	4,006	11,034	3,645	11,548	2,731	2,664	7,158
1971	71,214	58,331	22,935	609	3,704	18,623	48,278	4,476	4,014	11,338	3,772	11,797	2,696	2,747	7,437
1972	73,675	60,341	23,668	628	3,889	19,151	50,007	4,541	4,127	11,822	3,906	12,276	2,684	2,859	7,790
1973	76,790	63,058	24,893	642	4,097	20,154	51,897	4,656	4,291	12,315	4,046	12,857	2,663	2,923	8,146
1974	78,265	64,095	24,794	697	4,020	20,077	53,471	4,725	4,447	12,539	4,148	13,441	2,724	3,039	8,407
1975	76,945	62,259	22,600	752	3,525	18,323	54,345	4,542	4,430	12,630	4,165	13,892	2,748	3,179	8,758
1976	79,382	64,511	23,352	779	3,576	18,997	56,030	4,582	4,562	13,193	4,271	14,551	2,733	3,273	8,865
1977	82,471	67,344	24,346	813	3,851	19,682	58,125	4,713	4,723	13,792	4,467	15,302	2,727	3,377	9,023
1978	86,697	71,026	25,585	851	4,229	20,505	61,113	4,923	4,985	14,556	4,724	16,252	2,753	3,474	9,446
1979	89,823	73,876	26,461	958	4,463	21,040	63,363	5,136	5,221	14,972	4,975	17,112	2,773	3,541	9,633
1980	90,406	74,166	25,658	1,027	4,346	20,285	64,748	5,146	5,292	15,018	5,160	17,890	2,866	3,610	9,765
1981	91,156	75,126	25,497	1,139	4,188	20,170	65,659	5,165	5,376	15,172	5,298	18,619	2,772	3,640	9,619
1982	89,566	73,729	23,813	1,128	3,905	18,781	65,753	5,082	5,296	15,161	5,341	19,036	2,739	3,640	9,458
1983	90,200	74,330	23,334	952	3,948	18,434	66,866	4,954	5,286	15,595	5,468	19,694	2,774	3,662	9,434
1984	94,496	78,472	24,727	966	4,383	19,378	69,769	5,159	5,574	16,526	5,689	20,797	2,807	3,734	9,482
1985	97,519	81,125	24,859	927	4,673	19,260	72,660	5,238	5,736	17,336	5,955	21,999	2,875	3,832	9,687
1986	99,525	82,832	24,558	777	4,816	18,965	74,967	5,255	5,774	17,909	6,283	23,053	2,899	3,893	9,901
1987	102,200	85,190	24,708	717	4,967	19,024	77,492	5,372	5,865	18,462	6,547	24,235	2,943	3,967	10,100
1988	105,536	88,150	25,173	713	5,110	19,350	80,363	5,527	6,055	19,077	6,649	25,669	2,971	4,076	10,339
1989	108,413	90,644	25,326	700	5,200	19,426	83,087	5,648	6,271	19,580	6,724	27,096	2,988	4,175	10,606
1990p	110,330	92,035	25,004	735	5,205	19,064	85,326	5,838	6,361	19,790	6,833	28,209	3,086	4,284	10,925

40

Table 2-2 The Work and Earnings of America (continued)
Average weekly earnings

	Total private	Mining	Construction	Manufacturing	Transportation and public utilities	Wholesale trade	Retail trade	Finance, insurance, and real estate	Services
1964	$91.33	$117.74	$132.06	$102.97	$118.78	$102.36	$64.81	$85.77	$70.05
1965	95.45	123.52	138.38	107.53	125.14	106.27	66.65	88.85	73.60
1966	98.82	130.24	146.26	112.19	128.13	111.08	68.50	92.21	76.92
1967	101.84	135.89	154.95	114.49	130.82	115.85	70.86	95.70	80.30
1968	107.73	142.71	164.49	122.51	138.85	121.89	74.93	101.70	84.08
1969	114.61	154.80	181.54	129.51	147.74	129.74	78.67	108.56	90.62
1970	119.83	164.40	195.45	133.33	155.93	136.91	82.31	112.79	96.52
1971	127.31	172.14	211.67	142.44	168.82	143.68	87.51	118.02	103.04
1972	136.90	189.14	221.19	154.71	187.86	151.42	92.03	122.94	110.62
1973	145.39	201.40	235.89	166.46	203.31	159.74	96.45	129.34	117.49
1974	154.76	219.14	249.25	176.80	217.48	170.11	102.55	137.68	126.22
1975	163.53	249.31	266.08	190.79	233.44	182.42	108.63	147.89	134.73
1976	175.45	273.90	283.73	209.32	256.71	194.15	114.56	155.51	143.53
1977	189.00	301.20	295.65	228.90	278.90	208.76	121.54	165.42	153.59
1978	203.70	332.88	318.69	249.27	302.80	227.87	130.14	178.03	163.89
1979	219.91	365.07	342.99	269.34	325.58	247.65	138.83	190.92	175.36
1980	235.10	397.06	367.78	288.62	351.25	267.13	147.24	209.68	190.98
1981	255.20	438.75	399.26	318.00	382.18	290.75	157.99	228.73	209.16
1982	267.26	459.88	426.82	330.26	402.48	309.23	163.83	245.68	225.87
1983	280.70	479.40	442.97	354.08	420.81	328.25	171.13	263.68	239.04
1984	292.86	503.58	458.51	374.03	438.13	341.78	174.47	278.04	247.25
1985	299.09	519.93	464.46	386.37	450.30	351.08	174.81	289.20	256.49
1986	304.85	525.81	466.75	396.01	458.64	357.57	175.80	304.49	265.93
1987	312.50	531.70	480.44	406.31	471.58	365.30	178.80	316.37	276.03
1988	322.02	541.44	495.73	418.81	475.69	380.24	183.62	325.25	289.49
1989	334.24	569.75	512.41	430.09	490.53	394.82	188.72	341.53	306.11
1990p	346.04	601.97	524.49	442.27	503.76	411.48	195.26	357.64	321.44

p = Preliminary.
Source: U.S. Department of Labor.

Table 2-3   U.S. Unemployment
(percent; monthly data seasonally adjusted)

Year or month	All civilian workers	White Total	White Males Total	White Males 16–19 years	White Males 20 years and over	White Females Total	White Females 16–19 years	White Females 20 years and over	Black Total	Black Males Total	Black Males 16–19 years	Black Males 20 years and over	Black Females Total	Black Females 16–19 years	Black Females 20 years and over
											Black and other				
1948	3.8	3.5	3.4			3.8			5.9	5.8			6.1		
1949	5.9	5.6	5.6			5.7			8.9	9.6			7.9		
1950	5.3	4.9	4.7			5.3			9.0	9.4			8.4		
1951	3.3	3.1	2.6			4.2			5.3	4.9			6.1		
1952	3.0	2.8	2.5			3.3			5.4	5.2			5.7		
1953	2.9	2.7	2.5			3.1			4.5	4.8			4.1		
1954	5.5	5.0	4.8	13.4	4.4	5.5	10.4	5.1	9.9	10.3	14.4	9.9	9.2	20.6	8.4
1955	4.4	3.9	3.7	11.3	3.3	4.3	9.1	3.9	8.7	8.8	13.4	8.4	8.5	19.2	7.7
1956	4.1	3.6	3.4	10.5	3.0	4.2	9.7	3.7	8.3	7.9	15.0	7.4	8.9	22.8	7.8
1957	4.3	3.8	3.6	11.5	3.2	4.3	9.5	3.8	7.9	8.3	18.4	7.6	7.3	20.2	6.4
1958	6.8	6.1	6.1	15.7	5.5	6.2	12.7	5.6	12.6	13.7	26.8	12.7	10.8	28.4	9.5
1959	5.5	4.8	4.6	14.0	4.1	5.3	12.0	4.7	10.7	11.5	25.2	10.5	9.4	27.7	8.3
1960	5.5	5.0	4.8	14.0	4.2	5.3	12.7	4.6	10.2	10.7	24.0	9.6	9.4	24.8	8.3
1961	6.7	6.0	5.7	15.7	5.1	6.5	14.8	5.7	12.4	12.8	26.8	11.7	11.9	29.2	10.6
1962	5.5	4.9	4.6	13.7	4.0	5.5	12.8	4.7	10.9	10.9	22.0	10.0	11.0	30.2	9.6
1963	5.7	5.0	4.7	15.9	3.9	5.8	15.1	4.8	10.8	10.5	27.3	9.2	11.2	34.7	9.4
1964	5.2	4.6	4.1	14.7	3.4	5.5	14.9	4.6	9.6	8.9	24.3	7.7	10.7	31.6	9.0
1965	4.5	4.1	3.6	12.9	2.9	5.0	14.0	4.0	8.1	7.4	23.3	6.0	9.2	31.7	7.5
1966	3.8	3.4	2.8	10.5	2.2	4.3	12.1	3.3	7.3	6.3	21.3	4.9	8.7	31.3	6.6
1967	3.8	3.4	2.7	10.7	2.1	4.6	11.5	3.8	7.4	6.0	23.9	4.3	9.1	29.6	7.1
1968	3.6	3.2	2.6	10.1	2.0	4.3	12.1	3.4	6.7	5.6	22.1	3.9	8.3	28.7	6.3
1969	3.5	3.1	2.5	10.0	1.9	4.2	11.5	3.4	6.4	5.3	21.4	3.7	7.8	27.6	5.8
1970	4.9	4.5	4.0	13.7	3.2	5.4	13.4	4.4	8.2	7.3	25.0	5.6	9.3	34.5	6.9
1971	5.9	5.4	4.9	15.1	4.0	6.3	15.1	5.3	9.9	9.1	28.8	7.3	10.9	35.4	8.7
1972	5.6	5.1	4.5	14.2	3.6	5.9	14.2	4.9	10.0	8.9	29.7	6.9	11.4	38.4	8.8
											Black				
1972	5.6	5.1	4.5	14.2	3.6	5.9	14.2	4.9	10.4	9.3	31.7	7.0	11.8	40.5	9.0
1973	4.9	4.3	3.8	12.3	3.0	5.3	13.0	4.3	9.4	8.0	27.8	6.0	11.1	36.1	8.6
1974	5.6	5.0	4.4	13.5	3.5	6.1	14.5	5.1	10.5	9.8	33.1	7.4	11.3	37.4	8.8
1975	8.5	7.8	7.2	18.3	6.2	8.6	17.4	7.5	14.8	14.8	38.1	12.5	14.8	41.0	12.2
1976	7.7	7.0	6.4	17.3	5.4	7.9	16.4	6.8	14.0	13.7	37.5	11.4	14.3	41.6	11.7
1977	7.1	6.2	5.5	15.0	4.7	7.3	15.9	6.2	14.0	13.3	39.2	10.7	14.9	43.4	12.3
1978	6.1	5.2	4.6	13.5	3.7	6.2	14.4	5.2	12.8	11.8	36.7	9.3	13.8	40.8	11.2
1979	5.8	5.1	4.5	13.9	3.6	5.9	14.0	5.0	12.3	11.4	34.2	9.3	13.3	39.1	10.9
1980	7.1	6.3	6.1	16.2	5.3	6.5	14.8	5.6	14.3	14.5	37.5	12.4	14.0	39.8	11.9
1981	7.6	6.7	6.5	17.9	5.6	6.9	16.6	5.9	15.6	15.7	40.7	13.5	15.6	42.2	13.4
1982	9.7	8.6	8.8	21.7	7.8	8.3	19.0	7.3	18.9	20.1	48.9	17.8	17.6	47.1	15.4
1983	9.6	8.4	8.8	20.2	7.9	7.9	18.3	6.9	19.5	20.3	48.8	18.1	18.6	48.2	16.5
1984	7.5	6.5	6.4	16.8	5.7	6.5	15.2	5.8	15.9	16.4	42.7	14.3	15.4	42.6	13.5
1985	7.2	6.2	6.1	16.5	5.4	6.4	14.8	5.7	15.1	15.3	41.0	13.2	14.9	39.2	13.1
1986	7.0	6.0	6.0	16.3	5.3	6.1	14.9	5.4	14.5	14.8	39.3	12.9	14.2	39.2	12.4
1987	6.2	5.3	5.4	15.5	4.8	5.2	13.4	4.6	13.0	12.7	34.4	11.1	13.2	34.9	11.6
1988	5.5	4.7	4.7	13.9	4.1	4.7	12.3	4.1	11.7	11.7	32.7	10.1	11.7	32.0	10.4
1989	5.3	4.5	4.5	13.7	3.9	4.5	11.5	4.0	11.4	11.5	31.9	10.0	11.4	33.0	9.8
1990	5.5	4.7	4.8	14.2	4.3	4.6	12.6	4.1	11.3	11.8	32.1	10.4	10.8	30.0	9.6

Source: Department of Labor, Bureau of Labor Statistics.

Table 2-4 Jobs and Money: Pay and Employment in Various Occupations

This chart shows how many people are employed in various occupations and their median weekly earnings. Numbers are in thousands.

	1990					
	Both sexes		Men		Women	
Occupation	Number of workers	Median weekly earnings	Number of workers	Median weekly earnings	Number of workers	Median weekly earnings
Total, 16 years and over	85,082	$415	49,015	$485	36,068	$348
Managerial and professional specialty	22,858	608	12,263	731	10,595	511
Executive, administrative, and managerial	11,165	604	6,401	742	4,764	485
Administrators and officials, public administration	484	634	286	710	198	549
Administrators, protective services	54	606	43	[1]	12	[1]
Financial managers	455	688	252	837	202	558
Personnel and labor relations managers	117	684	51	881	66	604
Purchasing managers	109	738	80	789	29	[1]
Managers, marketing, advertising, and public relations	468	797	321	902	147	616
Administrators, education and related fields	474	724	243	819	231	588
Managers, medicine and health	158	636	55	788	103	592
Managers, properties and real estate	254	419	114	517	139	383
Management-related occupations	3,282	545	1,600	656	1,681	480
Accountants and auditors	1,186	533	550	644	636	483
Underwriters, and other financial officers	719	592	380	741	340	483
Management analysts	98	768	62	868	36	[1]
Personnel, training, and labor relations specialists	360	582	144	695	216	508
Buyers, wholesale and retail trade, except farm products	159	483	73	581	86	393
Construction inspectors	68	579	64	587	4	[1]
Inspectors and compliance officers, except construction	182	582	138	605	44	[1]
Professional specialty	11,693	610	5,863	720	5,831	534
Engineers, architects, and surveyors	1,866	809	1,708	818	158	725
Architects	76	695	58	731	17	[1]
Engineers	1,769	814	1,629	822	141	736
Aerospace engineers	104	830	97	855	7	[1]
Chemical engineers	67	890	58	920	8	[1]
Civil engineers	212	790	200	794	12	[1]
Electrical and electronic engineers	568	848	520	856	49	[1]
Industrial engineers	202	764	182	779	20	[1]
Mechanical engineers	296	805	284	811	12	[1]
Mathematical and computer scientists	808	734	510	803	298	631
Computer systems analysts and scientists	542	744	351	799	191	661
Operations and systems researchers and analysts	217	696	130	781	87	597
Natural scientists	357	661	261	691	96	613
Chemists, except biochemists	119	676	89	718	30	[1]
Biological and life scientists	74	602	43	[1]	32	[1]
Health diagnosing occupations	316	824	232	920	83	685
Physicians	266	892	198	978	68	802
Health assessment and treating occupations	1,662	600	258	663	1,404	596
Registered nurses	1,181	608	76	616	1,104	608
Pharmacists	117	794	73	811	44	[1]
Dietitians	71	454	7	[1]	64	457
Therapists	234	536	61	587	173	521
Inhalation therapists	50	516	21	[1]	29	[1]
Physical therapists	56	525	16	[1]	41	[1]
Therapists, n.e.c.	56	477	17	[1]	39	[1]
Physicians' assistants	60	510	41	[1]	19	[1]
Teachers, college and university	540	747	376	808	164	620
Teachers, except college and university	3,175	522	913	594	2,263	505
Teachers, prekindergarten and kindergarten	298	344	6	[1]	292	341
Teachers, elementary school	1,311	519	200	575	1,111	513
Teachers, secondary school	1,058	589	527	610	531	571
Teachers, special education	238	510	37	[1]	202	506
Counselors, educational and vocational	183	595	75	695	108	563
Librarians, archivists, and curators	148	493	28	[1]	120	484
Librarians	133	489	21	[1]	112	479
Social scientists and urban planners	241	603	125	677	116	515
Economists	89	689	54	769	36	[1]
Psychologists	119	553	52	605	68	514
Social, recreation, and religious workers	908	423	465	446	442	408
Social workers	496	445	163	483	333	427
Recreation workers	80	307	28	[1]	52	288
Clergy	267	433	246	441	22	[1]
Religious workers, n.e.c.	64	387	29	[1]	35	[1]
Lawyers and judges	417	1,052	306	1,184	111	834
Lawyers	390	1,045	285	1,178	105	875
Writers, artists, entertainers, and athletes	1,072	499	604	581	468	423
Technical writers	58	673	33	[1]	25	[1]
Designers	338	500	188	616	150	381
Actors and directors	59	594	36	[1]	23	[1]
Painters, sculptors, craft artists, and artist printmakers	70	412	38	[1]	33	[1]
Photographers	51	410	35	[1]	16	[1]

Table 2-4 Jobs and Money: Pay and Employment in Various Occupations (continued)

Occupation	Both sexes Number of workers	Both sexes Median weekly earnings	Men Number of workers	Men Median weekly earnings	Women Number of workers	Women Median weekly earnings
Editors and reporters	208	$513	108	$588	100	$452
Public relations specialists	134	581	56	623	79	524
Technical, sales, and administrative support	25,799	378	9,596	496	16,202	332
Technicians and related support	3,218	493	1,747	570	1,470	417
Health technologists and technicians	978	398	191	467	787	387
Clinical laboratory technologists and technicians	239	445	61	482	178	431
Health record technologists and technicians	70	342	5	(¹)	65	334
Radiologic technicians	97	481	24	(¹)	73	468
Licensed practical nurses	319	377	19	(¹)	299	377
Engineering and related technologists and technicians	895	509	730	532	165	398
Electrical and electronic technicians	339	533	286	552	53	449
Drafting occupations	247	499	204	520	43	(¹)
Surveying and mapping technicians	67	446	65	450	2	(¹)
Science technicians	203	475	143	501	60	400
Biological technicians	54	415	30	(¹)	24	(¹)
Chemical technicians	83	524	61	550	22	(¹)
Technicians, except health, engineering, and science	1,141	599	683	672	458	506
Airplane pilots and navigators	76	898	74	910	2	(¹)
Computer programmers	544	654	349	691	195	573
Legal assistants	194	475	39	(¹)	155	470
Sales occupations	8,197	401	4,666	505	3,531	292
Supervisors and proprietors	2,407	437	1,539	509	868	327
Sales representatives, finance and business services	1,558	514	870	639	687	418
Insurance sales	388	513	237	608	151	441
Real estate sales	341	507	161	686	180	405
Securities and financial services sales	225	707	164	805	61	528
Advertising and related sales	128	504	61	523	68	477
Sales occupations, other business services	475	469	247	598	228	376
Sales representatives, commodities, except retail	1,326	596	1,037	623	289	501
Sales workers, retail and personal services	2,885	258	1,210	336	1,676	219
Sales workers, motor vehicles and boats	242	464	222	479	19	(¹)
Sales workers, apparel	173	219	41	(¹)	132	211
Sales workers, furniture and home furnishings	99	345	57	413	42	(¹)
Sales workers, radio, television, hi-fi, and appliances	119	350	90	383	29	(¹)
Sales workers, hardware and building supplies	152	357	127	379	25	(¹)
Sales workers, parts	130	320	120	323	9	(¹)
Sales workers, other commodities	608	253	204	314	404	225
Sales counter clerks	101	269	33	(¹)	68	232
Cashiers	1,081	215	231	242	850	210
Street and door-to-door sales workers	114	311	45	(¹)	69	284
Administrative support, including clerical	14,384	350	3,183	440	11,202	332
Supervisors	745	497	322	595	424	448
General office	452	465	153	606	299	423
Financial records processing	87	494	23	(¹)	64	480
Distribution, scheduling, and adjusting clerks	160	545	113	558	47	(¹)
Computer equipment operators	688	374	242	446	446	348
Computer operators	681	374	240	450	441	348
Secretaries, stenographers, and typists	3,689	342	59	387	3,630	341
Secretaries	3,183	343	28	(¹)	3,154	343
Typists	470	327	23	(¹)	447	326
Information clerks	995	288	126	340	869	283
Interviewers	144	304	28	(¹)	116	300
Hotel clerks	64	234	23	(¹)	41	(¹)
Transportation ticket and reservation agents	99	394	41	(¹)	58	369
Receptionists	536	273	16	(¹)	520	272
Records processing, except financial	633	323	111	360	521	320
Order clerks	175	421	43	(¹)	132	415
Personnel clerks, except payroll and timekeeping	66	355	6	(¹)	60	352
Library clerks	58	281	7	(¹)	51	278
File clerks	188	283	32	(¹)	155	279
Records clerks	119	318	20	(¹)	99	316
Financial records processing	1,663	338	153	400	1,510	332
Bookkeepers, accounting, and auditing clerks	1,236	338	103	391	1,134	335
Payroll and timekeeping clerks	171	367	21	(¹)	150	355
Billing clerks	164	312	13	(¹)	151	307
Cost and rate clerks	56	346	11	(¹)	45	(¹)
Duplicating, mail and other office machine operators	55	290	22	(¹)	33	(¹)
Communications equipment operators	179	319	26	(¹)	153	313
Telephone operators	170	319	22	(¹)	148	313
Mail and message distributing	796	514	546	520	250	499
Postal clerks, except mail carriers	263	552	157	546	106	559
Mail carriers, postal service	306	554	241	562	65	525

44

	1990					
	Both sexes		Men		Women	
Occupation	Number of workers	Median weekly earnings	Number of workers	Median weekly earnings	Number of workers	Median weekly earnings
Mail clerks, except postal service	135	$300	76	$321	60	$268
Messengers	92	315	73	313	19	(¹)
Material recording, scheduling, and distributing clerks, n.e.c.	1,576	358	935	385	641	325
Dispatchers	201	381	93	480	107	325
Production coordinators	190	494	97	582	93	434
Traffic, shipping, and receiving clerks	468	323	345	339	122	288
Stock and inventory clerks	494	346	286	373	208	326
Weighers, measurers, and checkers	72	373	41	(¹)	32	(¹)
Expediters	91	325	33	(¹)	59	303
Adjusters and investigators	978	384	242	477	736	364
Insurance adjusters, examiners, and investigators	316	407	81	511	235	376
Investigators and adjusters, except insurance	464	379	116	458	348	358
Eligibility clerks, social welfare	82	359	9	(¹)	73	354
Bill and account collectors	117	366	37	(¹)	79	364
Miscellaneous administrative support occupations	2,388	319	398	388	1,990	311
General office clerks	553	323	109	355	444	319
Bank tellers	302	273	22	(¹)	280	270
Data-entry keyers	406	316	52	379	354	312
Statistical clerks	77	427	24	(¹)	53	373
Teachers' aides	232	246	7	(¹)	225	246
Service occupations	9,007	268	4,476	320	4,531	230
Private household	310	172	12	(¹)	298	171
Child care workers	139	132	2	(¹)	137	134
Cleaners and servants	142	190	7	(¹)	135	189
Protective services	1,738	468	1,523	477	216	405
Supervisors	171	615	156	637	16	(¹)
Police and detectives	87	645	77	676	9	(¹)
Firefighting and fire prevention	207	590	201	594	6	(¹)
Firefighting	195	595	192	596	3	(¹)
Police and detectives	809	507	700	512	109	483
Police and detectives, public service	465	559	411	569	54	519
Sheriffs, bailiffs, and other law enforcement officers	103	445	90	454	12	(¹)
Correctional institution officers	241	449	199	448	42	(¹)
Guards	550	304	466	309	85	263
Guards and police, except public service	521	307	450	310	71	274
Service occupations, except private household and protective	6,959	248	2,942	273	4,017	231
Food preparation and service occupations	2,645	220	1,263	243	1,382	206
Supervisors	222	285	95	346	127	245
Bartenders	170	248	81	276	89	226
Waiters and waitresses	596	208	150	266	446	194
Cooks, except short order	1,002	226	585	248	417	206
Food counter, fountain, and related occupations	99	184	32	(¹)	67	178
Kitchen workers, food preparation	58	215	15	(¹)	43	(¹)
Waiters' and waitresses' assistants	144	206	101	205	42	(¹)
Miscellaneous food preparation occupations	317	209	183	205	134	215
Health service occupations	1,470	263	164	300	1,306	260
Dental assistants	107	300	1	(¹)	106	300
Health aides, except nursing	320	287	57	314	263	281
Nursing aides, orderlies, and attendants	1,043	251	105	284	937	248
Cleaning and building service occupations	2,036	272	1,306	299	730	232
Supervisors	137	365	92	417	45	(¹)
Maids and housemen	423	220	98	279	325	211
Janitors and cleaners	1,437	280	1,079	294	358	248
Personal service occupations	808	252	209	297	599	239
Hairdressers and cosmetologists	240	247	26	(¹)	214	239
Attendants, amusement and recreation facilities	77	228	45	(¹)	32	(¹)
Public transportation attendants	51	635	10	(¹)	41	(¹)
Welfare service aides	57	253	7	(¹)	50	245
Child care workers	184	203	14	(¹)	169	200
Precision production, craft, and repair	11,062	477	10,169	488	893	316
Mechanics and repairers	3,808	476	3,669	477	139	459
Supervisors	238	586	220	594	18	(¹)
Mechanics and repairers, except supervisors	3,571	469	3,450	470	121	450
Vehicle and mobile equipment mechanics and repairers	1,422	425	1,411	425	10	(¹)
Automobile mechanics	649	393	646	393	3	(¹)
Bus, truck, and stationary engine mechanics	284	458	283	458	1	(¹)
Aircraft engine mechanics	102	576	100	582	2	(¹)
Automobile body and related repairers	138	403	138	403	—	—
Heavy equipment mechanics	153	509	151	511	1	(¹)
Industrial machinery repairers	491	480	475	482	16	(¹)
Electrical and electronic equipment repairers	633	563	576	576	56	499
Electronic repairers, communications and industrial equipment	151	472	137	485	14	(¹)

| | 1990 | | | | | |
| | Both sexes | | Men | | Women | |
Occupation	Number of workers	Median weekly earnings	Number of workers	Median weekly earnings	Number of workers	Median weekly earnings
Data processing equipment repairers	149	$585	135	$603	15	$(1)
Telephone line installers and repairers	61	602	56	611	5	(1)
Telephone installers and repairers	181	626	163	629	18	(1)
Miscellaneous electrical and electronic equipment repairers	57	502	53	510	4	(1)
Heating, air conditioning, and refrigeration mechanics	210	447	210	446	1	(1)
Miscellaneous mechanics and repairers	797	462	761	467	37	(1)
Office machine repairers	76	452	71	448	5	(1)
Millwrights	89	550	88	547	1	(1)
Construction trades	3,653	479	3,603	480	50	394
Supervisors	486	590	481	592	5	(1)
Construction trades, except supervisors	3,167	457	3,122	459	44	(1)
Brickmasons and stonemasons	134	506	134	506	—	—
Carpet installers	51	376	50	380	1	(1)
Carpenters	861	412	849	413	11	(1)
Drywall installers	110	443	108	440	1	(1)
Electricians	605	524	596	526	9	(1)
Electrical power installers and repairers	115	593	112	595	3	(1)
Painters, construction and maintenance	284	382	274	386	10	(1)
Plumbers, pipefitters, steamfitters, and apprentices	366	508	363	508	3	(1)
Concrete and terrazzo finishers	59	414	59	414	—	—
Insulation workers	51	436	50	431	1	(1)
Roofers	137	341	137	341	—	—
Structural metalworkers	52	569	52	569	—	—
Extractive occupations	142	582	141	584	1	(1)
Precision production occupations	3,459	470	2,755	508	703	300
Supervisors	1,306	546	1,104	586	202	363
Precision metalworking occupations	823	497	786	502	37	(1)
Tool and die makers	148	557	145	563	3	(1)
Machinists	464	486	448	491	16	(1)
Sheet metal workers	113	493	105	496	7	(1)
Precision woodworking occupations	54	356	47	(1)	8	(1)
Precision textile, apparel, and furnishings machine workers	118	296	58	356	61	249
Precision workers, assorted materials	448	313	194	376	255	291
Electrical and electronic equipment assemblers	278	298	93	342	185	286
Precision food production occupations	336	308	235	374	101	239
Butchers and meat cutters	221	314	172	378	49	(1)
Bakers	82	304	49	(1)	33	(1)
Precision inspectors, testers, and related workers	110	590	81	557	29	(1)
Inspectors, testers, and graders	102	504	76	549	26	(1)
Plant and system operators	263	546	251	553	11	(1)
Water and sewage treatment plant operators	58	467	57	466	1	(1)
Stationary engineers	110	562	105	567	4	(1)
Operators, fabricators, and laborers	14,932	339	11,257	378	3,675	262
Machine operators, assemblers, and inspectors	7,350	325	4,510	391	2,840	260
Machine operators and tenders, except precision	4,849	313	2,936	381	1,913	247
Metalworking and plastic working machine operators	421	403	352	430	69	311
Lathe and turning machine operators	55	406	51	428	4	(1)
Punching and stamping press machine operators	107	354	79	408	28	(1)
Grinding, abrading, buffing, and polishing machine operators	120	410	103	427	17	(1)
Metal and plastic processing machine operators	160	352	131	382	29	(1)
Molding and casting machine operators	94	326	70	379	24	(1)
Woodworking machine operators	149	295	131	297	18	(1)
Sawing machine operators	100	292	88	294	12	(1)
Printing machine operators	398	409	301	431	97	309
Printing machine operators	279	410	239	424	39	(1)
Textile, apparel, and furnishings machine operators	1,133	228	242	295	891	217
Winding and twisting machine operators	72	289	20	(1)	52	269
Textile sewing machine operators	663	214	78	255	585	211
Pressing machine operators	105	222	34	(1)	71	211
Laundering and dry cleaning machine operators	142	220	44	(1)	99	207
Miscellaneous textile machine operators	71	293	41	(1)	30	(1)
Machine operators, assorted materials	2,568	336	1,766	381	802	271
Packaging and filling machine operators	408	264	164	296	244	250
Mixing and blending machine operators	113	372	102	378	11	(1)
Separating, filtering, and clarifying machine operators	64	523	56	525	9	(1)
Painting and paint spraying machine operators	182	385	158	400	25	(1)
Furnace, kiln, and oven operators, exc. food	103	467	98	475	5	(1)
Slicing and cutting machine operators	189	319	148	357	41	(1)
Photographic process machine operators	77	315	39	(1)	38	(1)
Fabricators, assemblers, and hand working occupations	1,704	352	1,178	398	526	282
Welders and cutters	552	423	527	428	25	(1)
Assemblers	1,010	320	578	370	432	287
Production inspectors, testers, samplers, and weighers	797	363	396	461	402	300
Production inspectors, checkers, and examiners	646	375	316	483	330	304

Table 2-4   Jobs and Money: Pay and Employment in Various Occupations (continued)

| | 1990 | | | | | |
| | Both sexes | | Men | | Women | |
Occupation	Number of workers	Median weekly earnings	Number of workers	Median weekly earnings	Number of workers	Median weekly earnings
Production testers	55	$435	33	$(¹)	22	$(¹)
Graders and sorters, except agricultural	91	273	43	(¹)	48	(¹)
Transportation and material moving occupations	3,948	413	3,721	418	227	314
Motor vehicle operators	2,792	402	2,604	409	188	305
Supervisors, motor vehicle operators	65	521	53	552	12	(¹)
Truckdrivers, heavy	1,614	430	1,586	432	28	(¹)
Truckdrivers, light	570	321	533	323	38	(¹)
Drivers and sales workers	172	438	162	446	10	(¹)
Bus drivers	226	354	138	405	89	305
Taxicab drivers and chauffeurs	110	308	101	314	10	(¹)
Transportation occupations, except motor vehicles	159	686	156	686	3	(¹)
Rail transportation	107	717	104	716	3	(¹)
Water transportation occupations	52	547	52	550	—	—
Material moving equipment operators	996	415	961	417	35	(¹)
Operating engineers	215	504	213	506	2	(¹)
Crane and tower operators	91	477	89	479	2	(¹)
Excavating and loading machine operators	79	431	79	431	—	—
Grader, dozer, and scraper operators	86	409	85	409	1	(¹)
Industrial truck and tractor equipment operators	420	373	398	371	22	(¹)
Miscellaneous material moving equipment operators	68	404	60	422	8	(¹)
Handlers, equipment cleaners, helpers, and laborers	3,635	298	3,027	308	608	250
Helpers, construction and extractive occupations	117	277	113	279	4	(¹)
Helpers, construction trades	107	272	103	274	4	(¹)
Construction laborers	666	347	647	348	19	(¹)
Production helpers	74	314	64	313	10	(¹)
Freight, stock, and material handlers	1,053	288	857	302	196	227
Stock handlers and baggers	427	228	309	242	118	209
Machine feeders and offbearers	75	280	50	309	24	(¹)
Garage and service station related occupations	147	235	144	237	4	(¹)
Vehicle washers and equipment cleaners	176	249	152	251	24	(¹)
Hand packers and packagers	255	258	100	262	154	255
Laborers, except construction	1,112	309	918	320	194	258
Farming, forestry, and fishing	1,423	257	1,253	263	171	216
Farm operators and managers	69	348	58	360	11	(¹)
Farm managers	61	363	53	369	8	(¹)
Other agricultural and related occupations	1,265	250	1,109	256	156	212
Farm occupations except managerial	628	233	542	239	86	206
Farm workers	561	229	492	234	70	202
Related agricultural occupations	637	271	566	276	70	222
Supervisors, related agricultural	64	392	60	394	4	(¹)
Groundskeepers and gardeners, except farm	500	267	478	267	22	(¹)
Animal caretakers, except farm	52	228	21	(¹)	31	(¹)
Forestry and logging occupations	74	314	71	313	3	(¹)
Timber cutting and logging	53	314	52	313	1	(¹)

¹Data not shown where base is less than 50,000.
Note: n.e.c. is an abbreviation for "not elsewhere classified" and designates broad categories of occupations which cannot be more specifically identified.
Source: *Employment and Earnings.*

47

Chapter Three

WORKING WOMEN: THE STRIDES AND STUMBLES

HIGHLIGHTS AND TRENDS

• Over half of all women (58.0%) were in the labor force in 1990, employed or looking for work.

• The number of women in the labor force increased by 173% (from 16.7 million to 45.6 million) between 1947 and 1980. Since then, it has grown even more, to 56.7 million in 1990. About 53.6 million women were employed and 3.1 million were unemployed and looking for work in 1990.

• Today, women make up 45.1% of the labor force. By the start of the 21st century they will make up nearly half (47.3%).

• As women have moved into the labor force they've decided to have fewer children; the fertility rate for American women is now 1.8, compared to 3.7 in the late 1950s at the height of the baby boom.

• About half of all women (52%) with children under the age of 1 are working.

• Today, women-owned businesses are the fastest-growing segment of small business. The number of women-owned firms jumped from 1.9 million in 1977 to 4.4 million in 1987. About 32% of all small businesses are owned by women. Women-owned firms had sales of $68.8 billion in 1987, up from $37.4 billion in 1977.

• Even though more women are working, more women are living in poverty. About 25 million mothers and their children now live in poverty.

• Women earn 72 cents for every dollar men make, indicating that the wage gap between men and women has improved somewhat since 1955, when women made 65 cents for every dollar men did.

• Less than 11% of all women fit the stereotype of a housewife—a married woman, not in the labor force, with children at home.

• The number of women enrolled in undergraduate business programs more than doubled since 1970. Women now account for half of all under-graduate business students and about one third of all M.B.A.'s.

• About 40% of all managerial, executive, and administrative workers are women. There are about 4.8 million women managers, executives, and administrators, up from 2.2 million in 1972, when women were 27.5% of the total.

• Yet the single most common occupation for women is still secretarial.

WOMEN AT WORK IN THE 1990S

In the past few decades, women have been muscling in on the labor market. Between 1947 and 1990, the number of women in the labor force more than tripled, from 16.7 million to 56.7 million. In contrast, the number of men increased only 57% (from 44.3 million to 69.7 million).

Today 53.6 million women hold jobs and another 3.1 million are unemployed but looking for work. The greatest increase has been among those of childbearing age, forever altering the nature of the American family. During the 1970s the increase for women under 45 was more than twice the overall increase, and now even women with young children are entering the labor market in record numbers. Today 52% of all women with children less than a year old work outside the home, up from 39% in 1970; 79% of all single mothers with children less than 3 years old work. Over 25 million children lived in families in which the mother was away from home part of the working day, a fact that has been good for child-care centers and hard on their parents' pocketbooks. Americans now spend over $3 billion a year on day care.

The U.S. economy might be reeling from the effects of foreign competition, but when it comes to women workers the United States is holding its own. Only one country, Sweden, where 80% of all women are working or looking for work, has a higher labor-force participation rate. In Japan, the labor-force participation rate for women is 57.2%; in West Germany, the U.S.'s other major foreign competitor, about half of all women (50.4%) are employed or looking for work.

Nor is there any evidence that these trends represent a passing flirtation with the labor market. Nearly half of all working women (47%) regard their jobs as careers, according to one poll, up from 30% in 1970. The poll indicates that women are almost as career-oriented as men—only 57% of all men consider their work a career.

But, judging from the jobs women hold, many of their careers are in lower-paying service jobs. Women continue to be overrepresented in certain fields—for example, as hairdressers (87% are women), dental assistants (100%), waiters and waitresses (76.2%), receptionists (97.7%), secretaries (99.1%), bank tellers (92%), nurses (93%), librarians (85%), and cashiers (78.5%). They also continued to be underrepresented in traditionally male occupations—for example, as engineers (9.0%), lawyers (29.4%), police officers (12.3%), auto mechanics (1.0%), construction workers (1.75%), clergy (5.2%), and truck drivers (1.8%).

Besides changing the nature of the work force, women have also altered the nature of the American family. For most working women, the job now shares center stage with marriage and motherhood. Less than 11% of all women fit the stereotype of a housewife (a married woman, not in the labor force, with children at home) and women are waiting longer to get married. The average age for a woman's first marriage is now 23.6, up from 20.3 in 1960. The proportion of single women aged 25 to 34 has also tripled since 1970.

The need to balance a job with a family has given rise to "superwomen" who must do it all. Only one third of all women who work full-time hire household help. And most men are still not much use around the house, despite all the rhetoric about growing male sensitivity. Only about 14% of all husbands do half the housework—71% of married women have to do over three quarters of the work.

No wonder women are having fewer children. The average woman is now having only 1.8 children, down from 3.7 children during the baby boom of late 1950s. And those having children are waiting longer than ever before. Today 29% of all women aged 25 to 29 who have ever been married are childless; in 1960, only 12.6% were.

The stress of women working outside the home and rapidly changing sex roles also put new strains on family life. Although about 90% of all women will marry at least once, more marriages than ever before are ending in divorce. About half of all marriages end in divorce and the typical American marriage now lasts about seven years. Moreover, about 32% of all women aged 40 to 44 who have ever been married have gone through a divorce, up from 18% in 1970. The average age for a divorce is 33.7 for women and 34.4 for men.

And when a marriage breaks up, women suffer more than men, at least in economic terms. Currently about 33.6% of all households headed by women are living in poverty. That state of affairs is one major reason why 20.0% of all Americans under the age of 18, 45.1% of all black children, and 39.7% of Hispanic children are growing up in poverty.

INCOME

The number of married women with jobs jumped from 11.6 million in 1960 to 28.6 million today, in part because more families need an extra paycheck to make ends meet. The typical family with a woman working earns $36,431; families in which a wife does not work earn an average of only $24,556.

Yet the wage gap remains. Women earned only 72 cents for every dollar men made in 1990, indicating that the wage gap between men and women has improved slightly since 1955, when women made 65 cents for every dollar men made. The gap between men's and women's wages widened in the 1970s, when large numbers of women entered the labor market. Since then women's pay has been increasing, with younger women making the biggest gains.

The wage disparity has spawned a movement to equalize men's and women's pay for comparable jobs. Advocates argue that women in traditionally female-dominated occupations, such as nursing, are often paid less than men in male-dominated occupations, even though the jobs may require similar levels of education, skill, knowledge, and responsibility. To correct that problem, they have introduced legislation and brought suits against employers, trying to force them to equalize the pay of men and women for comparable jobs. Britain and Australia already have comparable-worth laws. And unions have also made comparable worth an important issue.

Opponents argue that deciding "comparable worth" is a task beyond the reach of law, and that the real net effect of the movement will be the institution of government wage control. Large business groups such as the National Association of Manufacturers and the Chamber of Commerce have been among those fighting the idea, saying that it would create a bureaucratic nightmare and cost businesses the right to set their own pay schedules. Their view is supported by the Bush administration, and no federal legislation mandating comparable worth is likely to pass in the near future.

Despite all the rhetoric about the "new woman," it should be remembered that some of the gains women have made over the last twenty years were simply a matter of recapturing ground that was lost during the 1950s, when women left the labor market for the home. For example, in 1947–1948, 1 in 10 medical degrees was awarded to a woman; that percentage fell to 1 in 20 about 10 years later. It wasn't until the mid-1970s that women were again earning as many medical degrees as in 1947–1948.

It would also be wrong to assume that women have traditionally stayed at home or survived only with the help of men. Many poorer, single, and minority women have always worked, with 39.7% of all black women working in 1890, compared with 16.3% of white women.

WOMEN IN BUSINESS AND MANAGEMENT

Twenty-five years ago, many parents sent their daughters to college to find husbands. Instead, the daughters found careers, becoming managers, executives, or entrepreneurs. Getting exact figures on women-owned businesses is difficult, but there is little doubt that women-owned businesses are one of the fastest-growing segments of the economy. The number of women-owned nonfarm sole proprietorships jumped from 1.9 million in 1977 to 4.4 million in 1987 (the most recent data available in the spring of 1991). About 32% of these businesses, which tend to be small, are owned by women. Women-owned businesses also nearly doubled their sales during this period, from $37.4 billion to $68.8 billion. Yet they still garnered only 13% of the total sales of all nonfarm sole proprietorships. (All of these figures understate the power of women-owned businesses, since there are no data on women-owned partnerships or corporations.)

The service industry, retail trade, finance, real estate, insurance, and other services account for about 9 out of every 10 women-owned businesses. Over half of all women-owned sole proprietorships are in the area of miscellaneous services (2,542,337). The next most popular industry is wholesale and retail (1,046,364), followed by finance, insurance, and real estate (502,146).

The fastest-growing sector for new women-owned businesses is in the traditionally male-dominated industries of mining, construction, and manufacturing. In that sector, women-owned businesses increased by 34.7% per year between 1977 and 1987.

Women are also moving into the corporate world in record numbers. The nation's 4.8 million female managerial, executive, and administrative workers accounted for 40% of all managers in 1990, a dramatic increase over 1972, when there were 2.2 million women in these fields, 27.5% of the total.

Women are no longer such an anomaly in America's corporate boardrooms. About two fifths of all major corporations have women on their board of directors, compared to only 13% in the mid-1970s. But only 3% to 4% of all directorships are held by women, despite the increasing number of women workers. Only 25% of all major corporations have more than one woman on their board.

Better opportunity for education is one major reason why more women are moving into executive suites or opening their own businesses. Today women get 35% of all doctorates, up from 9.6% in 1950. They get 32% of all M.D.'s (up from 5.5% in 1960), 40.2% of all law degrees (up from 2.5% in 1960), and 13% of all master's degrees in engineering (up from 0.4% in 1960). Finally, the number of women receiving undergraduate business degrees jumped from 114,865 (9.1%) in 1971 to 241,156 (46.5%) at the end of the 1980s. Nearly one third of all M.B.A.'s are now given to women, up from only 4% in 1970.

But despite all the good news, women have not moved into the highest levels of business and politics. About 17% of all state legislators are now women, up from 8% in 1975. But women make up only 6% of Congress, up from 4% in 1975. Similarly, *Fortune* estimates that the nation's largest 1,000 corporations have 3,993 male top executives or directors but only 19 women. Black women have fared worse than white women. Despite increasing numbers of black women earning M.B.A.'s, they still only account for 2% of all corporate managers, and there are only 20 black women corporate officers in America's 1,000 largest corporations.

One reason for the scarcity of top women executives is that the large numbers of women who got M.B.A.'s in the 1970s and 1980s haven't had time to work their way up the corporate ladder. Yet part of the problem is still sex discrimination. A survey by the *Harvard Business Review* indicated that more than half of all men felt uncomfortable working with women. One in five also thought women were temperamentally unfit for management. Perhaps because of these attitudes, half of those surveyed felt that women would never be wholly accepted in business.

Their pay, probably more than anything else, shows where women are. Only 2% of all women managers earn over $50,000 a year compared with 14% of all men. In 1990, women in executive, administrative, and managerial jobs had median weekly earnings of $485 a week, 65.4% of the $742 weekly earnings of men.

THE RICHEST WOMEN IN THE U.S.

Even the richest women have something in common with their more plebian counterparts—they are not as rich as the equivalent men. Only 62 women made the 1990 *Forbes* list of the 400 wealthiest Americans. The 5 wealthiest women were collectively worth a mere $8.6 billion, compared to the $19.6 billion of the 5 wealthiest men. And all of the 5 wealthiest women inherited their money, unlike 4 of the 5 wealthiest men, who built their fortunes from scratch. But, with business empires of at least $1 billion, the 5 wealthiest women in America don't have much to complain about:

1. and 2. Barbara Cox Anthony and Anne Cox Chambers

The two sisters own 98% of Cox Enterprises, which is worth over $5 billion, according to *Forbes,* simply because they are the daughters of James Cox, a former governor of Ohio who built a vast media empire. Cox Enterprises now owns 28 newspapers, 7 TV stations, a cable system with 1.5 million sub-scribers, and 13 radio stations. Barbara's son James is now running Cox Enterprises. Anne became the first woman bank director in Atlanta in 1973 and has served as U.S. ambassador to Belgium.

3. Jacqueline Mars Vogel

Jacqueline Mars Vogel shares the $6.8 billion Mars candy empire with three other family members. She serves on the board of directors.

4. Margaret Hunt Hill

The heiress of H. L. Hunt's fabulous Texas oil fortune managed to avoid her brothers' disastrous attempt to corner the world's silver market—a move that cost the Hunt brothers billions and eventually forced them into bankruptcy. She has withdrawn her shares from the family's oil trusts and controls assets, including her brother Hassie's trust, worth about $1 billion.

5. Joan Beverly Kroc

The widow of Ray Kroc, founder of the McDonald's fast food empire, is worth about $900 million.

Table 3-1   The Academic Revolution

(earned degrees conferred, by field of study and level of degree)

Level and field of study	1971	1980	1983	1984	1985	1986	1987	Percent Female 1971	1987
Bachelor's, total	839,730	929,417	969,510	974,309	979,477	987,823	991,339	43.4	51.5
Agriculture and natural resources	12,672	22,802	20,909	19,317	18,107	16,823	14,991	4.2	31.2
Architecture and environmental design	5,570	9,132	9,823	9,186	9,325	9,119	8,922	11.9	37.3
Area and ethnic studies	2,582	2,840	2,971	2,879	2,867	3,060	3,340	52.4	61.7
Business and management	114,865	185,361	226,893	230,031	233,351	238,160	241,156	9.1	46.5
Communications[1]	10,802	28,616	38,602	40,165	42,083	43,091	45,408	35.3	60.0
Computer and information sciences	2,388	11,154	24,510	32,172	38,878	41,889	39,664	13.6	34.6
Education	176,614	118,169	97,991	92,382	88,161	87,221	87,115	74.5	76.2
Engineering[1]	50,046	68,893	89,270	94,444	96,105	95,953	93,074	.8	13.7
Foreign languages	19,945	11,133	9,685	9,479	9,954	10,102	10,184	74.6	72.6
Health sciences	25,190	63,607	64,614	64,338	64,513	64,535	63,206	77.1	85.5
Home economics	11,167	18,411	16,705	16,316	15,555	15,288	14,942	97.3	92.5
Law	545	683	1,099	1,272	1,157	1,197	1,178	5.0	68.6
Letters	64,933	33,497	32,743	33,739	34,091	35,434	37,133	65.5	65.8
Liberal/general studies	5,461	20,069	18,524	18,815	19,191	19,248	21,365	29.0	56.4
Library and archival sciences	1,013	398	258	255	202	157	139	92.0	85.6
Life sciences	35,743	46,370	39,982	38,640	38,445	38,524	38,114	29.1	48.5
Mathematics	24,801	11,378	12,453	13,211	15,146	16,306	16,489	38.0	46.4
Military sciences	357	251	267	195	299	256	383	.3	6.8
Multi/interdisciplinary studies	8,306	14,404	17,282	16,734	15,727	15,700	16,402	28.4	53.7
Parks and recreation	1,621	5,753	5,198	4,752	4,593	4,433	4,107	34.7	60.2
Philosophy, religion, and theology	11,890	13,276	12,536	12,349	12,439	11,841	11,686	25.5	30.1
Physical sciences	21,412	23,410	23,405	23,671	23,732	21,731	19,974	13.8	28.4
Psychology	37,880	41,962	40,364	39,872	39,811	40,521	42,868	44.5	68.9
Protective services	2,045	15,015	12,579	12,654	12,510	12,704	12,930	9.2	38.3
Public affairs	6,252	18,422	16,290	14,396	13,838	13,878	14,161	60.2	68.0
Social sciences[2]	155,236	103,519	95,088	93,212	91,461	93,703	96,185	36.8	44.0
Visual and performing arts	30,394	40,892	39,469	39,833	37,936	36,949	36,223	59.7	61.9
Master's, total	230,509	298,081	289,921	[3]284,263	286,251	288,567	289,557	40.1	51.2
Agriculture and natural resources	2,457	3,976	4,254	4,178	3,928	3,801	3,523	5.9	30.1
Architecture and environmental design	1,705	3,139	3,357	3,223	3,275	3,260	3,142	13.8	34.0
Area and ethnic studies	1,032	852	826	888	879	927	851	38.3	46.9
Business and management	26,481	55,006	65,319	66,653	67,527	67,137	67,496	3.9	33.0
Communications[1]	1,856	3,082	3,604	3,656	3,669	3,823	3,937	34.6	59.2
Computer and information sciences	1,588	3,647	5,321	6,190	7,101	8,070	8,491	10.3	29.4
Education	88,952	103,951	84,853	77,187	76,137	76,353	75,501	56.2	74.0
Engineering[1]	16,443	16,243	19,350	[2]20,661	21,557	21,661	22,693	1.1	12.6
Foreign languages	4,755	2,236	1,759	1,773	1,724	1,721	1,746	65.5	70.4
Health sciences	5,445	15,068	17,068	17,443	17,383	18,624	18,426	55.9	78.9
Home economics	1,452	2,690	2,406	2,422	2,383	2,298	2,070	93.9	87.6
Law	955	1,817	2,091	1,802	1,796	1,924	1,943	4.8	26.8
Letters	11,148	6,807	5,767	5,818	5,934	6,291	6,123	60.2	65.0
Liberal/general studies	549	1,373	889	1,173	1,180	1,154	1,126	44.3	59.2
Library and archival sciences	7,001	5,374	3,979	3,805	3,893	3,626	3,815	81.3	79.1
Life sciences	5,728	6,510	5,696	5,406	5,059	5,013	4,954	33.6	48.7
Mathematics	5,191	2,860	2,837	2,741	2,882	3,159	3,321	29.2	39.1
Military sciences	2	46	110	127	119	83	83	—	2.4
Multi/interdisciplinary studies	1,157	3,579	2,930	3,148	3,184	3,104	3,041	10.9	42.0
Parks and recreation	218	647	565	[2]555	544	495	476	29.8	55.3
Philosophy, religion, and theology	4,036	5,126	5,873	6,259	5,519	5,630	5,989	27.1	34.5
Physical sciences	6,367	5,219	5,290	5,576	5,796	5,902	5,652	13.3	24.9
Psychology	4,431	7,806	8,378	8,002	8,408	8,293	8,204	37.2	65.2
Protective services	194	1,805	1,300	1,219	1,235	1,074	1,019	10.3	29.4
Public affairs	8,215	18,413	16,245	15,373	16,045	16,300	17,032	49.2	63.7
Social sciences[2]	16,476	12,101	11,112	10,465	10,380	10,428	10,397	28.5	39.5
Visual and performing arts	6,675	8,708	8,742	8,520	8,714	8,416	8,506	47.4	55.8

54

Table 3-1 The Academic Revolution (continued)

Level and field of study	1971	1980	1983	1984	1985	1986	1987	Percent Female 1971	Percent Female 1987
Doctorate, total	32,107	32,615	32,775	33,209	32,943	33,653	34,120	14.3	35.2
Agriculture and natural resources	1,086	991	1,149	1,172	1,213	1,158	1,049	2.9	17.0
Architecture and environmental design	36	79	97	84	89	73	92	8.3	28.3
Area and ethnic studies	144	151	153	139	137	157	132	16.7	44.7
Business and management	807	792	809	977	866	969	1,098	2.9	23.6
Communications[1]	145	193	214	219	234	223	275	13.1	42.5
Computer and information sciences	128	240	262	251	248	344	374	16.4	13.9
Education	6,403	7,941	7,551	7,473	7,151	7,110	6,909	21.2	54.9
Engineering[1]	3,638	2,507	2,831	2,981	3,230	3,410	3,820	.6	6.9
Foreign languages	781	549	488	462	437	448	441	38.0	58.3
Health sciences	459	771	1,155	1,163	1,199	1,241	1,213	16.3	53.5
Home economics	123	192	255	279	276	311	297	61.0	78.1
Law	20	40	72	121	105	54	120	—	34.2
Letters	1,857	1,500	1,176	1,215	1,239	1,215	1,181	28.0	56.4
Life sciences	3,645	3,636	3,341	3,437	3,432	3,358	3,423	16.3	35.0
Mathematics	1,199	724	698	695	699	742	725	7.8	17.4
Multi/interdisciplinary studies	80	295	387	378	285	319	276	13.8	37.0
Philosophy, religion, and theology	866	1,693	1,612	1,644	1,608	1,660	1,658	5.8	13.3
Physical sciences	4,390	3,089	3,269	3,306	3,403	3,551	3,672	5.6	17.3
Psychology	1,782	2,768	3,108	2,973	2,908	3,088	3,123	24.0	53.3
Public affairs	185	372	347	421	431	385	398	23.8	45.7
Social sciences[2]	3,659	3,219	2,931	2,911	2,851	2,955	2,916	13.9	30.5
Visual and performing arts	621	655	692	728	693	722	792	22.2	43.6
Other	53	218	178	180	209	160	136	28.3	50.0

—Represents zero.
[1]Includes technologies.
[2]Includes history.
[3]Data revised since originally published.
Source: U.S. National Center for Education Statistics, *Digest of Education Statistics,* annual.

Table 3-2 Women-owned Businesses

This table provides a snapshot of women-owned sole proprietorships in 1977 and 1987, the most recent year for which data are available. It provides a breakdown of women-owned businesses by industry and receipts.

Number of Businesses

Industry	1977 Total	1977 Women-owned	1977 Men-owned	1987 Total	1987 Women-owned	1987 Men-owned	Annual percentage change 1977–1987 Women-owned	Annual percentage change 1977–1987 Men-owned
All Industries	8,413,806	1,900,723	6,255,101	14,159,758	4,391,116	9,273,524	13.10	4.83
Mining, Construction, and Manufacturing	1,289,351	47,661	1,220,132	2,276,538	213,785	1,989,212	34.86	6.30
Transportation	385,322	23,631	352,886	672,770	86,484	555,958	26.60	5.75
Wholesale and Retail Trade	2,264,847	641,086	1,519,525	2,711,071	1,046,364	1,523,104	6.32	0.10
Finance, Insurance, and Real Estate	894,941	225,597	643,660	1,384,701	502,146	831,062	12.26	2.91
Services	3,302,537	936,713	2,284,937	7,114,678	2,542,337	4,374,188	17.14	9.14

Receipts (in Dollars)

Industry	1977 Total	1977 Women-owned	1977 Men-owned	1987 Total	1987 Women-owned	1987 Men-owned	Annual percent change 1977–87 Total	Annual percent change 1977–87 Women-owned	Annual percent change 1977–87 Men-owned
All Industries	482,158,952	37,407,923	435,706,618	506,417,185	67,191,243	418,326,102	0.50	7.96	−0.40
Mining, Construction, and Manufacturing	85,234,117	1,676,508	82,673,490	94,135,159	4,849,052	86,042,261	1.04	18.92	0.41
Transportation	20,623,177	954,648	19,266,227	24,478,590	2,854,214	20,122,952	1.87	19.90	0.44
Wholesale and Retail Trade	238,476,138	9,872,759	213,401,230	177,826,079	22,043,155	146,129,555	−2.54	1.09	−3.15
Finance, Insurance, and Real Estate	28,707,588	3,354,421	24,821,707	37,584,902	7,523,303	28,527,297	3.09	12.43	1.49
Services	100,729,633	11,248,143	87,601,456	172,392,456	29,921,518	137,504,037	7.11	16.60	5.70

Note: Both 1977 and 1987 data exclude agriculture. Data have been adjusted to 1982 dollars using the GNP deflator.
Source: Special tabulations prepared by the U.S. Department of the Treasury, Internal Revenue Service, under contract to the U.S. Small Business Administration, Office of Advocacy, unpublished data, various tabulations.

Chapter Four

MINORITIES: INCORPORATING THE AMERICAN DREAM

HIGHLIGHTS AND TRENDS

• After minority joblessness reached new heights in the 1982 recession, the job outlook for minorities improved. By 1990, black unemployment had dropped to 11.3% from 20.2% in November of 1982. The 1987 unemployment rate for Hispanics fell to 8.0%, down from a high of 16.3% in 1983.

• Minority businesses are one of the fastest-growing sectors of the economy. A 1990 U.S. Census Bureau study shows that there were 424,165 black-owned businesses in 1987, up 38% from 1982, and that the number of black-owned businesses with paid employees grew 87% to 70,815 in 1987 (the most recent data available).

• Generally, minorities continue to lag behind whites. For example, if blacks earned as much as other Americans, they would have had $401.4 billion worth of income in 1990. Yet actual black income was only $278 billion, resulting in an income gap of $123.4 billion.

• The average black family's income ($20,209) is only 56% of the average white family's, down from 1970, when black families earned 61% as much as white families. The average Hispanic family's income ($21,769) is 64% of a typical white family's, down from 67% in 1975. Adjusted for inflation, the average white family's income has increased 10% since 1970. But the average black family's income grew only 0.7% during that period.

• Black-owned businesses continue to be overshadowed by large corporations. In 1989, the top 100 black-owned corporations had combined sales of $6.8 billion, about 5% of the sales of General Motors, the largest company, and about $3.7 billion more than Wang Laboratories, the largest Asian-owned business. The combined sales of the 100 largest black companies would have put them 68th in the *Fortune* 500.

• The 500 largest Hispanic companies had sales of only $8.37 billion and employed 67,618 people in 1989, according to *Hispanic Business*. The combined sales of all 500 companies would have ranked them only 56th on the *Fortune* 500.

MINORITIES IN AMERICA

America has always been a country of minorities, a nation of immigrants and refugees. In 1920, when there were 105 million Americans, 14 million were foreign born and 10.5 million were black. Only a little more than half of the population was white and had American-born parents.

Today, the country is still a kaleidoscope of races, religious minorities, and ethnic groups. Of the 226,546,000 Americans counted in the 1980 census, there were 26,683,000 blacks (11.8%), and 14,609,000 Hispanics (6.4%). There were also some 806,000 Chinese (0.36%), 774,700 Filipinos (0.34%), 701,000 Japanese (0.31%), 361,500 Asian Indians (0.16%), 354,600 Koreans (0.16%), 261,700 Vietnamese (0.12%), and nearly 7,000,000 people who belonged to various other ethnic groups (3.1%).

In the year 2000, when there will be nearly 268 million Americans, the country will be 13.3% black, 9.4% Hispanic, 3.6% other, and 74.2% white non-Hispanic. The percentages do not add up to 100% because people of Spanish origin may be of any race, white, black, or Asian.

By the year 2080, the face of America will have changed dramatically. The number of white non-Hispanics will have fallen from 192 million in 1990 to only 176 million in 2080, while the number of Hispanics will have increased from 19.9 million to 59.6 million. The number of black Americans will grow from 31.4 million in 1990 to 55.7 million in 2080 while the number of members of other races will increase from 7.5 million to 23.4 million. In 2080, only 56.6% of the country will be white non-Hispanic. About one fifth of the population (19.2%) will be Hispanic, followed by 17.9% black, and 7.5% will be other races, including Asian.

A hundred years after the building of the Statue of Liberty, immigration is once again on the rise. During the 1970s the U.S. saw a new wave of immigration as more than 4.5 million people legally immigrated to the United States, the highest number since the 1910s, and the third-highest number for any decade in the nation's history. By 1980, 14 million Americans, 6.2% of the population, were foreign-born and 23 million people lived in households where a language other than English was spoken. Another 5.2 million legal immigrants arrived during the 1980s. Others arrived illegally. The U.S. Census Bureau estimates that there are about 3 million to 4 million illegal aliens living in the United States.

But, as might be expected in a country of immigrants, only a small minority can trace its history far back into America's past. Only about 2 million people, under 1% of the population, can say they are real indigenous Americans—American Indians.

As minorities and immigrants increase their share of the population, they will play an increasingly important role in the American economy and workplace. By the year 2000, Hispanics will account for 10.1% of the labor force, up from 5% in 1979 and 7.4% in 1988. Asians will hold 4.0% of all jobs, up from 2.3% in 1979 and 3.0% in 1988. The proportion of blacks will grow more slowly, hitting 11.7% in 2000, up from 10.2% in 1979 and 10.9% in 1988. Immigrants will account for about 21% of the growth in the labor force between now and the end of the century; blacks will produce 17% of the growth, Hispanics 27%, and Asians 10%.

But, as minorities and immigrants become increasingly important to the nation's future, their economic status has not shown dramatic improvement. Adjusted for inflation, the average black family earned $20,067 in 1970, and 33.5% of blacks lived in poverty. Between 1970 and 1982, the average black family's income dropped a whopping 15% to $17,473 and the number of blacks living in poverty increased to 35.6%. Since then, however, things have improved slightly. Today, the average black family's income has recovered to $20,209. Similarly the average Hispanic family's income dropped from $21,002 in 1975 to $20,919 in 1986 before recovering to $21,769 today.

If blacks earned as much as other Americans, they would have had $401.4 billion worth of income in 1990, yet actual black income was only $278 billion, resulting in an income gap of $123.4 billion. Moreover, minorities are falling further behind whites in the race for economic prosperity. In 1970, the average black family earned only 61% as much as the average white family. Today, they earn 56%. Similarly, Hispanics earned 66% of what the average white family made in 1975 but get only 64% as much money today. Adjusted for inflation, the average white family's income has increased 10% between 1970 and today, but the average black family's income grew only 0.7% during that period.

MINORITY-OWNED BUSINESSES

In the 1990s, minority business stands at the crossroads. During the 1970s and 1980s, minorities made some remarkable strides in business and politics. But much remains to be done, and many minority business will need the creativity they showed in the 1980s to survive the 1990s. A slumping economy and less help from Washington both spell trouble for many small, undercapitalized minority firms in the 1990s.

First the good news. Like the rest of America, minorities were bitten by the entrepreneurial bug during the 1980s. A 1990 U.S. Census Bureau study shows that there were 424,165 black-owned business in 1987, up 38% from 1982, and that the number of black-owned businesses with paid employees grew 87% to 70,815 in 1987 (the most recent data available). The number of black contractors with paid employees more than tripled and business-service firms owned by blacks tripled.

These numbers also show that black-owned businesses were one of the fastest-growing sectors of the economy. While the number of black-owned businesses increased 38%, the total number of new businesses grew only 14%. But black-owned businesses have a long way to go before they achieve real economic power. Only 3% of all American businesses were owned by blacks, and black-owned firms received only 1% of all business revenues. Most are still located in areas with large black populations that tend to be poorer than the average consumer, and most are much smaller than other businesses. Although the typical business takes in $146,000 a year, the average black business has only about $47,000 in sales.

The accomplishments and problems in minority-owned business are demonstrated by the state of some of the largest minority-owned businesses in America. The 500 largest Hispanic companies in America increased their sales slightly from $8.3 billion in 1988 to $8.35 billion in 1989, according to *Hispanic Business*. But that total was actually less than in 1986, when the Hispanic 500 earned $10 billion. Their combined sales would have ranked them only 56th on the *Fortune* 500.

The same story can be found in the largest black companies. In 1989 *Black Enterprise*'s top 100 black-owned companies had combined revenues of $6.8 billion, way up from $2.562 billion in 1984. All well and good, but those sales were only 5% of what General Motors, the largest company in the United States, sold in 1989 and the combined sales of the top 100 black companies would have only ranked them 68th in the *Fortune* 500.

At the same time, the 39 black-owned banks had assets of only $1.8 billion, the 30 black-owned insurance companies had $803 million in assets, and the 24 black-owned savings and loans associations had assets of $1.3 billion. In contrast, Citicorp had assets of $230.6 billion (over 128 times the assets of all black-owned banks) and Prudential of America had assets of $129.1 billion (over 161 times the assets of all black-owned insurance companies).

Moreover, many black-owned businesses are in some of the most volatile sectors of the economy. The number of black contractors doubled in the 1980s, but these builders now face a real estate slump and fewer new construction projects in the 1990s. Faced with dramatic changes in the financial services sector, nearly one third of all black-owned savings and loan associations went bankrupt or were sold to whites between 1986 and 1990. Auto dealers have more sales than any other type of black business ($2.2 billion), but with slumping auto sales, they also face tough times.

In 1989, these economic trends hit the 100 largest black-owned firms hard. *Black Enterprise* reports that 19 of the 100 largest black-owned companies in the industrial and service sectors went broke in 1989 alone. As a result, black firms were behaving much like their white counterparts: They were cutting operating costs, laying off employees and restructuring the debts they had accumulated during the boom years of the 1980s. Staff in the 100 largest black companies dropped 9% in 1989 to 39,565.

Yet there are many bright spots. During the 1980s, black entrepreneurs made increasing inroads into the entertainment and media businesses. Led by long-established black-owned firms such as Johnson Publishing (*Ebony* magazine), 11 of the top 100 black companies were in media, entertainment, or advertising in 1989.

Black advertising agencies also flexed their economic muscles. Collectively, the top 3 black-owned ad agencies had $32.6 million worth of billings in 1989. And black entrepreneurs in recent years also put together increasingly large deals. In 1987 TLC Group L.P. chairman Reginald F. Lewis put

Table 4-1   Black-owned Businesses

This chart provides a snapshot of black-owned business between 1977 and 1987, the most recent year for which data are available. It provides a breakdown of black-owned businesses by industry, and sales.

	1977		1987	
	Total number	Sales & receipts (in millions of dollars)	Total number	Sales & receipts (in millions of dollars)
All Industries	231,203	8,645	424,165	19,763
Construction	21,101	758	36,763	2,174
Manufacturing	4,243	614	8,004	1,023
Transportation & Public Utilities	23,061	509	36,958	1,573
Wholesale Trade	2,212	664	5,519	1,327
Retail Trade	55,428	3,352	66,229	5,890
Food Stores	10,679	786	8,952	1,001
Auto Dealers	5,002	1,106	3,690	2,156
Eating and Drinking Places	13,008	572	11,834	1,084
Finance, Insurance Real Estate	9,805	641	26,989	804
Other Services	101,739	1,890	209,547	6,120

Source: U.S. Department of Commerce, *1987 Survey of Minority-owned Business Enterprises,* July 1990.

together a $985 million leveraged buyout of Beatrice International Food Companies. In 1985, a syndicate of 10 black businessmen or companies, including Michael Jackson, O. J. Simpson, J. Bruce Llewellyn, Julius Erving, and Essence Communications (publisher of *Essence* magazine), put together a $65 million deal to buy one of the TV stations Capital Cities was forced to sell when it acquired ABC. In 1990, Magic Johnson and the publisher of *Black Enterprise,* Earl Graves, acquired a Pepsi bottling franchise in the Washington, D.C., area that *Business Week* estimates is worth about $60 million. The deal was important not only because of its size, but also because it was part of a larger deal to promote Pepsi's products. Magic Johnson agreed to do Pepsi commercials over the next 3 years for a $4.2 million payment and a new Pepsi bottling franchise, the first time a major athlete had asked a major sponsor that his compensation include a piece of the business he was promoting.

BUSINESS AND POLITICAL POWER

Rapid political changes are also forcing minority businesses to change the way they do business in the 1990s. During the 1970s and 1980s, federal, state, and local governments actively encouraged minority businesses. Executive orders requiring increased employment of minorities and women by government contractors have helped many minorities break into occupations from construction to investment banking. A number of federal laws and regulations required that a certain amount of business be given to minority companies. Under such requirements, about $5.3 billion in federal government contracts was given to small minority-owned businesses at the end of the 1980s, about 2.7% of all contracts.

Increased black political clout, following three decades of marching and lobbying, also has encouraged the growth of minority-owned businesses on the local level. Fueled in part by Jesse Jackson's presidential campaign, the number of black officeholders rose to 7,370 in 1990, up from only 1,400 in 1970. Even so, blacks hold only 1.4% of the nation's 490,800 elective offices. Black mayors govern 3 of the nation's 5 largest cities, and there are 316 black mayors nationwide, up from only 48 in 1973. These mayors run cities

Table 4-2   Top Black-owned Businesses

	Company	Location	Chief executive	Year started	Staff	Type of business	1989 sales*
1	TLC BEATRICE INTERNATIONAL HOLDINGS INC.	New York, New York	Reginald F. Lewis	1983	6,000	Processing & distribution of food products	1,514.000
2	JOHNSON PUBLISHING CO. INC.	Chicago, Illinois	John H. Johnson	1942	2,370	Publishing; broadcasting; cosmetics; hair care	241.327
3	PHILADELPHIA COCA-COLA BOTTLING CO. INC.	Philadelphia, Pennsylvania	J. Bruce Llewellyn	1985	985	Soft-drink bottling	240.000
4	H.J. RUSSELL & CO.	Atlanta, Georgia	Herman J. Russell	1958	668	Construction; communications; food & beverages	132.876
5	THE GORDY CO.	Los Angeles, California	Berry Gordy	1958	70	Entertainment	100.000
6	SOFT SHEEN PRODUCTS INC.	Chicago, Illinois	Edward G. Gardner	1964	565	Hair-care products manufacturer	87.200
7	TRANS JONES INC./JONES TRANSFER CO.	Monroe, Michigan	Gary L. White	1986	1,264	Transportation services	78.555
8	THE BING GROUP	Detroit, Michigan	David Bing	1980	170	Steel processing & distribution	73.883
9	THE MAXIMA CORP.	Rockville, Maryland	Joshua I. Smith	1978	918	Systems engineering & computer management	58.383
10	DICK GRIFFEY PRODUCTIONS	Hollywood, California	Dick Griffey	1975	86	Entertainment	50.162
11	NETWORK SOLUTIONS INC.	Herndon, Virginia	Emmitt J. McHenry	1979	480	Systems integration	48.800
12	INTEGRATED SYSTEMS ANALYSTS INC.	Arlington, Virginia	C. Michael Gooden	1980	640	Engineering & technical support services	48.710
13	ADVANCED CONSUMER MARKETING CORP.	Burlingame, California	Harry W. Brooks, Jr.	1984	427	Systems integration; mail-order products	47.800
14	COMMUNITY FOODS INC.	Baltimore, Maryland	Oscar A. Smith, Jr.	1970	450	Retail foods	47.200
15	YANCY MINERALS	Woodbridge, Connecticut	Earl J. Yancy	1977	8	Industrial metals, minerals, and coal distributor	45.000
15	CRESCENT DISTRIBUTING CO. INC.	Harahan, Louisiana	Stanley S. Scott	1988	165	Beer distributor	45.000
17	THE THACKER ORGANIZATION	Decatur, Georgia	Floyd G. Thacker	1970	98	Construction & engineering	42.100
18	GRANITE BROADCASTING CORP.	New York, New York	W. Don Cornwell	1988	350	TV broadcasting	38.611
19	ESSENCE COMMUNICATIONS INC.	New York, New York	Edward Lewis	1969	85	Publishing; TV production; direct-mail catalog sales	38.037
20	SYSTEMS MANAGEMENT AMERICAN CORP.	Norfolk, Virginia	Herman E. Valentine	1970	390	Computer systems integration	38.000

*In millions of dollars, to nearest thousand.
Source: *Black Enterprise*

Table 4-3   Top Black-owned Banks

Rank	Bank	Location	Chief executive	Year started	Employees	Assets*	Deposits*	Loans*
1	SEAWAY NATIONAL BANK OF CHICAGO	Chicago, Illinois	Walter E. Grady	1965	142	163.840	139.150	45.405
2	CITIZENS TRUST BANK	Atlanta, Georgia	I. Owen Funderburg	1921	157	126.486	116.557	51.520
3	INDUSTRIAL BANK OF WASHINGTON	Washington, D.C.	B. Doyle Mitchell	1934	97	121.982	110.653	60.044
4	INDEPENDENCE BANK OF CHICAGO	Chicago, Illinois	Alvin J. Boutte	1964	106	117.990	102.544	44.240
5	DREXEL NATIONAL BANK	Chicago, Illinois	Alvin J. Boutte	1989	86	108.919	100.298	36.896
6	FIRST INDEPENDENCE NATIONAL BANK OF DETROIT	Detroit, Michigan	Gerald E. Harrington	1970	96	100.607	89.741	33.898
7	FIRST TEXAS BANK	Dallas, Texas	William E. Stahnke	1975	67	95.550	85.357	54.866
8	MECHANICS AND FARMERS BANK	Durham, North Carolina	Julia W. Taylor	1908	96	92.108	81.354	51.388
9	HIGHLAND COMMUNITY BANK	Chicago, Illinois	George R. Brokemond	1970	70	74.041	66.838	12.987
10	BOSTON BANK OF COMMERCE	Boston, Massachusetts	Ronald A. Homer	1982	50	67.721	63.442	57.230

*In millions of dollars, to the nearest thousand.
Source: *Black Enterprise.*

with a combined population of over 18 million. There is no black in the U.S. Senate. But in 1989 L. Douglas Wilder was elected governor of Virginia, making him the first black to hold that office since Reconstruction, and Representative William H. Grey was named House Majority Whip, making him one of the most powerful men in Congress.

Increased political power is likely to translate into further help for black-owned business, especially on a local level. Like mayors in the 19th and early 20th centuries who were protective of their immigrant constituencies, black mayors are likely to be more sensitive to the desires of minority businesses. But black businesses will have to face the 1990s with much less help from Uncle Sam and local governments. Budget cutbacks in Washington are

Table 4-4   Largest Hispanic Companies

1989 Rank	Company	Type of business	1989 Sales ($M)
1	Bacardi Imports	Import/Dist. Rum/Wine	500.00
2	Goya Foods, Inc.	Hispanic Food Mfg./Mktg.	320.00
3	Sedano's Supermarkets	Supermarket Chain	198.24
4	Handy Andy Supermarkets	Supermarket Chain	155.74
5	Galeana Van Dyke Dodge	Auto Dealerships	141.93
6	Pizza Management, Inc.	Restaurant Chain	134.50
7	Frank Parra Chevrolet, Inc.	Auto Dealerships	125.75
8	Ancira Enterprises, Inc.	Auto Dealerships	117.65
9	Int'l Bancshares Corp.	Commercial Bank	114.88
10	Capital Bancorp	Commercial Bank	110.28

Source: *Hispanic Business*

also likely to hurt minority firms, which do nearly $5 billion worth of business with the federal government. Cutbacks in commercial lending by many banks, and troubles with many government loan-guarantee programs, mean it will be harder for many undercapitalized minority firms to find financing.

Worse from the standpoint of such businesses, the Supreme Court ruled in 1989 that nearly all affirmative-action programs by state and local governments that set aside a percentage of the contracts for minority-owned firms were unconstitutional. Since that decision, nearly 20 states and cities have suspended their affirmative-action programs, and 33 state and local governments face court challenges to their affirmative-action programs.

MINORITY MANAGERS

In the past decade, minorities have slowly moved into positions of corporate power. In 1990, there were over 1.9 million black managers and professionals, about 6.2% of the total, up from 2.4% in 1972. There were about 1.1 million Hispanic managers and professionals, about 3.6% of the total, up from 2.8% in 1983. The rapid growth of black managers and small-business owners during the 1980s has created many more affluent blacks in the 1990s. According to *Black Enterprise,* about 9.5% of all blacks have incomes over $50,000, a 1,000% increase over 1970, when only 0.1% of the black population earned that much.

Moreover, more blacks are moving into the top executive ranks. In 1989 Kenneth Chenault was named president of American Express's Consumer Card Group and in 1990 Richard Parsons became the head of New York's Dime Savings Bank. But the number of minority and women managers is still very small. According to the U.S. Equal Employment Opportunity Commission, white males hold 67.4% of all management jobs in firms with more than 100 employees. In contrast, white women hold 23.2% of the management jobs, black men 2.9%, black women 2%, Hispanic men 1%, Hispanic women 0.8%, and other minorities 2.7%.

Cuban-born Roberto C. Goizueta is the CEO of Coca-Cola, but no black heads a *Fortune* 500 company. Over two thirds (68%) of America's largest corporations don't have a black, Hispanic, or Asian on the board, and about 41% don't have a woman. Still, that's something of an improvement over 1980, when 83% were all-white and 64% had all-male directors.

TOP MINORITY ENTREPRENEURS

Wang Laboratories   One of the nation's most successful minority-owned companies in the 1970s, Wang fell on hard times in the mid-1980s and faces severe challenges in the 1990s. An Wang, a refugee from Communist China, revolutionized computer technology by inventing the magnetic memory core, and in 1951 he founded his own company. Sales were only $15,000 during the first year but grew at the astonishing rate of 40% a year for the next three decades. By 1983, with 40% ownership in Wang

Laboratories, Dr. Wang and his family were worth $1.6 billion, making him one of America's five wealthiest individuals.

But the company badly bungled its early lead in the market for word processors and office computers. Sales of Wang word processors dropped when other companies put out cheaper, more powerful personal computers, and the company's stock plummeted in 1985, when the value of the Wang family holdings dropped by $1 billion. Dr. An Wang returned to active management in 1985, working with his son, Fred, to revitalize the company. But Dr. Wang died in 1989 and, under Fred's management, the company lost $629 million the same year. Finally Fred Wang resigned in early 1990 and the company hired an outsider, Richard Miller, as CEO. He's slashed jobs and sold operations to cut down the company's huge debts. But sales are still slow.

John H. Johnson   After founding Johnson Publishing Company in 1942, John Johnson built it into the largest black-owned company in the United States, with sales of $241.3 million in 1989, up from $173.5 in 1986. The flagship of his empire is *Ebony* magazine, but his business is not limited to publishing. The company's Fashion Fair cosmetics have been selling well; it also has a book division and owns several radio stations.

Johnson created his media empire Horatio Alger–style. He and his mother moved north when he was 15 because there was no high school in his hometown in Arkansas. After working for a black-owned insurance company, he founded his first magazine, *Negro Digest.* Despite problems from white distributors who refused to carry the magazine, circulation quickly took off, reaching over 150,000 after Johnson convinced Eleanor Roosevelt to write an article called "If I Were a Negro."

Johnson's next project was *Ebony,* founded in 1945. The magazine was designed for returning black servicemen to meet the rising expectations of postwar blacks. The magazine has always emphasized articles about accomplished blacks, a fabulously successful editorial formula. By the 1980s the combined circulation of Johnson's magazines equaled half the number of black adults in America. Johnson also is the first black publisher to crack the white advertising market. Johnson is worth over $180 million.

Berry Gordy   In the late 1950s and 1960s Berry Gordy's Motown Record Corporation revolutionized the record business, rocking the whole country with the Motor City sound of Detroit. Back then, Gordy made money with the sound of the Supremes, the Marvelettes, and Marvin Gaye. But Gordy's success at Motown continued into the 1980s with such popular acts as Lionel Ritchie. Gordy started Motown with $800 he borrowed from his family and says he made $367 million from the company before selling it in 1988 to MCA and Boston Ventures for $61 million. Gordy still owns Jobete Music Publishing, a firm that holds the copyrights to nearly all the Motown hits, and his Gordy Company grossed more than $100 million in 1989.

Chapter Five
UNIONS: MORE LOSERS
THAN WINNERS

HIGHLIGHTS AND TRENDS

• Stagnant incomes, a declining manufacturing sector, foreign competition, high unemployment, deregulation, a changing work force, and a high-tech workplace have all meant trouble in the union hall.

• In 1960 one third of American workers belonged to unions; today, only 16.1% of the workforce, about 16.7 million people, carries union cards.

• Faced with foreign competition and financial troubles in its traditional power base—manufacturing and mining—organized labor is on the defensive. Strikes have declined dramatically, making the period between 1975 and 1991 the most peaceful in American labor history since 1945. More union workers have been forced to take lower wages and lesser benefits than nonunion workers every year since 1984. Wages for union members rose only 3.7% in 1989 compared to 5.1% for nonunion workers.

• This decline in unions' longstanding political and social power has forced them to conduct costly organizing drives and adopt new strategies. Even so, unions face a difficult future: wage increases for union employees are expected to average less than those for nonunion workers through the end of the decade.

• By the year 2000, as older union members retire, some forecasters say that only about 13% of the labor force will belong to unions, the lowest rate since 1930.

TOUGH TIMES IN THE UNION HALL

In short, organized labor is probably in the worst shape it's been in since the 1920s, thanks to a rapidly changing U.S. economy. Young people, part-time workers, women, service employees, and college-educated workers have historically not been part of unions, yet they are the fastest-growing segments of the labor force. Unions represent only 8% of all part-time workers, 7% of all service workers, and 15% of all women employees.

Manufacturing and construction, which have always been the backbone of union membership, now employ a smaller share of the labor force, while service jobs are increasing. Service workers, women, and professional and technical workers, many of whom work in offices or smaller businesses, have also been harder to organize than workers in the large industrial factories that once provided the bulk of union membership.

At the same time, foreign competition and deregulation have hurt union bargaining power. Airlines, faced with stiff competition following deregulation, and steel makers, faced with tough foreign competition, have successfully demanded reduced benefits and salaries from their employees. Costly work rules have also been abolished, increasing productivity and cutting union power on the factory floor. Many unionized firms in the trucking and construction industry have gone bankrupt or turned to nonunion labor, and as a result the number of unionized workers in those industries has been cut. In the trucking industry, for example, nearly 200,000 union jobs have been lost in the last decade. In the railroad industry 100,000 jobs were lost following deregulation.

Management has also developed increasingly sophisticated techniques for reducing the cost of union contracts. Some companies have terminated their pension funds and used the proceeds to diversify; others have used Chapter 11 bankruptcy proceedings to get rid of unions altogether.

Moreover, financial troubles in its traditional power base—manufacturing, construction, and mining—have put organized labor on the defensive. The United Auto Workers (UAW) lost 1 million members since 1979. Strikes have also declined dramatically, making the period between 1975 and 1991 the most peaceful in American labor history since 1945.

Since the 1981–1982 recession ended, unions have been forced to settle for less at the bargaining table.

In 1983, union leaders were forced to accept wage cuts or wage freezes for 56% of all manufacturing workers and 37% of all nonfarm workers who got a new union contract that year. In 1986, new union contracts were even worse: 60% of manufacturing workers covered by new contracts took cuts or freezes. Even in 1989, when the manufacturing sector was much stronger, 17% of manufacturing workers who received new union contracts had to take wage cuts or freezes.

The manufacturing sector was, of course, particularly hard hit in the 1980s, but union workers throughout the economy faced problems. Every year since 1984, union workers have been forced to accept lower wage increases than their nonunion counterparts. In 1989, wages for union workers rose 3.7%, not enough to keep pace with inflation. Meanwhile, wages for nonunion workers jumped 5.1%.

Union negotiators are increasingly forced to give back many of the gains they had made during the 1960s and 1970s. The number of contracts that provided for automatic cost of living increases fell from 59% in 1979 to 40%

in 1989. Benefits were also under attack. To cut the cost of heath care insurance, payroll deductions for health plans have increased by 12% and deductibles (the amount an employee must pay before medical bills are paid by insurance) rose 6.5%.

Simultaneously, a second industrial revolution in the workplace is bringing increased automation to the factory and office, reducing the number of jobs available and forcing unions into the difficult position of bargaining over technological development. Already some unions have made job security one of their top priorities. In 1984, for example, the United Auto Workers' contract with General Motors established a $1 billion job security fund for workers who had been laid off because of technological change, transfer of work to outside suppliers, or changes in the work force. But job security still remains an elusive goal. The 1990 contract between General Motors and the United Auto Workers forced the union to accept the fact that management will be laying off many more employees in the future.

To keep unions out, management has also been more willing to improve wages and working conditions of nonunion employees. And as the courts have made it harder for employers to fire workers, unions also have a harder time arguing they are the only institutions that can protect worker's rights.

The most notable growth area for an otherwise declining union movement is the trend towards unionizing government employees. By 1974, following a series of tough strikes and favorable legal decisions, there were 2.9 million government employees in unions, up from only 0.9 million in 1956. Of this total, 1.5 million worked for state and local governments; 1.4 million were federal employees. Then, once the momentum began to build, union membership skyrocketed, hitting over 6.5 million in 1990. Public employees now account for 26% of the AFL-CIO membership, up from 15% a decade ago.

But even this trend is unlikely to reverse the declining fortunes of organized labor. In an era of fiscal austerity, government employment has increased more slowly and the percentage of unionized government employees has remained stagnant (36.5%).

Finally, management has begun involving workers in the process of running businesses, putting unions in a new and often awkward position. A 1984 law provided for sweeping tax incentives for employee stock ownership plans. In other cases, where workers haven't become entrepreneurs, they've been brought into the management process through productivity committees. About one third of all companies with over 500 employees have participatory management programs and about 31% of all companies with more than 100 employees have profit-sharing plans. As unions become more involved in management, they may be forced to give up some of their anti-management posturing, a development that could improve productivity.

Table 5-1 Union Membership, 1930–1990
Total in all unions

Year	Membership (thousands)	Year	Membership (thousands)
1930*	3,401	1960	17,049
1931	3,310	1961	16,303
1932	3,050	1962	16,586
1933	2,689	1963	16,524
1934	3,088	1964	16,841
1935	3,584	1965	17,299
1936	3,989	1966	17,940
1937	7,001	1967	18,362
1938	8,034	1968†	20,721
1939	8,763	1969	20,776
1940	8,717	1970	21,248
1941	10,201	1971	21,327
1942	10,380	1972	21,657
1943	13,213	1973	22,276
1944	14,146	1974	22,809
1945	14,322	1975	22,361
1946	14,395	1976	22,662
1947	14,787	1977	22,456
1948	14,319	1978	22,880
1949	14,282	1979	22,618
1950	14,267	1980‡	20,095
1951	14,946	1981	NA
1952	15,892	1982	NA
1953	16,948	1983	17,717
1954	17,022	1984	17,340
1955	16,802	1985	16,996
1956	17,490	1986	16,975
1957	17,369	1987	16,913
1958	17,029	1988	17,002
1959	17,117	1989	16,960
		1990	16,740

*1930–1980, Dues paying members, employed and unemployed.
†1968–1987, Includes union members and employee associations.
‡1980–1987, From Current Population Survey, employed dues paying members of unions and employee associations.
Source: Bureau of Labor Statistics, U.S. Department of Labor.

NEW STRATEGIES FOR THE 1980s AND BEYOND

Faced with some of the toughest challenges in its history, organized labor has turned to new strategies. Realizing that service workers and office workers will have to be the rank and file of the future, unions have waged long and ultimately successful campaigns to organize office workers at such universities as Columbia, Yale, and the University of Cincinnati.

The Service Employees International Union (SEIU) has made organizing the service industry its primary goal. Its membership jumped from 537,000 in 1979 to 850,000 today. Another union, the American Federation of State, County and Municipal Employees, has increased membership by 200,000 over the last decade by recruiting service workers in the public sector.

In other cases, merger mania has hit the union halls. There were 38 union mergers between 1975 and 1984, the most in any period of American labor. In 1989, the Teamsters voted to re-enter the AFL-CIO. In each case, union leaders hoped that labor solidarity would increase their waning strength.

Unions are also following management's footsteps by bringing in outside consultants to wage sophisticated public-relations and organizing campaigns. One consulting group, Corporate Campaign, has built up a reputation as a union defender with slick PR campaigns designed to pressure companies into improving relations with unions.

For example, in the bitter battle over organizing the J. P. Stevens textile plants, Corporate Campaign got community and church groups to put pressure on directors of the company. These directors, who headed banks, insurance companies, and other large corporations, suddenly realized that the adverse publicity hurt their own corporate images. These outside directors forced J. P. Stevens to settle with the union. But the same tactics failed in a bitter strike by meatpackers against Hormel.

Despite new tactics and strategies, unions still face an uphill battle. The public still worries about union bureaucrats, union democracy, an aging union leadership, and the influence of organized crime in a few unions. (See the chapter "Crime.") Moreover, drives to organize service workers have proved to be costly and difficult. The battle to organize workers at Columbia University, for example, dragged out over 10 years.

Unions are also finding it increasingly tough convincing workers they can deliver on bread-and-butter issues. Wage increases in the 1990s are expected to be even lower than those for nonunion workers. By the year 2000, as older union members retire, some forecasters say that only about 13% of the labor force will belong to unions, the lowest rate since 1930.

Table 5-2   Union Members: Who They Are, What They Earn

This chart presents the social and economic characteristics of America's union members and compares them to nonunion workers. It shows what percentages of various groups belong to unions and the median weekly earnings of union and nonunion workers, as well as union membership in various occupations for 1983 and 1989.

(Annual averages of monthly data. Covers employed wage and salary workers 16 years old and over. Excludes self-employed workers whose businesses are incorporated although they technically qualify as wage and salary workers. Based on Current Population Survey.)

| | Employed wage and salary workers | | | | | | Median usual weekly earnings (dollars) | | | | | |
| | Total (in thousands) | | Union members (thousands) | | Percent union members | | Total | | Represented by unions | | Not represented by unions | |
	1983	1990	1983	1990	1983	1990	1983	1990	1983	1990	1983	1990
Total	88,290	103,905	17,717	16,740	20.1	16.1	313	415	383	507	288	390
16–24 years	19,290	18,337	1,749	1,178	9.1	6.4	210	269	275	343	203	263
25–34 years	25,978	30,972	5,097	4,336	19.6	14.0	321	408	376	479	304	395
35–44 years	18,722	26,411	4,648	5,323	24.8	20.2	369	487	407	534	339	463
45–54 years	13,150	16,558	3,554	3,685	27.0	22.3	366	488	402	553	335	453
55–64 years	9,201	9,279	2,474	2,008	26.9	21.6	346	456	390	514	316	418
65 years and over	1,934	2,348	196	209	10.1	8.9	260	343	330	491	238	317
Men	47,856	54,828	11,809	10,564	24.7	19.3	378	485	414	541	349	457
Women	40,433	49,077	5,908	6,175	14.6	12.6	252	348	307	444	237	326
White	77,046	89,120	14,844	13,798	19.3	15.5	319	427	391	518	295	402
Men	42,168	47,515	10,134	8,914	24.0	18.8	387	497	421	557	362	477
Women	34,877	41,605	4,710	4,884	13.5	11.7	254	355	313	456	240	335
Black	8,979	11,416	2,440	2,410	27.2	21.1	261	329	324	434	222	302
Men	4,477	5,541	1,420	1,350	31.7	24.4	293	360	360	471	244	318
Women	4,502	5,875	1,020	1,060	22.7	18.0	231	308	287	403	209	286
Hispanic	(NA)	8,181	(NA)	1,209	(NA)	14.8	(NA)	307	(NA)	422	245	288
Men	(NA)	4,869	(NA)	794	(NA)	16.3	(NA)	322	(NA)	460	(NA)	301
Women	(NA)	3,312	(NA)	415	(NA)	12.5	(NA)	280	(NA)	367	(NA)	266
Full-time workers	70,976	85,082	16,271	15,422	22.9	18.1	313	(NA)	383	(NA)	288	(NA)
Part-time workers	17,314	18,822	1,446	1,318	8.4	7.0	(X)	(X)	(X)	(X)	(X)	(X)
Occupations												
Managerial and professional	19,657	25,671	3,354	3,674	17.1	14.3	437	608	421	608	446	608
Technical sales and administrative support	28,024	33,292	3,377	3,462	12.1	10.4	281	378	341	455	270	365
Service occupations	12,875	14,400	1,971	1,989	15.3	13.8	205	268	299	412	182	241
Precision, production, craft and repair	10,542	11,616	3,466	3,011	32.9	25.9	377	477	450	582	322	422
Operators, fabricators, and laborers	15,416	17,114	5,452	4,514	35.4	26.4	275	339	361	460	226	300
Farming, forestry and fishing	1,775	1,812	98	89	5.4	4.9	196	257	287	373	189	251
Industries												
Agricultural wage and salary workers	1,446	1,530	49	29	3.4	1.9	198	260	(B)	(B)	195	259
Private nonagricultural wage and salary workers	71,225	84,610	11,933	10,227	16.8	12.1	307	403	385	493	286	386
Mining	869	675	180	121	20.7	18.0	481	565	470	583	488	553
Construction	4,109	5,122	1,131	1,073	27.5	21.0	348	458	510	642	296	407
Manufacturing	19,066	20,339	5,303	4,197	27.8	20.6	335	430	368	475	315	414
Transportation	5,142	6,124	2,182	1,934	42.4	31.6	417	415	445	571	386	485
Wholesale and retail trade	18,081	21,274	1,568	1,338	8.7	6.3	252	319	348	406	242	313
Finance, insurance and real estate	5,559	6,835	160	173	2.9	2.5	296	428	285	408	297	430
Services	18,400	24,241	1,410	1,391	7.7	5.7	272	378	303	418	268	373
Government	15,618	17,765	5,735	6,484	36.7	36.5	351	490	381	526	316	438

(B) Data not shown where base is less than 50,000.
(NA) Not available.
(X) Not applicable.
[1] Members of a labor union or an employee association similar to a labor union.
Source: U.S. Bureau of Labor Statistics, *Employment and Earnings*, annual.

Table 5-3 Work Stoppages Involving 1,000 Workers or More, 1947–1990

Year	Number of stoppages	Workers involved (thousands)	Days idle (thousands)
1947	270	1,629	25,720
1948	245	1,435	26,127
1949	262	2,537	43,420
1950	424	1,698	30,390
1951	415	1,462	15,070
1952	470	2,746	48,820
1953	437	1,623	18,130
1954	265	1,075	16,630
1955	363	2,055	21,180
1956	287	1,370	26,840
1957	279	887	10,340
1958	332	1,587	17,900
1959	245	1,381	60,850
1960	222	896	13,260
1961	195	1,031	10,140
1962	211	793	11,760
1963	181	512	10,020
1964	246	1,183	16,220
1965	268	999	15,140
1966	321	1,300	16,000
1967	381	2,192	31,320
1968	392	1,855	35,367
1969	412	1,576	29,397
1970	381	2,468	52,761
1971	298	2,516	35,538
1972	250	975	16,764
1973	317	1,400	16,260
1974	424	1,796	31,809
1975	235	965	17,563
1976	231	1,519	23,962
1977	298	1,212	21,258
1978	219	1,006	23,774
1979	235	1,021	20,409
1980	187	795	20,844
1981	145	729	16,908
1982	96	656	9,061
1983	81	909	17,461
1984	62	376	8,499
1985	54	324	7,079
1986	69	533	8,995
1987	46	174	4,469
1988	40	118	4,364
1989	51	452	16,996
1990	44	201	6,580.5

Source: *Current Wage Developments.*

Table 5-4 Biggest Unions in the U.S.

Union	Address	Membership
American Federation of Labor and Congress of Industrial Organizations Merged: 1955 President: Lane Kirkland	815 16th Street, N.W. Washington, D.C. 202-637-5000	14,500,000
National Education Association* Founded: 1857 President: Keith Geiger	1201 16th Street, N.W. Washington, D.C. 202-833-4000	2,000,000
International Brotherhood of Teamsters, Chauffeurs, Warehousemen and Helpers of America* Founded: 1903 President: William J. McCarthy	25 Louisiana Avenue, N.W. Washington, D.C. 202-624-6800	1,600,000
United Food and Commercial Workers International Union Founded: 1979 President: William H. Wynn	1775 K Street, N.W. Washington, D.C. 202-223-3111	1,300,000
American Federation of State, County and Municipal Employees Founded: 1936 President: Gerald W. McEntee	1625 L Street, N.W. Washington, D.C. 202-452-4800	1,200,000
International Union, United Automotive, Aerospace and Agricultural Implement Workers of America (United Auto Workers) Founded: 1935 President: Owen Bieber	8000 Jefferson Avenue Detroit, Michigan 313-926-5000	1,000,000
International Brotherhood of Electrical Workers Founded: 1891 President: John J. Barry	1125 15th Street, N.W. Washington, D.C. 202-833-7000	1,000,000
Service Employees International Union Founded: 1921 President: John J. Sweeney	1313 L Street, N.W. Washington, D.C. 202-898-3200	850,000
United Steelworkers of America Founded: 1936 President: Lynn Williams	5 Gateway Center Pittsburgh, Pennsylvania 412-562-2400	750,000
United Brotherhood of Carpenters and Joiners of America Founded: 1881 President: Sigurd Lucassen	101 Constitution Avenue, N.W. Washington, D.C. 202-546-6206	595,000
Communications Workers of America Founded: 1938 President: Morton Bahr	1925 K Street, N.W. Washington, D.C. 202-728-2300	700,000
American Federation of Teachers Founded: 1916 President: Albert Shanker	555 New Jersey Avenue, N.W. Washington, D.C. 202-879-4400	750,000
International Association of Machinists and Aerospace Workers Founded: 1888 President: George Kourpias	1300 Connecticut Avenue, N.W. Washington, D.C. 202-857-5200	826,875

Table 5-4   Biggest Unions in the U.S. (continued)

Union	Address	Membership
Laborers' International Union of North America Founded: 1903 President: Angelo Fosco	905 16th Street, N.W. Washington, D.C. 202-737-8320	450,000
International Union of Operating Engineers Founded: 1896 President: Larry L. Dugan	1125 17th Street, N.W. Washington, D.C. 202-429-9100	375,000
United Association of Journeymen and Apprentices of the Plumbing and Pipe Fitting Industry of the United States and Canada Founded: 1889 President: Marvin J. Boede	901 Massachusetts Avenue, N.W. Washington, D.C. 202-628-5823	325,000
American Postal Workers Union Founded: 1971 President: Moe Biller	1300 L St. N.W. Washington, D.C. 202-842-4200	365,000
Hotel Employees and Restaurant Employees International Union Founded: 1892 President: Edward T. Hanley	1219 28th Street, N.W. Washington, D.C. 202-393-4373	330,000
National Association of Letter Carriers of the United States of America Founded: 1889 President: Vincent R. Sombrotto	100 Indiana Avenue, N.W. Washington, D.C. 202-393-4695	315,281
Amalgamated Clothing and Textile Workers Union Founded: 1914 President: Jack Sheinkman	15 Union Square West New York, New York 212-242-0700	272,669
United Paperworkers International Union Founded: 1884 President: Wayne E. Glenn	3340 Perimeter Hill Drive Nashville, Tennessee 615-834-8590	230,000
International Ladies' Garment Workers' Union Founded: 1900 President: Jay Mazur	275 7th Avenue New York, New York 212-741-6161	175,000
Retail, Wholesale and Department Store Union Founded: 1937 President: Lenore Miller	30 East 29th Street New York, New York 212-684-5300	200,000
American Federation of Government Employees Founded: 1932 President: John Sturdivant	80 F Street, N.W. Washington, D.C. 202-737-8700	210,000
United Mine Workers of America* Founded: 1890 President: Richard Trumka	900 15th Street, N.W. Washington, D.C. 202-842-7200	186,000
American Federation of Musicians of the United States and Canada Founded: 1896 President: Jay Martin Emerson	1501 Broadway New York, New York 212-869-1330	206,000

*Independent unions. All other unions are members of the American Federation of Labor and Congress of Industrial Organizations.
Sources: U.S. Department of Labor and unions.

HIGHLIGHTS OF AMERICAN LABOR

1636   First labor dispute in America over money takes place in Maine, where fishermen strike over a proposal that would cost them a year in wages.

1648   The first American labor organization is formed by Boston shoe and barrel makers.

1734   New York maids form the first women's labor organization.

1786   Philadelphia printers hold the first authenticated strike in the United States. Their demand? A minimum wage of $6 a week.

1806   Members of the Philadelphia Journeymen Cordwainers strike to raise wages. As a result of that strike they become the first union to be tried and found guilty of a criminal conspiracy to raise wages.

1824   Women workers participate in a strike for the first time, one involving Pawtucket, Rhode Island, weavers.

1834   The first attempt to found a national labor federation in the U.S. is made when the National Trades Union is formed in New York City. The union, however, falls apart during the panic of 1837.

1847   The first state law limiting the workday to 10 hours is passed in New Hampshire.

1852   The first national organization of workers to endure to the present day, the National Typographical Union, is formed.

1863   New York mailmen form the first union for federal workers.

1868   An eight-hour workday for federal employees is declared.

1869   The Noble Order of the Knights of Labor is established. Unusual for the time is the fact that membership is open to both blacks and women. Knights, who have a socialist ideology, work in extreme secrecy until 1878 when they embark on a series of railroad strikes. By pushing for the eight-hour day, which is considered a revolutionary idea, they acquire 700,000 members by 1886, but decline thereafter because of the rise of the American Federation of Labor.

1869   The first black labor union, the Colored National Labor Union, is established.

1870   The first written contract between coal miners and operators is signed.

1874   The first use of the union label is introduced by Cigar Makers' International Union.

1875   American Express becomes the first private company to set up a pension plan.

1884   The Bureau of Labor is established in the Department of the Interior. It later becomes an independent agency without cabinet rank, is absorbed into the new Department of Commerce and Labor in 1903, and becomes, in 1913, the present Department of Labor, a cabinet-level position.

1886   The first convention of the American Federation of Labor takes place. Headed by Samuel Gompers, the union grows into the nation's largest, but is organized by crafts rather than by industry, making it difficult to organize some larger factories.

1886   On May 1, some 340,000 workers around the country go on strike for an eight-hour day, and in Chicago four strikers are killed. On May 4, a demonstration in Haymarket Square is held to protest their deaths and to support the eight-hour day. The rally is peaceful until police attempt to stop it; then a bomb explodes, killing seven policemen and four workers. The event becomes a labor cause célèbre and leads to the creation of May Day as a workers' holiday.

1888   The first federal labor relations law is passed, setting up arbitration and a presidential board of investigation for the railroad industry.

1890   The United Mine Workers union is formed. About a fifth of its early members are black.

1892   In one of the bloodiest strikes in U.S. history, workers at the Carnegie steel mills in Homestead, Pennsylvania, go on strike to protest wage cuts. During the six-month strike, four other Carnegie plants and several mills unrelated to the company are shut down. At one point Andrew Carnegie sends several boatloads of Pinkerton agents to retake the mill but they are attacked by the strikers, leaving four strikers and twelve Pinkerton guards dead. Eventually the strike fails and the union is ousted from most of the steel mills.

1900   The International Ladies' Garment Workers' Union is formed.

1905   The founding convention of the communist-oriented Industrial Workers of the World (the Wobblies) takes place. Under the leadership of Big Bill Haywood, the union picks up 100,000 members by 1917 (including the first mass unionization of migrant agricultural workers). The union is, however, effectively destroyed by the government for its opposition to the First World War. The Wobblies are the last powerful union in the United States to advocate a socialist revolution. Since then, large unions restrict their demands to economic goals—higher wages and benefits.

1911   In one of the worst industrial accidents in the country's history, a fire at the Triangle Shirtwaist Company in New York kills 146 workers. Most die because the garment-factory owners had locked the exits. The tragedy leads to the creation of the New York Factory Investigating Commission and the passage of a number of laws designed to improve factory conditions.

1933   Frances Perkins becomes the first woman secretary of labor and the first woman named to a cabinet-level position. She is also the first secretary of labor who has had a college education and the first who has never been a union member.

1935   The National Labor Relations Act (the Wagner Act) guarantees workers the right to organize unions and have collective bargaining. This act, along with section 7A of the National Industrial Recovery Act (1933), marks a new deal for organized labor and leads to explosive union growth. The Wagner Act also establishes the National

Labor Relations Board as a monitor for union organizing and collective bargaining.

1936   After the first large sit-down strike, the United Rubber Workers win recognition from the Goodyear Tire and Rubber Company.

1937   The United Auto Workers get a big break when General Motors recognizes the UAW as the bargaining agent for its workers.

1937   The United States Steel Corporation recognizes the Steel Workers Organizing Committee as the bargaining agent for its workers.

1937   In one of the bloodiest labor protests ever, 10 people are killed and 80 are wounded when police attack members of the Steel Workers Organizing Committee at the Republic Steel Corporation plant in South Chicago on Memorial Day.

1938   The Fair Labor Standards Act establishes the first minimum wage of 25 cents per hour. It also sets regulations on minimum work age and maximum work week and mandates time-and-a-half overtime pay for employees engaged in interstate commerce.

1941   The first union-shop agreement with a major auto company is signed between the United Auto Workers and Ford Motor Company after a 10-day strike.

1941   The AFL and the CIO issue a no-strike pledge effective for the duration of the war.

1941   Under pressure from black unionist A. Philip Randolph, who threatens a march on Washington to dramatize discrimination against black workers, President Roosevelt establishes a Fair Employment Practices Committee. Its mission is to ensure that workers employed in government or the defense industry are not discriminated against because of race, creed, color, or national origin.

1946   About 1.43% of all working time in the United States is lost because of strikes, the most in the country's history, as unions try to make up for the war years when they took no-strike pledges.

1947   The Labor Management Relations (Taft-Hartley) Act is passed over President Truman's veto. The act revises the Wagner Act and curbs the power of unions by prohibiting a list of unfair labor practices: the closed shop, secondary boycotts, and mass picketing. Taft-Hartley also encourages state right-to-work laws, establishes a cooling-off period before a strike can be called, requires unions to publish their finances, and allows employers to sue unions for broken contracts or damages inflicted during a strike.

1949 and 1950   Eleven unions charged with communist domination are expelled from the CIO.

1954   The longest major strike in the history of the United States begins on April 5 at the Wisconsin plumbing manufacturing plant of Kohler Company. The dispute is over whether employees can unionize and drags on until September 1, 1960. Eventually the company is cited for unfair labor practices. Almost all of the strikers are reinstated with $4.5 million back pay when the strike ends.

1955   The AFL and CIO settle their differences and agree to merge, forming the nation's largest union, with 16 million members and over 85% of all unionized workers.

1957   The AFL-CIO expels the Teamsters, the Bakery and Confectionery Workers and the Laundry, Dry Cleaning and Dye House Workers (a combined membership of 1.6 million) for union corruption.

1959   The longest strike ever in the steel industry begins on July 15 and ends on October 21, when a back-to-work injunction is invoked under the Taft-Hartley Act. In terms of employee time lost, the 116-day strike, which idled hundreds of thousands, is the largest strike in the history of the United States. Workers return to their jobs for the 80-day cooling-off period as required under Taft-Hartley and a new contract is finally signed in January 1960.

1962   A major step in the unionization of federal employees takes place when an executive order gives unions the right to engage in collective bargaining with federal agencies.

1970   The first massive work stoppage by federal employees occurs when 210,000 postal workers go on strike on March 18. An agreement is reached in two weeks after military units are summoned to handle the mail in New York City.

1970   Hawaii becomes the first state to grant state and local government employees the right to strike.

1972   A 35-year-long labor dispute, one of the longest in the history of labor relations, is settled by an agreement to phase out firemen's jobs on diesel freight locomotives gradually. The dispute between the United Transportation Union and major railroad companies began in 1937.

1974   Reflecting the increased importance of government employees in the labor movement, the AFL-CIO forms a new Public Employee Department. It includes 24 affiliated unions representing 2 million public workers, including Post Office employees.

1979   Lane Kirkland becomes president of the AFL-CIO, succeeding George Meany.

1980   Ronald Reagan becomes the first former union president to be elected president of the United States.

1980   After a 17-year-long battle, the Amalgamated Clothing and Textile Workers Union signs a collective bargaining agreement with J. P. Stevens & Co.

1981   President Reagan dismisses 8,590 members of the Professional Air Traffic Controllers Organization after they go on strike.

1982   A recession in smokestack industries hits the union movement hard. Economic troubles cost the AFL-CIO more than 400,000 dues-paying members and forces some unions to lay off members of their staffs.

1984   Organized labor's declining political clout becomes apparent when the candidate of organized labor, Walter Mondale, is clobbered by President Reagan, despite heavy union support.

1986   In some of the worst contracts ever negotiated by union leaders, 56% of all manufacturing workers covered by new labor contracts are forced to accept pay freezes or pay cuts.

1987   After decades of feuding, the Teamsters vote to rejoin the AFL-CIO.
        The reason: To shore up declining labor power by increased coopera-
        tion between unions. The Teamsters would add 1.7 million members
        to the AFL-CIO—enough people to cover 15% of the AFL-CIO's
        annual budget. Moreover, the Teamsters have a political action com-
        mittee with annual receipts of over $10 million that could help rein-
        force the unions' declining political clout.

1989   After seeing real hourly earnings in the private nonfarm sector fall by
        6.4% from 1979 to 1989, labor militancy increases. There are 51
        strikes involving nearly 452,000 workers, up from 1988's record low
        of only 40, involving 118,000 workers. But wages for union members
        increase only 3.7%, slower than for nonunion members, who saw
        their paychecks increase by 5.1%.

1990–1991   The Tribune Company, a major media company, gets tough
        with the unions at its New York Daily News, New York City's largest
        newspaper. Tribune management pays King and Ballow, a law firm
        known for its expertise in busting unions, nearly $10 million for
        advice. After millions' worth of concessions in 1986, management
        asks for more givebacks in 1990 and a strike begins on October 25th.
        But the unions leaders prevent the paper from being distributed at
        local newsstands and circulation plummets from nearly 1 million a
        day to only 350,000. After losing as much as $160 million during the
        five-month strike, the Tribune Company pays British media baron
        Robert Maxwell $60 million to take over the paper and assume long
        term liabilities—such as pensions and severance pay that total over
        $100 million. Tribune's disastrous get-tough strategy and its inability
        to put out a non-union paper indicates the difficulties of waging all-
        out war against well-organized unions. But the unions also come out
        badly bruised. To keep the paper from folding, Maxwell forces the
        unions to accept a contract that cuts 800 jobs. In the end, they get a
        contract that includes many of the same provisions that the Tribune
        company proposed before the strike.

1991   After settling a racketeering suit in 1989, the Teamsters are sched-
        uled to hold democratic elections under the supervision of a court-
        appointed trustee. Government prosecutors and rank-and-file union
        activists hope the election will break the power organized crime has
        held over the Teamsters since the 1930s.

PART II

The Haves

Chapter Six

MONEY: FROM WAMPUM TO PLASTIC

Economists, who have a hard time explaining what constitutes money in a money economy, have an even harder time coming up with a definition that applies to the whole history of money. Generally, they admit defeat and say money is just about anything people say it is. Even bankers, who know a lot about money, aren't any more precise. The American Bankers Association says money is "anything that can be used to buy goods and services."

Money, in short, can act as money because people believe in it. Greenback dollars don't buy goods and services because paper is so expensive. They have value because people have faith in their value. That faith, as well as a certain vagueness about what constitutes money, allows gold, silver, dollars, and checks to function as money. It also allows notes printed by banks and governments that will eventually go bankrupt to circulate as money.

Of course, precious metals, usually gold and silver, have been the most common forms of money. But thanks to faith, most anything will work as money, as long as you believe in it. At various times, such commodities as tobacco, shells, and whiskey have served as mediums of exchange. Today, little pieces of paper in the form of checks and currency, plastic credit cards, and even electronic impulses used to credit and debit accounts can also be classified as mediums of exchange, that is, as money.

But faith can only take you so far, especially in the world of finance. Faith may explain why money has assumed so many different forms. It doesn't explain the history of money and how it has transformed our economy.

Money, banking, and our financial system were created and developed over time in response to a simple practical problem: the need to get the most out of one's goods, services, and capital.

The early development of money was a vast improvement over barter, allowing merchants to exchange money or precious metals rather than cumbersome products. For the state, money meant that taxes could be paid in coins, or, when taxes didn't cover its expenses, a sovereign could mint more money to finance wars, new palaces, and any other sort of nonsense.

At the same time, banking made the growth of a money economy possible. The earliest banks, as noted below, performed two vital functions: they exchanged foreign currency, thus facilitating international trade, and they provided short-term credit for merchants and tradesmen, increasing production and trade. In this way, both money and banking made the economy more liquid. They allowed producers and governments to take commodities, land, fixed assets, or even goodwill and turn them into liquid assets—money, credit, or other instruments that could be easily exchanged or used to buy goods and services.

Over time the evolution of banking and money has helped create increasingly efficient markets and economies. The development of land banks allowed landlords to monetarize an illiquid asset—real estate—and use the money to invest in other businesses and expand their operations. Short-term loans allowed businesses to expand their operations or tide themselves over seasonal shortages in cash. But progress never moves in a straight line. Bankers, merchants, businesses, and especially governments occasionally display an alarming tendency to view money, banking, and finance as a kind of alchemy: a mysterious science that will somehow transpose future sales, not-yet-workable inventions, intangible hopes, vague schemes, visions of military might, soon-to-be-discovered El Dorados, rampant boosterism, and even revolutionary ardor into pure gold.

On this side of the history of money one finds government finance by the printing of paper money, speculation on Florida swamp land, the Tulip Bubble, and the 10,000 banks that failed in the early years of the Depression.

Such excesses help explain another basic theme running through the history of money, banking, and financial services: both banks and governments create money. Governments produce money by printing or coining money; banks accomplish the same feat either by issuing bank notes, as early American banks did, or by making loans and extending credit. Being in the business of manufacturing money, if you will, governments and banks have developed an uneasy but symbiotic relationship.

Speculative loans by banks have precipitated economic depressions, forcing governments to step in and regulate the financial industry. Similarly, and often with worse consequences, governments have discredited and delayed the development of key financial revolutions, such as paper money and central banks, by using them to finance disastrous spending sprees and harebrained economic policies. These excesses, in the public and private sector, go a long way toward explaining why the financial markets are the most heavily regulated sector of the American economy.

Here are a few key developments in the history of money and banking. (Key moments in the history of the stock exchanges can be found on page 272.)

7000 B.C.   Cattle are used as a medium of exchange. The relationship between money and cattle survives in our word *pecuniary,* which derives from the Latin word *pecus,* meaning "cow." In several other languages, the word for *money* is related to the word for *cattle* or some kind of domestic animal. Our word *fee* comes from the Anglo-Saxon *feoh,* meaning both money and cattle. Our words *capital, chattel,* and *cattle* are also all derived from the word *capitale.* During this period, grains such as wheat and barley are also used as mediums of exchange.

2000 B.C.   Bronze ingots, often in the shape of cows, appear and are used as a medium of exchange. Though less cumbersome than actual commodities, the ingots still must be weighted, unlike modern coins. The Chinese are reported to have made coins as early as 2250 B.C.

1000 B.C.   Purer metals such as gold and silver begin to replace bronze as mediums of exchange.

973 B.C.   King Solomon's fleet trades in the Red Sea and begins mining gold in Africa and Arabia.

800 B.C.   The forerunners of our modern coins appear. The Lydians of Asia Minor stamp ingots of electrum, a natural alloy of gold and silver, and each ingot bears a mark that shows its weight. This practice does away with the need for scales.

625 B.C.   The first coins are introduced into Greece. They are stamped with the likeness of an ear of wheat, perhaps as a reminder that grains were once used as a medium of exchange.

540 B.C.   Along with the creation of money come counterfeiters. On this date Polycrates of Samos cheats the Spartans with fake gold coins. Cheats also profit by raising the quantity of silver in relation to gold in coins.

4th century B.C.   The Greeks invent the bill of exchange. It allows a merchant to deposit a sum of money with his banker, who gives him a letter. When the merchant presents this letter to another banker in another city, the banker pays the money. The forerunner of a bank check, the bill of exchange facilitates travel and trade by allowing people to journey from one place to another without the danger or inconvenience of taking large sums of gold or coins.

3rd century B.C.   If money makes the economy more efficient by facilitating the exchange of goods and services, it also opens up even greater opportunities for fraud, inefficiency, and outright larceny. On a small scale, individuals and merchants often clip or shave small bits of gold off each coin before spending the money. But the biggest offenders are governments. As early as the Punic Wars, the Romans pioneer the idea of debased coinage by reducing the value of silver in their coins. The idea catches on and remains a common practice even today, when governments do the same thing with printing presses. In the short run, this technique allows kings to pay their debts by simply manufacturing money rather than by increasing taxes or curtailing spending. Over time, currency debasement causes inflation, since more money is chasing the same amount of goods. In extreme cases of hyperinflation or hyperdebasement, individuals and merchants stop accepting coins as payment.

6th to 11th centuries A.D.   The Dark Ages are bleak times for banking. Banking was widespread in the Mediterranean region during the Greek and Roman period, but it declines after the fall of the Roman Empire because of the decline of international trade, a radically reduced need to change foreign currencies, a decline of the money economy, and a falling demand for credit—that is, declines in the factors that led to the creation of banking in the first place. As trade revives, however, in the 11th century, banking reappears.

13th century   The Italians become Europe's bankers and banking houses play a major role in reviving European commerce and trade. Italian banking houses are prohibited from charging interest by church laws against usury but get around the rule by buying and selling bills of exchange at a discount. (The discount, or difference between the value of the bill of exchange and what the bank paid for it, produces a profit, just as a modern bank makes money by charging interest on loans.) But early banking is a perilous profession and many banking houses go broke in the highly profitable but risky business of loaning money to medieval princes. The Fugger family, for example, amasses a $50 million fortune but goes bankrupt with the fall of the Holy Roman Empire.

1492   Columbus discovers the New World. He doesn't make any money on his venture and dies poor. But Spain soon discovers vast treasures of silver and gold in Mexico and Latin America. Between 1500 and 1650 about 181 tons of gold and 16,000 tons of silver reach Europe from America. That capital helps finance Europe's growing dominance of the world's economy.

1558   Reflecting on the problem of creating a stable currency, Sir Thomas Gresham articulates a basic law of economics: bad money always drives out good. By this he means that debased money is spent while good money, with a higher value of gold and silver, is hoarded. Later, Gresham's law is applied to paper money. When governments print too much money, the paper often freely circulates, at reduced value, while precious metals and coins are hoarded.

17th century   Mints put serrated edges on coins so people can't shave bits of gold or silver off the sides of coins, thus reducing their weight. A common tactic is to put coins in a bag and shake them vigorously for several hours. The friction of the coins rubs off some gold dust, which is sold.

17th century   Lacking precious metals, the American colonists experiment with various commodities. In Massachusetts, corn and beaver skins are used as mediums of exchange. Indian currency of beads, or wampum, is made legal tender in 1637 by the Massachusetts Bay government, and in 1618 the Virginia colonists make tobacco legal tender. But these experiments run into problems. Wampum rapidly depreciates in value as the white man introduces one of his own inventions—counterfeit wampum. In Virginia, bumper crops of tobacco quickly depreciate the crop's value as money.

1652   The first colonial mint is established in the Massachusetts Bay Colony. The Crown is angered by colonists usurping the British monopoly on printing money, and royal decrees order the mints to close in the 1680s.

1658   The Riksbank of Stockholm becomes the first bank to issue bank notes.

1690   Failing with wampum, Massachusetts becomes the first colony to issue paper money. The experiment works until the colony prints far too much money, after which the currency declines dramatically in value. Other colonies make the same mistake, setting off high inflation. Worried about this fiscal mismanagement, Parliament prohibits paper money first in Massachusetts in 1751 and then in all the colonies in 1763. However, in Pennsylvania, where the money supply is controlled carefully, the experiment with paper money is successful.

1775   As one might expect in a country that started out as the result of a tax revolt, the first Continental Congress is opposed to financing the War of Independence with new taxes. The solution is to print money. As one delegate puts it, "Will I consent to load my constituents with taxes when we can send to our printer and get a wagon load of money, one quire of which will pay for the whole thing?" Obviously not. For the first two years, Congress restricts the amount of paper money issued, and the currency, known as continentals, holds its value. But after 1778, the printing presses move into high gear and by 1780 one dollar in specie is worth $80 in continentals. Eventually the U.S. government adopts a plan whereby all remaining continental currency is redeemed at the rate of $1 dollar in specie for $100 in paper.

1781   The first commercial bank is created when Congress gives Robert Morris, the superintendent of finance during the revolution, a charter to the Bank of North America. It is absorbed in the 1920s by the Pennsylvania Company.

1791   The issue of a central bank runs through American financial history. In the first battle over the creation of a central bank, James Madison and Alexander Hamilton debate the pros and cons. Madison, defending the idea of hard currency and attacking paper money as fiscally and economically irresponsible, argues that Congress doesn't have the power to charter a bank. He, like other opponents of the bank, believes that hard money is endangered by the speculative excesses of banks. But Congress is convinced by Hamilton's argument that banks increase productive capital by advancing credit, that banks help the government finance its programs, and that banks facilitate the payment of taxes. It charters the Bank of the United States as a central bank for twenty years with an authorized capital of $10 million, of which the federal government contributes $2 million. Investors snap up the stock when it goes on sale in July of 1791.

1792   As for most revolutionary governments, one of the first tasks of the new republic is to create its own money. In 1792 Congress sets up the first minting of U.S. coins and puts the U.S. on a bimetallic standard of gold and silver. Alexander Hamilton recommends the bimetallic standard to avoid the "evils of scanty circulation." But things don't work out the way Congress intends. The U.S. never functions on a bimetallic standard whereby both gold and silver circulate as money. Worse, U.S. coins or money are not widely circulated in the United States before the 1830s. During those years, foreign coins and paper money printed by private banks act as the country's money supply. Here's how Congress manages to accomplish exactly the opposite of what it intends: Worried about the states' past practices of printing worthless paper money, the Constitution of the United States gives the right to "coin Money" to the federal government and prohibits the states from issuing "bills of credit"—paper money. In 1792, when Congress gets around to setting up the money supply, it adopts the Spanish dollar as the unit of account, adopts a decimal system for smaller coins, decrees that gold or silver sold to the mint will be turned into coins, and puts the U.S. on a bimetallic standard with 15 ounces of silver equal to 1 ounce of gold. Congress also authorizes a ten-dollar gold eagle, a five-dollar gold piece, a two-dollar-and-fifty-cent piece, a gold dollar, a silver dollar, a half dollar, a quarter, a dime, a half dime, a cent, and a half cent. But the ratio overvalues silver. As a result, holders of gold sell gold only in the open market and only silver is brought to the mint to be coined. Since gold is not minted into coins and hence doesn't circulate, the U.S. operates on a de facto silver standard, like most of Europe. This state of affairs continues until 1834, when Congress changes the ratio. (See 1834.) Worse, very few American silver dollars circulate. The dollar minted in Philadelphia is slightly lighter than the Spanish silver dollar that is circulated in Latin America. But Spanish colonists discover that the U.S. dollar circulates just as well as the heavier and hence more valuable Spanish silver dollar. They bring Spanish silver dollars to the U.S., melt them down, and mint them into U.S. dollars for a profit. As a result the U.S. is forced to suspend coinage of silver dollars and foreign coins and paper money printed by private banks act as our currency.

19th century   The new country needs capital to develop frontier regions and banks appear almost as fast as saloons in frontier towns. Various state legislatures issue 29 bank charters by 1800, 90 by 1811, and 120 by 1816. These banks issue $100 million in notes in 1817, up from $45 million in 1812. Most play a major role in financing early development by proving needed capital. Some, however, simply print paper money. (See 1809.)

1804   The Farmers Bank of Maryland is the first bank to pay interest on bank deposits. Massachusetts banks begin paying interest on large deposits left in the 1810s, and in 1825 the country's central bank, the Bank of the United States, starts paying interest on specie deposits.

1809   The Farmers Exchange Bank of Gloucester, Rhode Island, earns the dubious distinction of becoming the first bank to fail in the United States. Founded in 1804, the bank began with only $3,000 in capital but issued hundreds of thousands of dollars worth of paper money. The owner had cashiers working overtime signing the bills the bank circulated as money and at another point the bank issued $648,000 in notes backed by only $86 in specie.

1811   After another debate between supporters of a central bank and hard-money proponents who oppose a central bank, Congress decides not to renew the charter of the Bank of the United States. Jefferson's party, the Democratic-Republicans, opposes the bank because it supports hard money and wants the government to accept only specie. In its view, the central bank encourages fiscal irresponsibility and the printing of paper money, which almost inevitably depreciates. Ending the bank's charter causes immediate economic and fiscal problems. When the War of 1812 starts, the U.S. no longer has a central bank to finance the war. Many state banks work their printing presses overtime and many bank notes circulate at a substantial discount. Banks also face temporary liquidity problems. Without a central bank they have no way of surviving temporary shortfalls that occur seasonally.

1816   The first savings banks, the Provident Institution for Savings in Boston and the Savings Fund Society in Philadelphia, are established. By the Civil War, traditional distinctions between American banks are well established. Savings banks encourage people to save and are required to hold a large portion of their assets as mortgages. National commercial banks are prohibited from making mortgages; their business is based on taking in demand deposits and making short-term business loans.

1816   Seeing the problems caused by unregulated state banks, the Democratic-Republicans reverse their earlier opposition to a central bank and Congress charters the Second Bank of the United States. With capital of $35 million it controls the money supply by collecting state bank notes and presenting them to the issuing bank for redemption in specie. That way it can loosen or tighten the money market. But political considerations force the bank to adopt a lenient policy and state banks continue on their merry way, printing money. This soon gets the central bank into trouble. By 1819 it has accumulated too many bank notes, and in order to avoid bankruptcy the Bank of the U.S. redeems the state bank notes for specie. This forces many banks into bankruptcy and throws the country into a depression. As a result of such actions, the bank irritates both the hard-money people, who feel it is too liberal, and the easy-money people, who think it is too conservative. These attacks grow after 1828, when Andrew Jackson is elected president. Jackson puts together a coalition of people who disagree on everything except their hatred of the central bank. With the backing of state banks (which favor easy money), hard-money supporters (who favor tight money policies and the return to specie), states'-rights proponents (who chafe at the idea of central power), free-market advocates (who call the bank a monopoly), and populist politicians (who view the bank as a rich man's tool), Jackson succeeds in preventing the bank's charter from being renewed in 1836 when it expires.

1834   Congress raises the coinage ratio to 16 ounces of silver for 1 ounce of gold. This and the California Gold Rush in 1849 push down the price of gold. As a result only gold is coined, effectively putting the U.S. on a gold standard. The change, however, does allow gold coins to circulate. But until the Civil War, the only paper money circulating in the United States is produced by private banks.

1836   The Specie Circular decrees that the government will only take gold and silver for public lands. This act, along with Jackson's destruction of the central bank, helps plunge the U.S. economy into a severe recession in 1837. Specie flows out of the U.S. to Britain, contracting the money supply, and there is no central bank to help banks and the economy make the transition.

1849   Gold is discovered in California; $450 million worth is mined during the next seven years.

1853   The New York Clearing House starts operations. The clearing-house allows banks to balance their accounts with each other when checks are drawn on one bank and deposited with another.

1853   When the U.S. changes the ratio of gold and silver in coins in 1834, U.S. coins go into mass circulation for the first time. But as gold drives silver out of circulation, smaller coins like the quarter are not widely circulated and the U.S. continues to exist without having small coins in mass circulation. To remedy this problem, which makes it hard to conduct business, the silver content of small coins is reduced in 1853. After that year, for the first time in American history, half dollars, quarters, and dimes circulate freely.

1857   Congress repeals the legal-tender status of foreign coins, ending the use of Spanish pieces of eight and other foreign coins as legal tender.

1862   Congress continues the American tradition of financing wars by printing money. It authorizes the issuance of $150 million in notes. By the end of the Civil War the North issues $430 million worth of greenbacks—which take their name from the green ink on the paper money. Inflation naturally follows. After the war, some of the money is withdrawn, leading to protests against the government for pursuing a hard-money policy. Eventually, Congress allows $346,681,016 worth of paper money to remain in circulation.

1864   Congress passes the National Bank Act, establishing nationally chartered banks and creating the office of the Comptroller of the Currency to regulate those banks. The act allows five or more people to obtain a banking charter from the Comptroller of the Currency. To end the abuses caused by state banks issuing too many bank notes, the act also levies a tax on paper money issued by state banks.

1873   The U.S. has been on a bimetallic standard of gold and silver in theory but in practice it has always been on either gold or silver. (See 1792 and 1834.) Recognizing this fact, Congress finally discontinues minting the silver dollar. However, large silver deposits are discovered at this time and the price of silver is dropping. Soon easy-money theorists push for a return to silver coinage, which would expand the money supply. It is in support of this crusade that the Democratic Party candidate for President, William Jennings Bryan, declares in an 1896 speech that "you shall not crucify mankind upon a cross of gold."

1876   The Supreme Court affirms the separation of commercial banking and investment banking by writing that "dealing in stocks is not expressly prohibited under the National Bank Act of 1864 but such a prohibition is implied from the failure to grant the power." Separation of commercial and investment banking conforms to the British theory that the two functions should be performed in separate financial institutions since investment banking is "risky" and commercial banking should involve the conservative use of "other people's money." But over the next forty years banks break down the separation. (See 1914.)

1900   The battle of gold versus silver is won by gold when the Congress passes the Gold Standard Act in 1900. It puts the U.S. officially on the gold standard instead of on a de facto gold standard. But what really kills the silver movement is the increasing importance of checking accounts and bank deposits. As they expand, the money supply doubles between 1900 and 1912, easing credit restrictions.

1913   After numerous financial panics, Congress finally consents to the creation of a central bank with the passage of the Federal Reserve Act of 1913. The final bill is a compromise between fiscal conservatives and agrarian populists who have long opposed a central bank. But the Federal Reserve System's supporters hope the bank will smooth out fluctuations in the money supply and prevent financial panics by making loans to banks through its Discount window. During the 1920s, the Federal Reserve learns that buying and selling government securities also affects the money supply. The banking acts of the 1930s strengthen the Federal Reserve by concentrating the power to buy and sell securities in the Federal Open Market Committee. (See the profile of Federal Reserve System, page 92.)

1914   By this time banks manage to break down most effective barriers between investment and commercial banking. Though the Supreme Court has affirmed the distinction for national banks, that is, banks chartered under the National Bank Act, states issue charters giving companies the authority to engage in both investment and commercial banking. When the Comptroller of the Currency rules that national banks should not underwrite securities, national banks form affiliates chartered under state law that act as investment bankers. Increasingly, investment bankers also accept deposits and expand their activities into commercial banking. (See 1927.)

1927   Congress passes the McFadden Act. Designed to make national
        banks more competitive with state banks, the law allows national
        banks to establish branches in the states where they are already locat-
        ed, providing that state law allows branch banking. It also allows real-
        estate loans and increases the amount of money that can be loaned to
        one borrower. This act formally gives national banks the power to
        underwrite "investment securities," something they have been doing
        for some time. (See 1876 and 1914.) Commercial banks capitalize on
        the new law by dominating the investment banking field and expand-
        ing their share of bond underwriting from 37% in 1927 to 61% in
        1930.

1932   The Great Depression causes the money supply to shrink by over one
        third. The Depression also touches off a national debate between
        proponents of hard money and easy money. The Roosevelt adminis-
        tration works to ease the money supply.

1932   Senate Banking Committee hearings criticize the banking industry,
        blaming banks and Wall Street for the Great Depression. The Com-
        mittee charges that banks encouraged rampant speculation by pro-
        viding loans for buying stocks on margin and for dubious real-estate
        ventures. Moreover, the committee also attacks affiliates of commer-
        cial banks that sold and underwrote stocks, saying they tricked the
        public into buying some nearly worthless public offerings and "devot-
        ed themselves . . . to perilous underwriting operations, stock specula-
        tion, and maintaining a market for the banks' own stock, often
        largely with the resources of parent banks." These charges and the
        publicity surrounding the Banking Committee hearings help create a
        political consensus for a reform of the banking and capital markets
        that will shape the nature of financial services during the next forty
        years. (See 1933.)

1933   Attacks on the banking system culminate with the passage of the
        Glass-Steagall Act. This law contains the following major provisions:
        (1) it divorces commercial banking institutions from investment
        banking institutions; (2) to protect depositors, many of whom lost
        their life savings when 10,000 banks failed between 1929 and 1933, it
        authorizes the establishment of the Federal Deposit Insurance Cor-
        poration (FDIC); (3) to curb the speculation of the Roaring Twen-
        ties, it restricts the extension of bank credit for speculation; (4) it
        restricts branch banking and group banking; (5) it regulates the inter-
        est paid on deposits; (6) it allows savings and industrial banks to join
        the Federal Reserve; and (7) it extends the open-market activities of
        the Federal Reserve.

1934   President Roosevelt takes the U.S. off the gold standard and the
        Gold Reserve Act of 1934 devalues the dollar. By lowering the
        amount of gold in the dollar from what it had been since 1837, the act
        effectively raises the price of gold from $20 to $35. The act also
        nationalizes gold. All gold imported or produced in the U.S. has to be
        bought by the U.S. Treasury. Moreover, Federal Reserve Banks have

to maintain 25% of their notes and deposits as gold certificates. These provisions are changed in the 1960s and 1970s. (See 1963, 1965, and 1971.)

1935 The Banking Act of 1935 revises the structure of the Federal Reserve, making it more independent from political pressure. The law also sets up the Open Market Committee at the Federal Reserve, allows the Fed to require higher reserves of member banks, requires state nonmember banks with deposits over $1 million to become members or forfeit their deposit insurance, and authorizes the Fed to make loans to member banks.

1944 The Bretton Woods Conference is held at Bretton Woods, New Hampshire, in July to deal with the economic problems of the world after World War II. Forty-four nations send representatives. They create the International Monetary Fund (IMF) and the International Bank For Reconstruction and Development (the World Bank). (See profile of IMF, page 96.)

1950 Ralph Scheider sets up Diners Club, allowing members to eat and pay later at 27 New York restaurants. It is the first credit-card company.

mid-1950s To satisfy complaints by large corporate borrowers that they are not earning enough interest on their deposits, banks issue certificates of deposit (CDs). In 1961 National City Bank of New York (later Citibank) announces it will issue negotiable CDs and a secondary market is created. The popularity of bank CDs is also aided in 1973 when interest-rate ceilings for large negotiable CDs with terms over 90 days are lifted.

1956 The Bank Holding Company Act gives the Federal Reserve the power to approve or disapprove the formation of a bank holding company. The Fed also must approve the acquisition of more than 5% interest in a bank by an existing bank holding company.

1958 Bank of America issues the BankAmericard, the first bank credit card.

1960 The Bank Merger Act makes bank mergers subject to approval by various federal agencies.

1962 The United States, the United Kingdom, West Germany, France, Belgium, the Netherlands, Italy, Sweden, Canada, and Japan meet and sign the General Arrangements to Borrow. This agreement makes $6.2 billion of additional credit available to the IMF. Following this agreement, the ten nations, which account for most of the world's trade, are called the Group of Ten. They still meet on a regular basis to solve problems of international finance and the Group of Ten often participates in IMF activities. The group is also called the Paris Club.

1963 Congress passes the first of a series of measures that will make silver less important for the nation's currency. In 1963, following a rise in the price of silver that threatens to cause the disappearance of silver coins, Congress eliminates the silver certificate and allows the Federal Reserve to issue one-dollar and two-dollar notes. In 1965, another step is taken when the silver dollar is eliminated. Half dollars are to be made out of an alloy of silver and copper; quarters and dimes will have no silver, only copper and nickel. In 1967, Congress passes a law stating that silver certificates cannot be redeemed in silver.

1965   Congress moves away from gold as a basis for banking and currency. It abolishes a requirement created by the Gold Reserve Act of 1934 that Federal Reserve deposits be backed by a 25% gold security. This helps solve the deficit in the balance of payments and allows gold to move out of the country. In 1968, Congress goes further and removes the gold cover from Federal Reserve notes. As a result of the legislation, which says that Federal Reserve notes will be supported by government bonds and commercial paper rather than by gold, gold is no longer a driving force in banking and in the U.S. monetary system. (See 1971.)

1970   Amendments to the Bank Holding Company Act allow banks to open and conduct nonbanking activities across state lines.

1971   President Nixon does away with the gold-dollar standard. The latter emerged from a 1944 agreement reached at Bretton Woods, New Hampshire, that tied all the world's currencies to the dollar and the dollar to gold. Under this system, the Treasury Department was committed to buying gold at $35 an ounce. For many years the agreement allowed the U.S. to inflate the money supply all it wanted while other countries had to take our dollars at artificially high exchange rates. But with a worsening balance of payments and rising government expenditures, foreigners demand gold. U.S. gold reserves drop and Nixon takes the country off the gold standard. Since gold no longer supports currency, in 1974 Congress allows Americans to freely buy and sell gold, ending the 1934 provision that nationalized gold.

1978   The International Banking Act provides for federal regulation of foreign banks in domestic financial markets.

1978   Banks and thrifts offer savings certificates tied to market interest rates.

1980   The Depository Institutions Deregulation and Monetary Control Act of 1980 phases out interest-rate ceilings over the next six years, allows money-market accounts, gives savings and loans more lending powers in the areas of commercial and consumer finance, and permits payment of interest on demand deposits (such as checking accounts).

1982   The Depository Institutions Act authorizes money-market accounts with $2,500 minimum balances, expands thrift lending power and makes provisions for failing thrifts, and allows interest-rate differentials paid by banks and thrifts to be phased out by 1984.

1982   BankAmerica acquires Charles Schwab & Co., the brokerage. Subsequently about 1,000 banks acquire discount brokerages, start their own operations, or make other arrangements to provide discount brokerage services.

1982   A commercial bank acquires a failed thrift for the first time. This opens the way for more commercial banks to acquire thrifts and helps blur the distinctions between the two.

1983   The minimum balance on money-market accounts is reduced to $1,000.

1983   Facing a third-world debt crisis and worries about U.S. banks that have loaned billions to nearly bankrupt developing countries, the chairman of the Federal Reserve, Paul Volcker, asks Congress to increase its support of the IMF. Congress does but also passes the International Lending Supervision Act of 1983. The Federal Reserve and other regulatory agencies are given greater powers to supervise international lending by U.S. banks.

1984   The Supreme Court upholds the right of banks to buy discount brokerage firms.

1985   The Supreme Court rules that regional pacts that permit interstate banking are constitutional. The ruling breaks down barriers to interstate banking by allowing the development of large regional banks but is a setback for large New York City banks, such as Citibank, which brought the suit. The rise of interstate banking is expected to reduce the number of banks and produce some giant regional banks. Mergers in the midwest, New England, and other areas where states have signed regional pacts have already produced super regional banks like SunTrust Banks, First Wachovia, NCNB, the Bank of New England, Fleet Financial, and the Bank of Boston. Other large banks, such as Chemical, have acquired banks in Texas, and Citibank already owns thrifts in California.

1986   In April the last restrictions on savings deposit rates—which had been set by the regulators at 5.5%—end. This means commercial banks and thrift institutions can pay any rate they choose on millions of accounts.

1989   Soon after taking office, President George Bush announces a plan to clean up the mess in the savings and loan industry. He says the plan, designed to assure that "the country won't have to face this problem again," would cost $73 billion, without interest. But within a year, the Administration is forced to double its estimate, and reliable outside estimates say the cost, with interest, will total over $500 billion, up from Reagan administration estimates of $17.5 billion in the early 1980s. The $500 billion bailout translates into $100 for every person on earth. It could pay the interest on the national debt for two years, buy 12 million Mercedes, and fund federal programs for AIDS for the next two and half centuries.

1990   The regulatory equivalent of the Berlin Wall falls when the Federal Reserve gives the J.P. Morgan bank the power to buy and sell securities. In 1933, the Glass-Steagall Act forced the J.P. Morgan financial empire to split up its banking and securities operations. The new rule breaks down one of the last major barriers between commercial banking and Wall Street created by the Roosevelt administration half a century ago. But a slump on Wall Street and financial problems in American banks will probably keep most banks from using their new power in the near future.

1990   The body count in the savings and loan crisis continues to rise. Over 200 thrifts have been closed or sold since October of 1988, and nearly 250 have been taken over by the government. But another 800 shaky thrifts may have to be shut down. The FBI and top government officials estimate that as much as one third of the losses are due to fraud. Over 300 savings and loan officials have been indicted and 202 convicted since early 1988; over 230 failed savings and loan associations are under investigation. But only $12 million has been recovered since August of 1989 in fraud cases brought by government agencies.

1991   President Bush proposes landmark legislation to reform America's banking and financial system by allowing banks to enter a wide range of new business such as insurance and securities. The package would: (1) Allow well-capitalized banks to have securities, mutual fund, and insurance affiliates; (2) Legalize nationwide banking; (3) Shore up the fund which insures bank deposits by charging higher premiums for undercapitalized banks, by increasing regulatory supervision of less well capitalized banks and by limiting insurance coverage to only one $100,000 checking or savings account per bank; (4) Restructure a byzantine system of bank regulation so that each bank has only one regulator, tie bank regulation more directly to a bank's capital and impose fewer regulations on better capitalized banks; (5) Set up a streamlined regulatory system where the Federal Reserve would regulate all state banks, a new department in the Treasury would regulate all national banks and thrift institutions and the FDIC would insure bank deposits, thus losing a number of its current regulatory functions. The proposals, which would create more competition between financial services firms, would improve the international competitiveness of American banks. But the reform measures would probably trigger a period of consolidation and mergers within the American financial system that could hurt the profitability of Wall Street firms and smaller banks. As a result, the proposal faces an uphill battle in Congress.

THE FEDERAL RESERVE SYSTEM

Ever since the 1790s, when Alexander Hamilton and James Madison debated the pros and cons of a central bank, no banking and financial issue has produced more political heat—or, it must be admitted, less economic sense.

The Federal Reserve System, created in 1913 as the nation's central bank, has in recent years been championed by Wall Street as the white knight that slew inflation. But the Federal Reserve's conservative approach to banking deregulation has caused some banks to attack this white knight for saddling the banking system with outmoded regulations. Other banks, of course, applaud the Federal Reserve's banking regulations as a way of keeping big

New York City banks off Main Street, Peoria. And populist politicians and bankrupt farmers, repeating arguments that go back to William Jennings Bryan and his "cross of gold" speech, blame the Federal Reserve's tight-money policies for causing the 1982 recession.

Reality, it must be said, doesn't quite support all these claims. The Federal Reserve System's policies, which are supposed to keep the economy on an even keel, haven't solved or created all the world's problems.

But there is little doubt why the Federal Reserve System gets so much criticism and praise. The Fed is the nation's most important financial institution. It is the nation's central banking system and its most important responsibility is control over monetary policy. The Federal Reserve also handles government deposits and debt issues, supervises and regulates banks that belong to the system, acts as a clearinghouse for checks and other instruments, and loans banks money as a lender of last resort. Economic statistics collected by the Federal Reserve are a key indicator of the nation's economic health.

One of its most important and difficult tasks is using the money supply to control economic growth. The Fed's defenders claim its policies have moderated the well-known economic shortcomings of Congress and the White House. Its critics blame the Fed for every recession in the last 70 years.

History, however, shows a record of mixed results. Consider, for example, how the Federal Reserve's policies have affected the money supply and the economy:

It wasn't until the 1920s that the Federal Reserve System understood the power of open-market operations—that is, buying and selling government securities—to regulate the money supply. Its first sales, however, were uncoordinated and actually contributed to problems in the financial markets. Later, after the crash of 1929, the Fed did little to increase the money supply by open-market operations. In those years the Fed not only failed to keep the nation's money supply growing at a steady, moderate, predictable rate, it actually allowed the money supply to collapse, shrinking by an astounding 35%!

In the 1960s and 1970s, the Keynesians in the Federal Reserve targeted interest rates as the key to economic growth and stability. The theory was that changes in the money supply were unpredictable in their effects, depending on such factors as the public's desire to spend or save. Since low interest rates would encourage investments, the Fed focused its policy on targeting the Federal Funds rate, which is the interest rate on overnight borrowing between member banks to obtain required reserves. In practice, however, tinkering with interest rates managed to accentuate cyclical swings of the economy and in many cases didn't lower interest rates. For example, when the Fed increased the money supply to lower interest rates, it increased inflation. Investors recognized that more money meant more inflation so they demanded even higher interest rates than the rates the Fed was trying to lower.

Under former Federal Reserve chairman Paul Volcker, the Fed announced in 1979 that it would control the money supply rather than

emphasizing interest rates. This decision, though actually never fully imple-
mented, has often been viewed as a turn away from Keynesian economics
toward a monetarist view. Volcker's overall effort to moderate the inflation-
ary growth of money worked dramatically, and while earning him a reputation for creating a "tight money" policy, it got him reappointed to a new
term in 1983 by President Reagan. Inflation during his tenure dropped from
13.3% in 1979 to only 1.9% in 1986.

But despite this success, the Fed's monetary policy has remained erratic.
At times M1 (currency in circulation, commercial bank demand deposits
such as checking, NOW accounts, automatic transfer from savings accounts,
nonbank traveler's checks, credit union share drafts, and mutual savings
bank demand deposits) fell dramatically while M2 (M1 plus overnight repurchase agreements issued by commercial banks, overnight Eurodollars, savings accounts, time deposits over $100,000, and money-market mutual-fund
shares) grew sharply. At other times, a stop-go money policy shocked the
economy. The erratic month-to-month implementation of the Fed's policy
served to keep interest rates higher than they would have been and pro-
longed the 1981–1982 recession.

While the Fed was grappling with the problems of controlling the money
supply, longtime chairman Paul Volcker was tiring of his job. In the summer
of 1987 he submitted his resignation and President Reagan appointed
economist Alan Greenspan to the job. A follower of the laissez-faire
philosopher Ayn Rand and a staunch supporter of free markets, Greenspan
served as head of Council of Economic Advisers under President Ford. He
was known for his anti-inflation stance, his opposition to large government
deficits, and his political acumen, three qualities he shared with Volcker.

Greenspan had little time to ease into his new post. Shortly after he was
appointed, the stock market crash of October 19 raised fears that the economy might face its worst financial crisis since 1929. By easing credit and making money available to the securities industry, the Fed helped avert a serious
crisis. Greenspan's handling of the crisis was widely applauded. But the
crash of 1987 was only the first of several major problems Greenspan faced.
As a bank regulator, Greenspan had to deal with the major financial problems at many of the nation's largest banks that surfaced in 1990 and 1991. In
the short term, he faced the challenge of making certain the financial system
survives billions of dollars worth of bad real estate loans, bankrupt leveraged buyouts, and shaky third-world debt. Over the long term, the challenge
included facing up to more fundamental regulatory problems created by
rapid changes in the international financial markets.

As if these problems weren't bad enough, the Federal Reserve faced even
tougher problems managing the nation's monetary policy. Greenspan loosened up the money supply after the crash of 1987, to make certain the economy survived the turmoil on Wall Street. The economy did, and the Fed
quickly shifted its emphasis to fighting inflation. In 1989 and 1990,
Greenspan raised interest rates and slowed the growth of the money supply
to its lowest levels since the 1950s. But critics complained that he pushed the
economy into a recession. After the Persian Gulf crisis, Greenspan was left

with the problem of bringing the economy out of a recession without reignit-
ing inflation. Approving this policy, President Bush appointed Greenspan to
a second term in 1991.

To influence the American economy, the Federal Reserve can affect
short-term interest rates and the money supply in three ways: (1) In its open
market operations, it can choose to buy or sell Government securities. When
it sells such securities, it removes money from the private economy, thereby
contracting the available supply of credit. When it buys such securities, it
creates the funds out of thin air, thus in effect "printing money at will," and
expanding the money supply. These open-market operations are the most
important way the Fed affects economic growth and the money supply. (2) It
can raise or lower the Discount rate at which it lends to the banks in its system, thus sending a loud and clear signal of its overall policy intentions.
Raising the Discount rate would make it more expensive for banks to buy
money and loan it out; lowering the Discount rate has the opposite effect.
(3) It can change the reserve requirements governing the amount of money
banks must keep in relation to their deposits; higher reserve requirements
mean "tighter" money since the banks will then have less available for loans.

As chairman, Greenspan is the most powerful man in the Federal Reserve
System. But the power of the chairman is by no means absolute. His most
important policies have to be approved by a majority of the Board of Governors of the Federal Reserve and have to be carried out through the structure
of the Federal Reserve. Here's how the system is structured and works:

The Structure of the Federal Reserve

The Federal Reserve System consists of five parts: (1) the Board of Governors in Washington, (2) the 12 Federal Reserve Banks and their 25 branches
and other facilities situated around the country, (3) the Federal Open Market Committee, (4) the Federal Advisory Council, and (5) the nation's financial institutions, including commercial banks, savings and loan associations,
mutual savings banks, and credit unions.

(1) The Board of Governors

The most powerful part of the Federal Reserve System is the Board of Governors. It's made up of seven members appointed by the President and
approved by the Senate. The board determines monetary and interest-rate
policies, monitors credit conditions, enforces various consumer-protection
laws such as the Truth in Lending Act, supervises Federal Reserve Banks,
and regulates banks belonging to the system. Though the other members of
the Board of Governors traditionally follow the lead of the chairman,
Greenspan will have to forge a working majority on the Board of Governors
to carry out his policies. The governors also sit on the Open Market Committee.

(2) The Federal Open Market Committee

One of the most important ways the Board of Governors influences credit conditions, monetary policy, and economic growth is through the Federal Open Market Committee. The committee is composed of the Board of Governors and the five presidents of the Reserve Banks. Greenspan, as chairman of the Board of Governors, heads the Open Market Committee. As noted above, the Open Market Committee buys and sells securities on the open market—hence its name—as a way of influencing credit conditions, controlling the money supply, and regulating economic growth. Selling securities takes money out of the economy, slows economic growth, and, by making money more scarce, raises interest rates. Buying has the opposite effect. Since the Federal Reserve is not funded by Congress, buying and selling securities also produces most of its income. Under the committee's direction, the Federal Reserve Bank of New York also buys and sells foreign currencies to help regulate the value of the dollar on foreign markets.

(3) The Federal Reserve Banks

There are Federal Reserve Banks in 12 cities and branches of these banks in 25. Each Reserve Bank has nine members on its Board of Directors. Under the supervision of the Board of Governors, the Reserve Banks set the interest rates for loans to banks that belong to Federal Reserve.

(4) The Federal Advisory Council

It confers with the Board of Governors and advises the board on general business conditions. The council is composed of 12 members, one from each Federal Reserve district. The council is required to meet in Washington at least four times a year but can meet more often if called by the Board of Governors.

(5) Member banks

The banks that belong to the system actually own it. They are required to subscribe 6% of its capital stock and in return receive a dividend of 6% a year on their investment. The Federal Reserve System regulates state-chartered banks that are members.

THE IMF

The International Monetary Fund was established in 1944 as a way of stabilizing the world's currency. But over the years it has become the closest thing to a worldwide central bank, acting as a creditor and regulator of third-world economies. How it got that way says a lot about the third-world debt crisis and economic relations between developed and developing nations.

In 1944, when representatives from 44 countries met at Bretton Woods,

New Hampshire, the specter of worldwide depression and war was still fresh in their minds. During the early 1930s nationalistic trade barriers and currency devaluations had helped deepen the worldwide depression. Finding a way of stabilizing the world's currency and allowing countries to solve temporary balance-of-payments deficits without restoring trade barriers and currency devaluations would, they hoped, prevent the recurrence of another worldwide depression.

Out of the Bretton Woods conference came an agreement to create the International Monetary Fund and the International Bank for Reconstruction and Development, usually known as the World Bank. The IMF was given the responsibility for maintaining orderly currency prices in international trade, while the World Bank was given the task of creating long-term investments to improve the world's economy.

In the beginning, a member of the IMF could borrow foreign currency from the IMF in exchange for its own currency if it had a balance-of-payments deficit—that is, if its imports exceeded exports. The borrowing country then had to repurchase the currency in three to five years. That way, the borrower could take care of a balance-of-payments problem without having to unduly depress its own economy, put up trade barriers, or devalue its currency and thus disrupt world trade. When the temporary loans were made, the IMF also negotiated with the borrowing country so that changes in its economic policy would solve the underlying balance-of-payments deficit.

Since the IMF was never intended to be a major lending institution or an agency for economic development, it was overshadowed in its early years by the World Bank. Later, in 1973, it appeared that the IMF's influence would decline even further. When the major powers abandoned fixed exchange rates and allowed their currencies to float that year, the IMF stood to lose its power over exchange rates.

But several measures made the IMF a more important lender and provider of international credit. In 1969, the IMF created special drawing rights and in 1974, with the support of the Federal Reserve and the U.S. Treasury, the IMF decided to expand its long-term and short-term lending. On one hand it moved to help countries whose balance-of-payments deficits were hurt by OPEC's price hikes; on the other, as private lending institutions reached their limits, the IMF stepped in by providing more funds and by coordinating debt renegotiations between countries and private lenders.

Since its creation, the IMF has made loan commitments totaling $140 billion. But, considering that the third world has over $1.3 trillion in outstanding loans, that amount is really inconsequential. The IMF's real power comes from the fact that commercial banks will not extend new loans or renegotiate old ones until the country has reached an agreement with the IMF.

Increased lending and a greater say over the economies of debtor nations, however, have led to growing criticism of the Fund. In the early 1980s, as a condition for obtaining new loans, the IMF ordered debtor countries to improve their trade balances and pushed for freer markets. The idea was that, by increasing exports and cutting imports, the debtor nations would earn the foreign currency they needed.

In some ways the strategy worked, at least for a while. Ten of the largest debtor nations improved their trade balances from only $2.9 billion in 1981–1982 to $45 billion by 1984. But the policy also created heavy political costs. To improve their trade balances, governments had to undertake austerity measures such as cutting price supports for food, cutting government services, slashing wages, and devaluing currency. Even though the bitter medicine was necessary for a long-term solution to the problem, it resulted in the short run in reduced living standards and fewer goods. These conditions provoked riots in several countries.

Faced with the prospect that IMF austerity could provoke political unrest, some third-world governments have talked more openly of a debt moratorium or outright default. They argue that the western countries need to provide more help for their economies and that the IMF should grant them more lenient terms for renewed debt. Only if their economies are allowed to grow, they say, can they generate the goods and services they need to pay off their debts.

Third-world critics also charge that the IMF is controlled by large western powers, promoting their interests more than those of poor, less-developed countries. To some degree that charge is correct. While the IMF is governed by its 151 member countries, power over the Fund's policy is based on money. Each member is allowed a basic 250 votes and additional votes are allotted according to a country's payment into the Fund, which in turn is proportional to the country's share of the world economy. That means large industrial nations effectively control the Fund's policies.

The debate over austerity versus a more lenient policy towards debtor nations was played out in the 1986 selection of a new head of the IMF. One candidate was Dutch finance minister H. Onno Ruding; the other, Michel Camdessus, a former head of France's central bank. Ruding hit the campaign trail for the IMF job as a fiscal conservative enjoying the support of private banks that had loaned billions to third-world debtors. Camdessus was known to be more sympathetic to the debtors' problems. He favored a policy that would promote economic growth rather than austerity.

Since Camdessus's election, the IMF and the industrialized nations have shifted their tactics away from austerity toward the notion that debtors need more lenient terms to deal with the problems.

In 1989, U.S. Treasury Secretary Nicholas Brady announced a plan to reschedule some debts, reduce others, and cut the interest payments on debts held by 19 severely indebted third-world countries, such as Mexico. The Brady plan was supposed to achieve several aims: By lowering debt claims, it would give third-world countries more money for economic development and help pull their economies out of a severe depression. Moreover, Brady hoped his plan would attract more foreign investment by reducing worries about the financial stability of third-world countries.

Since the Brady plan was announced, Mexico made a deal with commercial bankers that cut its outstanding debts by $6.8 billion and its debt-service payments by $22.5 billion—thus creating annual savings of about $1.4 billion that might be used to revive its crippled economy. By 1991, the Philippines, Costa Rica, Morocco, and Venezuela had all either concluded or were about to conclude similar agreements.

The World Bank estimates that the Brady plan would help reduce third-world debts by $30 billion to $35 billion, enough money to cut the annual debt service of the severely indebted countries by an estimated $6 billion a year between 1990 and 1993.

But the new policy isn't likely to solve the problem. Even if third-world economies were efficiently managed and based on policies that encouraged investment and growth—which they aren't—most of them would still be facing major problems. High energy costs following the oil embargo of 1973 wreaked havoc on many third-world economies. Later, in the 1980s, reduced prices for commodities and stagnant western economies reduced the demand for third-world exports and made it impossible for them to finance their debts. Add to those basic structural problems harebrained development schemes, extravagant arms purchases by dictators on the right and the left, rampant government corruption that diverts aid money to Swiss bank accounts, and capital flight. In the last decade at least $198 billion worth of capital has fled from 18 debtor countries to the west, making it harder for them to pay their debts and finance new development.

Table 6-1 Money Stock, Liquid Assets, and Debt, 1959–1990
(Averages of daily figures; billions of dollars, seasonally adjusted)

Year and month	M1 — Sum of currency, demand deposits, travelers checks, and other checkable deposits (OCDs)	M2 — M1 plus overnight RPs and Eurodollars, MMMF balances (general) purpose and broker/dealer), MMDAs, and savings and small time deposits	M3 — M2 plus large time deposits, term RPs, term Eurodollars, and institution-only MMMF balances	L — M3 plus other liquid assets	Debt[1] — Debt of domestic nonfinancial sectors (monthly average)	M1	M2	M3	Debt
December:									
1959	140.0	297.8	299.8	388.7	704.7				7.5
1960	140.7	312.4	315.3	403.7	739.5	0.5	4.9	5.2	4.9
1961	145.2	335.5	341.1	430.8	781.8	3.2	7.4	8.2	5.7
1962	147.9	362.7	371.5	466.1	833.9	1.9	8.1	8.9	6.7
1963	153.4	393.3	406.1	503.8	888.9	3.7	8.4	9.3	6.6
1964	160.4	424.8	442.5	540.4	952.0	4.6	8.0	9.0	7.1
1965	167.9	459.4	482.3	584.5	1,020.3	4.7	8.1	9.0	7.2
1966	172.1	480.0	505.1	614.8	1,087.8	2.5	4.5	4.7	6.6
1967	183.3	524.4	557.1	666.6	1,163.3	6.5	9.2	10.3	6.9
1968	197.5	566.4	606.3	729.0	1,256.7	7.7	8.0	8.8	8.0
1969	204.0	589.6	615.1	763.6	1,347.0	3.3	4.1	1.5	7.2
1970	214.5	628.1	677.4	816.3	1,437.1	5.1	6.5	10.1	6.7
1971	228.4	712.7	776.2	903.0	1,568.6	6.5	13.5	14.6	9.2
1972	249.3	805.2	886.0	1,023.0	1,723.8	9.2	13.0	14.1	9.9
1973	262.9	861.0	985.0	1,142.6	1,912.1	5.5	6.9	11.2	10.9
1974	274.4	908.6	1,070.4	1,250.3	2,083.6	4.4	5.5	8.7	9.0
1975	287.6	1,023.3	1,172.3	1,367.0	2,264.3	4.8	12.6	9.5	8.7
1976	306.4	1,163.7	1,311.8	1,516.6	2,503.0	6.5	13.7	11.9	10.5
1977	331.3	1,286.7	1,472.6	1,705.3	2,815.8	8.1	10.6	12.3	12.5
1978	358.5	1,389.0	1,646.6	1,910.7	3,188.5	8.2	8.0	11.8	13.2
1979	382.9	1,497.1	1,803.2	2,116.2	3,568.5	6.8	7.8	9.5	11.9
1980	408.9	1,629.9	1,987.5	2,324.2	3,904.1	6.8	8.9	10.2	9.4
1981	436.5	1,793.5	2,234.2	2,596.8	4,292.1	6.7	10.0	12.4	9.9
1982	474.5	1,953.1	2,441.9	2,851.6	4,685.9	8.7	8.9	9.3	9.2
1983	521.2	2,186.5	2,693.4	3,154.7	5,212.6	9.8	12.0	10.3	11.2
1984	552.1	2,371.6	2,982.8	3,524.1	5,961.9	5.9	8.5	10.7	14.4
1985	620.1	2,570.6	3,202.1	3,829.5	6,773.5	12.3	8.4	7.4	13.6
1986	724.7	2,814.2	3,494.5	4,135.5	7,636.2	16.9	9.5	9.1	12.7
1987	750.4	2,913.2	3,678.7	4,338.7	8,345.1	3.5	3.5	5.3	9.3
1988	787.5	3,072.4	3,918.3	4,676.1	9,107.6	4.9	5.5	6.5	9.1
1989	794.8	3,221.6	4,044.3	4,881.2	9,790.4	.9	4.9	3.2	7.5
1990	825.5	3,323.3	4,094.0			3.9	3.2	1.2	

Source: Board of Governors of the Federal Reserve.

100

Table 6-2　The Third World Debt Crisis

This table shows debts held by various third-world countries and provides several ways of looking at their debt burden. For example, it shows that Brazil's long term debt has skyrocketed from $5,128 million in 1970 to $101,356 million in 1988. These new debts are now equal to 30% of the country's GNP and require $11,686 million in annual interest payments. Making the annual payments on the debt takes 4.5% of Brazil's GNP, up from 1.6% of GNP in 1970. Worse, 42% of the money Brazil makes by exporting goods and services must be spent to pay off its debts. The countries are ranked in the chart by their per capita income, with the poorest countries listed first.

| | | Total long-term debt outstanding and disbursed | | | | Total interest payments on long-term debt (millions of dollars) | | Total long-term debt service as a percentage of | | | |
| | | Millions of dollars | | As a percentage of GNP | | | | GNP | | Exports of goods and services | |
		1970	1988	1970	1988	1970	1988	1970	1988	1970	1988
Low-income economies											
China and India											
Other low-income											
1	Mozambique	—	4,039	—	399.7	—	15	—	2.7	—	10.4
2	Ethiopia	169	2,790	9.5	50.6	6	78	1.2	4.3	11.4	37.4
3	Chad	33	300	9.9	33.2	0	4	0.9	0.7	4.2	2.7
4	Tanzania	265	4,100	20.7	140.1	8	41	1.6	3.0	6.3	17.8
5	Bangladesh	0	9,330	0.0	48.5	0	139	0.0	1.6	0.0	20.5
6	Malawi	122	1,193	43.2	85.9	4	29	2.3	4.6	7.8	19.0
7	Somalia	77	1,754	24.4	185.2	0	3	0.3	0.4	2.1	4.9
8	Zaire	311	7,013	9.1	118.0	9	98	1.1	2.8	4.4	6.9
9	Bhutan	—	68	—	27.9	—	1	—	0.5	—	—
10	Lao PDR	8	816	—	153.5	0	2	—	1.8	—	143.5
11	Nepal	3	1,088	0.3	34.6	0	19	0.3	1.2	3.2	8.5
12	Madagascar	89	3,317	10.4	192.7	2	81	0.8	9.3	3.7	39.0
13	Burkina Faso	21	805	6.6	43.4	0	14	0.7	2.0	7.1	11.9
14	Mali	238	1,928	71.4	100.8	0	15	0.2	2.5	1.4	14.2
15	Burundi	7	749	3.1	69.8	0	16	0.3	3.3	2.3	25.1
16	Uganda	138	1,438	7.3	34.3	5	20	0.5	1.0	2.9	14.0
17	Nigeria	567	28,967	4.3	102.5	28	1,411	0.7	7.0	7.1	25.7
18	Zambia	654	4,194	37.5	116.7	32	62	4.6	4.9	8.0	14.2
19	Niger	32	1,542	5.0	66.0	1	74	0.4	5.6	4.0	32.6
20	Rwanda	2	585	0.9	25.5	0	8	0.2	0.7	1.5	9.6
21	China	—	32,196	—	8.7	—	1,593	—	1.0	—	6.9
22	India	7,938	51,168	13.9	19.3	193	2,554	0.9	1.8	23.7	24.9
23	Pakistan	3,069	14,027	30.6	37.6	78	436	1.9	3.5	23.9	24.1
24	Kenya	406	4,869	26.3	58.5	17	194	3.0	5.7	9.1	25.3
25	Togo	40	1,067	16.0	81.6	1	68	1.0	7.0	3.1	18.3
26	Central African Rep.	24	584	13.5	53.3	1	7	1.7	1.1	5.1	5.9
27	Haiti	40	683	10.2	27.7	0	8	1.0	0.9	7.2	8.8
28	Benin	41	904	15.1	49.3	0	8	0.7	1.0	2.5	5.4
29	Ghana	498	2,270	22.9	44.6	12	64	1.2	4.0	5.5	20.6
30	Lesotho	8	270	7.7	36.5	0	7	0.5	3.0	4.5	5.2
31	Sri Lanka	317	4,253	16.1	61.6	12	125	2.1	4.8	11.0	17.6
32	Guinea	312	2,312	—	94.7	4	31	—	5.9	—	21.9
33	Yemen, PDR	1	1,970	—	199.4	0	31	—	10.8	0.0	46.5
34	Indonesia	2,914	45,655	30.0	61.7	46	2,918	1.7	11.5	13.9	39.6
35	Mauritania	27	1,823	13.9	196.2	0	33	1.8	11.9	3.4	21.6
36	Sudan	298	8,418	14.8	74.6	12	19	1.7	0.6	10.6	9.5
37	Afghanistan	—	—	—	—	—	—	—	—	—	—
38	Myanmar	106	4,217	—	—	3	39	—	—	—	—
39	Kampuchea, Dem.	—	—	—	—	—	—	—	—	—	—
40	Liberia	158	1,101	39.2	—	6	6	4.3	—	8.0	—
41	Sierra Leone	59	510	14.2	—	3	3	3.1	—	10.8	5.9
42	Viet Nam	—	—	—	—	—	—	—	—	—	—

Table 6-2 The Third World Debt Crisis (continued)

| | | Total long-term debt outstanding and disbursed | | | | Total interest payments on long-term debt (millions of dollars) | | Total long-term debt service as a percentage of | | | |
| | | Millions of dollars | | As a percentage of GNP | | | | GNP | | Exports of goods and services | |
		1970	1988	1970	1988	1970	1988	1970	1988	1970	1988
Middle-income economies											
Lower-middle-income											
43	Bolivia	491	4,651	49.3	114.9	7	95	2.6	5.6	12.6	32.9
44	Philippines	1,544	24,467	21.8	62.6	44	1,638	4.3	7.6	23.0	27.7
45	Yemen Arab Rep.	—	2,378	—	41.7	—	56	—	3.4	—	16.0
46	Senegal	131	3,019	15.5	63.6	2	117	1.1	5.2	4.0	19.3
47	Zimbabwe	229	2,281	15.5	37.3	5	150	0.6	8.2	2.3	27.9
48	Egypt, Arab Rep.	1,714	43,259	22.5	126.7	56	729	4.8	4.4	38.0	16.6
49	Dominican Rep.	353	3,334	23.9	77.3	13	151	2.7	5.8	15.3	14.4
50	Côte d'Ivoire	267	11,788	19.5	135.1	12	447	3.1	12.4	7.5	31.9
51	Papua New Guinea	209	2,129	33.4	64.2	10	153	4.8	15.6	24.5	30.9
52	Morocco	727	18,767	18.6	89.8	25	814	1.7	6.5	9.2	25.1
53	Honduras	109	2,837	15.6	68.3	4	128	1.4	7.2	4.9	28.6
54	Guatemala	120	2,244	6.5	28.3	7	104	1.6	4.5	8.2	27.2
55	Congo, People's Rep.	124	4,098	46.5	205.0	3	75	3.4	13.1	11.5	28.7
56	El Salvador	176	1,685	17.3	31.5	9	66	3.1	3.3	12.0	18.8
57	Thailand	726	16,905	10.2	29.7	33	1,184	2.3	6.0	14.0	15.7
58	Botswana	17	494	21.3	37.9	0	34	0.7	5.7	1.0	4.0
59	Cameroon	140	3,366	12.6	27.0	5	192	1.0	4.6	4.0	27.0
60	Jamaica	982	3,554	73.1	127.2	64	217	17.4	15.2	43.5	24.8
61	Ecuador	242	9,378	14.8	94.2	10	297	2.2	5.7	14.0	21.4
62	Colombia	1,580	15,392	22.5	42.1	59	1,213	2.8	8.0	19.3	42.3
63	Paraguay	112	2,119	19.2	36.4	4	114	1.8	5.0	11.8	24.6
64	Tunisia	541	6,121	38.6	64.2	18	380	4.7	11.5	19.7	25.5
65	Turkey	1,886	31,589	15.0	46.1	44	2,424	1.4	9.1	22.6	35.2
66	Peru	2,655	13,898	37.3	56.1	162	174	7.0	1.3	40.0	8.7
67	Jordan	119	3,955	22.9	94.0	2	239	0.9	19.6	3.6	31.9
68	Chile	2,568	16,121	32.1	79.3	104	1,019	3.9	7.9	24.5	19.1
69	Syrian Arab Rep.	233	3,685	10.8	25.0	6	119	1.7	2.6	11.3	21.1
70	Costa Rica	246	3,847	25.3	89.2	14	185	5.7	7.7	19.9	19.9
71	Mexico	5,966	88,665	16.2	52.4	283	7,590	3.5	8.2	44.3	43.5
72	Mauritius	32	709	14.3	37.1	2	43	1.4	7.7	3.2	10.4
73	Poland	—	33,661	—	51.1	—	829	—	2.5	—	10.0
74	Malaysia	440	18,441	10.8	56.3	25	1,498	2.0	16.5	4.5	22.3
75	Panama	194	3,625	19.5	81.2	7	4	3.1	0.2	7.7	0.2
76	Brazil	5,128	101,356	12.2	29.6	224	11,686	1.6	4.5	21.8	42.0
77	Angola	—	—	—	—	—	—	—	—	—	—
78	Lebanon	64	229	4.2	—	1	16	0.2	—	—	—
79	Nicaragua	147	6,744	19.5	—	7	73	3.1	—	10.6	—
Upper-middle-income											
80	South Africa	—	—	—	—	—	—	—	—	—	—
81	Algeria	945	23,229	19.8	46.6	10	1,809	0.9	12.7	4.0	77.0
82	Hungary	—	14,791	—	54.9	—	1,100	—	10.7	0.0	23.3
83	Uruguay	298	3,039	12.5	39.8	17	257	2.9	7.5	23.6	30.3
84	Argentina	5,171	49,544	23.8	58.6	338	2,803	5.1	4.9	51.7	36.0
85	Yugoslavia	2,053	19.341	15.0	38.9	104	1,401	3.5	6.4	19.7	17.6
86	Gabon	91	2,128	28.8	65.6	3	57	3.8	2.7	5.7	6.2
87	Venezuela	954	30,296	7.5	49.0	53	2,675	0.9	8.2	4.2	39.7
88	Trinidad and Tobago	101	1,718	13.3	43.2	6	88	2.1	3.7	4.6	9.2
89	Korea, Rep. of	1,991	27,376	22.3	16.2	76	2,081	3.1	4.8	20.4	11.5
90	Portugal	753	14,565	12.1	35.6	34	1,163	1.9	11.0	8.7	30.3
91	Greece	1,293	18.797	12.7	35.9	63	1,468	1.6	7.0	14.7	32.1
92	Oman	—	2,488	—	34.7	—	182	—	7.4	—	—
93	Libya	—	—	—	—	—	—	—	—	—	—
94	Iran, Islamic Rep.	—	—	—	—	—	—	—	—	—	—
95	Iraq	—	—	—	—	—	—	—	—	—	—
96	Romania	—	1,946	—	—	—	420	—	—	—	—

Source: World Bank.

102

Table 6-3   Consumer Price Index

This chart shows the consumer price index for various major types of expenditures, such as transportation and medical care. Using 1982 to 1984 as the base period, equal to 100, the index shows that the price of all items rose to 1.24 in 1989. That means it costs $1.24 to buy the same amount of goods and services you could buy in 1946 for 19 cents. The figures are for all urban consumers.

(1982–1984 = 100)

Year or month	All items	Food and beverages		Housing				Apparel and upkeep	Transportation	Medical care	Entertainment	Other goods and services	Energy
		Total*	Food	Total	Shelter	Fuel and other utilities	Household furnishings and operation						
1946	19.5		19.8					34.4	16.7	12.5			
1947	22.3		24.1					39.9	18.5	13.5			
1948	24.1		26.1					42.5	20.6	14.4			
1949	23.8		25.0					40.8	22.1	14.8			
1950	24.1		25.4					40.3	22.7	15.1			
1951	26.0		28.2					43.9	24.1	15.9			
1952	26.5		28.7					43.5	25.7	16.7			
1953	26.7		28.3	22.0	22.5			43.1	26.5	17.3			
1954	26.9		28.2	22.5	22.6			43.1	26.1	17.8			
1955	26.8		27.8	22.7	23.0			42.9	25.8	18.2			
1956	27.2		28.0	23.1	23.6			43.7	26.2	18.9			
1957	28.1		28.9	24.0	24.3			44.5	27.7	19.7			21.5
1958	28.9		30.2	24.5	24.8			44.6	28.6	20.6			21.5
1959	29.1		29.7	24.7	25.4			45.0	29.8	21.5			21.9
1960	29.6		30.0	25.2	26.0			45.7	29.8	22.3			22.4
1961	29.9		30.4	25.4	26.3			46.1	30.1	22.9			22.5
1962	30.2		30.6	25.8	26.3			46.3	30.8	23.5			22.6
1963	30.6		31.1	26.1	26.6			46.9	30.9	24.1			22.6
1964	31.0		31.5	26.5	26.6			47.3	31.4	24.6			22.5
1965	31.5		32.2	27.0	26.6			47.8	31.9	25.2			22.9
1966	32.4		33.8	27.8	26.7			49.0	32.3	26.3			23.3
1967	33.4	35.0	34.1	30.8	28.8	27.1	42.0	51.0	33.3	28.2	40.7	35.1	23.8
1968	34.8	36.2	35.3	32.0	30.1	27.4	43.6	53.7	34.3	29.9	43.0	36.9	24.2
1969	36.7	38.1	37.1	34.0	32.6	28.0	45.2	56.8	35.7	31.9	45.2	38.7	24.8
1970	38.8	40.1	39.2	36.4	35.5	29.1	46.8	59.2	37.5	34.0	47.5	40.9	25.5
1971	40.5	41.4	40.4	38.0	37.0	31.1	48.6	61.1	39.5	36.1	50.0	42.9	26.5
1972	41.8	43.1	42.1	39.4	38.7	32.5	49.7	62.3	39.9	37.3	51.5	44.7	27.2
1973	44.4	48.8	48.2	41.2	40.5	34.3	51.1	64.6	41.2	38.8	52.9	46.4	29.4
1974	49.3	55.5	55.1	45.8	44.4	40.7	56.8	69.4	45.8	42.4	56.9	49.8	38.1
1975	53.8	60.2	59.8	50.7	48.8	45.4	63.4	72.5	50.1	47.5	62.0	53.9	42.1
1976	56.9	62.1	61.6	53.8	51.5	49.4	67.3	75.2	55.1	52.0	65.1	57.0	45.1
1977	60.6	65.8	65.5	57.4	54.9	54.7	70.4	78.6	59.0	57.0	68.3	60.4	49.4
1978	65.2	72.2	72.0	62.4	60.5	58.5	74.7	81.4	61.7	61.8	71.9	64.3	52.5
1979	72.6	79.9	79.9	70.1	68.9	64.8	79.9	84.9	70.5	67.5	76.7	68.9	65.7
1980	82.4	86.7	86.8	81.1	81.0	75.4	86.3	90.9	83.1	74.9	83.6	75.2	86.0
1981	90.9	93.5	93.6	90.4	90.5	86.4	93.0	95.3	93.2	82.9	90.1	82.6	97.7
1982	96.5	97.3	97.4	96.9	96.9	94.9	98.0	97.8	97.0	92.5	96.0	91.1	99.2
1983	99.6	99.5	99.4	99.5	99.1	100.2	100.2	100.2	99.3	100.6	100.1	101.1	99.9
1984	103.9	103.2	103.2	103.6	104.0	104.8	101.9	102.1	103.7	106.8	103.8	107.9	100.9
1985	107.6	105.6	105.6	107.7	109.8	106.5	103.8	105.0	106.4	113.5	107.9	114.5	101.6
1986	109.6	109.1	109.0	110.9	115.8	104.1	105.2	105.9	102.3	122.0	111.6	121.4	88.2
1987	113.6	113.5	113.5	114.2	121.3	103.0	107.1	110.6	105.4	130.1	115.3	128.5	88.6
1988	118.3	118.2	118.2	118.5	127.1	104.4	109.4	115.4	108.7	138.6	120.3	137.0	89.3
1989	124.0	124.9	125.1	123.0	132.8	107.8	111.2	118.6	114.1	149.3	126.5	147.7	94.3
1990	130.7	132.1	132.4	128.5	140.0	111.6	113.3	124.1	120.5	162.8	132.4	159.0	102.1

*Includes alcoholic beverages, not shown separately.

Note: Data beginning 1978 are for all urban consumers; earlier data are for urban wage earners and clerical workers.

Data beginning 1983 incorporate a rental equivalence measure for homeowners' costs and therefore are not strictly comparable with earlier figures.

Source: Department of Labor, Bureau of Labor Statistics.

103

Table 6-4   The Rising Cost of Goods and Services

This chart shows changes in the consumer price indexes and lists the inflation or deflation rate for various types of goods and services. It shows, for example, that the cost of energy skyrocketed 30.9% in 1980 and then dropped 13.2% in 1986.

(percent changes in consumer price indexes, commodities and services, 1929–1986)

| | All items | | Commodities | | | | | | | | Services | | | | Energy† | |
| | | | Total | | Food | | Commodities less food | | | | Total | | Medical care services | | | |
Year	Dec. to Dec.*	Year to year	Dec. to Dec.*	Year to year	Dec. to Dec.*	Year to year	Dec. to Dec.*	Year to year			Dec. to Dec.*	Year to year	Dec. to Dec.*	Year to year	Dec. to Dec.*	Year to year
1929	0.6	0			2.5	1.2										
1933	.8	−5.1			6.9	−2.8										
1939	0	−1.4	−0.7	−2.0	−2.5	−2.5	0.5	−1.6			0	0	1.2	1.2		
1940	.7	.7	1.4	.7	2.5	1.7	.5	.5			.8	.8	0	0		
1941	9.9	5.0	13.3	6.7	15.7	9.2	10.7	5.4			2.4	.8	1.2	0		
1942	9.0	10.9	12.9	14.5	17.9	17.6	6.3	10.8			2.3	3.1	3.5	3.5		
1943	3.0	6.1	4.2	9.3	3.0	11.0	5.5	4.6			2.3	2.3	5.6	4.5		
1944	2.3	1.7	2.0	1.0	0	−1.2	4.7	5.3			2.2	2.2	3.2	4.3		
1945	2.2	2.3	2.9	3.0	3.5	2.4	3.3	4.2			.7	1.5	3.1	3.1		
1946	18.1	8.3	24.8	10.6	31.3	14.5	12.7	6.0			3.6	1.4	9.0	5.1		
1947	8.8	14.4	10.3	20.5	11.3	21.7	9.2	12.9			5.6	4.3	6.4	8.7		
1948	3.0	8.1	1.7	7.2	−.8	8.3	5.2	7.4			5.9	6.1	6.9	7.1		
1949	−2.1	−1.2	−4.1	−2.7	−3.9	−4.2	−4.6	−1.3			3.7	5.1	1.6	3.3		
1950	5.9	1.3	7.8	.7	9.8	1.6	5.5	−.3			3.6	3.0	4.0	2.4		
1951	6.0	7.9	5.9	9.0	7.1	11.0	4.9	7.6			5.2	5.3	5.3	4.7		
1952	.8	1.9	−.9	1.3	−1.0	1.8	−.6	.9			4.4	4.5	5.8	6.7		
1953	.7	.8	−.3	−.3	−1.1	−1.4	.3	.3			4.2	4.3	3.4	3.5		
1954	−.7	.7	−1.6	−.9	−1.8	−.4	−1.5	−1.2			2.0	3.1	2.6	3.4		
1955	.4	−.4	−.3	−.9	−.7	−1.4	0	−.6			2.0	2.0	3.2	2.6		
1956	3.0	1.5	2.6	1.0	2.9	.7	2.7	.9			3.4	2.5	3.8	3.8		
1957	2.9	3.3	2.8	3.2	2.8	3.2	2.0	2.9			4.2	4.3	4.8	4.3		
1958	1.8	2.8	1.2	2.1	2.4	4.5	.8	1.1			2.7	3.7	4.6	5.3	−0.9	0
1959	1.7	.7	.6	0	−1.0	−1.7	1.4	1.4			3.9	3.1	4.9	4.5	4.7	1.9
1960	1.4	1.7	1.2	.9	3.1	1.0	−.3	.6			2.5	3.4	3.7	4.3	1.3	2.3
1961	.7	1.0	0	.6	−.7	1.3	.8	.3			2.1	1.7	3.5	3.6	−1.3	.4
1962	1.3	1.0	.9	.9	1.3	.7	.6	.6			1.6	2.0	2.9	3.5	2.2	.4
1963	1.6	1.3	1.5	.9	2.0	1.6	1.4	.8			2.4	2.0	2.8	2.9	−.9	0
1964	1.0	1.3	.9	1.2	1.3	1.3	.3	.8			1.6	2.0	2.3	2.3	0	−.4
1965	1.9	1.6	1.4	1.1	3.5	2.2	.8	.8			2.7	2.3	3.6	3.2	1.8	1.8
1966	3.5	2.9	2.5	2.6	4.0	5.0	1.9	1.3			4.8	3.8	8.3	5.3	1.7	1.7
1967	3.0	3.1	2.5	1.9	1.2	.9	3.1	2.4			4.3	4.3	8.0	8.8	1.7	2.1
1968	4.7	4.2	4.0	3.5	4.4	3.5	3.6	3.6			5.8	5.2	7.1	7.3	1.7	1.7
1969	6.2	5.5	5.4	4.7	7.0	5.1	4.7	4.3			7.7	6.9	7.3	8.2	2.9	2.5
1970	5.6	5.7	3.9	4.5	2.3	5.7	4.7	4.1			8.1	8.0	8.1	7.0	4.8	2.8
1971	3.3	4.4	2.8	3.6	4.3	3.1	2.2	3.9			4.1	5.7	5.4	7.4	3.1	3.9
1972	3.4	3.2	3.4	3.0	4.6	4.2	2.6	2.2			3.4	3.8	3.7	3.5	2.6	2.6
1973	8.7	6.2	10.4	7.4	20.3	14.5	4.9	3.5			6.2	4.4	6.0	4.5	17.0	8.1
1974	12.3	11.0	12.8	11.9	12.0	14.3	13.2	10.7			11.4	9.2	13.2	10.4	21.6	29.6
1975	6.9	9.1	6.2	8.8	6.6	8.5	6.1	9.1			8.2	9.6	10.3	12.6	11.4	10.5
1976	4.9	5.8	3.3	4.3	.5	3.0	5.1	5.0			7.2	8.3	10.8	10.1	7.1	7.1
1977	6.7	6.5	6.1	5.8	8.1	6.3	4.8	5.5			8.0	7.7	9.0	9.9	7.2	9.5
1978	9.0	7.6	8.8	7.2	11.8	9.9	7.7	5.8			9.3	8.6	9.3	8.5	7.9	6.3
1979	13.3	11.3	13.0	11.3	10.2	11.0	14.3	11.6			13.6	11.0	10.5	9.8	37.5	25.1
1980	12.5	13.5	11.0	12.3	10.2	8.6	11.5	13.8			14.2	15.4	10.1	11.3	18.0	30.9
1981	8.9	10.3	6.0	8.4	4.3	7.8	6.7	8.6			13.0	13.1	12.6	10.7	11.9	13.6
1982	3.8	6.2	3.6	4.1	3.1	4.1	3.8	4.1			4.3	9.0	11.2	11.8	1.3	1.5
1983	3.8	3.2	2.9	2.9	2.7	2.1	3.1	3.2			4.8	3.5	6.2	8.7	−.5	.7
1984	3.9	4.3	2.7	3.4	3.8	3.8	2.1	3.1			5.4	5.2	5.8	6.0	.2	1.0
1985	3.8	3.6	2.5	2.1	2.6	2.3	2.4	2.0			5.1	5.1	6.8	6.1	1.8	.7
1986	1.1	1.9	−2.0	−.9	3.8	3.2	−5.3	−3.3			4.5	5.0	7.9	7.7	−19.7	−13.2
1987	4.4	3.6	4.6	3.2	3.5	4.1	5.1	2.6			4.3	4.2	5.6	6.6	8.2	.5
1988	4.4	4.1	3.8	3.5	5.2	4.1	3.2	3.3			4.8	4.6	6.9	6.4	.5	.8
1989	4.6	4.8	4.1	4.7	5.6	5.8	3.3	4.0			5.1	4.9	8.6	7.7	5.1	5.6
1990	6.1	5.4	6.6	5.2		7.4		4.8			5.7	5.5	9.9	9.3	18.1	8.3

*Changes from December to December are based on unadjusted indexes.
†Household fuels—gas (piped) electricity, fuel oil, etc.—and motor fuel. Motor oil, coolant, etc. also included through 1982.
Note: Data beginning 1978 are for all urban consumers; earlier data are for urban wage earners and clerical workers.
Source: Department of Labor, Bureau of Labor Statistics.

Table 6-5 Consumer Installment Credit Outstanding, 1950–1990

[amount outstanding (end of month); millions of dollars, seasonally adjusted]

Year and month	Total consumer credit	Installment credit					Noninstallment credit[4]
		Total	Automobile	Revolving[2]	Mobile home[3]	Other	
December:							
1950	23,295	15,166	6,035			9.131	8,129
1951	24,624	15,859	5,981			9,878	8,765
1952	29,766	20,121	7,651			12,470	9,645
1953	33,769	23,870	9,702			14,168	9,899
1954	35,027	24,470	9,755			14,715	10,557
1955	41,885	29,809	13,485			16,324	12,076
1956	45,503	32,660	14,499			18,161	12,843
1957	48,132	34,914	15,493			19,421	13,218
1958	48,356	34,736	14,267			20,469	13,620
1959	55,878	40,421	16,641			23,780	15,457
1960	60,035	44,335	18,108			26,227	15,700
1961	62,340	45,438	17,656			27,782	16,902
1962	68,231	50,375	20,001			30,374	17,856
1963	76,606	57,056	22,891			34,165	19,550
1964	85,989	64,674	25,865			38,809	21,315
1965	95,948	72,814	29,378			43,436	23,134
1966	101,839	78,162	31,024			47,138	23,677
1967	106,716	81,783	31,136			50,647	24,933
1968	117,231	90,112	34,352	2,022		53,738	27,119
1969	126,928	99,381	36,946	3,563		58,872	27,547
1970	131,600	103,905	36,348	4,900	2,433	60,224	27,695
1971	147,058	116,434	40,522	8,252	7,171	60,489	30,624
1972	166,009	131,258	47,835	9,391	9,468	64,564	34,751
1973	190,601	152,910	53,740	11,318	13,505	74,347	37,691
1974	199,365	162,203	54,241	13,232	14,582	80,148	37,162
1975	204,963	167,043	56,989	14,507	15,388	80,159	37,920
1976	228,162	187,782	66,821	16,595	15,738	88,628	40,380
1977	263,808	221,475	80,948	36,689	16,362	87,476	42,333
1978	308,272	261,976	98,739	45,202	16,921	101,114	46,296
1979	347,507	296,483	112,475	53,357	18,207	112,444	51,024
1980	350,269	298,154	111,991	55,111	18,736	112,317	52,115
1981	366,869	311,259	119,008	61,070	20,058	111,124	55,610
1982	383,132	325,805	125,945	66,454	22,604	110,802	57,327
1983	431,170	368,966	143,560	79,088	23,562	122,756	62,204
1984	511,315	442,602	173,564	100,280	25,861	142,897	68,713
1985	592,129	518,252	210,187	121,816	26,850	159,400	73,877
1986	649,112	573,017	247,428	135,851	27,096	162,642	76,095
1987	681,892	610,468	265,851	153,078	25,920	165,620	71,424
1988	731,521	664,701	284,556	174,057	25,201	180,887	66,820
1989	777,975	716,624	290,770	197,110	22,343	206,401	61,351
1990[5]	794,493	738,316	283,989	219,416	22,516	212,395	56,177

[1]Installment credit covers most short- and intermediate-term credit extended to individuals through regular business channels, usually to finance the purchase of consumer goods and services or to refinance debts incurred for such purposes, and scheduled to be repaid (or with the option of repayment) in two or more installments. Credit secured by real estate is generally excluded.

[2]Consists of credit cards at retailers, gasoline companies, and commercial banks, and check credit at commercial banks. Excludes 30-day charge credit held by travel and entertainment companies. Prior to 1968, included in "other," except gasoline companies included in noninstallment credit prior to 1971. Beginning 1977, includes open-end credit at retailers, previously included in "other." Also beginning 1977, some retail credit was reclassified from commercial into consumer credit.

[3]Not reported separately prior to July 1970.

[4]Noninstallment credit is credit scheduled to be repaid in a lump sum, including single-payment loans, charge accounts, and service credit. Because of inconsistencies in the data and infrequent benchmarking, series is no longer published by the Federal Reserve Board on a regular basis. Data are shown here as a general indication of trends.

[5]November data.

Source: Board of Governors of the Federal Reserve System.

Table 6-6   The Rise and Fall of the Dollar: Exchange Rates for Major Currencies
[currency units per U.S. dollar, except as noted]

Period	Belgium (franc)	Canada (dollar)	France (franc)	Germany (mark)	Italy (lira)	Japan (yen)
March 1973	39.408	0.9967	4.5156	2.8132	568.17	261.90
1967	49.689	1.0789	4.9206	3.9865	624.09	362.13
1968	49.936	1.0776	4.9529	3.9920	623.38	360.55
1969	50.142	1.0769	5.1999	3.9251	627.32	358.36
1970	49.656	1.0444	5.5288	3.6465	627.12	358.16
1971	48.598	1.0099	5.5100	3.4830	618.34	347.79
1972	44.020	.9907	5.0444	3.1886	583.70	303.13
1973	38.955	1.0002	4.4535	2.6715	582.41	271.31
1974	38.959	.9780	4.8107	2.5868	650.81	291.84
1975	36.800	1.0175	4.2877	2.4614	653.10	296.78
1976	38.609	.9863	4.7825	2.5185	833.58	296.45
1977	35.849	1.0633	4.9161	2.3236	882.78	268.62
1978	31.495	1.1405	4.5091	2.0097	849.13	210.39
1979	29.342	1.1713	4.2567	1.8343	831.11	219.02
1980	29.238	1.1693	4.2251	1.8175	856.21	226.63
1981	37.195	1.1990	5.4397	2.2632	1138.58	220.63
1982	45.781	1.2344	6.5794	2.4281	1354.00	249.06
1983	51.123	1.2325	7.6204	2.5539	1519.32	237.55
1984	57.752	1.2952	8.7356	2.8455	1756.11	237.46
1985	59.337	1.3659	8.9800	2.9420	1908.88	238.47
1986	44.664	1.3896	6.9257	2.1705	1491.16	168.35
1987	37.358	1.3259	6.0122	1.7981	1297.03	144.60
1988	36.785	1.2306	5.9595	1.7570	1302.39	128.17
1989	39.409	1.1842	6.3802	1.8808	1372.28	138.07
1990	33.424	1.1668	5.4467	1.6166	1198.27	145.00

Period	Netherlands (guilder)	Sweden (krona)	Switzerland (franc)	United Kingdom (pound)[1]	Multilateral trade-weighted value of the U.S. dollar (March 1973 = 100) Nominal	Real[2]
March 1973	2.8714	4.4294	3.2171	247.24	100.0	100.0
1967	3.6024	5.1621	4.3283	275.04	120.0	
1968	3.6198	5.1683	4.3163	239.35	122.1	
1969	3.6240	5.1701	4.3131	239.01	122.4	
1970	3.6166	5.1862	4.3106	239.59	121.1	
1971	3.4953	5.1051	4.1171	244.42	117.8	
1972	3.2098	4.7571	3.8186	250.34	109.1	
1973	2.7946	4.3619	3.1688	245.25	99.1	98.8
1974	2.6879	4.4387	2.9805	234.03	101.4	99.2
1975	2.5293	4.1531	2.5839	222.17	98.5	93.9
1976	2.6449	4.3580	2.5002	180.48	105.7	97.2
1977	2.4548	4.4802	2.4065	174.49	103.4	93.0
1978	2.1643	4.5207	1.7907	191.84	92.4	84.2
1979	2.0073	4.2893	1.6644	212.24	88.1	83.1
1980	1.9875	4.2310	1.6772	232.46	87.4	84.8
1981	2.4999	5.0660	1.9675	202.43	103.4	100.9
1982	2.6719	6.2839	2.0327	174.80	116.6	111.7
1983	2.8544	7.6718	2.1007	151.59	125.3	117.1
1984	3.2085	8.2708	2.3500	133.68	138.2	128.5
1985	3.3185	8.6032	2.4552	129.74	143.0	131.9
1986	2.4485	7.1273	1.7979	146.77	112.2	103.3
1987	2.0264	6.3469	1.4918	163.98	96.9	90.6
1988	1.9778	6.1370	1.4643	178.13	92.7	88.0
1989	2.1219	6.4559	1.6369	163.82	98.6	94.2
1990	1.8215	5.9231	1.3901	178.41	89.1	86.4

[1]Cents per unit of foreign currency.
[2]Adjusted by changes in consumer prices.
Source: Board of Governors of the Federal Reserve System.

Chapter Seven
MORE AND MORE: THE RICH IN AMERICA

HIGHLIGHTS AND TRENDS

• A Federal Reserve study of wealth, the first major government study of the rich in twenty years, found that "a surprisingly large percentage of all U.S. families [4%] were estimated to have a net worth of more than $500,000." The study found that almost 2% of all families (1,310,000) had a net worth of more than $1 million and that almost 0.5% of the families (320,000 households) had net financial assets (which exclude business, property, and housing assets) of at least $1 million.

• But becoming a millionaire is not the distinction it used to be. After adjusting for inflation, a million dollars in 1948 was worth only $621,000 in 1970; by 1990, it was down to a mere $185,000.

• America's millionaires control about $1 trillion in assets, about one third of the country's wealth. About $273 billion was controlled by the richest 400 Americans in September of 1990.

• Many of the wealthiest families—such as the du Ponts ($9 billion), the Mellons ($4+ billion) and the Rockefellers ($4+ billion)—are dynasties that were founded in the 19th century. One hundred eighty-three members of the *Forbes* list of the 400 wealthiest Americans inherited their wealth.

• Large fortunes continue to be made. The three richest men in the United States are all self-made men; 217 of *Forbes*'s 400 wealthiest Americans created their own fortunes. One, William Gates, the founder of Microsoft, joined the ranks of America's billionaires early in 1987 at the age of 30.

THE LAST BILLIONAIRES?

In the mid-1970s there were only two billionaires alive—insurance magnate John D. MacArthur and shipping tycoon Daniel Ludwig—and many people wondered if they might be the last of their breed.

But like the fish in New York's East River, billionaires have staged a comeback. There are more than 40 of them in *Forbes*'s 1987 list of the 400 richest Americans (almost double their number a year earlier) and in the 1990 list there were 66 billionaires. Though a billion dollars might not be worth what it was when John D. Rockefeller became the first American billionaire, there's little doubt that a billion (or a near billion) still leaves someone nicely off. Consider a list of the world's billionaires compiled by *Fortune* magazine (see Table 7-1 below).

Table 7-1 The World's 25 Richest Billionaires, 1990

Name, age	Home	Wealth US$ billions	Sources of wealth
Sultan Haji Hassanal Bolkiah Mu'izzadin Waddaulah, 44	Bandar Seri Begawan, Brunei	$25.0	Oil and gas resources; real estate around the world; foreign investments
King Fahd Bin Abdul-Aziz al Saud, 69 and family	Riyadh, Saudi Arabia	$18.0	Saudi Arabia's oil and gas resources
Forrest E. Mars, Sr., 86	Las Vegas, Nevada	$12.5	100% of Mars Inc.: M&M/Mars, Uncle Ben's Rice, Kal-Kan pet food, Mars Electronics
Forrest E. Mars, Jr., 59	McLean, Virginia		
John F. Mars, 54	Arlington, Virginia		
Jacqueline Mars Vogel, 50	Bedminster, New Jersey		
Queen Elizabeth II, 64	London, England	$11.7	The Crown Estates: 267,000 acres in England and Scotland; U.S. and European real estate; racehorses; art, stamp, silver, porcelain, and jewelry collections; vast stock portfolio
Samuel I. Newhouse, Jr., 62 Donald E. Newhouse, 60 and family	New York, New York	$11.5	100% of Advance Publications and Newhouse Broadcasting
Albert Reichmann, 62 Paul Reichmann, 61 Ralph Reichmann, 58	Toronto, Canada	$11.1	100% of Olympia & York Developments
Yoshiaki Tsutsumi, 56	Tokyo, Japan	$7.3	40% of Kokudo Keikaku, which owns 48.5% of land-rich Seibu Railway
Sam Moore Walton, 72 and family	Bentonville, Arkansas	$7.3	38.5% of Wal-Mart Stores Inc.
John Werner Kluge, 75	Charlottesville, Virginia	$7.0	97.4% of Metromedia Inc.; real estate; stockholdings; cash, lots of it
Tsai Wan-Lin, 65 Tsai Wan-Tsai, 61 and family	Taipei, Taiwan	$6.5	65% of Cathay Life Insurance; 60% of Cathay Construction
Kenneth Roy Thomson, 67 and family	Toronto, Canada	$6.2	69.2% of Thomson Corp.; 78.5% of Hudson's Bay Co.; 12.4% of Consolidated Talcorp; art; real estate
Gerald Grosvenor, 38 and family	London, England	$5.4	Real estate holdings including 300 acres in London's exclusive Mayfair and Belgravia districts; 100,000 acres of Scottish woodlands; 12,000 acres in Vancouver, British Columbia; a 10,000-acre Australian sheep station; commercial properties in Britain, Hawaii, and California; and holdings in Northern Ireland

Table 7-1   The World's 25 Richest Billionaires, 1990
(continued)

Name, age	Home	Wealth US$ billions	Sources of wealth
Sheikh Jaber Ahmed al Sabah, 64 and family	Kuwait	$4.8	Cash; vast foreign investments
Charles Koch, 54 David Koch, 50	Wichita, Kansas New York, New York	$4.7	80% of Koch Industries
Anne Cox Chambers, 70	Atlanta, Georgia	$4.5	96% of Cox Enterprises
Barbara Cox Anthony, 67	Honolulu, Hawaii		
Perry Bass, 76 Sid Richardson Bass, 47 Edward Perry Bass, 45 Robert Muse Bass, 42 Lee Marshall Bass, 33	Fort Worth, Texas	$4.5	Oil, real estate, investments in Walt Disney Co., Universal Health Services, and more
Jay Pritzker, 68 Robert Pritzker, 64 and family	Chicago, Illinois	$4.5	100% of Hyatt Corp., hotels and resorts; 100% of Marmon Group
Queen Beatrix, 51	The Hague, Netherlands	$4.4	Securities, including stock in Royal Dutch/Shell; jewels; real estate
Thomas Schmidheiny, 45	Zurich, Switzerland	$4.2	Nueva Holdings, construction supplies; Unotech, high-tech investing; SMH, watch manu-
Stephan Schmidheiny, 43	Hurden, Switzerland		facture; BBC/ABB and Landis & Gyr, electronics firm;
Alexander Schmidheiny, 39	Calistoga, California		Anova Holdings, packaging and real estate
Giovanni Agnelli, 69 and family	Turin, Italy	$4.0	39.4% of Fiat Group; real estate; art
Sheikh Rashid Bin Said al Maktoum, 80 and family	Dubai, United Arab Emirates	$4.0	Oil; vast foreign investments
Johanna Quandt, 68 and family	Wiesbaden, Germany	$4.0	67% of BMW; securities
Eugene Paul (J. Paul, Jr.) Getty, 58 Gordon Peter Getty, 56	London, England San Francisco, California	$3.8	Trusts; inheritance; investments
Mary Idema Pew, 68 Robert Pew, 66 Robert Pew, Jr., 39 Kate Pew Wolters, 33	Grand Rapids, Michigan	$3.8	Controlling interest in Steelcase Inc.; real estate

Source: *Fortune,* September 10, 1990

THE MYSTERIES OF WEALTH

Studying the rich is a national pastime. In fact, you could say that glitz, glamour, and glitter are big business—all because the American public has a seemingly inexhaustible interest in the rich and famous. Our fascination with the rich sells magazines such as *People* and it boosts the ratings of TV shows such as *Dallas*. Without the rich, an army of journalists, publicists, and gossip columnists would be reduced to penury or, even worse, forced to cover subjects such as the national debt.

Considering the amount of effort spent studying the rich, it is not surprising that journalists have uncovered a few facts. Reporters have already exposed the mysteries of how multimillionaire celebrities such as Michael Jackson decorate their game rooms, as well as the constant divorces, scandals, and drug deals that seem to afflict the rich. We even know a thing or two about how a pair of overweight Texas billionaires lost their shirts trying to buy all the silver in the world.

But for all that's said and written about the rich, it must be admitted that most of what we know is relatively trivial—at least from an economic standpoint. Even though the rich complain about constant press coverage, they have done an expert job of hiding their wealth from public scrutiny. In fact, any honest analysis of the rich must begin with the embarrassing admission that no one quite knows how rich the rich really are—even though this is a country where wealth is the most obvious sign of success. Even when reasonable estimates of wealth are available, it's often impossible to cut through the morass of paper corporations, holding companies, and offshore banks to figure out the exact holdings of the rich and superrich.

Lacking exact information, it's hard to know what to make of the rich. Are they a new aristocracy? Or are the rich the real backbone of the American economy, men and women transforming industries, creating new companies, wealth, and jobs? Do the great American dynasties—the Rockefellers, the du Ponts, the Fords, and the Hunts to name a few—really run the country, controlling Wall Street and the White House? Or are the rich an endangered species—a class threatened by an anonymous army of mediocre middle managers, technocrats, and government regulators hell-bent on driving the great industrial fortunes out of existence?

Table 7-2   Billion-Dollar Dynasties
Here are America's richest families:

Family	Holdings	Value
du Pont	Over 15% of E. I. du Pont de Nemours,	$5–9 billion
Mellon	Mellon Bank, etc; they no longer act together in investments	$4–5 billion
Bass	Four brothers and families have investments in Walt Disney, Taft Broadcasting, real estate, savings and loans, Bell & Howell American Medical International	$4–5.5 billion
Rockefeller	Exxon (oil), real estate, Chase Manhattan, etc.	$4 billion +
Getty	Four branches of the family that are not on good terms earned $3 billion from sale of Getty Oil to Texaco	$3 billion
Cargill, MacMillan	Cargill (grain trading)	$2.2 billion
Hearst	Hearst Corporation (media), real estate	$4 billion
Phipps	Steel, stocks, real estate	$1.8 billion
Haas	Levi Strauss	$2 billion+
Bronfman	Seagram Co.	$1.9 billion
Busch	Anheuser-Busch	$1.5 billion+
Ford	Ford Motor, real estate, etc	$1–1.5 billion
Chandler	Times Mirror Co.	$1 billion+

Sources: Various press reports.

AMERICA'S MILLIONAIRES: WHO ARE THEY AND WHAT DO THEY OWN?

Although the rich are secretive about their holdings, tracking the life and times of America's millionaires is helped by the fact that the Internal Revenue Service has a long-standing obsession with discovering large and preferably taxable fortunes. Based on tax returns, the IRS estimates that 941,000 Americans, about 0.5% of the population, have net assets worth a million dollars.

But these figures are probably understated. A 1986 Federal Reserve survey of wealth, the first major government study of the rich in twenty years, found that "a surprisingly large percentage of all U.S. families [4% in 1983] were estimated to have a net worth of more than $500,000." The study, found that almost 2% of all families (1,310,000) had a net worth of over $1 million and that 0.5% of the families (320,000 households) had net financial assets (excluding business, property, and housing assets) of at least $1 million. About 14% of all families surveyed had a net worth of at least $163,800, up from 1962, when only 6% were that wealthy.

But joining the Millionaires' Club of America is no longer quite the distinction it used to be. In terms of assets, only 13,000 Americans—one in 11,287—were worth a million in 1948.

Inflation has also played havoc with the value of a million dollars. As we noted, a million dollars in terms of its 1948 buying power was worth only $621,000 in 1970; by 1990, it was down to a mere $185,000.

And keeping up with the Rockefellers is getting harder and harder for America's nouveaux riches. In fact, many of the de rigueur status symbols of the truly wealthy have increased in cost faster than most basic necessities. In the 19th century, the first act of any self-respecting millionaire was to put a mansion on Fifth Avenue in Manhattan. But over the years, that prestigious address has gotten more expensive: the cost of a Fifth Avenue townhouse has skyrocketed from $55,000 in 1940 to $10 million or so today. Similarly, since 1940 the price of a painting by Jan Brueghel has gone from $2,000 to $560,000, a flawless diamond from $3,000 to $75,000, and a tin of caviar from $15 to $300. A van Gogh that you could pick up at the end of the 19th century for nothing sold for $82.5 million in 1990, the most ever paid for a painting up to that time.

But then, most millionaires can't afford that kind of conspicuous consumption. When you get down to it, someone worth a mere million has only joined the peasantry of the rich. In 1990 a man or woman had to be worth $260 million to make the real aristocracy of American money, the *Forbes* list of the 400 richest Americans. One of the richest men, John Kluge, was worth $7 billion; collectively the richest 400 Americans were worth $273 billion in 1990. In contrast, the 941,000 millionaires discovered by the IRS controlled about $2.7 trillion dollars in net assets.

No one would deny that $273 billion is a lot of money. In 1990, it was enough to buy all of the common stock in General Motors, IBM, Exxon, du Pont, and Procter & Gamble. It would pay for the $50 billion in illegal drugs Americans use every year for over four years running. With the $2.7 trillion owned by America's millionaires you could pay off a hefty chunk of the national debt, fight every American war from the Revolution to the Vietnam War, or buy all the assets of the 500 largest corporations in America. But is $2.7 trillion enough to buy real political and economic power? Is it enough to control the economy?

Certainly not. Even a couple of trillion dollars doesn't buy the kind of political and economic clout it used to. If the $2.7 trillion owned by American millionaires was nationalized and distributed to the public, every American would only receive a little over $10,800, not even enough to buy a BMW. And its even possible to lose a trillion dollars. The stock market dropped that much in value between August and November of 1987.

A PROFILE OF THE TOP EXECUTIVE

Throughout most of America's economic history, the surest way to the top of a major company was to start one, inherit one, or buy one. At the end of the 19th century there was little doubt that many big businesses were firmly controlled by a few powerful and often self-made entrepreneurs, men such as John D. Rockefeller and Andrew Carnegie.

Yet over the next half-century the path to corporate power changed dramatically. Stock ownership became more diffuse, making it harder for the great economic dynasties of the 19th century to hold onto their family fortunes. In established industries such as steel or, later on, the auto industry, entrepreneurs had little chance of raising the kind of capital they needed to start a new General Motors or U.S. Steel. And as the size of companies grew dramatically, huge corporate bureaucracies were created to run these firms.

The result was the rise of the modern manager. Unlike entrepreneurs such as Rockefeller or Carnegie, these men rarely owned large parts of the companies they ran. Their power was based on the separation of ownership and actual corporate power. Since the 1950s, most corporations have been run by professional managers. They set long-term strategies, plan acquisitions, and direct the companies' day-to-day operations, while the actual owners of the companies, the stockholders, have little power over the companies' direction. Nor are stockholders likely to interfere with the companies' management. Usually the chief executive officer (CEO) and top corporate executives of each company control the board of directors by appointing outside directors who are likely to do their bidding. Only in unusual cases do stockholders revolt and try to run their own slate of directors. Yet even then, management holds the upper hand in proxy fights because of its power to sway shareholders.

This is not to imply that professional managers are completely independent. Besides government regulators and unions, who often have the power to derail the best-laid plans, a company's creditors often are represented on the board of directors.

More importantly, Wall Street can signal its disapproval by cutting the price of the company's stock, making it harder for the company to secure new credit or financing. In the past few years, management's autonomy has been further eroded by corporate raiders. They've delivered a rude ultimatum to the management of many undervalued companies—either increase shareholder value or lose control of the company.

Yet even though American business bears little resemblance to the way companies were run in the 19th century, there are some similarities between the entrepreneurs who ran 19th-century corporations and today's professional managers. A survey of top CEOs by *Fortune* indicates that many of the values and characteristics of top executives of the past have survived and in fact thrived.

Like the proverbial 19th-century entrepreneurs who spent a lifetime building their companies, most American CEOs work long hours and spend most of their lives with one company. The majority (68%) work over 55 hours a week, and most (58%) take less than three weeks' vacation, about the same vacation time given to an assembly-line worker with seniority. About 33% have worked for only one company in their lives, and over half (57.6%) have only worked for two companies. Only 8.3% have worked for five or more companies.

And although family members have been replaced by managers in most large corporations, many of these managers have a large financial stake in the companies they run. Over half of all top CEOs (51.6%) own stock in their companies valued at over $1 million, 18% have stock valued at over $5 million, and 33% have stock valued at over $2.5 million.

Socially, America's captains of industry also have some resemblance to their 19th-century predecessors. America's top executives are still overwhelmingly male—only Katharine Graham of the Washington Post Company runs one of the 1,000 largest companies in America. And CEOs typically assumed their position at 50 years of age, about the same as in 1990, when they were 48.

But in other very important ways American managers are very different, reflecting the way business has changed. With top corporations becoming increasingly complex, American managers are better educated than ever before. Nearly 31% hold master's degrees, 12% have doctorates, and another 20.3% have spent some time in graduate school. Although most come from middle- or lower-middle-class backgrounds, many of them also attended elite schools. By 1980, Harvard could boast that its graduates made up 19% of the top three officers of *Fortune* 500 companies and that over 3,500 alumni headed U.S. corporations.

THE WITHERING AWAY OF INDIVIDUAL WEALTH?

No doubt the managerial revolution has profoundly transformed the nature of economic power. And, over time, the assets of most dynasties become widely dispersed, weakening their economic and political clout. But it would be wrong to conclude that the great industrial dynasties play only a minor role in the economy. A study in the late 1970s by Wharton School professor Edward Herman for the Twentieth Century Fund found that individual owners and families controlled 21% of the top 100 industrial corporations. About 16% of the largest 200 industrial corporations were controlled by individuals or families. Family- or owner-controlled corporations had assets of $95 billion, about 13.2% of the total assets of the top 200 corporations.

Today, a study of smaller public corporations or privately held companies would probably reveal that individual owners have even more power than owners of the largest corporations because it takes much less capital to control the companies. For example, privately owned companies make up about 98% of all companies, producing about one third of all the goods and services in the United States. Half of the country's billionaires get their wealth from privately owned companies, *Forbes* notes. The 400 largest private companies employ about 3 million people.

Moreover, there is no sign that the richest and most powerful families will fade from the scene. While it's true that a few wealthy families no longer control smokestack companies such as U.S. Steel, many families still control powerful empires in newly emerging high-tech industries or in the media. In the media, for example, Rupert Murdoch, the Newhouses, the Grahams, and the Chandlers all control far-flung empires.

WHAT THE RICH OWN

The difficulties of finding out what the rich own were revealed in 1986 when the Joint Economic Committee of Congress rushed out a study under the headline "The Rich Get Richer." The study, based on Federal Reserve figures, concluded that 0.5% of the population owned 35% of the nation's wealth, up from only 25.4% in 1963, when the last Federal Reserve study was undertaken. Most of the public (90%) owned only 28.2% of the wealth, down from 35% in 1963.

But then it was discovered that a mistake had been made. Someone had recorded one man's wealth as $200 million when it should have been $2 million. Oops.

The revised data indicate that 0.5% of population, who had an average net worth of over $2.5 million, controlled 26.9% of the nation's wealth, up only slightly from 1963 when the richest Americans owned 25.4%. Ninety percent of the households, on the other hand, were worth less than $206,340.

Those results were consistent with studies of American wealth made since the 1920s, most of which have shown that the wealthiest 1% of the population has controlled about one third of the wealth, and the wealthiest 0.5% about 20% to 25% of the nation's wealth. A 1983 Federal Reserve survey found that the top 0.5% held 19% of all assets and 31% of all financial assets. Financial assets, according to the Federal Reserve, do not include assets in business, property, and housing and include such things as stocks and bonds.

Moreover, several studies show that the number of very rich increased dramatically during the 1980s. A 1990 IRS study found that the number of Americans worth more than $500,000 jumped from 2.2 million in 1982 to 3.3 million in 1986. These people, who comprised just 1.6% of the nation's adult population, had a combined net worth of $3.8 trillion, about 28.9% of the personal wealth in the United States. Moreover, the number of millionaires jumped from 180,000 in 1976 to 475,000 in 1982 to 941,000 in 1986. These millionaires, who made up only 0.5% of the population, had a collective net worth of $2.7 trillion, about 20% of the nation's wealth.

Viewing the issue from another angle, the Center on Budget and Policy Priorities noted in a 1990 study that "the richest 1 percent of all Americans now receive nearly as much income after taxes as the bottom 40% of Americans combined. Stated another way, the richest 2.5 million people now have nearly as much income as the 100 million Americans with the lowest incomes."

Using data compiled by the Congressional Budget Office, the Center also found that the after-tax income for the top 1% of all Americans grew 87% between 1980 and 1990, the top 5%'s income jumped 51%, and the richest 20% grew 33%. In contrast, the poorest 20% lost 5% of their income, and the bottom 60% of all Americans had virtually no income gain during the 1980s.

A 1991 Census Department study also shows many American families did not benefit from the booming 1980s. This study found that American households had a median net worth of $35,752 in 1988, down from $37,012 in 1984. The net worth (assets minus debts) of the typical white household, $43,280, was more than 10 times the average black household, $4,170, and the typical married white couple was worth $62,390, much more than the average black couple, $17,640. About 26.2% of all American households were worth less than $5,000, and 56.9% were worth under $50,000. In contrast, 2.8% of all households were worth over $500,000, and about 25.3% had a net worth of over $100,000. The wealthiest 20% (those with incomes over $46,000) held 44.4% of the nation's wealth while the poorest 20% (those with incomes under $11,268) held 7% of the nation's net worth.

Other government studies indicate that because of their large timber, agricultural, and farming interests, about 3% of the population own about 55% of the land, or 95% of the land that is privately owned. And the top 0.5% own about 56% of all municipal bonds and 43% of all stock.

IS THERE ROOM AT THE TOP?

Absolutely. Despite the difficulties of cracking many markets dominated by huge corporations, new American fortunes are still being created. The three wealthiest men in America—former T.V. mogul John Kluge; Warren Buffett, the head of Berkshire Hathaway; and corporate raider Ronald Perelman—are all self-made men. Moreover, most of the CEOs of the nation's 500 largest companies were not born into great wealth. These executives might not found economic dynasties the size of a Rockefeller's, but while they head companies such as Exxon they have much more economic power than many of the nation's richest families.

How do they do it? Being in the right place at the right time helps. Many of the fortunes profiled below were created in emerging and developing industries. John D. Rockefeller made a billion dollars in the early days of the oil industry while David Packard made his billion-dollar fortune as a pioneer in the electronics industry. In 1987, William Gates III, the founder of the software firm Microsoft, became the first of the computer entrepreneurs who capitalized on the personal-computer revolution to become a billionaire. Gates was only 30. By 1990, at the ripe old age of 34, he was worth $2.5 billion.

More importantly, America's great entrepreneurs show a marked talent for shaping new industries in their own images. Rockefeller virtually invented big business with his Standard Oil Company, showing the importance of economies of scale. Henry Ford, Sr., wasn't the first auto manufacturer or even the most technically brilliant, but he was the first to mass-produce a car, thus lowering costs and allowing middle-class and working-class buyers to afford his Model T. Here's how they did it:

The Rockefellers Around the world, the Rockefeller name is better known than the names of most American presidents, thanks to a $4 billion plus fortune that was established by John D. Rockefeller and his brother William during the last half of the 19th century. Born on a modest farm in upstate New York, John D. started out as a commodity merchant. He got into the oil business in the 1860s, in the early days of the world's first oil boom, and by 1878 his company, Standard Oil, had a virtual monopoly on the oil business.

In creating his oil empire, Rockefeller created the first trust, which got around state laws prohibiting corporations from doing business in more than one state. Later, when the Sherman Antitrust Act forced him to dissolve the trust, he pioneered the use of the holding company to control his vast holdings. The growth of monopolistic power brought profits into the Rockefeller empire. By 1883, after gaining control of the market, Rockefeller was worth $40 million. His fortune grew to $200 million by 1897, and by 1913 he had become the country's first billionaire.

However, Rockefeller came under attack because of Standard Oil's economic power and ruthless tactics—competitors' refineries had a nasty habit of blowing up. To polish his tarnished reputation, Rockefeller spent the last third of his life giving away money—$531 million in all. His son John gave away another $544 million and other Rockefellers gave away hundreds of millions more. One of the family's foundations, the Rockefeller Brothers Fund, had assets of $220 million in 1986, and the dynasty has remained active in public life, philanthropy, and social causes.

But like all dynasties, the Rockefellers have had their problems. While David Rockefeller, the former head of Chase Manhattan Bank, is worth about $1 billion, many of the 87 other living Rockefellers have not done so well. Recently they were upset that some family assets, such as Rockefeller Center, were not producing enough income. To improve the cash flow to less affluent heirs, the family sold 51% of the Rockefeller Group (which owns the famous Rockefeller Center) in 1990 to the Japanese. Trust managers, reversing a long-standing policy of pursuing long-term capital gains, have invested the family's money in ventures likely to produce better short-term gains. The results should help the family avoid the kind of family feuds and costly litigation that have wrecked many other dynasties. But since David Rockefeller's retirement from Chase Manhattan, it's unlikely that any member of the family will emerge as a spokesman or spokeswoman for American business, ending a century-long tradition. The family is worth over $4 billion.

The Vanderbilts   The Vanderbilts made the first great industrial fortune of the latter half of the 19th century. In 1860, when John D. Rockefeller was still an unknown commodity merchant, Cornelius Vanderbilt was already 60, a successful shipping magnate worth a million dollars. But, at an age when most men were thinking of retiring, Vanderbilt was looking for new worlds to conquer. During the next 15 years he became one of the country's most powerful railroad magnates and Wall Street operatives. By the time of his death, in 1877, he was worth nearly $100 million, with most of that money invested in railroads. In a mere seven years after his death, his son had doubled the family fortune to $200 million.

A former sailor who never lost his taste for unprintable language, Cornelius Vanderbilt was an able manager who improved the equipment of the railroad lines he owned—such as the New York Central—and was an accomplished speculator in railroad stocks, doing battle with the likes of Jay Gould. He spent heavily to improve his railroad holdings. His son William turned New York Central into a powerful railroad line and consolidated the family holdings. William and the third generation of the dynasty also followed a familiar pattern by gaining admittance into high society, something that would have been impossible for the hard-swearing family patriarch.

Family holdings in the New York Central Railroad dwindled in the 20th century, and by the time the line went bankrupt in 1970 the family had few or no holdings in it. One family member, however, heiress Gloria Vanderbilt, showed the old entrepreneurial spirit by cashing in on the highly profitable fad in designer jeans.

The Mellons Family patriarch Judge Thomas Mellon grew wealthy in the mid 19th century from his law practice and real estate investments. In 1870 he founded the family bank, T. Mellon and Sons (later Mellon National Bank, now Mellon Bank), which financed much of Andrew Carnegie's growing steel empire, and his heirs played a major role in financing Pittsburgh's booming industrial economy. His youngest son Andrew invested in the aluminum industry, backing Alcoa as well as the Carborundum Company and Union Steel (sold for $30 million to U.S. Steel in 1902). The Mellon National Bank's most profitable investment, however, was in an oil company that became Gulf Oil Corporation.

Today, several family members have remained in the public eye. Mellon heir Richard Scaife has become the nation's largest financier of conservative causes. Paul Mellon, who failed with such ventures as the In-N-Out hamburger restaurant, has since devoted his life to art, amassing one of the largest collections in the United States. His French Impressionist collection alone is valued at over $100 million. He and his sister Ailsa spent nearly $100 million to build the east wing of the National Gallery of Art. In the late 1970s he donated another $200 million worth of art to Yale University. Various members of the family are probably worth well over $4 billion altogether, but no one has been either willing or able to consolidate the family holdings so that all the various trusts and family members act together. The Mellon Bank is no longer run by family members.

The Astors In New York the Astor family has long been synonymous with high society. Family wealth was created by John Jacob Astor, a financier, fur trader, and real estate investor. He got his start by selling whiskey, illegally, to the Indians in exchange for pelts. By the time of his death in 1848, his $20 million fortune made him the richest man in America. His son William continued buying New York real estate, earning him the title "landlord of New York." By 1875, when William died, the family was worth $40 million. In the third generation the family established its reign over high society, causing one minister to report that "not to have received an invitation to an Astor ball" was equivalent to being banned from high society. The Astors were famous for their parties; it was at the Cliveden estate of the British Astors where call girl Christine Keeler cavorted with the English elite, setting off the notorious Profumo affair. Today, the family has sold off most of its New York real estate, valued at $125 million in the late 1950s, and established a $50 million foundation, the Vincent Astor Foundation.

The Cabots   The family that defined "Boston brahmin" was the Cabots. The family first arrived in Boston in 1700 and by the early part of the 18th century had built up a merchant empire in the not-so-genteel trade of rum, slaves, and opium (thanks largely to the efforts of shipbuilder, pirate, and U.S. Senator George Cabot). But wealth sanitizes all sins, and in the 19th century the family attempted to recreate a European aristocracy in Boston. Intermarrying with the Lowells, Higginsons, Jacksons, and other top Boston families, they established a line of senators, governors, and capitalists, setting up the first cotton mill and providing money for the early railroads, copper mines, and the telephone. By the early 1900s a wit could note, "And this is good old Boston, / The home of the bean and the cod, / Where the Lowells talk to the Cabots / And the Cabots talk only to God." Today, with a family fortune estimated at $350 million, Louis W. Cabot is a director and former chairman of the Cabot Corporation, the world's largest producer of carbon black. Other family members sit as trustees on prominent universities, run mutual funds, or work as investment bankers.

The Bronfmans   The family arrived in Canada as Russian immigrants in 1889 and made money in hotels and saloons. When Prohibition hit Canada in 1916, they sold liquor through a mail-order business from Quebec, which was still wet. Later they supplied U.S. bootleggers and bought Seagram's in 1928.

Today, the family controls about 40% of Seagram Company, but not all family members have shared equally in the wealth. Samuel Bronfman ousted two nephews, Edward and Peter, in 1953. These two moved to Toronto, sold their stock for about $25 million and built up Edper Enterprises Ltd, a conglomerate with holdings valued at around $1 billion. In 1971, Sam's sons, Edgar and Charles Bronfman, took over the firm. Edgar, who became chairman in 1975, ran the American operations, and Charles, who became co-chairman in 1986, ran the overseas business.

In 1989, Edgar Bronfman, Jr., was named president and COO of the company at the age of 34. Edgar, who left home as a teen to produce movies, is now guiding Seagrams through troubled times in the 1990s. With liquor consumption down, Edgar, Jr., has been beefing up sales of nonalcoholic beverages, such as its Tropicana orange juice line and Soho natural soda. Profits tripled since 1981, but about three quarters of the company's profits come from its 20% stake in du Pont Co., acquired in

1980, and Seagrams is no longer the world's largest liquor company. It was surpassed in the 1980s by Grand Metropolitan, Plc. and Guinness, Plc. Edgar, Sr., is worth about $1.9 billion.

The Tisches   Laurence Tisch and his brother Preston Robert are two businessmen who have a reputation for having built up a $2.0 billion family fortune by purchasing distressed properties and turning them around. So in 1986, it was in character when they took charge of another pair of down-and-out businesses—CBS and the U.S. Postal Service. Laurence moved into the executive suites of Black Rock, as the CBS headquarters is known, as the CEO while Bob was named Postmaster General, a post he held until 1988. No one has ever managed to turn the U.S. Mail into an efficient, well-run organization. Still, brother Bob seems to have gotten the easier job.

The Tisches entered Black Rock in 1985 as white knights, when CBS was fighting takeover threats by Ted Turner and several others. Their Loews Corporation agreed to buy up a substantial stake in CBS to protect the company from outside takeovers and Laurence was put on the board. But by the fall of 1986, they had boosted their share of CBS to 25% and had ousted the company's chairman.

The CBS staff and the news division cheered when Laurence Tisch was named chairman. Ex-CEO Thomas Wyman had angered the news department and founder William Paley by cutting the news staff and axing such corporate perks as the company jet. CBS was foundering in the ratings, hadn't produced a hit to match NBC's top rated *Cosby Show,* and its once-vaunted news division was in a three-way ratings war with NBC and ABC. Paley, the news division, and board member Walter Cronkite all asserted that Tisch would restore the network to its former splendor.

But within months the white knight had his armor tarnished. The cost cutting that Wyman began continued under Tisch. Hundreds of employees, from pages and security guards to top managers, were fired. CBS Technology Center, an influential 50-year-old laboratory where the long-playing record and a prototype of color TV were developed, was shut down. And the news division, which believed it would be spared further cuts, was ordered to shave $30 million off its $300 million budget, forcing staff layoffs of 200 people, about 15% of its payroll.

The Tisches also angered the staff by breaking their promise not to sell off significant assets. The record division, publishing operations, and the magazine division were all quickly sold.

But while all these actions shocked CBS's staff, they didn't surprise people who knew the Tisch family. Cutting costs, buying distressed properties, and spinning off assets is what the Tisch brothers had always done. The brothers bought a New Jersey resort in 1946 and built it up to a 12-hotel chain by 1955. In 1960 they gained control over Loews Corporation and over the years turned it into a profitable conglomerate with $8.6 billion in 1986 revenues.

Laurence Tisch's cost-cutting philosophy may in fact be the best for

CBS in the short run. Paley ran a company that never worried about costs, and in fact never needed to as long as network advertising kept rising and CBS remained head and shoulders above its rivals in the entertainment and news ratings wars. With network ad revenues not even keeping up with inflation, the networks are keeping a sharper eye on budgets.

Still, network TV is an industry where a hit such as *The Cosby Show* can produce high ratings and huge profits. While the Tisches' cost cutting and asset sales boosted CBS's bottom line, it did nothing for the ratings. After spending the last half of the 1980s in third place and firing a string of programing directors, CBS is still a network searching for a new identity. In 1989 and 1990, the network illustrated a new willingness to gamble by paying billions for rights to professional sports. But after it bought the rights to major league baseball, industry insiders say that CBS lost as much as $100 million in the 1990 season, thanks in part to a weak economy and an unexpectedly short World Series. Still, there are some bright spots. CBS won the first week of the fall season in 1990, and many of its new shows did better than expected.

The Basses   This is one of the few families that has made the transition from Texas oil to Wall Street. The second-generation Bass brothers—Sid, Edward, Robert, Perry, and Lee—have built a $50 million oil fortune into a financial empire valued at least $4 billion.

The first Bass family millions were created by Sid Williams Richardson. He built up a $105 million fortune in the Texas oil fields during the Depression. Nephew Perry Bass was Richardson's partner, but when Richardson died, Perry was left with only a $12 million stake in their company. The bulk of Richardson's fortune went to the Sid W. Richardson Foundation.

So the Bass family started all over. They consolidated their assets in 1960 into Bass Brothers Enterprises, and in 1970 Sid Rainwater joined Bass Brothers Enterprises as an investment adviser. A former Yale classmate of Sid Bass, Rainwater helped the Basses put together hundreds of profitable deals.

One of their most profitable deals came in 1984 when they bought up a major stake in The Walt Disney Company, saving Disney from raiders who wanted to sell off the company's assets. When the new management brought in by the Basses turned the company around, the Disney investment earned the family over $850 million. In other cases they earned a reputation as shrewd corporate raiders. Rainwater and the Basses, for example, bought up a 10% stake in Texaco after its Getty Oil takeover deal was announced. Fearing a Bass takeover, Texaco bought their shares for $1.2 billion, leaving the Basses with a $450 million profit.

Over the years, family wealth has ballooned to more than $4 billion, while Rainwater has also amassed a $175 million personal fortune. In 1985 the brothers finally liquidated Bass Brothers Enterprises, their main investment company, and split the profits. Recently they have not worked together. Robert has made several highly publicized investments in the savings and loan industry. One of his newly acquired thrifts produced a $200 million profit in 1989, touching off a firestorm of protest in Congress that taxpayer money was being used to enrich wealthy corporate raiders. Robert is worth $1.5 billion. Brothers Edward ($1 billion), Lee ($1.4 billion) and Sid ($1.4 billion) are also doing quite nicely.

The Gettys   Unlike many of the other wildcatters who struck it rich in oil, Jean Paul Getty was well educated, having studied economics at Oxford. He joined his father George's successful Minnehoma Oil Company in 1914. With his father's backing he bought and sold leases, determined to make his first million in two years. By 1916, only one year behind schedule, Getty was a millionaire, and during the 1920s his fortune grew to $3 million, including a one-third interest in a company that would evolve into Getty Oil. However when his father died, Getty got only half a million dollars out of his father's $10 million estate because of his loose living. (Young Getty was already on his third of five wives by this point.)

Nonetheless, Getty, who got along no better with his own children, recovered from this setback and prospered during the Depression, buying new companies and real estate, including the $2.3 million Pierre Hotel in New York. His most profitable venture was in 1949. He purchased the right to an oil field between Saudi Arabia and Kuwait for $9.5 million. After investing $30 million, he hit an oil field that would eventually make him a billionaire. In 1967, Getty merged the Tidewater Oil Company and the Missouri Oil Company into the Getty Oil Company, which then had a value of $3 billion.

But wealth did not bring domestic bliss. One son committed suicide. Another became a drug addict. Son Gordon left the company in 1966 and sued his father to increase the dividends from Getty Oil. So when Jean Paul died, he left most of his money to the J. Paul Getty Museum. Without a trust set up by his mother, Sarah, Jean Paul Getty's five sons would have been left with little.

Gordon became the sole trustee of the family's trust in 1982, but the current generation has been unable to patch up the family feuds. Gordon decided Getty Oil was not producing enough revenues, and as head of the family trust he attempted to sell Getty Oil to an outsider, Pennzoil. But family members sued, opening the way for a much higher bid by Texaco. That put more money in the Getty family trust, but produced a legal nightmare. In 1988, the family trust was dissolved as part of a settlement to the Texaco takeover. Today, Gordon is worth about $1.3 billion, but spends most of his time composing music and conducting symphony orchestras.

LOSING A BILLION

Being rich is not as simple as making money. The trick is keeping it. In recent years, some of America's richest men have found that it's also possible to lose a billion dollars.

The Hunts and the Silver Crash

The Hunt brothers first became interested in silver in 1970 when silver was at a historic low, selling for only $1.50 an ounce. After a few initial purchases, they made a tidy profit when the metal went up to $3. As double-digit inflation hit, the Hunts saw silver as a hedge against both inflation and economic disaster. By 1973, the Hunts had taken delivery on 55 million ounces in silver, worth $160 million. But it wasn't until the late 1970s that they began their silver play in earnest. With Arab backers they bought 130 million ounces of silver and held silver contracts for 90 million ounces. Some traders believed it was possible to corner the silver market with only 200 million ounces, and naturally the price of silver began to rise, hitting $34.45 at the end of 1979 and climbing to $50 in January 1980. By this point, the Hunts had nearly $4.5 billion in silver, giving them a profit of $3.5 billion. But they didn't cash in their chips, and government regulators limited futures buying in an attempt to stabilize the market. Soon the price dropped, hitting $21 by March. With their margin calls at $10 million a day, the Hunts were in trouble, and they were eventually forced to announce that they wouldn't be able to meet their margin calls. To keep the market from crashing, Federal Reserve chairman Paul Volcker gave his approval to a $1.1 billion loan to bail out the Hunts.

The Hunts' losses from failing to sell at the right time were enormous. Their silver holdings had declined $4 billion from their peak in 1980, and the Hunts' silver play left them $1.5 billion in debt. Still, Bunker Hunt's only comment was, "A billion dollars isn't what it used to be."

The brothers finally sold their last silver holdings in 1985 for a $1 billion loss. By that time, everyone was saying the Hunts' billions weren't what they used to be. For several years the Hunts managed to pay their loans, but a dramatic drop in the price of oil soon threatened the very existence of the Hunt dynasty. For example, their speculative oil leases, once valued at over $2.27 billion, were rendered almost worthless by 1982. Placid Oil's assets had lost $1.35 billion in value in the 1980s and the value of their offshore oil rigs fell dramatically.

So, hounded by their creditors, the Hunts defaulted on their Penrod and Placid Oil loans in the spring of 1986. Efforts to restructure payments failed and the Hunts filed for protection under Chapter 11.

If one adds their silver losses ($1.5 billion) to the losses they've sustained in the oil business, the Hunts have lost an estimated $7.15 billion in less than six years, one of the largest transfers of personal wealth since the Czar was overthrown. Nor did Chapter 11 protect their personal assets. After years of litigation, the Hunt brothers were forced to sell off about $250 million worth of personal assets. In 1990, Herbert and Bunker estimated their personal net worth at about $1.5 million each. But other members of the family who stayed out of the silver debacle kept lots of loot. Sisters Caroline Rose Hunt and Margaret Hunt Hill are two of the richest people in the world, with assets valued at around $1.5 billion. Younger brother Lamar Hunt still owns the Kansas City Chiefs football team. Ray Lee Hunt and family, descendants of H. L. Hunt's second family, are worth $1 billion to $1.5 billion.

Taking big risks is in the family tradition. H. L. Hunt, the founder of the family fortune, was the quintessential Texas wildcatter. After making and losing a fortune speculating in cotton and timberland, he moved to the oil fields of El Dorado, Arkansas. There he used his photographic memory to become a professional gambler, making a tidy profit at the gaming tables of the tough boomtown. But in 1921, the local Ku Klux Klan labeled him a "moral degenerate" and threatened to burn down his saloon. So Hunt took up an even riskier profession—speculating in oil leases. His luck at the gaming tables stayed with him. By 1924 he was able to sell a 50% interest in his oil wells for $600,000, and during the 1930s he capitalized on the financial difficulties of another oilman to buy an East Texas field that became the site of the greatest oil discovery up to that time. Over the next 50 years, this field produced more than 4 billion barrels of oil.

After that discovery, Hunt built up his company, Hunt Oil, into the largest independent oil producer in the United States, and in the 1970s, before his death, he was worth $2 billion or $3 billion. His oil properties pumped out an income of over $1 million a week into the pockets of the old gambler.

Like many gamblers, Hunt was always a character, reminiscent of many other empire builders. He sired 15 children by three wives. Although he built a replica of George Washington's Mount Vernon mansion, he carried his lunch to work every day in a brown paper bag. H. L. Hunt also tried his hand as a novelist. His self-published novel *Alpaca* included the obligatory love story. But its real purpose was to describe Hunt's vision of a utopia—a mythical country where votes and political power are based on the amount of taxes a person pays.

Table 7-3   The Largest Privately Held Companies in America

To preserve family control over companies, many corporations have remained private. Private firms comprise 98% of all American businesses and account for about one third of the country's production. Some of these privately held corporations are run by outside managers but in many cases they are still run by entrepreneurs, families, owner-managers, or, in a few cases, by the employees. Buying out the stockholders and taking the company private has also been a way for families to preserve their control over companies.

Rank	Company	Sales (in millions)	Employees
1	Cargill	$44,000	55,000
2	Koch Industries	17,190	9,300
3	Continental Grain	14,850	14,500
4	RJR Nabisco	12,764	48,000
5	United Parcel Service	12,400	122,000
6	Southland	8,352	35,604
7	Mars	7,500	23,000
8	American Financial	7,286	53,000
9	RH Macy	7,270	76,000
10	Supermarkets General	6,299	52,300

Source: *Forbes.*

Henry Ross Perot

In just three short months Perot, the founder and chairman of Electronic Data Systems of Dallas, managed to lose $1.2 billion, losing $450 million in just one day, April 22, 1970.

This disaster began auspiciously enough in 1968, when Perot took EDS public. The stock soared to an all-time high of $162 a share in March of 1970, making Perot the richest man in America, worth an estimated $1.5 billion. But then the stock dropped drastically, to $85 in April, and tumbled to only $29 in May, leaving Perot worth a mere $270 million.

Since then he has bounced back nicely. In 1984, he sold his 46% of EDS to General Motors for $1 billion and received 11.3 million shares of class-E GM stock. In 1986 GM bought him out, and in 1988, Perot set up his own company, Perot Systems, to compete with EDS. Today Perot is worth about $2.1 billion. Looking back, he dismisses the $1 billion paper loss: "That was Mickey Mouse." (See the profile of Perot in the "Electronics" section.)

Daniel Ludwig

By the late 1960s this reclusive entrepreneur, who had only an eighth-grade education, built up a $2-3 billion fortune in shipping, real estate, and oil refining. Known for his conservative management, Ludwig, however, then embarked on one of the riskiest and most grandiose business ventures in the last 50 years—the development of a tract of land in the Amazon jungle that is larger than the state of Connecticut.

Ludwig bought 6,000 square miles of Amazon forest in 1968 for only $3 million. Over the next 15 years, he poured about $1.1 billion into his quixotic dream of developing the Amazon.

Like everything else Ludwig has done, the project, in the Jari Valley, was shrouded in secrecy. That secrecy fueled rumors of Indians held as slaves in his compounds, of a vast smuggling operation in gold and silver, and of a plan to turn the area into an American enclave that would eventually secede from Brazil.

The reality wasn't quite as strange, but certainly more grandiose. In vast stretches of jungle he built airstrips, thousands of miles of roads, a private railroad, hospitals, and a city for 35,000 people.

The plan was to build a lumber and paper business to provide these products during what Ludwig believed would soon be a worldwide shortage. But here he ran into trouble. He planted a Southeast Asian tree that grows about a foot a year, but it wouldn't grow in the thin Amazon soil. Then he had trouble with the Brazilian government, which refused to confirm his title to his land. That made it hard for him to get additional financing. In 1982, he finally threw in the towel. After selling the project for $280 million, he was left with an $820 million loss. Since then, he has given about $1.5 billion to the Swiss foundation he created to study cancer but is still worth over $1 billion. Not bad for someone who dropped out of junior high school and got started in business with only a $5,000 loan.

Table 7-4 The 20 Highest-paid Chief Executives in 1990

	Company	1990 salary and bonus	Long-term compensation	Total pay
		Thousands of dollars		
1. STEPHEN M. WOLF	UAL	$1,150	$17,151	$18,301
2. JOHN SCULLEY	Apple	2,199	14,531	16,730
3. PAUL B. FIREMAN	Reebok	14,822	—	14,822
4. DEAN L. BUNTROCK	Waste Management	1,582	10,708	12,290
5. LEON C. HIRSCH	U.S. Surgical	1,128	10,548	11,676
6. MICHAEL D. EISNER	Walt Disney	11,233	—	11,233
7. JOSEPH D. WILLIAMS	Warner-Lambert	1,585	6,898	8,483
8. DAVID O. MAXWELL	Federal National Mortgage	1,039	6,529	7,568
9. GEORGE V. GRUNE	Reader's Digest	1,192	6,271	7,463
10. P. ROY VAGELOS	Merck	2,092	5,050	7,142
11. RAND V. ARASKOG	ITT	3,844	3,179	7,023
12. RICHARD D. WOOD	Eli Lilly	1,781	5,104	6,885
13. DANIEL E. BURKE	Capital Cities/ABC	1,033	5,584	6,617
14. WILLIAM S. EDGERLY	State Street Boston	953	5,561	6,514
15. ROBERT P. LUCIANO	Schering-Plough	1,695	4,691	6,386
16. MARTIN S. DAVIS	Paramount Communications	3,646	2,614	6,260
17. JAMES E. PRESTON	Avon Products	1,188	5,061	6,249
18. ROBERTO C. GOIZUETA	Coca-Cola	3,142	3,100	6,242
19. H. WILLIAM LURTON	Jostens	880	5,099	5,979
20. ROBERT E. CAWTHORN	Rhone-Poulenc Rorer	1,054	4,835	5,889

Source: Business Week, May 6, 1991.

PART III

The Heavy Hand

Chapter Eight
GOVERNMENT: FOR GOOD OR BAD

HIGHLIGHTS AND TRENDS

• Federal, state, and local governments spent $2.0 trillion in 1990, an amount equal to about one third of the GNP.

• Per capita, federal government expenditures have increased from $280 in 1950 to $5,086 today, while state and local governments spend $3,015 on every person in the U.S., up from $184 in 1950.

• Federal, state, and local governments are the country's largest landlord, owning 39.1% of all land in the U.S., about 885 million acres.

• Federal, state, and local governments own equipment and buildings valued at $4.6 trillion, including the world's largest office building, the Pentagon.

• If federal, state, and local governments seceded from the Union and formed their own country with a GNP the size of today's government expenditures ($2.0 trillion), that country's government would have the fourth-largest GNP in the world.

• Between 1950 and 1991, outstanding debts of the federal government increased from $257 billion to $3.2 trillion.

• Per capita, the debt of all government agencies has increased from $1,856 in 1950 for each man, woman, and child in America to $12,800 today.

• To pay the interest on a $3.2 trillion debt, U.S. taxpayers forked over $286 billion in gross interest payments and $197.7 billion in net interest payments in 1991.

• Today net interest payments on the nation's debt will be large enough to pay for all the money the federal government spent on Medicare, education, training, and international affairs combined!

• If you've ever doubted the fact that big government hurts the competitiveness of American business, consider this: the interest on the national debt could pay for all the industrial equipment U.S. companies bought in 1987, 1988, and 1989.

THE STATE'S BUSINESS

The U.S. government can't quite boast, as one monarch once did, that it is "the only merchant in town." There's little doubt, however, that government is the country's largest business. Government expenditures equal about one third of the GNP. Put together, government agencies spend more money, employ more people, and own more land than any company or individual in the U.S. That makes big government the biggest business in America.

The sheer size of these expenditures and activities can boggle the mind. The $500 billion savings and loan bailout, the $3.2 trillion national debt, and $137.2 billion worth of new taxes between now and 1995 are only a few examples of how big government has a big impact on the future of the American economy. Unlike individual finances, which are counted in dollars, or corporate finances, which are counted in thousands or millions of dollars, government finances work on the level of billions and trillions of dollars—sums of money so monumental they become almost absurd. As one U.S. senator once quipped about the way Congress spends money, "A billion here, a billion there, and pretty soon you're talking about real money."

Because a billion dollars—let alone the idea of a three-trillion-dollar government debt—has almost no meaning to most people, this chapter, the first of four chapters on government and the business of power, is devoted to translating those figures into terms that can be understood. That we've devoted so much space to government indicates the magnitude of government power over the economy.

GOVERNMENT: WHAT IT OWNS

Land

Federal, state, and local governments are the country's largest landlord, owning 39.1% of all land in the U.S., about 885 million acres. Most of this, about 726.6 million acres, or 32.2% of all land, is owned by the federal government. The feds own 60% of the land in the Western part of the U.S., only 0.5% of the land in Connecticut, but 85% of the land in Nevada, 47.9% of the land in California, half of Oregon, and 61.4% of Utah, as well as the 400,000 caribou, 152,000 moose, and 64,000 wild horses and burros that live on these lands.

Federal-owned land would fill up an area the size of Delaware, Maryland, the District of Columbia, Virginia, West Virginia, North Carolina, South Carolina, Georgia, Florida, Kentucky, Tennessee, Alabama, Mississippi, Arkansas, Louisiana, Oklahoma, Texas, Maine, New Hampshire, Vermont, Massachusetts, Rhode Island, Connecticut, New York, New Jersey, Pennsylvania, Ohio, and Illinois.

If turned into a separate country, federal lands would constitute the sixth-largest country in the world.

Moreover, the federal government leases another 1.6 million acres, as well as 246 million square feet of office space, at a cost of $1.9 billion a year.

If you divide up all the 885 million acres owned by federal, state, and local governments, every man, woman, and child in the U.S. would get about 3.5 acres.

And, as you might expect from an enterprise that's primarily devoted to producing and pushing paper, the federal government owns a lot of trees. About 10 billion board feet of timber are cut every year on federal lands. The federal government owns 20 million acres of forest land in Idaho (39% of the state), 16 million acres in Oregon (27%), 20 million acres in California (20%), and 17 million acres in Montana (18%).

Precious Metals and Resources

The federal government owns some of the country's most valuable mineral and environmental resources: 80% of the shale reserves, a third of the coal, a third of its uranium, and large reserves of gold, silver, oil, copper, and molybdenum (an element used to strengthen and harden steel).

Equipment and Buildings

Federal, state, and local governments own equipment and buildings valued at $4.6 trillion; state and local government own about $3 trillion of this figure. If all the equipment and buildings owned by the federal, state, and local governments were sold off, every American would get about $18,200.

Among these holdings is the world's largest office building, the Pentagon. This 6.5-million-square-foot building houses 29,000 workers. The Pentagon receives 280,000 telephone calls a day on 44,000 telephones. Staffers walk down 17 miles of corridors, look out 7,748 windows, and eat at 2 restaurants, 6 cafeterias, and 10 snack bars.

Food

You could say that the government is the world's largest supermarket and commodities broker all rolled into one. To stabilize and support the price of farm goods, the Commodity Credit Corporation (owned by the federal government) buys various agricultural products, such as wheat, corn, and cheese. In 1988 it bought $12.2 billion worth of food and by the end of the year it owned $5.6 billion dollars worth of food: 123 million pounds of cheese, 123 million pounds of dried milk, 234 million pounds of butter and butter oil, 305 million bushels of wheat, 454 million bushels of sorghum, and 679 million bushels of corn.

WHAT THE GOVERNMENT DOES

Spend Money

Primarily the government collects money, lots of it, and then spends even more of it. Federal, state, and local governments spent $2 trillion in 1990.

Per-capita federal government expenditures have increased from $280 in 1950 to $5,086 today, while state and local governments spend $3,015 on every person in the U.S., up from $184 in 1950.

Spending by government agencies increased 3,079% between 1950 and 1990. In contrast, during this period, the population increased by 64% and the number of employed people paying taxes to finance big government only doubled. Our GNP (up 1,788% between 1950 and 1990) and corporate profits (up 688%), also grew at a much slower rate than taxes.

If federal, state, and local governments seceded from the Union and formed a country with a GNP the size of today's government expenditures, that government would have the fourth-largest GNP in the world—only the private sector of the U.S., the Soviet Union, and Japan would have a larger GNP.

Stay in Debt

As for most big spenders, the revenues of government agencies have not kept up with ever-growing expenditures. Between 1950 and 1991, outstanding debts of the federal government increased from $257 billion to $3.2 trillion.

The national debt increased from $1,856 in 1950 for each man, woman, and child in America to $12,800 in 1991. To pay the interest on this debt, U.S. taxpayers forked over $286 billion in gross interest payments in 1991 and $197.7 billion in net interest payments. In 1991, the interest payments would have been enough to pay for all federal spending on Medicare, education, training, and international affairs combined! Net interest payments would fund the salary of every federal bureaucrat for two years, and pay for all the industrial equipment U.S. companies bought in 1987, 1988, and 1989. In contrast to the $3.2 trillion in government debt, total consumer debt stood at $794 billion, nonfinancial corporations owed $2.1 trillion, and mortgage debt hit $3.7 trillion.

Employ People

One of the things governments do best is create bureaucracies. Today the federal government was by far the nation's largest employer, employing 3.3 million civilians. The largest private employer, General Motors, employs less than a third as many people, a mere 775,000 workers. State governments employed 4.2 million while local governments employed 10.9 million.

Overall, federal, state, and local governments employ 18.4 million people, about 16.6% of the nonagricultural labor force. Altogether, government employees form the 50th-largest country in the world. There are more government employees than the entire population of Australia. The number of government employees is larger than the combined populations of Maine, New Hampshire, Vermont, Massachusetts, Rhode Island, Connecticut, Oklahoma, and New Mexico.

But government bureaucracies aren't growing as fast as everyone imagines. Federal employment grew 44% between 1960 and 1990, less than total nonagricultural employment (104%) and about the same as the population (40%). But total government employment grew 120% between 1960 and 1990, from 8.8 million to 18.4 million, largely because state and local employment grew 149%.

And the life of a government bureaucrat isn't as easy as most people imagine. One government study found that 6,888 federal employees were bitten by dogs in an average year, proving the point that taxpayers aren't the only ones who get irritated with bureaucrats. But that wasn't the most common way federal employees hurt themselves on the job: "falls" (24,949 accidents), accidents while "handling materials" (24,608); "slipping, twisting and tripping" (18,781), and "striking against objects" (13,640) led the list. "Flying particles" (5,244 accidents), "vehicles" (4,173), "dust and gases" (3,667), "bites by other animals [not including dogs] and insects" (2,642) and "violence" (1,992) rounded off the list of the top ten hazards faced by federal employees. Strangely enough, the most hazardous duty in government is not at the CIA, the Pentagon, or the FBI, but at an obscure agency known as the Architect of the Capitol that includes the carpenters, electricians, and gardeners in the capital and the botanic gardens. Following that were the Panama Canal Commission, the Postal Service (bedeviled by 5,200 dog bites), and the Government Printing Office.

But all of these injuries are no joke, at least in terms of balancing the budget. The cost of workers' compensation claims for federal employees runs around $964 million a year.

Provide Social Services

Besides spending money and employing people, the government provides a bewildering array of social services, many of which involve giving away money. About 38.6 million people (only a little less than the population of Poland) collect Social Security, 10.9 million people (more than the population of Hungary) get Aid to Families with Dependent Children, 18.4 million people (more than the population of East Germany) get food stamps, and 22.9 million people (more than the population of North Korea) get Medicaid.

Per capita, government programs on the federal, state, and local levels spend $3,364 on various social-welfare programs. That figure includes $1,671 on social insurance, $826 on education, $447 on public aid, $192 on health and medical care, and $112 on veterans' benefits.

Unlike defense spending, which has declined as a percentage of GNP and total government spending, social-welfare programs have increased. For all levels of government, social-welfare expenditures increased as a percentage of the total budget from 38.4% in 1960 to 54% today. Most of this increase has occurred at the federal level, where half of the budget goes to social-welfare programs, up from 28.1% in 1960, and down from 54.6% in 1979. The percentage of local and state government money spent on social-welfare programs has actually dropped to 59.6% from 60.1% in 1960. As a percentage of GNP, social-welfare spending stands at 18.4%, up from 10.3% in 1960. Again, the federal government accounted for most of the increase as social-welfare spending is now 11% of the GNP, up from 4.9% in 1960.

Another major social program is Social Security. For the time being, the system is quite solvent. As the baby-boom generation moves into its peak earning years, the system will do something government agencies rarely do—rack up huge surpluses. But the system may start running a deficit after 2010 and by 2025 could be losing over $350 billion a year.

Thanks to all the money the federal government gives away, Washington is the biggest check writer in the U.S. Every year the federal government issues 650 million checks.

Other government agencies make certain you can drive to the bank to cash your government check. Government is responsible for building, repairing, and maintaining the 3.8 million miles of roads in the U.S. at a cost of $90.1 billion a year. Local and state police have to regulate cars that drive about 2.0 trillion miles each year and investigate the 20.8 million traffic accidents that occur each year. Add the 184 million motor-vehicle registrations that exist in the U.S., all of which have to be renewed every few years, and you have a monumental bureaucratic gridlock.

The job of picking up the nearly 150 million tons of garbage produced every year is so massive that no one even seems to know how much government money is spent on this problem. State and local governments, however, spend $21.3 billion on sewage and sanitation. New York City spent $1 million just cleaning up the trash produced by the celebration held on the 100th birthday of the Statue of Liberty. And that celebration didn't even rank as the biggest trash-producing day in the city's history. The sanitation department cleaned up a record 5,438 tons of garbage on the V-J Day celebration in 1945, 3,474 tons for a parade for John Glenn in 1962, and 3,249 tons in 1951 for General Douglas MacArthur. Not surprisingly, New York City's largest export is not clothes from its famous garment district, but recycled wastepaper.

And then there is the Postal Service, everyone's nominee for the least efficient government agency. It ships 160 billion pieces of mail each year, about 655 for every man, woman, and child.

Create Paperwork

Some government agencies don't ship paper, they create it. It's been estimated that small businesses fill out 850 million pages of government forms to comply with various federal edicts. Laid end to end, the paperwork would circle the earth nearly 6 times; stacked up in a federal office, it would rise 67 miles into the atmosphere.

Estimates of the cost of government paperwork vary, but all of them are alarming. The Commission on Federal Paperwork found that in 1977 the cost of filling out a mountain of federal paperwork was $25 billion to $32 billion for private industry. Today that estimate would mean private industry spent $52 billion to $69 billion to fill out paperwork, state and local governments spent $10.5 billion to $18.8 billion, individuals other than farmers spent $18.2 billion, and farmers spent $732.4 million. Overall, the cost of government paperwork amounted to about $1,046 for each American.

The Office of Management and Budget also estimates that the American public spent 1.7 billion hours filling out government forms. Depending on how one values the time spent on filling out government forms, the total costs could range from $17 billion to $34 billion and more.

Pay Politicians

Large sums of money are spent each year keeping America's political leaders fed and clothed. In the private and public sector an estimated $1.8 billion a year is spent on party politics and the electoral process.

It cost $3.2 billion to run the 100th Congress. Included in that cost is the pay for 11,604 staff members in the House of Representatives and 7,200 Senate employees. House members spent $176,853,600 for staff and $64,380,000 for offices; the Senate spent $104,030,000 for staff and $6,100,000 for offices. This, of course, was a big change from the first Congress, for which there were only 7 employees in the House and 6 employees in the Senate. Senators and congressmen were paid $6 a day plus a travel allowance of $6 for every 20 miles. It only cost $378,853 to run the first Congress—the 100th Congress spent over $8.7 million a day, 365 days a year.

Fight Crime

Government agencies are charged with solving the 20,700 murders, 92,500 rapes, 543,000 robberies, 3.2 million burglaries, and 1.4 million car thefts committed each year. To pay for all this protection, the taxpayers coughed up $45.6 billion. And when criminals are caught it costs the taxpayers more money. There are 603,928 Americans behind bars, a 53% increase since 1980. At that rate, there will be nearly 1.7 million Americans behind bars by the year 2000, 12.8 million by 2025. Already the tide is overflowing U.S. prisons. In 1985, prisons were forced to grant 18,617 prisoners early releases because they lacked the space.

Fight War

One of the main pastimes of governments has always been war. The total cost of American wars, from the American Revolution to the Vietnam conflict, assumed by the government has been $771.4 billion. The cost of wars between 1940 and 1990 was $698.5 billion, or about $2,790 for every living American. James Clayton of the University of Utah estimates that the cost of the Vietnam War reached $172 billion by 1988, the Korean War cost $69.5 billion, and spending for World War II hit $456.7 billion. In contrast, earlier American wars were strictly low-budget affairs. The American Revolution cost $170 million, the War of 1812 cost $120 million, and the Mexican War set back taxpayers only $120 million. The Civil War, which many military historians view as the first modern war, was also the first American war to cost over a billion dollars. Union spending was $6.8 billion. The Spanish-American War cost $2.4 billion, while total costs of World War I hit $63.3 billion, only enough money to keep the Pentagon running for a few months today. These figures include veterans' benefits and interest payments on war loans as well as the direct cost of buying weapons and supplies.

Preparing for a war can be even more expensive than actually waging one. The government spent about $3.4 trillion between 1976 and 1990, when the country was at peace, about 4.4 times what was spent in all the wars in American history up to that time.

Keeping the military going is also big business. Every day the military signs 52,000 contracts—the Air Force alone entered into 5 million contracts in 1985.

Military procurement remains one of the most complex systems known to man—which may explain why a lot of expensive weapons systems never work. Defense firms typically face over 44,000 specifications for a weapons system. The instructions on procurement runs to 32 volumes and take up six feet of shelf space. One Pentagon study found that regulations accounted for one third of procurement costs.

Play Big Brother

With all of its resources, the government is busy collecting information on all of us. Scattered throughout its massive bureaucracy are some 11,000 computers, which have access to over 4,000 data systems. These systems contain almost 4 billion records on individuals—20 dossiers for every American. But given the skill of your typical bureaucrat, many of these records may be inaccurate. The IRS estimates its employees enter about 20% of the information from tax returns incorrectly into computers. In the late 1970s, Congress's Office of Technology Assessment found that about 20% of the arrest records stored at the FBI's National Crime Information Center were inaccurate.

Table 8-1 Federal Receipts, Outlays, Surplus or Deficit, and Debt, 1929–1992
(billions of dollars; fiscal years)

	Total			On-budget			Off-budget			Gross Federal debt (end of period)		Adden-dum:
Fiscal year or period	Re-ceipts	Outlays	Surplus or deficit (−)	Re-ceipts	Outlays	Surplus or deficit (−)	Re-ceipts	Outlays	Surplus or deficit (−)	Total	Held by the public	Gross National Product
1929	3.9	3.1	0.7							[1]16.9		
1933	2.0	4.6	−2.6							[1]22.5		
1939	6.3	9.1	−2.8	5.8	9.2	−3.4	0.5	−0.0	0.5	48.2	41.4	88.4
1940	6.5	9.5	−2.9	6.0	9.5	−3.5	.6	−.0	.6	50.7	42.8	95.8
1941	8.7	13.7	−4.9	8.0	13.6	−5.6	.7	.0	.7	57.5	48.2	113.0
1942	14.6	35.1	−20.5	13.7	35.1	−21.3	.9	.1	.8	79.2	67.8	142.2
1943	24.0	78.6	−54.6	22.9	78.5	−55.6	1.1	.1	1.0	142.6	127.8	175.8
1944	43.7	91.3	−47.6	42.5	91.2	−48.7	1.3	.1	1.2	204.1	184.8	202.0
1945	45.2	92.7	−47.6	43.8	92.6	−48.7	1.3	.1	1.2	260.1	235.2	212.4
1946	39.3	55.2	−15.9	38.1	55.0	−17.0	1.2	.2	1.0	271.0	241.9	212.9
1947	38.5	34.5	4.0	37.1	34.2	2.9	1.5	.3	1.2	257.1	224.3	223.6
1948	41.6	29.8	11.8	39.9	29.4	10.5	1.6	.4	1.2	252.0	216.3	247.8
1949	39.4	38.8	.6	37.7	38.4	−.7	1.7	.4	1.3	252.6	214.3	263.9
1950	39.4	42.6	−3.1	37.3	42.0	−4.7	2.1	.5	1.6	256.9	219.0	266.8
1951	51.6	45.5	6.1	48.5	44.2	4.3	3.1	1.3	1.8	255.3	214.3	315.0
1952	66.2	67.7	−1.5	62.6	66.0	−3.4	3.6	1.7	1.9	259.1	214.8	342.4
1953	69.6	76.1	−6.5	65.5	73.8	−8.3	4.1	2.3	1.8	266.0	218.4	365.6
1954	69.7	70.9	−1.2	65.1	67.9	−2.8	4.6	2.9	1.7	270.8	224.5	369.5
1955	65.5	68.4	−3.0	60.4	64.5	−4.1	5.1	4.0	1.1	274.4	226.6	386.4
1956	74.6	70.6	3.9	68.2	65.7	2.5	6.4	5.0	1.5	272.7	222.2	418.1
1957	80.0	76.6	3.4	73.2	70.6	2.6	6.8	6.0	.8	272.3	219.3	440.5
1958	79.6	82.4	−2.8	71.6	74.9	−3.3	8.0	7.5	.5	279.7	226.3	450.2
1959	79.2	92.1	−12.8	71.0	83.1	−12.1	8.3	9.0	−.7	287.5	234.7	481.5
1960	92.5	92.2	.3	81.9	81.3	.5	10.6	10.9	−.2	290.5	236.8	506.7
1961	94.4	97.7	−3.3	82.3	86.0	−3.8	12.1	11.7	.4	292.6	238.4	518.2
1962	99.7	106.8	−7.1	87.4	93.3	−5.9	12.3	13.5	−1.3	302.9	248.0	557.7
1963	106.6	111.3	−4.8	92.4	96.4	−4.0	14.2	15.0	−.8	310.3	254.0	587.8
1964	112.6	118.5	−5.9	96.2	102.8	−6.5	16.4	15.7	.6	316.1	256.8	629.2
1965	116.8	118.2	−1.4	100.1	101.7	−1.6	16.7	16.5	.2	322.3	260.8	672.6
1966	130.8	134.5	−3.7	111.7	114.8	−3.1	19.1	19.7	−.6	328.5	263.7	739.0
1967	148.8	157.5	−8.6	124.4	137.0	−12.6	24.4	20.4	4.0	340.4	266.6	794.6
1968	153.0	178.1	−25.2	128.1	155.8	−27.7	24.9	22.3	2.6	368.7	289.5	849.4
1969	186.9	183.6	3.2	157.9	158.4	−.5	29.0	25.2	3.7	365.8	278.1	929.5
1970	192.8	195.6	−2.8	159.3	168.0	−8.7	33.5	27.6	5.9	380.9	283.2	990.2
1971	187.1	210.2	−23.0	151.3	177.3	−26.1	35.8	32.8	3.0	408.2	303.0	1,055.9
1972	207.3	230.7	−23.4	167.4	193.8	−26.4	39.9	36.9	3.1	435.9	322.4	1,153.1
1973	230.8	245.7	−14.9	184.7	200.1	−15.4	46.1	45.6	.5	466.3	340.9	1,281.4
1974	263.2	269.4	−6.1	209.3	217.3	−8.0	53.9	52.1	1.8	483.9	343.7	1,416.5
1975	279.1	332.3	−53.2	216.6	271.9	−55.3	62.5	60.4	2.0	541.9	394.7	1,522.5
1976	298.1	371.8	−73.7	231.7	302.2	−70.5	66.4	69.6	−3.2	629.0	477.4	1,698.2
Transition quarter	81.2	96.0	−14.7	63.2	76.6	−13.3	18.0	19.4	−1.4	643.6	495.5	448.7
1977	355.6	409.2	−53.6	278.7	328.5	−49.7	76.8	80.7	−3.9	706.4	549.1	1,933.0
1978	399.6	458.7	−59.2	314.2	369.1	−54.9	85.4	89.7	−4.3	776.6	607.1	2,171.8
1979	463.3	503.5	−40.2	365.3	403.5	−38.2	98.0	100.0	−2.0	828.9	639.8	2,447.8
1980	517.1	590.9	−73.8	403.9	476.6	−72.7	113.2	114.3	−1.1	908.5	709.3	2,670.6
1981	599.3	678.2	−78.9	469.1	543.0	−73.9	130.2	135.2	−5.0	994.3	784.8	2,986.4
1982	617.8	745.7	−127.9	474.3	594.3	−120.0	143.5	151.4	−7.9	1,136.8	919.2	3,139.1
1983	600.6	808.3	−207.8	453.2	661.2	−208.0	147.3	147.1	.2	1,371.2	1,131.0	3,321.9
1984	666.5	851.8	−185.3	500.4	686.0	−185.6	166.1	165.8	.3	1,564.1	1,300.0	3,687.7
1985	734.1	946.3	−212.3	547.9	769.5	−221.6	186.2	176.8	9.4	1,817.0	1,499.4	3,952.4
1986	769.1	990.3	−221.2	568.9	806.8	−237.9	200.2	183.5	16.7	2,120.1	1,736.2	4,180.8
1987	854.1	1,003.8	−149.7	640.7	810.0	−169.3	213.4	193.8	19.6	2,345.6	1,888.1	4,424.7
1988	909.0	1,064.1	−155.1	667.5	861.4	−193.9	241.5	202.7	38.8	2,600.8	2,050.3	4,780.4
1989	990.7	1,144.1	−153.4	727.0	933.2	−206.1	263.7	210.9	52.8	2,867.5	2,190.3	5,131.3
1990	1,031.3	1,251.7	−220.4	749.7	1,026.6	−277.0	281.7	225.1	56.6	3,206.3	2,410.4	5,405.6
1991[2]	1,091.4	1,409.6	−318.1	793.2	1,171.7	−378.5	298.3	237.9	60.4	3,617.8	2,717.6	5,615.8
1992[2]	1,165.0	1,445.9	−280.9	849.8	1,194.2	−344.4	315.3	251.7	63.6	4,021.1	2,995.4	5,985.5

[1]Not strictly comparable with later data.
[2]Estimates.
Note.—Through fiscal year 1976, the fiscal year was on a July 1–June 30 basis; beginning October 1976 (fiscal year 1977), the fiscal year is on an October 1–September 30 basis. The 3-month period from July 1, 1976 through September 30, 1976 is a separate fiscal period known as the transition quarter.
Refunds of receipts are excluded from receipts and outlays.
Sources: Department of Commerce (Bureau of Economic Analysis), Department of the Treasury, and Office of Management and Budget.

137

Table 8-2 Federal Receipts, Outlays, and Debt, Fiscal Years 1981–1992
(millions of dollars; fiscal years)

Description	Actual									Estimates	
	1981	1982	1983	1984	1985	1986	1988	1989	1990	1991	1992
RECEIPTS AND OUTLAYS:											
Total receipts	599,272	617,766	600,562	666,457	734,057	769,091	908,954	990,691	1,031,308	1,091,440	1,165,029
Total outlays	678,209	745,706	808,327	851,781	946,316	990,258	1,064,051	1,144,069	1,251,703	1,409,563	1,445,902
Total surplus or deficit (–)	–78,936	–127,940	–207,764	–185,324	–212,260	–221,167	–155,097	–153,378	–220,396	–318,123	–280,874
On-budget receipts	469,097	474,299	453,242	500,382	547,886	568,862	667,463	727,026	749,652	793,153	849,775
On-budget outlays	543,013	594,302	661,219	685,968	769,509	806,760	861,360	933,158	1,026,638	1,171,658	1,194,205
On-budget surplus or deficit (–)	–73,916	–120,003	–207,977	–185,586	–221,623	–237,898	–193,897	–206,132	–276,986	–378,505	–344,430
Off-budget receipts	130,176	143,467	147,320	166,075	186,171	200,228	241,491	263,666	281,656	298,287	315,254
Off-budget outlays	135,196	151,404	147,108	165,813	176,807	183,498	202,691	210,911	225,065	237,905	251,697
Off-budget surplus or deficit (–)	–5,020	–7,937	212	262	9,363	16,731	38,800	52,754	56,590	60,382	63,557
OUTSTANDING DEBT, END OF PERIOD:											
Gross Federal debt	994,298	1,136,798	1,371,164	1,564,110	1,816,974	2,120,082	2,600,760	2,867,538	3,206,336	3,617,837	4,021,124
Held by Government accounts	209,507	217,560	240,114	264,159	317,612	383,919	550,507	677,214	795,906	900,214	1,025,731
Held by the public	784,791	919,238	1,131,049	1,299,951	1,499,362	1,736,163	2,050,252	2,190,324	2,410,431	2,717,623	2,995,393
Federal Reserve System	124,466	134,497	155,527	155,122	169,806	190,855	229,218	220,088	234,410		
Other	660,325	784,741	975,522	1,144,829	1,329,556	1,545,308	1,821,034	1,970,236	2,176,021		
RECEIPTS: ON-BUDGET AND OFF-BUDGET	599,272	617,766	600,562	666,457	734,057	769,091	908,954	990,691	1,031,308	1,091,440	1,165,029
Individual income taxes	285,917	297,744	288,938	298,415	334,531	348,959	401,181	445,690	466,884	492,635	529,518
Corporation income taxes	61,137	49,207	37,022	56,893	61,331	63,143	94,508	103,291	93,507	95,866	101,913
Social insurance taxes and contributions	182,720	201,498	208,994	239,376	265,163	283,901	334,335	359,416	380,047	401,955	429,363
On-budget	52,545	58,031	61,674	73,301	78,992	83,673	92,845	95,751	98,392	103,668	114,109
Off-budget	130,176	143,467	147,320	166,075	186,171	200,228	241,491	263,666	281,656	298,287	315,254
Excise taxes	40,839	36,311	35,300	37,361	35,992	32,919	35,227	34,386	35,345	44,810	47,768
Estate and gift taxes	6,787	7,991	6,053	6,010	6,422	6,958	7,594	8,745	11,500	12,241	13,265
Customs duties and fees	8,083	8,854	8,655	11,370	12,079	13,327	16,198	16,334	16,707	17,698	19,295
Miscellaneous receipts:											
Deposits of earnings by Federal Reserve System	12,834	15,186	14,492	15,684	17,059	18,374	17,163	19,604	24,319	23,384	20,741
All other	956	975	1,108	1,347	1,480	1,510	2,747	3,225	2,997	2,852	3,166

OUTLAYS: ON-BUDGET AND OFF-BUDGET

Total	678,209	745,706	808,327	851,781	946,316	990,258	1,064,051	1,144,069	1,251,703	1,409,563	1,445,902
National defense	157,513	185,309	209,903	227,413	252,748	273,375	290,361	303,559	299,331	298,910	295,245
International affairs	13,104	12,300	11,848	15,876	16,176	14,152	10,471	9,573	13,764	16,953	17,814
General science, space, and technology	6,469	7,200	7,935	8,317	8,627	8,976	10,841	12,838	14,444	15,781	17,452
Energy	15,166	13,527	9,353	7,086	5,685	4,735	2,297	3,702	2,358	2,617	3,710
Natural resources and environment	13,568	12,998	12,672	12,593	13,357	13,639	14,606	16,182	17,067	18,821	19,545
Agriculture	11,323	15,944	22,901	13,613	25,565	31,449	17,210	16,919	17,958	15,857	15,261
Commerce and housing credit	8,206	6,256	6,681	6,917	4,229	4,890	18,815	29,211	67,147	119,506	92,788
On–budget	8,206	6,256	6,681	6,917	4,229	4,890	18,815	29,520	65,522	119,447	93,912
Off–budget								–310	1,626	59	–1,124
Transportation	23,379	20,625	21,334	23,669	25,838	28,117	27,272	27,608	29,485	31,469	32,707
Community and regional development	10,568	8,347	7,560	7,673	7,680	7,233	5,294	5,362	8,498	7,710	6,457
Education, training, employment, and social services	33,709	27,029	26,606	27,579	29,342	30,585	31,938	36,674	38,497	42,800	45,530
Health	26,866	27,445	28,641	30,417	33,542	35,936	44,487	48,390	57,716	71,188	81,260
Medicare	39,149	46,567	52,588	57,540	65,822	70,164	78,878	84,964	98,102	104,433	113,720
Income security	99,723	107,717	122,598	112,668	128,200	119,796	129,332	136,031	147,277	173,189	184,839
Social security	139,584	155,964	170,724	178,223	188,623	198,757	219,341	232,542	248,623	268,965	288,632
On–budget	670	844	19,993	7,056	5,189	8,072	4,852	5,069	3,625	5,127	5,847
Off–budget	138,914	155,120	150,731	171,167	183,434	190,684	214,489	227,473	244,998	263,837	282,785
Veterans benefits and services	22,991	23,958	24,846	25,614	26,292	26,356	29,428	30,066	29,112	31,483	33,001
Administration of justice	4,769	4,712	5,105	5,663	6,270	6,572	9,236	9,474	9,995	12,567	14,486
General government	11,429	10,914	11,235	11,817	11,588	12,564	9,464	9,017	10,724	11,169	13,183
Net interest	68,734	84,995	89,774	111,058	129,430	135,969	151,748	169,166	184,221	197,038	206,343
On–budget	71,022	87,065	91,619	114,368	133,548	140,298	159,164	180,561	200,212	217,202	230,076
Off–budget	–2,288	–2,071	–1,845	–3,310	–4,118	–4,329	–7,416	–11,395	–15,991	–20,164	–23,733
Allowances											
Undistributed offsetting receipts	–28,041	–26,099	–33,976	–31,957	–32,698	–33,007	–36,967	–37,212	–36,615	–39,093	–40,780
On–budget	–26,611	–24,453	–32,198	–29,913	–30,189	–30,150	–32,585	–32,354	–31,048	–33,266	–34,549
Off–budget	–1,430	–1,646	–1,778	–2,044	–2,509	–2,857	–4,382	–4,858	–5,567	–5,827	–6,231

Sources: Department of the Treasury and Office of Management and Budget.

139

Chapter Nine
POWER BROKERS

THE BUSINESS OF POWER

In 1868, when railroader speculator Jay Gould was in the middle of his battle with shipping magnate Cornelius Vanderbilt for control of the Erie Railroad, he and his partners decided that they needed help from the New York state legislature. So Gould packed his suitcases, carefully filling one of them with $500,000 in cash, and sneaked up to Albany, New York. There he set up his lobbying headquarters in a luxury hotel suite and began passing money to legislators in exchange for their support of a bill that would prevent Vanderbilt from taking over the railroad. A million dollars later, Gould won out.

"In a Republican district, I was a Republican," he told an investigating committee when asked to explain his tactics and his actions; "in a Democratic district, I was a Democrat; in a doubtful district I was doubtful; but I was always for Erie [the railroad he wanted to control]."

Today, doing business with government is a lot more complicated. Gould's pliant legislators have been replaced with vast bureaucracies and strict laws governing how politicians earn their money. But even though the rules have changed, the stakes haven't. Government regulators and legislators routinely make decisions that can save or ruin entire industries. In recent years, some industries, such as the chemical and auto industries, have seen a drastic growth in environmental regulations that have added billions to the cost of doing business. Other industries, such as the railroads and airlines, which grew fat under the protection of government regulations, have seen their industries deregulated, forcing them to deal with increased competition and lower rates.

As a result, the growth of big government in the last fifty years has created another big business—the business of influencing political decisions. About $1.8 billion is spent every year on party politics and the electoral process. There are somewhere between 2,000 and 5,000 political consulting firms that

140

earn about $100 million a year. Political advertising on television alone cost $225 million in 1988, up from $90 million in 1980, and it could hit $350 million in 1992. In 1984, Ronald Reagan spent $66.6 million to be reelected president; his opponent, Walter Mondale, spent even more ($67.4 million) to be clobbered. Four years later George Bush spent $75.4 million to win and Michael Dukakis wasted $72.4 million to lose. Candidates for the U.S. Senate in 1988 spent $201.1 million, with the average winner spending $3.7 million. Candidates for the House spent $256.5 million, with the average winner paying $358,992 (46% of which came from PACs) to convince voters he or she was the best person for the job. Today, there are nearly 4,300 political action committees (PACs). Incumbents in the Senate outspent their challengers 2.3 to 1 and raised an average of $1 million from PACs, far more than their challengers, who got only $286,149. Incumbents in the House meanwhile raised $427,117 for their 1988 election campaigns, nearly four times as much as the $118,654 the average challenger was able to raise. PAC spending for incumbents in the House was even more lopsided—$201,360 compared to only $27,519 for the average challenger. Not surprisingly, the power of big money allowed 99% of all House incumbents and 85% of all senators to win reelection in 1988. Even in 1990, when there was a widespread anti-incumbent backlash, 96% of all House members were reelected. Only one senator was defeated.

Once elected, politicians are hounded by a small army of lobbyists. In Washington, D.C., alone, there are more than 20,000 people employed as lobbyists, making lobbying the fourth-largest business in the nation's capital, after government, printing, and tourism. Over $60 million is spent each year by registered lobbyists. There are over 800 trade associations that keep headquarters in the city and there are innumerable public-relations people working around the clock to make certain the press prints nice stories about their particular causes or special interests. Even the government itself employs 19,000 PR people.

But these figures don't quite describe the size of the enterprise that is solely devoted to manipulating and influencing politics. There are the think tanks, lawyers (Washington has one lawyer for every 40 people, the most anywhere), the political consultants, the direct mailers (some political junk mailers have computerized lists of over 20 million people), the academics, and the large political contributors who lobby, mold opinions, set the tone of political campaigns, and help set policy. This, of course, only covers the political world of the nation's capital, Washington, D.C. Out in the hinterlands, lining the corridors of statehouses, city halls, and county courthouses, there is another army of influence peddlers, too vast to be enumerated.

THE LOBBYISTS

Until recently there was a well-defined business establishment in Washington. When the National Association of Manufacturers, the Council on Economic Development, the Business Council, or the Business Roundtable spoke up on issues, most members of Congress knew that they were listening to the voice of American business. They might disagree with these organizations, but no one doubted their power.

Since 1980, however, changing political winds, the retirement of the old political power brokers, and the emergence of a new breed of business leaders has begun to change how business protects its interests in Washington.

The change began in the late 1970s and early 1980s when prominent business power brokers like David Rockefeller (chairman of Chase Manhattan and of the Council on Foreign Relations), Irving Shapiro (chairman of du Pont and founder of the Business Roundtable), Reginald Jones (head of General Electric), John deButts (head of AT&T), Thomas Murphy (head of General Motors), and Henry Ford II (head of the Ford Motor Company) retired from their positions. Although these men never achieved the celebrity status that Ted Turner, Steven Jobs, or Lee Iacocca attained, they were far more powerful in Congress. They were the business leaders who pioneered a period of postwar cooperation between business and government, and their retirement left a power vacuum.

At the same time, long-term political and economic changes hurt the political and economic power of the old business establishment. As manufacturing and oil struggled through hard times, new entrepreneurs who were creating high-tech industries or executives who were revitalizing decaying manufacturing companies became more powerful. Many of these business leaders were from the West or the Sunbelt and had been long-time Reagan supporters. They opposed the kind of government intervention that the old guard had accepted. But unlike their predecessors, none of the new entrepreneurs or executives had the political experience of a David Rockefeller or an Irving Shapiro. As a result, the political power of business became more diffuse and decentralized at a time, ironically, when some business leaders were becoming household names and media celebrities.

Perhaps for that reason, professional lobbyists are becoming even more important in the power politics of the nation's capital. The number of lobbyists registered with the Secretary of the Senate increased from 5,662 in 1981 to 20,400 in 1986. In 1986, over $60.8 million was spent by registered lobbyists, up 25% from 1985, 45% from 1984, and more than double the amount spent on lobbying in 1975. The Center for Responsive Politics notes that PACs set up by lobbyists and lawyers contributed about $4.8 million to congressional candidates in 1988, with about 74% of the money going to incumbents. A more accurate figure of how much is spent on influencing politicians and government officials might be as high as $1.5 billion, including campaign contributions.

But numbers alone don't tell the power of Washington's lobbyists. As noted above, many of them are former government appointees or elected officials who have access to their former colleagues. As a result, lobbyists are playing an increasingly powerful role in the legislative process. Major legislation, including the Chrysler bailout bill, has been written in lobbyists' offices. Lobbyists have played a major role in getting committee assignments and subcommittee chairmanships for friendly members of Congress. Increasingly, lobbyists control political action committees or act as political consultants, making members of Congress more beholden to them. And, as in everything else that gets done in Washington, power and money take precedence over ideology. Many of Reagan's former employees now lobby the Bush administration.

No list of Washington power brokers and lobbyists could touch on all the power brokers for hire, but here are a few of the biggest names and most important special-interest groups.

The Gun Lobby

Led by the National Rifle Association, the gun lobby leads the fight against handgun restrictions. Following increased street crime and Martin Luther King's assassination in the 1960s, the NRA was unable to stop some handgun legislation, but beat back a number of antigun measures in the 1980s. One reason is its political clout. Besides being one of the biggest spending lobbyists on Capitol Hill, the gun lobby spends lots of money promoting the political careers of its friends. According to the first detailed study of PAC spending by industry and issues, published in 1990 by the Center for Responsive Politics (CRP), the gun lobby gave out $802,906 in PAC contributions during the 1987–88 election cycle, with the NRA contributing $772,756 to 237 candidates. In contrast, groups pushing for control of handguns spent only $87,900. But, as drug gangs push up crime rates and kill police with high-tech automatic weapons, the gun-control measures have gained in popularity.

The Oil Lobby

In the fight to protect the sacred oil depletion allowance the oil lobby has for decades been an unassailable power on Capitol Hill. In Washington the oil lobby maintains several organizations, the largest of which, the American Petroleum Institute, has a staff of 350 people and an annual budget of $50 million. CRP estimates that the energy and natural resource sectors contributed $10.4 million in the 1987–88 election cycle to congressional candidates, while a recent Common Cause study found that energy PACs gave $18.8 million between 1983 and 1988 to senators and representatives who were still in office in 1990. Thanks to this clout, the oil depletion allowance saved the oil industry about $5 billion a year until Congress ended it in the mid-1970s for major oil companies. Independent oil companies were, however, still allowed to use it and saved $1.5 billion through this device in 1985, according to the Treasury Department. Following the Persian Gulf crisis in the fall of 1990, the industry lobbied for government subsidies to improve domestic production and fought a public relations campaign against consumer groups angry about alleged price gouging.

The Defense Lobby

Led by McDonnell Douglas ($8.6 billion in defense contracts), General Dynamics ($7 billion), Lockheed ($2.7 billion), Boeing ($2.9 billion), General Electric ($5.8 billion), Raytheon ($3.8 billion), and other top contractors, the defense lobby is undoubtedly the most powerful in Congress, where a coalition of Southern Democrats and Republicans has protected it from every onslaught in the last 40 years. But a widening deficit, the fall of the Berlin Wall, and the apparent end of the cold war are making the military-industrial complex a tougher sell on Capitol Hill. Defense contractors are now lobbying to protect Star Wars and other programs set up during the Reagan years, with heavy PAC contributions, and hoping that the successful high-tech war against Iraq will help their cause. During the 1987–88 election, CRP estimates, defense industry PACs gave $7.2 million to congressional candidates, with 87% going to incumbents and 52% donated to Republicans. So-called peace groups, in contrast, contributed a mere $354,815. Current incumbents in the House of Representatives alone received over $6.2 million from defense PACs between 1983 and 1988, according to Common Cause.

The Environmental Lobby

Led by such groups as the Sierra Club ($286,904 in PAC contributions in 1988), various environmental and conservationist groups continue to push for new environmental legislation. Their major victories came in the 1970s, when they pushed through the legislation that created the Environmental Protection Agency and several major bills regulating the environment, toxic substances, and the workplace. But even in the 1980s their political clout has defeated Reagan-backed initiatives to curb increased regulation. In recent years the budget of the EPA has once again resumed its inexorable growth, and a new pro-environmental mood helped pass the Clean Air Act of 1990. But while CRP estimates that environmental groups gave $459,951 in PAC contributions in 1987–88, they were heavily outspent by PACs representing the chemical industry, which contributed $1,353,896.

The Union Lobby

Gone are the days when organized labor could count on the undivided support of major Democratic Party politicians and at least some influence on moderate Northeastern Republicans. Still, union PACs remain among the biggest-spending campaign contributors. With such powerful political fundraisers as the United Auto Workers PAC (spent $2.0 million in 1987–88) and the National Education Association PAC ($2.2 million), unions will provide massive support for Democratic Party candidates in 1992. About 91% of all union PAC money still goes to Democratic Party candidates. Between 1981 and 1988, union PACs spent $113.6 million. In contrast to the $37.6 million union PACs gave to congressional candidates in

1987–88, anti-union PACs such as the Right to Work PAC contributed only $447,878, according to CRP.

PACs

One of the most controversial and important changes in the business of power has been the development of PACs—political action committees. The growth of political action committees, so attacked these days by campaign-law reformers, was ironically a result of campaign reform. In 1971 Congress passed the first campaign reform law since the 1920s; organized labor, which invented political action committees, pushed through an exemption for its PACs. Following Watergate, when Congress limited individual contributions, PACs became a major way for high rollers to continue to contribute large sums of money.

The result was something that organized labor and campaign reformers have complained about ever since: the growth of corporate political action committees. Corporate PACs are increasing at a far faster rate than union PACs or PACs affiliated with trade and health organizations. From 1975 to 1990, the number of business PACs grew from 139 to 1,816, while union PACs went from 226 to 354. Spending has also been skyrocketing, with funding for PACs growing to $370 million in 1988, up from $138 million in 1979–80.

All that money has dramatically changed the business of power. Gone are the days when a presidential candidate would campaign from his porch. The average senator spent $3.6 million in 1988, up from $610,000 in 1976. Since this meant he had to raise $12,000 a week for six years, incumbents and challengers have become increasingly dependent on PAC money. Even though 1990 was an off year, House and Senate candidates received $279 million in contributions between 1988 and June of 1990, up from $270 million during a similar period in the 1987–88 election.

This massive flow of money has had a dramatic effect on who gets elected to Congress. Since PACs overwhelmingly favor incumbents, the gap between the money raised by incumbents and that raised by challengers has widened dramatically over the past two decades. In 1974, the average challenger for a House seat raised only $16,000 less than the incumbent, but by 1988 the average challenger was outspent by $264,000. This surely contributed to the fact that nearly 99% of all incumbents in the House were reelected in 1988, and many potential candidates did not even try to unseat the incumbents. In 1990, Senate incumbents were able to out-fundraise their challengers by a 5-to-1 margin. Many built up such massive war chests that 11 of the 32 senators up for reelection ran unopposed or against very weak candidates.

After the election, PAC money causes even greater problems, critics contend. Huge contributions from the savings and loan industry helped protect it from tougher laws and regulations. But more often the result is simple inaction. Pressed by competing special interests, Congress has increasingly adopted the strategy of doing nothing. Six years after the Ivan Boesky insid-

er-trading scandal, Congress still hasn't gotten around to passing legislation
that would define what constitutes insider trading. The business press has
been talking about a revolution in international finance for over a decade.
Yet Congress has let the banking and finance industry stumble along under
a regulatory system that was designed in the 1920s and early 1930s, long
before anyone had heard of computers, junk bonds, Euronotes, money markets, the Big Bang, or any of the other wonders of late-20th-century civilization.

The political paralysis has turned the budget deficit into the longest-run-
ning soap opera in Washington and played a key role in the savings and loan
scandal. Delays by the Reagan administration and the Democratic leadership in Congress helped boost the cost of the savings and loan bailout from
about $17 billion in 1983 to over $500 billion by 1991.

Another casualty has been voter confidence in Washington. A 1990 Louis
Harris and Associates poll found that only 15% of all Americans express a
"great deal" of confidence in Congress, and voter turnout for congressional
races has been dropping for nearly two decades. Politicians, however, are
trying to turn the PAC issue to their advantage. In the 1990 race for governor of California, both candidates ran negative ads attacking their opponent
for taking PAC money from savings and loans. No mention was made of the
other PAC money that helped finance these television-advertising blitzes.

Chapter Ten
REGULATION AND DEREGULATION: CHANGING THE RULES

HIGHLIGHTS AND TRENDS

- Red tape is making a comeback in the 1990s. After an experiment with deregulation in the late 1970s and early 1980s, Washington is once again increasing the budgets, staffs, and power of government regulators.
- Spending at 51 federal regulatory agencies hit $12.25 billion in 1991, up 769% from the $1.4 billion spent in 1970, according to budget data compiled by the Center for the Study of American Business at Washington University.
- The number of people employed in regulatory agencies has also increased 54% from 73,375 in 1970 to 113,311 in 1991.
- Some of the biggest increases have been in the financial sector of the economy. The staff of the SEC increased from 1,436 in 1970 to 2,598 in 1991 and the Commodity Futures Trading Commission rose from 180 to 613. Meanwhile staff at other banking and financial regulators increased from 6,219 in 1970 to 10,884 in 1991.
- Spending for financial regulators has also increased, according to the Center for the Study of American Business. The budget of the SEC jumped from $22 million in 1970 to an estimated $193 million in 1991; the CFTC increased from $2 million to $45 million; and other banking and financial regulators increased from $87 million to $1,218 million.
- Despite important measures to deregulate certain key industries (particularly communications, transportation, and finance) in the late 1970s and early 1980s, government regulation still imposes a huge tax on the economy. In 1989, the Council of Economic Advisors to the Bush administration estimated that government regulations cost American business at least $100 billion a year.
- Government paperwork also costs a bundle. The Commission on Feder-

al Paperwork found that in 1977 the cost of filling out the mountain of federal paperwork was $25 billion to $32 billion for private industry. In 1990 dollars that estimate would mean that private industry spent $54 billion to $69 billion to fill out forms. Overall, the cost of government paperwork amounted to about $1,046 for each American. The Office of Management and Budget estimated that the American public spent 1.7 billion hours filling out government forms. Depending on how one values the time spent on filling out government forms, the total costs could range from $17 billion to $34 billion and more.

REGULATING THE REGULATORS

Government is not only big business, it also has a big impact on how business can be done. Today, government is involved in nearly everything business does. Government regulations determine how our homes are built, how we do our jobs, the ingredients that go into the food we eat, how our products are transported to market, how our banks take care of our money, what kind of television we watch, the drugs we take, and even the number of maggots allowed in canned mushrooms. (By government decree, there can be no more than 20 maggots in 100 grams of canned mushrooms.)

There is little doubt that many of these regulations improve our health and safety by making sure companies sell safe products, avoid environmental pollution, and properly advertise their services. But there is also little doubt that regulations cost money. Often, critics complain, they cost more money than they're worth.

The Costs of Regulation

"Government regulation of business is one of the growth areas of the economy," economist Murray L. Weidenbaum tartly observes. His controversial study of regulatory costs for the Subcommittee on Economic Growth and Stabilization of Congress's Joint Economic Committee is probably the most influential look at regulatory costs made in the last decade. He found that business spent about $65.5 billion in 1976, or about $307 for every man, woman, and child, to comply with government regulations. The "direct and indirect compliance costs of Federal regulation . . . [are] about twenty times the administrative costs of $3 billion for regulatory agencies," Weidenbaum wrote more recently. In 1976, Weidenbaum found, paperwork alone cost businesses $18 billion; regulations requiring the inclusion of catalytic converters in cars to reduce air pollution added $666 to the cost of each car and increased fuel consumption by $3 billion (at a time when the economy was hurt by foreign cars and a fuel crisis); a myriad of zoning, land-use, building-code, and other government regulations on housing boosted the costs of new houses by $2,000 apiece (at a time when young couples were finding it increasingly difficult to afford the price of a home); regulations forced some businesses to close facilities and lay off workers (at a time when unemployment was edging toward new heights); and government equipment regulations forced companies to spend $10 billion on capital (at a time when this capital investment could have been used to boost declining productivity).

More recently, the Council of Economic Advisors for the Bush administration estimated that government regulations cost American business about $100 billion a year. How government regulators came to have such an important impact on the economy can be found in a century-long trend toward government regulation.

The Rise of the Regulators

The history of regulation is the history of economic crises—a history of problems that seemed to contemporary observers to have eluded the hidden regulator of Adam Smith's benevolent marketplace. In every case of increased government regulation during the past 150 years, the government has stepped in to protect the so-called "public interest" from alleged abuses—such as monopolies or "cutthroat" competition—that were thought to be disrupting the marketplace. The problem, which runs through the history of government regulation, is how industry and government ended up defining such a vague concept as "public interest." Quite often the result had little to offer the public.

The first attempts at government regulation were aimed at the railroads. Like later targets of government regulation, the railroad industry created problems that seemed to elude the mechanism of free-market competition. Because they were expensive to build, it made little sense to run two competing railroad lines through the same area, so railroad companies usually operated as monopolies, controlling the transportation costs of a certain region. As monopolies, 19th-century rail lines had the power to charge high rates or offer secret rebates to favored customers. These rebates gave some companies, such as Standard Oil, an edge in the market and allowed favored customers to destroy their rivals.

To control an industry that threatened to do away with a competitive marketplace, state legislatures began setting up railroad commissions. The Massachusetts Board of Railroad Commissioners, the first modern regulatory agency with a paid staff, was created in 1869. During the next few years, farmers and other customers who were angry about excessive rates forced the creation of other regulatory agencies. But the agencies soon ran into a problem that would bedevil attempts at regulation during the next century: either the agencies were hampered by court rulings that limited their powers or a lack of staff to carry out their mandates, or, more often, they quickly developed close relations with the very industries they were supposed to regulate.

Legislators recognized those problems, but strangely enough, the failure of one agency or set of regulations did not result in a reexamination of government regulation. Rather, legislators typically followed the most fundamental law of government intervention: if one regulation doesn't work, add another one, and if that doesn't work, create a new agency.

After it became obvious to everyone that the state railroad commissions had failed, Congress created the first federal regulatory agency in 1887—the Interstate Commerce Commission (ICC). Its mission was to set "just and reasonable rates" and to stop abuses such as rebates, pools, and rate discrimination.

The ICC was in principle a more promising way of regulating the railroads. In contrast to the crazy-quilt pattern of state commissions, each governing a section of a nationwide network, the ICC would be able to deal with the whole railroad system, not just a part of it. This obviously made more sense for both business—which wanted some form of regulation—and the public.

Unfortunately, the ICC soon became a prime example of how regulatory agencies thrive on an atmosphere of dull inefficiency. By the late 1890s the ICC's powers were gutted by Supreme Court rulings that reduced it to a mere information-gathering agency. Congress responded with a series of acts between 1903 and 1940 that were designed to give the agency some real power. These laws, however, satisfied no one. On one hand, industry continued attacking the agency for restricting its management prerogatives and for usurping the power to set rates. Consumers, on the other hand, attacked the agency for protecting the railroads at the expense of the public. Both, of course, were right. The commission set rates at levels that hurt the public and benefited industry. At the same time, its regulatory control over the industry prevented the railroads from vigorously responding to alternative forms of transportation such as trucking.

Given its track record, one would imagine that the ICC would have quickly disappeared. But instead of being disbanded as a bureaucratic failure, a menace to the consumer and industry, the ICC continued to grow and expand its powers. By the end of the Second World War it had control over not just railroads, but all interstate surface transportation—trains, trucks, buses, inland ships, freight forwarders, transportation brokers, and even a coal slurry line.

The fact that neither the public nor business liked the kind of regulation it was getting from the country's first regulatory agency should have set off alarm bells in Congress, but it didn't. The ICC became the model for a whole slew of regulatory agencies. The Federal Trade Commission was set up in 1914 to deal with the problem of growing monopolies that were threatening to do away with market competition. The Federal Power Commission (now called the Federal Energy Regulatory Commission) was created in 1920 to curb the monopolistic power of the utilities. The Radio Act of 1927 created the Federal Radio Commission; in 1934 the Federal Communications Commission replaced that agency and was also given the job of regulating the telecommunications industry, a job it inherited from the ICC.

The Great Depression set off another spurt in government regulation in the 1930s. As government agencies and Congress groped for ways to end the Great Depression and to eliminate some of the problems that had caused the stock-market crash, new regulatory agencies sprouted like weeds. Congress set up the Securities and Exchange Commission in 1934 to regulate Wall Street, the Federal Deposit Insurance Corporation in 1933, the

Federal Home Loan Bank Board in 1934, the Farm Credit Administration in 1933 to regulate the cooperative Farm Credit System, the Civil Aeronautics Board in 1938, and the National Labor Relations Board in 1935 to regulate collective bargaining, to name a few. The power of the Federal Reserve System, which had been regulating the banking industry since 1913, was also increased.

Only a few agencies were set up in the two decades following the New Deal—the Atomic Energy Commission (1946) and the Federal Aviation Agency (1958), now called the Federal Aviation Administration, were the two most important.

In 1960, looking back over the first 90 years of government regulation, it would have been safe to say that most government regulation had been economic. That is, it had been concerned with regulating the marketplace, for example, by setting rates for railroads or utilities.

However, a new era of government activism in the 1960s touched off a new alphabet soup of government regulators and a different type of government regulation. The Equal Employment Opportunity Commission was created to administer the Civil Rights Act of 1964. Following the passage of auto safety legislation in 1966, Congress created the National Highway Traffic Safety Administration as part of the Transportation Department to set auto safety and fuel efficiency standards. Also created was the Consumer Product Safety Commission (1972), as well as a number of landmark consumer laws, which were administered by already existing agencies.

During the same period, a growing environmental protection movement led to the establishment of the Environmental Protection Agency in 1970; the Occupational Safety and Health Administration in 1970 to regulate health and safety standards in the workplace; the Mining Enforcement and Safety Administration in 1973 (today the Mine Safety and Health Administration) to regulate mine safety and health; the Nuclear Regulatory Commission in 1974 to take over the regulatory functions of the Atomic Energy Commission, which was abolished; the Materials Transportation Bureau in 1975 to regulate the movement of hazardous material; and the Office of Surface Mining, Reclamation, and Enforcement in 1977 to regulate strip mining, just to name a few.

These new agencies represented a new turn in government regulation. Many of these agencies had social rather than strictly economic goals. Reflecting the social activism of American society and the federal government during the 1960s and 1970s, these agencies pursued social agendas such as ending racial discrimination or providing consumer education. Unlike earlier regulatory agencies that had been set up to protect the marketplace from monopolies and other forces that were threatening to destroy it, these new agencies were not so much concerned with preserving an orderly marketplace as they were in imposing moral and political values—clean air, small cars that produced less air pollution, truth in lending—on the workings of the marketplace.

As might be expected, the shift from economic regulation to social regulation also entailed widespread interference in the workings of the market and a dramatic growth in the cost of government regulation. Nearly every government regulatory agency, however, has followed the predictable and alarming patterns first established by the ICC. The regulators have been continually criticized by business, especially smaller businesses that do not have the resources to deal with the paperwork of the regulatory process. And, equally importantly, they haven't satisfied the critics who argue that many of these agencies soon developed very close ties with the industries they were supposed to regulate.

Yet, despite the low marks they have received from business and the public, regulatory agencies slowly managed to enlarge their powers at least until the middle of the 1970s. By that time, the pendulum was beginning to swing in the other direction. An ailing economy and a decline in the reforming zeal of the 1960s forced policymakers to reassess the role of government regulators. Their solution was deregulation.

For a time everyone liked the idea, even if they didn't agree on what deregulation meant. Republicans were for it. Democrats were for it. Conservatives were for it. Neoconservatives were for it. Neoliberals were for it. Jimmy Carter was for it. Ronald Reagan was for it. Unfortunately, as with most buzzwords, no one agreed on what deregulation meant. In the end, that confusion helped derail the fight for deregulation.

Deregulation

In what might be called the first wave of deregulation, Congress began passing a series of landmark laws deregulating the transportation, financial services, and aviation industries in the late 1970s. And then, after Ronald Reagan's 1980 election, he initiated another wave of deregulation by appointing officials who promised to get government out of the business of regulation whenever possible.

In some industries, the results were quite dramatic. Deregulation in the transportation industry allowed railroads more freedom to set rates. Deregulation touched off a revolution in the airline industry that lowered fares and attracted millions of new passengers. Banks and savings and loan associations were given new freedom to make loans and enter businesses that had been off-limits for half a century. A lax attitude toward antitrust laws during the 1980s allowed merger mania to flourish without fears of government interference. The breakup of AT&T forever changed the face of the telephone industry, and the cable television industry, which had been losing piles of money in the early 1980s, flourished after it was deregulated in 1984. Similarly, the FCC eased many restrictions on the broadcast television industry, a move that allowed each of the three major networks to be sold during the 1980s.

There is little doubt that popular resentment against growing red tape and big government helped push deregulation forward in the late 1970s and early 1980s. The popularity of President Reagan's "get the government off our backs" political message made it seem as if policymakers and the American public really embraced the idea that "the government that governs least, governs best."

In fact, the politics of deregulation were more complex.

Americans have a schizophrenic attitude toward government regulation. Most Americans have a knee-jerk reaction against big government, yet some of the same people support strong environmental and health regulations. The most successful attempts at deregulation have occurred in industries such as transportation and telecommunications in which long-term techno-logical changes have transformed the way the industries work. In these industries, deregulation began during the 1960s and 1970s and had little or nothing to do with a general political commitment to free-market policies. In contrast, deregulation has faced an uphill battle in the areas of environmen-tal and antitrust policies, about which the public is politically divided and in which powerful interest groups have managed to protect regulatory agen-cies. This diverse band of critics—ranging from small state banks to environ-mentalists—represents a powerful political bloc that frequently successfully fought deregulation.

Critics of deregulation were helped by several highly publicized fiascos that weakened political support for deregulation. Mismanagement of the EPA's superfund led to the ouster of several top Reagan appointees in 1982 and started a swing back toward more stringent environmental regulations that culminated in the Clean Air Act of 1990, the toughest piece of environ-mental legislation in over a decade. Worse, mistakes by government regula-tors and political interference by the White House and Congress allowed deregulation in the savings and loan industry to turn into a $500 billion fiasco.

As a result, the tide against government regulation turned in the mid-1980s. A comprehensive study of budgets at federal regulatory agencies by the Center for the Study of American Business found that Ronald Reagan reduced staff by 15% from 118,800 in 1980 to 101,280 in 1985. If you adjust for inflation and express the budgets in constant 1982 dollars, regulatory spending also dropped, from $7,310 million in 1980 to $7,122 million in 1985.

But since then, regulatory agencies have resumed their upward climb, with spending rising from $7,122 million in 1985 to $8,919 million in 1991 in constant 1982 dollars, the CSAB says. (Of course, the actual budgets, expressed in current dollars, were growing even more rapidly, from $7,942 million in 1985 to $12,246 million in 1991.) The number of employees is also on the rise, from 101,280 in 1985 to 113,311 in 1991. That's still below the level when Reagan took office in 1980, but way above the 73,375 people employed by federal regulators in 1970.

Such increases are likely to continue. George Bush, who calls himself "the environmental president," supported the Clean Air Act of 1990, and has boosted spending on environmental regulation by nearly $500 million since taking office. Concerns about the stability of the financial system, safety in the airline industry, and the quality of American food have also resulted in the administration's increasing budgets and staffing levels at agencies regu-lating finance, airlines, food, antitrust laws, and the pharmaceutical industry.

Yet, it would be wrong to dismiss deregulation as a brief respite from the ever-growing power of big government. Deregulation during the 1980s has had a lasting impact on a number of industries. Here's a quick tour of how government regulations affect several key industries in the 1990s:

Banking

Today's banking industry looks very little like the banking industry of the 1970s, thanks to widespread changes in the financial markets and a series of new regulations.

The first key piece of legislation deregulating the banking industry was passed in March of 1980. The Depository Institutions Deregulation and Monetary Control Act allowed money market accounts, let banks pay interest on demand deposits (such as checking accounts), and gave savings and loan associations new powers to make commercial, corporate, and business loans of up to 5% of their assets. Such loans had been illegal in the past. But the increased competition between commercial banks and thrifts led many depositors to move their money out of the savings and loan industry. So Congress passed the Garn–St. Germain Depository Institutions Act in 1982. To make thrifts more competitive, they were allowed to make commercial loans of up to 10% of their assets and to make direct investments in nonresidential personal property. To help federal regulators deal with troubled banks, the act also allowed government officials to make interstate and intrastate bank mergers.

Other important changes were to follow. New state laws and Supreme Court decisions broke down the barriers against interstate banking that had kept the nation's largest banks out of many markets. In 1986, federal regulators ended the last restrictions on the interest rates that banks could pay their customers on savings deposits. Federal regulators gave banks the right to underwrite municipal securities and, in 1990, gave the J. P. Morgan bank the right to buy and sell securities. This ended one of the most important regulatory features of American finance. For over half a century banks had been barred from selling stocks, and Wall Street firms were kept out of the banking industry.

These new rules had a number of far-reaching affects. One was increased competition between banks and other financial institutions. Banks were allowed to set up discount brokerages and sell insurance. Savings and loan associations made loans to commercial real estate developers, traditionally the preserve of commercial banks. Large corporations, which once raised most of their short-term debt from commercial banks, now turned to foreign banks and Wall Street firms. Securities firms such as Merrill Lynch offered certificates of deposit and sold lines of credit; finance companies, especially subsidiaries of large auto makers, moved into the auto-loan market. Sears and other retailers, which were once content to sell power tools and lawn chairs, now peddle credit cards and stocks.

Meanwhile large commercial banks aggressively expanded into markets they had traditionally ignored. Competing with local banks around the country, they bought up out-of-state banks and set up large regional or national banking systems. Battling Wall Street and foreign banks, they aggressively expanded their foreign operations, set up investment banking units, invested in leveraged buyouts, and even bought London-based securities firms. Eyeing the profits earned by thrifts and finance companies that provided financial services to the average American, they issued more credit cards and made more consumer loans than ever before. And they came up with new ways of maximizing their profits and capital. For example, by selling securities backed by mortgages, car loans, credit card receivables, and student loans, commercial banks could turn over their money much faster and produce higher returns on their capital.

New banking regulations encouraged many of these changes. Yet the driving force behind the revolution in American finance was the marketplace, not Congress or Washington bureaucrats. As with a number of other industries that were deregulated during the 1980s, changes in the banking industry reflected a new era in American and global finance. Since 1970, the amount of currency, stocks, and bonds flowing through the international financial system has grown 3,500% to over $2 trillion a day. Over time, this vast flow of money, seeking the highest possible rates of return, dramatically changed the business of money.

On one hand, the vast flows of capital through the international financial system tied together banks all around the globe. On the other hand, this tidal wave of money helped level regulatory barriers. During the 1970s and 1980s, old regulations governing the world's three most important financial markets, Japan, Britain, and the United States, were significantly changed. In Japan, new rules helped Japanese banks expand into the American market, where they grabbed about 14% of the business, and in London, the so-called Big Bang that deregulated the London Stock Exchange in 1986 allowed American banks to buy British securities firms.

Many of the regulatory changes in the U.S. banking system were designed to help American banks compete more effectively in the national and international financial markets. For example, Regulation Q, which limited interest rates on savings accounts to 5.5%, was abolished so that banks could effectively compete with money market firms that offered consumers much higher rates of return. Regulators allowed thrifts to invest in risky commercial real estate so they could afford to attract new deposits by paying high interest rates. Federal regulators, who had allowed Wall Street firms into some of the areas once dominated by commercial banks, also let banks invest in leveraged buyouts and set up investment banking operations.

Not all of these experiments ended happily. A series of disastrous regulatory policies in the thrift industry helped turn $17 billion worth of problems during the early 1980s into a $500 billion fiasco. (See "Banking" in Part VI and Chapter 15 on crime for a discussion of the savings and loan fiasco.) Risky investments in leveraged buyouts by banks and insurance companies have also sparked widespread fears about the solvency of the whole financial system.

But all the talk about how deregulation has affected the banking industry shouldn't obscure one important fact: Banking is still one of the most heavily regulated industries in the United States. There are four main agencies that regulate banks and thrifts on the federal level; locally there is at least one agency that regulates banks and thrifts. And more agencies are being created all the time.

The Federal Home Loan Bank Board (FHLB) used to run the Federal Savings and Loan Insurance Corp., which insured deposits at thrifts and regulated savings and loan institutions. But FSLIC went broke. In 1989, the FHLB was given a new name, the Federal Home Loan Bank System, and many its old powers were transferred to new agencies. The Savings Association Insurance Fund, which is run by FDIC, now insures deposits and regulates thrifts. The Resolution Trust Corp. was set up to manage bankrupt thrifts and sell their assets (as much as $150 billion worth of property will be sold by the RTC during the 1990s). The Office of Thrift Supervision, a separate office in the Treasury Department, also was set up to regulate thrifts, and the Federal Housing Finance Board, another new independent agency, runs the 12 regional banks that used to be operated by the Federal Home Loan Bank Board. These regional banks act as a kind of Federal Reserve for the thrift industry.

Confused? Well, that's part of the problem. The alphabet soup of government regulators hampers banks and isn't a very efficient way of protecting the public. For example, after Congress relaxed the thrift industry's regulation in the early 1980s, many thrifts switched their charters from state to federal, so that they would be faced with less red tape. Naturally, this upset local officials. California legislators, who had long collected hefty campaign contributions from the thrift industry, worried that the thrifts would shower their campaign contributions on Washington instead of Sacramento. So they passed a new law making the state thrift rules even more lenient than the federal rules. Of course, taxpayers all around the country got to pick up the bill when dozens of these thrifts went broke in the late 1980s, and after federal regulators tightened their control over the thrifts in the early 1990s, some S&Ls switched their charters to the more lenient states.

Many top government regulators also argue that it's time for a change. Outgoing FDIC Chairman William Seidman notes that "the American banking and financial industry is in need of thorough reorganization if we are going to be competitive in the world." To address that problem, President Bush proposed landmark legislation in early 1991 that would radically reform America's banking and financial system. The package would:

1. Allow well-capitalized banks to have securities, mutual fund, and insurance affiliates;
2. Legalize nationwide banking;
3. Shore up the fund that insures bank deposits by charging higher premiums for undercapitalized banks, by increasing regulatory supervision of less well capitalized banks, and by limiting insurance coverage to only one $100,000 checking or savings account per bank;

4. Restructure a byzantine system of bank regulation so that each bank had only one regulator, tie bank regulation more directly to a bank's capital, and impose fewer regulations on better capitalized banks;
5. Set up a streamlined regulatory system where the Federal Reserve would regulate all state banks, a new department in the Treasury would regulate all national banks and thrift institutions, and the FDIC would insure bank deposits, thus losing a number of its current regulatory functions.

The proposals, which would create more competition between financial services firms, would improve the international competitiveness of American banks. But it's unlikely that Congress will pass any landmark legislation in the near future. Pointing to the record number of bank failures and the savings and loan bailout, critics argue for more, not less, regulation. Meanwhile, the financial services sector is divided on which direction to go. The reform measures would probably trigger a period of consolidation and mergers within the American financial system that could hurt the profitability of Wall Street firms and smaller banks. Larger banks want to end the barriers that prevent them from setting up branches all around the country; smaller state bank will battle any law creating a nationwide banking system. Securities companies like deregulation when it allows them to take business away from commercial banks; they oppose it when banks say they should be allowed on Wall Street.

Nor will change be easy. Most analysts argue that there are simply too many banks and companies in the financial services industry. They believe the industry is due for a consolidation even if no new laws are passed. The Controller of the Currency, for example, estimated in 1990 that existing competition between financial institutions will reduce the number of banks to about 11,000 by 1993. New legislation to abolish limits on interstate banking would reduce the number of banks even further by forcing many smaller banks out of business. But big banks are also likely to undergo some difficult times. Many analysts are forecasting a wave of mergers that may even include some of the nation's largest banks.

Still, doing nothing could create even more serious problems for American banking. E. Gerald Corrigan, president of the Federal Reserve Bank of New York, noted in 1990: "While the data may suggest that U.S. firms are still quite capable of holding their own in an international context, there is no doubt in my mind that as a group their position has slipped . . . [in part because] . . . the U.S. banking system is simply out of step with the rest of the world, and more importantly, it is out of step with the reality of the marketplace."

Broadcasting and Communications

No aspect of deregulation touched the hearts and minds of America more directly than the changing rules governing broadcasting. During the 1980s, the Federal Communications Commission (FCC) dramatically altered its stance on media ownership. Individual owners are now allowed to own 12 stations, up from 7; transferring licenses has become easier and the old rule prohibiting a buyer from reselling a station within three years after purchase has been rescinded. A relaxed attitude toward concentration of individual ownership made the merger between Capital Cities Communications and ABC possible, as well as raising the once-unthinkable possibility of a hostile takeover of a major network.

At the same time, the FCC has moved to get out of the business of regulating programming. The Fairness Doctrine, which required broadcasters to air opposing viewpoints, has been abolished. The FCC has also changed rules to allow cartoons based on toys, ended the requirement that broadcasters show a certain amount of informative children's programming, and eliminated rules that regulated the time and frequency of TV commercials.

More important, Congress passed the Cable Television Deregulation Act in 1984. This legislation allowed cable companies to set their own rates and freed them from state and city agencies that had previously controlled the types of programming aired and the rates local systems could charge. Between 1987 and 1990, rates jumped by 25%, twice as fast as inflation. Moreover, the lax antitrust policies allowed cable operators to embark on a wave of acquisitions, creating a web of vertically and horizontally integrated media empires. Though the three major networks (ABC, CBS, and NBC) are prohibited from owning more than a small share of the programming shown on network television, cable operators have bought stakes in many of the nation's largest cable channels, including CNN, HBO, and MTV.

But, as in many other industries, problems created by deregulation have pushed the pendulum back toward regulation. Critics attacked local television stations for showing too many ads on children's programming and for buying cartoons designed to promote toys. Congress agreed and in 1990 passed new legislation limiting the number of ads on children's programming.

The cable industry, under fire for poor service, rate gouging, sleazy programming, and monopolistic practices, may be next. Several bills are pending before Congress which would curb rate hikes, force cable operators to stop using strong-arm tactics against program suppliers, and break up some of the largest cable monopolies. The nation's largest cable operator, Tele-Communications Inc., takes the threat of new regulations so seriously that it is planning to break up its operations into two smaller companies that would be immune to antitrust action.

But rapid changes in the national and international media markets are likely to force policymakers to abolish some government regulations. In the 1970s, the FCC passed rules that limited the amount of programming the three major networks could own, believing that their monopoly over the airwaves would otherwise allow them to control the television production industry. However, with the rise of cable and other media, the three major broadcasting networks have lost much of their power. The networks, which face slumping audiences and profits, argue that they should be able to expand into the lucrative network programming business by buying Hollywood studios, producing more television programming, and selling reruns of hit network shows (the *Cosby* show brought in more than $500 million in syndication). Most analysts believed the FCC will abolish these rules, known as the financial interest and syndication rules, in 1991. But in the end, the networks didn't get everything they wanted. The new 1991 rules let the networks produce only 40% of all prime-time shows inhouse, and the rules expanded but still limited their ability to profit from the lucrative domestic market for reruns of network programing. Like a number of other so-called attempts at deregulation, these new rules are even more complicated than the old.

Still these modest changes bring the world of government regulation a little closer to changes in the American and international television marketplace.

Over the past decade, huge media conglomerates have been buying up publishing, cable, motion picture, home video, satellite television, and record companies. Sony, for example, now sells television sets that show programs made by its motion picture studio (Columbia Pictures) and tape players that play its tapes from Columbia Records, another subsidiary. Another conglomerate, Time-Warner, owns magazines that write articles about movies made by Time-Warner that are based on books published by Time-Warner. Eventually, the movies are shown on cable systems and pay-cable channels that are owned by guess who? Time-Warner.

Realizing that integrated media giants are the wave of the future, ABC and NBC are doing what they can to exploit loopholes in the regulations limiting their ability to produce television programs. ABC, for example, owns several cable networks, including ESPN, and has a division that produces programming for cable and foreign markets. Since few thought foreign markets or cable programming would be very important in the early 1970s, the networks are allowed to produce programming for those markets, which are now growing faster than any other part of the television business.

Beyond television programming issues, government regulators will have to face up to even larger technological changes. Sometime in the early part of the next century, a relatively new technology called fiber optics will allow hundreds of different video channels, computer data bases, telephone lines, movies, music, computer games, and many services to travel over one line into the home. When that happens, the old regulatory system based on phone companies providing phone service, cable companies supplying cable television, and broadcast television stations beaming out a steady diet of sitcoms and game shows will be obsolete. Will government regulators let phone companies into the business of making movies and television programs? Will phone companies be limited to owning the wire into the house, with other companies controlling the entertainment and information that flows through it? Or will regulators require the phone company to bring one wire into the house for phone service and cable companies to bring in another for video? What about network television? Will ABC, CBS, and NBC be just three channels among many? Stay tuned.

Transportation

In many ways, transportation was a model of deregulation in the 1980s. Landmark legislation in the late 1970s and early 1980s changed regulations that had governed the industry for decades. Freight railroads were given new freedom to set rates by the Railroad Revitalization and Regulatory Reform Act of 1976 and the Staggers Rail Act of 1980. That helped railroads more effectively compete against the trucking industry, which had been stealing its business for decades. A lax attitude toward antitrust laws also allowed a wave of mergers in the railroad industry, which produced larger, more financially stable carriers. With improved economic prospects, the rail industry spent more than $100 billion during the 1980s on track and equipment and by the end of the decade hauled a record amount of freight. The railroads' share of the nation's freight traffic has fallen dramatically since 1950, when it was 56%, but the recent rule changes have helped it hold its share at about 37% in the 1980s.

The passenger railroads were given new life. The Northeast Rail Service Act of 1981 allowed Conrail to cut unprofitable runs, reduce its work force, transfer local commuter services to local governments, and more aggressively market its services. After 1981, Conrail, a government-owned line that was created out of the wreckage of Penn Central, began to record profits. In 1987 it was sold for $1.9 billion to private investors.

Meanwhile, the Motor Carrier Reform Act of 1980 eased rules governing trucking and made it easier for new firms to enter the market. (For example, the average price of an ICC license dropped from $398,000 in 1975 to only $4,900 in 1982). Since then, increased competition has produced a wider range of services and dramatically reduced the nation's freight bill. In 1990 the U.S. Department of Commerce estimated that the nation saved about $30 billion a year in truck and rail bills because of deregulation.

But the most dramatic change in the transportation industry was probably made in the airlines sector. The Airline Deregulation Act of 1978 made it easier for new airlines to enter the business, allowed carriers to change the routes they offered, and in 1982 allowed them to set their own fares. As new airlines like People Express entered the markets with discount fare plans, the airline industry embarked on a decade of mergers, labor strife, and fare wars. A decade of increased competition cut fares by 20% between 1978 and 1988.

But by the early 1990s, the industry was under attack by regulators for safety and performance. Delays at many of the nation's overcrowded airports are at record levels. The average airplane is older than ever before, 12.8 years compared to 9 years in 1979, and critics charge that the industry is cutting corners on safety. In 1990, the U.S. Attorney in Brooklyn indicted Eastern Airlines for falsifying maintenance reports on its aircraft.

Consumer critics are also wondering if deregulation was worth all the trouble. Many of the new companies that entered the airline business soon went bankrupt or were bought by larger carriers. By the late 1980s, many major airports were dominated by one or two carriers and these airlines were often able to charge higher fares. A 1989 General Accounting Office study found that fares were 27% higher at airports where one or two companies had a virtual monopoly over air travel.

A decade of fare wars and merger mania has also taken its toll on the industry's bottom line. The 35 largest carriers are weighted down with $12 billion worth of debt and $1.9 billion worth of annual interest payments. During the 1980s, many airlines survived the fare wars by cutting labor costs. But a decade of labor strife has left unions in an extremely combative mood and made it harder for management to win new concessions. As a result, Bush administration officials are putting more pressure on the airlines to improve safety and are looking for ways to preserve as much competition as possible.

Antitrust

Antitrust is the only area in which Reagan appointees may have made a greater impact than the FCC has by its deregulation of broadcasting and telecommunications. They dropped the government's 13-year suit to break up IBM and inaugurated a program whereby the government could intervene on the side of corporations sued for violating antitrust laws. Their most important stand, however, has been on the issue of merger mania. With only a few exceptions, no actions have been taken against the megamergers sweeping Wall Street. Justice Department antitrust actions against a few key mergers would have stopped the movement and prevented the restructuring of several major industries. Between 1981 and 1987, the U.S. Justice Department received 10,723 merger notifications. Only 26 were challenged.

But the Reagan administration's antitrust policy fell into a pattern that plagued most of its deregulatory measures. Top administrators eased government enforcement, but no major legislation was passed. Some of the antitrust proposals offered by the Justice Department were so controversial they have never been given to Congress. The Reagan administration's last program to reform antitrust laws, submitted in February of 1986, provoked opposition from business lobbies, consumer groups, and powerful members of Congress. Even before the legislative package was made public, the laws were pronounced dead on arrival by the largely sympathetic business press.

Since then, the Bush administration has put new emphasis on enforcing antitrust legislation. With more staff and higher budgets, antitrust officials started taking a closer look at mergers and probing price fixing in a number of important areas, including cable television, health care, oil, and airlines. But the tougher policy isn't simply a return to the old style of trust busting. Bush administration officials are especially interested in applying antitrust laws in ways that can help American companies fight off foreign competitors. For example, regulators are investigating cozy ties between Japanese auto makers and their Japanese suppliers, and looking into allegations that financial ties between foreign auto makers and their suppliers cut U.S. companies out of the market. Similarly, the U.S. is investigating possible antitrust violations by Japanese construction firms that are suspected of rigging bids for work at the U.S. naval base near Tokyo.

Environment

The same problem of great expectations and failed plans also plagued the overhaul of environmental regulations. While some environmental regulations have helped clean up the environment, others have placed heavy costs on small businesses. For example, in the foundry industry, 80% of the 4,000 foundries in the U.S. employ fewer than 100 workers. When these small firms began to go out of business, about a third of them blamed EPA regulations for their demise.

The Reagan appointees to the Environmental Protection Agency raised hopes among business leaders that such regulations might be changed. The EPA is the best example of Reagan's approach to regulation—do away with regulation by appointing long-time critics of government regulation to enforce those regulations. Rita Lavelle, appointed to head the EPA's Superfund to clean up toxic waste dumps, was a former public-relations employee for a subsidiary of Aerojet-General Corporation, a firm that environmentalists had attacked as one of California's biggest polluters. The chief of staff had been a lobbyist for paper companies and Manville Corporation, a company that went bankrupt because of asbestos-related lawsuits, and the assistant administrator for air, noise, and radiation was a lobbyist for the paper company Crown Zellerbach Corporation, another company that had faced problems with environmental regulations. Heading up this band of anti-EPA regulators was Anne (Gorsuch) Burford, a Colorado colleague of James Watt. Burford helped cut the agency's budget and reduce the number of antipollution cases brought by the agency.

But then everything came apart. Like many of Reagan's appointees, the new EPA regulators misjudged the political climate and moved too far too fast in an effort to favor industry. In 1982 a scandal erupted over the agency's management of the Superfund program. Critics charged that the EPA had been lax in enforcing toxic-waste law, that it made secret deals with companies accused of pollution, that agency employees had profited from conflicts of interest, and that political hit lists were used to terminate dissidents within the agency.

After that, the emphasis swung back toward more environmental regulation. Adjusted for inflation, spending for environmental regulation grew modestly in the early years of the Reagan era, increasing from $1,915 million in 1980 to $2,238 million in 1985, according to the Center for the Study of American Business. That was a big change from the 1970s, when spending for environmental regulation more than quadrupled. Similarly, Reagan held the line on staffing at environmental agencies during his first five years, allowing the number of employees to grow only from 14,318 to 14,657. But, by 1991, employment has increased to 20,258 and the cost of environmental regulation hit $4,485 million.

George Bush, who calls himself "the environmental president," has boosted spending on environmental regulation by nearly $500 million since taking office, more than for any other regulatory area. Bush also supported the Clean Air Act of 1990, the most significant, and toughest, piece of environmental legislation since the 1970s. Environmentalists praised the bill for measures they believe will reduce the number of cancer cases, end smog alerts in major cities, and cut respiratory diseases like emphysema. But the bill will cost industry about $25 billion a year by the end of the 1990s.

Over time, refineries must produce gas that burns with fewer pollutants, cities must cut smog levels, manufacturing plants must reduce emissions of 189 toxic chemicals, auto makers will be required to produce cars with fewer emissions, and plants must cut emissions that cause acid rain. These provisions will raise the price of cars, gas, and electricity and force layoffs in the coal industry. Benefits will include lower health care bills and a cleaner environment, which is good news for tourism and travel.

WHO OWNED WHOM

Nobody likes to give up business, yet sometimes the government forces the issue. And sometimes the result is companies spinning off other companies that become powerhouses in their own right. Here are some examples of government-created companies and the parents that grudgingly let them go:

Parent	*Offspring*
1. American Telephone & Telegraph In 1984, the company divested itself of the 22 wholly-owned Bell operating companies. These companies were organized into 7 regional holding companies.	American Information Technologies Bell Atlantic BellSouth NYNEX Pacific Telesis Group Southwestern Bell U S WEST
2. CBS In 1970, after the FCC barred major broadcasters from owning cable-TV companies, Viacom was spun off.	Viacom International
3. United Aircraft (now UAL) In 1934, following government hearings and passage of a law prohibiting air-mail contractors from being associated with aviation manufacturing companies, United Aircraft was forced to split up into 3 companies, including United Airlines.	Boeing Pratt & Whitney
4. J. P. Morgan Company (now part of Morgan Guranty Trust Company of New York) The Glass-Steagall Act in 1933 erected a Chinese wall between the functions of investment and commercial banking. J. P. Morgan's investment house was spun off; others were divested.	Morgan Stanley

5. Standard Oil Company of New Jersey (now Exxon)

In 1911, the U.S. Supreme Court sustained a lower court decision that the company was in violation of anti-trust laws, and it was broken up into 34 companies.

Anglo-American Oil
Atlantic Refining
Borne-Scrymser
Buckeye Pipe Line
Chesebrough Manufacturing
Colonial Oil
Continental Oil
Crescent Pipe Line
Cumberland Pipe Line
Eureka Pipe Line
Galena-Signal Oil
Indian Pipe Line
National Transit
New York Transit
Northern Pipe Line
Ohio Oil Company
Prairie Oil and Gas
Solar Refining
South Penn Oil
Southern Pipe Line
South Western Pennsylvania Pipelines
Standard Oil (California)
Standard Oil (Indiana)
Standard Oil (Kansas)
Standard Oil (Kentucky)
Standard Oil (Nebraska)
Standard Oil (New York)
Standard Oil (Ohio)
Swan and Finch
Union Tank Line
Vacuum Oil
Washington Oil
Waters-Pierce Oil

Chapter Eleven

TAXES: ONE OF THE INEVITABLES

HIGHLIGHTS AND TRENDS

• It doesn't take a rocket scientist to figure out why taxes are the toughest political problem facing big government in the 1990s. Huge government deficits racked up during the 1980s threaten to put Washington and many state and local governments into Chapter 11. Lawmakers must cut popular government programs or increase taxes. But Americans, who already pay over $1.9 trillion, are refusing to support any more tax increases. No wonder. The $1.9 trillion in tax revenues for federal, state, and local governments represents a 1,251% jump from 1960. During that period, state and local tax revenues jumped 1,484% from $50 billion to $792 billion. Those whopping tax hikes meant that every man, woman, and child in the U.S. paid an average of $7,592 in federal, state, and local taxes in 1990, up from an average of a mere $629 in 1960.

• Between 1967 and June of 1990, receipts from federal personal income taxes jumped 745%, Social Security and other social insurance taxes rocketed 999%, and corporate taxes grew 307%. Total tax receipts grew 722%, much faster than consumer prices (390%).

• Federal tax revenues hit 20.3% of the GNP in 1990, up only slightly from 1970, when they accounted for 19.5%. But state and local taxes have risen so fast that the total share taken by government set a record 34.9%, up from 30.2% in 1970.

• Budget cutbacks have curbed the power of the IRS to audit taxpayers; about 1.1 million tax returns are audited, only 1%, down from 1.7 million (2.2%) in 1970.

TAXES: WHO CREATES THEM AND WHO PAYS THEM

Few people understand taxes, but almost everyone hates them, primarily because they keep going up and up. As federal, state, and local governments embarked on a period of proliferating expenses, ranging from increased social services payments to newer and better bombs, taxes rose dramatically. But figuring out exactly how much they've gone up is no easy matter. Over the last 50 years, federal, state, and local governments have increasingly moved some large programs "off budget," established programs that are funded by insurance trusts, created public authorities and set up quasi-government agencies that are not included in the budget. These accounting tricks not only hide the real tax bill, they also allow the White House and Congress to avoid difficult decisions on cutting spending or raising taxes.

But even after all the smoke and mirrors, one thing is clear: Taxes have increased dramatically. Between 1967 and June 1990, total federal, state, and local tax receipts, including social insurance taxes, jumped 722%. Personal income taxes collected by Washington grew 745%, and social insurance contributions increased a whopping 999%.

A sign of our heavy tax bills was found on your calendar. May 8 was designated by the Washington-based nonprofit Tax Foundation as "Tax Freedom Day" in 1991.

On that day, the average American finally got to keep some of the fruits of his or her labors. From January 1 through May 8, every penny of income was confiscated by federal, state, and local tax men—which is another way of saying that more than one third of U.S. annual earnings is grabbed by big government. For many Americans, of course, Tax Freedom Day comes much later.

If history is any guide, Tax Freedom Day will probably be celebrated even later in the year as the 1990s roll on. In 1950, in the wake of the New Deal and in the midst of the Fair Deal, Tax Freedom Day could have been marked more than a month earlier than it is today. The average taxpayer's share of all government taxes was fully paid by April 3. Since then it has advanced through the calendar, reaching May 8 in 1991.

The result has been a kind of permanent tax revolt. In the late 1970s, a California tax revolt forced public officials to put a cap on property taxes. In 1980, Ronald Reagan was swept into office with a promise to get the government off the backs and out of the wallets of middle-class voters. George Bush's pledge of "no new taxes" helped him come from behind in the polls to defeat Michael Dukakis in 1988.

Much of this discontent can be traced to the structure of government finances.

The most popular federal program is undoubtedly Social Security. Unlike most other social-welfare programs, which are intended to benefit the poor, this program also benefits middle-class voters and their parents. Yet since Social Security is financed by a payroll tax, its burden falls heavily on small business and the average worker.

Locally, the situation is even more obvious. For the most part, middle-income families still depend on the public education system. Yet school districts primarily finance schools through the property taxes that fall mainly on middle-income homeowners or on renters, who pay property taxes indirectly as a part of their rent. Similarly, the state and local governments—which finance police and fire departments, education, garbage pickup, road repair, and other programs popular with middle-class taxpayers—still get two thirds of their revenues from either property taxes (which account for three quarters of local government tax revenue) or sales taxes (which account for nearly half of all state tax receipts and one seventh of all local taxes). Both taxes, levied at a fixed rate regardless of income, are felt immediately, directly, and painfully, by middle-income voters. Faced with rising tax bills on their homes or rising sales taxes at the stores, middle-class homeowners have become increasingly fed up with a system of government financing that costs more but seems to deliver less of the local sanitation, police, and educational services they need.

A few numbers illustrate how the fastest-growing taxes also fall hardest on working-class, middle-income, and upper-middle-income families. For example, property tax revenues collected by state and local governments increased 706% from $16.4 billion in 1960 to $132.2 billion today. Sales taxes have climbed 1,224% from 11.8 billion in 1960 to $156.3 billion and social insurance taxes (primarily Social Security taxes) jumped 2,183% from $21.9 billion in 1960 to $499.9 billion. By comparison the population has increased only 114% and the cost of living 341%.

These problems have made taxes one of the most politically important issues of the 1990s, with both Republicans and Democrats vying for the hearts and minds of disgruntled taxpayers. But perhaps a more important problem, and, unfortunately, one that has been given less serious attention, is how taxes affect the economy. To understand that, it's worth taking a look at the development of government taxes.

TAXES: THE HISTORY OF A DISAGREEABLE INSTITUTION

Like the evolution of life, the evolution of taxation is a progression from the simple to the complex. However, unlike the evolution of people from the apes, there is little reason to believe that the social evolution of the tax system has followed a trajectory from a primitive, less intelligent system to a complex, more rational system.

In the relatively underdeveloped colonial economy of the U.S., the tax system was based on poll taxes, import and export duties, and faculty taxes on the income of various tradesmen. Following the revolution, Congress depended heavily on custom duties and on an internal revenue system based on excises on liquor, carriages, sugar, snuff, and other commodities. However, taxes on the sale of liquor and other commodities proved to be highly unpopular, leading to a bloody tax revolt known as the Whiskey Rebellion in 1794. (See "Tax Revolts" below.) Under political pressure, Congress abolished such taxes by 1817.

After 1817 and for most of the 19th century, Congress relied on customs duties and the sale of public lands. Only during the Civil War, when faced with the need for vast new revenues, did Congress turn to an income tax. This tax, which expired in 1872, brought in $310 million in 1866, the most collected until 1911, several years after a corporate income tax was established. An 1894 income tax law was declared unconstitutional in 1895.

The simplicity of the early tax system had its virtues and its drawbacks, illustrating the ironclad law that any tax policy, by transferring money from the private to the public sector, will affect the economy, benefiting some groups and hurting, at least temporarily, other groups. In the 18th and 19th centuries, the reliance on excise taxes and duties meant that most of the tax burden fell on the lower and middle classes, who paid out a higher proportion of their income in taxes than did the rich.

However, regressive tax systems, when coupled with a booming investment climate, encouraged capital spending by giving the wealthy more money to invest. Some economists believe that as much as $156 million was put into capital investment as a result of federal tax policies between 1790 and 1860. Moreover, such tax policies were possible only if government spending was kept to a bare minimum—it accounted for only 1% or 2% of the GNP before the Civil War and only 2% to 4% between 1866 and 1914. Today, government spending is over a third of the GNP.

The same income inequality that helped spur investment and a booming 19th-century development also created political pressure on government to devise a tax system that was not so biased against the lower and middle classes and to raise revenues to finance more social-welfare programs. In 1909, a Republican Congress put through the first corporate income tax system—a 1% tax on corporate profits. In 1913, a progressive income tax was established for individuals.

During the next half-century, three trends guided the development of the tax system. One was an ever-increasing tendency to raise the tax rates. For example, the tax rate for a single person with an income of $5,000 increased from 0.4% in 1913 to 16.7% in 1967, raising the tax bill from $20 in 1913 to $856 in 1967. Similarly, the tax rates for someone earning $1 million a year soared from 6% in 1930 to 90% in 1943 and then fell thereafter down to 70.2% by 1970.

The second trend had already become familiar under earlier tax systems: the desire of special interests to lobby for tax breaks. Just as various industries had lobbied, usually successfully, for favors under the tariff and excise taxes, special interests soon began feeding on the income tax code. Rates for various tax brackets increased and the IRS began taxing new types of income, but special interests also managed to get new tax deductions. The result was a kind of Rube Goldberg device that few people understood, forcing 15 million Americans each year to use professionals to prepare their taxes.

The complexity and seemingly unfair nature of the income tax system also touched off a third major aspect of postwar debates about taxes—political pressure for tax simplification and reduction. Every administration since Eisenhower's has discussed proposals to simplify taxes. Unfortunately, unlike the other two trends, this one led to little action. One result of the failure to reform and simplify the tax system was ever-growing complexity. A system of tax deductions means, however, that taxes and tax deductions have become a way for governments to regulate the economy.

TAXES: THE HIDDEN REGULATOR

As it developed in the 20th century, the tax system was not only a way of raising more and more money for social programs, it was also a way for government to intervene in the marketplace. By raising or lowering taxes through an increasingly Byzantine system of tax breaks and loopholes, the tax system became a hidden regulator of the economy—perhaps the most powerful regulator in Washington, determining which goods and services would be financed or subsidized partially by tax deductions.

Over time, almost every sector of America was given tax breaks. In an attempt to equalize income distribution, tax rates were raised for higher earners. For middle-class homeowners (and, of course, for the ever-powerful real estate industry), there were interest deductions on mortgages; for manufacturers, there were investment tax credits; for the timber industry, lower tax rates; for the oil patch, the oil depletion allowance; for multinationals, foreign tax credits; and so forth until Congress, in its attempt to regulate the economy through taxation, had created the most complicated system known to humanity.

In 1871, the tax code filled one page. Today IRS rulings on obscure subsections fill thousands of pages. As an illustration of how bad things have gotten, the so-called Tax Reform Law of 1986 covers 876 pages. The bill did simplify and reduce taxes for several million Americans, but overall this dismal excuse for tax reform is so complicated that Americans spent an estimated extra 10 million hours working on tax returns in 1987!

That's good news, of course, for accountants and tax lawyers, but bad news for the concept of tax reform. It also means the government is going to stay in the business of regulating the economy through tax policies.

Supporters of government regulation by tax deduction have long claimed that the tax system should reflect the social policy priorities of Congress and the White House. That sounds fine in theory. In practice the results have often been less than beneficial. Take, for example, the two most notorious tax shelters, the oil depletion allowance and accelerated depreciation for real estate.

Thanks to real estate tax shelters, many real estate deals were structured around tax write-offs, not cash flows or the market for commercial properties. Fueled by billions of dollars worth of tax-shelter money, real estate developers built a lot of office buildings. Unfortunately, no one was building office tenants, at least at the same rate or with quite as many tax deductions. The vacancy rate in many cities, such as Houston and Los Angeles, hit 25% in 1985. In 1986, when Congress cut off the flow of tax dollars to real estate shelters, there were problems, and the real estate industry faced the difficult prospect of withdrawing from decades of government subsidies.

The famous oil depletion allowance had the same effect before it was finally abolished. It encouraged oil production, but by keeping oil prices low it encouraged auto makers to make gas guzzlers. When OPEC finally turned off the spigot, the economy, drivers, and the auto industry faced the trauma of adjusting to higher energy costs.

The moral is not that real estate shelters or oil depletion allowances are unjustified. Both produced certain benefits, not only to the industry but to the whole economy. However, they did this at the cost of increasing govern-ment interference in the economy. Tax subsidies given by Congress allow an industry to pursue investment strategies that are very different from those that would have been allowed by the free market. Cheap oil, made possible by government tax deductions—which are really subsidies—prods industry into producing larger cars and works against the use of other energy sources. Accelerated depreciation schedules on real estate prompt developers to put up buildings that would not be profitable if no such subsidies existed. Money spent on these buildings is money that is not spent on factory modernization or in other sectors of the economy.

Faced with how the government tax system is changing the working of the economy, the Reagan administration moved to support tax reform and sim-plification. Unfortunately, what we got was neither.

It now takes the average taxpayer 17 hours to keep the records and pre-pare a 1040 tax return with a few of the most common schedules; more than 35 hours if the return includes business income and losses from rental prop-erty or a tax shelter. IRS agents have to ask a taxpayer 42 questions just to figure out if the person should be considered a head of household. Not sur-prisingly more Americans than ever must use an accountant to figure out their taxes.

Like most earlier tax codes, the 1986 tax law hasn't accomplished many of the things Congress intended. It was supposed to reduce individual taxes and increase corporate taxes. In fact, corporate taxes have been about $100 bil-lion less than expected, and individual taxes actually have gone up.

Since then, Washington has been making the tax system even more com-plex (a code word for more costly). Bills passed to reduce the deficit in 1989 and 1990 added obscure provisions that would affect taxes on most Ameri-cans, as well as a number of special interest groups. In 1989 changes in obscure rules increased taxes for banks, takeovers, junk bonds, chemical companies, oil, airline tickets, cruise ships, and, of course, the average American. Meanwhile tax breaks were given to various programs to increase research, corporate funding of employees' tuition, low-income housing, and alternative energy courses.

In 1990, Congress and the White House agreed to cut spending by $331.4 billion over 5 years while hiking taxes and user fees by $137.2 billion. The bill raised taxes for gasoline ($25 billion over five years), telephone service ($13.1 billion), booze ($8.8 billion), income taxes ($11.2 billion), air travel ($11.9 billion), luxury goods ($1.5 billion), and Medicare ($26.9 billion). Income tax rates for the highest earners were increased from 28% to 31%, and exemptions were phased out for singles earning over $100,000 and joint filers with more than $150,000 in income. But Congress handed out tax breaks to energy companies, lower-income workers, small businesses, research, low-income housing, and some Medicaid beneficiaries.

THE INTERNAL REVENUE SERVICE

Easily the most hated government agency, the Internal Revenue Service is facing hard times of late. The number of returns increased to 190 million in 1990, up from 143 million in 1980, while the agency's full-time employment only increased from 85,500 in 1980 to 114,000 in 1986. And the paperwork just keeps growing.

To keep up with the work, the IRS decided to go high-tech and spend $10.7 billion on a modernization program. But, as in every other kind of tax reform the government has attempted, the results were disastrous. In 1985, a new computer system, installed to improve efficiency, caused unprecedented backlogs, forcing the government to pay $42.8 million more in interest on late refunds. In some IRS offices, workers simply threw away returns that couldn't be processed. Tapes containing $185 million in tax records disappeared for 11 days.

Now, even though some of the bugs are out of the computer system, the long-term outlook for the agency is far from rosy. Even though the IRS says it takes about three years to become effective on the job, only about 25% of its employees stay that long. As a result, IRS studies have found that about 20% of the information typed in the agency's records by keypunch operators is wrong and the agency loses 2 million returns each year. The number of returns audited has also fallen drastically, from 2.3% in 1975 to 2.0% in 1980, and to about 1% today. Only 1.1 million returns are now audited, down from 1.8 million in 1975.

The IRS's lack of staff and inability to collect taxes has become so bad that over 8% of all tax returns understate the amount due. Some accountants say that each percentage point of taxpayer noncompliance costs the government about $25 billion, and even IRS Commissioner Fred Goldberg, Jr., admits that he could collect $40 billion more taxes if he had enough staff. Various IRS studies estimate that nearly $100 billion worth of income goes unreported each year.

The IRS Audit

With the number of audits declining, many taxpayers seem to believe that their problems with audits are over. Not so. But the chances of being audited vary with the type of form filed and its reported income. The IRS audits only 1 in 100 returns filed by someone making less than $25,000, but it scrutinizes 1 in 55 for those making over $50,000. It checks one in 76 businesses with sales under $25,000, but one in 26 making over 100,000. Tax returns for partnerships have a 1 in 139 chance of being audited; small corporations face a 1 in 152 rate. The IRS is increasingly turning to high tech in its war against tax fraud. Currently, IRS computers sort high-income taxpayers into two categories and apply a formula the IRS calls the "discriminant function," or DIF. This formula flags returns that have higher- or lower-than-average deductions, use of tax shelters, types of income, and other factors. The formula rates each return and assigns it a score for each factor; those returns with the highest scores get audited.

About 75% of all audited returns are selected this way, but another 15% are selected by computers that match documents. In these cases, a bank might say a person received $3,000 in interest payments, but the taxpayer failed to report it as income.

Knowing exactly how the DIF formula works would be a gold mine to anyone seeking to avoid audits. But the IRS isn't about to release the workings of this top-secret formula, which in the wrong hands would be a formula for tax fraud. Only 12 agency employees know the formula, which is kept in top-secret vaults. However, it is known that the IRS leans toward auditing forms with certain characteristics. The most common one is, perhaps, the extensive use of tax shelters. But the IRS also goes after returns that show higher-than-average charitable donations, medical costs, and business expenses; large numbers of adult dependents; apparent underreporting of business income; and deductions for hobbies, sideline businesses, home offices, and rental and vacation homes.

TAX FRAUD

As the tax system has grown more and more complex, taxpayers have increasingly resorted to tax fraud, threatening the integrity of the entire system. Tax fraud has grown from $29 billion in 1973 to $100 billion in 1991. Only 81.6% of the taxes owed are now collected. Here are some of the biggest tax-fraud cases:

The Markowitz Case

The largest tax-fraud case ever prosecuted was masterminded by a financial promoter and part-owner of the Washington Capitals hockey team, Edward Markowitz. He tricked more than 100 investors into putting money in his tax-sheltered partnerships. The shelters supposedly involved legitimate buying and selling of government securities, but in fact Markowitz forged documents showing fictitious trades that made it seem as if his partnerships suffered enormous losses between 1979 and 1983. A number of celebrities, including Woody Allen, Bill Murray, Erica Jong, Peter Boyle, and Dick Cavett, put up a total of $20 million that netted them $445 million in false deductions. But the IRS, which has been stepping up its investigations of tax shelters, cracked down on the scam. In April of 1985, Markowitz was convicted, and the investors, who thought they were investing in a legal tax shelter, now owe nearly a half-billion dollars in back taxes and interest.

The Annenberg Case

The biggest individual tax-fraud case until the 1980s involved Moe Annenberg, an immigrant with ties to organized crime who had built up a multimillion-dollar newspaper empire. The linchpin of this empire was the Nation-wide News Service, a telephone and telegraph wire service with a monopoly on horse-racing information that served bookies in 39 states. But it wasn't Annenberg's ties to illegal betting and organized crime that got him into trouble. President Roosevelt, angry with attacks on the New Deal by Annenberg-owned newspapers, unleashed a massive IRS investigation. In 1940, Annenberg was convicted of $9.6 million in income tax evasion. Despite this disaster, his son Walter managed to salvage his father's busi-ness, turning it into a billion-dollar media empire. (See the profile in the "Magazines" section.)

The Newhouse Case

In probably the largest estate tax case ever filed, the IRS wanted $914 mil-lion from the Newhouse family for taxes and penalties from the estate of Samuel Newhouse, who died in 1979. About $305 million is for fraud penal-ties. But the IRS doesn't always win. In a 100-page opinion issued in March of 1990, a federal judge sided with the family, who argued they only owed $47 million.

TAX REVOLTS

As might be imagined in a country that can trace its origins to a successful tax revolt, America's history is full of tax protests. Some protests, like the Boston Tea Party and the Proposition 13 movement in California, have involved many people and shaped the very course of our history. Others, like Henry David Thoreau's tax protest against the Mexican War, have been private protests, matters of intellectual conviction.

Boston Tea Party

The British imposed a vast and heavy burden of taxes on American colonists, but thanks to a lax and fairly corrupt government bureaucracy few of these taxes and trading regulations were ever enforced. However, follow-ing the Seven Years' War (1756–1763), the British decided to get tough with the colonists and make them pay for some of the costs of running the empire. The Townshend Acts of 1767 imposed duties on vital colonial imports and in 1773, angered by the fact that the British East India Compa-ny was seeking a monopoly on tea sales to the colonies, 150 Boston radicals dressed as Indians dumped 342 cases of tea into the Boston Harbor. The cost of the lost tea was 18,000 pounds sterling, but the eventual result was the loss of the colonies.

The fact that the American Revolution began as a tax revolt, however, caused problems for the early revolutionary government. It managed to col-lect only $5.8 million from the colonies during the war and General George Washington was forced to spend a great deal of time requesting funds and supplies.

The Whiskey Rebellion

In 1794, President Washington sent in 13,000 troops when some 3,000 Pennsylvania farmers revolted instead of paying an excise tax on liquor. As a result, Congress gradually turned away from using excise taxes to finance the government, abolishing most of them in 1802 and the rest in 1817.

Proposition 13

California's famous tax revolt actually resulted from an earlier attempt to reform the property tax system. After a corrupt San Francisco property tax assessor was sent to jail for taking bribes from corporations in exchange for lower property taxes, the state legislature reformed the property tax code. The legislators believed that home owners were being overtaxed, and so the new law required that all properties be taxed at the same rate. In fact, however, the reverse was true. For political reasons, local governments had always kept taxes on homes low by undervaluing the homes. So, property taxes on homes skyrocketed. In the 1970s, Howard Jarvis, a long-time conservative activist, capitalized on the discontent by organizing one of the largest mass tax protests in recent years. He and Paul Gann collected 1 million signatures to get Proposition 13 on the ballot. Local politicians howled, saying mandated property tax cuts would cripple government and force it to eliminate essential services. No matter. The voters wanted lower taxes and Proposition 13 passed in 1978 by a two-to-one margin. The movement spread to other states, and popular sentiment for lower taxes helped push Congress toward reducing income taxes.

In the short run, Proposition 13 did not cause a fiscal crisis in California, as everyone predicted. Government budgets had been running a surplus—thanks to rising taxes. There were only minor cuts in services. But home owners never received much of a tax cut since the $6.15 billion tax relief created by Jarvis's formula rewarded business and corporate property owners first, wealthy home owners second, and poorer households last. Rental tenants got nothing. However, 10 years after it was passed political pressure was building to repeal Proposition 13 in order to increase social services and improve the educational system. And in 1990, California voters passed Proposition III, which increased gas taxes.

The Tax Revolt of 1990

As Congress struggled to reduce the budget in the fall of 1990, another grass-roots tax rebellion was brewing. In Oregon, antitax activists were pushing a proposition that would put a cap on property taxes. In Massachusetts, there was a measure to repeal a 1989 hike of 15% in the state income tax. Colorado was considering a constitutional amendment to cap property taxes. Illinois debated a measure that would require 60% of the state legislature, not a simple majority, to approve new taxes. In California, the home of Proposition 13, a new proposition would require a two-thirds

Table 11-1   Tax Freedom Day, Selected Years 1950–1991

The economists for the Tax Foundation each year estimate the number of days the average American must work to satisfy all federal, state, and local tax obligations. In 1991, taxes consumed 128 work days—from January 1 to May 8 to pay his or her tax bills.

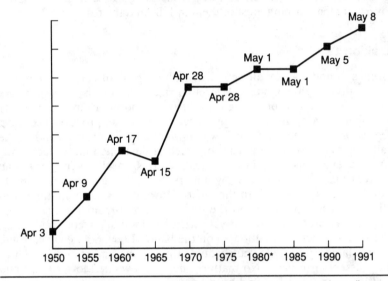

* Leap year causes the calendar date of Tax Freedom Day to appear one day earlier.
Source: Tax Foundation.

vote by the legislature or all voters to pass new taxes. Fights against tax hikes could also be found in Washington, New Jersey, North Dakota, Nevada, and Maryland. And this was only the beginning. Tax hikes of over $137.2 billion between 1991 and 1995 should fuel even more antitax revolts.

Table 11-2   Tax Freedom Day by State, Calendar Year 1991

State	Tax Freedom Day	Number of Days	Rank
United States	May 8	128	—
Alabama	April 25	115	50
Alaska	May 11	131	10
Arizona	May 7	127	21
Arkansas	April 26	116	49
California	May 7	127	22
Colorado	May 2	122	38
Connecticut	May 17	137	4
Delaware	May 21	141	3
Dist. of Columbia	May 26	146	2
Florida	May 4	124	32
Georgia	May 3	123	35
Hawaii	May 16	136	5
Idaho	April 28	118	47
Illinois	May 9	129	16
Indiana	May 2	122	36
Iowa	May 7	127	23
Kansas	May 5	125	29
Kentucky	April 29	119	43
Louisiana	May 4	124	33
Maine	May 8	128	19
Maryland	May 11	131	12
Massachusetts	May 8	128	18
Michigan	May 12	132	8
Minnesota	May 14	134	6
Mississippi	April 24	114	51
Missouri	April 28	118	46
Montana	May 4	124	31
Nebraska	May 7	127	25
Nevada	May 8	128	17
New Hampshire	April 29	119	44
New Jersey	May 14	134	7
New Mexico	May 7	127	20
New York	May 26	146	1
North Carolina	May 3	123	34
North Dakota	May 6	126	27
Ohio	May 6	126	26
Oklahoma	May 2	122	37
Oregon	May 10	130	15
Pennsylvania	May 7	127	24
Rhode Island	May 12	132	9
South Carolina	May 1	121	41
South Dakota	April 28	118	48
Tennessee	April 29	119	45
Texas	May 5	125	30
Utah	May 1	121	40
Vermont	May 10	130	13
Virginia	May 2	122	39
Washington	May 10	130	14
West Virginia	May 1	121	42
Wisconsin	May 11	131	11
Wyoming	May 6	126	28

Source: Tax Foundation.

Table 11-3   Tax Freedom Day by State, Calendar Year 1991

Legend:
- May 9 or later
- May 8 or earlier

NH April 29 #44
VT May 10 #13
ME May 8 #19
MA May 8 #18
RI May 12 #9
CT May 17 #4
NJ May 14 #7
NY May 26 #1
PA May 7 #24
DE May 21 #3
MD May 11 #12
DC May 26 #2
WV May 1 #42
VA May 2 #39
NC May 3 #34
SC May 1 #41
OH May 6 #26
KY April 29 #43
TN April 29 #45
GA May 3 #35
AL April 25 #50
FL May 4 #32
IN May 2 #36
IL May 9 #16
MI May 12 #8
WI May 11 #11
MN May 14 #6
IA May 7 #23
MO April 28 #46
AR April 26 #49
MS April 24 #51
LA May 4 #33
ND May 6 #27
SD April 28 #48
NE May 7 #25
KS May 5 #29
OK May 2 #37
TX May 5 #30
MT May 4 #31
WY May 6 #28
CO May 2 #38
NM May 7 #20
HI May 16 #5
ID April 28 #47
UT May 1 #40
AZ May 7 #21
WA May 10 #14
OR May 10 #15
NV May 8 #17
CA May 7 #22
AK May 11 #10

Source: Tax Foundation.

178

Table 11-4 Government Finance Around the World

This table shows how the U.S. and other countries finance their governments. It shows that while the U.S. raises only 8.1% of its tax revenues from corporate taxes, Japan raises 22.9%.

(percent distribution of tax receipts by type of tax)

Country and year		Total[1]	Income and profits taxes[2] Total[3]	Indi-vidual	Cor-porate	Social security contributions Total[4]	Em-ployees	Em-ployers	Taxes on goods and services[5] Total[3]	General con-sumption taxes[6]	Taxes on spe-cific goods, serv-ices[7]
United States:	1980	100.0	47.0	36.9	10.2	26.2	10.0	15.5	16.6	6.6	7.8
	1986	100.0	42.4	35.4	7.0	29.8	11.5	17.3	17.5	7.6	7.5
	1987	100.0	44.3	36.2	8.1	28.8	11.1	16.6	16.7	7.4	7.2
Canada:	1980	100.0	46.6	34.1	11.6	10.5	3.7	6.6	32.5	11.5	13.0
	1986	100.0	45.8	37.0	8.0	13.7	4.7	8.8	29.5	14.5	11.1
	1987	100.0	47.3	38.7	8.0	13.3	4.6	8.5	28.9	14.1	11.2
France:	1980	100.0	18.1	12.9	5.1	42.7	11.1	28.4	30.4	21.0	8.4
	1986	100.0	17.9	12.8	5.0	42.9	11.9	27.5	29.3	19.4	8.9
	1987	100.0	18.0	12.7	5.2	43.0	12.3	27.2	29.3	19.5	8.9
Italy:	1980	100.0	31.1	23.1	7.8	38.0	6.9	28.4	26.5	15.6	9.7
	1986	100.0	36.2	27.8	10.6	34.4	6.7	24.4	26.1	14.7	10.3
	1987	100.0	36.1	26.3	10.5	34.3	6.7	24.1	26.4	14.6	10.3
Japan:	1980	100.0	46.1	24.3	21.8	29.1	10.2	14.8	16.3	—	14.1
	1986	100.0	45.7	25.0	20.7	29.8	10.8	15.4	13.3	—	11.4
	1987	100.0	47.0	24.0	22.9	28.6	10.2	14.8	12.9	—	11.1
Netherlands:	1980	100.0	32.8	26.3	6.6	38.1	15.7	17.8	25.2	15.8	7.3
	1986	100.0	27.5	20.2	7.3	42.9	18.0	17.8	25.8	16.4	7.2
	1987	100.0	27.4	19.7	7.7	42.7	18.8	17.0	26.0	16.4	7.4
Sweden:	1980	100.0	43.5	41.0	2.5	28.8	—	27.6	24.0	13.4	9.2
	1986	100.0	42.7	38.0	4.7	25.1	—	24.1	24.7	13.3	10.2
	1987	100.0	41.3	37.2	4.1	24.2	—	23.3	24.1	13.3	9.8
United Kingdom:	1980	100.0	37.8	29.4	8.4	16.6	6.4	9.8	29.4	14.5	13.3
	1986	100.0	38.3	28.0	10.3	18.0	8.4	9.2	31.0	15.5	13.7
	1987	100.0	37.2	26.6	10.6	18.1	8.3	9.4	31.4	16.1	13.6
West Germany:	1980	100.0	35.1	29.6	5.5	34.4	15.3	18.5	27.1	16.6	9.3
	1986	100.0	34.5	28.6	6.0	37.2	16.1	19.1	25.2	15.3	8.6
	1987	100.0	34.0	29.0	5.0	37.3	16.1	19.1	25.4	15.7	8.6

—Represents zero.
[1]Includes property taxes, employer payroll taxes other than Social Security contributions, and miscellaneous taxes, not shown separately.
[2]Includes taxes on capital gains.
[3]Includes other taxes, not shown separately.
[4]Includes contributions of self-employed, not shown separately.
[5]Taxes on the production, sales, transfer, leasing, and delivery of goods and services and rendering of services.
[6]Primarily value-added and sales taxes.
[7]For example, excise taxes on alcohol, tobacco, and gasoline.
Source: Organization for Economic Cooperation and Development, Paris, France, *Revenue Statistics of OECD Member Countries,* annual.

179

Table 11-5 A Tax Tour: The Tax Bill Around the World

This chart shows the tax revenues in other major countries. America's per-capita tax bill is higher than those of such countries as Italy but lower than those of such countries as Japan and Sweden. As a percentage of gross domestic product (GDP), the U.S. tax bill is, however, lower than every country listed here.

Country	Tax revenues, 1987 Total (bil. dol.)	Tax revenues, 1987 Per capita (dol.)	Percent change in total tax revenue as expressed in national currency 1980–1982	1983–1984	1984–1985	1985–1986	1986–1987	Tax revenues as percent of GDP 1980	1984	1985	1986	1987
United States	1,316.1	5,396	46.5	11.1	9.8	5.4	10.1	29.5	28.4	29.2	28.9	30.0
Australia	64.6	3,975	80.4	16.8	10.9	12.6	13.8	29.0	30.7	30.4	31.0	31.3
Austria	49.6	6,550	41.8	9.6	7.3	5.1	2.8	41.2	42.4	43.1	42.9	42.3
Belgium	65.8	6,665	47.0	9.8	7.3	3.8	4.9	43.5	46.3	46.5	45.8	46.1
Canada	146.5	5,710	59.1	8.9	7.5	7.1	12.8	31.6	32.9	32.9	33.2	34.5
Denmark	52.6	10,257	77.4	12.9	12.2	12.2	6.4	45.5	47.6	49.0	51.0	52.0
Finland	32.1	6,515	95.1	17.6	12.8	10.6	3.0	33.0	35.5	36.8	38.1	35.9
France	394.9	7,099	78.4	11.4	7.5	6.7	6.5	41.7	44.6	44.5	44.1	44.8
Greece	17.6	1,764	223.3	29.6	22.4	25.5	17.1	29.4	34.9	35.2	36.8	37.4
Ireland	11.7	3,307	112.2	13.5	5.2	8.4	7.5	34.0	39.0	38.4	39.5	39.9
Italy	273.9	4,778	139.2	11.5	10.6	15.7	9.7	30.2	34.8	34.4	36.1	36.2
Japan	727.5	5,959	43.5	7.4	8.2	7.4	9.4	25.5	27.4	28.0	28.9	30.2
Luxembourg	3.0	8,084	68.8	6.5	9.2	3.9	4.4	40.9	43.2	43.6	42.8	43.8
Netherlands	102.9	7,012	21.7	1.1	4.3	5.0	5.7	45.8	45.0	44.9	45.9	48.0
New Zealand	13.5	4,076	100.5	13.6	19.0	21.8	23.3	33.1	32.9	33.9	34.9	38.6
Norway	39.9	9,546	77.3	10.7	14.8	7.9	4.8	47.1	45.8	47.6	49.9	48.3
Portugal	11.6	1,185	209.3	19.9	22.8	32.4	10.3	28.7	32.2	31.6	33.4	31.4
Spain	95.5	2,459	121.7	18.4	10.5	22.0	19.1	24.1	29.2	29.1	31.0	33.0
Sweden	89.9	10,707	68.0	11.3	9.6	15.0	13.9	49.4	50.3	50.6	53.7	56.7
Switzerland	54.7	8,267	39.2	7.1	5.8	8.5	3.1	30.8	32.3	32.0	32.5	32.0
Turkey	16.4	315	477.4	32.0	71.8	65.2	57.0	21.7	17.3	19.7	22.8	24.1
United Kingdom	253.4	4,451	64.4	7.7	9.3	8.8	6.7	35.3	37.8	37.8	38.5	37.5
West Germany	420.7	6,880	23.6	5.3	5.6	4.6	4.0	38.0	37.5	38.0	37.6	37.6

Source: Organization for Economic Cooperation and Development, Paris, France, *Revenue Statistics of OECD Member Countries*, annual.

PART IV

The Business of Business

Chapter Twelve

SERVICES: PRODUCTS ARE PASSÉ

HIGHLIGHTS AND TRENDS

• Today over 75% of all American workers are employed in service-producing industries. That stands in sharp contrast to the beginning of the 20th century, when about 73% of the population worked in agriculture and blue-collar occupations, or even 1952, when 58.6% were employed in services.

• By the end of the century, manufacturing, mining, and construction will only account for 21% of nonagricultural jobs, down from 32.2% in 1972. Meanwhile, service jobs will comprise nearly four fifths of all jobs (79%), up from 67.8% in 1972.

• Services have been the only bright spot in America's ballooning trade deficit. Services ran a $28.2 billion trade surplus in 1989.

• The nonagricultural sector of the economy produced about 39.9 million jobs between 1970 and 1990—38.1 million of them in the service sector.

• The services boom is likely to continue. Most of the 18.1 million new jobs created between now and the year 2000 will be service jobs. The U.S. Department of Labor indicates that 16.7 million service jobs will be created between 1988 and 2000, with such jobs totaling 96.4 million at the turn of the century. Meanwhile, manufacturing jobs will drop 1.6% to 19.1 million in 2000.

• A lot of new service jobs won't pay as well as the blue-collar jobs that once made up the backbone of the economy. Take the new jobs expected to be created between now and 2000 for salespersons (730,000), more than any other occupation. But salesworkers earned only an average of $258 a week in 1990. Similarly, 7 out of the 10 largest job-producing occupations— salesworkers, waiters, janitors, clerks, nurse's aides, receptionists, and secretaries—pay less than the average weekly wage of $415.

• The economy, however, is producing well-paying jobs too. Some 479,000 new managerial and executive jobs, which pay $516 a week, will be created. Another 613,000 new jobs will open up for registered nurses, who earn $608 a week.

THE NEW SERVICE ECONOMY

A hundred years ago, only a lunatic might have imagined an economy in which over 75% of all workers were not involved in the production of food, housing, and manufactured products.

But that's exactly the kind of economy we have.

Even more surprising, this strange economy works, at least part of the time.

For the first time in history, most Americans don't produce the things we all need to survive. Few grow food, build homes and offices, mine raw materials, or manufacture goods. They produce services.

With over half of the labor force working in offices, we are accustomed to the idea that services are an important part of the economy. But to get an idea how unusual the service economy is, it's worth remembering that in 1900 about 73% of the population worked in agriculture and blue-collar occupations. Today, the figure is nearly reversed, with 77.1% of all nonagricultural employees in service-producing industries. About 25.4 million Americans produce goods—working in manufacturing, construction, or mining. Over three times as many (85.4 million) work in service-producing industries. Only 3.3 million Americans have jobs in agriculture. And services will be even more important in the future. Just about all of the jobs expected to be created in America will be in the service sector.

Services Serve the Economy

If the service economy does not produce goods, what does it do? Unlike manufacturing, mining, construction, farming, and other goods-producing industries, service industries are hard to define. Indeed, service-producing industries are a mixed bag. Education is a service industry; so is banking. The esoteric business of dredging rivers to improve trout fishing is a service, as is the more mundane job of driving a truck. All government agencies, from the Central Intelligence Agency to the Parks Department, are part of the service sector, as are wholesale and retail trade, communications, public utilities, health care, education, repair and maintenance, transportation, insurance, banking, finance, advertising, consultants, lawyers, engineering firms, nonprofit organizations, hotels, barber shops, data processing, employment agencies, restaurants, bars, and headhunters.

Some sections of the service sector—such as prostitution—are among the world's oldest businesses. Others, such as data processing, are only possible in a modern industrial economy. Although it's tempting to dismiss the service economy as producing only paperwork, modern economies that rely on high technology and information would not be possible without service industries.

In fact, service industries make the production of goods possible. Services such as banking arrange complicated financing for multinational corporations that are wealthier than many countries. Service workers educate the people who run those corporations. Service workers do market research, helping companies to produce new products. Service workers transport these products to the market. Service workers create advertisements to show how these products will make you sexier, wealthier, and wiser.

That's not all. Service workers repair products when they break and file lawsuits if a product isn't all it's cracked up to be. Service workers even dispose of the trash produced by other service workers.

The growth of services is also a reflection of long-term social as well as economic changes. As more and more women enter the labor force, service industries care for their children and prepare meals for families too busy to cook at home. With the decline of the extended family, government and health services care for the elderly, the disabled, and the poor.

And service industries make the so-called consumer society possible. Increasingly affluent workers turn to a variety of financial services to invest their money and to other services, such as recreation and travel, when they want to spend their money. In fact, such services as advertising and retail sales create the very psychology of consumerism.

The State of the Service Industries

How the service economy affects the economic health of the American economy is the subject of a widespread and often confusing debate. Some pop economists say services will save the country from the decline of manufacturing; others argue, just as vehemently, that the rise of the service economy will produce a period of slower economic growth, declining productivity, and stagnant wages.

In fact, neither position makes much sense. Service industries are no panacea for a healthy manufacturing, construction, and farm economy. A declining manufacturing sector hurts the future of rapidly growing service industries dependent on manufacturing concerns.

Since some service occupations pay worse than many manufacturing or construction jobs, critics have charged that the continuing shift of jobs to the service sector could help drag down consumer incomes. As noted, seven of the 10 occupations expected to produce most of the jobs—salesworkers, waiters, janitors, clerks, nurse's aides, receptionists, and secretaries—are all service jobs that pay less than the average weekly wage.

Fortunately, the second-highest number of jobs will be created in registered nursing, an occupation where salaried employees earn $608 a week. And the economy will be creating many well-paying jobs for managers and truck drivers.

A more worrisome problem is productivity in the service sector. Companies have spent tens of billions of dollars on computers and other equipment to automate their offices, yet productivity in service-producing industries has shown virtually no improvement since 1979. That dismal showing held down productivity and, as a result, wages, for the entire economy. If no gains are made in service-sector productivity, some forecasters believe that the GNP will grow less than 3% a year between now and 1995, with per-capita income growing only 1.5%. (See the chapter "Trade, Productivity, and Staying Ahead" for a discussion of how low productivity is holding down our incomes.)

Also remember that service jobs are just as vulnerable to technological displacement and foreign competition as manufacturing jobs have been. Moreover, lower wages in other countries have caused employers to move some office jobs overseas. For example, newspaper articles contained in one computer database are keyed into the computer by Chinese workers who can't even read English. Likewise, a recent study of the Office of Technology Assessment of the U.S. Congress estimates that even more service companies will move overseas to find cheap wages. Data-entry clerks in the Caribbean earn weekly wages of only $15 to $60; clerks in China might earn only $2 a week. Indian workers, for example, enter data into computers for only 10% to 15% of what it would cost to do the job with American workers.

Such statistics contradict those who imagine services will ensure economic prosperity. However, it's also wrong to blame the economy's recent woes on services, as others have done.

A popular myth that emerged from the tough 1981–1982 recession was that the decline of manufacturing and the rise of services are relatively recent phenomena. In fact, if you define a service economy as one in which more than half of the workers are employed in service-producing industries, then the U.S. has been a service economy since 1950. Yet the growth of the service economy didn't wreck the whole economy. Wages for both manufacturing and services grew rapidly during the 1950s and 1960s, when both service and manufacturing pay increased by about $9,500. Moreover, the gap between service and manufacturing pay is shrinking, indicating that the problems with the U.S. economy are not simply the fault of the service sector.

Services have also been growing faster than manufacturing for some time. Between 1960 and 1981, service employment grew 3.2% a year while manufacturing grew 1% a year. The service sector created 17 million of the 19 million new jobs produced in the 1970s.

The nonagricultural sector of the economy produced about 39.9 million jobs between 1970 and 1990—38.1 million of them were in the service sector.

THE CREATION OF THE MODERN OFFICE

2nd century A.D.   Becoming a paper pusher becomes possible when the Chinese invent paper, manufacturing it with some unknown type of plant fiber. The Arabs introduce paper to Europe in the 9th century. Paper made from wood pulp does not appear until the 14th century.

1564   The pencil is invented shortly after the discovery of graphite in England.

1750   The eraser is invented around this time by Magalhaens, a Portuguese physicist, making it possible for a paper pusher to erase his or her mistakes.

mid-18th century   The word *bureaucracy* is coined by Frenchman Vincent de Gournay. Derived from the Latin *burrus,* referring to the dark-brown cloth used to cover a writing desk or bureau, and from the Greek *kratein,* meaning "to rule," the new word means "government by desk." Gournay coins the word to refer to the novel phenomenon of clerks working in government or private offices at desks in contrast to the older system whereby aristocrats worked out of their estates. From the beginning, the word has a pejorative connotation. Gournay suggests these new bureaucrats suffer from excessive zeal, a disease he calls *bureaumania.*

1773   The first duplicating machine is invented by James Watt, the famous British inventor of the steam engine, so he can handle the paperwork at his factory.

1802   A Frenchman, Descroissilles, invents the coffeepot, making the coffee break possible. The first coffeehouses appeared in 1554 in Constantinople.

1806   An Englishman, R. Wedgewood, invents carbon paper.

1808   An Italian, Pellegrine Turri, builds the first typewriter for the Countess Caroline Frantoni, who is blind, so they can send each other letters. A Danish pastor, Malling Hansen, markets the first typewriter in 1870. The first electric typewriter is built by Dr. Thaddeus Cahill in 1901, but IBM popularizes electric typewriters by marketing the Electromatic in 1933.

1820   An Englishman named S. K. Brewer announces that he has invented the envelope. Though a few earlier envelopes have been found, most letters were folded and mailed without an envelope.

1875   The first want ads for typists appear. The pay is $10 to $20 a week, which is considered good pay at the time.

1875   The first commercial telephone is connected at the Cambridge, Massachusetts, Board of Waterworks. Employees can only call one other party—the Board's branch office. By the 1980s there are 151 million telephones in America.

1884   Fountain pens are reported as early as the 17th century. In 1884 Lewis Waterman founds the first fountain pen factory.

1900   The paper clip is invented by a Norwegian, Johann Waaler.

1911   An American, Willis Carrier, invents the air conditioner.

1913   The first U.S. crossword puzzle is published. It is written by journalist Arthur Wynne. The crossword puzzle soon becomes a favorite way of wasting time in offices.

1925   Scotch tape is invented by Dick Drew of the Minnesota Mining and Manufacturing Company (3M) as a masking tape for painting cars in two tones. The product gets its name because the original tape only has adhesive on the edges. Auto workers think the company is trying to save money by scrimping on adhesive so they call the tape "Scotch tape," after the frugal citizens of Scotland. The first clear or cellulose Scotch tape appears in 1930.

1938   Lazlo Biro, a Hungarian journalist, invents the ballpoint pen. Ballpoint pens first go on sale at Gimbel's at $12.50 apiece in 1945 and sell out on the first day. Banks, however, suggest that signatures made using the new ballpoint pen may not be legal.

1954   The first electronic computer used in business goes into service at J. Lyons & Co. in London. The same year the computer Univac I starts operations at the GE Appliance Park.

1959   Revolutionizing the art of creating paperwork, Xerox introduces its first office copier, the Xerox 914. It only makes six copies a minute. The Xerox machine, which was invented by Chester Carlson in 1938, was the first to use dry photocopying on untreated paper. Carlson has trouble finding someone to sell his invention but in 1947, after 20 companies refused to develop his patents, Haloid, a small company that eventually becomes Xerox, signs an agreement.

1959   Digital Equipment Corporation produces the first minicomputer, setting off a trend toward smaller and smaller computers that eventually opens up the market for small office computers.

1972   The first pocket calculator is developed by Texas Instruments.

1979   Apple introduces the first mass-market personal computer, touching off a revolution in office technology.

1989   But the revolution in office technology doesn't cut down on the need for paper pushers. The number of "deskworkers" hits 41.2 million (37.3% of the labor force), up from 34 million only five years earlier.

1990   Over one third of all workplaces have a personal computer, up from 14.8% in 1984. There are nearly 14 million P.C.s in use, far more than manual typewriters (1.1 million), or even electric typewriters (11.7 million).

Chapter Thirteen
MANUFACTURING:
THE RUSTING OF AMERICA

HIGHLIGHTS AND TRENDS

• American manufacturing faces the 1990s after a decade of turmoil and decline. Only 17.3% of all nonagricultural workers were employed in manufacturing in 1990, down from 22.4% in 1980, 27.3% in 1970, and 35.2% in 1947. Manufacturing's share of the GNP has also been sagging, dropping from 28.1% in 1947 to about 20% today.

• The decline of manufacturing has been a major contributor to the trade deficit of the United States. Americans imported $105.5 billion more merchandise in 1990 than they exported, with 38% of that deficit ($40.5 billion) in goods from Japan. In contrast, the U.S. had a positive trade balance of $10.9 billion in 1975.

• Even with improvement in the economy, the country's factories face an uncertain future. Few economists believe that the auto industry will ever again produce the 9.6 million cars it did in 1973 or that the steel industry will ever again employ 602,000 workers, as it did in 1974.

• Declining American competitiveness has hurt the manufacturing sector. About 9.7 million experienced American workers lost their jobs because of plant closings or employment cutbacks between 1979 and 1987, according to a 1990 study. Two fifths of these jobs, 4.27 million, were lost in the manufacturing sector even though manufacturing employs 17.5% of all nonagricultural workers.

• About 16% of these experienced workers who lost their jobs between 1983 and 1987 remained unemployed; another 14.5% left the labor force.

• About 29.8% of the 1.2 million displaced manufacturing workers who eventually found full-time work suffered wage cuts of more than 20%. About half (48.8%) of all steelworkers who found new full-time jobs earned 20% less than before. Another 15.9% of manufacturing workers were hit with earning cuts of 1% to 20% at their new jobs. About 158,000 now work part time or started their own businesses. But not all displaced manufacturing workers were hurt by the layoffs. About 26.3% of those who found full-time work were earning more at their new jobs.

• One explanation for employment problems in American manufacturing is simple: American companies are failing to match the productivity improvements of their toughest competitors. U.S. productivity in the manufacturing sector as measured by output per hour grew only 2.2% between 1973 and 1985, down from a 3.2% increase between 1960 and 1973. That was way below Japan's growth rate of 10.3% a year between 1960 and 1973 and 5.6% between 1973 and 1985. As a result, U.S. productivity growth between 1960 and 1985 lagged way behind the average 5.4% annual rate of increase in productivity of its 11 major industrial competitors. While U.S. manufacturing productivity grew only 2.7% a year between 1960 and 1985, productivity grew 8.0% in Japan, 5.5% in France, 3.4% in Canada, 4.8% in Germany, 5.4% in Italy, 3.5% in the United Kingdom, 6.5% in Belgium, 4.8% in Denmark, 6.2% in the Netherlands, 3.2% in Norway, and 4.7% in Sweden.

• Since then, U.S. manufacturers have made a modest comeback in the productivity race. After 1985, U.S. manufacturing productivity grew at an average rate of 3.3% a year, faster than Canada (1.9%), France (2.8%), Germany (1.9%), or Italy (2.1%). But it lagged behind the United Kingdom (4.9%) and its chief foreign competitor, Japan (5.7%).

THE CRISIS IN AMERICAN MANUFACTURING

In 1870 more than half of all American workers (53%) could be found down on the farm. But by 1920 more Americans (11.2 million) were employed in manufacturing than in agriculture (10.8 million), and in the 1930s, as the Dust Bowl forced thousands of farmers into the cities, it finally became apparent that the U.S. was no longer a rural, agricultural nation. By 1960 there were 16.8 million Americans employed in manufacturing, more than three times the 5.5 million employed in agriculture. Manufacturing accounted for 28% of GNP compared to only 4% for agriculture.

But in the late 1970s and early 1980s disaster struck. During the recession of 1982, American manufacturing underwent its own Dust Bowl, a Rust Bowl that rocked the boardrooms of the old industrial giants. U.S. auto makers sold only 5.7 million cars in 1982, the worst slump since the 1950s, producing long lines at the unemployment office. In Michigan, unemployment hit 14.2% in 1982, and in some cities, such as Flint where 20,000 auto workers were laid off, nearly a quarter of the labor force was out of work.

Like the Dust Bowl 50 years earlier, the crisis of American manufacturing also supposedly heralded a new economic era—the rise of the service economy. Faced with the declining prospects at home, tens of thousands of laid-off blue-collar workers migrated from the old industrial heartland of the midwest and northeast into service jobs in the more prosperous western and southern states, just as the farmers put their possessions in Model T's and fled the Dust Bowl during the 1930s.

That migration marked more than an economic change; it was a major political change. Just as manufacturing made the midwest and northeast states dominant economic and political powers in the first half of the 20th century, the Rust Bowl sapped those states, shifting economic power toward the west and the Sunbelt. Not surprisingly, the last five presidents to be elected to office—Johnson, Nixon, Carter, Reagan, and Bush—were from the west or the south. In contrast, organized labor, with its traditional base in manufacturing, was weakened. The last three presidential candidates backed by labor were defeated, despite millions of dollars in contributions.

The spectacle of rusty steel mills, idle auto plants, and U.S. manufacturers moving their factories overseas touched off a long-overdue debate over the future of the American economy. Unfortunately, this debate, like most discussions of the American economy, produced more heat than light.

As the media descended on the industrial heartland, looking for the best disaster story since the eruption of Mount St. Helens, some of the most pessimistic pundits began predicting that the heyday of manufacturing was long gone. Soon, it was said, we'd have an economy whose principal products were fast food, unemployment checks, and paperwork.

A few went even further, having the temerity to suggest that this wasn't such a bad development, and that services, not manufacturing, were the wave of the future. Soon those unemployed blue-collar workers would find new service jobs and go back to work as white-collar workers. They could become data processors. After all, who needs a dirty, smelly factory when you can work in a nice clean office?

But, as usual, the economy confounded the forecasters. American manufacturing was able to battle itself off the ropes in the late 1980s. A drop in the U.S. dollar in 1985 and improved manufacturing productivity boosted sales and employment. Exports jumped 11% in 1987 and a whopping 29% in 1988. This boosted employment by 715,000 jobs and helped profits, which leapt from a paltry $58 billion in 1982 to $91.8 billion in 1990.

Also, it would be a mistake to overemphasize the growth of the service economy. Some of the drastic growth in the service industry is simply because the cost of services has increased faster than the cost of goods. For example, half of all consumer spending (54.2%) in 1990 was for services, up from the 36.6% spent in 1955. But when you adjust for inflation in the service industry, the service economy's share of consumer spending has been virtually unchanged since 1979 and has grown only about 9 percentage points, rather than 18, since 1955.

Some economists would also argue that manufacturing has only declined in current dollars, not in real dollars—that is, not in dollars that are adjusted for inflation. In 1970, manufacturing accounted for 21% of GNP; by 1988, it hit 23% in constant 1982 dollars.

Even those alarmed by manufacturing's declining share of GNP argue that the future of manufacturing remains vital to the American economy. Although manufacturing only employs 17.3% of all nonagricultural workers, it still calls the shots for most of the economy. Spending for durable and nondurable goods, for example, accounts for nearly half of all personal consumption. As a result, cyclical swings in the economy are still touched off by declines in the manufacturing sector. Moreover, the service sector, traditionally less affected by economic cycles of boom and bust, is now more closely tied to the profitability of manufacturing. If you imagine that GM's biggest supplier is a steel maker or a tire manufacturer, you're wrong. It's Blue Cross and Blue Shield. Also, two of the fastest-growing areas of the service economy are business services and health services. These industries would have a hard time if there were no manufacturing companies to buy their services.

Does this mean American manufacturing is in fine shape? No. After-tax profits of American manufacturers dropped 18% between 1981 and 1990, from $101.3 billion to only $91.8 billion. About 1.2 million jobs were lost in the manufacturing sector between 1980 and 1990. Productivity gains in the manufacturing sector have been only half those of Japan. Making American manufacturers more competitive at home and in the international markets will dominate economic debates for the next decade.

The human effects of a declining manufacturing sector are readily apparent. A 1990 study by the Bureau of Labor Statistics found that about 9.7 million Americans lost their jobs because of plant closings or employment cutbacks between the start of 1979 and 1987. Of the 4.6 million workers displaced between 1983 and 1987, about 44% (1.8 million) were in the manufacturing sector, even though manufacturing employs less than one fifth of all workers.

Many of the experienced manufacturing workers did not find new work and their skills have been lost to the economy. About 15.9% of the workers who had held the same job for at least three years before being laid off remained unemployed; another 14.5% left the labor force.

And many of the workers who found work saw sharp cuts in their paychecks. About 28% of the 1.2 million displaced manufacturing workers who eventually found full-time work suffered wage cuts of more than 20%. About half (48.8%) of all steelworkers who found new full-time jobs earned 20% less than before. About 16% of all reemployed manufacturing workers were hit with earning cuts of 1% to 20% at their new jobs. Another 158,000 started their own businesses or found part-time work.

But not all displaced manufacturing workers were hurt by the layoffs. About 55.3% of those who found full-time work were earning more at their new jobs.

A simple explanation for the employment problems in American manufacturing can be found in American productivity. As previously noted, U.S. productivity in the manufacturing sector as measured by output per hour grew a mere 2.2% between 1973 and 1985, down from a 3.2% increase between 1960 and 1973. Meanwhile, Japan's growth rate was much higher, 10.3% and 5.6% for the respective periods, and productivity growth in the U.S. was falling behind that of all its major industrial competitors.

In recent years, U.S. manufacturers have gotten back in the race. Between 1985 and 1988, the most recent year when comparable international statistics were available, U.S. manufacturing productivity increased at an average rate of 3.3% a year. This was faster than Canada (1.9%), France (2.8%), Germany (1.9%), or Italy (2.1%), but slower than the United Kingdom (4.9%) and the U.S.'s chief foreign competitor, Japan (5.7%). But in 1989, U.S. manufacturing productivity grew only 2.0%, and it rose only 2.4% in 1990.

Part of the improved productivity in American manufacturing can be traced to its responses to some of its wrenching problems. To hold down prices, companies have slashed corporate bureaucracies, shut down aging plants, and forced wage concessions from unions. Few economists believe the auto industry will ever again produce the 9.6 million cars it did during the early 1970s or that the steel industry will ever again employ 602,000 workers, but many manufacturers won't have to return to the good old days. Ford Motor Company, for example, cut costs and in the late 1980s was producing record profits in a stagnant auto market.

Thanks in part to that tough medicine, U.S. factories once again were showing signs of life between 1987 and 1990. Aided by a falling dollar, rising exports, and a strong economy, some manufacturers were resuming U.S. production. U.S. factories were operating at 83% in 1990, up from 70.3% in the dog days of 1982.

But the manufacturing sector may have a harder time keeping up the good work. A stronger dollar and a global recession hurt exports in 1991. This time the slowdown is not likely to be as painful as the 1982 recession, or as hard on many local communities in the Midwest, which are no longer so dependent on manufacturing plants for their livelihood. Still, a number of long-term measures need to be taken to improve the international competitiveness of American manufacturing into the 21st century. The tax system will have to become more supportive of capital investment; labor will have to make concessions on work rules and costs; management is going to have to learn that long-term investments in technology are the best way to increase profits for shareholders; the U.S. will have to increase pressure on foreign countries to open their markets to American goods. Perhaps most important, all of these solutions are going to take time. Lowering the taxes on capital gains or giving investment tax credits for three years and then taking them away because they don't solve all the world's problems are not the ways to promote long-term investment. (See the chapter "Trade, Productivity, and Staying Ahead" for a complete discussion of how American companies are fighting to improve their competitive position.)

Table 13-1   Value of Shipments in Selected Manufacturing Industries

The following table gives a sense of how individual industries have fared by showing the value of shipments for individual industries. It shows that many industries, particularly primary metals (which includes the steel industry) and farm machinery, have still not recovered from the crisis of 1981 and 1982 while other industries, such as office- and computing-machine manufacturers (which includes computers) and electronic-component manufacturers, grew even during the worst recession since the 1930s.

(in billions of dollars)

Industry	1978	1980	1982	1985	1989	1990
Shipments, total	1,522.9	1,852.2	1,908.3	2,341.2	2,781.4	2,860.3
Durable goods	814.2	930.6	920.3	1,243.8	1,472.0	1,485.2
Stone, clay, and glass products	41.7	46.1	44.0	57.3	64.8	63.9
Primary metals	118.1	133.9	107.0	125.8	145.4	137.1
Fabricated metal products	101.3	116.2	114.0	169.0	162.6	168.6
Machinery excluding electrical	143.2	180.7	180.6	212.6	266.0	267.4
Engines and turbines	12.4	13.7	12.8	15.1		
Farm machinery and equipment	11.9	15.1	11.8	10.4		
Construction, mining, and material handling equipment	28.9	33.6	34.5	33.6		
Office and computing machines	21.0	32.4	40.4	55.5		
Electrical machinery	100.5	128.6	141.1	185.5	239.6	245.7
Electrical transmission & distribution	17.9	21.3	21.9	24.9		
Household appliances	11.5	12.9	12.1	17.1		
Radio and TV	7.9	8.1	7.8	11.2		
Communication equipment	17.9	27.6	31.3	62.5		
Electronic components	17.9	27.6	31.3	38.9		
Transportation equipment	188.8	186.5	195.1	313.4	372.9	378.5
Motor vehicles and parts	132.0	104.6	112.2	203.4		
Aircraft, missiles, and parts	37.5	58.5	63.6	90.6		
Instruments and related products	33.7	44.1	46.7	56.7	77.0	79.6
Scientific and engineering equipment	19.2	25.6	28.0	37.3		
Photographic goods	11.5	15.9	16.6	17.2		

Industry	1978	1980	1982	1985	1989	1990
Nondurable goods	708.7	922.1	988.0	1,097.4	1,309.3	1,375.1
Food and kindred products	216.0	256.2	277.3	296.1	388.1	406.1
Meat products	55.6	63.0	66.2	67.6		
Fat and oils	16.2	18.2	15.4	13.7		
Beverages	26.6	33.0	40.3	45.2		
Tobacco products	10.0	12.2	14.5	20.6	24.1	26.2
Textile mill products	42.3	47.3	47.2	52.6	63.5	60.4
Paper and allied products	57.0	72.8	79.0	97.6	130.4	131.2
Paper, pulp, paperboard, and mill products	24.0	31.8	33.5	41.8		
Paperboard containers	14.5	17.2	18.4	21.4		
Chemical & allied products	129.4	162.5	172.8	214.3	255.5	265.7
Industrial inorganic chemicals	44.8	57.3	55.8	71.6		
Drugs, soaps, and toiletries	34.2	41.9	48.6	56.1		
Petroleum and coal products	103.9	198.7	206.4	194.0	138.5	169.6
Rubber and plastic products	43.2	47.3	50.2	48.2	95.8	90.1

Source: U.S. Department of Commerce.

Table 13-2 Manufacturing Profits

(billions of dollars; quarterly data at seasonally adjusted annual rates)

Corporate profits with inventory valuation adjustment and without capital consumption adjustment

Year	Total manufac-turing	Durable goods Total	Pri-mary metal indus-tries	Fabri-cated metal prod-ucts	Machin-ery, except electri-cal	Electric and elec-tronic equip-ment	Motor vehicles and equip-ment	Other	Nondurable goods Total	Food and kindred prod-ucts	Chemi-cals and allied prod-ucts	Petro-leum and coal prod-ucts	Other
1929	5.2	2.6							2.6				
1933	−.4	−.4							.0				
1939	3.3	1.7							1.7				
1940	5.5	3.1							2.4				
1941	9.5	6.4							3.1				
1942	11.8	7.2							4.6				
1943	13.8	8.1							5.7				
1944	13.2	7.4							5.9				
1945	9.7	4.5							5.2				
1946	9.0	2.4							6.6				
1947	13.6	5.8							7.8				
1948	17.6	7.5	1.6	0.8	1.2	0.7	1.4	1.8	10.0	1.9	1.7	2.8	3.7
1949	16.2	8.1	1.5	.7	1.3	.8	2.1	1.7	8.1	1.6	1.8	1.9	2.8
1950	20.9	12.0	2.3	1.1	1.6	1.2	3.1	2.6	8.9	1.6	2.3	2.3	2.7
1951	24.6	13.2	3.1	1.3	2.3	1.3	2.4	2.8	11.4	1.4	2.8	2.7	4.4
1952	21.7	11.7	1.9	1.0	2.3	1.5	2.4	2.6	9.9	1.7	2.3	2.3	3.6
1953	22.0	11.9	2.5	1.0	1.9	1.4	2.6	2.6	10.1	1.8	2.2	2.8	3.3
1954	19.9	10.5	1.7	.9	1.7	1.2	2.1	2.9	9.4	1.6	2.2	2.7	2.9
1955	26.0	14.3	2.9	1.1	1.7	1.1	4.1	3.5	11.8	2.2	3.0	3.0	3.6
1956	24.7	12.8	3.0	1.1	2.1	1.2	2.2	3.2	11.9	1.8	2.8	3.3	4.1
1957	24.0	13.3	3.0	1.1	2.0	1.5	2.6	3.1	10.7	1.8	2.8	2.6	3.6
1958	19.4	9.3	1.9	.9	1.4	1.3	0.9	2.9	10.0	2.1	2.5	2.1	3.3
1959	26.4	13.7	2.3	1.1	2.1	1.7	3.0	3.5	12.7	2.4	3.5	2.5	4.3
1960	23.6	11.6	2.0	.8	1.8	1.3	3.0	2.7	12.0	2.2	3.1	2.5	4.2
1961	23.3	11.4	1.6	1.0	1.9	1.3	2.5	3.1	11.9	2.3	3.2	2.2	4.1
1962	26.0	14.0	1.6	1.1	2.3	1.5	4.0	3.5	12.0	2.3	3.2	2.2	4.3
1963	29.3	16.3	2.0	1.3	2.5	1.6	4.9	4.0	13.1	2.7	3.6	2.1	4.6
1964	32.3	17.9	2.5	1.4	3.3	1.7	4.7	4.4	14.4	2.7	4.0	2.4	5.3
1965	39.3	23.0	3.1	2.0	3.9	2.7	6.2	5.1	16.3	2.8	4.6	2.9	6.0
1966	41.9	23.8	3.6	2.4	4.5	3.0	5.1	5.2	18.1	3.2	4.9	3.2	6.8
1967	38.6	21.0	2.7	2.4	4.1	2.9	3.9	4.9	17.6	3.2	4.3	3.9	6.3
1968	41.4	22.2	1.9	2.3	4.1	2.8	5.5	5.7	19.1	3.2	5.2	3.7	7.0
1969	36.7	19.0	1.4	2.0	3.7	2.3	4.8	4.9	17.7	3.0	4.6	3.3	6.9
1970	26.7	10.2	0.8	1.1	3.0	1.2	1.2	2.9	16.5	3.2	3.9	3.5	5.9
1971	34.3	16.4	.7	1.5	2.9	1.9	5.1	4.3	17.9	3.5	4.5	3.6	6.4
1972	40.8	22.5	1.6	2.1	4.3	2.8	5.9	5.8	18.3	2.9	5.2	3.0	7.2
1973	46.2	24.7	2.3	2.6	4.7	3.0	5.8	6.2	21.6	2.5	6.0	5.2	7.9
1974	39.8	14.6	4.9	1.6	3.1	.3	0.7	4.0	25.2	2.5	5.1	10.7	7.0
1975	53.6	19.8	2.7	3.1	4.8	2.4	2.0	4.8	33.8	8.8	6.4	9.5	9.1
1976	70.9	31.3	2.0	3.9	6.7	3.7	7.2	7.9	39.6	7.1	8.2	13.1	11.2
1977	80.6	38.6	1.3	4.4	8.9	5.8	9.4	8.8	42.0	6.9	7.8	12.9	14.4
1978	88.7	44.6	3.5	4.9	9.6	6.7	8.9	10.9	44.0	6.2	8.2	14.7	14.9
1979	87.5	37.3	3.6	5.2	9.1	5.2	4.7	9.5	50.2	5.8	7.2	22.5	14.7
1980	77.1	21.3	2.5	4.3	7.7	4.7	−2.5	4.5	55.8	6.1	5.4	31.4	12.9
1981	88.5	21.0	3.1	4.4	8.6	4.1	.1	.7	67.5	8.7	8.2	36.5	14.1
1982	58.0	2.1	−4.9	2.4	4.1	1.7	−.8	−.4	55.9	7.0	5.2	29.1	14.5
1983	70.1	17.2	−4.9	3.0	3.1	3.7	5.1	7.2	53.0	7.2	6.7	21.4	17.7
1984	88.8	38.1	−.6	4.7	6.2	5.5	9.0	13.3	50.7	6.7	8.0	17.2	18.8
1985	79.7	28.5	−1.4	4.6	3.2	3.6	7.2	11.3	51.2	8.3	6.2	17.5	19.2
1986	59.5	30.8	2.6	4.8	3.0	2.9	4.1	13.3	28.7	7.8	7.6	−7.6	20.9
1987	86.7	41.0	2.8	5.1	6.3	6.2	2.8	17.8	45.7	11.1	15.6	−2.6	21.6
1988	106.5	42.8	6.3	6.3	7.0	6.7	1.5	14.9	63.7	14.5	21.9	4.4	22.9
1989	96.1	37.1	6.2	6.7	4.7	7.4	−1.9	13.9	59.0	14.0	21.7	.3	23.1
1990ᵖ	91.8	33.5	4.3	5.5	6.9	7.3	−6.0	15.6	58.3	14.3	21.9	2.9	19.2

ᵖPreliminary figures.
Source: U.S. Department of Commerce, Bureau of Economic Analysis.

Table 13-3 Displaced Workers
(in thousands)

Industry and class of worker	Total 1979–83	Total 1981–85	Total 1983–87	Workers displaced during 1983–87 period		
				Employed	Unemployed	Not in labor force
Total, 20 years and over	5,091	5,130	4,629	71.5	13.8	14.7
Nonagricultural private wage and salary	4,700	4,772	4,443	71.5	13.7	14.8
Mining	150	175	215	68.8	13.0	18.1
Construction	401	316	390	70.8	21.5	7.7
Manufacturing	2,483	2,550	1,791	69.6	15.9	14.5
Durable goods	1,675	1,691	1,230	70.0	15.9	14.0
Lumber and wood	81	104	68	NA	NA	NA
Furniture and fixtures	65	63	42	NA	NA	NA
Stone, clay, and glass	75	87	32	NA	NA	NA
Primary metals	219	235	142	64.1	10.6	24.6
Fabricated metals	173	187	159	66.0	14.5	18.9
Machinery, except electric	396	361	299	79.3	12.4	8.7
Electrical machinery	195	255	200	70.0	14.0	16.0
Transportation equipment	354	260	199	61.3	30.2	8.5
Autos	224	148	118	51.7	39.8	8.5
Other	130	112	80	75.0	16.3	8.8
Professional and photographic equipment	54	73	50	NA	NA	NA
Other durable goods	62	66	40	NA	NA	NA
Nondurable goods	808	859	561	68.8	15.9	15.5
Food and kindred products	175	178	131	71.0	19.1	9.9
Textile mill products	80	123	52	NA	NA	NA
Apparel and other finished textiles	132	171	128	69.5	8.6	21.9
Paper and allied products	60	39	36	NA	NA	NA
Printing and publishing	103	94	52	NA	NA	NA
Chemicals and allied products	110	98	71	NA	NA	NA
Rubber and miscellaneous products	100	67	37	NA	NA	NA
Other nondurable goods	49	88	55	NA	NA	NA
Transportation and public utilities	336	386	292	73.3	14.7	12.3
Transportation	280	303	228	72.4	13.6	14.0
Communication and public utilities	56	83	64	NA	NA	NA
Wholesale and retail trade	732	689	930	73.4	7.4	19.1
Wholesale trade	234	294	232	79.3	8.6	11.6
Retail trade	498	395	698	71.3	7.0	21.6
Finance, insurance, and real estate	93	107	250	78.0	6.4	15.2
Services	506	540	574	71.8	14.6	13.6
Professional services	187	198	252	71.8	11.5	16.7
Other	318	342	322	71.7	17.1	11.2
Agriculture wage and salary	100	141	46	78.3	19.6	2.2
Government	248	172	136	72.1	14.7	13.2
Self-employed and unpaid family workers	25	33	4	NA	NA	NA

NA = Not available.
Source: *Monthly Labor Review,* May 1990.

Table 13-4   The 30 Industries Adding the Most Jobs in the 1980s
(numbers in thousands)

Rank	Industry	SIC	Employees		Change	
			1979	1989	Number	Percent
1	Eating and drinking places	58	4,513.1	6,369.9	1,856.8	41.1
2	Miscellaneous business services*	739	1,277.5	2,256.5	979.0	76.6
3	Grocery stores	541	2,001.9	2,889.1	887.2	44.3
4	Hospitals	806	2,608.4	3,490.7	882.3	33.8
5	Personnel supply services	736	526.5	1,351.2	824.7	156.6
6	Hotels, motels, and tourist courts	701	1,019.9	1,548.9	529.0	51.9
7	Computer and data-processing services	737	270.8	763.4	492.6	181.9
8	Offices of physicians	801	716.8	1,206.8	490.0	68.4
9	Legal services	81	459.9	896.3	436.4	94.9
10	Nursing and personal care facilities	805	950.8	1,384.2	433.4	45.6
11	Miscellaneous shopping goods stores	594	568.5	905.4	336.9	59.3
12	Services to buildings	734	487.0	807.6	320.6	65.8
13	Machinery, equipment, and supplies	508	1,260.8	1,574.0	313.2	24.8
14	Trucking and trucking terminals	421.3	1,248.8	1,537.7	288.9	23.1
15	Colleges and universities	822	716.9	990.9	274.0	38.2
16	Amusement and recreation services	79	712.0	975.6	263.6	37.0
17	Engineering and architectural services	891	515.0	756.1	241.1	46.8
18	Insurance agents, brokers, and service	64	430.1	659.8	229.7	53.4
19	Residential care*	836	201.1	426.4	225.3	112.0
20	Accounting, auditing, and bookkeeping	893	299.0	520.4	221.4	74.0
21	Outpatient care facilities*	808	113.0	317.3	204.3	180.8
22	Air transportation	451.2	390.9	595.0	204.1	52.2
23	Commercial and stock savings banks	602	1,369.3	1,572.8	203.5	14.9
24	Individual and family services*	832	161.0	353.1	192.1	119.3
25	Real estate agents and managers	653	360.2	550.6	190.4	52.9
26	Groceries and related products	514	648.4	837.9	189.8	29.3
27	Offices of dentists	802	322.0	511.6	189.6	58.9
28	Department stores	531	1,878.1	2,056.2	178.1	9.5
29	Security brokers and dealers	621	164.7	336.5	171.8	104.3
30	Savings and loan associations	612	236.0	402.8	166.8	70.7

*Although published monthly estimates begin in 1982, the previously unpublished annual average for 1979 was computed and used for these comparisons.

Note: Figures shown for 1979 and 1989 are annual averages from the CES program. Industries are compared at the three-digit Standard Industrial Classification (SIC) level, unless the CES program only publishes monthly estimates at the two-digit level.

Source: *Monthly Labor Review,* September 1990.

195

Chapter Fourteen

SMALL BUSINESS: WINGING IT

HIGHLIGHTS AND TRENDS

• The 1970s and 1980s saw a resurgence of the entrepreneurial spirit, with the number of self-employed Americans increasing by 53% since 1970. Until 1970, the number of self-employed Americans had been decreasing, largely due to the decline of the small farm.

• Today there are some 20 million small businesses in America, most of which are sole proprietorships or partnerships. The nation's 14.5 million sole proprietorships had $611 billion in receipts in 1987.

• Another indication of a growing entrepreneurial spirit is the fact that more businesses than ever before are being started. The number of businesses incorporated every year has more than doubled since 1975. Dun & Bradstreet estimates that 675,565 new corporations were created in 1989, up from only 264,209 in 1975.

• These new businesses are one of the most dynamic sectors of the economy, producing more jobs and wealth. For example, small businesses that employ fewer than 100 people are creating jobs faster than larger businesses. Between 1976 and 1986, small businesses with fewer than 100 employees increased their payrolls by 43%, and businesses with under 500 employees increased their employees by 57%. In contrast, employment at firms with more than 500 employees grew by about 42%.

• Today about 55% of Americans are employed in industries dominated by small companies (trucking, restaurants, construction, etc.). Moreover, employment in industries dominated by small business has grown much faster than industries where firms tend to be large, such as the auto and steel industries. In 1988, small business–dominated industries increased their payrolls by 3.2%, much faster than the 1.4% increase in sectors of the economy dominated by large companies.

• Presidents of small and medium-sized companies earn modest salaries and bonuses compared to the top executives in large companies. The average compensation for presidents of small businesses employing fewer than 250 employees is $75,650. The average compensation for presidents of companies with revenues under $1 million is $76,000; it is $102,000 for presidents of companies with $1 million to $2 million in revenues; $151,000 for presidents of companies in the $2 million to $5 million class; and $173,000 for presidents of companies earning $5 million to $10 million. In contrast, CEOs of companies with sales over $6 billion have an average annual compensation of over $1.2 million.

• For statistical purposes, the federal government defines a small business as one that employs fewer than 500 people. Most small businesses are partnerships or sole proprietorships, but they can also be corporations. Except where otherwise noted, we have followed the federal government's definition.

THE STATE OF SMALL BUSINESS

The 1980s was the decade of the entrepreneur. Dun & Bradstreet estimates that 676,565 new businesses were incorporated in 1989, up from 662,047 in 1985, 533,520 in 1980, and 264,209 in 1970. The economic record of the last 10 years also illustrates that bigger is not necessarily better, at least in terms of putting people to work. The number of self-employed Americans has been growing faster than wage- and salary-paying employment. Moreover, the Small Business Administration estimates that small businesses have been creating jobs faster than bigger companies. Between 1976 and 1982, firms employing fewer than 20 people created 38.5% of all new jobs, while firms employing fewer than 100 people created over half (52.6%) of all new jobs. During the economic slowdown between 1980 and 1982, small firms with fewer than 20 employees created over 2.3 million jobs, or about 232% of all the new jobs during those recession years! In contrast, firms with more than 500 employees lost 900,000 jobs!

Between 1976 and 1986, employment at small businesses with fewer than 100 employees grew by 43%, and businesses with under 500 employees increased their employees by 57%. But at the same time, firms with more than 500 employees increased their payrolls only about 42%.

Today about 55% of Americans hold jobs in industries dominated by small companies, such as trucking, restaurants, and construction. And in industries dominated by small business, employment has grown much faster than in industries where firms tend to be large, such as the auto and steel industries. Small business–dominated industries increased their payrolls in 1989 by 3.2%, a significantly greater rate than the 1.4% increase in sectors of the economy dominated by large companies.

But if small businesses are becoming one of the most dynamic sectors of the economy, government statisticians don't pay them a lot of attention. Most statistics for small businesses date from 1987, and even those data are wildly inconsistent. The U.S. Labor Department notes that there were about 8.8 million self-employed people in 1990. But business filed 20 million tax returns with the IRS, and the Small Business Administration estimates that nearly all of them were filed by small businesses, typically by small corporations, sole proprietorships or partnerships. In 1987 about 6.7 million of the nation's 13 million sole proprietorships had sales under $10,000. Only 42,800 sole proprietorships (0.3%) had sales over $1 million.

A 1987 study of small businesses done by Sheldon Haber, Enrique Lamas, and Jules Lichtenstein estimates that there were 12.84 million business owners and some 13.53 million businesses. There were 8.77 million male entrepreneurs who owned 9.15 million businesses and 4.17 million women business owners who ran 4.38 million firms. Just to put those numbers in perspective: about 11.9% of all Americans working outside agriculture own a business. About 9.5% of all male workers operate a business full-time; 3.2% of all women have a full-time business.

About 65.3% of all male business owners operate their businesses full-time, compared to 37% of all female business owners. And, as you might guess from the large number of part-time businesses, the median earnings for small businesses are, well, small. Male business owners earned $14,787 and females earned $4,894. Men who ran their businesses as side operations to supplement income from other jobs had median earnings of $4,784 while male entrepreneurs who worked full-time at their businesses earned $15,600. The average man who worked full-time and had a business that was large enough to support a full-time employee earned even more, $20,039. In contrast, the average woman owner who was substantially engaged in running a business earned only $4,894 and the average woman owner who had a full-time employee earned $12,079.

Overall, about 28.5 million business owners, paid and unpaid family members, and paid employees work in privately held companies. That's about 36.6% of everyone who works in the private sector. Just as a point of comparison, the 500 largest industrial corporations employ about 14 million people.

But despite the resurgence of small business and its economic importance, there is little reason to believe that the U.S. economy is on its way back to the good old days of mom-and-pop stores and small factories. Nationwide statistics indicate that the business of America is still big business. As mentioned above, over half of America's 13 million sole proprietorships are very small businesses indeed, with under $10,000 a year in sales. IRS statistics indicate that smaller corporations with sales under $1 million a year make up 84% of the country's corporations. Yet smaller corporations bring in only $590 billion in sales, about 7% of the total corporate receipts.

Similarly, in 1987, the most recent year for which comparable statistics are available, the *Fortune* 500 had $1,879.5 trillion in sales while the nation's 1.6 million partnerships had only $578 billion in sales. That same year, nonfarm sole proprietorships totaled 13.1 million, but they had $611 billion in business receipts, less than a third of the receipts of the 500 largest industrial corporations. All the partnerships in the U.S. had assets of $1.3 trillion while the 500 largest corporations had $1.7 trillion in assets.

In 1988, the nation's manufacturing corporations had $2.4 trillion in total assets. About 70% of those assets were controlled by corporations with more than $1 billion in assets; only 6% of all assets were controlled by small-er corporations with less than $10 million in assets. These smaller manufac-turing corporations earned $11.4 billion in profits, about 7% of the $154.9 billion in profits earned by all manufacturing corporations. Corporations with $1 billion or more in assets earned $112.4 billion, 73% of all manufac-turing profits.

Small-business owners also face huge risks. New businesses are opening at record rates, but they're also going out of business at an alarming rate. Busi-ness failures grew from 11,742 in 1980 to 57,067 in 1985 and 61,183 in 1986. The failure rate per 10,000 business skyrocketed from 36 in 1973 to 120 in 1986. The number of failures fell to 49,719 in 1989, and the failure rate has since declined to about 98 per 10,000. But an economic slowdown in 1990, which boosted the number of failures to 60,409, and a credit crunch in the banking industry are expected to boost the rate of business failures back to record levels in 1991 and 1992. And these statistics understate the number of business failures. About 9 out of 10 businesses close their doors voluntarily without filing for bankruptcy and thus do not appear in Dun and Brad-street's statistics of business failures. About half (53%) of all new businesses go bankrupt within the first five years of operation, two thirds by the end of the seventh year, according to Dun & Bradstreet.

Studies indicate that about 90% of all businesses fail because of manageri-al inexperience or incompetence. Managerial problems result in inadequate sales in nearly 60% of failed businesses and in excessive operating expenses in another 30%. As these alarming statistics indicate, having a good idea isn't enough. You also need to know the basics of marketing, accounting, finance, and taxes to make your business survive over the long haul.

After all those dismal statistics on business failures, it's worth remember-ing that small businesses have done a remarkable job of adapting to a rapid-ly changing economy. In fact, they've responded faster to changes in the market than many larger firms. Take, for instance, deregulated industries such as the airlines, trucking, transportation, shipping, finance, and telecom-munications, to name a few. In these industries, government regulations tra-ditionally fixed rates, made it difficult for new firms to enter the industry, and generally restricted free-market competition. However, in the late 1970s and early 1980s Congress passed a series of laws that deregulated those industries and opened the way for renewed competition. Almost immediate-ly, small businesses responded to the challenge and the opportunities of a competitive marketplace. In the deregulated industries of financial services and transportation, new business starts increased by 12.3% between 1980 and 1984, faster than the 8.2% increase for the whole economy. The Small Business Administration estimates that most of those new business (84%) were small, with fewer than 500 employees.

Small businesses have also been on the cutting edge of developing new technology. Even though large companies spend most of the research and development money, small companies frequently offer the kind of entrepreneurial environment that allows them to produce more technologi-cal advances and innovations for their money, as the early years of Silicon

Valley confirmed. However, to quantify the ability of small and large companies to create technological advances, the SBA undertook a study of the various inventions that were marketed in 1982. To compare large and small companies, the SBA tallied the number of innovations made by firms employing fewer than 500 people and the innovations made by larger firms. The innovations rate (or the number of innovations for every million employees employed by small or larger businesses) was higher for small business. Small businesses produced 36.2 innovations for every million people employed; larger companies produced 31.0 innovations per million employees. That small business accounted for 16.8% more innovations is especially startling if you remember that larger firms spend 96% of the research and development money in the U.S.

The Small Business Administration hasn't updated that study, but the data point up an important lesson. During the 1980s, small businesses responded quicker to technological change and new markets than many of their larger competitors. As a result they produced more jobs and helped change the course of many industries. In the 1990s, an economic slowdown and difficulties in obtaining credit will hurt many small businesses. But for all the problems they face, their ability to adapt quickly to new economic conditions will be a key factor in America's ability to respond to foreign competition and rapidly changing international markets.

Table 14-1   Earnings of Small-Business Owners

This chart shows the median earnings of business owners. For example, it shows the median income for male business owners was $14,787 in 1983, the most recent year for which statistics are available.

(in thousands)

Category	Men	Women
Business owners, including owners of a side business	$14,787	$4,894
Owners of a side business	4,784	(1)
Business owners, excluding owners of a side business	15,600	4,894
Unincorporated business owners[2]	13,520	3,767
Sole proprietors	12,235	3,671
Partners[3]	20,216	(1)
Incorporated business owners[3]	24,012	9,302
Paid employees only	20,039	12,079

[1]Fewer than 50 observations.
[2]Excludes partners of noncasual businesses who could not be distinguished from incorporated owners of noncasual businesses.
[3]Excludes incorporated owners of noncasual businesses who could not be distinguished from partners of noncasual businesses.
Source: *Monthly Labor Review*, May 1987.

Table 14-2   Business Formation and Business Failure

This chart shows the country's rising entrepreneurial spirit, as well as the problems faced by many businesses. The chart lists the number of new business formations and the number of failures. The index on the left side of the chart shows that new businesses have recently been formed at record rates compared to earlier years. But the business failure rate per 10,000 businesses is also growing, skyrocketing from 27.8 businesses per 10,000 in 1979 to 98.0 in 1988.

				Business failures					
				Number of failures			Amount of current liabilities (millions of dollars)		
	Index of net business formation (1967 = 100)	New business incorporations (number)	Business failure rate		Liability size class			Liability size class	
Year				Total	Under $100,000	$100,000 and over	Total	Under $100,000	$100,000 and over
1945			4.2	809	759	50	30.2	11.4	18.8
1946		132,916	5.2	1,129	1,003	126	67.3	15.7	51.6
1947		112,897	14.3	3,474	3,103	371	204.6	63.7	140.9
1948	101.1	96,346	20.4	5,250	4,853	397	234.6	93.9	140.7
1949	83.7	85,640	34.4	9,246	8,708	538	306.1	161.4	146.7
1950	87.7	93,092	34.3	9,162	8,746	416	248.3	151.2	97.1
1951	86.7	83,778	30.7	8,058	7,626	432	259.5	131.6	128.0
1952	90.8	92,946	28.7	7,611	7,061	530	283.3	131.9	151.4
1953	89.7	102,706	33.2	8,862	8,075	787	394.2	167.5	226.6
1954	88.8	117,411	42.0	11,086	10,226	860	462.6	211.4	251.2
1955	96.6	139,915	41.6	10,969	10,113	856	449.4	206.4	243.0
1956	94.6	141,163	48.0	12,686	11,615	1,071	562.7	239.8	322.9
1957	90.3	137,112	51.7	13,739	12,547	1,192	615.3	267.1	348.2
1958	90.2	150,781	55.9	14,964	13,499	1,465	728.3	297.6	430.7
1959	97.9	193,067	51.8	14,053	12,707	1,346	692.8	278.9	413.9
1960	94.5	182,713	57.0	15,445	13,650	1,795	938.6	327.2	611.4
1961	90.8	181,535	64.4	17,075	15,006	2,069	1,090.1	370.1	720.0
1962	92.6	182,057	60.8	15,782	13,772	2,010	1,213.6	346.5	867.1
1963	94.4	186,404	56.3	14,374	12,192	2,182	1,352.6	321.0	1,031.6
1964	98.2	197,724	53.2	13,501	11,346	2,155	1,329.2	313.6	1,015.6
1965	99.8	203,897	53.3	13,514	11,340	2,174	1,321.7	321.7	1,000.0
1966	99.3	200,010	51.6	13,061	10,833	2,228	1,385.7	321.5	1,064.1
1967	100.0	206,569	49.0	12,364	10,144	2,220	1,265.2	297.9	967.3
1968	108.3	233,635	38.6	9,636	7,829	1,807	941.0	241.1	699.9
1969	115.8	274,267	37.3	9,154	7,192	1,962	1,142.1	231.3	910.8
1970	108.8	264,209	43.8	10,748	8,019	2,729	1,887.8	269.3	1,618.4
1971	111.1	287,577	41.7	10,326	7,611	2,715	1,916.9	271.3	1,645.6
1972	119.3	316,601	38.3	9,566	7,040	2,526	2,000.2	258.8	1,741.5
1973	119.1	329,358	36.4	9,345	6,627	2,718	2,298.6	235.6	2,063.0
1974	113.2	319,149	38.4	9,915	6,733	3,182	3,053.1	256.9	2,796.3
1975	109.9	326,345	42.6	11,432	7,504	3,928	4,380.2	298.6	4,081.6
1976	120.4	375,766	34.8	9,628	6,176	3,452	3,011.3	257.8	2,753.4
1977	130.8	436,170	28.4	7,919	4,861	3,058	3,095.3	208.3	2,887.0
1978	138.1	478,019	23.9	6,619	3,712	2,907	2,656.0	164.7	2,491.3
1979	138.3	524,565	27.8	7,564	3,930	3,634	2,667.4	179.9	2,487.5
1980	129.9	533,520	42.1	11,742	5,682	6,060	4,635.1	272.5	4,362.6
1981	124.8	581,242	61.3	16,794	8,233	8,561	6,955.2	405.8	6,549.3
1982	116.4	566,942	89.0	24,908	11,509	13,399	15,610.8	541.7	15,069.1
1983	117.5	600,400	110.0	31,334	15,509	15,825	16,072.9	635.1	15,437.8
1984	121.3	634,991	107.0	52,078	19,618	32,460	29,268.6	409.8	28,858.8
1985	120.9	662,047	115.0	57,253	36,551	20,702	36,808.8	790.8	36,018.0
1986	120.4	702,738	120.0	61,616	38,908	22,708	44,724.0	838.3	43,885.7
1987	121.2	685,572	102.0	61,622	39,372	22,250	36,369.9	753.6	35,616.3
1988	124.1	685,095	98.0	57,097	38,300	18,797	39,573.0	686.9	38,886.1
1989	124.8	676,565	65.0	50,361	33,304	17,057	42,797.5	670.6	42,126.9
1990ᵖ	120.7			60,409	40,401	20,008	65,303.3	727.7	64,575.6

ᵖPreliminary figures.
Sources: Department of Commerce (Bureau of Economic Analysis) and The Dun & Bradstreet Corporation.

Table 14-3 Big Business and Small Business

The following chart shows the structure of the U.S. economy. It shows, for example, that large firms with over 500 employees account for only 0.2% of all businesses but earn 65.1% of all net incomes.

(percentages)

| | | | **Employment size of business** | | | | |
	Total	1–19	20–99	Under 100	100–499	Under 500	500 or more
Firms	100	88	10.5	98.5	1.3	99.8	0.2
Employees	100	21	20	41	12	53	47
Receipts	100	17	16	33	12	45	55
Assets	100	9	13	22	13	35	65
Net income	100	16.5	10.2	26.7	8.2	34.9	65.1

Source: U.S. Small Business Administration, *The State of Small Business: A Report of the President, 1986.*

Chapter Fifteen

CRIME: OFFERS SOME CAN'T REFUSE

HIGHLIGHTS AND TRENDS

• Rising street crime forces taxpayers to spend $45 billion a year on the criminal justice system and another $21 billion on private security measures. Even so, the average American stands an 83% chance of being a victim of a violent crime during his or her life.

• Worldwide, the U.S. State Department estimates that the illegal drug industry has $300 billion in sales and about $240 billion in profits.

• Employee theft and shoplifting cost stores as much as $27 billion a year. Surveys indicate that about 43% of lost inventory is due to employee theft, 30% to shoplifting, 23% to poor paperwork control, and 4% to vendor theft. These losses force retailers to spend about 0.42% of sales revenues on security.

• The so-called underground economy, made up of untaxed legal and illegal income, might be as large as 10% of GNP, or about $550 billion.

• In contrast to the few hundred dollars a mugger might steal in a night of violence, organized crime pulls in about $50 billion a year, according to a 1986 study by the President's Commission on Organized Crime.

• Estimates of white-collar crime range from $40 billion a year to over $100 billion.

THE BUSINESS OF CRIME

The 19th-century French novelist Honoré de Balzac once claimed that behind every fortune there was a crime. And, although there is little evidence to suggest that most businesses or individuals are dangerously or systematically dishonest, crime has always been a very important, though poorly understood, part of the economy. As early as the 18th century,

Americans considered smuggling and tax evasion to be legitimate enterprises, almost patriotic duties. This tradition continued in the 19th century,
when American merchants profited from the booming Chinese opium trade,
and on a more popular level in the 1920s, when millions ignored Prohibition.
In the Roaring '80s, some 10% to 25% of the population admitted to using
drugs on the job; another 25% to cheating on their taxes.

All of this is part of the economy of crime, a booming underground marketplace whose dimensions and effects remain obscure. Individually, crooks
may be deviant characters, violent, unpredictable, and even colorful. But as
a group, the elements that make up booming underground economy of
crime adhere quite closely to the laws of the marketplace. As in other businesses, they try to capitalize on technological change. (A revolution in the
international financial system during the 1980s offered people like Ivan
Boesky and Dennis Levine new ways to profit from securities fraud and
insider trading.) They must obey the laws of supply and demand (a glut of
cocaine during the mid-1980s cut the wholesale price of cocaine in half) and
fight foreign competitors (the New York Mafia, which once had a virtual
monopoly over the city's lucrative $15 billion to $25 billion drug trade, has
now lost 60% of the heroin market place to Asian organized crime groups).

In fact, the business of crime in the 1990s is adapting to many of the same
trends that are reshaping the face of the American economy. More than
ever before, crime is a global business, linking street addicts in American
cities with peasants in Bolivia and bankers in Switzerland. It is a big business, with only four cartels supplying virtually all the cocaine that reaches
America, and increasingly a high-tech business, in which crooks use computers to steal trade secrets and launder money. Not surprisingly, many of the
most successful entrepreneurs in the business of crime are experts in government regulation and high finance who use foreign financial markets and
bank secrecy laws in offshore havens to avoid taxes, carry out complex
investment scams, and launder drug money. What follows is a survey of that
business, from crime in the streets to crime in the suites.

Crime in the Streets

The odds of living a crime-free life are not good. In an average year, over 35
million crimes are committed in the United States, including 4.5 million
assaults, 141,000 rapes, and over 20,000 murders: about one killing in every
25 minutes. Contrary to popular belief, most of these slayings are not just
random acts of violence. The largest number of murders are committed by
acquaintances (35%), friends or lovers (11.3%), or spouses (9.3%). Only
23.3% are committed by strangers.

Over time, these numbers add up to some frightening statistics. Americans stand an 83% chance of being a victim of a violent crime at some point
in their lives; 52% will be victimized more than once, according to a 1987
Justice Department study. As noted, chances for Americans to be murdered
are quite high: 1 in 133. About three quarters of all Americans (74%) will be
victims of an assault or attempted assault, 40% will be injured by a robber or

assailant, and 99% will be victims of a theft. Rapists will rape or try to rape one of every 12 women. Three out of every four houses will be burglarized during a 20-year period. One in five households will have its car stolen during a 20-year period.

Not surprisingly, given these numbers, state, local, and federal government agencies spend more than $45 billion a year on the criminal justice system, which includes more than 17,000 police departments, 1.4 million employees, and a prison system that holds over 676,000 inmates. Private business and individuals spend another $21 billion to stop crime.

Drug Abuse

A major factor in the increase in street crime has been drug abuse. The use of drugs such as marijuana, cocaine, and heroin has skyrocketed in the last 20 years. Government statistics show that 54% to 82% of all men arrested for serious crimes in 14 major cities tested positive for drug use. San Diego had the highest level of crooks using drugs (82%), followed by Philadelphia (80%), New York (78%), and Chicago (78%). Even in Kansas City, which had the best record, over half of all those arrested (54%) tested positive. And government studies indicate the problem is getting worse. About 18% of those arrested in Washington, D.C. tested positive for cocaine in 1983; today, 62% have cocaine in their bloodstream.

Overall, rising drug-related crimes reflect the growing business of selling illegal drugs. The House Select Committee on Narcotics estimates that the drug trade has been increasing by $10 billion a year since 1979.

About 20 million people use marijuana regularly; between 5 and 6 million people use cocaine regularly; a half-million are addicted to heroin. In addition, about 15 million people are addicted to alcohol, according to the National Institute on Alcohol Abuse and Alcoholism.

But there is a lot of evidence to suggest that drug abuse may be falling. The percentage of high school students who had tried an illegal drug increased from 55.2% in the late 1970s to 65.6% in 1981. Since then, however, the news has improved. Today, about 50.9% have tried marijuana, cocaine, or another drug during the past year. Moreover, the number of current users of marijuana aged 18 to 25 declined from 25.2% in 1974 to 15.5% in the late 1980s. Young cocaine users also declined from 2.5% to 1.9%, but heroin users increased from 3.1% to 4.5%.

Still, the international drug cartels can count on a huge market for their products. About 30% of adults over the age of 26 say they have used marijuana, 6.6% have used hallucinogens, 9.9% have used cocaine, 1.1% have used heroin, and a whopping 88.6% have used alcohol.

Drugs on the Job

As one might expect, the growth of the illegal drug industry has spilled out of the streets into the workplace. Various studies estimate that 10% to 25% of the work force has abused drugs on the job, and a 1990 federal government study estimates that the cost of drug abuse tops $60 billion a year. That makes drug abuse one of the most expensive health hazards in America. By way of comparison, the American Cancer Society estimates that cancer costs about $70 billion a year.

But private estimates of the cost of drug abuse are even higher, up to $100 billion. These studies point out that drug users are three times more likely to be injured on the job and that drug abuse has been associated with some major accidents. Since 1975, about 50 train wrecks and accidents, which resulted in 37 deaths, 80 injuries, and $34 million worth of damages, were attributable to drug or alcohol abuse.

To avoid higher costs of health insurance and job-related accidents, many employers have resorted to drug testing. The U.S. Department of Labor estimates that about 3.9 million job applicants each year are tested for drugs and that about 50% of all Fortune 500 corporations have drug-testing programs. The retail industry, where 24.4% of all job applicants tested positive, had the highest incidence of drug abuse, followed by wholesale (17.4%), mining (12.7%), nondurable goods (12.7%), construction (11.9%), durable goods (11.2%), transportation (9.9%), miscellaneous services (9.9%), finance, insurance, and real estate (6.7%), and communications and utilities (5.5%). Overall, it's believed that nearly 20 million employees used drugs on a regular basis.

But drug-testing programs have come under fire, often because of inaccurate drug tests. Critics note that in 1984 the Army admitted it had mishandled half of the 60,000 tests it had given; others attack the growth of drug tests as an unconstitutional invasion of privacy. "Trying to stop organized crime's multimillion-dollar drug business by creating a police state in federal office buildings would be virtually ineffective and would create one crime to stop another," Representative Charles Schumer of New York says.

Widespread drug abuse has forced employers to spend more money on drug treatment programs. One study by the U.S. Bureau of Labor Statistics of 84 million workers estimates that companies employing 20 million workers offer some form of assistance for drug problems, triple the number that were offered in 1983.

But despite all that has been said and written about cocaine, crack, and heroin, alcoholism remains the most costly addiction in America. Health problems and lost productivity caused by alcoholism cost the economy $117 billion a year. It's believed that alcohol causes about 105,000 deaths a year, including 20,282 from auto accidents and over 57,000 from cirrhosis of the liver and other diseases.

The Worldwide Drug Trade

Over the past 20 years, the U.S., Europe, and other developed countries have been inundated by a flood of illegal drugs. There was heroin and opium from Afghanistan, Iran, Mexico, and the Golden Triangle (parts of Thailand, Burma, and Laos); cocaine from Colombia, Peru, and Bolivia; marijuana from the Caribbean, Mexico, Asia, and Africa. The exact dimensions of this traffic remains obscure, but the U.S. State Department estimates that the worldwide drug trade produces over $300 billion a year in revenues and nearly $240 billion in profits.

Those involved don't always live up to the stereotypes of a street junkie or Mafia thug. In Bolivia, where 32,000 to 38,000 hectares are used to produce cocaine, the drug traffic is so lucrative that two military coups in the early 1980s have been indirectly traced to feuds over cocaine profits. In Afghanistan, one of the world's largest opium and heroin producers, the tribesmen used the profits of their trade to fight the Soviet army. "We must grow and sell opium to fight our holy war against the Russian nonbelievers," the brother of a leading rebel commander and a major owner of opium fields told *The New York Times*. And here at home, the traffic has even corrupted some straitlaced bankers. In 1990, several top executives at BCCI, the world's 9th largest private bank, were convicted of laundering millions of dollars in drug profits for cocaine smugglers and deposed Panamanian dictator Colonel Manuel Noriega. Worldwide, the DEA estimates that banks launder nearly $300 billion a year in drug money.

But even the drug business can't escape the laws of supply and demand. Increased demand, as previously noted, undoubtedly caused many countries to increase their production. But increased demand was only part of the story. In a good example of how supply-side economics works, problems in the third world also helped increased drug production. International experts on the drug economy say it's no accident that drug production skyrocketed in the 1970s and early 1980s, as prices for basic agricultural commodities and metals fell on the world market, destroying the economies of many third world countries. As prices for Colombian coffee fell over 33% and Peruvian copper dropped 50% between 1980 and 1986, cocaine production in these countries doubled and then tripled. Soon, revenues from drugs became one of the few growth industries in the third world. Countries with some of the worst economic problems—Mexico, Colombia, Peru, and Bolivia—became some of the largest drug producers. Eduardo Crawley, editor of *Latin American Newsletters,* notes that Peru gets about $1.3 billion to $2.8 billion a year in export earnings, while Colombia ends up with $7 billion to $15 billion in net profits.

Increasingly, these operations have taken on the attributes of a large-scale multinational company, in which the agricultural workers on the bottom make low wages and the executives at the top earn huge profits. The average peasant, who gets only $2.10 for a kilogram of coca leaves, makes no more than $1,000 a year, while a top-level wholesaler can get $20,000 for a kilo, producing $75 billion to $110 billion in worldwide sales for the top four Colombian cartels. Moreover, like the late Ferdinand Marcos and other rich third world leaders who transfer billions into Swiss bank accounts, the wealthy cocaine executives move about 90% of their revenues out of the third world into the offshore banking system.

Like copper, coffee, and other third world industries, the drug cartels are also battling a chronic problem of overproduction. Demand for drugs in the U.S. slowed after 1982, but more and more drugs continued to pour across the border. Naturally, that forced dealers to cut prices and increase the purity of the drugs they sold—a fact that explains the introduction of more potent forms of cocaine like crack. Today, the wholesale price of a kilo of cocaine is about half what it was in the early 1980s.

The result: a good old-fashioned shakeout in the drug market. As major producers slashed prices, small fry were forced out of business, unable to afford the expensive arms and political protection it now takes to run an international drug cartel. In Colombia, for example, there were hundreds of small cocaine producers and smugglers in the 1960s. But in the 1980s, the cost of protection and the need to control a huge smuggling ring forced over 250 small drug-producing family enterprises to combine into one major cartel, the Medellin cartel. Today, the DEA claims that most of the 200 Colombian groups that distribute most of the cocaine in America are associated with the four main cartels, the Cali, Medellin, Bogota, and North Atlantic Coast. These groups now produce so much cocaine that David Westrate, assistant administrator of the Drug Enforcement Administration, says they have been forced to expand into Europe and are now "showing interest in Japan."

Meanwhile, oversupply and increased competition have forced American dealers to resort to even more violent methods of protecting their markets. Hence, a dramatic rise in violent gangland wars and a booming market for semi-automatic weapons. Just as high unemployment rates in many Latin American countries forced millions of Hispanics to migrate illegally to the U.S., economic problems in the third world have spilled over into the streets of America.

Still, drug dealers aren't going into Chapter 11. When the DEA cracked down on the export of chemicals needed to refine coca leaves into cocaine, the cartel built its own chemical-processing plants and established sophisticated techniques for buying chemicals on the black markets. Similarly, the Colombian cartels now operate as sophisticated multinational organizations, with a complex division of labor. Miami-based IRS agents say the cartels have hired specialists in money laundering and separated their banking operations from their smuggling and distribution subsidiaries. That way, the police won't be able to get at cartel bank accounts when they arrest a dealer or smuggler.

Of course, Peruvian peasants aren't the only farmers looking for a way to end their economic woes. One prominent Montana rancher and former Republic state committeeman turned to pot farming when he was unable to pay off $2 million in farm loans. After spending $200 cultivating each plant, he was able to sell the pot it produced for over $4,000. He told CBS News that he would have been able to pay off all his debts in two years if he hadn't been caught. Lured by similar profits, U.S. marijuana farmers now produce nearly 5,100 tons of pot each year, up 50% since 1981. In the nation's agribusiness center, marijuana is the largest cash crop. In California 5.6 million cultivated cannabis plants weighing 2,548 tons were destroyed. About 5,737 pot farmers were arrested in 1989, up from 4,941 in 1984.

Drug factories are also popping up all over the country. Traditionally, illicit drugs such as cocaine and heroin were manufactured abroad because it was too difficult to smuggle the bulky raw materials into the country. It takes about 500 kilograms of dry coca leaf to produce one kilogram of cocaine HCl. But that way of doing business is changing as more drugs are grown in the U.S. and it becomes harder to smuggle drugs into the U.S. In 1985 police discovered one laboratory in upstate New York that was equipped to produce 1,000 pounds of cocaine a week from partially processed leaves, enough to supply about a third of the U.S. market. The police have also uncovered a $225-million-a-year heroin factory in Arizona, the first one ever found in the U.S. A sign of that trend is that the number of drug labs seized by federal authorities increased from 226 in 1983 to 810 in 1988.

Solutions to the problem are not easy. Even without high-level government corruption, Latin American and Asian countries would still have trouble stopping the drug trade. Because those countries are faced with huge foreign debts, crops such as opium, cocaine, and marijuana (in the case of Jamaica) play an important role in keeping them solvent on the international market and in paying for badly needed imports. After years of paying little attention to the problem of laundering money through the international financial system, U.S. authorities finally made it one of their top priorities in the 1980s. Agreements were signed with several notorious centers for laundering drug profits, including Switzerland and Panama, so that U.S. investigators can get some information on numbered accounts used to launder drug profits. But much more needs to be done in this area, as drug dealers have moved their banking to offshore havens that have maintained tight secrecy rules. Worse from the standpoint of enforcement, havens like Switzerland that opened their books during the late 1980s for drug investigations still won't provide information for prosecuting tax-evasion cases, the easiest way to convict top-level smugglers. Finally, on the lowest level of the international drug trade, far away from the powerful cocaine generals and the illicit drugs-for-arms deals, are the poor Asian and Latin American peasants who grow the crops. Opium and cocaine provide them with far more income than any other cash crop, especially on the currently depressed international market for commodities. Any plan to curb the international drug trade must provide them with an equally lucrative way of making a living.

Table 15-1 provides a survey of this huge business, based upon information culled from several government agencies. It lists the leading producers of various kinds of drugs and their market share, revenues, profit margins, and profits, wherever such information is available.

Table 15-1 The Illegal Drug Market

TOTAL DRUG REVENUES

Worldwide revenues	Worldwide profits	U.S. revenues
$300,000,000,000	$240,000,000,000	$150,000,000,000

Profit margins

Over 90%

The value of a pound of cocaine increases four to five times from the time it moves from the foreign wholesale market to the time it reaches the domestic wholesale market, adding $1.6 billion in value to the product.

The value of total marijuana production increases by about $6 billion as it moves from foreign to domestic wholesalers.

Heroin increases some 30 to 40 times in value as it moves from the foreign to the domestic wholesale market.

Cost of fighting drug smuggling

$7.6 billion in U.S. government spending and over $60 billion in health care and lost productivity

Why it's so hard to stop drug smuggling

Each year 25 million passengers enter the U.S. on commercial airlines; 115 million people come into the U.S. from the Mexican border; 48,000 commercial vessels landed in U.S. ports; 100 million letters and parcels enter the U.S. from overseas.

THE MARIJUANA MARKET

Revenues from the sale of marijuana

$10 billion–$33 billion

Americans who used marijuana at least once in the past month

1982	1989
20.0 million	18 million

Marijuana prices

	1983	1985	1989
Commercial-grade			
Wholesale (pound)	$350–600	$300–600	$300–2,800
Retail (ounce)	$40–65	$50–100	$20–250
Sinsemilla			
Wholesale (pound)	$1,000–2,000	$1,200–2,000	$700–4,000
Retail (ounce)	$100–150	$120–200	$100–$600

Marijuana growers

	Quantity (metric tons)		
	1984	1986	1989
Domestic growers	1,700	2,100	5,000
Mexico	2,500–3,000	3,000–4,000	49,590
Colombia	4,100–7,500	2,200–3,900	2,800
Jamaica	1,500–2,250	1,100–1,700	190
Belize	1,100	500	66

Table 15-1   The Illegal Drug Market (continued)

THE COCAINE MARKET

Revenues from the sale of cocaine

$76 billion–$181 billion.

U.S. cocaine consumption (pounds)

1982	1985
68,355	159,422 (+133%)

Americans who used cocaine at least once in the past month

1982	1989
4.2 million	5.8 million

Cocaine prices

	1983	1986	1989	1990
Wholesale (kilogram)	$45,000–55,000	$22,000–45,000	$18,000–25,000	$20,000–35,000
Retail (gram)	$100–125	$80–120	$60+	NA

Cocaine growers

While Peru produced more of the coca leaf used to process cocaine in 1989, Colombia continued to dominate the final stage of cocaine production and supplied about 75% of the cocaine reaching the U.S. market, compared to 5% for Peru. It takes about 500 kilograms of dry leaf to produce one kilogram of cocaine.

Country	Coca leaf produced (metric tons) 1989	Net Export earnings
Peru	124,408	$1.3–2.8 billion
Bolivia	65,998	1.4–2 billion
Colombia	33,487	7–15 billion
Ecuador	270	NA

THE MARKET FOR HEROIN AND OPIATES

Revenues from the sale of heroin

$14–30 billion

Foreign wholesale price (pound), 1989.	$11,000
Domestic wholesale price (pound), 1989.	$150,000–$170,000
Domestic retail price (pound), 1989.	$2,300,000

Opium production (metric tons)

Country	1983	1986	1989
Afghanistan	400–575	500–800	585
Iran	400–600	200–400	300
Pakistan	45–60	140–160	130
Mexico	17	20–40	85
Myanmar	600	700–1,100	2,625
Thailand	35	20–25	50
Laos	35	100–290	85

Table 15-1   The Illegal Drug Market (continued)

Heroin and opium addicts, here and in the countries that produce opiates

U.S.	600,000 heroin addicts
Thailand	300,000–500,000 opium and heroin addicts
Pakistan	400,000–500,000 heroin addicts
India	500,000 heroin addicts
India	500,000 chronic opium users
Iran	100,000 heroin addicts and 500,000 opium users
Afghanistan	100,000–125,000 chronic opium users
Malaysia	250,000–350,000 heroin addicts
Hong Kong	50,000 heroin addicts

THE HASHISH MARKET

	Production in major source countries (metric tons)		Market share, 1985 and 1986
	1984	1986	
Lebanon	350–400	600	25–30%
Afghanistan	200–400	200–400	Pakistan/Afghanistan:
Pakistan	200	200	
			60–65%
Morocco	60–225	30–60	5%
Total	810–1,225	1,030–1,260	

Sources: National Institute on Drug Abuse, National Narcotics Intelligence Consumers Committee, Drug Enforcement Administration; U.S. Congress, Office of Technology Assessment, U.S. Department of State.

Employee Theft and Shoplifting

Few crimes hit retailers harder than employee theft and shoplifting. Employee theft and shoplifting produce a sea of red ink. The U.S. Commerce Department estimates that employee theft costs American business about $40 billion a year, while the National Institute of Justice puts the loss at $5 billion to $10 billion.

Today, shoplifting costs U.S. retailers about $27 billion a year, or as much as 2% of their sales. To stop the losses, the retail industry spends about half a billion a year on security. Surveys indicate that about 43% of lost inventory is due to employee theft, 30% to shoplifting, 23% to poor paperwork control, and 4% to vendor theft.

The Underground Economy

There is a vast economy that is not mentioned in government statistics—the underground economy. The very name sounds mysterious, like a secret criminal society, but a large part of the underground economy is really quite mundane. What economists mean by the underground economy is simply income that should be taxed but isn't. This income comes from two sources. Part of the underground economy is money from criminal activities such as drugs, loan-sharking, or numbers rackets and the rest is legitimate income such as wages and tips that isn't reported on tax returns.

James O'Leary at the U.S. Trust Co. believes that the underground economy is a growth industry. His self-described "guesstimates" of the underground economy suggest that it grew from about 5.7% of disposable income (about $52.5 billion) in the early 1970s to a whopping 21% of disposable income—about $558.4 billion in 1984. Since then, other estimates have pegged the underground economy at anywhere from 10% to 20% of the GNP, or between $550 billion and $1.1 trillion dollars.

The IRS comes up with somewhat different figures, but agrees that the underground economy is one of the fastest growing parts of American business. In 1965, the IRS believed that about $15.5 billion worth of taxes weren't paid each year. By 1982, the IRS estimated that Americans failed to report about $260 billion worth of income, thus avoiding $86.3 billion in taxes. More recently, IRS Commissioner Fred T. Goldberg said tax fraud totaled $100 billion in 1990 and could hit $110.1 billion to $127 billion in 1992. In 1987, the IRS believed that some of the biggest tax cheats were small businesses. Sole proprietorships, it was alleged, underpaid their federal taxes by about 23%, costing the government $16.6 billion. Large corporations reportedly avoided about $15.8 billion, while small corporations were said to have underpaid their taxes by $5.2 billion. Other private studies, however, actually place the tax gap much higher. If you include state and local taxes, tax fraud in America may top $200 billion a year.

Most studies suggest that the largest part of the underground economy is legitimate income that is hidden from the tax collector. This income comes from such mundane sources as unreported tips, profits, capital gains, and even state income tax refunds that were not reported to the government. But all of this tax fraud adds up. About 50% to 75% of the underground economy is legitimate income that was not reported to the IRS. The illegal part of the underground economy—income from drugs, prostitution, illegal gambling, etc.—accounts for the rest.

Organized Crime

Just as big business took over many major industries in the early 20th century, organized crime has moved into the most lucrative areas of criminal activity—drug smuggling, gambling, racketeering, counterfeiting, and union corruption. Organized crime doesn't publish an annual report and estimates of its income vary widely, but profits for the American and Sicilian Mafia may total as much as $170 billion a year.

The rise of modern American organized crime can be traced to the prohibition against alcohol in the 1920s, when mobsters began setting up the first modern criminal organizations. At that time, the Italian Mafia was somewhat moribund. Its leadership responded to Prohibition with the same lack of imagination many established corporations show when faced with major economic changes. In the immigrant ghettos around the country, there had always been people who made their own wine, beer, and distilled liquor. So the older generation of mobsters simply expanded on this cottage industry, producing the proverbial bathtub gin.

Lucky Luciano, Meyer Lansky, and Arnold Rothstein (whom baseball fans know as the gambler who attempted to fix the 1919 World Series) realized there was a better way. They openly derided the Mafia's old-world methods, and applied modern American know-how to the business of crime. Like good business executives, they recognized the importance of understanding the market and the American consumer. So, taking a page from marketing specialists, Rothstein decided they should target upscale consumers, who could pay high prices and afford to visit mob-owned speakeasies.

But Rothstein knew that upscale consumers would not pay top prices for bathtub gin. So he decided to import real liquor. Rothstein and his partners bought English companies and arranged to import Canadian whisky through Seagrams. They set up a vast importing and exporting company that was vertically and horizontally integrated, a kind of General Motors of crime. Like 19th-century robber barons, they ruthlessly expanded, constantly seeking economies of scale. If they needed to bottle more booze, they bought bottling plants and printing factories to produce counterfeit Seagrams labels. They acquired ships and warehouses, built hidden breweries, established connections with French Champagne producers, created a kind of headhunting outfit that recruited unemployed distillers, and even bought up distilleries in the U.S. that were producing legal alcohol for medical needs. They then had the legal distillers illegally increase production, bottling the surplus in the mob's bottling plants, fitting the bottles with counterfeit labels from the mob's printing factories, and shipping the goods through the mob's trucking fleet to the mob's speakeasies. Later, the money was moved overseas, where it could be used to buy still more booze.

"We became a big business corporation employing hundreds of people," Meyer Lansky remembered many years later. "I had to read lots of books about how to run such an organization. . . . We had to hire accountants and other administrators."

But the Rothstein organization wasn't the only gang to apply modern business methods to the rackets. During the 1920s, modern organized crime groups were also established in Chicago, Detroit, and a number of other major cities. Bloody gang wars frequently broke out between rival mobs, but by the late 1920s mob leaders realized the need for a nationwide crime syndicate. "We were in a business like the Ford Motor Company," Lansky explained. "Shooting and killing was an inefficient way of doing business. Ford salesmen don't shoot Chevrolet salesman."

After several faltering attempts in the late 1920s, a national syndicate was finally established in the early 1930s. It divided the country into territories, one for each family, much like a bottling franchise that gives a local bottler rights to produce and sell a soft drink inside its territory without competition from outside interests. Disputes were to be mediated by a national commission, thus avoiding the bloody gangland fights that had produced bad publicity and—worse—government investigations during the 1920s.

In the 1930s the mob also diversified into legitimate businesses with heavy investments in Las Vegas, Hollywood, and the garment and construction industries. And as the mob grew in size, it began to behave more and more like a multinational corporation. After a meeting with twenty other top mobsters who underwrote a chain of posh hotels for him in Cuba, Meyer Lansky offered Cuban dictator Fulgencio Batista a share of the profits. With Batista on the mob's payroll, the huge profits from the mob's gambling operations were not taxed.

Over time, the mob's growing financial size helped produce a division of labor in the top ranks. Just as modern corporations rely on executives with special expertise to head different subsidiaries, mobsters began specializing in labor racketeering, drugs, or political corruption. Frank Costello, for example, specialized in municipal graft, bribing congressmen, mayors, and cops to secure lucrative contracts or to protect the mob from government investigations. Others, such as Meyer Lansky, made most of their money as silent partners in legitimate businesses and casinos, while shunning more risky ventures like drug smuggling. Union graft was another popular specialty. By taking over Teamster locals in New Jersey, they were able to make millions by bilking truckers out of pension funds and signing "sweetheart contracts" that lowered wages in exchange for bribes and kickbacks.

As an enterprise, the development of a national syndicate and a nationwide industry had a number of advantages. Although bloody turf wars still broke out, they were never as violent as the gangland wars in the 1920s. The creation of a loosely organized national syndicate to mediate disputes also helped shape an enterprise in which local families established profitable niches and specialties—labor, municipal graft, loan sharking, drugs, money laundering, illegally dumping of toxic wastes—that did not compete with other families' activities. Over time, this division of areas made it easier to keep the peace.

The success of this organization created a kind of revolution in the business of crime. Just as a few huge corporations now dominate most major industries, organized crime developed a virtual monopoly over some of the most lucrative areas of criminal activity—drug smuggling, gambling, racketeering, counterfeiting, and union corruption. The mob doesn't file financial statements with the SEC, but a study by the WEFA Group for the President's Commission on Organized Crime in 1986 estimated that organized crime takes in at least $50 billion a year, or about 1.13% of U.S. gross national product. That means organized crime made as much money as all the U.S. metal producers (iron, steel, aluminum, copper, etc.) or America's textile and apparel industry. And organized crime is also a big employer. WEFA believes that organized crime groups employ at least "281,487 people as members and associates, with the estimated number of crime-related jobs ranging to over 520,000."

All these activities hit consumers right in the pocket. Various studies indicate that the cost of organized crime adds 2% to the cost of construction, warehousing, trucking, and waste hauling, about 1% to the price of clothes, 0.5% to prices in the wholesale and retail trade, and 0.2% to the cost of banking services and real estate.

These small percentage increases don't sound like much, but they add up. In New York, mob control of the concrete industry reportedly added $1.4 million to the cost of 26 construction jobs, including $184,000 to the cost of BankAmerica headquarters on 45th Street in Manhattan. Nationwide, U.S. citizens paid an estimated $6.5 billion in higher taxes to compensate for the fact that organized crime is so skillful at avoiding the IRS. The WEFA researchers estimated that as a result of increased taxes and higher prices caused by organized crime, the output of the U.S. economy was cut by $18.2 billion dollars. Over 400,000 jobs were lost, and consumer prices were 0.3% higher than was necessary. On a personal level, WEFA estimates the cost of organized crime reduces the income of the average American by $77 each year.

More recent estimates suggest that the profits are even bigger. The FBI says the mob earns $100 billion to $140 billion a year in profits. To launder this dirty money into legitimate assets, organized crime has bought banks, bribed bank employees, and used major securities firms like E.F. Hutton to launder billions of dollars. European investigators add that another $72 billion worth of profits from the Italian Mafia is laundered through European banks.

Table 15-2   The Mob's Marketplace

The chart below estimates the income of organized crime. The data column on the left shows the market share of organized crime in various industries, such as prostitution. The center column contains midrange estimates of total criminal receipts from each industry and the right column shows estimates of net income. Profits are very high because the profit margins on many of the mob's products and services are very high.

	Organized crime's share	Total criminal gross receipts (midrange) (millions of dollars)	Total criminal net income (midrange) (millions of dollars)
Heroin	100%	9.066	7.706
Cocaine	100%	13.046	12.552
Marijuana	100%	8.536	7.305
Loan-sharking	100%	7.015	7.015
Illegal gambling	42%	2.348	1.878
Prostitution	20%	3.332	2.665
Household and personal theft	20%	1.713	0.895
Shoplifting and employee theft	50%	4.879	3.049
Trucking cargo theft	100%	0.874	0.607
Air cargo theft	100%	0.041	0.035
Railroad cargo theft	100%	0.035	0.024
Bank robbery	0%	0.000	0.000
Business robbery	0%	0.000	0.000
Nonresidential burglary	0%	0.000	0.000
Fraud arson	50%	0.253	0.202
Bank embezzlement	0%	0.000	0.000
Counterfeiting	30%	0.020	0.018
Cigarette smuggling	100%	0.290	0.232
Total		51.449	44.185

Sources: THE WEFA GROUP, formerly Wharton Econometric Forecasting Associates, Inc., and President's Commission on Organized Crime, 1986.

During most of the 1980s, these huge profits brought the mob unwanted attention from government prosecutors and other organized crime groups. In 1984 alone, there were 3,118 indictments against organized crime figures, resulting in 2,194 convictions, with another 4,190 indictments in 1985 and 3,530 convictions or plea bargains. These cases resulted in $15 million worth of fines, and courts seized $387 million in contraband and assets.

This crackdown, which has put heads of crime families in New York, Kansas City, New Orleans, Milwaukee, and Cleveland behind bars, has hurt older families and will hasten a long-term shift in power from La Cosa Nostra and the Mafia to newer organized crime groups. Asian crime groups managed to capture about 60% of the heroin market, thanks in part to the sophisticated money-laundering operations they run out of Hong Kong, and the Colombians moved in on the cocaine trade. There have been signs in 1990 that the Mafia and the Colombians are increasingly working together. The Medellin Cartel, it seems, hope to use the Sicilian Mafia's expertise in the heroin trade to crack the lucrative European market.

At the same time, the mob, has pushed into new markets. During the 1980s, mob con artists set up scams that contributed to the collapse of 22 savings and loan associations. Even Wall Street wasn't safe. In one case, the so-called Euroscam affair, two colorful con artists with longstanding ties to New York and Las Vegas organized crime groups set up dozens of boiler rooms in America and Europe that bilked tens of thousands of investors out of over $1 billion.

In the 1990s, the rapidly changing structure of global finance and the prospect of European unification in 1992 offers even greater opportunities for financial crime. "We are about to see the golden age of Mafia Inc.," says Pino Arlacchi, a premier expert on Mafia finances. Already mob money has fueled rampant speculation on the Milan stock market and the mob has moved into the business of selling counterfeit securities. Even more worrisome, the mob's growing financial sophistication has allowed it more effectively to launder its dirty money into legitimate businesses. A 1989 Italian report says the huge profits from the mob's drug operations have bought tens of billions of dollars worth of companies, ranging from banks and movie studios to vineyards and securities firms.

Europeans worry that the mob's power over legitimate businesses and the financial system will become even larger after 1992, when European unification will end customs checks at borders and allow the mob to move money and goods easily throughout the European community. "The Mafia bosses in their dark double-breasted suits are getting ready for 1992," warned Carlo Azeglio Ciampi, head of Italy's central bank, in a 1989 report detailing the mob's growing economic clout.

Counterfeiting

Any mention of counterfeiting makes most people think of someone printing nice crisp currency. But counterfeit money is really small potatoes compared to the booming business of counterfeiting everything from Rubik's

Cubes to bootleg Bruce Springsteen tapes. The cost of counterfeited products to the economy range from the 1983 House Energy and Commerce Committee's estimate of $20 billion year to the estimate of $60 billion by the Counterfeit Intelligence Bureau in London. The U.S. International Trade Commission and the U.S. Chamber of Commerce say that counterfeiting costs U.S. business about $8 billion to $20 billion a year, up from only $3 billion in 1978. In contrast only about $90 million a year worth of counterfeit U.S. currency is seized each year.

Products routinely counterfeited are chemicals, computers, drugs, fertilizers, pesticides, medical devices, military hardware, foods, tape cassettes, Gucci shoes, and expensive watches. The Recording Industry Association of America says the U.S. music industry loses $300 million a year on illegal or counterfeit recordings, or about 7% of its sales. Organized crime operations earn nearly $750 million counterfeiting credit cards and have a major share of the $500-million-a-year industry in counterfeiting airline tickets.

Most counterfeit goods sold in the U.S. are produced overseas, especially in Asia; only about 20% of them are made in the U.S.A. Consumers who buy counterfeit goods often get stuck with shoddy goods, as anyone who has ever bought a bootleg album can tell you. In other cases counterfeit goods have posed a direct threat to the consumer's health. A million fake birth control pills hit the U.S. market in 1984, causing heavy bleeding in some women, and, in 1982, surgeons got a scare when a counterfeit and defective part was found in pumps used to keep hearts beating during open-heart surgery. In other cases, bogus parts have caused helicopter crashes, auto wrecks, and even construction accidents.

In the counterfeit-money business, foreign producers are starting to beat out U.S. counterfeiters with better quality and better business methods. Just as the Japanese have earned a reputation for producing better cars, the Italians now produce the best bogus bills. Their technique is simple. To get around the problem of imitating the paper used in U.S. currency, counterfeiters in Milan take a $1 bill, bleach it, and then print a $100 bill over it. Presto. A $99 profit.

Overseas counterfeiters also have better distribution networks and printing techniques, thanks to their experience in counterfeiting European currency that is multicolored and hence harder to duplicate. Already the flood of foreign counterfeit money is causing problems. Even though the Treasury Department has changed U.S. currency to make it harder to copy, some foreign banks will no longer change $100 bills. Government officials believe that U.S. crooks will fight back with a new generation of color photocopy machines. And if that fails? Well there's always protectionism and quotas. . . .

Credit-Card Fraud

A crime with a rosy future is credit-card fraud. As the economy shifts more and more toward a cashless society, credit-card fraud has skyrocketed, costing banks and consumers more than $700 million a year. Consumers are generally protected by a federal law that limits individual liability, but they eventually end up footing the bill through higher interest payments and annual credit-card fees.

Union Corruption

Union corruption illustrates how crime can tarnish the good name of an entire enterprise. Thanks to union corruption, a poll by the Conference Board found that only 12% of the American public thought unions were well managed—Congress and the Pentagon were the only two institutions to get lower ratings.

Of course, like most corporations, most unions are honest. Federal investigators estimate that organized crime influences only 400 of the 70,000 union locals in the U.S. But corrupt union leaders can earn big profits. The President's Commission on Organized Crime found that "organized crime can use unions in four principal ways: First, it can convert union resources—members' dues, union assets, or worker benefit funds—to its own use. Second, it can use unions to exact payoffs from businesses in the form of sweetheart contracts or strike insurance. Third, it can use the union as a way to influence an entire market. This last use may generate the kind of payoffs that come from the sweetheart deal or a strike insurance. Indeed, these rackets may be part of a general market corruption scheme. Finally, organized crime can use unions as a means of access to and protection from the political and governmental process."

Union corruption is heavily concentrated in only a few mob-dominated unions. The dubious distinction of being the nation's most corrupt union falls to the Teamsters, one of the nation's most politically powerful unions with 1.7 million members. Close behind them in racketeering, if not in size, are the Laborers' International Union of North America; the Hotel Employees and Restaurant Employees International Union; and the International Longshoremen's Association. According to the FBI, these unions are "substantially influenced and/or controlled by organized crime."

Analysts cite many reasons for the rise of corruption and organized crime influence in unions. One of the most important is that once mobsters and corrupt officials establish themselves in the ranks of a union bureaucracy, they are difficult to remove unless the union has a strong tradition of union democracy. As a result, unions with a strong commitment to union democracy, such as the United Auto Workers, have been free from the taint of corruption and organized crime ties; others, such as the Teamsters, with its history of corruption, keep a tight control over union members and allow little dissent. In the past, Teamsters dissidents have been beaten or threatened.

An equally important factor in union corruption and the influence of organized crime is simply the kind of marketplace in which a business or union operates. In trucking, restaurants, construction, shipping, and other industries dominated by small businesses, businesses and unions have been more vulnerable to racketeers. Unions have used racketeers to provide the muscle needed to control those anarchic industries while employers, being small and vulnerable, have been less able to resist the power of racketeers. Not surprisingly, the four most corrupt unions—the Teamsters, the International Longshoremen's Association, the Hotel Employees and Restaurant Employees International Union, and the Laborers' International Union (a construction-trades union)—are in those industries. In contrast, unions in large, established industries, such as the UAW and the Steel Workers, have been less vulnerable in part because of the size of the industries. Finally, unions in industries that rely on white-collar workers, such as airline pilots, have more sophisticated members and have been less vulnerable to racketeering.

Business itself has played an important role in the rise of union corruption by agreeing to do business with mobsters. In some cases, businesses have worked with mob-run unions to keep wages and benefits low. In the 1970s, the Teamsters allegedly negotiated favorable contracts—so-called sweetheart contracts—with dozens of companies that kept down wages in return for kickbacks to union leaders. In some cases, though, there is a fine line between businesses' sanctioning agreements that hurt their employees and businesses' being blackmailed into agreements that help only a few union bosses. In 1980, for example, Douglas LaChance, the president of the Newspaper and Mail Deliverers Union, was convicted of taking $330,000 in illegal payments to ensure labor peace.

Money Laundering

In the fall of 1989, a group of high-powered coke dealers and experts on international finance got into rented limousines for a drive to a hot bachelor party. Everyone was in a very festive mood until their chauffeurs, who were really DEA and customs agents, pulled into a Tampa, Florida parking lot and announced that everyone was under arrest.

The arrests capped a two-year investigation into money laundering by the Medellin cocaine cartel, an investigation that government investigators code named *C-Chase,* after the c-notes or hundred dollar bills that drug dealers launder through the American and off-shore banks. By the start of 1991, C-Chase had produced 85 arrests and ongoing investigations into money laundering by 42 major U.S. banks. More importantly, C-Chase and the BCCI case provided an inside look at the increasingly profitable marriage between high finance and international drug cartels.

One of those arrested on route to the mock bachelor party was Amjad Awan, the assistant director for the Latin American division of BCCI, the world's ninth largest private bank. Over the past few years, Awan had acted as the private banker for then Panamanian dictator Colonel Noriega, handing a $25 million secret account at BCCI that Noriega used to launder bribes and kickbacks from drug dealers around the world.

Awan and his bank were convicted in 1990 of money laundering, but the business of laundering money lives on. Over the past ten years, providing financial services to crooks, particularly multinational criminal organizations, has been one of the fastest growing parts of the underground economy. Like other big businesses, very few large criminal organizations would be able to function without financial services. On the most basic level, money laundering allows crooks to enjoy the fruits of their labor without having to worry about IRS or government investigators. But as crime becomes more complex and sophisticated, financial services also play a key role in the commission of the crime. For example, Colombian cartels use dummy corporations and the international financial system to make it appear that a legitimate chemical company is ordering the chemicals needed to process cocaine. Similarly, Tommy Quinn and Arnold Kimmes, two expert con artists with longstanding ties to New York and Las Vegas crime families, used American banks and European financial experts to hide their control over dummy corporations and securities firms that manipulated the penny stock market over a ten-year period during the 1980s. Thanks to that subterfuge, they were able to bilk thousands of investors in over 80 countries out of over $1 billion.

Like every other aspect of high finance, money laundering has changed dramatically during the last decade. In the late 1970s and 1980s, most federal investigations into money laundering focused on American banks, who often ignored the Bank Secrecy Act of 1970 that required all banks to file a currency transaction report whenever cash deposits larger than $10,000 were made. By the start of 1986, 21 banks had been penalized for laundering money, including the following major cases:

- Chemical Bank was the first bank prosecuted for laundering money. In 1977 the bank and three executives were charged with laundering $8.5 million for several narcotics dealers. The bank pleaded guilty to 200 misdemeanors and was fined a mere $200,000 plus court costs, even though it had allowed a multimillion-dollar drug business to flourish.
- In the so-called pizza connection case, La Cosa Nostra members distributed heroin through New York pizza parlors and sent the cash (about $25 million in $5 to $20 denominations) overseas to Bermuda, Switzerland, and Italy where, after being laundered, it was used to buy more heroin. The money was first deposited and wired overseas through an account at Merrill Lynch, but the brokerage firm soon became suspicious and stopped all deposits. Then the operation began depositing money at E. F. Hutton & Co., which was more cooperative. Ever anxious to please, E. F. Hutton executives arranged for large cash deposits at Bankers Trust and helped soothe the suspicions of bank employees. Finally, when Hutton officials were served with grand-jury subpoenas, they warned associates of Franco Della Torre, the man who made the deposits, even though government agents had asked Hutton officials not to contact him. After the warning the company that received the money in Switzerland was deregistered and Della Torre made no further deposits. E. F. Hutton eventually pled guilty to money-laundering charges.
- In the Great American Bank case, this Dade County, Florida, bank laundered $94 million for three narcotics organizations. Even though the bank treated the drug smugglers as valuable customers and allowed them to process such large amounts of cash, it was fined only $500,000.

- In the Eduardo Orozco case, 11 different banks helped him launder $151 million for cocaine and heroin dealers. Of these, only one bank contacted law-enforcement officials about its suspicions. A major portion of this money—about $97 million—was deposited in cardboard boxes at Deak-Perera, a currency exchange based in New York.
- In 1986. The Bank of New England, the second-largest financial institution in the region, was fined $1.24 million for not reporting 31 cash transactions totaling $817,000. That same year the Bank of America received civil penalties of $4.7 million and Texas Commerce Bancshares was hit with $1.9 million in civil fines for not reporting cash transactions.

Today, however, the largest money-laundering operations operate out of the international financial system. Like many other aspects of the business of crime, the use of the international financial system illustrates that crooks are extremely adept at exploiting legitimate economic activities and technological change. During the last two decades, vast sums of money have moved out of the highly regulated Western economies into deregulated, offshore banking and financial havens in places like Switzerland, Panama, Hong Kong, and the Bahamas. Sophisticated computer and telecommunications systems allow major banks and corporations to move billions of dollars through these havens each day. Their attraction is very simple and quite legitimate: banks and other financial institutions don't have to worry about costly and bothersome government rules imposed by many American, Japanese, and European regulators.

This lack of government control over the international markets, which has been such a blessing for legitimate financial institutions, has also created an explosion of financial crime. While government regulators and police are forced to confine the pursuit of their investigations within the borders of their homelands, the new world of international finance lets crooks move their profits and operations anywhere in the world. They can press a button on a computer on Wall Street and within seconds move millions of dollars into an account in an offshore financial haven in the Bahamas, Switzerland, or Hong Kong. Press another button and the money is moved to a numbered account in the South Pacific. Here, you don't have to worry about income taxes and silly rules against securities fraud.

As a result, U.S. government investigators contend these offshore havens play a key role in the international drug industry ($300 billion worldwide), capital flight and corruption in the third world ($660 billion since 1976), tax fraud ($100 billion a year in America alone), securities fraud and insider trading ($10 billion in the U.S.), the business of laundering money for the Mafia (the American and Sicilian Mafia produces over $170 billion a year in profits that must be laundered), the black-market arms trade (offshore bank accounts were used in the Iran/Contra affair and in several recent cases where technology used to make nuclear bombs was sold to third world countries), the savings and loan debacle (law suits filed around the country allege corrupt bank executives moved several billion dollars into secret offshore bank accounts), political corruption (offshore bank accounts were used in

Watergate and the recent HUD and Pentagon corruption scandals), and crimes by multinational corporations (the IRS is currently conducting the largest investigation in its history into multinational corporations, particularly Japanese banks and large electronics firms, who are believed to have used offshore centers to avoid tens, maybe even hundreds of billions of dollars worth of taxes).

In fact, government investigators say a list of crimes committed in offshore banking havens reads like highlights from the history of infamy. Offshore bank accounts were used to launder money or hide assets in the Robert Vesco affair, the Vatican bank scandal, Watergate, the Nugan Hand bankruptcy, the recent insider trading scandals, the savings and loan debacle, the P-2 scandal, the Guinness Brewery stock scandal, the Iran/Contra affair, the Marcos racketeering case, and the drug charges against Noriega.

To fight back against crooks using the international financial system, government investigators are turning to high-tech surveillance to track international money flows and international cooperation.

In a dramatic departure from the past, the Swiss and a few other offshore havens signed treaties during the late 1980s that allow American authorities limited access to information on some secret bank accounts.

But much yet remains to be done. U.S. authorities must still prove that an offshore account was used to launder drug money or defraud investors before foreign authorities will let them look at the financial data. Unfortunately, investigators often need the bank data to make their case. Worse, from the standpoint of enforcement, few offshore havens will cooperate with tax fraud investigations, which are typically the easiest way to convict top-level drug lords.

Banking and Securities Fraud

Rapid changes in the American and international financial system also opened up new opportunities for securities fraud and bank fraud during the 1980s and early 1990s. One classic case of how good crooks are at exploiting economic change is the savings and loan industry. In the early 1980s, government regulators allowed thrifts to enter many new businesses and abolished a number of government regulations. Fair enough. Many of the old regulations had been obsolete for decades.

But no one made much of an attempt to make certain that the newly deregulated thrifts would use their freedom wisely. Real estate developers bought thrifts so they could have a private piggy bank to finance office buildings and condos no one needed. Con artists set up loan scams and used thrifts to launder money. Thrift executives cooked the books and paid themselves huge bonuses when their banks were actually losing money. By the time, federal regulators moved in to end the mess, the cost of the bailout had ballooned from $17 billion in 1983 to over $325 billion in 1990. (See Banking section for a complete discussion of the events that wrecked the savings and loan industry.)

Just how much money fraud cost the taxpayers is hard to say. Government regulators estimate that fraud played a role in the collapse of at least 30% of all thrifts, and various studies contend that fraud cost taxpayers anywhere between $5 billion and $20 billion. (Organized crime operators set up scams that contributed to the collapse of Texas thrifts with over $10 billion worth of assets.) But, whatever the exact cost, there is little doubt that fraud was rampant. Regulators have sent over 21,000 possible cases of fraud to prosecutors for criminal action, but federal agencies only have the resources to investigate a small percentage of the cases. Between 1988 and the fall of 1990, the Justice Department brought 328 criminal indictments and won 231 convictions, with 78% of those resulting in prison terms. These convicted criminals were ordered to pay $57 million, but most of this money has not been paid. (Defendants were ordered to pay $8.9 million in 1988 and 1989, but by the summer of 1990 had paid the government only $23,700.) At the start of 1991, the FBI was investigating 234 failed thrifts and the Justice Department had 654 pending investigations. Thirty savings and loan executives had been sued for civil damages since October of 1988, but the government had recovered only $12 million.

Rapid changes in the securities markets also produced a boom in securities fraud during the 1980s. Ivan Boesky, for example, drew on his understanding of "the legitimate rackets," as Al Capone once described American business, to set up the largest insider-trading scam in the history of the United States. Boesky secured his place in the history of financial crime by taking advantage of rapid changes in American finance.

Back in the 1970s, no one imagined that Boesky would achieve much of anything, good or bad. Like many geniuses, Old Testament prophets, and successful crooks, the young Boesky was something of an underachiever. He drifted through three schools before finally receiving a law degree from Detroit University. After coming to New York in 1966, Boesky bounced around from one Wall Street firm to another. He was fired from one securities company, Kalb Vooris, after losing $20,000 on one deal and got into trouble with the SEC in the mid-1970s for violating securities laws. "Ivan the Bum," his father-in-law, a wealthy Chicago real estate developer, called him.

But times were changing on Wall Street, offering Ivan the Bum a chance to make a name for himself. High inflation and a sluggish economy—the legacy of shortsighted and stupid economic policies during the 1960s and 1970s—kept stock prices low in the 1970s and early 1980s. That meant you could buy a company's stock for less money than it cost to build a comparable operation. The takeover boom was born. American companies spent $1.3 trillion on takeovers during the 1980s.

Ivan Boesky was one of the first to move into risk arbitrage, the business of speculating on takeover stocks. He first became infatuated with the idea of speculating on takeover stocks as early as 1967, during another outbreak of merger mania, and by 1975, he had formed his own firm. Over the next eleven years, until he settled insider trading charges with the SEC, Boesky expertly exploited every opportunity—legal and not so legal—offered by merger mania and the revolution on Wall Street.

At the heart of his success was one of the basic laws of crime or stock speculation: reduce your risks. Like Meyer Lansky, Boesky realized that the most profitable crimes are well organized. So he worked with a number of investment bankers, brokerage firms, and investors who were also active in the takeover boom. Boesky paid investment bankers like Dennis Levine and Martin Siegel cash for tips on pending deals and set up elaborate arrangements to avoid securities laws. In one case he used offshore accounts to help executives at Guinness Plc. manipulate the London stock market, so that Guinness could win a takeover battle for Distiller's Corp. (In return, Guinness agreed to invest $100 million in Boesky's risk arbitrage fund.) In other cases, he bought stock for clients of Michael Milken, the head of the junk bond division at Drexel Burnham Lambert, so that Milken could complete huge takeovers. (In return, Milken agreed to cover all Boesky's potential losses and raised hundreds of millions of dollars in junk bond financing for Boesky's operations.)

These cozy relationships benefited almost everyone involved, except those investors and people outside the network. Milken and Drexel were able to use Boesky to buy up stock before a takeover was announced. Because Boesky already owned a large block of stock, it was easier for one of Drexel's clients to take over a company. Boesky also got investors for his arbitrage fund and received hot tips on takeover stocks. In other cases, he avoided taxes and SEC rules on capital requirements by having Drexel "park" his stocks, that is, have Drexel appear to own stock that he secretly controlled.

All of this was illegal. But Boesky's gamble that he could avoid prosecution was not as big as one might think. Before the 1980s, the SEC rarely enforced rules on insider trading or parking stocks. True, SEC Chairman John Shad, who had spent eighteen years running the mergers and corporate financing department at E.F. Hutton, followed through on his 1981 promise to crack down on insider trading with "hobnail boots." Yet budget constraints crippled the SEC's ability to regulate one of the biggest bull markets in American history. While trading volume on the exchanges grew 133% from 16.0 billion in 1980 to 37.2 billion in 1985, the period when Boesky was committing most of his crimes, only 25 new SEC employees were hired.

Boesky also had a lot of bad luck, which helped government investigators crack the case. One of the investment bankers who provided Boesky with tips, Dennis Levine, had been trading through dummy corporations in offshore accounts since 1978. He contacted his Swiss bankers in the Bahamas only by pay phone outside his office and left strict instructions about how to conduct his trades. They were not to copy any of his trades and were supposed to use a lot of different brokerage firms. But they used only one brokerage firm, Merrill Lynch, and, seeing the success Levine had, began copying his trades.

In 1985, Merrill Lynch received an anonymous letter from Venezuela. Government investigators believe that the letter writer saw a broker at Merrill Lynch's Venezuelan office copying Levine's trades and became angry when he or she was not allowed to trade on Levine's information. Merrill Lynch followed up on the letter and handed over the information to the

SEC. The SEC traced the trades to a secret account in the Bahamas, where the matter might have died. But after being threatened with SEC action against its U.S. assets, Bank Leu broke with tradition and let the SEC look at Levine's accounts. Levine then tried to cover up the mess, but eventually agreed to cooperate. If the Merrill Lynch investigator hadn't pursued the anonymous tip, if Dennis Levine's partners in crime at his Swiss bank had followed his instructions, if the Swiss bank had refused to give up Levine's name, and if Levine hadn't later agreed to cooperate, Boesky's bet that he would never be caught might have paid off.

Seeing the writing on the wall, Boesky became a government informant after the Levine case was filed in 1986. Over the next four years, government investigators advanced slowly through dozens of investigations that eventually resulted in successful criminal or civil suits against Dennis Levine, Ivan Boesky, Martin Siegel, Boyd Jefferies, Kidder Peabody, Princeton/Newport Partners, Salim Lewis, and Paul Bilzerian.

The largest came in 1989, when Drexel Burnham Lambert, faced with the prospect of a racketeering suit, agreed to pay $650 million to settle a 184-page SEC complaint, the most wide-ranging insider trading suit ever filed. Milken, who was also named in the SEC suit and in a separate criminal case, initially maintained his innocence but eventually also settled the charges by agreeing to pay $600 million to fines. In the fall of 1990, he was sentenced to ten years in prison. The sentence, one of the toughest ever meted out to a white collar criminal, could be reduced if Milken agrees to cooperate with government investigations into savings and loan associations and other financial institutions who bought junk bonds from Drexel. (See profiles of Milken and Drexel in the bond section and a list of the major cases at the end of this chapter.)

By the early 1990s, Boesky and Levine were out of jail, but the investigation they helped launch drags on. Many of Milken's bonds were sold to savings and loan associations who eventually went bankrupt. Since 1990, government investigators have been focusing on thrifts and insurance companies that bought bonds from him. In the fall of 1990, the investigation reached a new stage when the FDIC filed $6.8 billion in claims in bankruptcy court against Drexel Burnham Lambert for its role in the savings and loan scandal, charging the firm has "willfully plundered" more than 40 failed institutions "through bribery, coercion, extortion, fraud, and other illegal means."

Despite the success of this investigation, securities fraud is alive and well in the 1990s. The North American Securities' Administrators Association (NASAA), a group of state regulators, estimate that securities fraud is a $10 billion a year investment. Thanks to rapid changes in the international financial markets, one of the fast-growing areas for stock fraud is overseas. In a 1990 report issued last summer by the NASAA notes that 87 international investment scams set up in 1988 and 1989 have bilked Americans out of over $1.1 billion. The international scams capitalized on the fact that many Americans are interested in investment prospects in Europe, foreign stock exchanges, and Eastern Europe. Unfortunately, many prospective investors don't realize that many of these foreign markets are very poorly regulated and that con artists operating out of foreign countries can easily avoid U.S. regulators.

Corporate Crime

Crime in the suites—white-collar and corporate crime—rarely has the immediate, devastating effects of a rape or a murder; nonetheless, the economic consequences are great. In perhaps the best study of the problem, the U.S. Chamber of Commerce estimated in 1974 that the cost of white-collar crime was over $40 billion a year. Corporate crime has also affected a wide segment of the business community. Amitai Etzioni, a visiting professor at Harvard Business School, notes that two thirds of the Fortune 500 companies were convicted of serious crimes between 1975 and 1985, and a 1982 survey by *U.S. News & World Report* found that "of America's 500 largest corporations, 115 have been convicted in the last decade of at least one major crime or have paid civil penalties for serious misbehavior. Those findings confirmed earlier studies, such as a 1975 survey of federal court action that found that 60% of the largest corporations had at least one action brought against them in 1975 or 1976, with 42% facing multiple charges.

Getting an accurate tally of the total costs of corporate crime is difficult because it covers a number of areas that have never been fully studied. Price fixing adds billions to the cost of goods and services. Water pollution caused by U.S. corporations in violation of federal laws could cost the economy $10 billion a year. The Office of Technology Assessment believes it could cost as much as $100 billion to clean up the 32,000 toxic waste dumps in the U.S. A study by the Congressional Research Service estimates that discrimination costs minorities about $37.6 billion in lost jobs or inequitable salaries. About $30 billion to $50 billion might be lost in treating occupational diseases such as asbestosis. Wasteful car repairs cost about $9 billion a year while deceptive grocery labeling costs around $14 billion. In the late 1970s, the American Management Association estimated that commercial bribery and kickbacks ranged from $3.5 billion to $10 billion a year. Another billion dollars was spent in the 1970s by about 500 U.S. companies to bribe foreign officials.

Like other crimes, many corporate crimes can be explained by economic changes or market pressure. For example, many of the recent Pentagon procurement scandals can actually be traced to reforms made in the way Washington bought weapons in the mid-1980s. Under strict new procurement policies, companies were forced to bear the initial research and design costs on many big projects. Such costs can total billions of dollars. Competitive bidding has increased, and contracts changed to make companies responsible for cost overruns. Cost-plus contracts, which encouraged defense contractors to bid low for a project, knowing that they could eventually earn hefty profits even if they ran billions over budget, were reduced dramatically.

The new guidelines were good for taxpayers but hard on contractors, who had to assume new risks. In earlier years, the defense companies would have simply walked into the offices of top Pentagon officials and talked out their problems. More than likely, the bureaucrat sitting on the other side of the conference table had worked for a defense contractor before going to work for the Pentagon and hoped to return to the private sector after leaving government service. An accommodation was usually reached.

But the Reagan administration had staffed the top levels of the Pentagon with people who had little experience with the nuts and bolts of actually producing weapons. Defense contractors found that they couldn't get appointments to see top officials and when they did get in the door, they were unable to talk to anyone in power who actually understood their problems.

At the same time, the new competitive rules concerning contracts made access to top government officials more important than ever. Competition meant that a company had to spend tens of millions of its own money to develop a weapon system. A company that had access to inside information about the bidding process and its competitors could cut those risks and win huge contracts. A company that didn't have access could lose its shirt.

In its quest for information and access to top officials, the defense industry discovered consultants. Consultants, who were often former bureaucrats themselves, could provide access to top officials. Others acted as go-betweens serving middle-level Defense Department officials and the companies. In exchange for cash or the hope of getting high-paying executive positions after leaving the Pentagon, the middle-level bureaucrats were only too happy to provide inside information about contracts and bids. At the same time, top Reagan officials lacked the expertise in procurement to see the problem until it was too late.

Changing markets also help to explain the rash of oil spills and fires at chemical refineries in the late 1980s and early 1990s. *The Wall Street Journal* notes that environmental problems were one of the unintended fallouts of merger mania in the early 1980s. Faced with falling oil prices and corporate raiders in the early 1980s, many large oil companies underwent a massive restructuring. Some companies acquired in takeover battles had to cut staff to pay off their debts; others laid off employees after taking on huge debts for stock buyback programs that were designed to protect them from a takeover. Unfortunately, safety programs were often shortchanged and many experienced middle-level managers, who knew how to avoid spills and environmental problems, were axed. The result came back to haunt the industry with the Exxon *Valdez* oil tanker spill, which ruined miles of pristine Alaskan coastline and cost the company $1.7 billion in 1989 alone.

Here are a few of the most famous corporate scandals:

The Robert Vesco Case

Son of an auto worker and a high school dropout, Vesco built up a financial empire in the 1960s by using other people's money to take over companies. Using his New Jersey-based company, International Controls Corporation (ICC), he set up an international shell game of offshore companies, highly leveraged deals, and shady finances to build ICC in only four years into the 688th largest company in the U.S. In 1970, he managed to take over the foundering Investors Overseas Services, Ltd., and over the next few years the SEC accused him of pilfering $224 million. However, the SEC had been watching him. Denver oilman John King filed a $1 billion suit against him for using illegal funds to gain control of U.S. companies, and, in 1971, Vesco was arrested in Switzerland. But the CIA, under orders from the Nixon administration, had him released. Once released, Vesco bribed the governments of Costa Rica and later the Bahamas to prevent his extradition. Vesco became a major figure in the Watergate scandal when it was reported that he gave a $200,000 contribution to the Committee to Re-elect the President in an attempt to block the SEC investigation. Subsequently, narcotics agents linked him to international drug deals, and he was eventually thrown out of the Bahamas for his alleged involvement in drug smuggling. Currently Vesco's exact location is unknown, though he was spotted in Cuba by reporters for NBC, fueling speculation that he was either receiving medical treatment or operating his drug operations from Havana. Former Attorney General John Mitchell and former Secretary of Commerce Maurice Stans were acquitted in 1974 of attempting to block the SEC investigation of Vesco in exchange for the campaign contributions.

The Michele Sindona Case

After beginning his business career as a seller of art books, the Italian financier Michele Sindona applied the art of fraud to divert illegally as much as $225 million from his Italian holdings to overseas banks. By 1972, using his expertise as a tax lawyer and accountant, Sindona acquired the Franklin National Bank (the 19th largest bank in the U.S.) and built up an empire of banks and industries scattered around the world that was valued at $450 million. However, when the Franklin Bank collapsed in 1974, Sindona's empire came unglued. Losses from his illegal banking practices at the Franklin and other banks totaled several hundred million dollars. The powerful Vatican bank lost millions in its dealings with him. As Sindona's creditors filed lawsuits, the lawyer Giorgio Ambrosoli, appointed by the Italian courts to liquidate his holdings, was murdered on Sindona's orders, apparently because Ambrosoli discovered evidence of fraud. Subsequent investigations led to Sindona's conviction for the murder of Ambrosoli in a U.S. trial and a conviction by Italian courts for fraud. These trials also revealed that Sindona had a tangled web of associations with organized crime figures and P2, an Italian lodge whose illegal activities and links with top Italian politicians touched off the biggest political scandal in postwar Italian history. In 1986 Sindona was poisoned while in prison, touching off speculation that he was murdered to prevent other top political leaders from being hurt by the scandal. His last words were, "They have poisoned me."

The Charles Ponzi Case

The famous Ponzi scheme began in 1919, when this former messenger placed an ad in the paper saying investors in his Securities Exchange Company would earn a 50% profit in only a month and a half. Guaranteed or your money back. That sounded pretty good to thousands of investors and within six months 20,000 investors had coughed up $10 million. Ponzi claimed he was earning investors huge profits by buying International Postal Reply Coupons and then selling them in countries with higher exchange rates, thus profiting from the fluctuating currency markets. A constant flow of new investment money allowed him to buy up the Hanover Trust Company and achieve national fame as a Horatio Alger figure. However, in 1920 it was revealed that none of the investors' money had been invested and Ponzi was shipped off to federal prison. Most investors never got any money back.

That, however, didn't quite end his investment career. He was later indicted for larceny in Massachusetts and for fraud for speculating in Florida swampland. After being deported to Italy he moved to Brazil. He failed at running a hot dog stand in Brazil, but managed to make a modest living giving language lessons—it is easy to see him explaining how to conjugate verbs like *steal* and *defraud*.

Table 15-3   The Wall Street Insider Trading Scandals

Name and occupation	Civil and criminal charges	Status
Dennis B. Levine Former investment banker with Drexel Burnham Lambert	1986 civil and criminal charges of insider trading. Set up a ring of lawyers and investment bankers who illegally traded on inside information. Also gave Ivan Boesky inside tips on mergers being handled by members of the ring before they were announced to the public. By illegally trading in 54 securities Levine made $12.6 million in profits.	In 1986 settled SEC civil charges by paying $11.6 million. Pled guilty to criminal charges and sentenced to 2 years in jail. As a key government witness, Levine helped investigators bring charges against David S. Brown, Ilan K. Reich, Ira B. Sokolow, Robert M. Wilkis, Randall Cecola, and Ivan Boesky.
David S. Brown Former investment banker with Goldman, Sachs	1986 civil and criminal charges of insider trading. Member of the Dennis Levine insider trading ring. Passed information to Sokolow, who relayed it to Levine. Levine made $1.8 million on the information.	Settled SEC charges by paying $145,790 in profits. Pled guilty and sentenced to 30 days in jail.
Ilan Reich lawyer formerly with Wachtell, Lipton, Rosen & Katz	1986 civil and criminal charges of insider trading. Member of the Dennis Levine insider trading ring. Passed information on 12 deals to Levine, allowing him to make $1.7 million in illegal profits. Also supplied information to Wilkis.	Settled SEC charges by paying $485,000 in fines. Pled guilty and sentenced to 1 year and 1 day in jail.
Ira B. Sokolow Former investment banker with Shearson Lehman Brothers	1986 civil and criminal charges of insider trading. Member of the Dennis Levine insider trading ring. Passed inside information to Levine that allowed Levine to make more than $499,595. Levine paid Sokolow more than $80,000 for the information.	Settled SEC charges by paying $210,000 in profits and fines. Pled guilty and sentenced to 1 year and 1 day in jail.
Robert M. Wilkis Former investment banker with Lazard Freres	1986 civil and criminal charges of insider trading. Member of the Dennis Levine insider trading ring.	Settled SEC charges by paying $3.3 million in profits and fined. Pled guilty and sentenced to 1 year and 1 day in jail.
Randall D. Cecola Former analyst at Lazard Freres	1986 civil charges of insider trading. Member of the Dennis Levine insider trading ring.	Gave up $21,800 to settle SEC suit.

Table 15-3   The Wall Street Insider Trading Scandals (continued)

Name and occupation	Civil and criminal charges	Status
Ivan F. Boesky Former stock speculator, headed Ivan F. Boesky Corp.	1986 civil charges of insider trading. 1987 criminal charges of filing false documents with the SEC. Worked with a number of top Wall Street professionals to trade on inside information, and violated a variety of securities laws. He agreed to cooperate with a wide-ranging government investigation in the summer of 1986 after being confronted with evidence supplied by Dennis Levine. The SEC alleges that he made $50 million in insider trading profits.	In 1986 settled SEC civil charges by paying $100 million. Pled guilty to criminal charges in 1987 and sentenced to 3 years in jail. As a key government witness, Boesky helped investigators bring cases against Michael Milken, Boyd L. Jefferies, John A. Mulheren Jr., Martin A. Siegel, and Drexel Burnham Lambert. Released from jail in April, 1990.
Drexel Burnham Lambert	1988 SEC civil charges and 1989 criminal charges. The 184-page SEC civil complaint alleged that Drexel, Milken, and others had traded on inside information, manipulated the stock market, defrauded Drexel's own clients, and violated numerous other securities laws in one of the largest cases of white collar crime ever filed by the SEC.	Settled SEC and criminal charges by paying $650 million. In 1990 declared bankruptcy, and went out of business.
Michael R. Milken Former Drexel Burnham Lambert executive.	1988 civil and criminal charges of violating various securities laws. Used his power over the junk bond market to create a network of people such as Ivan Boesky who violated securities laws and illegally profited from corporate takeovers. In 1990, the FDIC charged that Milken's employer, Drexel Burnham Lambert, was part of a $6.8 billion conspiracy to defraud the savings and loan industry.	After fighting the government investigation for 3 years, he pled guilty in 1990 to conspiracy, aiding in filing of false documents and 4 other felonies. Sentenced to 10 years in jail, he has agreed to cooperate with government investigations into sales of junk bonds to savings and loans and other investors. Also paid $600 million in fines and damages to settle criminal and SEC civil charges.
Martin A. Siegel Former investment banker with Kidder Peabody and Drexel Burnham Lambert.	1987 civil and criminal charges of insider trading. Sold Boesky inside information in exchange for bags of cash. Boesky made over $33 million on information supplied by Siegel	Pled guilty and settled SEC civil suit. Sentenced to 2 months in jail and paid $9.2 million to settle the SEC suit. As a cooperative government witness, Siegel helped investigators bring cases against Robert A. Freeman and his former employer, Kidder Peabody.
Robert A. Freeman Former head of arbitrage at Goldman, Sachs	1990 criminal and civil insider trading charges based on evidence supplied by government witness Siegel.	Pled guilty and sentenced to 4 months in jail. Fined $1 million.
Boyd L. Jefferies Former head of Jefferies & Co.	1987 civil and criminal charges of keeping false records. His company, which operated as a kind of private stock exchange, helped traders buy and sell large blocks of stocks when the regular exchanges were closed; its clients included many corporate raiders. With Boesky's help, investigators were able to show that Jefferies had helped Boesky, Paul A. Bilzerian, and other speculators carry out schemes to manipulate stock prices and violate securities laws.	Settled SEC charges and pled guilty to keeping false records. Sentenced to 5 years probation. Fined $250,000. Cooperated with investigators and provided evidence that led to cases against Salim B. Lewis, Paul A. Bilzerian, and James T. Sherwin.
Salim B. Lewis Former head of S.B. Lewis & Co.	Civil and criminal charges of market manipulation. 1988 criminal charges allege that Lewis and his company manipulated the price of Fireman's Fund Corp. in 1986 when American Express was planning an offering of stock and warrants.	Settled SEC charges and pled guilty to criminal charges. Received 3 months probation and fined $250,000. His company S.B. Lewis & Co. was fined another $400,000.
Paul A. Bilzerian Corporate raider and former head of Singer & Co.	1988 criminal charges of filing false information with the SEC in his takeover of Singer.	Convicted after jury trial and sentenced to 4 years in jail. Fined $1.5 million.

231

Table 15-3   The Wall Street Insider Trading Scandals (continued)

Name and occupation	Civil and criminal charges	Status

James T. Sherwin
  Vice Chairman of
  GAF Corp.
	1988 criminal charges of market manipulation when GAF sold its stake in Union Carbide Corp.	Convicted in jury trial and sentenced to 4 months in jail. Reversed on appeal in 1991.

GAF Corp.	1988 criminal charges of market manipulation in the Sherwin case.	GAF convicted after a jury trial. Fined $2 million. Reversed on appeal.
Kidder Peabody	1987 SEC charges of insider trading and other securities violations. The SEC alleged the company earned $13.7 million by trading on inside information in six securities over a 2-year period, and that it parked stocks for Boesky.	Paid $25 million to settle SEC suit.

James Sutton Regan
  Managing General Partner
  Princeton/Newport Partners
	Indicted for racketeering and fraud with 5 others in 1988. The government alleged that the defendants had created fictitious tax loses and had manipulated stock prices with "rigged" trades with Drexel Burnham Lambert and other securities firms. This landmark case was the first time prosecutors had used RICO statutes against white collar crime on Wall Street. It sparked a vigorous legal debate over the government's successful attempt to freeze the defendants' assets in Princeton/Newport Partners, even though they had not yet been convicted of any crime and PNP was not a defendant in the case. After a judge granted the freeze, PNP was forced to close its doors. The application of RICO against PNP and the devastating impact on PNP's ability to operate later pushed Drexel Burnham Lambert to negotiate a settlement with the government investigators.	Sentenced to 6 months in jail and fined $275,000. The conviction was partially reversed on appeal in 1991.

Bruce Lee Newberg
  former trader
  Drexel Burnham Lambert
	Charged in James Regan case.	Sentenced to 3 months jail Fined $165,000 and ordered to give up $200,000. Partially reversed on appeal.

Steven Barry Smotrich
  Controller
  Princeton/Newport Partners
	Charged in James Regan case.	Sentenced to 3 months jail. Partially reversed on appeal.

Paul Berkman
  General Partner
  Princeton/Newport Partners
	Charged in James Regan case.	Sentenced to 3 months jail. Fined $100,000. Partially reversed on appeal.

Charles Zarzecki
  General Partner
  Princeton/Newport Partners
	Charged in James Regan case.	Sentenced to 3 months jail. Fined $165,000 and ordered to forfeit $1.4 million. Partially reversed on appeal.

Jack Z. Rabinowitz
  General Partner
  Princeton/Newport Partners
	Charged in James Regan case.	Sentenced to 3 months jail. Fined $50,000. Partially reversed on appeal.

Chapter Sixteen

DEALS AND MERGERS: BIGGER IS BETTER?

HIGHLIGHTS AND TRENDS

• Merger mania is over, but the controversy over its legacy—high levels of corporate debt, the collapse of several financial institutions with large junk bond portfolios, and a depression in the junk bond market—is likely to keep economists arguing over its impact on the American economy for many years to come.

• As takeover fever on Wall Street mounted during the 1980s, the number of deals jumped from 1,558 (valued at $33 billion) in 1980 to 3,484 ($146 billion) in 1985, 4,000 deals (a record $236.4 billion) in 1988, 3,415 deals ($231 billion) in 1989, and 3,590 ($158.8 billion) in 1990. Altogether, 34,702 deals, valued at $1.5 trillion, were completed between 1980 and 1990.

• Many of these deals can be traced to innovative methods of financing mergers and acquisitions during the 1980s. Drexel Burnham Lambert and Michael Milken, the head of Drexel's junk bond department, built up a $300 billion market for junk bonds (the high-yield, highly speculative bonds that were used to finance many deals). Junk bonds and the growing willingness of large banks to lend money for takeover deals allowed the number of leveraged buyouts (LBOs) to jump from 11 ($0.24 billion) in 1980 to 388 ($61.58 billion) in 1989 before slumping to only 219 ($14.77 billion) in 1990.

• Throughout the decade corporations also sold off subsidiaries and shuffled assets at record speed: Divestitures jumped from 104 ($5.1 billion) in 1980 to 1,273 ($83.2 billion) in 1988 and 1,119 ($60.8 billion) in 1989 before falling to 1,119 ($53.7 billion) in 1990.

• The global supermarket for corporate assets was equally hot. Foreign corporations completed 42 acquisitions of American companies that were valued at over $1 billion during the 1980s; American companies, meanwhile, bought assets in Europe to prepare for 1992. More recently, in the fall of

1990, the Japanese electronics giant Matsushita negotiated a $6.1-billion deal to acquire MCA, the motion picture and amusement park company.

• As the decade wore on, takeover artists were able to carry out some of the largest deals in the history of America. Only 12 transactions worth more than $1 billion were completed between 1969 and 1980, but between 1982 and 1990 there were 232 $1-billion deals with a total value of $562 billion. There were a record 42 deals valued at over $1 billion (total value $96.4 billion) in 1988, 35 deals were valued at $117.5 billion in 1989, and 33 in 1990 ($73.4 billion).

• But in late 1989 and 1990, the takeover market collapsed. Several highly leveraged companies defaulted on their junk bonds, and the junk bond market plunged. Few analysts believe the hostile-takeover market will recover at any time in the near future.

LET'S MAKE A DEAL

"Let's Make a Deal" became the theme song of the 1980s as American business took its assets to the market. Mergers, acquisitions, and leveraged buy-outs reached unprecedented levels in the 1980s, totaling $1.5 trillion between 1980 and 1990 with over three quarters of that figure spent after 1985. In 1990, deals totaled $158.8 billion, down from 1988's record $236.4 billion.

In the feverish pace of merger mania, some of the biggest deals in the history of American business were put together. Only 12 transactions worth more than $1 billion were completed between 1969 and 1980, but in 1985 alone, 26 billion-dollar deals were put together. In fact, in 1985, when General Electric announced its plan to swallow RCA in a $6.4-billion deal that would produce the sixth-largest industrial company in the U.S., a billion-dollar merger wasn't even enough to put you in the top 20 deals. And that was only the beginning. In 1988, 42 billion-dollar deals were completed and 1989 saw 35 billion-dollar deals, including the largest LBO ever, the $24.7-billion buyout of RJR Nabisco, Inc. Forty-seven of the 50 largest mergers in U.S. history have been completed since 1984. Even in 1990 there were 33, valued at $73.4 billion.

But, as any historian of financial markets knows, a speculative boom is almost always followed by a bust. In 1989, when dealmakers were completing the $24.7-billion RJR Nabisco deal, the largest in American history, the takeover market was already shaky. Campeau Corp., a Canadian retailer, ended up in bankruptcy court along with several other companies that had built up huge corporate empires with billions of dollars worth of junk bonds. As investors worried about the how companies would pay off all these debts, the junk bond market took a nosedive, losing 40% of its value between the start of 1989 and September of 1990 before staging a rally in early 1991.

By 1991, the collapse of the takeover boom had brought down some of the biggest success stories of the 1980s. Drexel Burnham Lambert, the securities firm that built up the junk bond market to a $300 billion business, was forced to pay $650 million to settle securities fraud charges in 1989, and a year later announced that it was broke. Its star employee, Michael Milken, who was once known as the king of junk bonds, was forced to pay $600 million for securities law violations and pled guilty to criminal charges. He is now serving a 10-year jail sentence.

Today, the market for hostile takeovers is almost dead. But the debate over its legacy is still heating up. Critics complain that a decade of takeover speculation left American corporations saddled with huge debts and hamstrung their ability to compete in the global marketplace. Even worse, the collapse of the junk bond market has hurt a number of financial institutions. Several savings and loan associations with large junk bond holdings have collapsed, leaving federal regulators holding billions of dollars worth of junk bonds that were worth only 20% to 30% of their face value. Pension funds and several insurance companies that bought junk bonds have also taken a big hit. But these problems might only be a prelude for more serious bloodletting. U.S. banks hold over $55 billion worth of loans that were used to finance leveraged buyouts or mergers. To understand how takeover speculation in the 1980s is likely to affect the American economy in the 1990s, it's worth considering a little history.

Merger Mania

The most recent urge to merge hit American business in 1980 and 1981 when oil prices hit the skids, dropping the price for stocks of oil companies to absurdly low levels—and making them attractive to takeover attempts. These companies had assets worth 2 and sometimes 3 times as much as the stock. Since many analysts believed oil prices would eventually recover, buying these low-priced stocks was much like buying oil at $5 a barrel.

Take Conoco: Savvy raiders noticed that Conoco had domestic reserves of 400 million barrels of oil, lots of North Sea oil, and a subsidiary that was the second-largest coal producer in the U.S. Yet while Conoco's assets were worth over $140 a share, its stock was only selling for about $50 on Wall Street.

That was the kind of bargain few cash-rich companies could resist. During 1980 and 1981, some of the country's largest corporations—Seagram, du Pont, and Mobil—began wooing Conoco shareholders in a multi-billion-dollar takeover battle that touched off merger mania. Du Pont, which rode into the fray as a white knight, finally won the right to buy Conoco for $8 billion—the most expensive merger completed up to that time.

Other undervalued oil companies, such as Marathon (whose stock was trading at $68 despite assets of $210 a share in 1981) and Getty (with stock trading at $72 even though it had assets worth $250 a share), also fell to merger mania. U.S. Steel acquired Marathon for $6.6 billion and Texaco got Getty for $10.1 billion. Between 1980 and 1989, $153 billion worth of deals were put together in the energy sector.

But the oil patch wasn't the only part of the economy affected. No industry was spared.

• In the food industry, Philip Morris gobbled up General Foods for $5.6 billion. R. J. Reynolds paid $4.9 billion for Nabisco, and then in 1989 Kohlberg Kravis Roberts & Co. cooked up a $24.7-billion LBO of RJR

Nabisco, Inc. Total acquisitions in the food and tobacco industry during the 1980s: $120 billion.

• In retail, Safeway, the nation's largest supermarket chain, went private for $4.3 billion while Macy's managers took the department-store firm private for $3.6 billion. Total deals in the retail sector during the 1980s: $87.7 billion.

• In electronics, General Electric plugged into RCA, producing an industrial, financial, and electronics powerhouse with $35.2 billion in revenue in 1986. By the end of the 1980s, $35.1 billion worth of mergers had been completed in the electric and electronics industry.

• In the health-care industry, Baxter Travenol bought American Hospital Supply for $3.7 billion and Monsanto bought Searle for $2.7 billion, and Bristol-Myers Co. bought Squibb for $12.5 billion. Total health-care deals: $84.1 billion.

• In television, two of the major networks got new owners as Capital Cities took over ABC for $3.5 billion and General Electric took over NBC's parent company, RCA. Rupert Murdoch moved toward his goal of setting up a fourth network by buying Metromedia's television stations for $2 billion. Total media deals in the 1980s: $89.2 billion.

• Failing to buy a TV empire from CBS, Ted Turner went to the movies, buying MGM/UA for $1.5 billion. Later, Sony Corp. acquired Columbia Pictures Entertainment, Inc., for $3.5 billion, while Time and Warner scripted a $12.6-billion merger. The total for entertainment deals in the 1980s, which does not include the Time-Warner deal because it was not completed by January, 1990, was $24.2 billion.

• In telecommunications, Southwestern Bell spent $1.2 billion for Metromedia's cellular phone division and ITT sold off its telecommunications division for $1.5 billion. Over $27.5 billion worth of mergers were completed in the utilities sector.

• In chemicals, the West German company Hoechst paid $2.8 billion for Celanese. In 1989 alone, Sterling Drug was bought by Eastman Kodak for $5.1 billion, Borg Warner was sold to GE Plastics, and Firestone Tire & Rubber was sold to Bridgestone for $2.66 billion. By the end of the decade, nearly 30% of the manufacturing capacity of the chemical industry was owned by foreign companies, and over $38 billion worth of deals had been completed.

• Banks such as SunTrust Banks, First Wachovia, NCNB, the Bank of New England, Fleet Financial, and the Bank of Boston created regional banking empires by buying up banks in other states. The takeover spree drove up bank stocks in some states in anticipation of outside takeovers, and by the start of 1990, $77.4 billion worth of deals for banks were finalized.

• On Wall Street, General Electric bought Kidder, Peabody & Co. in 1986. In 1981 alone, Sears acquired Dean Witter, Prudential Insurance took over the Bache Group, American Express gobbled up Shearson Lehman, and Philbro bought up Salomon Brothers. Equitable Life took over Donaldson, Lufkin & Jenrette in 1984. Deals for nonbank financial companies totaled $49.4 billion.

• Even aerospace went into orbit. In Detroit, General Motors spent $5.0 billion to take over Hughes Aircraft, a major defense contractor.

One factor fueling the takeover frenzy was a revolution in how corporate takeovers were financed. In the 1970s, a bond trader at Drexel Burnham Lambert named Michael Milken (see Drexel Box) began investing in bonds that had been issued by financially troubled companies. These bonds, known as fallen angels, traded at a hefty discount because the companies that issued them were bankrupt or had poor credit ratings. But despite their poor credit ratings, many of the companies were servicing their debts. A careful investor who focused on the company's real financial prospects, not its bad credit rating, could make lots of money, Milken contended.

In the late 1970s and early 1980s, Milken and Drexel took this idea one step further. Traditionally, only the largest and most financially secure American corporations were given investment-grade credit ratings, allowing them to issue corporate bonds or get bank loans. Milken got around that problem by advising companies to issue high-yield, below-investment-grade bonds. These bonds became known as junk bonds because companies that issued them had poor credit ratings. But, as with the fallen angels, Milken was soon able to argue to investors that a credit rating wasn't everything. With the financing from junk bonds, small and medium-sized companies were able to expand their operations and meet the payments on their debts. Bond buyers liked the high interest rates and the fact that before 1988, as Milken had predicted, there were few defaults.

Exploiting the lure of high interest rates and giving assurances that the bonds were safer than their credit ratings might suggest, Milken was able to set up a network of junk bond investors. This group, which included insurance companies, corporate raiders, longtime clients, and even savings and loan associations, opened up a new pool of capital that could be used for more speculative investments. In 1984, junk bonds were used for the first time to finance a hostile takeover bid by T. Boone Pickens for Gulf. By the end of the 1980s, more than $300 billion worth of junk bonds had been issued.

Junk bonds enabled corporate raiders to raise large sums of money very quickly and finance highly leveraged transactions that would have been impossible only a few years earlier. Armed with junk bonds, you didn't have to be an industrial giant like General Motors or General Electric to play merger mania. Pantry Pride managed to swallow Revlon, which was three times its size, for $2.7 billion. Billion-dollar takeovers—even the $24.7-billion leveraged buyout of RJR Nabisco, Inc.—were possible.

But the rise of junk bonds wasn't the only factor fueling takeover fever. As with all speculative booms, each successful deal touched off a new round of speculation. Other companies drooled over the huge fees Drexel was getting by helping corporate raiders raise junk bond financing, and soon a huge business grew up around mergers and acquisitions. Other Wall Street firms set up or expanded operations specializing in takeovers, junk bond financing, and risk arbitrage (i.e., speculating in takeover stocks). A study of just 39 deals in 1986 found that Wall Street firms earned over $615 million in fees. Lawyers specializing in corporate law were earning $250 to $500 an hour, and arbitrageurs like Ivan Boesky were earning $50 million to $100 million a year speculating in takeover stocks.

In many ways, the takeover market fed upon itself as a kind of self-fulfilling prophecy. Battalions of investment bankers and lawyers were constantly suggesting possible corporate takeovers to their clients. Corporate raiders, using borrowed money, had to find takeover targets to cover their interest costs. Arbitrageurs helped fuel the fever by buying up stocks that might be put in play. Everyone made money as long as the fever lasted.

The Restructuring of American Business

Over time, merger mania had a dramatic effect on the face of American business. As some companies fought vicious takeover battles to enlarge their corporate domains, others sold off the corporate fat. Through the 1980s, corporate America sold assets and subsidiaries at a record-breaking pace. In 1990 there were 1,119 divestitures of a total of $53.7 billion, down from the record year of 1988, when 1,273 divestitures sold for $83.2 billion. Between 1980 and the end of 1990, companies sold off subsidiaries for $438.1 billion.

Even companies such as ITT, long the leader of corporate expansion, were cutting fat. Since 1980, ITT has sold off more than 100 businesses, including its European telecommunications operations. But ITT wasn't alone. Gulf + Western, which once specialized in buying up everything in sight, agreed in 1985 to sell nearly half of its businesses to Wickes Companies for about $1 billion. Then, in 1989, it sold off its financial services operations. With a new name, Paramount Communications, the company has refocused its energies on media, entertainment, and publishing.

But selling off assets was in no way incompatible with pursuing a strategy of corporate mergers. General Electric, for example, was buying and selling companies at a frantic pace. In the 1980s it has bought 24 companies for $8.5 billion and sold off 22 for $4 billion.

Other companies went private in record numbers. Leveraged buyouts—a process in which a group, usually the management or a large shareholder, buys out the other stockholders or owners using borrowed funds—also hit record numbers. Frequently, the company's assets serve as security for the loans and quite often the new owners take the company private.

In 1989 there were a record 388 leveraged buyouts worth a total of $61.58 billion, up from 11 leveraged buyouts worth $0.24 billion in 1980. Between 1980 and 1990 there were a total of 2,615 leveraged buyouts worth $254.8 billion.

Of course, greed and the creation of a huge industry devoted to merger mania helped keep the takeover market flying high. But it would be wrong to view merger mania as an outbreak of financial madness. Many of the excesses of the 1980s reflected rapid changes in the American and global economy. Faced with increased foreign competition, rapid technological change, declining profit rates, and rampant inflation in the early 1980s, many businesses had to change the way they operated.

It's no accident, for example, that many of the largest deals during the decade were put together in the most troubled sectors of the economy: energy ($153 billion), mining ($31.5 billion), transportation equipment ($44.8 billion), paper ($37 billion), and apparel and textiles ($24.5 billion). In these industries, poor earnings had driven down stock prices, allowing corporate raiders to purchase a company's assets for less money than it would cost to build a new factory.

Many mergers also took place in industries that were undergoing rapid change. Companies that acquired banks ($77 billion), insurance firms ($45 billion), nonbank financial interests ($49 billion), and transportation concerns ($42 billion) were moving into industries that were deregulated in the late 1970s and early 1980s. Other industries, such as the media ($89 billion) and computer production and development ($35 billion), attracted attention because they were undergoing rapid technological change that opened up new markets and offered hope for higher profits.

On a global scale, the supermarket of corporate assets reflected widespread changes in international production and trade. In the U.S. and abroad, huge multinationals continued to expand their operations around the world by purchasing subsidiaries that would aid their international operations. Sony Corp., for example, acquired Columbia Pictures and CBS Records because these two companies could supply "software" (movies or records) that could be played on Sony's "hardware" (tape decks, record players, televisions, or stereos). Abroad, U.S. and other foreign companies bought up companies in the European Common Market, hoping to capitalize on the market's unification in 1992. KPMG Peat Marwick estimates that foreign companies acquired over $50 billion worth of European companies in 1989 alone, including a $1.4-billion deal made by PepsiCo., Inc., to acquire the Walkers Crisps and Smiths Crisps units of BSN SA in France.

Closer to home, the need to improve stagnant profits and boost poor returns on equity helps explain why leveraged buyouts hit record numbers. LBOs leave the company saddled with debt, but can produce quick profits. LBO proponents say the heavy load of debt forces the new owners (often the old management) to sell off inefficient assets, reduce costs, cut wages, and generally do the kinds of things that are avoided when things are going well. Eventually, if all goes well, the company will emerge from the debt crisis leaner and meaner. Then the owners can sell the more efficient company or take it public again for huge profits. For example, in 1982 former Treasury Secretary William Simon led a group of investors who bought Gibson Greetings, Inc., for $80 million, using only $1 million of their own money. Then, 18 months later, they took the company public. Over time, Simon's company, Wesray, has made about $200 million on the deal. In another case, Metromedia owner John Kluge took his company private in 1984 for $1.1 billion. Then he sold off Metromedia's television stations, cellular phone properties, and other assets. By 1990, the profits from the Metromedia LBO had made Kluge one of the richest men in America, worth over $7 billion.

Do These Deals Work?

The urge to merge is, of course, nothing new. At the turn of the century, the U.S. economy was hit with its first wave of merger mania, as the investment bankers of the period put together the megadeals that created such industrial giants as U.S. Steel, Anaconda Copper, du Pont, American Tobacco, Allis-Chalmers, and American Smelting and Refining. Between 1898 and 1902, over 2,653 companies disappeared in merger deals worth about $6.3 billion. Another period of merger mania hit the economy in the 1920s when the cost of mergers reached about two thirds of what was spent on capital and equipment in 1928 and 1929. In the late 1960s, go-go conglomerates like Ling-Temco-Vought assembled huge, and often ill-defined, corporate empires.

During the height of merger mania, many analysts argued that some industries, such as energy, mining, and financial services, needed to be restructured by mergers or leveraged buyouts. Economist Michael C. Jensen, for example, wrote, "Shareholders and the economy would gain enormously if companies in industries . . . such as energy, airlines, broadcasting, and cable TV, felt the pressure of potential hostile takeovers. Otherwise, managers are free to waste resources on marginal enterprises, rather than paying out excess cash to shareholders." He points out that shareholders benefited to the tune of $17 billion in the Gulf, Getty, and Conoco takeovers.

There is also little doubt that merger mania helped fuel the great bull market of the 1980s. W. T. Grimm & Co. concluded that from 1981 to 1986 shareholder wealth increased $118.4 billion as a result of mergers, selloffs, leveraged buyouts, and takeover bids for companies. An SEC study found that the value of stock increased by $54 billion as a result of successful tender offers.

But as the 1980s wore on, the problems with merger mania became more apparent. As the total value of corporate bonds outstanding jumped from $819 billion in 1985 to $1,602 billion in 1990, many companies had trouble paying their debts. Interest payments as a percentage of after-tax profits climbed from 19% in the 1960s to 53% in the 1970s. By the end of the 1980s, the interest burden had more than doubled to 118% of after-tax profits.

One of the first to fall was a steel maker, LTV. In 1984 LTV acquired Republic Steel for $486.4 million, hoping to become a larger, more efficient steel producer. Instead, the deal pushed it into bankruptcy court in 1986. Soon others followed suit. The Midwest drugstore chain Revco DS went broke in 1988, only two years after completing a $1.3-billion LBO, and in 1989 Campeau Corp. filed for bankruptcy, unable to pay the debt on its $6.5-billion LBO of Federated Department Stores in 1988. That same year, Hillsborough Holdings, which had spent $2.4 billion for a building-material maker, Jim Walter Corp., also defaulted on its debts.

By the early 1990s, corporate bankruptcies had hit record levels. In 1989, when all the basic economic data indicated that the economy was booming, companies with $72.7 billion worth of assets went broke, up from a paltry $5.7 billion in 1983. More bad news followed in 1990, when $55.7 billion worth of bankruptcies were declared in the first half of the year.

Problems also developed in the $300-billion junk bond market. Drexel and Milken had lured investors into the junk bond market by claiming that only 2% of these bonds defaulted. But a 1990 study by the Bond Investors Association showed that nearly 34% of the junk bonds issued in 1977 and 1978 were not paid off in full. The BIA predicted that 38% of the junk bond debt would never be paid back and that $40 billion worth of junk bonds would default before 1993.

By now, the overleveraged economy had come back to haunt the Wall Street bankers who profited so handsomely from merger mania. The slow-down in the takeover market after the stock market crash in 1987 brought the merger boom to an end. Investment banking, junk bond, and arbitrage trading departments at Wall Street firms suffered massive layoffs. Many lawyers and accountants who specialized in mergers were also fired or reas-signed to the bankruptcy litigation, which quickly became one of the most profitable specialties in the legal profession. Worse, the collapse of the junk bond market pushed Drexel into bankruptcy in 1990 and bloodied a number of other firms. First Boston got stuck with $429 million worth of Campeau's debt when the retailer went broke, wiping out the $80 million in fees it had made advising Campeau on some of its ill-fated deals. Shearson Lehman Hutton, meanwhile, got stuck with a $500 million loan to Prime Computer after the junk bond market crashed, and its reputation was hurt when it came out on the wrong side of the battle for RJR Nabisco. Between 1989 and early 1990, American Express had to inject more than $1.2 billion worth of capital into Shearson to keep it afloat.

But Wall Street wasn't the only part of the financial system left with a bad hangover from merger mania. Stock prices for major banks plunged to new lows as investors became increasingly worried about the $55 billion worth of outstanding loans commercial banks made to finance takeovers and lever-aged buyouts. Savings and loan associations, which held over $7 billion worth of junk bonds, posted record losses in 1989, and several insurance companies that were heavy buyers of junk bonds had severe financial prob-lems. By the start of 1991, several of Milken's largest clients in the thrift and insurance field, such as Lincoln Savings & Loan, had either gone broke or were racking up hundreds of millions of dollars worth of losses.

The record bankruptcies and financial problems created by merger mania were especially worrisome because they emerged in late 1989 and 1990, when the economy was healthier than it had been for years. If companies were going bankrupt and banks were having financial problems when unem-ployment was low and the economy strong, what would happen if the coun-try slipped into a recession?

Even more bothersome is the long-range impact of merger mania. Many American corporations spent the 1980s trying to produce short-term results so that they could avoid being taken over by corporate raiders. The $1 tril-lion spent on buying and selling corporate assets between 1985 and 1989 was far more money than the $801 billion spent by American manufacturing companies on new plants and equipment during the same period.

Moreover, some evidence suggests that American corporations reduced their expenditures for research and development after taking on huge amounts of debt to finance mergers or LBOs. A study by the National Science Foundation of the 200 companies that spend the most on research and development found that the 24 companies that merged or underwent LBOs reduced their research spending by 8.3% in real terms in 1986 and 1987, a period when the other companies increased theirs by 5.4%. A more recent, smaller survey of 72 firms by the NSF confirmed those findings. It found that between 1988 and 1990, the 21 firms that were involved in takeovers or LBOs reduced their research spending by 0.2% (a 3 to 5% reduction if you adjust for inflation). The other companies increased such spending by 6.8%.

Similarly, University of Chicago financier Professor Steven Kaplan, who happened to believe that LBOs produced higher profits, admitted that they may have hurt capital spending. After studying the 76 large LBOs between 1980 and 1986, Kaplan concluded that companies in the same industries that had not undergone LBOs invested 36% more in capital spending in the first year, 33% more in the second, and 64% more in the third year than the companies that had been bought out.

Moreover, heavy borrowing by the U.S. government and private corporations during the 1980s has increased the cost of capital for U.S. businesses, making it harder for them to compete internationally. A 1990 study by the Office of Technology Assessment for Congress found that American businesses have to spend more for long-term capital than their toughest competitors, Japanese firms: "Each year from 1977 to 1988, the cost of capital in America averaged 3.4 percentage points higher than the cost of capital in Japan for investments in machinery and equipment with a physical life of 20 years; 4.9 percentage points higher for a factory with a physical life of 40 years; and 8 percentage points higher for a research and development project with a 10-year payoff." Not surprisingly, Japan spends about 30% of its gross domestic product on capital formation, compared to about 20% for the U.S.

Merger mania was also hard on organized labor since many mergers took place in the most troubled sectors of the economy, which tended to be heavily unionized. AFL-CIO President Lane Kirkland estimated that merger mania during the 1980s pushed about 90,000 union members out of jobs.

But such problems shouldn't overshadow some of its positive impact. Reshuffling assets has helped a number of companies like General Electric produce record profits. Selling off the dogs allowed companies to get rid of subsidiaries they weren't equipped to manage and buy companies that fit into their strategic plans. The new owners can often take a previously unprofitable business and turn it around. A study by Frederic M. Scherer, a Swarthmore College economist, indicated that 14 out of 15 subsidiaries sold between 1970 and 1982 did better on their own.

These positive features have helped keep the business of mergers and acquisitions alive. Though the collapse of the junk bond market has nearly killed the hostile-takeover market and slowed the number of other deals, many companies still find good reasons to buy and sell assets. As in the 1980s, large multinational corporations that want to crack foreign markets in the 1990s are still on the prowl for likely takeover targets. The Japanese bought 61 companies in the first half of 1990, up from 42 during a similar period during 1989, and Wall Street investment bankers are also greedily eyeing hundreds of state-owned Eastern European companies that are slated to be sold. Nearly $30 billion worth of state-owned enterprises will be sold by the end of the 1990s.

Of course, if you aren't interested in buying the wreckage of the fall of communism, there is always the wreckage of merger mania. Many of the people who made money on the takeover boom are already making hefty fees advising bankrupt companies or buying cheap junk bonds. Many Wall Street firms, which can get between $75,000 and $250,000 a month advising financially troubled clients, are competing with one another for the right to bail out companies from one another's failed deals. One of the biggest firms, Shearson Lehman Hutton, is advising Campeau on how to work its way out of the financial problems created by the Federated LBO, and First Boston, another powerhouse in the workout field, is advising half a dozen clients on how they can survive bad deals put together by Drexel. No one seems to mind that the geniuses at First Boston put together the Federated mess to begin with or that Shearson has lots of financial problems of its own.

Similarly, Weil Gotshall & Manges, which was one of the biggest legal advisers during the takeover boom of the 1980s, started the 1990s as the bankruptcy counsel for Drexel, earning $2.1 million in fees for three months' work. Even corporate raider Carl Icahn hopes to make money from other people's problems. He invested over $800 million on cheap junk bonds in the first 4 months of 1990, hoping their value had already hit rock bottom.

Table 16-1   Total Merger and Acquisition Activity, 1980–1990

	No. of deals	Value ($ billion)
1980	1,558	$32.8
1981	2,328	69.5
1982	2,298	60.7
1983	2,393	52.7
1984	3,175	126.1
1985	3,484	146.0
1986	4,446	205.8
1987	4,015	178.3
1988	4,000	236.4
1989	3,415	231.4
1990	3,590	158.8

Source: M&A Data Base. ADP/MLR

Table 16-2   Divestitures, 1980–1990

	No. of deals	Value ($ billion)
1980	104	$5.1
1981	476	10.2
1982	562	8.4
1983	661	12.9
1984	793	30.6
1985	1,039	43.5
1986	1,419	72.4
1987	1,219	57.7
1988	1,273	83.2
1989	1,119	60.8
1990	1,119	53.7

Source: M&A Data Base. ADP/MLR

Table 16-3   Leveraged Buyouts, 1980–1990

	No. of deals	Value ($ billion)
1980	11	$0.24
1981	100	3.87
1982	164	3.45
1983	231	4.52
1984	254	18.72
1985	255	19.67
1986	337	45.16
1987	279	36.23
1988	377	46.56
1989	388	61.58
1990	219	14.77

Source: M&A Data Base. ADP/MLR

Chapter Seventeen
TRADE, PRODUCTIVITY, AND STAYING AHEAD: WORLD WAR III?

HIGHLIGHTS AND TRENDS

- The days when the American economy could thumb its nose at the rest of the world are over. In 1950, U.S. exports and imports of goods and services were under 5% of GNP; today exports account for 13.1% of our GNP, and imports total 15.1%. Exports accounted for nearly half (49.3%) of America's GNP growth in 1989, and a downturn in foreign demand for American products could badly hurt the American economy in the 1990s. The U.S. Department of Commerce estimates that a 5% drop in U.S. exports would cut real GNP growth by one fifth.
- Meanwhile, the globalization of production has made American companies increasingly dependent on the health of their foreign subsidiaries. American companies increased their foreign investments from $56.6 billion in 1967 to $322.2 billion in 1987 and $373.4 billion in 1989. Similarly, Europe increased its foreign investments from $45.1 billion in 1967 to $524.5 in 1987, and Japan's foreign investments jumped from $1.5 billion to $77.0 billion during that period.
- The globalization of production has also increased the amount of foreign investment in America, making more and more American workers dependent on the economic fortunes of foreign countries. Between 1983 and 1989, foreign companies spent $263.1 billion acquiring U.S. companies or establishing subsidiaries in America.
- In 1989 alone, foreign companies acquired 645 U.S. companies, which employed 679,106 workers and owned 310,598 acres of land. Foreign firms also established 456 businesses, employing 13,088 workers and owning 269,205 acres of land. Foreign investors now own about $2 trillion worth of assets, and employ 3.7 million Americans.

• But despite the headlines about Japan buying up the whole world, Japan was not the largest foreign investor in the United States between 1983 and 1989. Japan's $49.8 billion investments ran a very distant second to the $81.1 billion spent by companies from the United Kingdom. By the start of the 1990s, foreign companies had invested $400.8 billion in the U.S., up from $184.6 billion in 1985.

• But adjusting to the new global economy has not been easy. Because American companies and individuals are less productive, save less money, and invest less money in new equipment and long-term research, the United States has fallen dangerously behind many of its key economic competitors.

• One troubling measure of America's economic problems is its trade deficit, which hit a record $152 billion in 1987, before recovering slightly to $109 billion in 1989. U.S. productivity in the manufacturing sector as measured by output per hour grew only 2.2% between 1973 and 1985, down from a 3.2% increase between 1960 and 1973. That was way below Japan's growth rate of 10.3% a year between 1960 and 1973 and 5.6% between 1973 and 1985. As a result, U.S. productivity growth between 1960 and 1985 lagged way behind the 5.4% annual growth in productivity of 11 major foreign competitors.

• Since then, U.S. manufacturers have made a modest comeback in the productivity race. In the second half of the 1980s, U.S. manufacturing productivity grew at an average rate of 3.3% a year, faster than in Canada (1.9%), France, (2.8%), Germany (1.9%), and Italy (2.1%). But it lagged behind productivity growth in the United Kingdom (4.9%) and America's chief foreign competitor, Japan (5.7%).

• The increased competitiveness of some American companies have also helped reduce the trade deficit in the early 1990s. The U.S. trade deficit fell to $5 billion in June of 1990, the lowest monthly level in 7 years, and totalled only $105 billion in 1990, way down from the $152-billion record in 1987. Even better, the U.S. was finally running a $1.7 billion surplus with European countries, up from a $21-billion deficit in 1987. Also encouraging was the fact that foreign countries were buying American capital goods in record numbers, producing a $37-billion surplus, up from $2 billion in 1987.

• Another bright spot in the trade picture has been services. The American surplus in services jumped from $2.5 billion in 1977 to $28.2 billion in 1989.

TRADING FOR DOLLARS: THE IMPORTANCE OF STAYING COMPETITIVE

The old "buy American" slogan makes less sense all the time. The average auto worker who has just been laid off by General Motors will have a hard time determining which products he should buy or boycott if he wants to help American industry. He could drive his Plymouth Lazer (made in Japan) on Firestone (owned by the Japanese) tires to a temp job he found at Manpower, Inc. (owned by a U.K. company). Later, with all the money he gets from temp work, he can buy a six-pack of Lone Star beer (Australian), watch an MGM movie (Italian), read a book on finding a new job that was published by Doubleday (German), take a trip to New York City to visit Rockefeller Center (half-owned by the Japanese), redecorate the living room with new furniture from Bloomingdale's (Canadian), listen to a Bruce Springsteen album from Columbia Records (Japanese), invest in Treasury bonds from First Boston (owned by the Swiss), or buy a new Ford (many of its parts were made overseas) that runs quite nicely on Texaco gas (Saudi Arabian).

Alternatively, he could always buy a car from a foreign auto maker (foreign car subsidiaries employ 56,000 Americans), insure it through a foreign insurance company (foreign insurers have 111,000 Americans on the payroll), drive it to a foreign-owned store (64,000 Americans work in such stores), and buy a new foreign stereo (foreign companies that make electrical and electronic goods provide weekly paychecks for 225,000 Americans). In fact, if everyone got really serious about buying American, 3.7 million Americans employed by foreign companies would be out of work.

Welcome to the new global order. As these examples suggest, the days when the American economy could thumb its nose at the rest of the world are gone. In 1950, when America first flexed its muscles as a global economic power, foreign trade accounted for only 5% of real GNP; today the amount of goods imported and exported to and from the United States each year tops $1.2 trillion dollars, about 28% of our GNP. American companies have invested $373.4 billion in foreign countries, and U.S.-based subsidiaries of foreign companies control $1.1 trillion worth of assets. More than ever before, Main Street is dependent on foreign trade for jobs and economic prosperity.

But adjusting to the new global order hasn't been easy for many sectors of the American economy. Thousands of farmers went broke in the early 1980s, when foreign demand for American agricultural products collapsed. The survivors, however, harvested decent profits in the late 1980s and the early 1990s, when Russia started buying record amounts of corn.

Increased foreign competition also forced manufacturing companies to lay off millions of workers in the early 1980s. But an export boom for American manufactured goods in the late 1980s created 715,000 new factory jobs and helped boost manufacturing profits from an anemic $58 billion in 1985 to $98 billion in 1988.

For most of the 1970s and 1980s, it seemed as if this turmoil reflected a long-term decline in America's economic power. In the 1960s American goods were known for their quality and innovation. Today the roles are exactly reversed. Many American consumers looking for quality prefer Japanese products, and American companies no longer dominate the global markets for many important high-tech goods. Since 1975, for example, America's share of the global machine-tool market has fallen from 17.6% to 6.7%. The U.S. once had 73% of the fiber-optics market; now it has 41.9%. Similarly, its market shares for semiconductors (60% in 1975, but only 36% today), d-ram chips (95.8% down to only 20%), and supercomputers (100% down to 76%) are also tumbling.

The problem has already created its own buzzword—*competitiveness.* Many manufacturing companies are in trouble, but studying competitiveness, talking about competitiveness, and making political hay on competitiveness is a growth industry. Republicans and Democrats have formed a special Congressional Caucus on Competitiveness. Foundations of all political stripes are issuing reports on the subject. Every presidential candidate has his or her own surefire method of restoring competitiveness. But most of the discussion has produced more heat, in the form of political posturing, than enlightened solutions.

Congress, for example, debated the problem, studied the problem, and then came up with a solution that will make everything much worse—protectionism. Meanwhile, foreign and U.S. companies prepared for the end of free trade. The Japanese, for instance, moved some of their manufacturing operations to the U.S., setting up auto factories, electronics manufacturing firms, and other operations. Between 1983 and 1989, the Japanese invested over $49.8 billion in American factories, real estate, and companies. The Japanese now own at least a 10% stake in American companies with assets of over $164 billion. These companies employ 289,300 Americans and have annual sales of over $200 billion.

But if Japanese investment created some jobs, Congress's faddish preoccupation with protectionism has little chance of helping the job market or solving America's economic woes. Why? Protectionist legislation ignores the real causes of the trade deficit.

THE TRADE DEFICIT THAT WON'T GO AWAY

After all that's been written about the growing trade deficit, it's easy to imagine that the problem has been with us for some time, like death and taxes. Despite the rising cost of foreign oil, the U.S. held a narrow surplus throughout most of the 1970s.

What ended all of that was a combination of events that, taken together, spelled disaster. The dollar rose to record highs, pricing many U.S. goods out of the world market.

But the dollar wasn't the only culprit. American manufacturers had survived a strong dollar during the 1950s; however, in the 1980s American leadership in technology and productivity was gone, making U.S. companies more vulnerable to foreign competition. At the same time, a strong economy helped worsen the trade deficit. In 1984 and 1985, as the economy emerged from the worst recession since the 1930s, consumers created a strong demand for foreign products, especially electronics, but the economies of our trading partners did not show the same growth, and demand for U.S. exports remained sluggish. On top of that, the seemingly unsolvable debt crisis of third-world countries continued to hurt the market for U.S. exports.

The result was record-breaking trade deficits during the mid-1980s: $118 billion in 1985, $138 billion in 1986, and $152 billion in 1987. These deficits declined in the late 1980s, as the dollar weakened and American manufacturing was able to battle itself off the ropes with better productivity and improved management. Even so, a few numbers indicate the U.S. economy has a long way to go before it is really competitive in the new global order:

- The deficit in manufactured goods increased to about $124.6 billion in 1986, up from a surplus of $27.7 billion in 1980. By 1989 the deficit still totaled $92.4 billion.
- The trade outlook in agricultural goods, traditionally among the country's largest exports, worsened. In 1986 agricultural exports totaled only $5.3 billion, the lowest in 10 years. The 1989 surplus ($20.6 billion) is still below 1981's record ($26.6 billion).
- In smokestack industries—motor vehicles, iron, steel, primary copper, aluminum, lead, zinc, industrial machinery, farm machinery, and machine tools—the trade deficit grew from $21.5 billion in 1980 to over $65 billion in 1985.
- The picture wasn't even bright in high-tech industries. The trade surplus in high-tech products declined from $26 billion in 1980 to only $7 billion in 1988.
- Between 1982 and 1986, U.S. exports of manufactured goods increased a paltry 12% while imports surged 95%. Then, between 1989 and 1986, exports jumped 59% and imports surged 28%.

Region by region, the outlook wasn't any better. In 1989 the U.S. managed to have a trade deficit with every industrialized country except the United Kingdom, Australia, Ireland, Belgium, and the Netherlands.

- In 1989 the U.S. ran a trade deficit with developed industrialized nations ($55.3 billion), South America ($8.7 billion), the old communist bloc countries ($3.0 billion), and Africa ($6.6 billion).
- Our trade deficit with Japan increased from $19 billion in 1982 to $49.0 billion in 1989. Japan bought 12.2% of our exports—making it the second-largest buyer of U.S. exports—but supplied 19.8% of our imports, more than any other nation. As a result, the U.S. ran a larger trade deficit with Japan than with any other country.
- In 1986 the U.S. had a huge trade deficit of $26.4 billion with the 12 members of the European Economic Community, having had a surplus of $5.9 billion in 1982. But in 1989 the U.S. closed the trade gap and ran a slight surplus of $1.2 billion.
- The U.S. trade deficit with Canada jumped from $13.1 billion in 1982 to $23.3 billion in 1986, before the deficit was reduced to $9.1 billion in 1989.
- The U.S. trade deficits with the newly industrializing East Asian countries of Hong Kong, Singapore, South Korea, and Taiwan more than tripled from $8.2 billion in 1982 to $30.8 billion in 1986, before dropping to $24.3 billion in 1989.
- Even communist countries were winning the trade war. Our trade balance with China dropped from a $410 surplus in 1982 to a $2.1-billion deficit in 1986. The U.S. trade surplus with the U.S.S.R. dropped from $2.3 billion

in 1982 to only $642 in 1986, and our trade balance with Eastern European countries slipped from a $102-million surplus in 1982 to a deficit of $859 million in 1986. In 1989 the U.S. still ran a deficit of $3 billion with these countries.

- Despite the plunging price of oil, the U.S. trade balance with the Middle East dropped from a $3.5-billion surplus in 1982 to a $179 million deficit in 1986, and a $4.0-billion deficit in 1989.

Evidence of declining competitiveness can be found in almost any department store. Many popular consumer goods are no longer produced in the U.S. and foreign companies are capturing significant shares of the domestic market. By 1986, imports supplied 13.5% of the U.S. market, up from 10.2% in only four years. Nearly one third of all new cars sold were imports in 1990 (30%), compared to 15.3% in 1970. Imported steel has 18% of the market, up from 8% in 1973.

But those industries are only a few of those faced with an invasion of foreign goods. In computers (where the U.S. market share dropped from 94% in 1979 to 66% in 1989) color t.v. sets (92% to 74%), household appliances (92% to 87%), machine tools (77% to 64%), tires (88% to 79%), and cement (90% to only 30% in 1989), American industries have been losing the battle against foreign competition.

PROTECTIONISM

Protectionism seems at first glance to be such a simple solution to such a tough problem. With protectionism, beleaguered industries wouldn't have to reduce labor costs, spend money to modernize factories, improve productivity, or change shortsighted management policies. No national policy to promote industrial development by reducing taxes on capital gains or investments would be necessary. All you would need to do is simply raise tariffs and price foreign goods out of the market.

Sounds almost too good to be true, doesn't it? Well, it is. Protectionism has been tried before, with disastrous results. In the Great Depression, the attempt to cut foreign products out of the U.S. market touched off a trade war that reduced world trade, deepening the worldwide recession.

Today, the effects of protectionism would probably be even worse than in the 1930s. Currently the U.S. is more heavily dependent upon overseas trade. A recent U.S. Census Department study estimates that one out of every nine manufacturing jobs depends upon foreign trade. Exports accounted for nearly half (49.3%) of America's GNP growth in 1989, and a downturn in foreign demand for American products could badly hurt the American economy in the 1990s. The U.S. Department of Commerce estimates that a 5% drop in U.S. exports would cut real GNP growth by one fifth. Moreover, many of the same industries facing tough foreign competition are also those that account for a large share of America's exports. Nine of the 25 largest import products were also among the 25 largest export products. Motor vehicles and car bodies, for example, were America's leading import *and* its fifth-largest export. As a result, any attempt to restrict imports to protect the auto industry and other industries would trigger a trade war that would only cut down our exports of products from these industries.

Moreover, many U.S. companies have huge overseas operations that would be hurt by protectionist legislation, which would force those companies to lay off U.S. workers. American companies increased their foreign investments from $56.6 billion in 1967 to $322.2 billion in 1987 and $373.4 billion in 1989. Many of these companies have subsidiaries that export products to the U.S. The largest exporters from Taiwan, for example, are Sears, J.C. Penney, and K-Mart. Overall 15% of our imports come from foreign affiliates of U.S. companies. Those affiliates export over $80 billion in goods each year that could be cut off by protectionist legislation. Many of those companies are also in industries that are already struggling with foreign competition and the loss of those imports would make it harder for them to raise capital to compete with foreign companies. For example, in the auto industry General Motors imports $7.2 billion (8% of U.S. sales), Ford imports $6.3 billion (13%), and Chrysler imports $4.5 billion (25%) worth of goods from foreign affiliates.

Protectionism also increases the profits of many foreign companies. For example, quotas on many popular products have boosted the prices of foreign imports and given foreign companies higher profits—money they can use to improve their factories and become even tougher competitors. Foreign companies earned an extra $10 billion in profits thanks to quotas, in such key industries as apparel ($3.5 billion), steel ($2.8 billion), automobiles ($2.5 billion), and machine tools ($320 million).

Finally, protectionism is no more than a tax on U.S. consumers. Quotas and protectionist legislation already cost consumers $49.9 billion a year, according to economists Gary Hufbauer and Howard Rosen. Protectionist legislation increases the cost of textiles and apparel by $27 billion, carbon steel by $6.8 billion, and autos by $5.8 billion. These higher prices, of course, decrease the amount of money saved by the American public and reduce the capital available for modernization of U.S. plants and companies.

Worse, protectionist barriers are being raised all around the world. The Institute of International Economics believes that these trade barriers cut exports by $200 billion a year and reduce imports by more than $250 billion. If all these barriers were eliminated, the institute believes, worldwide trade would increase by about $330 billion a year—enough money to pay off the third-world debt in about 4 years.

There is also little evidence to suggest that protectionism has helped our big industrial losers anyway. The steel industry, for example, has enjoyed significant protection from imports in the last 20 years, yet its competitive position is weaker than ever. In 1984 President Reagan proposed even more protectionism with a measure that would limit imports to 18.5% of domestic consumption, but shortly after the program was passed a Federal Trade Commission study estimated the proposal would cost about $1.1 billion and save only 9,951 jobs, at a cost of about $185,000 a job! And even with this billion-dollar gift, employment in the steel industry continues to drop, with no end in sight.

And protectionism is, at best, a short-term solution. Much of the blame—for the practices of American management, labor, and government—can be found on our own side of the protectionist barrier.

PROBLEMS IN THE FACTORY: PRODUCTIVITY

Faced with massive layoffs in many manufacturing industries, American labor has launched a campaign against foreign competition. Demonstrating auto workers have smashed Japanese cars with sledgehammers and union leaders want legislation to restrict imports of foreign cars. Auto makers have put through rules that have forced employees driving foreign cars to take the least desirable parking spaces. Bob Hope and other stars have appeared on T.V. with appeals to "buy American."

Yet many economists and executives believe that American productivity, not Japanese business, is the real villain. For example, workers in one of Toyota's Japanese plants can produce a car in about 16 hours, but it takes GM 31 hours of labor for each car. Yet the Toyota cars average only 0.45 defects per car, while the GM cars have 1.35 defects.

The same problems can be found in statistics of productivity for the whole American economy.

U.S. productivity in the manufacturing sector as measured by output per hour grew only 2.2% between 1973 and 1985, down from a 3.2% increase between 1960 and 1973. That was way below Japan's growth rate of 10.3% a year between 1960 and 1973 and 5.6% between 1973 and 1985. As a result, U.S. productivity growth between 1960 and 1985 lagged way behind the 5.4% annual growth in productivity of 11 major foreign competitors. While U.S. manufacturing productivity grew only 2.7% a year between 1960 and 1985, productivity grew 8.0% in Japan, 5.5% in France, 3.4% in Canada, 4.8% in Germany, 5.4% in Italy, 3.5% in the United Kingdom, 6.5% in Belgium, 4.8% in Denmark, 6.2% in the Netherlands, 3.2% in Norway, and 4.7% in Sweden.

Since then, the U.S. has shown some improvement. Between 1985 and 1988, the most recent year when comparable international statistics were available, U.S. manufacturing productivity grew at an average rate of 3.3% a year, faster than Canada (1.9%), France, (2.8%), Germany (1.9%), and Italy (2.1%). But it lagged behind the United Kingdom (4.9%) and its chief foreign competitor, Japan (5.7%). In 1989, U.S. competitiveness weakened even further, as manufacturing productivity grew only 2.0%, and it rose only 2.4% in 1990.

Those are the depressing numbers. But what happens to productivity is more than an idle statistical game. If everything else remains the same, increased output from labor and capital means there is more money to pay workers and shareholders. To illustrate how productivity affects a country's standard of living, the American Productivity Center did a study comparing what would have happened to our standard of living if the U.S. had maintained its high levels of productivity growth. Let's assume labor productivity never slowed down, as it did after 1965. Instead, labor productivity continued growing at the 1948 to 1965 rate—3.2% a year for the whole economy. In that case the average worker would have produced $56,704 of goods and services yearly. Now, let's assume labor productivity only grew 0.9% a year during those 20 years, as it did between 1979 and 1985. Then the average worker would have produced only $33,728 in goods and services yearly. In short, America's failure to sustain a high rate of productivity costs every worker $10,000 to $20,000 a year in higher living standards.

The notion that improved productivity will improve wages isn't just an academic theory. Increased productivity allowed Japanese wages to grow 4.2% a year faster than inflation between 1970 and 1980, 1.8% a year between 1980 and 1985, and 3.7% a year between 1985 and 1988. Meanwhile, real wages for U.S. workers increased only 0.8% a year in the 1970s, 0.4% annually in the first half of the 1980s, and they actually fell 0.1% a year between 1985 and 1988. Higher productivity also did wonders for Japanese shareholders. If, for example, you compare the performance of U.S. and Japanese stocks between the end of the 1960s and the mid-1980s, Japanese companies' stocks outperformed American stocks, producing much higher yields.

And decreased productivity has its human costs in layoffs, plant shutdowns, and unemployment. A 1990 study by the Bureau of Labor Statistics found that about 9.7 million Americans lost their jobs because of plant closings or employment cutbacks between the start of 1979 and 1987. Of the 4.6 million workers displaced between 1983 and 1987, about 15.9% remained unemployed and 14.5% left the labor force. Many of the manufacturing workers who found new employment were forced to accept lower wages. About 28% of the 1.2 million displaced manufacturing workers who eventually found jobs suffered wage cuts of over 20%, and another 16% saw their wages drop by 1 to 20%. And in some high-paying manufacturing sectors, the news was even worse. About half (48.8%) of the displaced steel workers earned 20% less when they found a new job.

Yet it would be a mistake to blame the decline of American manufacturing entirely on labor productivity or imagine that simple solutions such as cutting wages will have much effect. Increased automation has made labor costs a smaller part of the cost of doing business. Also, if lowering wages were the only way for the U.S. to regain its edge, then the solution might be worse than the problem. American business has long known that its welfare ultimately depends on having workers who make enough to buy its products. Since relatively high wages in the postwar world have made a boom in consumer goods possible, a concerted attack on the income levels of American workers would be much like killing the goose that laid the golden egg. No solution to the problem of foreign competition can come without improved management and changes in the way America allocates its resources.

PROBLEMS IN THE FACTORY: MANAGEMENT

Management, for all its talk about regaining competitiveness in the international marketplace, isn't putting its money where its mouth is. Consider the following facts:

- Many American corporations spent the 1980s trying to produce short-term results so that they could avoid being taken over by corporate raiders. The $1 trillion spent on buying and selling corporate assets between 1985 and 1989 is far more money than the $801 billion spent by American manufacturing companies on new plants and equipment during the same period.
- The $1.5 trillion worth of mergers and leveraged buyouts between 1980 and the end of 1990 also left many corporations heavily in debt. The value of corporate bonds outstanding jumped from $819 billion in 1985 to $1.6 trillion in 1990, making it difficult for many companies to invest in new factories. Interest payments as a percentage of after-tax profits climbed from 19% in the 1960s to 53% in the 1970s. By the end of the 1980s, the interest burden had more than doubled, to 118% of after-tax profits.
- The private investment in plants and equipment totals about 10% of GNP in the U.S.; it is 17% in Japan. The average U.S. factory is much older—17 years, compared to 10 years in Japan.
- There is a growing body of evidence suggesting that merger mania and the financial excesses of the 1980s hurt the competitive position of U.S. companies. A study by the National Science Foundation of the 200 companies that spend the most on research and development found that the 24 companies that merged or underwent an LBO reduced their research spending by 8.3% in real terms in 1986 and 1987, a period when the other companies increased theirs by 5.4%. A more recent, smaller survey of 72 firms by the NSF confirms those findings. It found that, between 1988 and 1990, the 21 firms that were involved in takeovers or LBOs reduced their research spending by 0.2% (a 3 to 5% reduction if you adjust for inflation). The other companies increased such spending by 6.8%.
- The U.S. developed robot technology but today it has the worst record of any industrialized nation for applying new robot technology.

In the late 1970s, American management was also slow to adopt techniques that could cut costs. While Japanese managers cut costs by reducing inventories of parts, Americans kept their capital tied up in warehouses of parts and supplies. Remember the GM and Toyota plants where it took 31 hours for the GM plant to build a car and Toyota only 16? Well, the Toyota plant also did a much better job with inventory control. The Toyota factory was so efficiently run that it kept only 2 hours' worth of spare parts on hand. The GM plant, meanwhile, inventoried 2 weeks' worth of parts.

American managers also deserve low marks for their quality control. For example, most American managers checked the quality of goods as they left the plant. However, by this time many goods had already been repaired or worked on several times, adding huge hidden costs. Japanese managers, however, worked to make certain the job was done right the first time. That not only cut costs but also improved quality.

Starting in the early 1980s, management scrambled to regain its competitive edge. Aging, unprofitable plants were closed. Layers of middle management were sent packing. Job classifications that required one worker to plug in a piece of equipment and another to run it were done away with. A million-plus manufacturing jobs were slashed.

Some of the results have been encouraging. GM and Toyota, for example, collaborated on a new car plant in Fremont, California, in 1987. This plant doesn't perform quite as well as the Toyota plant in Japan, but is far more efficient than the GM factory mentioned above. In Fremont, it takes only 19 hours to assemble a car, the quality rate is higher (0.45 defects per car is the same as Toyota's Japanese plant and much better than the 1.35 at GM), and the plant keeps only 2 days' worth of parts on stock.

The impact of similar ventures can be seen in trade statistics for the whole country. The U.S. trade deficit fell to $5 billion in June of 1990, the lowest monthly level in 7 years and totalled $105 billion in 1990, way down from the $152-billion record in 1987. Even better, the U.S. was running a $1.7 billion surplus with European countries, up from a $21-billion deficit in 1987. Also encouraging was the fact that foreign countries were buying American capital goods in record numbers, producing a $37-billion surplus, up from $2 billion in 1987.

Unfortunately, much remains to be done. Productivity has not improved in services despite a $150-billion investment in computers, telecommunications, and other high-tech equipment in the last few years. Recent Labor Department figures show that Canada has replaced the U.S. as the world's most productive nation. And closing plants, laying off workers, restructuring operations, and moving factories overseas may improve profits for a few years, but they are not long-term solutions.

PUTTING CAPITAL BACK TO WORK

No improvement in productivity can take place until businesses are able to afford new equipment and factories. But U.S. companies face much higher costs to finance new capital than many of our major competitors. A 1990 study for Congress by the Office of Technology Assessment estimates that American businesses have to spend more for long-term capital than their toughest competitor, Japan: "Each year from 1977 to 1988, the cost of capital in America averaged 3.4 percentage points higher than the cost of capital in Japan for investments in machinery and equipment with a physical life of 20 years; 4.9 percentage points higher for a factory with a physical life of 40 years, and 8 percentage points higher for a research and development project with a 10-year payoff." Not surprisingly, Japan spends about 30% of its gross domestic product on capital formation, compared to about 20% for the U.S.

Why is it so much more expensive to finance new investments in the U.S.? Huge federal deficits, which have kept interest rates high, are one problem. If Congress would forget about protectionist legislation and start worrying about the deficit it could dramatically improve the ability of American companies to finance new factories and capital.

Congress could also cut the cost of capital by reducing heavy-handed government regulation of the financial markets and by passing tax laws designed to encourage private savings. Right now, Americans have one of the lowest savings rates in the world. Americans save about 5.6% of their disposable income; the Japanese save 15.3%, the Canadians 10.4%, and the Germans 12.2%. U.S. savings are only 15.1% of our gross domestic product; savings account for 33% of GDP in Japan, 24% in Germany, and 21.1% in Canada.

In recent years, American consumers have been living beyond their means and cutting back on savings to buy more foreign goods than they export. These lower savings rates force American companies to pay high interest rates for scarce capital, hurting their ability to modernize plants. At the same time, the trade deficit puts more money in foreign hands, making it easier for foreigners to improve their competitive positions.

Increased private savings would help the trade deficit in the short run—since consumers would be buying fewer foreign goods on credit. In the long run it would help productivity—since increased savings would make capital less scarce and hence less expensive.

Of course, even a policy that encourages new investment and technology is not enough. American management is going to have to improve the way it uses high technology. GM, for example, spent millions building a high-tech plant in Hamtramck, Michigan, but the robots spray-painted each other instead of the cars and the company had to ship the cars to a 57-year-old plant to be repainted.

A plea for consistency in formulating public policy is always in order. Criticizing American business for its short-term outlook is a popular pastime in Washington. Corporate America has forgotten about long-term investment in the pursuit of short-term gains, the standard refrain goes.

Fair enough. But what's really needed is some consistency in Washington. There is no single solution to the problems facing American industry. The tax system will have to become more supportive of capital investment. Labor will have to make concessions on work rules and costs; management is going to have to make a long-term commitment to becoming competitive. All that takes time. But Congress continues to change its mind every few years. A few years ago it gave U.S. companies investment tax credits. Then, a few years later, it took them away because investment tax credits didn't solve all the world's problems. Congress needs to give up this short-term outlook and follow its own advice to American business—adopt a long-term, consistent policy. That way American companies can make long-term investment decisions without worrying about Congress upsetting their plans next year.

Table 17-1 The U.S. and Its Competitors
(numbers in thousands)

Employment status and country	1980	1981	1982	1983	1984	1985	1986	1987	1988	1989
Labor force										
United States	106,940	108,670	110,204	111,550	113,544	115,461	117,834	119,865	121,669	123,869
Canada	11,573	11,899	11,926	12,109	12,316	12,532	12,746	13,011	13,275	13,503
Australia	6,693	6,810	6,910	6,997	7,135	7,300	7,588	7,758	7,974	8,237
Japan	55,740	56,320	56,980	58,110	58,480	58,820	59,410	60,050	60,860	61,920
France	22,800	22,950	23,160	23,140	23,300	23,360	23,440	23,550	23,590	23,750
Germany	27,260	27,540	27,710	27,670	27,800	28,020	28,240	28,380	28,580	28,790
Italy	21,120	21,320	21,410	21,590	21,670	21,800	22,290	22,350	22,660	22,530
Netherlands	5,860	6,080	6,140	6,170	6,260	6,280	6,370	6,540	6,560	6,650
Sweden	4,312	4,327	4,350	4,369	4,385	4,418	4,443	4,480	4,540	4,599
United Kingdom	26,520	26,590	26,560	26,590	27,010	27,210	27,380	27,720	28,150	28,250
Participation rate[1]										
United States	63.8	63.9	64.0	64.0	64.4	64.8	65.3	65.6	65.9	66.5
Canada	64.1	64.8	64.1	64.4	64.8	65.3	65.7	66.2	66.7	67.0
Australia	62.1	61.9	61.7	61.4	61.5	61.6	62.8	63.0	63.3	64.2
Japan	62.6	62.6	62.7	63.1	62.7	62.3	62.1	61.9	61.9	62.2
France	57.2	57.1	57.1	56.6	56.6	56.3	56.1	55.9	55.5	55.5
Germany	54.7	54.7	54.6	54.3	54.4	54.7	54.9	55.0	54.9	55.0
Italy	48.2	48.3	47.7	47.5	47.3	47.2	47.8	47.6	47.4	47.1
Netherlands	55.3	56.6	56.5	56.1	56.2	55.7	55.9	56.7	56.3	56.7
Sweden	66.9	66.8	66.8	66.7	66.6	66.9	67.0	67.1	67.6	68.1
United Kingdom	62.5	62.2	61.9	61.6	62.1	62.2	62.3	62.7	63.5	63.6
Employed										
United States	99,303	100,397	99,526	100,834	105,005	107,150	109,597	112,440	114,968	117,342
Canada	10,708	11,001	10,618	10,675	10,932	11,221	11,531	11,861	12,245	12,486
Australia	6,284	6,416	6,415	6,300	6,494	6,697	6,974	7,129	7,398	7,728
Japan	54,600	55,060	55,620	56,550	56,870	57,260	57,740	58,320	59,310	60,500
France	21,330	21,200	21,240	21,170	20,980	20,920	20,950	21,020	21,180	21,440
Germany	26,490	26,450	26,150	25,770	25,830	26,010	26,380	26,580	26,770	27,140
Italy	20,200	20,280	20,250	20,320	20,390	20,490	20,610	20,590	20,870	20,770
Netherlands	5,510	5,510	5,510	5,410	5,490	5,640	5,730	5,890	5,940	6,050
Sweden	4,226	4,219	4,213	4,218	4,249	4,293	4,326	4,396	4,467	4,538
United Kingdom	24,670	23,800	23,560	23,450	23,830	24,150	24,300	24,860	25,740	26,270
Employment-population ratio[2]										
United States	59.2	59.0	57.8	57.9	59.5	60.1	60.7	61.5	62.3	63.0
Canada	59.3	59.9	57.1	56.8	57.5	58.5	59.4	60.4	61.6	62.0
Australia	58.3	58.4	57.3	55.3	56.0	56.5	57.7	57.9	58.7	60.2
Japan	61.3	61.2	61.2	61.4	61.0	60.6	60.4	60.1	60.4	60.8
France	53.5	52.8	52.3	51.8	51.0	50.4	50.2	49.9	49.8	50.1
Germany	53.1	52.5	51.6	50.6	50.5	50.7	51.3	51.5	51.5	51.9
Italy	46.1	45.9	45.2	44.7	44.5	44.4	44.2	43.8	43.7	43.4
Netherlands	52.0	51.6	50.7	49.2	49.3	50.0	50.2	51.1	51.0	51.5
Sweden	65.6	65.1	64.7	64.4	64.5	65.0	65.2	65.8	66.5	67.2
United Kingdom	58.1	55.7	54.9	54.3	54.8	55.2	55.2	56.2	58.1	59.2
Unemployed										
United States	7,637	8,273	10,678	10,717	8,539	8,312	8,237	7,425	6,701	6,528
Canada	865	898	1,308	1,434	1,384	1,311	1,215	1,150	1,031	1,018
Australia	409	394	495	697	641	603	613	629	576	509
Japan	1,140	1,260	1,360	1,560	1,610	1,560	1,670	1,730	1,550	1,420
France	1,470	1,750	1,920	1,970	2,320	2,440	2,490	2,530	2,410	2,310
Germany	770	1,090	1,560	1,900	1,970	2,010	1,860	1,800	1,810	1,650
Italy	920	1,040	1,160	1,270	1,280	1,310	1,680	1,760	1,790	1,760
Netherlands	350	540	630	760	770	640	640	650	620	600
Sweden	86	108	137	151	136	125	117	84	73	61
United Kingdom	1,850	2,790	3,000	3,140	3,180	3,060	3,080	2,860	2,410	1,980
Unemployment rate										
United States	7.1	7.6	9.7	9.6	7.5	7.2	7.0	6.2	5.5	5.3
Canada	7.5	7.5	11.0	11.8	11.2	10.5	9.5	8.8	7.8	7.5
Australia	6.1	5.8	7.2	10.0	9.0	8.3	8.1	8.1	7.2	6.2
Japan	2.0	2.2	2.4	2.7	2.8	2.6	2.8	2.9	2.5	2.3
France	6.4	7.6	8.3	8.5	10.0	10.4	10.6	10.7	10.2	9.7
Germany	2.8	4.0	5.6	6.9	7.1	7.2	6.6	6.3	6.3	5.7
Italy	4.4	4.9	5.4	5.9	5.9	6.0	7.5	7.9	7.9	7.8
Netherlands	6.0	8.9	10.3	12.3	12.3	10.2	10.0	9.9	9.5	9.0
Sweden	2.0	2.5	3.1	3.5	3.1	2.8	2.6	1.9	1.6	1.3
United Kingdom	7.0	10.5	11.3	11.8	11.8	11.2	11.2	10.3	8.6	7.0

[1]Labor force as a percent of the civilian working-age population.
[2]Employment as a percent of the civilian working-age population.
Note: See "Notes on the data" for information on breaks in series for Germany, Italy, the Netherlands, and Sweden.
Source: *Monthly Labor Review*

257

Table 17-2   Growth Rates in Real Gross National Product, 1961–1990

(percent change)

Area and country	1961–65 annual average	1966–70 annual average	1971–75 annual average	1976–83 annual average	1984	1985	1986	1987	1988	1989	1990[1]
OECD countries[2]	5.3	4.6	3.0	2.8	4.8	3.4	2.7	3.4	4.4	3.4	2.8
United States	4.6	3.0	2.2	2.5	6.8	3.4	2.7	3.4	4.5	2.5	.9
Canada	5.3	4.6	5.2	2.7	6.3	4.7	3.3	4.0	4.4	3.0	1.1
Japan	12.4	11.0	4.3	4.4	5.1	4.9	2.5	4.6	5.7	4.9	6.1
European Community[3]	4.9	4.6	2.9	2.3	2.5	2.4	2.7	2.7	3.9	3.5	2.9
France	5.9	5.4	4.0	2.5	1.3	1.9	2.5	2.2	3.8	3.6	2.5
West Germany	4.7	4.2	2.1	2.4	3.3	1.9	2.3	1.6	3.7	3.9	4.2
Italy	4.8	6.6	2.4	3.3	3.0	2.6	2.5	3.0	4.2	3.2	2.6
United Kingdom	3.2	2.5	2.1	1.7	2.1	3.6	3.9	4.7	4.6	2.2	1.6
U.S.S.R.	4.8	5.0	3.0	2.0	1.2	.9	3.5	1.9	2.2	1.4	–3.0
Eastern Europe	3.9	3.8	4.9	1.2	3.0	.5	2.5	.0	1.5	–.3	–4.0
China	–.2	8.3	7.4	6.7	14.6	12.7	8.3	11.0	10.8	3.9	4.4

[1]Estimates.
[2]OECD (Organization for Economic Cooperation and Development) includes Australia, Austria, Belgium, Denmark, Finland, France, West Germany, Greece, Iceland, Ireland, Italy, Luxembourg, Netherlands, New Zealand, Norway, Portugal, Spain, Sweden, Switzerland, Turkey, and United Kingdom, not shown separately.
[3]Includes Belgium, Denmark, Greece, Ireland, Luxembourg, Netherlands, Portugal, and Spain, not shown separately.
Sources: Department of Commerce, International Monetary Fund, Organization for Economic Cooperation and Development, and Council of Economic Advisers.

TRADE TRIVIA

1492   Columbus's arrival in the New World in 1492 leads to the discovery of a number of plants and foods that will eventually help feed Europe: corn, sweet potatoes, peppers, allspice, plantains, pineapples, and turtle meat.

1585   Jesuit missionaries introduce deep-fried cooking (tempura) to Japan.

1608   The first usable shipment of American goods sent to Europe is a cargo of pitch, tar, soap, ashes, and glass shipped from Jamestown in 1608. Even so, Captain Christopher Newport is not upset with his modest cargo. Twice before, he has carried back worthless mica with him to England, thinking it is gold.

1619   The first slave is imported to the U.S., to the Virginia colony of Jamestown, by a Dutch pirate. Eventually 10 million Africans are imported to the New World.

1630   At the first Thanksgiving dinner, British colonists discover popcorn, an old American Indian staple. It is not served in a paper sack or a cardboard tub; the Indians bring the popped kernels to the colonists in a deerskin sack.

1638   Honeybees are imported into the U.S. Native Americans call them the "white man's flies" and they spread all over the country. Later, western pioneers believe they are indigenous to the country.

late 1700s   Trading recipes: Thomas Jefferson imports french fries to America after growing fond of them while serving as ambassador to France. He also popularizes the idea of eating spaghetti and the habit of eating steak with french fries.

1930   Despite a petition signed by 1,028 economists who attack the idea of restricting trade, Congress passes the Smoot-Hawley tariff bill, raising tariffs to their highest level in history. The idea is to revive the economy by restricting imports. But other countries pass similar bills and, as world trade drops, the Depression gets much worse, causing even more unemployment.

1958   The Hula Hoop fad hits the U.S. and is quickly exported overseas. Worldwide sales eventually hit over 100 million. In England, TV stations broadcast live instructions to teach straitlaced British citizens how to get into the swing of things. The "huru hoopu," as it translates in Japan, spreads through the Land of the Rising Sun to "every yard, vacant lot and alley," according to one newspaper account. But following reports of back injuries and the death of one girl who is run over by a car while chasing her run-away "huru hoopu," Tokyo police ban the toy from the city's streets. By the end of the year, the fad fades and sales drop. Phillips Petroleum, which has sold plastic to the hoop makers, advises companies to punch holes in unsold hoops and try to pass them off as lawn showers.

1968   Worldwide trade and commerce is so important that a study by French economist Jean-Jacques Servan-Shreiber notes that the production of multinational companies around the world is exceeded only by the GNP of the U.S. and the Soviet Union.

1980   One of the few successful communist-bloc imports is Rubik's Cube. Invented by a Hungarian architectural professor, it becomes a fad in his own country before being imported to the U.S. under a licensing agreement with the Ideal Toy Company. Sales of the cube reach 10 million by 1981, with nearly twice as many counterfeit versions sold. The object is to arrange all the colors so that each side of the cube is one color, no easy task when you consider that there are 43,252,003,274,489,856,000 possible patterns.

1980s   The breadbasket of the world: Every American farmer produces enough to feed himself, 8 foreigners, and 45 Americans.

1986   A mounting trade deficit makes the U.S. the largest debtor in the world. Its net debt, the difference in value between foreign holdings in the U.S. and American investments abroad, reaches $107.4 billion in 1985, more than that of Brazil ($94.1 billion) or Mexico ($93.1 billion). Japan is the world's largest creditor nation with net assets of $129.8 billion. Only 5 years earlier, the U.S. was the world's largest creditor nation, with net assets of $140.7 billion.

Table 17-3 Labor Costs Around the World

The U.S. is not the most expensive labor market in the world. Here are hourly labor costs, including benefits, around the world.

Switzerland	$14.01
West Germany	13.85
U.S.	13.29
Sweden	12.53
Italy	10.82
France	10.49
Japan	7.76
United Kingdom	7.67
Greece	4.04
South Korea	1.53

Source: Business International Corporation.

Table 17-4 United States Merchandise Trade, 1970–1989

(domestic and foreign merchandise, f.a.s.; general imports, customs value; millions of dollars)

	Total merchandise			Manufactured goods			Agricultural products		
	Exports	Imports	Balance	Exports	Imports	Balance	Exports	Imports	Balance
1970	43,762.0	40,355.6	3,406.4	31,720.1	27,332.0	4,388.1	7,349.0	5,767.4	1,581.6
1971	44,718.9	46,169.7	(1,450.8)	32,904.6	32,103.7	800.9	7,785.8	5,765.5	2,020.3
1972	50,466.6	56,364.8	(5,898.2)	36,503.2	39,710.0	(3,206.8)	9,505.0	6,512.8	2,992.2
1973	72,495.8	70,472.7	2,023.1	48,467.7	47,130.6	1,337.1	17,861.3	8,491.6	9,369.7
1974	100,036.0	102,559.3	(2,523.3)	68,512.6	57,829.7	10,682.9	22,259.8	10,380.4	11,879.4
1975	109,316.8	98,502.9	10,813.9	76,869.5	54,004.0	22,865.5	22,095.5	9,471.9	12,623.6
1976	116,984.2	123,477.1	(6,492.9)	83,120.2	67,631.8	15,488.4	23,281.7	11,179.3	12,102.4
1977	123,243.4	151,038.5	(27,795.1)	88,901.7	80,504.0	8,397.7	24,234.2	13,597.7	10,636.5
1978	145,932.0	174,756.8	(28,824.8)	103,633.8	104,334.4	(700.6)	29,776.8	14,961.6	14,815.2
1979	186,527.6	209,458.3	(22,930.7)	132,745.4	117,130.9	15,614.5	35,212.9	16,879.5	18,333.4
1980	225,722.3	245,261.9	(19,539.6)	160,651.4	132,986.5	27,664.9	41,757.1	17,446.0	24,311.1
1981	238,685.9	260,981.8	(22,295.9)	171,749.3	149,752.1	21,997.2	43,813.6	17,182.4	26,631.2
1982	216,441.6	243,951.9	(27,510.3)	155,305.4	151,727.9	3,577.5	37,010.1	15,714.2	21,295.9
1983	205,638.6	258,047.8	(52,409.2)	148,466.8	171,189.3	(22,722.5)	36,455.8	16,533.0	19,922.8
1983	205,638.6	258,047.8	(52,409.2)	148,664.7	170,865.2	(22,200.5)	36,192.7	15,990.1	20,202.6
1984	223,998.7	330,681.2	(106,682.5)	164,071.3	230,909.6	(66,838.3)	37,950.4	19,337.3	18,613.0
1985	218,828.0	336,536.2	(117,708.2)	168,025.0	257,477.6	(89,452.6)	29,320.0	19,525.7	9,794.3
1986	227,158.5	365,437.7	(138,279.2)	179,818.6	296,652.7	(116,834.1)	26,322.7	20,946.1	5,376.6
1987	254,121.9	406,241.0	(152,119.1)	199,883.5	324,443.9	(124,560.4)	28,754.1	20,343.6	8,410.5
1988	322,426.4	440,952.3	(118,525.9)	255,638.7	361,381.0	(105,742.3)	37,210.8	20,750.9	16,459.9
1989	363,811.5	473,210.8	(109,399.3)	287,017.5	379,425.4	(92,407.9)	41,727.0	21,133.8	20,593.3

Note: Compiled from official statistics of the U.S. Department of Commerce.
Includes revisions to 1988 and 1989 data.
Data for 1983–1988 are estimated, based on the Harmonized System of commodity classification.
Data before 1983 are on a Schedule A/E basis and have been adjusted to match the 1990 trade definitions as closely as possible. Parentheses indicate negative values.

Chapter Eighteen
THE STOCK MARKET

HIGHLIGHTS AND TRENDS

Over the last decade, you couldn't have asked for a sweeter deal than the stock market. "Bull market" hardly seems like an adequate description for the leaps and bounds the stock market took when it roared back to life in mid-1982. Not since the market climbed out of the pits in 1932 had the Dow Jones Industrial Average doubled faster. Other, broader indexes soared as well. Records were routinely broken as, in the first three months of 1987 alone, the DJIA rose more than 400 points to above 2,400. By August it had cracked 2,700. But by late August the market was losing ground and on October 19 plunged an incredible 508 points, the biggest drop ever. More than $500 billion dollars in asset value was erased overnight, bringing total losses for a two-month period to more than $1 trillion.

But even the scary meltdown proved to be no more than a "correction," as the market returned not just to life but to record heights. By July 1990, the DJIA had soared to within a fraction of the 3,000 mark. Then, with the eruption of the Persian Gulf crisis adding to concerns about the tumbling Tokyo market, U.S. stocks sold off sharply and analysts outdid themselves with pessimistic predictions. Curse that Saddam Hussein! But in April 1991 the DJIA fooled the gloomsters again and cracked 3,000.

No one can say for sure just why the market went into its wild gyrations in October 1987 that saw the biggest daily gains and losses at any time in market history. Our trade and budget deficit problems were long with us, and the dipping dollar at the time wasn't brand-new either. The fact that the market could do so, however, had much to do with changes in the market itself. One major change is technological. The computerization of trading has accelerated the buying and selling of stock to a mind-boggling level and made the market more sensitive to the whims and wants of the powerful portfolio managers for big institutions, such as pension, insurance, and mutual funds, as well as private investment groups and the equity traders at major banks and brokerages. Also, computers have spawned trading in so-called stock-index futures (see page 299). After the October 19 debacle, a lot of people blamed futures for helping precipitate the crash.

Institutions worldwide had some $12 trillion dollars in the capital markets by 1990 that they could shift around as their fingers danced across computer-panel keys. Every day the institutions made 80% of stock trades though they controlled only about a third of the equity on the U.S. exchanges. The computer dance became the whirl of a dancing dervish. Daily volume on the New York Stock Exchange soared to more than 600 million shares, double the previous record. That's astounding considering that in the 1970s 30 million would have tested the Big Board's limits.

While we wonder what the market will do next, it's instructive to look at what happened with the market from the outset of the bull market in 1982 to the jitters in late 1990. The terrific bull markets of yore were based on epic events: war and peace, depression and recovery. This time around, the two big pushes behind the market drive were declining interest rates and lower inflation. Humbled and battered by more than a decade of climbing inflation, the stock market came back to health after a dose of the elixir disinflation. Waning inflation results in lower interest rates. As interest rates came down, corporate earnings growth became more important to investors.

The market also capitalized on a few lucky breaks. One was a hemorrhaging in oil prices, which seemed only just after the way the OPEC price hikes of the early 1970s knocked inflation in the U.S. into double digits and were a big factor in the market battering of 1974. The drop in oil prices—from $32 a barrel to $13 by the end of 1986—helped push long-term interest rates down to 8% by the end of 1986, from 12% a year earlier.

Moreover, the market benefited from takeover-hungry corporations, takeover-fearful companies that bought up their own stock, and the mad dash for mutual funds that created new demand. Also, the new markets in stock options and futures made stocks hotter. Finally, legions of foreign investors lusted after U.S. stocks in what has been called "globalization" or "internationalization" of the marketplace.

The Japanese, in particular, with their huge trade surpluses, invested heavily in everything American from stocks and bonds to real estate. Four Japanese brokerage firms—Nomura Securities, Daiwa Securities, Nikko Securities, and Yamaichi—came on so strong that there was talk that Wall Street might eventually go the way of the consumer electronics industry.

In London, the much-touted deregulation of its Stock Exchange, or "Big Bang" as it was dubbed, shook up that domestic market and added to the fierceness of the global competition and also the problems (see "Problems in the Global Village," below).

The joker in the deck was the U.S. dollar. From the late 1970s to the mid-1980s, the dollar had an extraordinary upsurge compared with other currencies. To everyone's dismay, that created severe economic dislocations, including an apparent severing of the link between the growth of the money supply and the GNP. The economy was sluggish but the money supply grew like kudzu in lush tropical soil. The result wasn't hard to find. The strong dollar made U.S. goods costlier, putting American companies at a serious disadvantage, and the trade deficit ballooned. Some fallout, though, helped the market. The overseas trade surplus resulted in more U.S. stock buying by foreigners.

The market got another boost in the fall of 1985 when the U.S., Japan, Britain, West Germany, and France agreed to bring the dollar down. Then Fed Chairman Paul A. Volcker backed the plan, which meant the Fed wouldn't raise interest rates, which, in effect, would have caused the dollar to go higher. The Dow went to 1550 by January 1986, a 250-point jump from the time of the announcement in late September.

So what happened? In 1987, the Reagan administration pushed the dollar lower. A declining dollar usually spurs the economy by making U.S. goods more competitive but it also adds to inflation as the prices of imports rise. Concern developed that the dollar sank too low. Meanwhile, the market wasn't getting the titanic boost from corporate raiders that it had in 1985 and 1986. (See the chapter "Deals and Mergers.") And by 1987, stocks were at their highest price levels compared to the value of assets since 1971.

Even so, U.S. stocks still looked good when compared to a lot of foreign stocks, especially Japanese stocks. Price-earnings multiples in Japan were around 50 times earnings versus 16 in the U.S., based on Merrill Lynch's 1987 earnings estimate for the Standard & Poor's 500 Composite Stock Index (S&P 500). Dividend yields in the U.S. in the first half of 1987 were 3% versus less than 1% in Japan. That's one reason the U.S. stock market remained strong in the face of mediocre corporate earnings and a horrific trade debt, even after the October 1987 "correction."

But all along, there were serious problems with the size of the U.S. budget deficit and the whopping trade imbalance. Meanwhile, Wall Street firms became bloated with bright young M.B.A.'s as they grasped for more and more. Cautious money managers were scoffed at. Consumers and companies overreached. Time and again, events that might have resulted in big selloffs didn't: the insider-trading scandals, the Iranian arms deal, the Latin debt problem, the Persian Gulf crisis.

What finally happened was that everything came together: fears over war, unstable oil prices, the bleak U.S. trade and budget deficits, an incredibly low dollar, financial innovations that made markets more efficient but also more susceptible to change, and the electronic-market global village we've created in which what adversely affects the exchanges in London, Hong Kong, or Tokyo affects New York's exchanges and vice versa.

No one, of course, can say for sure what will happen with the market. If the U.S. goes into future recessions still laden with excessive debt, the Fed may once again feel it has to inflate the economy to stave off depression. But if inflation isn't severe and the debt is pared down, there may be "corrections" in a market that rebounds. Whatever happens, a lot of stockholders will remember the sickening feeling they had when the market whipped wildly about like a flag in a hurricane. But then the market was never meant to be considered a sure thing. About the only thing certain about the market is what J. P. Morgan noted: "It will fluctuate."

PROBLEMS IN THE GLOBAL VILLAGE

The pundits use such expressions as "globalization" and "a one-world marketplace" when bantering about securities markets. To be sure, the global village is with us, thanks to deregulation and technological innovation.

Today, the world's competing financial centers—New York, London, Tokyo, Paris, Frankfurt—are getting rid of constraining regulations. As a result, more trading is done in unregulated international markets, especially Euroequities and Eurobonds, which live only in computer memories and phone links between customers and dealers. A tremendous amount of securities—some $12 trillion a year—freely crosses borders. (More than $600 billion a day is traded in the foreign exchange market.) Investors literally can now scan the globe for the highest rates of return at the cheapest cost.

This speedy growth of international securities markets, like a bucket of cold water thrown on Rip van Winkle, awakened a lot of domestic stock exchanges. But the rapid changes have brought about some new wrinkles for the van Winkles, especially in the form of ruthless competition and related problems.

The prime example of how things can get botched in a headlong race to deregulate a market is the London market. In October 1986, London's "Big Bang" was the most sweeping deregulation of any major financial marketplace. Fixed commissions on domestic equities and government bonds were done away with. Likewise, the distinction between brokers for individual clients and wholesalers disappeared. The result was heady expectations altered by cutthroat competition.

Brokers, who no longer enjoyed the certainty of fixed commissions, needed a lot more capital for trade. The London stock exchange's membership was opened to anyone, regardless of nationality. With that, the supposed gold rush was on. Foreign banks and securities firms elbowed their way into the city like lemmings anxious to race off a cliff.

What happened? Competition became fierce. Losses mounted, especially after the market crash of 1987. In 1988, London exchange member firms lost some $800 million in trading British shares. The next year saw another loss of more than $250 million. Banks such as Chase Manhattan and Citicorp licked their wounds and shut down their operations. Others pared their operations.

Meanwhile, Paris and Frankfurt started trying to lure away trade and end the London market's dominance of the little-regulated Euromarkets. A more serious challenge was mounted from the U.S. The Securities and Exchange Commission introduced Rule 144a, which allowed institutional investors to buy securities that hadn't gone through the expensive, time-consuming process of registration with the SEC. The aim was to encourage foreign as well as U.S. issuers to sell more stocks and bonds in the U.S. rather than the Euromarkets. Japan mounted a challenge too, as the government tried to put more zip in Tokyo's bond market.

Another problem that internationalization brought on was Americans being blamed by Japanese for the severe decline in the Tokyo stock market, which saw the Nikkei 225-share average plunge from a record 38,915 on December 19, 1989, to 28,002 on April 2, 1990. Bearish institutional investors sold futures in the market rather than the actual shares. As the price of the futures fell, the market was pulled down. As the value of the institutions' portfolios decreased, they sold more futures to protect themselves, thus perpetuating the drop. When sales of futures outstrip shares, the futures are discounted on the cash market.

As they watched what was happening, American investment houses in Tokyo saw a terrific opportunity to arbitrage through program trades. Americans bought Nikkei futures. At the same time, they sold the underlying shares. Normally, this would have brought the futures and cash market back into line. The Nikkei, though, wasn't liquid enough to handle the transactions easily. As the American sell orders on the exchange floor mounted, the index collapsed. The upshot was that program traders now had to keep their arbitrage for buying rather than selling underlying shares.

PROGRAM TRADING

In effect, program trading is letting the big guys stack the market against the little investor, dangerously turning the stock market into a gigantic crap shoot. Even if the practice didn't directly cause the U.S. stock market's stomach-churning 508-point drop on October 19, 1987, it may well have exacerbated it.

The biggest concern of the early 1990s was a practice called "self-frontrunning." Here a major brokerage house manipulated both futures and stock markets within a very short time in order to make a quick buck for itself while sending prices hurtling scarily in both directions, to the distress of just about everyone else.

Practitioners defend it as a legitimate way of doing business. Opposers see it as a way of scalping the market.

The controversy arises from the complexity of index arbitrage, which involves computer-driven trading based on minute-to-minute fluctuations in the price of the stock market in New York and the futures markets in Chicago. By attempting to profit from the discrepancies, institutional investors and investment firms speedily push vast sums of cash in and out of both markets. Transactions involve the buying or selling of hundreds of different stocks listed in an index, as well as an offsetting buy or sell of the futures contract based on the index.

Instead of banning the practice, the Big Board made the practice more difficult to implement. Access of those computerized trades to the NYSE's electronic order delivery system was limited. Moreover, all program trades were blocked on days when the Dow Jones Industrial Average moves 50 points up or down.

MARKET HIGHLIGHTS

1792 Twenty-four brokers form the first organized stock market in America under a buttonwood tree at what is now 68 Wall Street.

1793 An outdoor "curb market" is created and will last some 125 years.

1817 The name New York Stock and Exchange Board is adopted for an indoor market.

1830 The Exchange has its dullest day—31 shares traded.

1830 Outdoor trading in unlisted securities begins on Wall Street.

1867 Stock tickers are introduced.

1868 Exchange memberships are sold. Previously, each member had a reserved seat for life.

1869 Gold speculation results in "Black Friday."

1878 The first telephones are introduced at the Exchange.

1886 The Exchange has its first million-share day—1.2 million shares are traded.

1895 The Exchange recommends that listed or traded companies issue annual income statements and balance sheets to shareholders.

1908 E. S. Mendels forms the New York Curb Agency, the first departure from informal curb trading.

1914 The Exchange closes from July 31 to December 11 for World War I.

1921 Curb trading is moved indoors to 86 Trinity Place.

1929 The stock market crashes—16.4 million shares are traded.

1933 The Exchange closes to March 14 for a bank holiday.

1933 The Securities Act of 1933 seeks to provide full disclosure to investors and prohibit securities sales fraud.

1934 The Securities Exchange Act of 1934 creates the Securities and Exchange Commission to oversee regulation of securities trading.

1938 William McChesney Martin, Jr., is elected the first salaried president of the Exchange.

1939 The Maloney Act creates the National Association of Securities Dealers to regulate the over-the-counter (OTC) market.

1942 A record low price of $650 is paid for a seat on the Curb market.

1953 The Curb market becomes the American Stock Exchange (Amex).

1958 Mary G. Roebling becomes the first woman governor of Amex.

1964 National Association of Securities Dealers (NASD) is born and the OTC market takes on its current contours. Previously, a dealer could never be sure the price at which a stock was offered was its lowest selling price.

1969 A record $350,000 is paid for an Amex seat.

1977 Lynne Greenberg is the first woman broker to work on the Amex floor and Ginger Ketchum becomes the first woman specialist.

1982 The Big Board has its first 100-million-share day (132.7 million shares traded) on August 18.

1985 The 50 billionth share is traded on Big Board.

1986 On July 7 the stock market falls nearly 62 points, the largest drop ever up to this time.

1987   On September 21 a seat sells for a record $1.15 million.

1987   On October 19 the stock market falls 508 points, the largest drop ever up to *this* time.

NASDAQ   One of the more intriguing developments in the marketplace is what has happened with NASDAQ, the National Association of Securities Dealers Automated Quotations. Founded in 1971, NASDAQ has no trading floor but it offered computerized listings in 1990 of more than 4,706 issues worth more than $310.8 billion. What it has done is make the over-the-counter market—once disdained as the Casbah of the securities industry, the haven for insignificant, risky, or even shady stocks—respectable.

NASDAQ is the fastest-growing securities market and, right after the Big Board, the second-largest in the nation. Since 1976, annual share volume has exceeded 39 billion, and dollar volume of trading in 1990 passed the $1.325 billion mark. In preparing to participate in the global market, the National Association of Securities Dealers and the London Stock Exchange have agreed to share quotations in a two-year pilot project.

Once victims of Big Board and Amex snobbery, NASDAQ officials contend that now hundreds of their companies could find their way onto the Big Board or the Amex but don't want to do so. NASDAQ membership has grown to more than 4,100 companies from 2,500 in the last decade. Largely due to mergers and acquisitions during that period, the membership of the New York Stock Exchange (NYSE) has grown only slightly, to 1,769, while the number of members of the Amex was 859 in 1990, after several years' decline.

In the past decade, NASDAQ's trading volume has increased more than 1,500% to more than 33 billion shares a year. Daily trading volume on the NASDAQ market exceeded the NYSE's for the first time in May of 1983 and has done so on other occasions. In some quarters there has even been talk that NASDAQ will run the Big Board and Amex out of business someday.

NASDAQ's sophisticated, computerized network electronically links investors in the U.S. and abroad to brokers and dealers. The NASDAQ system receives and stores price and volume data on more than 5,000 domestic and foreign securities and transmits the data to the national and international financial services industry, the financial press, and investors.

NASDAQ gives so-called insider quotations, the highest bids and lowest asks on all its securities. And for the 600 companies listed on its National Market System, introduced in 1981, it offers information on the last sale and running volume, available within 90 seconds of the trade.

NASDAQ's appeal is obvious. For one, membership is comparatively cheap: about $5,000, or about a third of what the Amex charges and about a sixth of the Big Board's ante. Also, it doesn't have disclosure rules beyond those imposed by the SEC. Moreover, a lot of corporate chieftains are enamored of NASDAQ's market-making army compared with the

Table 18-1   NASDAQ Trading Volume

Year	Share volume (millions)	Average daily volume (millions)	Dollar volume (millions)
1990	33,380	131.9	452,430
1989	33,530	133.1	431,381
1988	31,070	122.8	347,089
1987	37,890	149.8	499,854
1986	28,737	113.6	378,216
1985	20,699	82.1	233,454
1984	15,159	59.9	153,454
1983	15,909	62.8	188,285
1982	8,432	33.3	84,189
1981	7,823	30.9	71,057

single floor specialist found at the Exchange. Some companies, for instance, have hundreds of dealers making market in their stock.

Something else NASDAQ has done is make both the Amex and the Big Board more competitive. Touchy about NASDAQ's technological sophistication, the exchanges continue to apply more automation to their business.

The October 1987 market collapse, however, pointed out NASDAQ weaknesses. Some dealers dropped out during the market fall. So NASDAQ proposed a rule that, with certain exceptions, would suspend for 30 days a market maker who withdraws bid and asked quotations in a stock. Also, because of customer complaints about not being able to get through phone lines, NASDAQ moved to increase the number of small trades executed automatically by computers, eliminating the need for a phone conversation between securities dealers in such trades. For complex reasons mainly related to blue chips and foreign-driven demand for U.S. stocks in the past few years, NASDAQ had not performed up to the level of the Standard & Poor's and Dow Jones indexes. This has been especially true of the smaller OTC stocks. And in the market collapse in the fall of 1987, these issues fell more sharply than the blue chips did.

ARBITRAGE

Arbitrageurs: What they do is really pretty simple, but trying to doing it well is something else again. It involves simultaneous purchases and sales of an asset, such as a commodity or currency, in two or more markets between which there are price discrepancies. Arbs want to profit from the price difference; in effect, the arbs lessen or eliminate that difference.

The breed got a bad name in 1986–1987 when Ivan Boesky, king of the "merger arbs," got nailed for a staggering $100 million fine in the early days of the insider-trading scandals that rocked Wall Street. But merger arbitrageurs were always considered the Mississippi riverboat gamblers of the trade. The two markets being "arbitraged" in a merger are the stock market on the one hand and the buyer's private market (offer price) on the other. The arb gambles substantial sums purchasing one stock and selling another short when a merger is in the works. (The arb may short the acquirer in a cash deal too if he expects investors to punish the stock because the company is paying a rich premium for the target.) If the merger comes off, the arb makes a profit. If the deal sours, the price of the stock the arb bought can drop sharply and the short stock can rise, producing a hefty loss.

WHO OWNS STOCK?

Not surprisingly, a profile of today's typical stockholder sounds pretty much like a Dewar's profile, perhaps minus the exotic hobby of white water chess playing. He or she lives in a metropolitan area, is mid-fortyish, is well educated, uses a broker, and had a portfolio in 1985 that was valued at about $6,200.

According to the latest Big Board survey, more than 47 million Americans own stock in publicly traded companies or mutual funds. Ownership is pretty much split between men and women. The median age for adult shareholders is 45 and 45% of them hold college degrees.

Most investors—nearly 60%—have white-collar jobs, while only about 16% are blue-collar workers. Housewives, retirees, and the unemployed make up the rest. Three quarters of them have incomes above $25,000 a year.

Portfolio sizes varied greatly, of course, but 45% of investors had portfolios valued under $5,000, while 12% have portfolios with values in excess of $50,000. The median portfolio value was about $6,200.

Nearly 65% of shareowners have IRA or Keogh accounts.

Not surprisingly, more than 60% of shareholders use brokers, and about 40% of investors are introduced to the market these days through brokers. The second most popular way of getting acquainted with the market is through employee stock purchase plans (25%).

Metropolises where more than a million shareholders live are New York, Los Angeles, Chicago, Washington, Boston, and Philadelphia. New York, with 2.5 million, has the most.

**Table 18–2   Securities Industry Personnel
(includes all levels of personnel)**

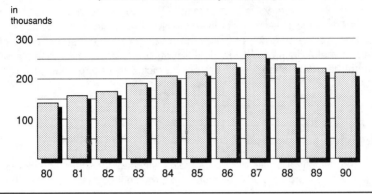

Source: Securities Industry Association.

RECORD SEAT PRICE

A record $1 million was paid for a seat on the Big Board on April 23, 1987. But records in the 1987 market were as long-lived as snowflakes in the Caribbean. The very next day a seat brought $1.1 million. On September 21, 1987, a seat fetched $1.15 million. In August 1978 a seat could be had for only $50,000. The earliest price of a seat was $25. There are 1,366 seats on the Big Board. Seats on the Amex in the first quarter of 1987 were selling for about a third of the NYSE record price. The cheapest seats around—about $8,200—were on the Cincinnati Stock Exchange.

The prices of seats have always been as stable as oil prices. In 1985, for instance, Big Board prices fluctuated between a low of $310,000 in January and a high of $480,000 in December. The lowest price ever in this century was $17,000, paid in 1942.

Merrill Lynch   In April 1987, Merrill Lynch & Co., one of the nation's biggest retail brokerage houses, issued a stunning admission. The company said it had lost $275 million from mortgage-securities dealings. Within months that figure increased to a whopping $377 million, an accounting trick having accounted for the earlier number. The chastened Merrill blamed an unauthorized series of transactions, and a few heads rolled. Critics, though, put some of the blame for the loss on Merrill's rush to expand its presence in the mortgage-securities business by trading in a risky way in hopes of reaping bigger profits.

While that wasn't business as usual at Merrill, bad news was. Only weeks earlier, a key London executive who was highly successful in mergers and acquisitions was swept up in an insider-trading scandal.

The company also didn't look good selling its 25% stake in a Hong Kong brokerage house after taking five years to learn that a joint venture in non–Hong Kong issues didn't pan out. Finally, Merrill's name was bandied around in the press as former CEO Donald T. Regan was bounced from his White House job as chief of staff as a result of the Contragate scandal.

While the company couldn't be held accountable for Regan's problems at the White House, he could be blamed for some of Merrill's woes. Regan was the architect of Merrill's expansion and diversification program, which ran into runaway costs. This controversial and ambitious strategy, undertaken in the late 1970s, called for creating a full-service firm offering everything from securities brokerage and investment banking to life insurance and real estate. Soon after Regan left, corporate profits tumbled and morale tumbled too. Moreover, the return on equity, an important gauge of an investment firm's performance, fell to 9.5% from Merrill's historic target of 15%.

The only trend emerging from most of the bad news was that there had to be some tinkering with the "full financial services" approach to the businesses. Indeed, that began happening.

Creating a separate partnership for the real estate business was part of a restructuring at Merrill, the first major reshaping of the full-service concept. Moreover, the retail brokerage operation was streamlined, including stepped-up efforts to become less reliant on income from commissions, which go up and down with market swings. The firm revised its commission structure, giving high performers bigger commissions and lower percentages to lower performers. Also, the "financial consultants," as brokers were dubbed, got greater incentives to sell fee-producing services, such as mutual funds and insurance.

In the fall of 1990, Merrill announced yet another reorganization, which would dissolve its two operating units and create six divisions, resulting in hundreds of layoffs. The new divisions were private client, which focused on retail and related business; asset management; insurance; investment banking; debt markets; and equity markets.

One area in which Merrill mostly won was in beefing up its once second-rate investment banking unit. Merrill ranked first in the first quarter of 1990 in initial public offerings of common stock, moved into second place in 1986 as an underwriter of junk bonds, and, using its own capital to finance mergers and acquisitions, forged ahead in merchant banking.

Also, the company has done remarkably well with life insurance. Since 1981, Merrill has ranked among the top 15 life insurance companies, using brokers—ahem, "financial consultants"—who draw on the resources of 130 insurance specialists to sell the product.

Despite the company's successes, those who keep an eye cocked on the blunders expect more of them. For instance, Perrin Long, a widely respected analyst with Lipper Analytical Securities Corporation, has stated that the company should concentrate on what the company knows best—the retail brokerage business. "The more they move into capital markets, the more opportunity for problems and unpleasant surprises that will impact earnings," he says.

Indeed, the company, which traces its roots back to 1885, has changed a lot more in recent years than it probably did at any other time in its history. The famed Merrill and Lynch of the corporate title were Charles Merrill and Edmund C. Lynch. Merrill was the son of a small-town Florida doctor who studied at Amherst and Michigan and played a summer of semipro baseball before winding up in the brokerage business. Lynch was a graduate of Johns Hopkins who was selling soda-fountain equipment when he met Merrill at a New York YMCA where they were lodging.

Merrill talked Lynch into joining him in the brokerage business. The two formed a partnership in 1914 and made a powerful team. Merrill set up the business deals and Lynch hammered out ironclad contracts so that nothing went wrong with them. It was Merrill, probably more than anyone else, who held the belief that stocks should be made available to everyone and thus tapped among the American public a vast reservoir of funds that could be channeled into securities investments.

Merrill was also among those who sensed that the stock market was heading for a great crash in the late 1920s. On March 31, 1928, he wrote his customers, "Now is the time to get out of debt. Sell enough securities to lighten your obligations or pay them off entirely . . . we do advise in no uncertain terms that you take advantage of present high prices and put your own financial house in order."

Merrill heeded his own advice, which enabled Merrill Lynch to weather the Depression better than most securities firms. Meanwhile, the company grew and picked up additional partners through mergers and acquisitions. Today the company has worldwide operations with some 450 branches and 10,000 or so financial consultants.

Table 18-3　Eight-Year Comparison of U.S. Stock Exchanges

	Companies			Issues			Share volume (millions)		
Year	NYSE	Amex	NASDAQ	NYSE	Amex	NASDAQ	NYSE	Amex	NASDAQ
1990	1,769	859	4,132	2,284	1,063	4,706	39,665	3,329	33,380
1989	1,719	859	4,293	2,241	1,068	4,963	41,699	3,125	33,530
1988	1,681	896	4,451	2,234	1,101	5,144	40,850	2,515	31,070
1987	1,609	863	4,706	2,244	1,077	5,537	47,801	3,506	37,890
1986	1,573	796	4,417	2,257	957	5,189	35,680	2,979	28,737
1985	1,540	783	4,136	2,298	940	4,784	27,511	2,101	20,699
1984	1,543	792	4,097	2,319	930	4,723	23,071	1,545	15,159
1983	1,550	822	3,901	2,325	948	4,467	21,590	2,081	15,909

WALL STREET—A BRIEF HISTORY

Wall Street, aptly enough, took its name from a stockade Dutch colonists erected in 1653 as protection against assault by Indians and the English, who apparently could be as fierce as today's SEC regulators going after insider traders. Expansion soon leveled the wall, the only trace being the famed narrow lane bearing that name.

Wall Street was a commercial hub linking the ports on the Hudson and East Rivers, where most imports entered the colony. In 1725, securities joined the furs, tobacco, spices, currencies, molasses, gunpowder, and assorted whatnots being traded there.

George Washington was inaugurated in 1789 at Wall Street's Federal Hall, only steps from offices where merchants specialized in lottery tickets, insurance, and commodities brokerage. High on Washington's new presidential agenda was footing the debt of the War of Independence. Thus, he issued $80 million in government bonds. In 1791, Alexander Hamilton, the first Secretary of the Treasury, added to the number of securities available when he established the Bank of the United States and made a public share offering.

Investors usually bought the new securities through coffee shops or newspaper ads; the local press recorded fluctuations in stock prices and trading volume. Soon clever merchants kept securities on hand and sold them over the counter in their stores (and gave a name to the over-the-counter market).

Recognizing a need, the merchants organized an auction where they sold off stocks and bonds, much like the auctioning of bales of cotton or casks of sugar. The noon auction was at 22 Wall Street, or the Stock Exchange Office as it came to be known. Securities were turned over to the auctioneers by an agent or broker for the owner of the securities. Both the broker and the auctioneer took commissions from the price the shares brought. Not surprisingly, discounting cropped up. After the auction, some astute men dealt in the same securities sold at the noon auction, but they made the prices more attractive by taking smaller commissions.

To make trading easier and to try to stave off the discounters, 24 brokers met on May 17, 1792. They signed an accord known as the Buttonwood Tree Agreement, by which they pledged to avoid public auction and set the broker's commission at 1/4 of one percent. The group met for a while beneath a buttonwood tree outside 68 Wall Street, but they soon moved to the Tonine Coffee House at the corner of Wall and William Streets and then to their own quarters at 40 Wall.

At the end of the War of 1812 between America and Great Britain, trade between the two countries became dynamic. Besides its ports, New York City also had an edge in becoming the nation's economic center in that Manhattan had the greatest concentration of banks that could finance such trade and commerce. By 1817 there were a dozen banks in New York, and along Wall Street was a concentration of distinguished financial institutions. Among them were Union Bank (No. 17), the Manhattan Bank (No. 23), the Bank of America and the Bank of New York (both at No. 29), City Bank (No. 31), National Insurance Company (No. 47) and Glove Insurance Company (No. 55).

The stock market was so strong by 1817 that brokers agreed to meet regularly at set hours. A constitution creating the New York Stock and Exchange Board was drafted and a room for the exchange was rented at 40 Wall Street. Rules and regulations were established and candidates for admission were voted upon by other members, each of whom placed a black ball or white ball in a box. Losers were blackballed. Among the new regulations: members were subject to fines of 6 to 25 cents for being absent or for not wearing their hats, and even the sale of fictitious contracts was forbidden.

During the 1820s and 1830s, trading expanded in federal securities; in state and private bonds to finance roads, bridges, and canals; in municipal borrowing for water, sewerage, and lighting systems; and in the stocks of banks and insurance companies. Daily trading soared from 100 shares in 1827 to 5,000 in 1834. In 1863, a name—the New York Stock Exchange— was finally adopted for what was to become known as "the Big Board."

Not all the brokers went indoors. Most remained on the street, offering to buy or sell shares in the newer and smaller companies being founded. Such "curbstone brokers" were among the first to offer turnpike and canal shares. The "curbstone" sobriquet was descriptive of what went on. Brokers in the street sent orders by means of hand signals to assistants who either stood or perched precariously in windows of surrounding buildings furiously giving their own signals until the trading was over.

Brokerage activity picked up after Connecticut became the first state to pass a general incorporation law, which made it possible to organize companies and float stock with minimum difficulty. The Mexican War of 1846–1848 and the California Gold Rush heated up the economy. Dozens of new banks and shipping companies were formed. In the boom year 1856, more than a million shares were traded just on the outdoor market.

The crash of 1857 temporarily decimated the brokerage business, but the short-lived depression was replaced by a spectacular Civil War boom, from which emerged a new kind of curb trading. During the war years, curb traders established more than a dozen exchanges of their own, such as the nation's busiest market of the era, the New York Gold Exchange.

During ensuing decades, increased regulation was imposed on curb traders and there was increased pressure to move indoors. A site was located on Trinity Place, on the west side of Trinity Church. The New York Curb Market, as it was then known, moved inside in 1921, coinciding with the great bull market of the 1920s. By 1929, a seat sold for a high of $254,000, up from $3,750 in 1921.

The prosperity, of course, skidded to a halt with the market crash of 1929. Nor did the Curb benefit when the economy finally picked up with the prosperity induced by World War II. In 1942, average daily volume dropped to 89,000 shares and a seat sold for $650. The Curb's business picked up with the postwar boom, and to celebrate its new prosperity, the exchange was given a new name, the American Stock Exchange.

One of the results of the higher standards imposed on the curb market was losing some stocks and brokers to the emerging over-the-counter market. The OTC market, however, remained more or less a stepchild until NAS-DAQ came on like gangbusters in the 1980s (see "NASDAQ," page 267). *Competition* became one of the familiar words in the securities industry.

Internationalization was the other buzzword. Street talk of the coming of a global market has seen U.S. securities exchanges seeking to link up electronically with foreign markets. The Big Board extended trading hours to attract more European business. The Tokyo Exchange began admitting foreign firms to membership and other foreign stock exchanges began loosening up their requirements so foreign firms could participate in them.

DOW JONES INDUSTRIAL AVERAGE

Charles Henry Dow, *The Wall Street Journal*'s first editor, was also the granddaddy of all those daily stock-market indexes. In 1884 he came up with the first average of U.S. stock prices. Its descendant, today's Dow Jones Industrial Average, tracks the prices of 30 leading blue-chip stocks; while it's by no means the most comprehensive stock-market indicator, it's by far the most widely followed.

Dow, the son of a Connecticut farmer, also provided the foundation for the "Dow theory," which holds that a major trend in the stock market must be confirmed by similar movements in both the Dow Jones Industrial Average and the Dow Jones Transportation Average. Unless both indexes reach new highs (or lows), the theory holds, no significant new trend is confirmed.

The Dow Jones Transportation Average used to be known as the Dow Jones Railroad Average. In 1896, when following "the rails" was crucial to the U.S. economy, the average covered 20 such stocks. In contrast, the Dow Jones Industrial Average then had only a dozen stocks, representing all other types of businesses. The number was increased to 20 stocks in 1916 and to 30 in 1928.

As with all stock-market indicators, the "Dow theory" is less than infallible, but it's still watched by so many traditionalists that a lot of people put a lot of stock in it.

BULLS AND BEARS

Just about everyone seems to know that a bull market goes up and a bear market goes down. But how did the nicknames originate? One theory holds that they reflect the way the two beasts fight. A battling bull slashes upward with his horns, while a bear slashes down with his paws. Maybe. According to a Merrill Lynch spokesperson, the earliest known reference was in 1709 in the English magazine *The Tatler.* An essayist wrote that someone who "ensures a real value upon an imaginary thing is said to sell a bear." *Bull* has been around since at least 1773, when a British stock exchange member wrote, "I know not why the jobber who contracts to buy is styled a bull except that he appears, when a loser, as surly as that animal."

STOCK

A stock is a security, a certificate proving ownership in a publicly held company. Stocks are available to the general public. They make you a part owner and let you vote in the election of directors. The types of stock are described below:

Shares of *common stock* are the majority of shares outstanding. There are two kinds, growth stocks and income stocks. Growth stocks show the ability to grow faster than the average stock. Usually they have low dividend payments to shareholders but the trade-off is the anticipated higher appreciation rate. Income stocks tend to be slower-growing than growth stocks, but they tend to pay higher dividends.

Preferred stock is like a bond in that it has a permanent, specified dividend and a definite rate of return. Also, such stock is more secure than common stock. If a company goes bankrupt or is liquidated, bondholders get their money first, but next in the pecking order come holders of preferred stock and then holders of common stock.

Penny stocks are highly speculative stocks. Some people consider them to be stocks selling for $2 or less a share while others extend the range up to $5.

Stock grants ownership in a corporation and is represented by shares that are a claim on the company's earnings and assets. *Common stock* normally lets the shareholder vote in the election of directors and in other matters that come up at the stockholders' meetings. *Preferred stock* may not give voting rights but gives the holder prior claim to assets and earnings; dividends are paid to holders of preferred stock before they are paid to those holding common stock. A corporation can issue other classes of stock, each with a set of contractual rights.

Blue-chip stocks are considered safe stocks and are generally high-priced and low-yielding. They are stocks in well-known companies with track records of profit growth, dividend payments, and good management, products, and services—for example, General Electric and International Business Machines.

A *stock option* is the right to buy a given stock (a *call*), or to sell it (a *put*), at a specified price during a defined period of time, generally three months. Investors buy and sell options in order to speculate on stock price changes or to protect or "hedge" against the risk of such price changes.

The *margin* is the amount of his or her own capital put up by the investor to help finance a securities holding. The Federal Reserve's initial margin requirement on qualified stocks was reduced to 50% from 65% on January 3, 1974. An investor wanting to buy $5,000 worth of stocks has to put up at least $2,500 in cash or in securities having a loan value of $2,500.

STOCK INDEXES AND AVERAGES

Stock indexes and averages measure and report value changes in representative stock groupings. They can be broad-based (made up of a lot of stocks and representative of a market) or narrow-based (made up of a smaller group of stocks and meant to reflect a sector of the market or an industry).

Selected indexes and averages are used as the underlying values of stock-index futures, index options, or options on index futures; they let investors hedge against getting hurt too badly from general market movement. There are a lot of averages and indexes. Among the most common are those described below:

The *Amex Major Market Index* is an average of 20 blue-chip industrial stocks and options in which high-priced stocks have more influence than low-priced stocks. The American Stock Exchange came up with this index to replicate the Dow Jones Industrial Average in measuring representative performance of the stocks of major industrial companies. (See "Dow Jones Industrial Average," page 275.) This index consists of stocks on the Big Board, 15 of which are part of the DJIA. Futures on the index are traded on the Chicago Board of Trade.

The *Amex Market Value Index* measures the collective performance of more than 800 stocks traded on the Amex, representing all major industry groups. Higher-priced stocks have more influence than lower-priced stocks. The index includes stocks, warrants, and American depository receipts. (A warrant entitles the holder to buy a certain amount of common stock at a specified price, usually higher than the market price at the time of issuance, for a period of years or to perpetuity. American depository receipts, or *ADR*s, are given to Americans instead of share certificates when they buy shares of foreign-based companies in overseas markets; they are receipts held by U.S. banks and they entitle the holder to all dividends and capital gains.) Options are listed on the Amex.

Barron's Group Stock Averages are averages of stocks in more than 30 industrial groups, adjusted for splits and large dividends since 1937. Futures and options aren't traded.

The *New York Stock Exchange Composite Stock Index* relates all Big Board stocks to a total market value as of December 31, 1965, adjusted for capitalization changes. Higher-priced stocks carry more weight than lower-priced stocks. The base value of the index is $50. Futures and futures options are traded on the NYSE's New York Futures Exchange. Index options are traded on the Big Board. Similarly, the *New York Stock Exchange Telephone Index* consists of the eight common stocks of companies that constituted AT&T before it was broken up. Index options in the Telephone Index are listed on the Big Board. Other NYSE subindexes are *Financial, Industrial, Transportation,* and *Utility.*

Standard & Poor's 500 Composite Stock Index (S&P 500) reflects alterations in the total market value of 500 stocks relative to the base period 1941–1943. Higher-priced stocks carry more value than lower-priced stocks. Most of the stocks are on the Big Board; some are on the Amex or are over-the-counter stocks. There are 400 industrials, 60 transportation and utilities stocks, and 40 financial issues. The index represents some 80% of the market value of all stocks traded on the NYSE. Index options are traded on the Chicago Board of Trade. Options are traded on the Chicago Mercantile Exchange.

The *NASDAQ-OTC Price Index* is based on the National Association of Securities Dealers Automated Quotations (see "NASDAQ," page 267) with higher-priced stocks having more influence than lower-priced stocks. It represents all U.S. over-the-counter stocks except those traded on exchanges and those that only have one market maker. It was introduced on February 5, 1971, with a base value of 100. Futures and options aren't traded.

The *Value Line Composite Index* reflects price changes of a cross-section of stocks. The index is the equally weighted geometric average of some 1,700 Amex, Big Board, and OTC stocks tracked by the Value Line Investment Survey, an investment service that ranks hundreds of stocks for performance and safety. Options are traded on the Philadelphia Stock Exchange and futures on the Kansas City Board of Trade.

The *Wilshire 5000 Equity Index* represents the value in billions of dollars of all Amex, Big Board, and OTC stocks for which quotes are available, some 5,000 stocks, as prepared by Wilshire Associates of Santa Monica, California. Changes are measured against a base value established December 31, 1980. Options and futures aren't traded in it.

Table 18-4 Common Stock Prices and Yields, 1949–1989

Common stock prices[1]

| Year or month | New York Stock Exchange indexes (Dec. 31, 1965 = 50)[2] | | | | | Dow Jones industrial average[3] | Standard & Poor's composite index (1941–43 = 10)[4] | Common stock yields (percent)[5] | |
	Composite	Industrial	Transportation	Utility	Finance			Dividend-price ratio[6]	Earnings-price ratio[7]
1949	9.02					179.48	15.23	6.59	15.48
1950	10.87					216.31	18.40	6.57	13.99
1951	13.08					257.64	22.34	6.13	11.82
1952	13.81					270.76	24.50	5.80	9.47
1953	13.67					275.97	24.73	5.80	10.26
1954	16.19					333.94	29.69	4.95	8.57
1955	21.54					442.72	40.49	4.08	7.95
1956	24.40					493.01	46.62	4.09	7.55
1957	23.67					475.71	44.38	4.35	7.89
1958	24.56					491.66	46.24	3.97	6.23
1959	30.73					632.12	57.38	3.23	5.78
1960	30.01					618.04	55.85	3.47	5.90
1961	35.37					691.55	66.27	2.98	4.62
1962	33.49					639.76	62.38	3.37	5.82
1963	37.51					714.81	69.87	3.17	5.50
1964	43.76					834.05	81.37	3.01	5.32
1965	47.39					910.88	88.17	3.00	5.59
1966	46.15	46.18	50.26	45.41	44.45	873.60	85.26	3.40	6.63
1967	50.77	51.97	53.51	45.43	49.82	879.12	91.93	3.20	5.73
1968	55.37	58.00	50.58	44.19	65.85	906.00	98.70	3.07	5.67
1969	54.67	57.44	46.96	42.80	70.49	876.72	97.84	3.24	6.08
1970	45.72	48.03	32.14	37.24	60.00	753.19	83.22	3.83	6.45
1971	54.22	57.92	44.35	39.53	70.38	884.76	98.29	3.14	5.41
1972	60.29	65.73	50.17	38.48	78.35	950.71	109.20	2.84	5.50
1973	57.42	63.08	37.74	37.69	70.12	923.88	107.43	3.06	7.12
1974	43.84	48.08	31.89	29.79	49.67	759.37	82.85	4.47	11.59
1975	45.73	50.52	31.10	31.50	47.14	802.49	86.16	4.31	9.15
1976	54.46	60.44	39.57	36.97	52.94	974.92	102.01	3.77	8.90
1977	53.69	57.86	41.09	40.92	55.25	894.63	98.20	4.62	10.79
1978	53.70	58.23	43.50	39.22	56.65	820.23	96.02	5.28	12.03
1979	58.32	64.76	47.34	38.20	61.42	844.40	103.01	5.47	13.46
1980	68.10	78.70	60.61	37.35	64.25	891.41	118.78	5.26	12.66
1981	74.02	85.44	72.61	38.91	73.52	932.92	128.05	5.20	11.96
1982	68.93	78.18	60.41	39.75	71.99	884.36	119.71	5.81	11.60
1983	92.63	107.45	89.36	47.00	95.34	1,190.34	160.41	4.40	8.03
1984	92.46	108.01	85.63	46.44	89.28	1,178.48	160.46	4.64	10.02
1985	108.09	123.79	104.11	56.75	114.21	1,328.23	186.84	4.25	8.12
1986	136.00	155.85	119.87	71.36	147.20	1,792.76	236.34	3.49	6.09
1987	161.70	195.31	140.39	74.30	146.48	2,275.99	286.83	3.08	5.48
1988	149.91	180.95	134.12	71.77	127.26	2,060.82	265.79	3.64	8.01
1989	180.02	216.23	175.28	87.43	151.88	2,508.91	322.84	3.45	
1988: Jan	140.55	168.47	121.20	70.01	119.40	1,947.35	250.48	3.66	
Feb	145.13	173.44	126.09	72.89	124.36	1,980.65	258.13	3.56	
Mar	149.88	181.57	135.15	71.16	125.27	2,044.31	265.74	3.48	7.18
Apr	148.46	180.88	133.43	69.40	121.67	2,036.13	262.61	3.57	
May	144.99	176.02	127.63	68.65	120.35	1,988.91	256.12	3.80	
June	152.72	184.92	136.02	72.25	129.04	2,104.94	270.68	3.58	7.92
July	152.12	184.09	136.49	71.50	129.99	2,104.22	269.05	3.65	
Aug	149.25	179.72	132.53	70.67	130.77	2,051.29	263.73	3.75	
Sept	151.47	182.18	136.27	71.83	133.15	2,080.06	267.97	3.69	8.36
Oct	156.36	188.58	141.93	74.19	134.66	2,144.31	277.40	3.61	
Nov	152.67	183.79	138.60	73.83	129.61	2,099.04	271.02	3.70	
Dec	155.35	187.75	144.07	74.81	128.83	2,148.58	276.51	3.68	8.56
1989: Jan	160.40	194.62	153.09	75.87	132.26	2,234.68	285.41	3.64	
Feb	165.08	200.00	162.66	77.84	137.19	2,304.30	294.01	3.59	
Mar	164.60	199.20	160.14	77.66	137.91	2,283.11	292.71	3.68	8.46
Apr	169.38	204.81	164.32	79.69	143.26	2,348.91	302.25	3.59	
May	175.30	211.51	168.89	84.07	146.59	2,439.55	313.93	3.52	
June	180.76	216.75	173.47	87.90	154.08	2,494.90	323.73	3.44	7.93
July	185.15	221.74	179.32	90.40	157.78	2,554.03	331.93	3.38	
Aug	192.94	231.32	197.52	92.91	164.86	2,691.11	346.61	3.28	
Sept	193.02	230.86	202.02	93.44	165.51	2,693.41	347.33	3.29	6.80
Oct	192.49	229.40	190.36	94.67	166.55	2,692.01	347.40	3.29	
Nov	188.50	224.38	174.26	94.95	160.89	2,642.49	340.22	3.39	
Dec	192.67	230.12	177.25	99.73	155.63	2,728.47	348.57	3.33	

[1]Averages of daily closing prices, except New York Stock Exchange data through May 1964, are averages of weekly closing prices.
[2]Includes all the stocks (more than 1,500) listed on the New York Stock Exchange.
[3]Includes 30 stocks.
[4]Includes 500 stocks.
[5]Standard & Poor's series, based on 500 stocks in the composite index.
[6]Aggregate cash dividends (based on latest known annual rate) divided by aggregate market value based on Wednesday closing prices. Monthly data are averages of weekly figures; annual data are averages of monthly figures.
[7]Quarterly data are ratio of earnings (after taxes) for 4 quarters ending with particular quarter to price index for last day of that quarter. Annual ratios are averages of quarterly ratios.
Note.—All data relate to stocks listed on the New York Stock Exchange.
Sources: New York Stock Exchange, Dow Jones & Co., Inc., and Standard & Poor's Corporation.

U.S. EXCHANGES

American Stock Exchange, Inc.
  86 Trinity Place
  New York, New York 10006

Boston Stock Exchange, Inc.
  One Boston Place
  Boston, Massachusetts 02108

Cincinnati Stock Exchange
  205 Dixie Terminal Building
  Cincinnati, Ohio 45202

Intermountain Stock Exchange
  373 South Main Street
  Salt Lake City, Utah 84111

Midwest Stock Exchange, Inc.
  440 South LaSalle Street
  Chicago, Illinois 60605

New York Stock Exchange, Inc.
  11 Wall Street
  New York, New York 10005

Pacific Stock Exchange, Inc.
  301 Pine Street
  San Francisco, California 94104
  233 South Beaudry
  Los Angeles, California 90012

Philadelphia Stock Exchange, Inc.
  Philadelphia Stock Exchange Building
  1900 Market Street
  Philadelphia, Pennsylvania 19103

Spokane Stock Exchange
  225 Peyton Building
  Spokane, Washington 99201

FOREIGN EXCHANGES

Australia

Sydney Stock Exchange
  Tower Building
  Australia Square
  P.O. Box H67
  Sydney, New South Wales 2000

Belgium

Brussels Stock Exchange
  Palais de la Bourse
  1000 Brussels

Canada

Alberta Stock Exchange
  300–5th Avenue S.W.
  Calgary, Alberta T2P 3C4

Bourse de Montréal
  The Stock Exchange Tower
  800 Victoria Square
  Montreal, Quebec H4Z 1A9

Toronto Stock Exchange
  2 First Canadian Place
  Toronto, Ontario M5X 1J2

Vancouver Stock Exchange
  Stock Exchange Tower
  P.O. Box 10333
  609 Granville Street
  Vancouver, B.C. V7Y 1H1

Winnipeg Stock Exchange
  303–167 Lombard Avenue
  Winnipeg, Manitoba R3B OT6

France

Bourse de Paris—Paris Stock Exchange
  Palais de la Bourse
  75002 Paris

Germany

Frankfurter Wertpapierbore—Frankfurt Exchange
  Borsenplatz 6
  6000 Frankfurt am Main 1

Hong Kong

Stock Exchange of Hong Kong
  One Exchange Square
  Hong Kong

Japan

Tokyo Stock Exchange
  1-1 Nihonbashi Kayaba-cho-z-chome
  Cho-Ku, Tokyo 103

The Netherlands

Amsterdamse Effectenbeurs—Amsterdam Stock Exchange
  Beursplein 5
  1012 JW Amsterdam

Switzerland

Geneva Stock Exchange
  Rue de la Confédération 8
  CH-1204 Geneva

Zürich Stock Exchange
  Boersenkommissariat, Bleicherweg 5
  CH-8001 Zürich

United Kingdom

The International Stock Exchange of the United Kingdom
and the Republic of Ireland Limited
  Old Broad Street
  London EC 2N 1HP

Chapter Nineteen
BONDS

HIGHLIGHTS AND TRENDS

The bond industry was booming in recent years, but a lot of people don't realize just how big the market was. Daily trading volume in government bonds alone was over $100 billion. "The bond market is an invisible giant and the stock market is a visible dwarf by comparison," said Byron Klapper, managing director, Fitch Investor Services Inc., a monitor of corporate and municipal bond ratings. As interest rates broke out of their past staid patterns, bond prices and yields fluctuated more wildly than those of stocks. It wasn't uncommon for a $1,000 bond to rise or fall $30 in a single day's trading, versus $1.25 just a few years ago. Like stocks, bonds respond to the major influences on the economy at large. Multibillion-dollar leveraged buyouts, plunging and rising oil prices, a lackluster Sunbelt, revitalized industrial cities, frantic takeover activity, and new types of corporate restructuring have all had a major effect on the bond market in recent years. And, like the stock market, the bond market has undergone an internationalization, with a lot of foreign buyers scrambling for attractive offerings. (See "Problems in the Global Village," page 264.) But by 1987, the bull market in bonds appeared to have died out: in the first three quarters of 1987 the market had one of its worst performances ever, due largely to the nosediving dollar. Then came a rebound after the stock market crash in October, as security-conscious money managers found U.S. government–backed bonds appealing. Even so, the volatility of the market worried many. In 1990, even though interest rates were down, bond investors had a bumpy time trying to ride prices upward. There were delays in anticipated Federal Reserve rate cuts. With war uncertainties, short term notes rose faster than long term bonds. Municipal bond investors did well but the recession threatened the quality of state and local government credit. The junk bond market, which collapsed in 1989, worsened as defaults increased.

THE MARKETPLACE

In 1990, U.S. corporations sold $313.9 billion worth of new issues in the domestic market, about the same as 1989. Falling interest rates in the 1980s spurred the refunding of high-coupon debt and lured new issuers, especially issuers of speculative or junk bonds. Municipal bonds picked up slowly but gathered momentum following the rush to beat anticipated tax reforms under the new federal tax act in 1986. By the end of 1987, municipal new issues totaled some $101 billion, down $46 billion from 1986, according to Securities Data Company Bond Buyer. U.S. government securities have dumped $200 billion of debt on the market annually since 1985. Indeed, the trading of U.S. government securities became the world's fastest-growing area of internationalization. Fueled by the enormous federal debt, average daily volume of such securities has skyrocketed to about $250 billion, compared with $180.4 million on the New York Stock Exchange. The market swell was abetted by deregulation of financial markets overseas and 1984 U.S. legislation permitting foreign investors to buy the securities tax-free. Japan's trade surpluses resulted in tremendous excess capital flowing into U.S. securities. All of that dampened, of course, after the market meltdown in October 1987. The market continued strong after Fed chairman Alan Greenspan noted on November 28, 1990, that the economy had entered a "meaningful downturn."

TYPES OF BONDS

Bonds are basically IOUs whereby the issuer (seller) promises to pay the face value (or principal amount or par value) of the bond on a specific date, or maturity date. The issuer compensates the bondholder for the use of his or her money by paying interest, usually semiannually, at a fixed percentage rate during the term of the bond, or each year the bond is held. The interest rate is the bond's coupon. Once considered a preserve of the very rich, bonds gave rise to the term "coupon clipper" as a sobriquet for those lucky enough to live handsomely by clipping their coupons and presenting them for payment.

The following are descriptions of taxable bonds:

Convertible bonds give owners the option of exchanging their bonds for common shares in the company. The number of shares is arrived at by dividing the bond's conversion price into par ($1,000). If the conversion price is $50, that means the bond converts into 20 shares.

Debentures are the most common type of taxable bonds. Debenture holders are general creditors of the corporate bond issuer. The bonds are secured by all corporate assets not otherwise pledged. Convertible bonds are examples of debentures.

Equipment trust certificates are issued in the name of a transportation company that leases equipment (freight cars, locomotives, aircraft, barges, truck trailers) from a bank. Usually a second bank acts as the trustee for bondholders. When lease payments are made, the first bank forwards funds to the trustee bank to make interest payments and for the redemption of bonds.

First mortgage bonds are among the more desirable forms of a bond issue. These bonds are the result of a bond issuer's designating certain corporate property as collateral for the issue as a way of adding additional security to it.

Flower bonds are a nice way of sidestepping some estate taxes. They can be acquired at significant discounts below par but are acceptable at par value in payment of estate taxes if the deceased was the holder at the time of death.

GNMA (Ginnie Mae) certificates are shares in pools of mortgages backed by the Government National Mortgage Association (Ginnie Mae). As monthly mortgage payments are made, the proceeds are divided among bondholders until the mortgages are paid off. The payments include both interest and principal. Similar are certificates issued by the Federal Home Loan Mortgage Corporation (Freddie Macs) and the Federal National Mortgage Association (Fannie Maes).

Income bonds are rarely issued today and, for good reason, aren't taken seriously by investors—they only pay off if the corporation operates at a profit.

Senior and subordinated bonds: Companies having more than one bond issue outstanding usually designate the seniority of the issues. Subordinated bonds are second to the senior issue in terms of interest payments and redemption. They become important if a company winds up in such serious trouble that it may be forced out of business.

Sinking fund bonds are designated to retire in specific numbers each year until final maturity. Normally selected by random lot, the bonds can be redeemed at par value, at a premium over par, or at a discount below par. Redemption of the bonds, usually by a trust company or trustee bank, normally starts 5 to 10 years after the bonds are issued.

Zero-coupon bonds include corporate bonds, municipal bonds, treasury bonds, and even deposit certificates from banks or savings and loans. Instead of making periodic interest payments, issuers defer the interest until maturity. Hence, these bonds are sold deeply discounted from the face value. Because they don't actually pay interest yearly, "zeros" fall more dramatically than other bonds when interest rates rise and they rise more quickly when interest rates fall.

Municipal bonds, or "tax-free" bonds, are issued by cities, counties, states, and agencies created by such governments. There are more than 20,000 issuers that have created more than 80,000 bond issues. Such bonds are usually exempt from federal taxation and usually free of city and state taxes if the investor lives in the state where the bond is issued. The Tax Reform Act of 1986 created a new class of municipals, known as "taxable municipals," which are subject to federal taxation.

The types of municipal bonds are described below:

General obligation bonds are the largest group and are backed by the full faith and credit of the issuer, including its taxing and borrowing powers. "GO bonds," as they're known, are paid back with general revenue and borrowings.

Revenue bonds are issued to fund specific projects that will generate revenues. They are paid off with the revenues collected from the bridge or tunnel or whatever project is developed with the proceeds of the bond issue.

Industrial development bonds are issued by state and local governments anxious to lure business to their regions. Many of them are now taxable under the Tax Reform Act of 1986. The proceeds are used to raise money to construct plants, industrial parks, or whatever the governments feel they can build that can be leased to private industry. The quality of the bonds generally depends on the quality of the corporations taking advantage of the new facilities.

Redevelopment agency bonds, or "tax allocation bonds," are often used to construct commercial projects such as shopping centers. They are secured by a share of property taxes generated by the developed property.

Airport bonds come in two types. The first is for general usage, such as for construction projects. The second is issued for facilities that will be leased to an airline; in this case, the security is the leasing contract with the airline, which means the quality of the bonds depends on the financial health of the particular airline, many of which don't have enviable health records.

JUNK BONDS

While bonds picked up a head of steam in recent years, junk bonds came on like gangbusters and barely flinched even when Ivan Boesky gave the business an even more unsavory image than it already had. Not until the stock market crashed in the fall of 1987 and fears of a recession set in did the business hit tough times. Quite simply, junk bonds are risky business, "speculative-grade" bonds with ratings at or below BB + or Ba1, respectively, according to the major rating services, Standard & Poor's and Moody's Investors Service. A lot of investors expect the risk to be offset by the high yield, which may be twice as much as that of AAA corporate bonds.

The bonds caught on with pension funds, mutual funds, and other investors attracted by their consistently outperforming blue chips and their low 1.5% default rate for the decade from the mid-1970s to the mid-1980s. An unprecedented one quarter of the junk bonds issued in 1986 were connected to leveraged buyouts, as corporate raiders made them a stock in trade. The underwriting of junk bonds soared from $2 billion in 1982 to $48 billion in 1986. By 1987, junk bonds accounted for some $145 billion of the $550 billion corporate bonds outstanding. The junk bond market eventually hit $300 billion.

While junk bonds came under a lot of criticism, they also had plenty of defenders. Out of the 23,000 companies in the U.S. with sales over $25 million, only some 800 are considered investment-grade. That leaves most of the others few options for funding corporate growth. A lot of them have turned to junk bonds, which has spurred growth in some quarters.

Junk bonds became big business largely because of one firm, Drexel Burnham Lambert. And that was because of senior executive vice president Michael Milken, who recognized that only a small fraction of companies issuing such bonds failed to make interest or principal payments on schedule. So, judging by the bonds' track records, anybody with a diversified portfolio could reasonably gamble on handsome gains offset by minuscule default losses. Drexel and Milken rode the market hard until the insider-trading scandals of 1986–1987 cast uncertainty over both Drexel's and Milken's futures.

Now, however, there is ever increasing worry about defaults. The bulk of all junk bonds were issued since 1985 and a lot of them were for the extra-risky leveraged buyouts. Thus, nobody knows what's going to happen in the near future. But one thing for certain is that there will be defaults on billions of dollars' worth of junk. By 1991, the default and restructuring rate was 10%, and yields were a record 20.5%, as people shunned them.

RATINGS AGENTS

Rating the securities racing onto the marketplace is often devilishly complex these days—and lucrative. The nation's two major credit ratings agencies, Standard & Poor's and Moody's Investors Service, are capitalizing on the boom. Not only do they make a lot of money ($1,000 for rating the simplest government bond offering to $125,000 for a complex commercial mortgage obligation), they are becoming ever more powerful.

It's not unusual for political leaders to consult with them about the soundness of everything from a contemplated municipal bond offering to a political candidate. Good ratings are like money in the bank, and when a rating slips folks tend to take it hard. When S&P devalued the credit rating of the government of Denmark, for instance, it touched off a fierce debate in the Danish Parliament. And according to one tale, when the rater lowered the rating of a Japanese company's bonds, the chairman attempted hara-kiri.

The raters have no government mandate to do their job, nor do they have subpoena powers or any other official authority. They simply study all the information they can get and then express their opinions in the form of letter and number symbols. The rating doesn't mean the raters have performed an audit or even that they back up the authenticity of the information provided them upon which a rating is based. "A credit rating is not a recommendation to purchase, sell, or hold a particular security," S&P cautions.

Indeed, frequently the raters have been slow in changing their ratings, even after a company issued bad news. Nonetheless, in 1986 a record 364 corporate and international ratings affecting $217 billion of debt were downgraded by S&P. Moody's downgraded ratings of 246 corporations, affecting $197 billion in debt, during the same year.

The scope of the business is staggering. S&P, for instance, has been assigning ratings to corporate bonds since 1923, to municipal bonds since 1940, and to commercial paper since 1969. It rates some 2,000 domestic and foreign companies; 8,000 municipal, state, national, and supranational entities; and 1,300 commercial-paper-issuing entities (banks and corporations).

Moody's, which began issuing ratings for railroad bonds in 1909, expanded to industrials and public utilities in 1913 and to municipals in 1918. Today, the rater rates 19,000 long-term debt issues in global markets, 28,000 municipals, and 2,000 commercial-paper-issuing entities.

A bond's quality is measured by the safety of both its interest and principal payments. Though Moody's and S&P's letter ratings differ somewhat, the ratings descend from AAA for the most secure to C for the least secure in S&P's grading, and from Aaa to C in Moody's.

S&P	Moody's
AAA	Aaa
AA	Aa
A	A
BBB	Baa
BB	Ba
B	B
CCC	Caa
CC	Ca
C	C

C and D ratings are given to bonds no longer paying interest. C is for income bonds and D is for all other types. An NR indicates that the bond isn't rated because the rater doesn't rate that type of bond, because the rater lacks enough information to rate it, or because the bond issuer didn't request a rating.

S&P assigns a plus (+) or a minus (−) sign to some ratings ranging from AA to CCC in order to reflect a bond's relative standing within its category.

U.S. GOVERNMENT SECURITIES

U.S. government securities are generally the safest investments around. They consist of three types of debt obligation that are used to finance various federal projects: *Treasury bills,* or "T-bills," with maturities up to a year; *Treasury notes,* which generally mature in 1 to 7 years; and *U.S. government bonds,* which mature in 7 to 25 years. They can be purchased without charge directly from Federal Reserve Banks or the Bureau of Public Debt, Securities Transactions Branch, Washington, D.C. In addition, T-bills and notes can be bought for a fee from certain brokerage houses, government securities dealers, and commercial banks. And there are a lot of federal issues to buy. Annually, the federal government creates more than $200 billion in debt. But compared to other foreign government issues, those of the U.S. have such attractive yields that international trading in U.S. government securities has become the fastest-growing international market. Spurred by the ballooning U.S. federal debt, daily volume in U.S. Treasury securities has soared to some $100 billion.

T-bills make up most of government financing and are issued in five denominations ranging from $10,000 to $1 million. The investor's return is the difference between what was paid for the bill and its face value at the time of maturity. The Treasury sells them at a discount through auctions. Weekly auctions are held for bills with three- and six-month maturities. Monthly auctions are held for the other two kinds of bills, those with nine-month and one-year maturities.

Treasury notes and bonds have longer maturities than do T-bills. Notes mature within one to seven years. Bonds have maturities longer than seven years and aren't redeemable prior to the maturity date, except when there is a "call" provision whereby the bond is redeemable by the Treasury before the maturity date. Some 20 other government agencies issue debentures and notes to finance their operations; since only a few are backed by the federal government, they generally offer higher interest rates than Treasury issues. The widest-known issuers are the Government National Mortgage Association (Ginnie Mae) and the Federal National Mortgage Association (Fannie Mae).

BOND HISTORY

Nobody seems quite sure of the origins of the term *bond,* but it could have had something to do with the practice in the Middle Ages of securing a debt by giving one's bond. Kings and governments, recognizing that taxes couldn't meet all their financial demands, sought a way of making money available to the crown. Government or "crown" bonds, similar to the government bonds we have now, appeared in England, France, and the Netherlands in the 17th century. For example, the Antwerp Bourse was a major financial center where royal bonds, city bonds, and even royally guaranteed private bonds were routinely traded. But because of the ban on usury, interest was disguised.

The first bonds in England considered to be modern were the public issue of William III in 1693. By then, Parliament was strong enough to back up the issue.

Table 19-1   Bond Yields and Interest Rates, 1929–1989

(percent per annum)

Year and month	U.S. Treasury securities Bills (new issues)[1] 3-month	6-month	Constant maturities[2] 3-year	10-year	Corporate bonds (Moody's) Aaa[3]	Baa	High-grade municipal bonds (Standard & Poor's)	New-home mortgage yields[4]	Commercial paper, 6 months[5]	Prime rate charged by banks[6]	Discount rate, Federal Reserve Bank of New York[6]	Federal funds rate[7]
1929					4.73	5.90	4.27		5.85	5.50–6.00	5.16	
1933	0.515				4.49	7.76	4.71		1.73	1.50–4.00	2.56	
1939	.023				3.01	4.96	2.76		.59	1.50	1.00	
1940	.014				2.84	4.75	2.50		.56	1.50	1.00	
1941	.103				2.77	4.33	2.10		.53	1.50	1.00	
1942	.326				2.83	4.28	2.36		.66	1.50	[8]1.00	
1943	.373				2.73	3.91	2.06		.69	1.50	[8]1.00	
1944	.375				2.72	3.61	1.86		.73	1.50	[8]1.00	
1945	.375				2.62	3.29	1.67		.75	1.50	[8]1.00	
1946	.375				2.53	3.05	1.64		.81	1.50	[8]1.00	
1947	.594				2.61	3.24	2.01		1.03	1.50–1.75	1.00	
1948	1.040				2.82	3.47	2.40		1.44	1.75–2.00	1.34	
1949	1.102				2.66	3.42	2.21		1.49	2.00	1.50	
1950	1.218				2.62	3.24	1.98		1.45	2.07	1.59	
1951	1.552				2.86	3.41	2.00		2.16	2.56	1.75	
1952	1.766				2.96	3.52	2.19		2.33	3.00	1.75	
1953	1.931		2.47	2.85	3.20	3.74	2.72		2.52	3.17	1.99	
1954	.953		1.63	2.40	2.90	3.51	2.37		1.58	3.05	1.60	
1955	1.753		2.47	2.82	3.06	3.53	2.53		2.18	3.16	1.89	1.78
1956	2.658		3.19	3.18	3.36	3.88	2.93		3.31	3.77	2.77	2.73
1957	3.267		3.98	3.65	3.89	4.71	3.60		3.81	4.20	3.12	3.11
1958	1.839		2.84	3.32	3.79	4.73	3.56		2.46	3.83	2.15	1.57
1959	3.405	3.832	4.46	4.33	4.38	5.05	3.95		3.97	4.48	3.36	3.30
1960	2.928	3.247	3.98	4.12	4.41	5.19	3.73		3.85	4.82	3.53	3.22
1961	2.378	2.605	3.54	3.88	4.35	5.08	3.46		2.97	4.50	3.00	1.96
1962	2.778	2.908	3.47	3.95	4.33	5.02	3.18		3.26	4.50	3.00	2.68
1963	3.157	3.253	3.67	4.00	4.26	4.86	3.23	5.89	3.55	4.50	3.23	3.18
1964	3.549	3.686	4.03	4.19	4.40	4.83	3.22	5.82	3.97	4.50	3.55	3.50
1965	3.954	4.055	4.22	4.28	4.49	4.87	3.27	5.81	4.38	4.54	4.04	4.07
1966	4.881	5.082	5.23	4.92	5.13	5.67	3.82	6.25	5.55	5.63	4.50	5.11
1967	4.321	4.630	5.03	5.07	5.51	6.23	3.98	6.46	5.10	5.61	4.19	4.22
1968	5.339	5.470	5.68	5.65	6.18	6.94	4.51	6.97	5.90	6.30	5.16	5.66
1969	6.677	6.853	7.02	6.67	7.03	7.81	5.81	7.80	7.83	7.96	5.87	8.20
1970	6.458	6.562	7.29	7.35	8.04	9.11	6.51	8.45	7.71	7.91	5.95	7.18
1971	4.348	4.511	5.65	6.16	7.39	8.56	5.70	7.74	5.11	5.72	4.88	4.66
1972	4.071	4.466	5.72	6.21	7.21	8.16	5.27	7.60	4.73	5.25	4.50	4.43
1973	7.041	7.178	6.95	6.84	7.44	8.24	5.18	7.96	8.15	8.03	6.44	8.73
1974	7.886	7.926	7.82	7.56	8.57	9.50	6.09	8.92	9.84	10.81	7.83	10.50
1975	5.838	6.122	7.49	7.99	8.83	10.61	6.89	9.00	6.32	7.86	6.25	5.82
1976	4.989	5.266	6.77	7.61	8.43	9.75	6.49	9.00	5.34	6.84	5.50	5.04
1977	5.265	5.510	6.69	7.42	8.02	8.97	5.56	9.02	5.61	6.83	5.46	5.54
1978	7.221	7.572	8.29	8.41	8.73	9.49	5.90	9.56	7.99	9.06	7.46	7.93
1979	10.041	10.017	9.71	9.44	9.63	10.69	6.39	10.78	10.91	12.67	10.28	11.19
1980	11.506	11.374	11.55	11.46	11.94	13.67	8.51	12.66	12.29	15.27	11.77	13.36
1981	14.029	13.776	14.44	13.91	14.17	16.04	11.23	14.70	14.76	18.87	13.42	16.38
1982	10.686	11.084	12.92	13.00	13.79	16.11	11.57	15.14	11.89	14.86	11.02	12.26
1983	8.63	8.75	10.45	11.10	12.04	13.55	9.47	12.57	8.89	10.79	8.50	9.09
1984	9.58	9.80	11.89	12.44	12.71	14.19	10.15	12.38	10.16	12.04	8.80	10.23
1985	7.48	7.66	9.64	10.62	11.37	12.72	9.18	11.55	8.01	9.93	7.69	8.10
1986	5.98	6.03	7.06	7.68	9.02	10.39	7.38	10.17	6.39	8.33	6.33	6.81
1987	5.82	6.05	7.68	8.39	9.38	10.58	7.73	9.31	6.85	8.21	5.66	6.66
1988	6.69	6.92	8.26	8.85	9.71	10.83	7.76	9.19	7.68	9.32	6.20	7.57
1989	8.12	8.04	8.55	8.49	9.26	10.18	7.24	10.13	8.80	10.87	6.93	9.21
										High-low	High-low	
1984:												
Jan	8.93	9.06	10.93	11.67	12.20	13.65	9.61	12.29	9.18	11.00-11.00	8.50- 8.50	9.56
Feb	9.03	9.13	11.05	11.84	12.08	13.59	9.63	12.23	9.31	11.00-11.00	8.50- 8.50	9.59
Mar	9.44	9.58	11.59	12.32	12.57	13.99	9.92	12.02	9.86	11.50-11.00	8.50- 8.50	9.91
Apr	9.69	9.83	11.98	12.63	12.81	14.31	9.98	12.04	10.22	12.00-11.50	9.00- 8.50	10.29
May	9.90	10.31	12.75	13.41	13.28	14.74	10.55	12.18	10.87	12.50-12.00	9.00- 9.00	10.32
June	9.94	10.55	13.18	13.56	13.55	15.05	10.71	12.10	11.23	13.00-12.50	9.00- 9.00	11.06
July	10.13	10.58	13.08	13.36	13.44	15.15	10.50	12.50	11.34	13.00-13.00	9.00- 9.00	11.23
Aug	10.49	10.65	12.50	12.72	12.87	14.63	10.03	12.43	11.16	13.00-13.00	9.00- 9.00	11.64
Sept	10.41	10.51	12.34	12.52	12.66	14.35	10.17	12.53	10.94	13.00-12.75	9.00- 9.00	11.30
Oct	9.97	10.05	11.85	12.16	12.63	13.94	10.34	12.77	10.16	12.75-12.00	9.00- 9.00	9.99
Nov	8.79	8.99	10.90	11.57	12.29	13.48	10.27	12.75	9.06	12.00-11.25	9.00- 8.50	9.43
Dec	8.16	8.36	10.56	11.50	12.13	13.40	10.04	12.55	8.55	11.25-10.75	8.50- 8.00	8.38

[1]Rate on new issues within period; bank-discount basis.
[2]Yields on the more actively traded issues adjusted to constant maturities by the Treasury Department.
[3]Series excludes public utility issues for January 17, 1984, through October 11, 1984, due to lack of appropriate issues.
[4]Effective rate (in the primary market) on conventional mortgages, reflecting fees and charges as well as contract rate and assuming, on the average, repayment at end of 10 years. Rates beginning January 1973 not strictly comparable with prior rates. (This series now published by the Federal Housing Finance Board; it was formerly published by the Department of the Treasury [Office of Thrift Supervision] and by the Federal Home Loan Bank Board.)
[5]Bank-discount basis; prior to November 1979, data are for 4–6 months paper.

Table 19-1 Bond Yields and Interest Rates, 1929–1989 (continued)

(percent per annum)

Year and month	U.S. Treasury securities Bills (new issues)[1]		Constant maturities[2]		Corporate bonds (Moody's)		High-grade municipal bonds (Standard & Poor's)[3]	New-home mortgage yields[4]	Commercial paper, 6 months[5]	Prime rate charged by banks[6]	Discount rate, Federal Reserve Bank of New York[6]	Federal funds rate[7]
	3-month	6-month	3-year	10-year	Aaa[3]	Baa				High-low	High-low	
1985:												
Jan	7.76	8.03	10.43	11.38	12.08	13.26	9.55	12.27	8.15	10.75-10.50	8.00- 8.00	8.35
Feb	8.22	8.34	10.55	11.51	12.13	13.23	9.66	12.21	8.69	10.50-10.50	8.00- 8.00	8.50
Mar	8.57	8.92	11.05	11.86	12.56	13.69	9.79	11.92	9.23	10.50-10.50	8.00- 8.00	8.58
Apr	8.00	8.31	10.49	11.43	12.23	13.51	9.48	12.05	8.47	10.50-10.50	8.00- 8.00	8.27
May	7.56	7.75	9.75	10.85	11.72	13.15	9.08	12.01	7.88	10.50-10.00	8.00- 7.50	7.97
June	7.01	7.16	9.05	10.16	10.94	12.40	8.78	11.75	7.38	10.00- 9.50	7.50- 7.50	7.53
July	7.05	7.16	9.18	10.31	10.97	12.43	8.90	11.34	7.57	9.50- 9.50	7.50- 7.50	7.88
Aug	7.18	7.35	9.31	10.33	11.05	12.50	9.18	11.24	7.74	9.50- 9.50	7.50- 7.50	7.90
Sept	7.08	7.27	9.37	10.37	11.07	12.48	9.37	11.17	7.86	9.50- 9.50	7.50- 7.50	7.92
Oct	7.17	7.32	9.25	10.24	11.02	12.36	9.24	11.09	7.79	9.50- 9.50	7.50- 7.50	7.99
Nov	7.20	7.26	8.88	9.78	10.55	11.99	8.64	11.01	7.69	9.50- 9.50	7.50- 7.50	8.05
Dec	7.07	7.09	8.40	9.26	10.16	11.58	8.51	10.94	7.62	9.50- 9.50	7.50- 7.50	8.27
1986:												
Jan	7.04	7.13	8.41	9.19	10.05	11.44	8.06	10.89	7.62	9.50- 9.50	7.50- 7.50	8.14
Feb	7.03	7.08	8.10	8.70	9.67	11.11	7.44	10.68	7.54	9.50- 9.50	7.50- 7.50	7.86
Mar	6.59	6.60	7.30	7.78	9.00	10.49	7.07	10.50	7.08	9.50- 9.00	7.50- 7.00	7.48
Apr	6.06	6.07	6.86	7.30	8.79	10.19	7.32	10.27	6.47	9.00- 8.50	7.00- 6.50	6.99
May	6.12	6.16	7.27	7.71	9.09	10.29	7.67	10.22	6.53	8.50- 8.50	6.50- 6.50	6.85
June	6.21	6.28	7.41	7.80	9.13	10.34	7.98	10.15	6.63	8.50- 8.50	6.50- 6.50	6.92
July	5.84	5.85	6.86	7.30	8.88	10.16	7.62	10.30	6.24	8.50- 8.00	6.50- 6.00	6.56
Aug	5.57	5.58	6.49	7.17	8.72	10.18	7.31	10.26	5.83	8.00- 7.50	6.00- 5.50	6.17
Sept	5.19	5.31	6.62	7.45	8.89	10.21	7.14	10.17	5.61	7.50- 7.50	5.50- 5.50	5.89
Oct	5.18	5.26	6.56	7.43	8.86	10.24	7.12	10.02	5.61	7.50- 7.50	5.50- 5.50	5.85
Nov	5.35	5.42	6.46	7.25	8.68	10.07	6.86	9.91	5.69	7.50- 7.50	5.50- 5.50	6.04
Dec	5.49	5.53	6.43	7.11	8.49	9.97	6.93	9.69	5.88	7.50- 7.50	5.50- 5.50	6.91
1987:												
Jan	5.45	5.47	6.41	7.08	8.36	9.72	6.63	9.51	5.76	7.50- 7.50	5.50- 5.50	6.43
Feb	5.59	5.60	6.56	7.25	8.38	9.65	6.66	9.23	5.99	7.50- 7.50	5.50- 5.50	6.10
Mar	5.56	5.56	6.58	7.25	8.36	9.61	6.71	9.14	6.10	7.50- 7.50	5.50- 5.50	6.13
Apr	5.76	5.93	7.32	8.02	8.85	10.04	7.62	9.21	6.50	7.75- 7.75	5.50- 5.50	6.37
May	5.75	6.11	8.02	8.61	9.33	10.51	8.10	9.37	7.04	8.25- 8.00	5.50- 5.50	6.85
June	5.69	5.99	7.82	8.40	9.32	10.52	7.89	9.45	7.00	8.25- 8.25	5.50- 5.50	6.73
July	5.78	5.86	7.74	8.45	9.42	10.61	7.83	9.41	6.72	8.25- 8.25	5.50- 5.50	6.58
Aug	6.00	6.14	8.03	8.76	9.67	10.80	7.90	9.38	6.81	8.25- 8.25	5.50- 5.50	6.73
Sept	6.32	6.57	8.67	9.42	10.18	11.31	8.36	9.37	7.55	8.75- 8.25	6.00- 5.50	7.22
Oct	6.40	6.86	8.75	9.52	10.52	11.62	8.84	9.25	7.96	9.25- 8.75	6.00- 6.00	7.29
Nov	5.81	6.23	7.99	8.86	10.01	11.23	8.09	9.30	7.17	9.00- 8.75	6.00- 6.00	6.69
Dec	5.80	6.36	8.13	8.99	10.11	11.29	8.07	9.15	7.49	8.75- 8.75	6.00- 6.00	6.77
1988:												
Jan	5.90	6.31	7.87	8.67	9.88	11.07	7.81	9.10	6.92	8.75- 8.75	6.00- 6.00	6.83
Feb	5.69	5.96	7.38	8.21	9.40	10.62	7.55	9.12	6.58	8.75- 8.50	6.00- 6.00	6.58
Mar	5.69	5.91	7.50	8.37	9.39	10.57	7.80	9.15	6.64	8.50- 8.50	6.00- 6.00	6.58
Apr	5.92	6.21	7.83	8.72	9.67	10.90	7.91	9.13	6.92	8.50- 8.50	6.00- 6.00	6.87
May	6.27	6.53	8.24	9.09	9.90	11.04	8.01	8.95	7.31	9.00- 8.50	6.00- 6.00	7.09
June	6.50	6.76	8.22	8.92	9.86	11.00	7.86	9.26	7.53	9.00- 9.00	6.00- 6.00	7.51
July	6.73	6.97	8.44	9.06	9.96	11.11	7.87	9.17	7.90	9.50- 9.00	6.00- 6.00	7.75
Aug	7.02	7.36	8.77	9.26	10.11	11.21	7.86	9.06	8.36	10.00- 9.50	6.50- 6.00	8.01
Sept	7.23	7.43	8.57	8.98	9.82	10.90	7.71	9.26	8.23	10.00-10.00	6.50- 6.50	8.19
Oct	7.34	7.50	8.43	8.80	9.51	10.41	7.54	9.10	8.24	10.00-10.00	6.50- 6.50	8.30
Nov	7.68	7.76	8.72	8.96	9.45	10.48	7.58	9.43	8.55	10.50-10.00	6.50- 6.50	8.35
Dec	8.09	8.24	9.11	9.11	9.57	10.65	7.66	9.39	8.97	10.50-10.50	6.50- 6.50	8.76
1989:												
Jan	8.29	8.38	9.20	9.09	9.62	10.65	7.41	9.52	9.02	10.50-10.50	6.50- 6.50	9.12
Feb	8.48	8.49	9.32	9.17	9.64	10.61	7.47	9.82	9.35	11.50-10.50	7.00- 6.50	9.36
Mar	8.83	8.87	9.61	9.36	9.80	10.67	7.61	9.99	9.97	11.50-11.50	7.00- 7.00	9.85
Apr	8.70	8.73	9.40	9.18	9.79	10.61	7.49	10.17	9.78	11.50-11.50	7.00- 7.00	9.84
May	8.40	8.39	8.98	8.86	9.57	10.46	7.25	10.18	9.29	11.50-11.00	7.00- 7.00	9.81
June	8.22	8.00	8.37	8.28	9.10	10.03	6.97	10.42	8.80	11.50-11.00	7.00- 7.00	9.53
July	7.92	7.63	7.83	8.02	8.93	9.87	6.97	10.48	8.35	11.00-10.50	7.00- 7.00	9.24
Aug	7.91	7.72	8.13	8.11	8.96	9.88	7.08	10.22	8.32	10.50-10.50	7.00- 7.00	8.99
Sept	7.72	7.74	8.26	8.19	9.01	9.91	7.27	10.24	8.50	10.50-10.50	7.00- 7.00	9.02
Oct	7.63	7.61	8.02	8.01	8.92	9.81	7.22	10.11	8.24	10.50-10.50	7.00- 7.00	8.84
Nov	7.65	7.46	7.80	7.87	8.89	9.81	7.13	10.09	8.00	10.50-10.50	7.00- 7.00	8.55
Dec	7.64	7.45	7.77	7.84	8.86	9.82	7.01	10.07	7.93	10.50-10.50	7.00- 7.00	8.45

[6]For monthly data, high and low for the period. Prime rate for 1929–33 and 1947–48 are ranges of the rate in effect during the period.

[7]Since July 19, 1975, the daily effective rate is an average of the rates on a given day weighted by the volume of transactions at these rates. Prior to that date, the daily effective rate was the rate considered most representative of the day's transactions, usually the one at which most transactions occurred.

[8]From October 30, 1942, to April 24, 1946, a preferential rate of 0.50 percent was in effect for advances secured by Government securities maturing in 1 year or less.

Sources: Department of the Treasury, Board of Governors of the Federal Reserve System, Federal Housing Finance Board, Moody's Investors Service, and Standard & Poor's Corporation.

Chapter Twenty
FUTURES MARKETS

In the movie *Trading Places,* the streetwise Eddie Murphy sits in the posh offices of a firm speculating in futures, about to become head of the company for the owners' devious reasons. Amidst the trappings of gentility, the owners explain how the business works. The savvy Murphy picks right up on it: "You guys is bookies!"

Gambling it is—at least for the speculators. (Producers, such as farmers, may be using the futures market to hedge their basic economic position.) The risks in such speculation are so extreme that futures aren't for the faint-hearted. There are so many variables involved that playing the futures market can be a frantic roller-coaster ride that leads to big rewards—or huge losses. Futures markets are actually auctions and clearinghouses for the latest information about supply and demand for an ever-expanding list of commodities. That list now includes a hodgepodge of such items as agricultural products, metals, petroleum, foreign currencies, and domestic stock indexes. The market grew like crazy, especially in financial futures—contracts based on financial instruments such as Treasury bonds and Treasury notes whose prices fluctuate with changes in interest, as well as contracts based on stock indexes. (See "Stock Index Futures," page 299.) Nearly two thirds of a million futures contracts are now bought and sold on an average day. The volume of trade for fiscal 1985–1986 hit 213.6 million, more than double what it was in 1980. In 1990, it was 276 million contracts.

CONTRACTS

There are two kinds of futures contracts: those that call for the physical delivery of what is traded and those that call for a cash settlement in whatever month is specified. Very few contracts actually are delivered, since few investors want to take delivery of $1 million worth of Treasury bills or 10,000 bushels of wheat. But the fact that buyers can take or make delivery of most commodities helps keep futures prices and the cash market value of the commodities in line.

MARGINS

Understanding margins is essential to knowing the futures business. The term *margins* as used in futures trading is very different from the term as used in buying securities, in which it has to do with the down payment and money borrowed from a broker to buy stocks. The futures deposit is quite simply a deposit of good-faith money that can be drawn by the brokerage house to cover trading losses. Usually margins are 5–10% of the value of a futures contract. Futures accounts are debited or credited each day for the full amount of the day's change. If the futures price moves adversely, the investor must put up more money; if the change is favorable, he or she can take cash out of the account.

LEVERAGE

Risk is what futures trading is all about and study after study has shown that most amateurs who enter the market get bloodied. Gains and losses are often enormous and the reason is leverage. Only a relatively small amount of money (known as the initial margin) is required to buy or sell a futures contract. The smaller the margin in relation to the value of the futures contract, the greater the leverage. For instance, a margin deposit of $1,250 could let an investor buy $25,000 worth of soybeans, or $6,000 could purchase a futures contract covering $100,000 worth of stock.

OPTIONS

The revolution in financial options started with options on individual stocks, when the Chicago Board Options Exchange created centralized exchange trading of the two most common options: a *call*, which gives the buyer the right to buy 100 shares of a stock at a particular price within a given period, and its opposite number, a *put*, which gives the buyer the right to sell the stock at the specified price. But the business exploded when trading began on overall stock indexes, thereby giving traders a single instrument that enabled them to bet, in effect, on the entire stock market. The Chicago Board Options Exchange's business soared from $448 million in 1978 to the multibillion-dollar level it has reached today. The appeal of options is that they provide limited risk with theoretically unlimited profit opportunities. For example, with a limited investment, the buyer of a call can participate fully in the movement of a stock or an entire market. The most he can lose is the initial premium he paid for the option. (He often does.)

THE PLAYERS

The players are speculators and hedgers. *Speculators* try to anticipate price changes and profit through the sale and purchase or purchase and sale of a commodity or futures contract. Speculators are going up against either other speculators, who think prices are going in an opposite direction, or hedgers, who are trying to ward off risk.

Hedging is basically an insurance, a way of trying to protect yourself against the risk of an unfavorable price change. To guarantee a known price level, hedgers buy and sell in the futures market, weeks or months in advance, something they intend to buy or sell in the cash market. Say a dentist knows he needs to buy gold in eight months, but he fears that the price of gold will go up. He is concerned also because he is quoting prices to patients based on what the price of gold is now. To hold today's price of, say, $450 an ounce for delivery in eight months, he buys a futures contract at that price. If the price rises to $465 eight months later, the dentist pays his supplier that much to get the gold, but the extra $15 an ounce will be offset by his $15-an-ounce profit when his futures contract is sold. If the price of gold had dropped, his loss would have been made up by buying cheaper gold on the cash market.

Floor traders buy and sell for their own accounts and, like specialists and market makers at stock exchanges, help provide market liquidity. If a hedger or speculator won't immediately buy or sell a certain contract, usually an independent floor trader will, in the hopes of making a small gain within minutes or even seconds, say, from a quarter-of-a-cent change in the contract price.

THE HISTORY OF FUTURES

The people frantically waving and shouting on the trading floor of a futures exchange aren't bent on driving the place into chaos. Actually, their antics are what the futures markets are all about—replacing chaos with order, a system that dates back centuries.

It evolved from a market system that goes back to ancient Greece and Rome, where marketplaces with fixed times for trading utilized bartering, currency systems, and even contracting for future delivery. The Agora of Athens started as such a marketplace and evolved into a vast, busy commercial hub as Athens became the center of political and maritime power. At the pinnacle of the Roman Empire, there were nearly 20 trading centers distributing the wealth of commodities imported from across the Empire.

Although commerce was disrupted in the Dark Ages, the fundamentals of the marketplace survived in the form of medieval fairs. Such fairs were promoted by *pieds poudres,* or "men with dusty feet," who traveled across the land. Gradually, some fairs began specializing in trade between different nations. In 1215, the Magna Carta guaranteed the right of foreign merchants to travel freely to and from English fairs. Although most trading was for cash for immediate delivery, contracting for later delivery of merchandise began.

In America, before the central grain markets were created in the mid-19th century, it was each buyer and seller for himself and there was no method for competitive bidding. Every autumn, America's farmers hauled their harvests to cities, towns, and transportation hubs in search of buyers. The supplies of grain usually far outstripped the needs of millers. The resultant gluts drove prices abysmally low so that disgusted farmers, lacking storage facilities, often wound up dumping what they couldn't sell right in the street or in nearby rivers and lakes. In the spring, there were shortages of that same wheat and corn.

Out of this mess emerged the first central markets, the forerunners of today's futures markets. Imaginative farmers and merchants began making contracts for forward deliveries, which assured them of having a buyer or seller for their commodities. Such forwarding contracts were in effect in Chicago shortly after the city's founding in 1833. In 1848, the Chicago Board of Trade was formed and forward contracting as well as cash trades were practiced.

But while forward contracts found a buyer a seller or vice versa, they did nothing about the risk of unforeseen price changes due to crop failures, transportation problems, or economic conditions. Thus, hedging (see page 294) arose to diminish the risk.

Today, the exchanges cover a plethora of "commodities." As well as farmers and grain dealers, participants include bond dealers, mortgage bankers, multinational corporations, savings and loan associations, and individual speculators. Thanks to high-tech communications, there is a global futures market. Futures prices set through competitive bidding are instantaneously relayed around the world. A South Dakota farmer, a Hong Kong exporter, a broker in London, and a New York speculator all have access to the latest market-derived price quotations.

FUTURES EXCHANGES

Most futures exchanges are not-for-profit membership associations. Membership is restricted and belongs to individuals, although companies, partnerships, and cooperatives may be registered for certain membership privileges. Some exchanges have of late offered special membership or trading privileges. The Chicago Board of Trade, for instance, has associate members who trade in designated markets, such as financial-instrument futures.

American Stock Exchange
  86 Trinity Place
  New York, New York 10006
    Offers include options on 135 stocks and 20 over-the-counter securities,
    Treasury bills, Treasury notes, two broad-based stock indexes (the
    Major Market Index and the Institutional Index), and three narrow-
    based stock indexes: in computer technology, oil, and airlines.

Amex Commodities Corporation
  86 Trinity Place
  New York, New York 10006
    A subsidiary of the Amex offering cash-settled options on gold bullion.

Chicago Board of Trade
  141 West Jackson Boulevard
  Chicago, Illinois 60604
    The world's largest futures exchange is a nonprofit association provid-
    ing a marketplace that includes agricultural, financial, metals, and
    stock-index futures and futures options in corn, silver, soybeans,
    Treasury bills, and Treasury notes.

Chicago Board Options Exchange
  400 South LaSalle Street
  Chicago, Illinois 60605
    The world's largest options marketplace and the only one exclusively
    for options trading. In addition to puts and calls on 159 of the most
    widely held and active stocks, it includes options on the Standard &
    Poor's 100 and 500 Stock Indexes, three U.S. T-bonds, three U.S.
    T-notes, and six foreign currencies.

Chicago Mercantile Exchange
  30 South Wacker Drive
  Chicago, Illinois 60606
    Second to the CBT in trading volume, the CME is the world's largest
    facility for futures with a membership of 2,725 traders. The most active
    contract is Standard & Poor's 500 Stock Index futures. Other futures
    traded include options on currencies, three short-term interest rate
    T-bills, Eurodollars, cattle and hogs, lumber, and pork bellies. The
    three divisions of the exchange include the CME, International Mone-
    tary Market, and Index and Options Market.

Chicago Rice and Cotton Exchange
  444 West Jackson Boulevard
  Chicago, Illinois 60606
    Formerly the New Orleans Commodity Exchange, the CRCE lists
    rough rice futures, which are traded on the floor of the Chicago Board
    of Trade, and short-staple cotton futures traded on the floor of the
    MidAmerica Commodity Exchange.

Coffee, Sugar and Cocoa Exchange
  4 World Trade Center
  New York, New York 10048
    The world's leading marketplace for futures contracts on world and
    domestic sugar, coffee, and cocoa as well as options on those commodi-
    ties, and the inflation-futures contract, the CIP-W, is based on the U.S.
    consumer price index.

Commodity Exchange
  4 World Trade Center
  New York, New York 10048
    The world's leading gold-futures exchange and the third-biggest com-
    modity exchange in the U.S. Contracts traded include gold, silver, cop-
    per, and aluminum futures and options on gold, silver, and copper
    futures.

Kansas City Board of Trade
  4800 Main Street, Suite 303
  Kansas City, Missouri 64112
    The world's primary marketplace for futures and options in hard red
    winter wheat and the first U.S. exchange to trade futures based on a
    stock market index, the Value Line Composite Index.

MidAmerica Commodity Exchange
  444 West Jackson Boulevard
  Chicago, Illinois 60606
    An affiliate of the Chicago Board of Trade, the MidAm offers futures
    contracts on financial instruments, foreign currencies, gold, grain, live-
    stock, metals, soybeans, and wheat. Many contracts are smaller versions of
    contracts traded elsewhere, with inherently smaller margin requirements.

Minneapolis Grain Exchange
  400 South Fourth Street
  Minneapolis, Minnesota 55415
    Offers future contracts for hard red spring wheat and white wheat
    futures and options on hard red spring wheat.

New York Cotton Exchange
  4 World Trade Center
  New York, New York 10048
    The oldest exchange in New York, it offers futures contracts on cotton,
    frozen concentrated orange juice (FCOJ), and liquid propane gas as
    well as options on cotton and FCOJ futures. The Financial Instrument
    Exchange division offers futures contracts on the U.S. Dollar Index and
    European Currency Units, with trading privileges open to all 1,300
    qualified Commodity Exchange floor traders.

New York Futures Exchange
  20 Broad Street
  New York, New York 10005
    A subsidiary of the New York Stock Exchange, NYFE contracts
    include NYSE Composite Stock Index futures and options on futures
    and Commodity Research Bureau Futures Price Index futures.

New York Mercantile Exchange
  4 World Trade Center
  New York, New York 10048
    Maintains a futures market for No. 2 heating oil, unleaded gasoline,
    light sweet crude oil, platinum, and palladium and is adding options on
    several energy contracts starting with crude oil.

New York Stock Exchange
  11 Wall Street
  New York, New York 10005
    The world's leading stock exchange offers stocks on more than 1,500
    companies and options on its NYSE Composite Stock Index.

Pacific Stock Exchange
   301 Pine Street
   San Francisco, California 94104
   233 South Beaudry
   Los Angeles, California 90012
      Has equity trading floors in Los Angeles and San Francisco. It offers
      some 1,300 securities and offers options on 86 stocks and one index, the
      PSE Technology Index.

Philadelphia Board of Trade
   1900 Market Street
   Philadelphia, Pennsylvania 19103
      The subsidiary of the Philadelphia Stock Exchange offers futures con-
      tracts in deutsche marks, Swiss francs, Canadian dollars, British pounds,
      Japanese yen, French francs, European Currency Units, and the
      National Over-the-Counter Index and options on actual Eurodollars.

Philadelphia Stock Exchange
   1900 Market Street
   Philadelphia, Pennsylvania 19103
      The nation's oldest securities exchange offers more than 1,200 equity
      securities, 87 stock options, seven foreign currency options and three
      index options (Value Line, National OTC, and Gold/Silver). The for-
      eign currency options program is the largest of its kind, offering options
      on deutsche marks, Swiss francs, Canadian dollars, British pounds,
      Japanese yen, French francs, and European Currency Units.

STOCK INDEX FUTURES

For years, the hottest craps game around was stock index futures. In 1987, the average daily volume of trading in the most popular contract, the Standard & Poor's 500 stock index futures contract, hit about $12 billion, nearly double the volume two years earlier. The October 1987 market meltdown and recession jitters, however, dampened six years of explosive growth. Also, the possibility that stock index futures and options were accessories to the market crash didn't help their image. In 1990, the average daily volume for S&P's 500 was $48 million.

A lot of folks have always considered commodity trading as gambling. After all, only 4% of all commodities traded are actually delivered. The rest are tossed around like chips in Vegas. But in 1905, Justice Oliver Wendell Holmes found a way of telling the commodities market from the casino. He noted there was an obligation to make or take delivery of the commodity, even if the delivery was moot in most cases.

Who knows what the good Justice would think about stock index futures, which were introduced on the Chicago Mercantile Exchange in 1982. Instead of prices of bushels of wheat or piles of pork bellies, traders bet on how a group of stocks will move. The most widely used group is the S&P 500. In a terraced pit about half the size of a tennis court, more than 500 traders elbow and gouge one another as they fight for position to trade the S&P Index, which became the fastest-growing futures contract ever. There's little wonder why. To buy $1 million in stock index futures one only had to put down $100,000, or a fifth of what one would have had to put down to buy $1 million in stock.

(The difference in margins between stocks and futures goes back to 1934, when President Roosevelt proposed raising margins on both. Ever inconsistent, Congress raised them for securities but ignored futures.)

A combination of the explosion in volume in stock and bonds markets in 1986 and 1987 and deregulation loosened the Chicago exchange's hammerlock on the most popular financial contracts. New contracts sprouted up on options exchanges and over-the-counter markets.

One result of all this is concern that the small shareholder is getting the short shrift. One study has substantiated what everybody suspected: professional traders who use stock index options and futures have occasionally dominated the stock market, at times creating wild swings in stock prices. The pros predicted that the Dow would experience 100-point rises or slides as a result of being zapped by Chicago.

As we witnessed in 1987, that's exactly what happened and, by all accounts, greatly contributed to the market craziness that saw the DJIA plummet 508 points on October 19. Critics blamed those market gyrations on traders engaging in something called "program trading." (See page 265.) Massive blocks of stock are traded—with the assistance of computers—as investors try to profit from the price difference between stock index futures or options and the actual cash value of the stocks that make up the index. As a kind of insurance for their portfolios when the market drops, big institutional traders sell stock index futures. If the index keeps falling below the contracted price, the traders profit and offset the loss in the value of the stock.

Table 20-1   Commodities Contracts*

1972

1.	Soybeans	Chicago Board of Trade	4,043,474
2.	Pork bellies	Chicago Mercantile Exchange	2,057,064
3.	Corn	Chicago Board of Trade	1,942,120
4.	Live cattle	Chicago Mercantile Exchange	1,370,471
5.	Soybean oil	Chicago Board of Trade	1,110,776
6.	Sugar	New York Coffee and Sugar Exchange	875,178
7.	Wheat	Chicago Board of Trade	855,813
8.	Silver	Commodity Exchange	815,166
9.	Silver	Chicago Board of Trade	813,492
10.	Soybean meal	Chicago Board of Trade	630,916
		Total, all contracts	18,332,055

1977

1.	Soybeans	Chicago Board of Trade	7,906,130
2.	Corn	Chicago Board of Trade	5,021,827
3.	Silver	Commodity Exchange	3,573,301
4.	Live cattle	Chicago Mercantile Exchange	2,830,517
5.	Soybean oil	Chicago Board of Trade	2,825,046
6.	Soybean meal	Chicago Board of Trade	2,373,453
7.	Silver	Chicago Board of Trade	2,257,069
8.	Wheat	Chicago Board of Trade	1,820,790
9.	Pork bellies	Chicago Mercantile Exchange	1,258,730
10.	Live hogs	Chicago Mercantile Exchange	1,307,712
		Total, all contracts	42,980,318

1982

1.	T-bonds	Chicago Board of Trade	16,739,695
2.	Gold	Commodity Exchange	12,269,448
3.	Soybeans	Chicago Board of Trade	9,165,520
4.	Corn	Chicago Board of Trade	7,948,257
5.	T-bills	Chicago Mercantile Exchange	6,598,848
6.	Live cattle	Chicago Mercantile Exchange	4,440,992
7.	Wheat	Chicago Board of Trade	4,031,584
8.	Live hogs	Chicago Mercantile Exchange	3,580,974
9.	Soybean oil	Chicago Board of Trade	3,049,313
10.	S&P 500	Chicago Mercantile Exchange	2,935,532
		Total, all contracts	112,400,879

1987

1.	T-bonds	Chicago Board of Trade	66,941,474
2.	Eurodollar	Chicago Mercantile Exchange	20,416,216
3.	S&P 500 Index	Chicago Mercantile Exchange	10,044,573
4.	Crude Oil	New York Mercantile	14,581,614
5.	Gold (100 oz)	Commodities Exchange	16,239,805
6.	Soybeans	Chicago Board of Trade	7,378,780
7.	Corn	Chicago Board of Trade	7,253,212
8.	Deutsche Mark	Chicago Mercantile Exchange	6,037,048
9.	Japanese Yen	Chicago Mercantile Exchange	5,358,556
10.	Swiss Franc	Chicago Mercantile Exchange	5,286,276
		Total, all contracts	104,364,496

*For information on exchanges where commodities are traded, see "Futures Exchanges," above.
Source: Futures Industry Association, Inc.

Table 20-2 Volume of Futures Trading, 1960–1990
(millions of contracts traded)

Millions of
contracts
traded

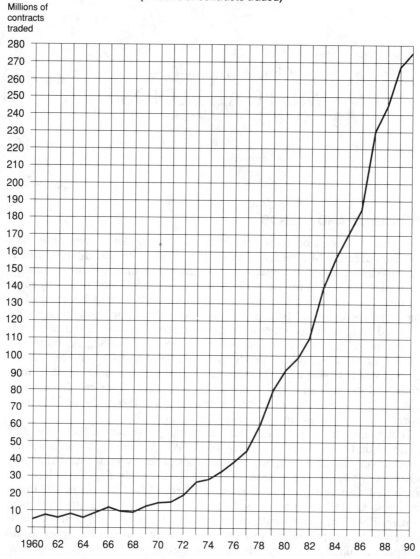

Source: Futures Industry Association, Inc.

Chapter Twenty-One
MUTUAL FUNDS

HIGHLIGHTS AND TRENDS

The 1980s may well be remembered as the decade Americans went mad over mutual funds. Mutual funds entered the 1990s as the third-largest financial vehicles in terms of assets, after commercial banks and life insurance companies. Starting in the early 1980s, when investors turned to money-market funds as the nation slid into a recession, funds started booming. The coming of the universal IRA in 1981 to boost the nation's low savings rate attracted legions of investors to mutuals. (IRA accounts in mutual funds grew to more than 17 million in 1990 from 500,000 in 1982.) As bond and equity funds flourished, new products, such as global stock and bond funds, Ginnie Maes, government income funds, foreign currency funds, index funds, and variable annuities, were introduced. (The funds caught on overseas too. By the beginning of 1989, mutual fund assets outside the U.S. were more than $850 billion, up from $141 billion in 1983.)

Though mutual funds became familiar to many investors in the 1980s, they aren't all that new. After the end of World War II, when they had total net assets of only about $1 billion, mutual funds probably grew faster than any other major financial institution in the U.S. In the 1980s they exploded. The combined assets of mutual funds soared from $58.4 billion in 1980 to a whopping $370.6 billion at the end of 1984 to a staggering trillion dollars in January 1990. The growth patterns of different types of funds largely reflected declining short-term interest rates and the bullish stock market. Bond and income funds grew mainly because investors were attracted by the relatively high returns from longer-term securities compared with those from short-term securities. Particularly hot were funds focusing on the securities of the federal government and the Government National Mortgage Association. But as go the markets, so go the funds. During the week of Black Monday (October 19, 1987), a lot of investors bailed out of mutual funds; more than $8 billion was diverted into money markets alone as world stock markets lost a scary one third of their value before recovering.

HOW FUNDS WORK

The industry is made up of investment companies that sell shares in one or more mutual funds, each of which simply consists of a pool of financial assets. Investors buy shares and get the benefits (or share the losses) of how the collective securities perform. Fund shares, which rise and fall depending upon the value of the assets, are sold publicly and are redeemable anytime. Because funds closely follow the market, investors gamble on the canniness of the fund manager to make the fund perform well. The manager determines the makeup of the fund portfolio, or assets, which can consist of stocks, bonds, gold, government securities, or whatever else falls within the fund's stated purpose. For example, bond funds are made up mostly of corporate or municipal bonds and are meant to provide regular income rather than growth. Income funds have the same goal as bond funds but include in their portfolios high-interest or dividend-paying government securities, common and preferred stock, and bonds. Equity-fund portfolios are made up primarily of common stocks and are meant to provide growth rather than dividends. Money-market mutual funds are made up of short-term market vehicles such as commercial paper, federal government securities, and bank certificates of deposit. Short-term municipal bond funds are like money-market funds, but their investments are mostly tax-exempt municipal securities.

THE PLAYERS

In the 1980s, there were hundreds of funds and more popping up all the time. Sometimes it seems as if there's one for just about everybody and maybe there is. Some funds' assets, for instance, are energy company stocks; others buy only stocks in companies headquartered in a particular state, such as Ohio, or a specific country, say, Germany. Then there have been proposals for Muslim and cemetery company funds, and a junk-bond fund for nonresident aliens. Still others reflect a heightened social conscience. (See the box on page 304.) Investors can buy shares from a lot of different sources: brokerage houses, insurance agencies, financial planners, unions, and even retailers. In 1986, the department store chain K Mart started offering funds at outlets in New Jersey. For years, Merrill Lynch's funds comprised the biggest group, but the most noteworthy is the maverick Fidelity Investments, now the largest family of funds and undoubtedly one of the most aggressive. (See the profile on page 305.)

TRENDS

The old saw about the past being a predictor of the future is what analysts generally cling to when talking about where mutual funds are going. As goes the market, so go most funds. Even with the tax changes knocking out a lot of IRA money that would have gone into mutual funds, the industry is expected to thrive and become more competitive over the next few years. With marketing efforts being stepped up by a lot of funds, a proliferation of specialized funds, and more retailers and others reaching out for customers, increasing numbers of individual investors are expected to open accounts. Moreover, trusts, pension funds, and other institutions are expected to continue turning to the funds, especially money-market funds, for liquidity or investments. Increased regulation, of course, can have a major impact on the industry. If banks, for instance, are allowed to sponsor and sell mutual-fund shares, competition will be hotter than ever. Money-market funds may become less enticing if reserve requirements that would reduce their yields are imposed. Nonetheless, the federal Office of Service Industries concludes that if there are no dramatic regulatory changes, "the mutual fund industry will grow at a strong rate over the next few years."

"ETHICAL" FUNDS

There are mutual funds for people who want to see their funds do good as well as do well. More than $50 billion is believed to be invested in funds with specific ethical considerations as the hallmark of their portfolios. One reason for the boom is state and city employees who say they want their pension funds invested in such a fashion. The practice isn't brand new, having become especially noticeable in the 1940s when union and government-agency fund managers wouldn't invest in companies with what they regarded as unfair labor records. Today, one of the major considerations of such funds is the elimination of apartheid in South Africa; other concerns include the environment, housing, nuclear power, and medical-care and weapons expenditures. Few funds agree, though, on precisely what is or is not "socially responsible" investing.

Probably the best-known such funds were formed in the 1970s—Calvert Social Investment, Dreyfus Third Century, and Pax World. Calvert invests in stocks of companies in the businesses of protecting the environment and providing renewable energy applications while shunning weapon makers and those engaged in nuclear power or with South African holdings. Dreyfus seeks out firms with environmental concerns and enforcers of strong quality and occupational safety codes. Pax World invests in food, housing, and medical-care companies while steering clear of gambling, liquor, tobacco, and weapons companies.

Do the ethical funds pay off other than in psychic soothing? The answer is yes—at least sometimes. "Ethical" fund managers don't get off the hook just because their portfolios purport to carry extra moral weight. A survey of such funds by Lipper Analytical Securities Corporation showed in 1985 that they produced an average yield of 25.24% compared to the average fund's yield of 24.95%. "No one wants to invest in anything that's morally irresponsible," a municipal union official told Financial World. "But people want to make money. You won't get that many do-gooders to invest if they can't make a fair return."

Fidelity Investments   In 1946 Edward C. Johnson II, a Harvard-educated lawyer, took over management of a privately held, Boston-based mutual fund that apparently was on its last legs. One of the oldest mutual-fund organizations in the nation, Fidelity had barely $3 million in assets. A cool, aloof man, Johnson—"Mister Johnson" to his employees—broke a pattern of investing in blue chips. Instead, he sought out strong stocks with the potential for good growth. The strategy paid off. Twenty years later, Fidelity had $4 billion more in assets and the company's tough relentlessness earned it the sobriquet "the Green Bay Packers of the fund league" in Adam Smith's *The Money Game.* By 1990, just one of Fidelity's funds, the outstanding Magellan Fund, had assets of $13.9 billion.

Today, Fidelity is still based in Boston and still privately held but is now run by the Mister's son, Edward C. III. More than ever, the company is known for its aggressiveness, innovativeness, and enviable track record. But after the stock market collapse in October 1987, the company faced tough challenges. The public became discouraged with mutual funds. Fidelity's sales pace was cut in half. And many customers were disappointed in the service during the market meltdown.

Fidelity has under its umbrella more than 100 portfolio funds compared with the fewer than a dozen held by most companies. Fidelity, for instance, has funds that specialize in turnaround companies, high-growth opportunities, out-of-favor issues, and over-the-counter stocks. One of the company's more controversial innovations was its sector funds, which have been compared to roulette wheels because they can be played 32 different ways. Rather than diversifying by buying stocks in different industries, Fidelity urged investors in sector funds to put all their shares in an industry they thought would do well and then switch to another industry when they thought the time was ripe.

Well before the competition, Fidelity invested heavily and smartly in advertising, technology, and a big support staff. It spent $50 million a year or so promoting its funds, more money than Anheuser-Busch has shelled out for its Bud Light TV campaign. And it had a huge service operation. Put in place a decade ago, it consisted by 1987, for example, of a sales and service force of 400 in Boston, a 650-person operation in Dallas, and a 100-person office in Salt Lake City. Even so, customers reported lengthy delays during the market panic as they tried to make changes in their holdings.

The delays were surprising because the telephone network had handled more than a call a second 24 hours a day. On the April 15, 1986, deadline for opening a tax-deductible IRA, Fidelity had a staggering 140,000 phone calls (double the usual number) and signed up an incredible 50,000 new accounts. In addition, Fidelity funds were pushed through a network of 36 discount brokerage houses as well as banks, and after having stopped dealing with unaffiliated brokers in the late 1970s, the company dealt with them again. Moreover, Fidelity continued pouring money into staff and technology to maintain its momentum. For instance, its street-level Investor Centers, where customers buy funds, trade stocks, or get money from their accounts, were supposed to be within an hour's drive of many people making $50,000 or more a year. Fidelity expected them to be within an hour's reach of 92% of that sought-after group by the early 1990s.

Fidelity's legions of fund managers and security analysts visited some 10,000 U.S. and overseas companies annually. Analysts were recruited fresh out of business school so that Fidelity's way of doing business was the only one they learned. They measured their results on a daily basis against how the stocks in their groups performed in the market. Within a year or so an analyst might be assigned to manage a portfolio of stocks within a certain industry, an opportunity that eluded many an analyst elsewhere for decades.

In recent years, some of the portfolio managers did very well and Fidelity went out of its way to advertise its winners. But others didn't perform as well and Fidelity didn't carve out a piece of its whopping ad budget to call attention to the mediocre to poorly performing funds. "On the average, they were average to above average," A. Michael Lipper, president of Lipper Analytical Securities, of Fidelity's overall performance, said before the stock market crashed in October 1987.

What Fidelity had was the amazing Peter Lynch and his amazing Magellan Fund. The spectacular performance of this fund, the best track record of any mutual fund over the past decade, tended to lend a magic to all of Fidelity's funds. Lynch's strategy sounded pretty simple. His 1,500-stock portfolio was largely made up of three categories: companies that were not doing very well but that potentially would do better, small profitable companies growing bigger, and undervalued companies with a wealth in assets. Magellan, however, had gotten so enormous (some $9 billion in total assets before the market crash in 1987) that it had some trouble outperforming stock market averages. Then again, Lynch's departure from Magellan in May 1990 could become a troublesome element if the fund doesn't do as well under his successor, Morris Smith. But Fidelity wasn't banking on Magellan to hit all its home runs. "We have so many funds, the odds are in our favor that we should have another doing very well," an executive noted.

Chapter Twenty-Two
INSURANCE

HIGHLIGHTS AND TRENDS

Insurance is really our "insecurity security." The market touches on just about everything from being out of work to losing everything in a flood. Dancers get their legs insured, ski resorts insure their slopes, and companies get their boards insured—when they can. No wonder. The thought of not being insured against just about every accident, stupid decision, or freak of nature can make one tremble. The cost of motor-vehicle accidents alone is some $76 billion a year. Robberies, burglaries, larcenies, and motor-vehicle thefts result in another $11 billion a year in losses. Fires consume an estimated $7.75 billion annually in property losses. The list goes on.

What it all means is that insurance is obviously big business. But it hasn't been a very good one. Property and casualty carriers had record underwriting losses in 1990, resulting in a sharp drop in the availability and affordability of some classes of liability insurance and a continuous clamor for a change in the liability system. The industry, though, has had a big hand in creating its own problems. Lured by the sky-high interest rates of the first half of the decade, a lot of property and casualty insurers abandoned their traditionally conservative underwriting practices and pumped premium money into high-interest investments including real estate and junk bonds. The result for a while was investment earnings that more than offset the flood of red ink that hit the insurance-writing business. Then came the downturn in real estate and a loss of confidence in junk bonds. But don't weep for underwriters. During the 10 years from 1976 to 1985, the property and casualty insurance industry lost about $81.3 billion on underwriting but earned $119.8 billion on investment income.

Since the late 1970s the industry has been devastated by ferocious competition, exorbitant civil-damage awards, plunging premiums, and other problems. Moving further into the personal-finance business, insurers have acquired several brokerage houses and developed new investment-oriented life insurance products. Also, some life and health insurers acquired hospitals and other health-care providers.

INTERNATIONALIZATION OF THE MARKETPLACE

Insurers are part of the increasing internationalization of financial services. By the beginning of 1986, 22 U.S. life insurance companies were owned by foreign-based corporations, a trend that is expected to continue. For their part, U.S. life insurance companies are making their presence felt abroad; life, health, and annuity premiums from operations abroad totaled $1.2 billion in 1985. While such income at this time is small, it is still greater than the life insurance income generated by 27 of the 50 states.

LIFE INSURANCE

About 65% of the U.S. population is covered by life insurance. Ordinary life insurance totaling $3.3 billion represents 54% of all life insurance. Group life insurance accounts for 42% of life coverage. Annual income now payable or committed to be paid is more than $23.9 billion.

Life insurance carriers in the U.S. are divided into two types of companies: stock companies (those owned by shareholders) and mutual life insurance companies (those owned by policyholders). Like others in the insurance industry, life insurance carriers are worried about the long-term prospect of banks moving into their line of business, either by direct underwriting or by acquiring insurance companies. To hedge against what strikes many insurers as the inevitability of such competition as well as to find new markets, life insurance carriers have introduced such innovative products as variable life insurance, which gives policyholders the opportunity to earn capital gains on their insurance investment; universal life insurance, which combines the low-cost protection of term insurance with a savings portion that is invested in a tax-deferred account earning money-market interest rates; and flexible premium variable life insurance, which contains elements of both variable and the universal insurance. Life insurers have also entered the real estate market and financing.

Table 22-1　Trends: Life Insurance
(in billions of dollars except as noted)

| | | | | | | | Percent change | | |
| | | | | | | | Compound annual | Annual | |
Item	1985	1986	1987	1988	1989[1]	1990[2]	1985–88	1988–89	1989–90
Premium receipts	155.9	194.1	213.0	229.1	247.4	265.2	13.7	8.0	7.2
New life insurance purchases[3]	1,231.2	1,308.8	1,352.5	1,406.9	1,446.3	1,482.5	4.6	2.8	2.5
Life insurance in force[3]	6,053.1	6,720.3	7,452.5	8,020.2	8,742.0	9,511.3	9.8	9.0	8.8
Total benefits paid	66.5	68.3	71.4	74.1	77.7	81.2	3.7	4.8	4.6
Life insurance assets	825.9	937.6	1,044.5	1,166.9	1,285.9	1,414.5	12.2	10.2	10.0
Employment (SIC 6311)[4]	559.3	578.3	578.1	576.5	575.8	575.0	1.0	–0.1	–0.1

[1]Estimated.
[2]Forecast.
[3]Excludes foreign business.
[4]Employees on payroll only.
　Source: American Council of Life Insurance; U.S. Department of Labor, Bureau of Labor Statistics. Estimates and forecasts by the U.S. Department of Commerce, International Trade Administration.

Table 22-2 The 10 Biggest Insurance Companies
(by assets, 1988)

U.S.	World
1. Prudential	1. Prudential
2. Metropolitan Life	2. Metropolitan
3. Equitable Life	3. Nippon Life
4. Aetna	4. Aetna
5. Teachers Insurance	5. Equitable Life
6. New York Life	6. Dai-Ichi Mutual
7. Connecticut General Life	7. CIGNA
8. Travelers	8. Travelers
9. John Hancock	9. Sumitomo Life
10. Northwestern Mutual Life	10. Prudential Corporation (U.K.)

Source: Various press accounts.

PROPERTY AND CASUALTY INSURANCE

After cutthroat competition from 1979 to 1984, when companies fought for premiums to pump into high-yield investments, premiums started to rise and continued to rise in 1990.

Meanwhile, there continue to be insurance availability problems. The areas include pollution, day-care, municipal, earthquake, liquor, motor-carrier, and corporate directors' and officers' liability insurance. Some of the problems are the result of bankruptcy by some specialty insurers, especially in liquor and motor-carrier liability. Affordability problems have hit the space satellite industry and parts of the medical community, including nurse-midwives. Insurance adequacy problems have abated for many businesses, except pharmaceutical companies and businesses dealing with hazardous waste.

Aware of the problems, more than 40 states have passed tort reform measures that reduce liability exposure in the expectation of making insurance cheaper and more available for businesses, professionals, government groups, and nonprofit organizations. The insurance industry is banking that federal legislation will further ease the situation.

Table 22-3 Trends: Property/Casualty Insurance
(in billions of dollars except as noted)

							Percent change		
							Compound annual	Annual	
Item	1985	1986	1987	1988	1989[1]	1990[2]	1985–88	1988–89	1989–90
Net written premiums	144.2	176.6	193.2	202.0	207.6	216.9	11.9	2.8	4.5
Underwriting gain (loss)	(22.6)	(13.7)	(7.1)	(8.4)	(16.6)	(22.7)	—	—	—
Net investment income	19.5	21.9	24.0	27.7	29.7	32.4	12.4	7.2	9.1
Operating earnings after taxes	(3.3)	6.6	11.0	12.9	8.6	6.4	—	(33.3)	(25.6)
Assets	311.4	374.1	426.7	476.9	522.2	569.2	15.3	9.5	9.0
Policyholders' surplus	75.5	94.3	104.0	118.2	128.8	138.6	16.1	9.0	7.6
Employment (000) (SIC 633)	474.9	499.6	526.2	540.2	547.5	555.7	4.4	1.4	1.5

[1]Estimated.
[2]Forecast.
Source: A. M. Best Company, *Best's Aggregates and Averages;* U.S. Department of Labor, Bureau of Labor Statistics. Estimates and forecasts by U.S. Department of Commerce, International Trade Administration.

Table 22-4   The 10 Costliest Fires in the U.S.

The San Francisco fire of 1906 was the costliest in the U.S. The estimated loss at the time was $350 million but, in 1982 dollars, that was equal to about $4 billion.

Rank	Date	Place	Property destroyed	Estimated loss (dollars)
1.	April 18, 1906	San Francisco	28,000 buildings	350,000,000
2.	October 8–10, 1871	Chicago	17,340 buildings	175,000,000
3.	November 12, 1984	Tinker AFB, Oklahoma	Jet engine repair facility	138,000,000
4.	July 23, 1984	Romeoville, Illinois	Oil refinery	100,000,000
5.	June 6, 1982	Falls Township, Pennsylvania	Retail distribution center	100,000,000
6.	November 25, 1982	Minneapolis	Bank building	91,000,000
7.	November 9, 1872	Boston	776 buildings	75,000,000
8.	September 1, 1979	Deer Park, Texas	Tank ship	70,000,000
9.	November 28, 1981	Lynn, Massachusetts	31 buildings	70,000,000
10.	April 16, 1947	Texas City, Texas	Waterfront industrial area	67,000,000

Source: Insurance Information Institute.

HISTORY

The earliest known insurance seems to date back to Babylonian days, when ships were insured. In the fourth millennium there were "bottomry" contracts, which insured ships and didn't have to be paid back if the ships went down.

In ancient Rome, there was burial insurance in effect through burial societies that paid their members' funeral costs from monthly dues.

It wasn't until the Great Fire of London in 1666 that fire insurance became widespread. Some 14,000 buildings were destroyed and 200,000 people were left homeless. During the same century, as a result of gatherings of shippers and insurers at Edward Lloyd's coffee shop, Lloyd's of London started as an organized group of underwriters accepting maritime risks.

Insurance came to the New World in 1735 when a short-lived fire insurance company was founded. The first to succeed was the Philadelphia Contributorship, or "Hand in Hand" as it was known, which was started in 1752 by Benjamin Franklin. The first life insurance company, the Corporation for Relief of Distressed Presbyterian Ministers and of the Poor and Distressed Widows and Children of Presbyterian Ministers, was established in 1759 in Philadelphia.

Life insurance agents came into existence in 1830 when the New York Life Insurance and Trust Company was formed and began employing the first such agents. By 1869 there were so many of them that they formed their first organization.

Introduction of the automobile was swiftly followed by car insurance. The first auto liability policy was issued in 1887 to Gilbert Loomis of Westfield, Connecticut. The cost was $7.50 per $1,000 of liability.

The first group life insurance for employees was started in 1911. In 1917,

Table 22-5   The 10 Costliest U.S. Civil Disorders

Rioting in Miami, Florida, in May 1980 resulted in the costliest insured losses on record stemming from civil disorders. Of the ten costliest, all except the one in Miami and a disturbance in New York City resulting from a massive power outage were racial riots in the 1960s.

Rank	Date	Location	Estimated loss (dollars)
1.	May 17–19, 1980	Miami	65,250,000
2.	August 11–17, 1965	Los Angeles	44,000,000
3.	July 23, 1967	Detroit	41,500,000
4.	July 13–14, 1977	New York City	28,000,000
5.	April 4–9, 1968	Washington, D.C.	24,000,000
6.	July 12, 1967	Newark	15,000,000
7.	April 6–9, 1968	Baltimore	14,000,000
8.	April 4–11, 1968	Chicago	13,000,000
9.	April 4–11, 1968	New York City	4,200,000
10.	April 4–11, 1968	Pittsburgh	2,000,000

Source: Insurance Information Institute.

life insurance for World War I servicemen was offered by the government under the War Risk Insurance Act. In 1940, legislation providing insurance for World War II service personnel was enacted by Congress, and in 1965, as a result of the Vietnam War, the insurance was provided again.

The Social Security Act was enacted in 1935. Amended at various times, the act provided benefits for survivors and dependents and for disabled workers and their dependents. It also was amended so it covered more jobs, lowered the minimum retirement age, revised contribution schedules, increased the earnings base, and in 1965, established Medicare, a health insurance program for people 65 and over.

WORKER'S COMPENSATION

Worker's compensation goes back to the 17th-century pirates, who recognized hazardous duty when they saw it.

A typical buccaneer comp schedule called for payment of 100 pieces of eight and a slave for the loss of an eye; 400 and four slaves for a left leg; 500 and four slaves for a left arm or right leg; and 600 and six slaves for a right arm. Anybody who lost a hand was out of luck. He was expected to have it replaced by a hook, which was actually considered something of an advantage because it made a good tool.

PERILS

Watch out for perils. Most property insurance policies exclude losses caused by certain perils, including rebellion, civil war, and enemy attack.

TYPES OF LIFE INSURANCE

Adjustable allows the policyholder to shift back and forth between term and whole life insurance and even to change the premium amounts paid for the policy.

Endowment insures a life for a certain period of time, such as 20 or 30 years, or to a certain age, such as 65. If the insured lives to the end of the time period, he or she receives the face amount of the policy. Essentially a savings plan as much as insurance, it gives less coverage than term or whole life insurance for the same price.

Term covers the insured for a specific time period. It requires the policyholder to pay only for the cost of protection against death. Because it usually does not build up an investment fund or have a cash value at the end of the period, premiums are lower than for whole life or endowment insurance.

Universal separates the cost of term insurance from the investment value of the policy. The cash value of the policy is set up as a fund that earns investment income, which is drawn on for the cost of term insurance. The policy is flexible in that as age and income change, a policyholder can increase or decrease premium payments and coverage or shift a portion of premiums into a savings account without penalty.

Variable lets the insured choose from among several ways of investing the value of the policy, such as common stocks or other potentially high-yielding investments. To reflect the rise or fall of the investment's performance, this insurance often comes with provisions for changes in policy cash values and death benefits.

Whole offers protection in case the insured dies and also builds up cash value. Premiums can be paid in a lump sum at the beginning of the contract, over a limited period such as 10 or 20 years, or throughout the life of the insured. This insurance typically yields a cash value that can be used as a security for borrowing or that can be taken as a cash payment at a certain age. Premiums are much higher than for term insurance.

KIDNAPPING

The 1932 kidnapping-murder of Charles A. Lindbergh, Jr., the 20-month-old son of the famous aviator, led to a new kind of insurance—kidnap and ransom insurance. Such policies reimburse ransom or extortion payments up to a certain limit, usually $1 million. Today, such policies are usually taken out by companies on key executives. Payments may now also cover rewards and other expenses, such as the interest on bank loans taken to raise the ransom. Such policies may also cover damage done by an extortionist as a means of coercion, such as contamination of a food product. The policy would cover any product recall as well as damages from the contamination.

LLOYD'S OF LONDON

Most folks contemplating sophisticated, big-time insurers think of Lloyd's of London. But Lloyd's isn't an insurance company in the usual sense but a marketplace with individual underwriting members. As a corporation, Lloyd's doesn't issue policies but sets standards for its members. Actual policies are prepared by Lloyd's Policy Signing Office but signed by individuals who will share in any losses. Worldwide, Lloyd's is organized into several hundred syndicates, each having from several to more than 500 participants. An underwriter manages each syndicate, determining which of the insurance applications brokers submit should be accepted. Americans involved with Lloyd's are primarily buyers of reinsurance, which is sharing the risk for part of the premium fee paid by the insured. Reinsurance allows insurers to take on clients whose coverage would be too great a burden for one insurer to carry.

Chapter Twenty-Three

PENSIONS

HIGHLIGHTS AND TRENDS

Remember all the talk about letting everybody stay on the job beyond age 70? It conjured up visions of vast legions crying in their beer at having to get out of the rat race as they approached their 65th birthdays. Well, maybe some folks do, but the reality is that about 70% of all employees quit work before age 65, about twice as many as in the mid-1970s.

A big reason is pensions, which, when combined with Social Security benefits, give a lot of folks an alternative to work. (In 1984, average monthly pensions for those with 30 years of service at age 65 ranged from $400 for those who had earned $15,000 a year to over $900 for those who had earned $40,000. Employees with 20 years of service received $263 to $623, respectively.)

After climbing for 30 years, the number of Americans with pension coverage declined in 1985 to 43% from 45% in 1981, the Employee Benefit Research Institute reported and has plateaued since then. Moreover, the 65-and-older population is expected to double by the year 2010, thus adding to the strains on and uncertainty of Social Security (See the chapter "Social Security.") What all this means is that pension plans will increasingly be of greater importance to Americans.

THE MONEY

There is a lot of money in pensions, but the amount being placed in them is diminishing. Employee benefit assets of just the nation's private pension trusts as of June 30, 1990 were $1,417 trillion, up from $1,250 trillion in 1989. In 1989, $667 billion of the assets were in equity, $319.8 billion in bonds, and $263.6 in cash and other assets.

Of the top 200 funds listed in the authoritative *Pension & Investment Age* in 1987, corporate funds showed the smallest increase—15.2%, to $445.9 billion. That reflected a downturn in contributions, but it also showed how mergers, acquisitions, and terminations of overfunded plans had thinned their ranks. Twelve company funds dropped out of the 200 while only four corporate funds moved into the ranking, leaving 108 corporate funds among the 200.

The top 11 union funds in 1989 saw their assets jump to $42 billion from $36 billion in 1982. Assets of the 13 largest miscellaneous funds, such as the World Bank, United Nations, and church funds, were $131 billion, up from $94 billion in 1987. The 25 largest public funds in the group increased to $487.5 billion from $435.9 billion in 1987.

THE PLAYERS

Cashing in on the lucrative portfolio-management business is the business of those who bill themselves as investment advisers. Fifteen years ago, the breed was hard to come by. Now, of course, they're breeding like jackrabbits. The Securities and Exchange Commission calculates that at least 300 new ones go into the business every month, and that meant more than 15,000 of them for 1990. Thus, as the flow of pension dollars winds down, the competition to get those dollars is greater than ever.

Even so, the biggest—and usually those who have been around the longest—wind up managing the mostest. As of January 1, 1990, the 100 biggest money managers had total assets under their belts of more than a trillion dollars. Insurance companies and their subsidiaries had 38%, banks and trust companies and their subsidiaries 36%, and independents 26%.

HISTORY

The nation's first pension plan was established in 1759 for widows and children of Presbyterian ministers. A century later, the first pension plan covering workers was created for retired New York City policemen. Before 1930, only about 15% of nonfarm U.S. workers were covered by pension plans. Now nearly half are covered.

TYPES OF PENSION PLANS

There are two major types of pension plans: single-employer plans, which are usually established by the employer, and multiemployer plans, which usually cover union workers and are set up by the workers and the union as a result of collective bargaining.

Defined contribution plans: The employer pays a specific amount—a percentage of salary or profits—into a pension fund. Employees may also make voluntary or mandatory contributions. The payments accumulate with investment and interest earnings in separate participant accounts.

Defined benefit plans: The benefit is determined in advance based on a benefit formula, such as payment for each year of service, or a percentage of annual salary, or average earnings over a specified number of years.

Profit-sharing plans: Employees share in an employer's profits and thus have an incentive for increased productivity. Profit-sharing plans provide supplemental income to employees and their families at death, disability, retirement, or employment termination.

401(k) cash or deferred arrangement plans: A 401(k) plan lets an employee place a portion of his or her compensation in a profit-sharing, stock bonus, or pension plan and the employee defers income tax until the money is withdrawn.

Individual retirement accounts: These were established by Congress in 1974 for workers who did not have employer-sponsored pension plans. In 1981 they were expanded to cover all U.S. workers who wanted to set aside up to $2,000 a year (the limit was $4,000 for a working couple and $2,250 for a worker with a nonworking spouse) on a tax-deferred basis. The 1986 tax law limits IRA deductions to those who aren't covered by employer-paid pension plans. All taxpayers may contribute to IRAs and have dividends and interest accumulate tax-free.

Rollovers: Individuals can roll over account balances from one IRA to another and from a qualified employer's pension plan to an IRA. To avoid tax penalties, the transfer of assets from one account to another must be done within 60 days.

Keoghs: Keogh plans are for employees of unincorporated businesses or self-employed people. The maximum that may be invested each year in such a pension plan depends on income but can be up to $30,000.

Table 23-1   Largest Miscellaneous Funds, 1989

Fund	($ millions)
TIAA-CREF	81,000
University of California	12,900
United Nations Joint Staff	8,414
Federal Retirement Thrift	4,319
Illinois State Universities	3,845
United Methodist Church	3,566
World Bank	3,292
Tennessee Valley Authority	3,090
Southern Baptist	2,559
Presbyterian Church	2,400
Nat'l Rural Electric Co-op	2,304
Episcopal Church	1,837
Evangelical Lutheran	1,782
Total	131,308

Source: *Pensions & Investments,* January 1991.

Table 23-2   Largest Public Pension Funds by Assets, 1989

Fund	($ millions)
California Employees	54,000
New York City	45,422
New York State & Local	44,238
California State Teachers	30,335
New York State Teachers	28,130
New Jersey	24,526
Texas Teachers	23,500
Wisconsin State Board	20,033
Ohio Public Employees	19,305
Florida State Board	18,700
Ohio State Teachers	18,059
State of Michigan	17,948
North Carolina	16,791
Pennsylvania Schools	15,430
Washington State Board	12,660
Minnesota State Board	12,343
Oregon Public Employees	11,178
Maryland State Systems	11,065
Virginia Supplemental	10,244
Pennsylvania Employees	9,504
Los Angeles County	9,359
Colorado Employees	9,227
Georgia Teachers	8,908
Illinois Teachers	8,475
Tennessee Consolidated	8,075
Total	487,455

Source: *Pensions & Investments,* January 1991.

Table 23-3   Largest Union Funds, 1989

Fund	($ millions)
Teamsters, Central States	9,849
Teamsters, Western	9,084
UMWA	5,300
Nat'l Electrical Contractors	3,675
Hospital/Healthcare	2,241
Bakery & Confectionery	2,175
Operating Engineers	2,154
Southern California UFCW	2,133
Boilermaker/Blacksmith	2,132
I.A.M. National Pension	1,695
Plumbers National HQ	1,615
Total	42,054

Source: *Pensions & Investments,* January 1991.

Chapter Twenty-Four
SOCIAL SECURITY

HIGHLIGHTS AND TRENDS

People keep predicting bankruptcy for the Social Security system. Seems logical, right? After all, in the mid-1970s Social Security began paying out more than it took in. (Contributions between 1973 and 1983 grew at a *12%* annual rate but benefits increased at a *13%* annual rate.) But what happened? Big rate increases. That will most likely be the pattern from here on in. As recently as 1963, the maximum Social Security tax was $174 a year. In the 1970s the maximum was $895 a year. Today it's more than triple that amount ($4,085), and while politicians seldom mention it, Social Security had a surplus of $62.7 billion at the end of 1990. The Congressional Budget Office projected a total surplus between 1991 and 1994 of $336.4 billion.

Most people think of Social Security as retirement insurance and that's the way we'll treat it here. But it also includes survivors' insurance, disability insurance, Medicare for the aged and disabled, black lung benefits, Supplemental Security Income, unemployment compensation, and public assistance and welfare services.

Congress has also bolstered the plan by upping the eligibility requirements. By 1990, people will have to work 10 years, up from 8.5, to become eligible. Moreover, early retirement benefits are gradually decreasing, while the age at which anyone can receive full retirement benefits will rise to 67 by the year 2022. Also, high-income people on Social Security have been paying taxes on benefits since 1984.

The big problem, however, lies with today's young workers. Right now there are 3.4 employed people shelling out Social Security money to support each retiree. That will decrease to 2 workers slaving away to support one retiree. And unless someone figures out a reasonable solution, the doomsayers may not be too far off the mark. But it will be the work force that goes bankrupt trying to keep Social Security from going bankrupt. When the system started, there were few payouts. The average U.S. male industrial worker died at age 62.

HOW IS SOCIAL SECURITY FUNDED?

Social Security is a pay-as-you-go operation. The taxes collected each year are intended to cover benefits and administrative costs paid out that year and to provide a small amount as a contingency fund. The tax rate went to 7.65% in 1990 from 7.51%. The maximum taxable earnings are now $53,400.

Self-employed people pay higher tax rates since they don't have employers to share the tax load. The self-employed tax rate increased to 15.3% in 1990, from 14.10%.

Chapter Twenty-Five

REAL ESTATE

HIGHLIGHTS AND TRENDS

Commercial

For the past few years, the market for commercial real estate has been in its worst shape since the Depression. By 1987, office building vacancies were 16.9% in downtown areas and 20.9% in the suburbs. The reason: oversaturation. The 1980s saw the greatest construction boom of the century. From 1981 to 1987, some 300 million square feet of office space was built each year, enough for five Manhattans. Even with the 18% interest rates of the early 1980s, money didn't stay away. Pension funds, insurance companies, banks, syndicators, and foreigners threw cash into commercial real estate ventures as if there was no tomorrow. Wall Streeters packaged properties into real estate partnerships, investment trusts, and zero-coupon real estate bonds. "If it's flat, develop it," the saying went. Then most developers shuddered and saw what an ill-conceived boom it was. With few exceptions, office rents in cities that support skyscrapers dropped 25% to 40%. Even places once thought immune to real estate recession, such as San Francisco, Chicago, Salt Lake City, Phoenix, and Dallas, suffered. By 1990, the nation's top 15 cities had an average commercial vacancy rate of about 16%, or quadruple what it was in 1981. The rates ranged from a high of about 31% in Phoenix to a low of just over 9% in Washington, D.C. New York's 16.3% didn't look so good when compared with the mere 2% in vacancies it had in 1981.

The reasons aren't hard to find. The oil industry's long slump obviously hurt markets in the southwest, but, more to the point, sharply lower inflation hit a lot of developers hard across the nation. Many of them had continued building with the same abandon they had in the 1970s when they could bank on inflation outstripping their costs. Another factor is the new tax law, which makes it tougher to carry high-vacancy buildings. Also, a lot of those Wall Street real estate packages were based on fantasy accounting when it came to appraisals, inflation expectations, projected occupancy rates, and rent rolls. Solving the overcapacity problem will take years.

Housing

Residential real estate's prospects look robust compared with those in the commercial market. Still, whatever happened to the hot housing market that economists were predicting? Sure there are megabuck people lined up in Beverly Hills and Bel Air itching to drop $20 million for fancy digs and others willing to pay $2 million or so for houses they tear down and replace with something more to their liking. But what about the rest of Americans? The economists' scenario went like this: As mortgage rates drifted down from their 15% peak in 1981 and hit 10%, the market would go crazy. Starts would hit 2 million or so, matching or bettering starts in the 1970s. Well, the magic 10% came and sure enough there was a spurt but it petered out. The more sober 1989 estimate for housing starts was about 1.38 million, a far cry from the anticipated boom.

The major reason is that the decline in mortgage rates wasn't that dramatic. Indeed, after discounting for inflation, mortgage rates actually rose over the last few years. Also, household formations, which are what really drive housing demand, fell to about one million in 1986, down 600,000 from a year earlier. Another big problem, of course, is the cost of housing these days. In many instances, price increases offset the gains from more favorable mortgage rates. After all, the price of an average house has fallen to $115,000 from $123,300 in 1987, but that is still out of the reach of a lot of average Americans. But talking average costs is often talking nonsense. Trends in housing prices have always been regional. An eight-room condo in Manhattan bought for $500,000 in 1981 fetches over $1 million today, while a $600,000 hacienda bought in Houston at the same time is now worth about $200,000 less. And a $400,000 château in Mobile bought in 1981 is still worth about $400,000.

Hotels

The outlook is as bleak as it is for office buildings. Nonetheless, construction contracts for new hotel rooms totaled $6.8 billion in 1988 while the occupancy rate fell below 65%—and that at a time when the break-even point rose to about 67%. Average room rates were $54.13 in 1989.

Shopping Centers

From 1984 to 1987, nearly as much money was spent constructing shopping centers as was spent constructing office buildings. Most of the problem properties are in the smaller strip centers along U.S. highways.

TRIVIA

• The Manhattan office market—the largest in the U.S.—consists of some 215 million square feet of space.

• With 55,000 hotel rooms, Orlando, Florida, home of Walt Disney World, ranks after only New York and Los Angeles in terms of such accommodations.

• The $250-million-a-year business of leasing furnished offices is nothing new, but lately major companies such as GTE and ITT find it cheaper to lease than to set up small branch offices for a few people. Support services include everything from telecopiers to secretaries.

• Americans spend more than $80 billion a year fixing up their properties. Painting is the leading expenditure, with roofing coming next.

• Regional differences in "nice neighborhoods" makes a tremendous difference in housing prices—some $400,000. A survey by Better Homes and Gardens Real Estate Service determined that the average price of a three-bedroom home in a desirable neighborhood ranges from $475,000 in Wilton, Connecticut, down to $62,000 in Knoxville, Tennessee.

BRAINY BUILDINGS

Computers are making buildings smart. (Some of them, anyway.) The wedding of architecture and high tech has resulted in elevators that tell passengers in a soothing voice not only that they are going up or down but what the weather is like. Lights go on in offices when someone walks in and they shut off soon after the person leaves. Doors are monitored to see whether they are locked, and temperatures are monitored for the right temperateness. Lobby directories not only cross-reference companies and employees but some offer everything from calendars of sports and art events to airport maps and public-transportation guides. Some smart buildings: One Financial Plaza, Chicago; CityPalace, Hartford; Grand Financial Plaza, Los Angeles. Analysts saw the market grow to $3 billion a year by 1990, when there were more than 1,500 brainy buildings in the U.S.

THE FIRST SKYSCRAPER

The first skyscraper? Until lately, Chicago's nine-story Home Insurance Company Building in Chicago held the title. Now that's disputed. For decades, the building was considered the first of all the tall buildings held up by a skeleton of steel columns and beams rather than massive masonry walls, thus qualifying it as the first skyscraper. Now it turns out that Home Insurance was given the title by a powerful group of Chicago architects who were out to cheat Minneapolis architect Leroy S. Buffington, the patent holder on building skeletal-framed big buildings. To avoid paying royalty fees and to break the patent, the Chicago architects discredited Buffington. Instead of one of Buffington's buildings, they nominated the Home Insurance Company Building as the first innovative high building. When poor Buffington proposed a breathtaking "cloudscraper" 28 stories high, he was met with derision. Now nobody seems sure what to designate as the first skyscraper.

JAPANESE REAL ESTATE INVESTMENT

Canadians remain the biggest foreign owners of U.S. real estate, but the Japanese will soon surpass them if they continue buying the way they have for the past few years. While Americans complained about sky-rocketing real estate costs, the strong yen made U.S. properties a bargain that sent Japanese scrambling into the U.S. market. The Japanese, for instance, own about a quarter of downtown Los Angeles. (Half of downtown L.A. is owned by foreigners, as well as 39% of Houston's office space, 21% of Manhattan's financial district, and 12% of Washington.) In 1986, the Japanese invested an estimated $4.1 billion in the U.S. market and a lot more in 1987. Shuwa Investment Corporation stunned the industry by alone buying $1.8 billion in real estate within 12 months. In 1988, Japanese investment in hotels and resort properties alone exceeded $3.5 billion.

Donald Trump   To trump up attention to himself while a student at the Wharton School, Donald Trump roamed around the campus wearing maroon suits with matching shoes. Later he did much the same thing by naming buildings after himself, and he became a celebrity as he elbowed his way into New York's glitzy world of the rich and powerful. Though never the largest of the nation's real estate developers, his Trump Organization certainly was the best known.

Trump got his initial stake in the business the old-fashioned way. He inherited it. His father Fred was a shrewd real estate builder who developed modest apartment complexes and created a tidy fortune of more than $40 million. For a while, "the Donald" had uncanny instincts for

---

CLOUDSCRAPERS

To hear architects these days, skyscrapers are old-fashioned. We're moving into the era of superskyscrapers as the Ramseses of our time demand colossi that will make their imprint on our megalopolises. Look at the 110-story Sears Tower, currently the world's tallest skyscraper. But that's nothing. Folks at the Council on Tall Buildings and Urban Habitat at Lehigh University in Bethlehem, Pennsylvania, talk of the potential for cloud-level buildings a mile tall, or nearly four times as tall as the Sears Tower. Of course, such structures would have to cope with winds of 90 miles per hour or more, which could set them swaying like ships in a gale, creating havoc with everything that wasn't nailed down and quite literally making everybody in them seasick. Engineers are toying with braces and other alternatives to provide the necessary rigidity. Builders of New York's World Trade Center solved the sway problem by placing spongelike pads in the structure to absorb vibrations. Builders of Citicorp's New York headquarters got around it by using an 800,000-pound weight that shifts about on a high floor to counter the effects of wind.

Not everybody's into the "edifice complex." Take Norwest Corporation's new headquarters in Minneapolis. Built by Gerald D. Hines Interests and designed by Cesar Pelli, the 773-foot structure is $2^{1}/_{2}$ feet shorter than the IDS Tower, the city's biggest building.

---

being in the right place at the right time. He created a $1.5 billion empire that was largely based on *chutzpah* and junk bonds.

His first major development converted the old Commodore Hotel into the 1,407-room Grand Hyatt Hotel. The 1975 project, undertaken in the middle of New York's fiscal crisis, included negotiations with city officials, many of whom were politically influential friends of his father. The result was a generous 40-year tax abatement of the hotel, the first awarded in Manhattan for a commercial property. When the hotel opened in 1982, the city had made a comeback and the hotel was in hot demand.

After that, he netted some $142 million when he sold condos in Trump Tower in Manhattan. He picked up another $130 million selling apartments in Trump Parc on Central Park South. Then, of course, there were the condo towers in West Palm Beach and, among other things, some 22,000 housing units in New York and New Jersey that he owned or controlled. He became a powerhouse as a casino operator in Atlantic City when he gained control over three gambling establishments. He also made big bucks as a greenmailer, garnering some $122 million in profits from selling holdings in Allegis Corporation, Holiday Corporation, and Bally Manufacturing Corporation. Putting what he did in some kind of perspective, he said, "It's like a great Monopoly game."

There was a bit of unintended irony in the statement since he was playing with paper money too, and the game caught up to him in 1990. "The Donald" overreached himself. By 1990, the wave he rode of easy credit, hot junk bonds, and escalating asset values was over. His cash flow turned negative and the junk bonds he stood on looked junkier than ever. Creditors squeezed him, and he began selling off major holdings and even suffered the indignity of being put on an allowance by his creditors. Meanwhile, until they found him boring, gossip columnists had a field day charting the B-movie-like melodrama of his failing marriage, which paralleled his crumbling business empire.

The Reichmanns   The Reichmann brothers may well make up the richest family in the world, but few people outside the real estate business know who they are. Their company, Olympia & York, controls some $18 billion worth of assets in North American real estate, manufacturing, and natural resources. Along the way, Olympia & York pulled off one of the most significant Manhattan real estate transactions ever with the creation of the World Financial Center, the biggest development project in New York since Rockefeller Center. Well before the project was completed in 1987, the complex was 95% leased—and that at a time when most of the rest of New York's commercial real estate agents were increasingly jittery as the commercial vacancy rate approached 10%.

Paul, Albert, and Ralph Reichmann were born in Vienna, the sons of an egg exporter. With the onslaught of Nazism, the family fled first to Paris and then to Tangiers. In 1956 they moved to Toronto where they imported steel and tile. They backed into the real estate business when they sought bids for the construction of a warehouse. The bids seemed high, so they built it themselves. They built some warehouses for others, and finally branched out so that they built up a lot of Toronto itself.

In 1976, the brothers took their biggest gamble. They decided real estate in financially troubled New York City was grossly undervalued. So they paid $320 million for a portfolio of eight office buildings formerly owned by the Uris family. Within a few years, the properties were worth about $2.25 billion. Now Olympia & York is engaged in a real estate project in London on Canary Wharf. The $7.86 billion development is the biggest real estate project in Europe.

Orthodox Jews, the Reichmanns strictly observe their faith. They see that construction stops on their projects at sunset on Fridays. It is even said that, in order to keep their buildings open on the Sabbath, they transfer ownership of them each Friday to a *Shabbes goy*.

SILICON VALLEY REAL ESTATE

As go computers, so go land values. At least that's the way it goes in the San Jose, California, area, known as "Silicon Valley." Once the land of microchips and honey, the valley suffered from oversupply and reduced demand in its once-lucrative real estate market. The problem, of course, was trouble in the computer industry. In its halcyon days, computer companies flocked here, turning the valley into the West Coast high-tech capital. (The Boston area remained the undisputed East Coast capital.) Silicon Valley was the driving force behind the booming Sunbelt. By 1984, two industries, electronic components (mostly semiconductor chips) and office and computing machines, provided almost half of San Jose's 294,000 manufacturing jobs. By 1990, speculative research and development space made up two thirds of the more than 150 million square feet of industrial inventory. The vacancy rate was more than 30%. Rents declined and land sales fell off as much as 25% in certain locations.

POSH APARTMENTS

Manhattan now has a category of apartments called "super luxury." Take Metropolitan Tower, where one-bedroom units start around $350,000—not including stiff monthly maintenance charges. To lure the superrich, there are such amenities as a separate floor of bedrooms for bodyguards and maids ($125,000 per room), a waiting room off the parking garage for chauffeurs, a private dining club, and a communications room replete with stock quotes.

Table 25-1 Most Expensive Office Space
(asking rent per square foot)

Manhattan (midtown)	$67.00
Boston	55.00
Washington, D.C.	52.00
Beverly Hills	51.60
Manhattan (downtown)	49.75
Chicago	49.31
Los Angeles	45.00
San Francisco	40.00
Dallas	40.00
Miami	35.00

Source: Cushman & Wakefield, third quarter 1990.

The Widget Makers: Industries in America

The business of America is business—and so it is, from advertising to pet food to wholesale merchants. Whenever possible, major industries are profiled according to the same format. This is the basic information you will find under each heading:

The Market: a brief summary of who buys the goods and services produced by this industry and how the industry affects the whole economy.

The Money: a summary of money made by this industry—its revenues and, where possible, profits.

The Players: a scorecard of the companies involved in this industry—how many companies are in the industry, some of the largest companies, and, where possible, what share of the market they hold.

The People: who is employed by this industry and, where possible, how much they earn.

Trends and Forecast: a brief summary of where the industry has been and where it is going through the end of this decade.

ADVERTISING

THE MARKET

Advertising has become like weather. It's everywhere—on billboards, cabs, radio, TV, magazines, and newspapers. Look up in the sky and the Goodyear Blimp might float by. If anyone can be held accountable for creating the world's first consumer-oriented economy, it's the adman.

THE MONEY AND THE PLAYERS

U.S. advertising spending topped $100 billion for the first time ever in 1986 and jumped to $128.6 billion in 1990. By the end of 1991, advertising spending is expected to grow to $132 billion. Worldwide spending rose to $266 billion in 1990, up from $158.1 billion in 1985.

Large companies continue to spend a hefty share of all advertising dollars. The hundred biggest advertisers spent $34 billion in 1989, up from $22.5 billion in 1984. The largest U.S. advertising agencies handled $90 billion in client advertising money (billings) and had $12.7 billion in gross income. Indicating the growing importance of international markets in the media business, the largest U.S. agencies had $36.0 billion in billings overseas and $5.2 billion in gross income. The next most powerful country was Japan (with $24.2 billion in billings), followed by the U.K. ($11.5 billion), France ($10 billion), and Germany ($5.8 billion).

Here's how companies spend their money plugging their products:

Newspaper advertising is projected to hit $35.4 billion in 1992, up from $32.3 billion in 1989 and $25.2 billion in 1985.

Television advertising is projected to reach $34.1 billion in 1992, up from $26.8 billion in 1989 and $20.8 billion in 1985.

Direct-mail advertising hit $21.9 billion in 1989, after reaching $17.1 billion in 1986 and $15.5 billion in 1985.

Magazine advertising was projected to hit $11.7 billion in 1992, up from $5.2 billion in 1985.

Radio advertising is projected to grow to $10.2 billion in 1992, up from $8.2 billion in 1989 and $6.5 billion in 1985. (See the separate sections "Magazines," "Newspapers," "Radio," and "Television and Cable.")

THE PEOPLE

There are 237,000 people employed in advertising today, up from 153,000 in 1980.

TRENDS AND FORECAST

In the mid-1980s, merger mania hit Madison Avenue. In 1986, for instance, 26 of the 100 largest U.S. ad agencies changed ownership. Then in 1987, the 123-year-old J. Walter Thompson was swallowed up by the British WPP Group.

In the 1990s, Madison Avenue is still recovering from the turmoil of the 1980s. Merger mania, new technologies, growing international markets, and tighter advertising budgets all changed the business of peddling products.

A few numbers indicate the turmoil in the media business: Between 1980 and 1990, 11 of the 15 largest advertising agencies changed ownership. Nearly one third of the nation's 100 largest advertisers were merged into larger companies. Eleven of the 20 top broadcasting companies merged or were acquired by a new owner. All three major television networks were sold. By the end of the decade, over $89 billion worth of mergers had been completed in the media industry.

Meanwhile, advertisers had an even tougher time deciding how to sell their products. Back in the early 1970s, television advertisers had the simple task of choosing between the three major networks. Now, there was Fox

Broadcasting, Rupert Murdoch's fourth network, superstations such as Turner Broadcasting System, independent television stations (local stations not affiliated with any of the three major networks), local cable systems (which have set up large regional networks to sell advertising time on their systems), dozens of cable channel networks (CNN, the Discovery Channel, Black Entertainment Network, etc., which offer advertisers a great way to reach a niche audience), regional sports networks (a cheaper way to sell products during sporting events), or even taped movies for VCRs (advertisers bet the viewers won't fast-forward through the sales pitch at the start of the tape). And advertisers could buy air time on shows in first-run syndication in which television producers sell shows like "Wheel of Fortune" directly to local stations.

But more is not always better. Media fragmentation reduced mass audiences on network television and made it harder to sell detergent and Big Macs to millions of people. Huge mergers among some of the nation's largest advertisers left these corporations with heavy debts and reduced their advertising budgets. This particularly hurt some large newspapers, which lost revenues from highly leveraged department stores that were acquired by corporate raiders.

Advertising revenues have also slowed. After jumping 13.9% in the low-inflation year of 1983 and 15.8% in 1984, they rose only 8.3% in 1985, and haven't returned to double-digit increases since then. The year 1990 was one of the weakest advertising markets since the 1970s, and an economic slowdown cut advertising spending in 1991. Analysts expect total advertising to grow only 3% to 4% that year.

Add up all those problems and you can understand why merger mania swept Madison Avenue. As profit margins at major agencies dropped from about 16% in 1976 to well under 12% a decade later, ad agencies struggled to cut costs and add new clients. The new mega-agencies say their acquisitions will build up their market shares at a time when total advertising revenues are growing slowly. They also argue that their bigger multinational operations can better serve multinational companies, providing advertising, research, consulting, marketing, and even public relations services around the world.

Not everyone thinks bigger is better. Worried about potential conflicts of interest resulting from a single mega-agency handling their products and those of their competitors, some companies took their business to smaller agencies. Ted Bates, for example, lost about $80 million in business from Colgate-Palmolive and another $65 million from Warner-Lambert soon after its merger with Saatchi & Saatchi.

Charles and Maurice Saatchi spent the 1980s building Saatchi & Saatchi into the world's second largest mega-agency. But disappointing earnings in 1988 and 1989 forced the company to change its ways. The Saatchi brothers agreed to sell their consulting operation, brought in a new management team, and are trying to refocus the company on advertising.

With a weaker economy in 1991, no one expects advertising revenues to pick up steam at any time in the near future. As a result, the turmoil of the 1980s has spilled over into the 1990s. Some agencies are likely to expand their international operations, creating even bigger multinational mega-

Table A-1   U.S. Advertising Expenditures, 1950–1990

(billions of dollars)

Year	Newspapers	Direct mail	Magazines	Business papers	Television	Radio	All other	Total
1950	2,070	803	478	251	171	605	1,322	5,700
1951	2,251	924	535	292	332	606	1,480	6,420
1952	2,464	1,024	575	365	454	624	1,634	7,140
1953	2,632	1,099	627	395	606	611	1,770	7,740
1954	2,685	1,202	629	408	809	559	1,858	8,150
1955	3,077	1,299	691	446	1,035	545	2,057	9,150
1956	3,223	1,419	758	496	1,225	567	2,222	9,910
1957	3,268	1,471	777	568	1,286	618	2,282	10,270
1958	3,176	1,589	734	525	1,387	620	2,279	10,310
1959	3,526	1,688	832	569	1,529	656	2,470	11,270
1960	3,681	1,830	909	609	1,627	693	2,611	11,960
1961	3,601	1,850	895	578	1,691	683	2,562	11,860
1962	3,659	1,933	942	597	1,897	736	2,666	12,430
1963	3,780	2,078	1,002	615	2,032	789	2,804	13,100
1964	4,120	2,184	1,074	623	2,289	846	3,014	14,150
1965	4,426	2,324	1,161	671	2,515	917	3,236	15,250
1966	4,865	2,461	1,254	712	2,823	1,010	3,505	16,630
1967	4,910	2,488	1,245	707	2,909	1,048	3,563	16,870
1968	5,232	2,612	1,283	714	3,231	1,190	3,828	18,090
1969	5,714	2,670	1,344	752	3,585	1,264	4,091	19,420
1970	5,704	2,766	1,292	740	3,596	1,308	4,144	19,550
1971	6,167	3,067	1,370	720	3,534	1,445	4,397	20,700
1972	6,938	3,420	1,440	781	4,091	1,612	4,928	23,210
1973	7,481	3,698	1,448	865	4,460	1,723	5,305	24,980
1974	7,842	4,054	1,504	900	4,854	1,837	5,629	26,620
1975	8,234	4,124	1,465	919	5,263	1,980	5,915	27,900
1976	9,618	4,786	1,789	1,035	6,721	2,330	7,021	33,300
1977	10,751	5,164	2,162	1,221	7,612	2,634	7,896	37,440
1978	12,214	5,987	2,597	1,400	8,955	3,052	9,125	43,330
1979	13,863	6,653	2,932	1,575	10,154	3,310	10,293	48,780
1980	14,794	7,596	3,149	1,674	11,424	3,702	11,211	53,550
1981	16,528	8,944	3,533	1,841	12,811	4,230	12,543	60,430
1982	17,694	10,319	3,710	1,876	14,566	4,670	13,745	66,580
1983	20,582	11,795	4,233	1,990	16,542	5,210	15,498	75,850
1984	23,522	13,800	4,932	2,270	19,670	5,817	17,809	87,820
1985	25,170	15,500	5,155	2,375	20,770	6,490	19,290	94,750
1986	26,990	17,145	5,317	2,382	23,185	6,949	20,772	102,140
1987	29,412	19,111	5,607	2,458	23,904	7,206	21,952	109,650
1988	31,197	21,115	6,072	2,610	25,686	7,798	23,572	118,050
1989	32,368	21,945	6,716	2,763	26,891	8,323	24,924	123,930
1990	32,281	23,370	6,803	2,875	28,405	8,726	26,180	128,640

Source: McCann-Erickson, Inc.

Table A-2   How Companies Spend Ad Dollars: U.S. Advertising Expenditures, Percentages of Total, 1950–1990

This chart provides a percentage breakdown of how advertisers spend their money. It shows that some media, such as television, have been increasing their share of advertising dollars while newspapers and magazines have been losing their shares of the market.

Year	Newspapers	Direct mail	Magazines	Business papers	TV	Radio	All other
1950	36.3%	14.1%	8.4%	4.4%	3.0%	10.6%	23.2%
1960	30.8	15.3	7.6	5.1	13.6	5.8	21.8
1970	29.2	14.1	6.6	3.8	18.4	6.7	21.2
1975	29.5	14.8	5.3	3.3	18.9	7.1	21.2
1980	27.6	14.2	5.9	3.1	21.3	6.9	20.9
1985	26.6	16.4	5.4	2.5	21.9	6.8	20.4
1989	26.1	17.7	5.4	2.2	21.7	6.8	20.1
1990	25.1	18.2	5.3	2.2	22.1	6.8	20.3

Source: McCann-Erickson, Inc.

agencies, or to struggle to make these far-flung operations make money. Others, reflecting the increasing fragmentation of the media, will look for profitable niches and specialties. All of them will have to cope with an advertising market which is expected to grow only 3% to 4% in 1991.

Table A-3   Top 25 Advertisers

Rank	Advertiser	Ad spending (in millions of dollars)
1	Philip Morris Cos.	$2,072.0
2	Procter & Gamble Co.	1,779.3
3	Sears, Roebuck & Co.	1,432.1
4	General Motors Corp.	1,363.8
5	Grand Metropolitan PLC	823.3
6	PepsiCo Inc.	786.1
7	McDonald's Corp.	774.4
8	Eastman Kodak Co.	718.8
9	RJR Nabisco	703.5
10	Kellogg Co.	611.6
11	Nestle SA	608.4
12	Unilever NV	604.1
13	Ford Motor Co.	602.1
14	Anheuser-Busch Cos.	591.5
15	Warner-Lambert Co.	585.9
16	AT&T Co.	567.7
17	Time Warner	567.5
18	K mart Corp.	561.4
19	Chrysler Corp.	532.5
20	Johnson & Johnson	487.1
21	General Mills	471.0
22	American Home Products Corp.	456.1
23	Bristol-Myers Squibb Co.	451.6
24	Ralston Purina Co.	429.5
25	Toyota Motor Corp.	417.6

Source: *Ad Age*

Table A-4   Top 10 Advertising Organizations

Rank	Agency	Worldwide gross income (millions of dollars)
1	WPP Group	$2,712.0
2	Saatchi & Saatchi Co.	1,729.3
3	Interpublic Group of Cos.	1,649.8
4	Omnicom Group	1,335.5
5	Dentsu Inc.	1,254.8
6	Young & Rubicam	1,073.6
7	Eurocom Group	748.5
8	Hakuhodo	586.3
9	Grey Advertising	583.3
10	Foote, Cone & Belding Communications	536.2

Source: *Ad Age*

J. Walter Thompson   Modern advertising all started here. Though no longer the world's biggest, JWT is the world's oldest ad agency.

Founder James Walter Thompson got his start after the Civil War when he joined the Carlton & Smith agency in New York in 1868. A decade later, when the original owner decided he'd rather sell books than advertise other people's products, Thompson bought the agency for $1,300 and even managed to come up with a new name for it.

Thompson pioneered many of the aspects of modern advertising that we now take for granted. For instance, he established magazines as a medium for advertising and was the first to recognize the importance of women's magazines. By the end of the 19th century, he'd established a virtual monopoly on magazine advertising. His agency also moved from simply selling space in newspapers and magazines to planning advertising and marketing campaigns. By 1916, the company had 177 employees and served clients that spent $3 million a year on advertising.

But Thompson made one big mistake. He decided the advertising business had peaked and sold out to a group of employees.

The new owners continued Thompson's tradition of innovation. Under Stanley Resor and Helen Landsdowne, the agency was one of the earliest to rely on research, testimonial advertising, and photography. It expanded overseas and hired some of the best copywriters in the business. Radio commercials boosted revenues, helping the agency survive the Depression, and, in 1947, JWT became the first agency ever to handle a $100 million campaign.

In the 1950s and 1960s, however, the agency ignored creative changes sweeping the ad world under the influence of television. Acquiring a reputation as an old, stodgy giant, JWT slipped behind other companies, losing its rank as the world's largest ad agency.

Against that background, Don Johnston took over as CEO in 1974. He struggled to rebuild JWT's reputation and its profitability. Creativity has improved but profits haven't. Profit margins have lagged behind those in the rest of the industry, falling from 8.9% in 1978 to only 3.4% in 1986, about one third the industry average. Worse, 1986 earnings were down by one third. In 1987, the British WPP Group took over Thompson, and Johnston left. J. Walter Thompson, which celebrated its 125th anniversary in 1990, now illustrates the power of international markets over advertising. The agency had $4.6 billion in billings worldwide in 1990; less than half ($1.79 billion) comes from the U.S.

SALT

Few things are as bothersome as a saltshaker that doesn't shake in damp weather. Thus, the Morton Salt Company folks knew they were onto something when they wanted to market their salt that ran free even on the lousiest days. The salt came in a nice but unexciting cylindrical blue box with a little spout. Great. But how could they let people know their salt didn't turn into a brick whenever it rained? Fortunately, they turned to the ad agency N. W. Ayer. In 1914, Morton introduced the box with the Morton Umbrella Girl whose box of salt, under her arm, is open with the salt flowing out. The slogan: "When It Rains It Pours." The moral, apparently, is that for some people you have to draw pictures.

POLITICAL BUTTONS AND PINUPS: A $3 BILLION BUSINESS

Self-promotion has come a long way. As early as 1807, the American Manufacturing Concern (now called Falcon Rule) was producing rulers, yardsticks, cribbage boards, paint stirrers, and paperweights that had companies' names printed on them. These businesses then distributed the merchandise to their customers free of charge. In 1828, Andrew Jackson became the first president to use political campaign buttons. And in 1840, a New York insurance agent noticed that his posters stayed up a lot longer if he added calendars to them.

Today, such specialty advertising is big business: about $3.1 billion a year, according to the Specialty Advertising Association. Some 6,000 companies manufacture or distribute specialty items—pens, cups, T-shirts, calendars, and just about any sort of gizmo that can display an advertising slogan. The most popular items are "wearables" such as T-shirts, which account for 19.3% of all sales, followed by writing instruments (16.5%) and calendars (12.1%).

SELLING BIG GOVERNMENT

Convincing someone to spend a night in Paris is one thing, selling several years in an Army barracks is another. But the federal government still tries, spending $309.5 million a year touting the virtues of everything from the Postal Service and the Army to the Statue of Liberty.

That makes Uncle Sam the country's 36th-largest advertiser. But government advertising is being hurt by the fall of the Berlin Wall. Joint armed services advertising dropped by $5 million to only $23.3 million in 1989. The budget for Army advertising fell (to $5.8 million), as did that of the Marine Corps (to $4.2 million). Both the Navy ($10.2 million) and the Air Force ($3.7 million) increased their advertising, but all the services expect cuts in the early 1990s. Huge deficits have also hurt other agencies. The Post Office spent $49.1 million in 1989 advertising its stamps, an easy way to raise revenues. But its advertising budget is expected to total only $35 million in 1991. Like many other mass marketers, Uncle Sam spends a hefty amount of his budget ($57 million) on network television.

FIRSTS IN ADVERTISING

3000 B.C.   The oldest surviving advertisement is a "wanted" poster for a runaway slave found in Thebes, Egypt. Until the 15th century, word of mouth, town criers, and posters advertising goods in marketplaces are the main forms of advertising.

1450   The dawn of printing also spawns a revolution in advertising. The invention of movable type allows advertisers to print flyers that can be posted in public places or put in books, pamphlets, and, later, newspapers.

1477   The first advertisement in English appears. It is for a prayer book.

1625   The first newspaper ad appears in the back of a London newspaper.

1670s   The *London Gazette* becomes the first newspaper to put out a special advertising supplement.

1704   The first regular American newspaper, the weekly *Boston News-Letter,* has the first paid ad in the colonies.

1741   The first magazine ad in America appears in Benjamin Franklin's *General Magazine.* Benjamin Franklin also improves the visual impact of early ads by using large headlines and surrounding the ads with extra white space.

1841   Volney B. Palmer starts the first ad agency in Philadelphia. He charges newspapers a 25% commission for selling advertising space to companies. By the start of the Civil War, his agents adopt the practice of holding out until right before printing deadlines, forcing publishers to lower ad rates. This allows agents to get 30% commissions.

19th century   Many firms spurn advertising because it can hurt their credit ratings. Banks believe firms that have to drum up business are confessing weak finances. The most popular products to advertise are patent medicines, a $75-million-a-year business by 1900.

1891   George Batten founds the first full-service advertising agency in New York, offering his clients such services as copy, art, production, and ad placement. Before this most agents only placed ads, but did not prepare them.

1893   The modern advertising agency system is established when the American Newspaper Publishers Association adopts a resolution giving independent advertising agencies a discount on rates and allowing no discounts on space sold directly to advertisers. This allows an ad agency to buy, say, $10,000 worth of space from a newspaper chain for $8,500, bill its client for $10,000, and pocket the difference, $1,500. The same system is now used in other media, such as radio and television.

1900　Some suggest that records for the new gramophone should include advertisements for such things as baking soda. The idea doesn't catch on.

1901　Ernest Elmo Calkins and Ralph Holden found Calkins & Holden. The company is sometimes considered the first modern ad agency because it creates advertising campaigns—rather than simply placing ads prepared by its clients—and sets up a typographical department. Doing its own graphics and layout is a revolutionary development in a period when other agencies let newspapers set and design ads as the papers see fit. Other agencies that pioneer the practice of preparing ad material are J. Walter Thompson Co., Lord & Thomas, Pettengill & Co., and N. W. Ayer. Agencies charge a 15% commission for this service in addition to the cost of materials and discounts they receive from the publications in which the ad is placed.

FIRST COMMERCIALS

Joseph Bulova, who made the famous watches bearing his name, was the first businessman to advertise on radio and TV. In 1926, the first radio spot came over Pittsburgh station KDKA when an announcer gave the time and then said, "B-U-L-O-V-A, Bulova watch time." In 1941, Bulova again made history when his company paid $9 for a 20-second TV commercial during a Dodgers baseball game.

AGRICULTURE

THE MARKET AND THE MONEY

If you want proof that success can be bad for business, consider American agriculture.

No doubt American farms are the most productive in the world. Every farm worker produces enough food for 79 other people, and that allows Americans to be some of the best-fed people in the world. In the course of a year, the average American eats about 115 pounds of meat, 44.5 pounds of chicken, 12.6 pounds of turkey, 93.4 pounds of fresh fruit, 17.2 pounds of ice cream, 23.6 pounds of cheese, 4.5 pounds of butter, 62.7 pounds of fats and oils, 89.8 pounds of fresh vegetables, 81 pounds of potatoes, 61.7 pounds of sugar, 127.5 pounds of wheat flour, 14.3 pounds of rice, 6.9 pounds of coffee, and 6.8 pounds of peanuts, just to name a few of the farm products sold in America. No wonder the diet industry does $10 billion worth of business every year.

All that production should add up to money in the bank, right? Wrong. The 1980s have produced a bitter harvest of rising farm foreclosures, sagging farm exports, growing farm debt, and declining profits.

Farm revenues declined from $166.3 billion in 1981 to only $156.5 billion in 1986, before recovering to $192 billion in 1990. Net income dropped from $27.4 billion in 1979 to only $12.7 billion in 1983 before recovering to $47 billion in 1990. Also, between 1981 and 1986, American farmers were losing their status as the breadbasket of the world. By 1986, the trade surplus in agricultural goods ($5.4 billion) was only a little more than one fifth of what it was in 1981 ($26.6 billion). But exports have since jumped from $26 billion in 1986 to $41 billion in 1989.

THE PLAYERS

The farm crisis, which began in the 1920s, has dramatically transformed the landscape of American agriculture. Today the U.S. has 2,172,920 farms that cultivate 991,473 acres—less than the amount of land cultivated in 1950 (1.2 billion acres). Today's average farm is 456 acres, more than twice the size of the 213-acre average farm in 1950. The big money needed to run a high-production, mechanized American farm has forced many small producers out of business and, over the past 50 years, polarized the industry into a few large producers and many small farms. Today 72% of farms have sales under $50,000, yet they produce less than 15% of gross farm revenues and only 0.5% of all profits—as measured by net farm income. On the other end of the scale only 1.3% of all farms have sales over $500,000. Yet they produce 31.3% of all farm revenues and 45.9% of all net farm income. The larger farms with over half a million in farm sales also receive a disproportionate share of government payments. They received 9% of all government aid while small farms with less than $50,000 in farm sales—72.9% of the total—received only 17.9%.

THE PEOPLE

Life on the farm is getting less crowded all the time. There are only 5.3 million people living on farms and 2.8 million employed on farms, down from 23 million and 9.9 million, respectively, in 1950. Some 928,000 of the farm workers are hired hands; the rest (1.7 million) are family members. Most farm owners (85%) are male and about 94% of all farm owners are white non-Hispanics. Less than 1% of all farmland is held by either blacks or Hispanics, with other minority groups holding even smaller proportions.

TRENDS AND FORECAST

Entering the 1990s, American agriculture has partially recovered from its worst economic crisis since the 1930s. Farm debt has dropped, and farm income is on the rise. But many of the problems of the last decade still shape the future of American farming. A few numbers illustrate many of the key issues:

- Farm debt problems have improved but remain a potentially explosive issue, particularly for marginal producers. During the 1970s and early 1980s, farm debt quadrupled, hitting $206.4 billion in 1983 and producing a wave of foreclosures. Since then, the debt load has dropped to about $144 billion, but a recession could hurt farm exports and produce more financial problems in 1991 and 1992.
- During the first half of the 1980s, thousands of farms were foreclosed. The foreclosed farm land was enough to cover an area the size of Delaware and Maryland combined. Naturally, as this land was placed on the auction block, the value of farm assets tumbled from a peak of $1,049 billion in 1982 to only $841 billion in 1986 and the average value of farm land dropped from $823 an acre to only $547 an acre. Since then a recovery in the farm belt has boosted the price per acre back to about $600, and total farm assets now top $1 trillion.
- The crisis in American agriculture during the 1980s made American farmers dangerously dependent on government aid. Over half of all farm profits in 1987 were directly attributable to $22.4 billion in government subsidies. Since then, government subsidies dropped to only $9 billion, but if farmers run into more problems during the early 1990s, Washington can hardly afford a new farm bailout. Another problem is who gets the farm subsidies. One General Accounting Office study found that almost two thirds of direct federal farm subsidies went to farmers with light debt and few if any financial problems.
- What happens on the farm has a major impact on banks and financial institutions around the country. Banks, government agencies, insurance companies, and all other lenders lost about $11 billion from bad farm loans just between 1984 and 1986.
- The average farm gets only 25 cents of every dollar spent in grocery stores.
- One problem that has plagued American agriculture since World War II is overproduction. In 1986, U.S. agriculture had an excess capacity of about 9%—meaning that there were 60 million acres of farm land producing crops that exceeded demand. For seven major crops—wheat, corn, soybeans, cotton, sorghum, barley, and oats—the level of excess capacity was a whopping 22%. About 31.1% of all wheat produced by American farmers in 1986, 782 million bushels, exceeded demand.
- Excess production made it impossible for many farmers to make a profit on their crops. For example it cost the average farmer about $2.04 to produce a bushel of wheat in 1986 but he or she could only sell it for about $1.40, producing a loss of about $75 an acre of land cultivated. Wheat

farmers spent $109 an acre to plant an acre of wheat but could only sell an acre of crops for $69.

• The problem of overproduction eased after 1986, thanks to several droughts, growing foreign demand for agricultural products, and a weaker dollar. Easing cold-war tensions and economic reforms behind the old Iron Curtain created new demand for American agricultural products, particularly from the Soviet Union. The USSR purchased 17 million metric tons of corn in 1990. As a result, America's agricultural trade surplus jumped from only $5.4 billion in 1986 to $26.6 billion in 1989, as exports increased from $26 billion in 1986 to $41.7 billion in 1989. This increased demand, coupled with several droughts that cut supplies, pushed up prices by 25%.

At the start of the 1990s, American farmers were financially stronger than they'd been since the mid-1960s. The value of farm land has increased by over $100 billion since 1986, and profit margins have improved. While prices for agricultural commodities had increased, lower oil prices in the late 1980s cut production costs from $142.7 billion 1984 to only $140 billion in 1989.

But many of the same old problems still worry farmers in the 1990s. A stronger dollar and a global economic slowdown could cut farm profits, making it hard for many farmers to service their debts. Overproduction, which has created a kind of perpetual crisis in American agriculture for over 40 years, has been temporarily tamed by drought and the end of the cold war. But weak foreign demand, a few big harvests, and higher fuel costs could quickly reverse a farm recovery into a recession, just as these same problems did in the early 1980s. Though no one expects the problems of the 1980s to be repeated in the early 1990s, farm profits are likely to drop in 1991 and 1992, placing more pressure on smaller, less efficient farms.

THE LANDLORDS

There are some 2.3 billion acres of land in America, enough for every man, woman, and child to have just under 10 acres. About 3% of the population owns 55% of the total land and about 95% of the privately owned land in the U.S., according to a survey by the U.S. Department of Agriculture. As few as 568 corporations control, directly or indirectly, about 300 million acres or 23% of the land in the U.S. Eight oil companies have about 65 million acres.

The biggest landlord is government. The federal government owns about 34% of all land; state and local governments own 6%. Individuals and corporations control about 58%. American Indians, who once had it all, now control only 2% of the land.

Of the 1.3 billion acres of land in private hands, about 63% is agricultural or ranch land. Timber interests control another large but undetermined chunk. About 25 million acres, or only 1% of all land, is used by the nation's 47 million to 58 million home owners. Golf courses take up 1.2 million acres.

FARM EQUIPMENT

The Market and the Money

The value of farm machinery sold dropped from nearly $12 billion in 1979 to a paltry $6.3 billion in 1987, before a modest recovery in the farm sector boosted shipments to $9.2 billion in 1990 and an estimated $9.7 billion in 1991.

The Players

The farm-equipment slump has prompted several famous manufacturers to leave the business. Wisconsin's Allis-Chalmers, New York's Sperry, and Chicago's International Harvester (now called Navistar International) all sold their farm-machinery operations to competitors. Those sales set off a trend toward consolidation and produced huge layoffs. There are only two U.S. tractor makers today, down from a dozen in 1951. At the same time, imports are grabbing more of the market, 24% in 1990, up from 10.6% in 1981. Still, the U.S. exports about $3.4 billion worth of farm equipment a year.

The People

Faced with a depression on the farm, employment in this industry dropped from 140,000 in 1979 to only 64,600 in 1991.

The Forecast

Farm-machinery manufacturers face tough foreign competition and rising gas prices in the 1990s as farmers find it hard to finance new equipment, look for continued contraction until the farm economy starts growing some profits.

Navistar International Corporation

CEO: James C. Cotting	455 North Cityfront Plaza Drive
Employees: 14,070	Chicago, Illinois 60611
Assets: $3.8 billion	312-836-2000

	1990	1989	1985	1980
Revenues (millions of dollars):	3,854	4,241	3,508	6,312
Net income (millions of dollars):	(11.0)	87	113	(370)
Share earnings (dollars)	—	0.23	0.77	—

What it does: The biggest maker of medium- and heavy-duty trucks in North America. The agricultural equipment operations were sold in 1985 to Tenneco, Inc., for $4.93 billion.

Navistar—once known as International Harvester—no longer makes farm products, which says a lot about the state of the farm-equipment industry.

The company's history goes back to Cyrus Hall McCormick, the son of a farmer, whiskey distiller, and unsuccessful inventor of farm equipment. But succeeding where his father failed, Cyrus invented the reaper in 1831. Farmers loved reapers and the McCormicks went on to create a vertically integrated company in the 19th century, with franchised dealers, a pioneering regional office network, and timber tracts and sawmills to produce the raw materials they needed to manufacture their machines.

In 1902, during the height of a merger mania, the McCormick family business and other major farm-equipment manufacturers merged into International Harvester, capitalized at $120 million. The firm, which controlled 85% of the market, wasn't profitable, earning only 1% on its assets. In 1906 it was reorganized with the old McCormick firm at its core and Cyrus McCormick, Jr., as its head.

Over the years, International Harvester helped transform American agriculture. Its products helped create the high-tech farm, allowing vast tracts of land to be settled and brought into production with a very small labor force. And, as the company grew and prospered, so did the McCormicks.

Like many other powerful 19th-century family dynasties, the McCormicks invested in media in order to have a voice in public opinion. During the Civil War, dynasty founder Cyrus McCormick purchased the *Chicago Times* in order to bombard readers with his unpopular pro-south views. Grandnephew Robert R. McCormick, following in this tradition of the irascible superrich newspaper publisher, gained control of the *Chicago Tribune* in 1914 and eventually radio and TV stations. His opposition to World War I, strong attacks on the New Deal, and accusations that President Truman was soft on communism kept him in the center of controversy all his life. Another McCormick, Anne Blaine "Nancy" Harrison, purchased the then-liberal *New Republic* and financed liberal movements, such as Henry Wallace's 1948 presidential bid. She sold *The New Republic* in 1974.

But in recent years, International Harvester fell on hard times. A devastating 1979 strike and a slump in the farm economy put the company in dire financial straits—revenues dropped from $8.3 billion in 1979 to only $3.6 billion in 1983. In 1985, the company sold farm operations and the name International Harvester to Tenneco, Inc., for $301 million in cash and $187 million in preferred stock.

With a new name, Navistar, the Chicago-based company has restructured its finances and hopes to be far away from the farm-equipment business that once caused it so much trouble. After paring unprofitable operations, it boosted net income to $259 million in 1988, up from a $61 million loss in 1984. Today it is the largest producer of medium- and heavy-duty trucks in North America. But its net income dropped to $87 million in 1989 and the company lost money in 1990. If the economy continues to slow and farm profits drop, Navistar will suffer.

The House of Cargill   What's the biggest privately held company in the U.S.? The answer is Cargill. The name of this secretive $44-billion-a-year food and grain conglomerate is not a household word, but it is the nation's top grain exporter, largest egg producer, a major beef packer, and number-three wheat miller. A giant in soybeans, salt (it owns Leslie), cocoa and coffee trading, and corn syrup (it can produce 1.5 billion pounds of corn syrup a year), Cargill exports about 10% of the American grain that goes overseas each year. All told, you have a company with more revenues than du Pont or Texaco in 1985.

The giant grain exporter has long been closely held by the Cargill and MacMillan families. William Cargill started the company with one grain elevator after the Civil War, and rode the growing farm economy into a crop storage powerhouse. Acting as a middleman, storing and trading grain, the company had $2.2 billion in annual revenues as early as 1971.

But in the 1970s as the U.S. farm-export business took off, so did Cargill. Revenues shot up to $28.5 billion by 1981 and hit $44 billion in 1989, the latest years for which figures are available. The company moves grain and food around the world in its armada of 430 barges, 23 ships, 6,500 railcars and 340 grain elevators. But it's also diversified into more than 40 businesses in 50 countries, including steel mills, and it employs 50,000 people worldwide.

Most of that growth can be traced to a family policy of simply plowing profits back into the business. Since 1981, Cargill has reinvested 87% of its cash flow—only 3% of profits have been paid out in dividends.

Like the other major grain exporters—Continental, Bunge Corporation, and Louis Dreyfus—Cargill has always been privately held and has closely held its financial data. The company has been hurt by declining U.S. agricultural exports in the 1980s, but apparently not too badly. After buying a financially troubled packing company, MBPXL, which made Cargill the nation's second-largest beef packer, Cargill patiently invested millions in the troubled company until the business started turning around. That same persistence has tided the company through the current farm crisis. Cargill still handles 25% of the world's grain trade, employs 50,000 people, and racks up $260 million a year in profits. That success has boosted the fortunes of the Cargill and MacMillan families, who own the entire company, to about $2.2 billion.

AIRLINES

THE MARKET

Airline travel has taken off, with the number of passengers growing from 208 million on major airlines in 1982 to 350 million passengers on 6.6 million commercial flights in 1986. Travelers flew 481 billion miles in 1990, making the airplane second only to the car as the most popular way to get around.

THE MONEY

The airline industry was a $77 billion business in 1990, up from only $36.4 billion in 1982, a bad recession year for the industry.

But as airlines battled each other with lower fares, more passengers and revenues haven't always translated into bigger profits. Airlines lost over $1.8 billion in 1987, and although the industry flew into $2.4 billion worth of profits in 1989, more turbulent weather is on the horizon. One major airline, Eastern, has already gone out of business. Continental and Pan Am filed for bankruptcy protection in 1990 and several other carriers, such as TWA, face severe financial problems. Rising fuel costs, $12 billion worth of debts in the 35 largest carriers, and $1.9 billion a year worth of annual interest payments indicate that the industry is already flying on one engine. Losses, which hit $2 billion in 1990, will remain at least as high in 1991.

THE PLAYERS

There are some 230 commercial air carriers, but the 10 largest hold about 96% of the market. Only American West, American, Continental, Delta, Federal Express, Northwest, Pan American, Southwest, TWA, United and USAir/Piedmont have more than $1 billion a year in revenues.

THE PEOPLE

About 644,000 people were employed by the airline industry in 1990, up from 361,000 in 1980.

DEREGULATION

Most of the industry's successes as well as many of its problems can be traced to deregulation. In 1977 a federal agency, the Civil Aeronautics Board (CAB), regulated which airlines could fly which routes and how much they could charge for tickets. The result was a fat and happy industry, with airlines posting nice profits, union members earning hefty salaries, and consumers paying through the nose.

After removing most federal restrictions on airlines providing air-cargo service in 1977, Congress passed and President Carter signed the Airline Deregulation Act in 1978. This act gave airlines more freedom to determine what routes they could fly and phased out government control over airfares on December 31, 1982. The 1984 Civil Aeronautics Board Sunset Act transferred the remaining regulatory functions of the Civil Aeronautics Board to the Department of Transportation in 1985. The CAB, which had been the main federal regulator of the airlines industry, no longer exists.

Deregulation quickly touched off an industry-wide revolution. Several low-cost airlines, most notably People Express, entered the market, starting fare wars. Lower airfares attracted many new passengers but also put a crimp on industry profits. With increased competition and reduced profit margins, unions were forced to accept salary cuts or fewer benefits. Most analysts expect only a few major carriers to emerge from the industry-wide dogfight for larger market shares. Deregulation prompted 77 new airlines to enter the industry, but by 1990, 60 of the new companies had folded or been bought by larger airlines. As a result, the industry has come full circle. After a decade of deregulation, a few large carriers still dominate the market.

TRENDS AND FORECAST

The Federal Aviation Administration sees over 650 million passengers and 26.4 million commercial flights by 1997. But the industry will have to fly through a lot of stormy weather between now and the end of the 1990s. It is already under attack by regulators for safety and performance. Delays at many of the nation's overcrowded airports are at record levels. The average airplane is older than ever before, 12.8 years compared to 9 years in 1979, and critics charge that the industry is cutting corners on safety. In 1990, the U.S. Attorney in Brooklyn indicted Eastern Airlines for falsifying maintenance reports on its aircraft.

Consumer critics are also wondering if deregulation was worth all the trouble. If you adjust for inflation, there is little doubt that a decade of increased competition cut fares by 20% between 1978 and 1988. But many of the new companies went out of business or were bought by larger carriers. So, as competition decreased in the late 1980s, prices increased. As the 1980s wore on, one or two major carriers provided most of the service in major airports and as a result were often able to charge higher fares. A 1989 General Accounting Office study found that fares were 27% higher at the airports where one or two companies had a virtual monopoly over air travel. The industry's economic problems produced a new wave of fare discounts in 1991, but over the long term fewer carriers will mean higher prices.

A decade of fare wars and merger mania has also left its toll on the industry's bottom line. The 35 largest carriers are weighted down with $12 billion worth of debt and $1.9 billion worth of annual interest payments. During the 1980s, many airlines survived the fare wars by cutting labor costs. But a decade of labor strife has left unions in an extremely combative mood and made it harder for management to win new concessions. After years of fighting Frank Lorenzo, unions at Eastern were willing to let the airline go bankrupt rather than agree to another round of cutbacks. Look for a few more crash landings and an industry dominated by fewer carriers.

Continental Airline Holding

President and CEO: Hollis Harris   333 Clay Street
Employees: 65,000   Houston, Texas 77002
Assets: $4.7 billion   713-658-9588

	1990	1989	1985	1980
Revenues (millions of dollars):	6,231	6,685	1,944	291
Net income (millions of dollars):	(2,343.9)	(886)	49	5
Share earnings (dollars):	—	—	2.49	0.64

What it does: Continental Airlines Holding (formerly Texas Air Corp.) owns Continental Airlines, the 6th largest carrier. It filed for bankruptcy protection in 1990.

The rise and fall of Frank Lorenzo is the story of the whole airline industry since deregulation.

Lorenzo's path to power was a simple one: relentless acquisitions and tough bargaining with unions to cut costs. Beginning in 1980, he snapped up

Eastern Air Lines, Continental Airlines, People Express, and Frontier. He started New York Air in 1981. In 1986 alone, he bought 14% of the U.S. air travel market to boost his share to 20%.

At the same time, he straight-armed unions. In 1980, he established an industry union-busting trend by setting up New York Air as a separate subsidiary so the company wouldn't be bound by the union contracts of its small predecessor, Texas International. When Lorenzo bought Continental Airlines, he broke his labor contracts, fired two thirds of his employees, and paid those who survived about two thirds less money. Not surprisingly, airline unions helped Carl Icahn beat Lorenzo's bid for TWA.

Lorenzo thrived by lowering fares and by reducing labor costs. But the revolution in air travel he helped get off the ground also wrecked his rapidly growing empire. Lorenzo took on $3.4 billion in debt after acquiring Eastern Airlines in early 1986. Then he promised to pay $300 million for People Express and the assets of the bankrupt airline Frontier. By 1987 he had $5.2 billion in long-term debt and many unhappy employees. Desperate for cash, Lorenzo sold off Eastern Airlines' profitable New York-to-Washington shuttle to Donald Trump, and labor unions began attacking Lorenzo for stripping the company of its most valuable assets. Sick of his dictatorial management, the unions went on strike and Lorenzo filed for bankruptcy, believing it would help him break the unions and keep control over the airline. But a U.S. bankruptcy judge in New York City named an outside trustee to run the airline in 1990 and issued several stinging opinions attacking Lorenzo's management of the company. Eventually Lorenzo was forced to repay over $200 million in assets that he had moved into other companies. Realizing the end was in sight, he sold his stocks to Scandinavian Airline System for $30.5 million. The deal, of course, was typical Lorenzo. Continental badly needed cash, but most of the $52.5 million SAS agreed to pump into the airline went to Lorenzo and his cronies. Stockholders, bondholders, and workers didn't fare so well. Lorenzo got $14 a share for his stock while it was trading at $6. By the end of 1990 Eastern had gone out of business, and mounting losses forced Continental to file for bankruptcy protection.

William P. Lear   When William P. Lear turned his attention to the business that made his name synonymous with corporate jets, he was already a wealthy inventor and businessman who had a string of patents to his credit.

In the 1920s, he had invented the first workable car radio while working in Chicago as a design engineer at Galvin Manufacturing Company, which made radio chassis. Galvin's owner, Paul Galvin, capitalized on the invention and changed the name of his company to Motorola. By 1931, Lear wasn't yet 30 years old but his radio patent royalties alone totaled $35,000.

He bought his own plane, which set off a new spate of Lear inventions. The first was an automatic navigation system using radio signals. Until then pilots navigated by keeping a lookout for landmarks and following railroad tracks. The Learoscope, as it was called, became the industry standard. Then he invented a compact, lightweight automatic pilot that could be fitted in fighter planes.

Wanting to get more return than just royalties, Lear launched Lear, Inc., in Grand Rapids, Michigan, to make aircraft instruments. During the Second World War, the company filled more than $100 million in defense contracts. The company grew after the war and Lear became very rich, but he ran into trouble with the directors of his own company when he proposed building a corporate jet. The directors vetoed the notion, saying it couldn't be done and, even if it could be built, nobody would buy the thing.

Lear promptly sold his 23% of the company and set up Lear Jet, Inc., in Wichita, Kansas. By the time the first glistening Lear Jet soared into the skies, Lear had sunk $8 million into development. His plane was an eight-passenger jet that climbed to 40,000 feet in less than 6½ minutes, about twice as fast as any other plane. By standardizing such things as headroom and interiors, he held the price to a relatively modest $649,000. Customers loved it. Sales the first year were $52 million, establishing Lear as the biggest jet aircraft maker in the world.

At age 65, Lear tried to retire but he was too restless. Soon he had set up shop to design a steam-powered car. That didn't prove feasible so he set to work on an improved corporate jet. He died in 1978 at age 76 trying to bring another of his ideas to fruition.

APPAREL

THE MARKET

The jingoistic "Buy America" advertising campaign, which saw movie stars urging everyone to shell out their hard-earned money for something U.S.-made, missed the point. U.S. manufacturers, or anybody else for that matter, must have quality products made as efficiently as possible if they want to compete. The clothing industry, which has been buffeted by import tides as well as tough domestic competition for more than a decade, seems finally to be learning that. There's more concern with automation, offshore manufacturing, and turnaround time. Overall, the industry expanded by 5% in 1987, the second annual gain after a slump from mid-1984 through 1985.

The apparel market, of course, touches everyone. Take men, for instance. Each year, they buy some 12.5 million suits, 18 million bathing suits, 564 million knit shirts and sweatshirts, 31 million sweaters, and 11.6 million team sports uniforms. Not surprisingly, women buy more. For example, women buy about 254 million shirts and blouses, 32.5 million bathing suits, 105.6 million sweaters, and 152 million dresses. Then, of course, there are the billion or so articles of clothing ranging from rompers to down coats for children.

THE MONEY

More than $213 billion a year is spent for clothing and shoes. But due to intense domestic and import competition, clothing prices have increased only moderately in recent years. Some $5.8 billion worth of dresses are shipped by American manufacturers each year, for example, and $4.0 billion worth of blouses and $4.1 billion worth of women's suits and coats. Annually, another $3.0 billion worth of men's suits and coats, $1.5 billion worth of work clothes for men and boys, and $5.5 billion worth of trousers are shipped. Shipments of men's skiwear alone are valued at some $41 million a year. The children's clothing market is big too: some $3.6 billion in shipments of dresses and blouses, coats and suits.

THE PLAYERS

With few exceptions, such as Levi Strauss & Co., most clothing manufacturers are small operations. The domestic apparel industry consists of some 15,000 firms utilizing about 21,000 facilities located in every state. Most of the firms produce a narrow range of products. Frequently, they are under contract to a large retailer or a larger, more diversified apparel firm. Most of the industry—60%—is found in New York, California, Pennsylvania, and New Jersey. High-fashion and tailored clothing producers are located in the mid-Atlantic cities and in California. Companies with large production runs, such as jeans concerns, are usually located in the south and southwest. Increasingly, U.S. apparel companies are opening manufacturing facilities in the Caribbean and elsewhere because of cheap labor costs. Others are contracting out to independent producers to make their products. The major designer and marketer of women's clothing, Liz Claiborne, Inc., for example, has more than 80% of its merchandise made overseas.

THE PEOPLE

About 1.0 million people are employed in this industry and most of the workers—about 77%—are women, a greater percentage than in any other manufacturing sector. More than half belong to unions, with the bulk of them represented by two unions, the International Ladies Garment Workers Union and the Amalgamated Clothing and Textile Workers Union. The average salary is about $6.85 an hour, or only about half the average wage paid by U.S. manufacturing overall. The low wages reflect foreign competition from big textile and apparel exporters such as Hong Kong, South Korea, the People's Republic of China, and Taiwan, nations where the hourly wage ranges from 20 cents to $1.

THE OUTLOOK

In light of spiraling imports, U.S. apparel makers are trying to take advantage of their one big advantage: their closeness to the marketplace. They are becoming more automated and shortening their lead times from fibers to shipments to retailers. Computerized reorder systems hold inventory costs down and cut delivery time. Also, they are increasingly holding down costs by setting up foreign manufacturing operations or contracting out to off-shore manufacturers. But America still ran a trade deficit of $22.5 billion in apparel in 1990 and many apparel manufacturers were hurt by bankruptcies and financial troubles of several major department stores. A slowdown in consumer spending for clothes is also bad news. Consumers spent 6.3% of their personal income on clothes in 1980, but only 5.8% in 1990. A sluggish economy in 1991 could further trim spending.

MANNEQUINS

Mannequins aren't dummies. They're clever sales promotion pieces that reflect the times. In the 1950s, Marilyn Monroe mannequins were hot. Then mannequins were shaped like Twiggy and, for a while, like Jackie O. For the 1980s, a lot were built like Joan Collins. Mannequins generally stand 5 feet 10 inches tall and are a size 6 or 8. (Male mannequins usually are a size 38 or 40.) At $700 apiece and with large clothing chains and department stores buying thousands each year, mannequins are a $1.2 billion business.

SUNGLASSES

OK, what's the "essential accessory," as *Time* magazine has called this item, that Jacqueline Onassis and Jack Nicholson never seem to go without? The answer is sunglasses. But they aren't the only folks who walk around in the dark. The U.S. retail market accounts for more than 175 million pairs of sunglasses sold annually, making it a $1.4 billion market. Domestic production, though, only accounts for 10% of the market, with shades from Hong Kong, Korea, and Taiwan dominating among the imports. When the Sunglass Association of America established "the All-Time Sunglass Hall of Fame" in 1984, the first person inducted was General Douglas MacArthur.

Reebok   When they aren't driving around in BMWs, yuppies must be running and jumping about in Reeboks. Reeboks, of course, are those graceless things that resemble nurse's shoes but aren't. They're athletic shoes and they're worth a lot of money to Reebok International Ltd. and its chairman Paul Fireman, who owned about 15% of the company's stock.

A Boston businessman, Mr. Fireman was smart enough in 1979 to license the American rights to the brand name and designs of Reebok, which has shod British runners since 1895. He had some success in the

U.S. launching the shoes but ran out of cash. In 1981, the British firm Pentland Industries bought 55% of Reebok USA for $78,000.

But soon thereafter, Reebok scored big by cashing in on the fitness craze. Revenues jumped from $13 million in 1983 to $1.4 billion in 1987, while profits leaped from $1 million to $165 million. Profits dropped in 1988, but the company diversified into other areas, cut costs and introduced a number of successful new products. Revenues bounced back to $2.16 billion in 1990, while profits hit $177 million. Fireman, with a salary of $14.8 million, became America's fourth highest paid executive in 1990.

THE TUXEDO

The tuxedo business turned out smartly in the 1980s. In the 1960s and 1970s, the tux was well on its way to becoming a museum piece, a casualty of the convention-defying lifestyle in which a wedding party was as likely to be barefoot in the park as dressed up in church. But formality came back into vogue and sales of tuxedos topped $100 million a year, up from $65 million in 1981. Prices ranged from $139 for polyester blends to $3,500 for tailored cashmere or silk numbers.

Oddly enough, this symbol of establishment elegance started out as a snub of high society. A young wag, Griswold Lorillard, scion of the tobacco fortune, raised the hackles of his social set in 1886 by showing up at the exclusive country club at Tuxedo Park, New York, wearing not just a red waistcoat but also a jacket with the tailcoat cut short, like a suit jacket. But comfort beat out convention and soon everybody copied Lorillard's style.

SHOES

Americans spend some $31 billion a year for more than 991 million pairs of shoes. Women and girls buy about two thirds of all shoes sold, the average woman buying five pairs a year. The average price of a pair of shoes is about $31, with the price of athletic shoes running about $30.

Levi Strauss   How many companies can boast that they've made a success of a garment "guaranteed to shrink, wrinkle and fade"? Well, the San Francisco-based Levi Strauss & Co. can.

Levi Strauss had some tough times in the 1980s and, for a while, it looked as if this company might go the way of its guarantee. The problem was heady success making management think it could do just about anything.

The jeans craze of the 1970s had zipped up Levi Strauss's sales to dizzying levels. Arrogantly, the company diversified into hats, leather accessories, and even several lines of fashion and designer apparel. Then management ticked off the 12,000 small retailers who made up the backbone of Levi Strauss's distribution network in 1981 when the company added J.C. Penney and Sears to its outlets.

Well, a lot of those businesses never worked out, and jeans sales slumped. (International sales, for instance, plunged to $601 million in 1984 from $820 million in 1982.) Hence, chief executive officer Robert Haas, the great-great-grandnephew of the company's founder, sold off or shut down many of the new lines of business, closed some 40 factories, and pared the work force from 48,000 to 36,000. Moreover, the Haas family retook control of the company in a $1.7 billion leveraged buyout to head off corporate raiders.

Today, the company's future lies in doing what it did so well in the past: making jeans and other apparel, such as shirts, slacks, and women's tops under the Levi brand. Unlike many LBOs, this one is doing great. About three quarters of the debt has been paid off, and revenues now top $3.6 billion. A number of new products, like its Dockers line, have also made the company less dependent on jeans.

The company was founded by Levi Strauss, an enterprising German-Jewish immigrant who landed in California with the idea of catering to gold miners' needs. Among the supplies he wanted to sell was canvas for tents. To Strauss's dismay, the tent market seemed to have been saturated. With the kind of brainstorm that separates a troubled tent maker from a true entrepreneur, Strauss decided to make his canvas into pants, which, as can be imagined, were quite durable. You can also imagine how desperate the miners were.

In 1872, Strauss's pants became even more durable after he took up Jacob Davis, a Russian-Jewish immigrant and a tailor, on his offer to buy a half share in the rights to sell his pants. Davis's genius was in putting rivets at stress points in pants to keep them from ripping. Strauss paid half Davis's $136 patent application fee for the riveting innovation as a way of buying in. Davis came to San Francisco and the company was soon churning out the products, which have changed little in more than a century. The first denim overalls were called 501 Double X, after the lot number and weight of the denim used.

When he died in 1902, the prosperous bachelor Levi Strauss left most of his estate to his nephews, Abraham, Jacob, Louis, and Sigmund Stern. Besides making jeans, they acted as wholesalers to retailers for other apparel makers, such as underwear and shirt makers. When San Francisco was leveled by the earthquake of 1906, the company continued paying its 350 employees until they could return to work and also gave its retailers no-interest loans to rebuild their businesses.

In 1927, Walter Haas, Sr., who had married into the Stern family, became head of the company, which he ran successfully through World War II, primarily as a wholesaler as well as a jeans manufacturer. It wasn't until 1948, when his sons, Walter and Peter, were running the business, that Levi Strauss gambled by moving out of wholesaling, which actually was the bulk of the business. The gamble paid off. By the late 1950s, annual sales reached about $50 million, up from some $8 million during the war years. In 1971, the company went public with the sale of 1,396,000 shares, or 13% of the stock, at $47 a share. The offering, one of the biggest ever, was sold out within a day. Today, sales are more than $2.7 billion annually.

L. L. BEAN

Success just kind of sneaked up on Leon "L. L." Bean. Until age 40, he spent more time hunting and fishing than he did at the little haberdashery he ran in Freeport, Maine, with his brother, Ervin. But then in 1912 he wanted a better hunting boot and designed it himself. It had a rubber shoe bottom and a nice leather ankle section. He dubbed it the Maine Hunting Shoe. Then, from somewhere, Bean got ambition. He made some more pairs in the basement and sold them through the mail. Soon it seemed as if everybody wanted them. Bean stocked some more outdoors goods and they sold too. He sent out a catalog, describing what he had to offer. Catalog and retail store sales topped $1 million by 1937. Business was so good that in 1951 Bean, who was then 79 years old, figured the store should stay open 24 hours a day. Grandson Leon Groman took over after Bean died in 1967 and business has been better than ever.

APPLIANCES

THE MARKET AND THE MONEY

Major household appliance manufacturers cooked up over $16.9 billion worth of revenues in 1990, up from $15.3 billion in 1984.

THE PEOPLE

The household appliance industry employs 110,000 people. Average hourly earnings for production workers are $10.87 and the annual payroll for the industry is $2.2 billion.

THE FORECAST

The appliance industry remains heavily dependent on certain important sectors of the economy, primarily housing starts, interest rates, and consumer spending. On the plus side, the 25-to-44 age group, which traditionally buys more appliances than anyone else, is growing rapidly. But the economy is showing signs of slowing down, housing starts are dropping, and consumer spending is sluggish. Sales slowed in 1990 and may drop further in 1991.

General Electric Company

Chairman and CEO: John F. Welch, Jr.
Employees: 295,000
Assets: $153.9 billion

3135 Easton Turnpike
Fairfield, Connecticut 06431
203-373-2211

	1990	1989	1985	1980
Revenues (millions of dollars):	58,414	53,884	28,285	24,949
Net income (millions of dollars):	4,303	3,939	2,336	1,514
Share earnings (dollars):	4.85	4.36	2.57	1.67

What it does: It makes light bulbs and GE and Hotpoint appliances; it is a defense and aerospace company that produces such things as aircraft engines, radar, and space satellites; it is a manufacturer of industrial equipment such as motors, turbines, construction equipment, and factory automation equipment; it is a builder of nuclear power plants; it is a producer of medical equipment; it is a financial services powerhouse through its ownership of Kidder, Peabody & Co., the investment banker, and the General Electric Credit Corporation; it runs General Electric Information Services Company; and, through its ownership of RCA, it runs NBC.

Thanks to Thomas Alva Edison, General Electric turned a little invention like the light bulb into an industrial empire. The company began in 1878 as Edison Electric Light Company and became General Electric in 1892. Edison left in 1894 to start a mining venture that soon went bust, but his successors made money on a list of inventions like electric elevators, the electric chair, the toaster, electric ranges, electrical equipment, electric motors, various appliances under the GE and Hotpoint label, and of course, light bulbs.

Always an influential leader in technology, GE is now becoming a test case on the direction of American manufacturing and big business. Under CEO John Welch, the company has undergone a wrenching change, keeping only the most profitable of its traditional product lines and shedding others to move into financial services and high tech. The company spent $1.1 billion to add financial services by buying Employers Reinsurance in 1984, and $600 million to buy the investment banking firm of Kidder, Peabody & Co. Its $6.4 billion acquisition of RCA in 1986 was the costliest nonoil merger up to that time. Meanwhile, Welch sold off $5.9 billion worth of businesses that didn't fit into his vision of GE as a high-tech and financial services powerhouse, including GE's small appliances operations and three mining and petroleum companies. Welch automated factories, moved manufacturing operations overseas, and axed tens of thousands of employees. (The layoffs earned Welch the nickname "Neutron Jack," after the neutron bomb that leaves a factory standing but wipes out the work force.) But between 1979 and 1989, earnings per share jumped 11% a year, while profits and revenues more than doubled. In 1981, when Welch took control, GE was the 10th largest company in terms of market capitalization. It is now number 3, behind IBM and Exxon, and Welch dreams of making GE number 1.

The changes have already paid dividends. General Electric Financial Services has made the company less dependent on manufacturing and boosted earnings. In 1989, financial services provided 23% of the company's revenues and 14% of its profits. David Tice, a Dallas based newsletter writer, believes that financial services have accounted for 24% of the company's earnings and 31% of its earnings growth between 1985 and the start of 1990.

But despite the company's remarkable growth, GE's stock hasn't performed up to management's expectations. In 1989, to bolster the price of its shares, the company announced in a 5-year, $10 billion plan to repurchase its stock. Another potential problem could be its financial services arm. Kidder Peabody hasn't lived up to GE expectations. Some analysts say its other financial operations are some of the best managed in the business, but worry that an economic slowdown could affect GE the same way it has major banks and other financial institutions. Also, the company's broadcasting operations may be in for a slump. After half a decade on top of the ratings game, NBC's hit programs like "The Cosby Show" are showing their age. Keeping the electricity in GE's television programs and financial services should keep Welch busy.

JACUZZIS

No, the Jacuzzi spa wasn't invented as a sybaritic place for yuppies to soak after jogging. Candido Jacuzzi came up with the tub as a form of home therapy for his son Kenny, who suffered from acute arthritis as a boy. Candido got the idea in the 1950s from whirlpool baths at a hospital where he took his son for hydrotherapy treatments. Since Candido's family made pumps and filters for industrial uses as well as swimming pools, making the Jacuzzi wasn't far afield from what their company already did. The firm then began marketing it to other arthritic sufferers through medical supply stores. Then athletes discovered the pleasure of soaking in the swirling hot tubs. It wasn't until 1968, however, that the Jacuzzi company integrated all the water pumps and jets and concealed them in the walls of a self-contained tub. Thus, the Jacuzzi could be made aesthetically appealing, and the market boomed. Richard Nixon, for instance, installed one at the White House during Watergate so he could try to soak some of his troubles away. In 1979, the Jacuzzi family sold the business to Kidde, Inc., for $70 million. (Kidde itself was acquired by Hanson Trust [U.K.] in 1987.)

HOOVER

In 1907, W. H. "Boss" Hoover was impressed when his wife's weird cousin, J. Murray Spangler, demonstrated a contraption he had invented. A janitor as well as inventor, Spangler wanted to make his job easier at the Canton, Ohio, department store where he worked. To sweep up, he made a vacuum cleaner out of an old fan motor, a soap box, a broom handle, and a pillowcase that collected the dirt.

An astute businessman and former railroad president, Hoover knew the saddlery business in which he was currently involved was doomed by the automobile. So he formed the Electric Suction Sweeper Company and, in

1908, began producing a refined model of Spangler's vacuum cleaner. The machine was originally sold in hardware stores, but then salesmen were hired and the company began advertising. The big pitch was a demonstration in the home, which almost always resulted in a sale. Following the First World War, door-to-door selling wasn't what it used to be and the company went back to selling through dealers. Hoover has been owned by Chicago Pacific since 1985.

AUTOMOBILES

THE MARKET

Every year, Americans hit the road in a big way—driving an estimated 1.9 trillion miles. There are 121.5 million cars and 50.2 million trucks and buses rumbling around U.S. roads, about one third of the world's 515 million motor vehicles.

In 1990, Americans bought 9.5 million new cars and 4.7 million trucks, below the 1986 record of 16.3 million. American consumers are projected to buy 9.7 million new cars in 1992 and 10.5 million in 1995. Foreign auto makers sold 2.9 million cars in 1990. They should sell 2.9 million in 1992 and 2.9 million in 1995. About 4.8 million trucks and buses will be sold in 1992 and another 5 million in 1995.

THE MONEY

Keeping the car on the road for those 1.9 trillion miles adds up to a big auto bill. Consumers spend over $382 billion at auto dealers on cars, trucks, equipment, and repairs each year. On the factory level, U.S. auto makers shipped $253 billion worth of motor vehicles in 1990. But those figures don't exhaust the impact of the auto industry on the U.S. economy. Federal, state, and local government spends about $75 billion a year on highways. Each year drivers spend another $81.9 billion on auto insurance and $131.7 billion on repairs and parking at the nation's service stations. Gas to keep the old clunker and the rest of the transportation industry going costs $99.1 billion, while tires and accessories cost another $35 billion. The average U.S. car cost $16,575 and the average import about $14,800.

THE PLAYERS

Worldwide, 175 car makers produce 50 million cars, trucks and buses. Here in the U.S., Americans are driving fewer U.S.-made cars. Detroit auto makers produced 85% of all new cars sold in the U.S. in 1970, only 74% in 1985, and about 68% today.

The big four, General Motors, Ford, Chrysler, and American Motors, became the big three in 1986, when Chrysler agreed to acquire American Motors. GM holds 35.5% of the American car market, and Ford has a 20.8% share of the market while Chrysler has 9.2%. The largest foreign producers are Honda (9.2%), Toyota (8.4%), and Nissan (4.9%). Japanese auto makers have captured 32% of the U.S. market, and Europeans have 4.2%.

THE PEOPLE

There were 802,000 people employed in the motor vehicle and equipment manufacturing industry in 1990, down from a peak of 924,000 in 1978. The average U.S. auto worker earns $19.79 an hour.

TRENDS AND FORECASTS

Detroit's future was on the line in the 1980s. A lot of buyers decided U.S. cars weren't worth the price and imports grabbed a growing share of the auto market. So, to fight back, Detroit went into the cost-cutting business. For example, even though sales increased by only 3% between 1980 and 1983, the three largest auto makers cut costs so dramatically that they were able to turn a $4 billion loss in 1980 into $6 billion in profits in 1983. More moderate labor pacts have saved auto companies about $6 billion; other savings came from closing 47 facilities and moving operations overseas.

Detroit also embarked on a major quality improvement program, with Chrysler and Ford both claiming gains of 40% to 50%. Auto makers spent billions a year in advertising how good their cars really were. And, just in case the consumer wouldn't believe Madison Avenue, auto makers sweetened the pot with low-cost auto loans. (All three auto makers have moved heavily into financial services. General Motors Acceptance Corporation, for example, is now the fourth-largest nongovernment U.S. financial institution.)

But consumers still weren't convinced. U.S. Commerce Department surveys show that 13% of all American consumers won't even consider buying an American car. Other studies indicate the public doesn't think American cars have improved relative to imports. Worse, most consumers don't realize that many of Detroit's cars are now competitively priced. As a result, even though a weaker dollar has hurt some foreign car makers, Detroit's market share has continued to slip. General Motors had about half the car market in 1979; today it holds only 34.7%. In fact, despite all the progress they made during the 1980s, American auto makers seem to have accepted the idea that less can be more. In the fall of 1990, General Motors took a $2.1 billion charge to close 7 plants and lay off 20,000 workers. The move, which produced a $2 billion loss in the third quarter, indicates that GM's new chairman, Robert C. Stempel, believed the car maker would never dominate the car market the way it once had. The future depends on making higher profits from fewer plants, as Ford did so successfully in the 1980s.

Higher oil prices in the fall of 1990 also hurt the auto makers and created new worries about their short-term prospects. Ford reported its worst earnings in more than a decade, and Chrysler was once again struggling to cut huge losses. By the start of 1991, one third of all U.S. auto plants were idle. The U.S. Commerce Department believes that cost cutting and improved quality will allow North American car makers to improve their market share to about 73% by 1994, but many analysts believe that projection is optimistic. At any rate, an economic slowdown should cut sales by about 5% in 1991.

THE BIG THREE

General Motors Corporation
Chairman: Robert C. Stempel   3044 General Motors Boulevard
Employees: 761,400   Detroit, Michigan 48202
Assets: $180.2 billion   313-556-5000

	1990	1989	1985	1980
Revenues (millions of dollars):	126,017	124,993	96,372	57,729
Net income (millions of dollars):	(1,986)	4,224	3,999	(763)
Share earnings (dollars):	—	6.33	6.14	—

What it does: The nation's largest car maker; owner of Delco; a defense and aerospace giant through its subsidiary Hughes Aircraft; a major player in the data processing industry through its subsidiary Electronic Data Systems; joint owner of a robotics company; a financial services power through the General Motors Acceptance Corporation.

At GM, numbers tell the story. The largest auto maker in the world as well as the world's largest industrial corporation, GM is more powerful than many countries. Only 21 countries have a gross domestic product larger than GM's sales; most countries, such as South Africa, Austria, Hungary, and Venezuela, have had a smaller GDP.

Even so, GM has acquired the reputation of a comatose giant, a symbol of what's wrong with American management and labor. Between 1980 and 1986, GM spent $41.5 billion to modernize its plants, and between 1987 and 1991 it cut some $13 billion in costs. Yet GM's competitive position has actu-

Table A-5   New Car Sales, 1972–1994
(thousands of vehicles)

Year	Domestic	Imports	Total
1972	9,237	1,623	10,860
1975	7,053	1,587	8,640
1980	6,581	2,398	8,979
1985	8,196	2,816	11,012
1988	7,484	3,056	10,540
1990	6,604	2,896	9,500
1992[1]	6,776	2,924	9,700
1994[1]	7,584	2,916	10,500

[1]Forecast.
Sources: *Ward's Automotive Reports*, U.S. Department of Commerce.

ally deteriorated. The company that once controlled half the American car market now has about 35.5% of all sales.

It wasn't always that way, of course. The creation of General Motors is an example of a large producer in a related industry taking advantage of new technology. William Crapo Durant ran Buick Motor and was the nation's largest carriage and wagon manufacturer when he founded GM in 1908. Over the next eight years, GM expanded by buying up Olds Motor Works, Oakland Motor Car (later Pontiac), Cadillac Motors and Chevrolet.

Durant left the company for good in 1920 and the du Ponts, who owned 28% of GM's stock, assumed financial control. Under Pierre du Pont and then Alfred P. Sloan Jr., the company also established a marketing and management formula that would make it the most successful corporation in the world. Sloan established a distinctive marketing strategy that catapulted GM past Ford Motor Company for the title of the world's largest auto producer. Ford had captured 60% of the market by producing inexpensive mass-built cars, but in the 1920s consumers wanted more than just a black box on wheels. By improving comfort, power, convenience, and style, GM captured a larger share of the market. GM also grew by making certain to differentiate the styling on each of its cars and by targeting a specific group of consumers with each car—Cadillacs for the rich, Chevrolets for the masses.

The formula was one of the most successful in the history of American industry. So, when hard times hit the auto industry in the early 1980s, many thought that GM would be the U.S. car company best positioned to survive. It was spending the most on new plants, was the furthest along in converting to small cars, and had the resources to be strongly positioned in the market when demand finally revived. While losing $763 million in 1981, the company's first loss since 1921, GM still embarked on an enormous capital spending program for new plants and equipment. GM also survived the tough times in the early 1980s with less pain than other U.S. auto makers. While American Motors lost $746 million between 1980 and 1983, Ford lost $3.26 billion between 1980 and 1982, and Chrysler lost $3.35 billion between 1979 and 1982, GM lost money only one year and actually made $533.6 million between 1980 and 1982.

This apparent strength became a real weakness, at least in the short run. Under Chairman Roger Smith the company embarked on an expensive strategy to position itself for the 21st century. GM diversified into defense, high tech, and financial services with purchases of Hughes Aircraft for $5 billion in 1985, the computer service company Electronic Data Systems (EDS) for $1 billion in cash and 11.3 million shares of GM class-E stock in 1984, and various financial services companies, and with joint ventures such as GMF Robotics in 1982. It spent billions to automate its factories and embarked on the Saturn project to build a small, fuel-efficient car. The company also diversified into financial services to help its bottom line. By 1989, financing and insurance operations produced 9% of GM's sales and 21% of its profits.

But GM still produced far more cars than customers wanted to buy. Faced with 1 million unsold cars in the summer of 1986, the company announced massive layoffs and plant closures. Then GM announced another wave of cutbacks in the fall of 1990. It took a $2.1 billion charge to shut down 7 of its 38 production plants and announced that nearly 20,000 workers would be laid off by 1993.

Still, abandoning its lavish plans is not necessarily a setback for GM. By cutting excess capacity, GM has finally realized that even the world's largest company cannot ignore a simple reality: sales of U.S. autos are not likely to reach earlier levels at any time in the near future. Adapting the company's goals and strategies to a stagnant market for American autos will eventually boost profits and lower costs.

In fact, cutbacks and a few successes leave GM positioned for new growth later in the 1990s. GM's European operations lost $2.2 billion between 1980 and 1986, but by 1989, sales hit $19.7 billion and profits totalled $1.8 billion. The Saturn project, conceived in 1983 as a car that would salvage GM's future, took 7 years and cost $3.5 billion before the first car rolled into the showrooms in the fall of 1990. No one expects the car to be as successful as GM once hoped, and many analysts believe the company will not be able to recoup its investment before the end of the 1990s. Although initial public reaction has been positive, the company lost nearly $2 billion in 1990.

Ford Motor Company

Chairman and CEO: Harold Poling   P.O. Box 1899
Employees: 370,400   Dearborn, Michigan 48121
Assets: $173,663 billion   313-322-3000

	1990	1989	1985	1980
Revenues (millions of dollars):	98,275	96,146	52,774	37,086
Net income (millions of dollars):	860	3,835	2,515	(1,543)
Share earnings (dollars):	1.86	8.22	4.55	—

What it does: World's second-biggest maker of cars and trucks.

Ever since Henry Ford continued producing black, stripped-down Model T's when car buyers wanted more whistles and bells, Ford has been number two in the auto industry. But in 1986, 1987, and 1988 Ford earned more in profits than GM. It was the first time since 1924 that the perennial number two had beaten GM on the bottom line. Though Ford is not likely to rack up more sales than GM at any time in the near future, the company has been proving that less can be more, at least when it comes to profits.

Responding to hard times in the auto industry, Ford laid off 50,000 workers in the 1980s and cut the number of its assembly plants. It led the industry trend toward producing more and more cars and parts overseas. That cut costs and improved quality, which had fallen far below the high standards once set by Henry Ford, Sr. The company cites studies saying it improved quality by 50%. And, with sleek space-age design on such top-selling cars as the Ford Taurus, the company has once again emerged as an industry innovator rather than a perennial number two.

Ford's recent problems and stunning revival, however, are consistent with the company's history.

The founder of this dynasty, Henry Ford, was almost a stereotype of the inventor and mechanic who builds an industrial empire with a new product. Born on a farm, he worked as a mechanic, repairing watches, power plants, and steam tractors before working for his lifelong friend Thomas Alva Edison. But all the time he was working on the internal combustion engine, producing his first engine in 1896 and his first car in the same year. Ford's first company broke up because he concentrated on building a larger and faster car than was commercially viable. Next, he incorporated as Ford Motor Company and set about building the world's first economy car. In 1907 he cut the cost of his car to $700 from $850, and he cut it to $350 in 1916 after building Michigan's largest industrial plant in Highland Park.

This plant fulfilled Ford's dream of building a universal car. Ford Motor became the first manufacturer to produce a single model with a standardized chassis made of interchangeable parts that was produced on an assembly line. (Before this, every part was individually fitted into the car and each part and car was different.) Lowered costs allowed middle-class buyers and farmers to enter the car market for the first time. But a major labor problem erupted—there was discontent due to the monotony of the assembly line. Ford held it off by raising wages to $5 a day, about twice the pay of the highest-paid skilled workers. He also distributed about $12 million under a pioneering profit-sharing plan. These moves made him a national hero and an often-mentioned presidential contender in 1920 and 1924.

Production at the Ford plant boomed, increasing to 730,000 by 1916. There were over 7,000 dealers affiliated with the company, with at least one in every town with more than 2,000 people.

But Ford proved to be an erratic manager. In 1916 he financed a boatload of socialists and anarchists who sailed to Europe in an unsuccessful attempt to negotiate a settlement to the First World War. Then, in 1920, after blaming Jews for the failure of his Senate bid, Ford's paper, the *Dearborn Independent,* launched weekly anti-Semitic attacks, touching off boycotts of his cars.

Meanwhile, General Motors took the title of the world's largest auto maker from Ford Motor. By the beginning of the Second World War the company teetered on the brink of disaster. Ford ran the company without even the most primitive financial standards and a huge hunk of Ford Motor's more than $680 million in cash was in bank accounts bearing no interest. There was virtually no cost accounting—no one, for example, had any exact figure for how much it cost to produce a car or exactly how much money the company was making or losing. Ford's right-hand man in charge of daily operations was Harry Bennett, a former prize fighter who relied on spies and a vast army of sycophants to run the company.

The future looked no better. The company was losing $10 million a month right after World War II and the only family heir was Henry Ford II, the founder's grandson, who had been thrown out of college for cheating on a term paper.

Realizing that Henry Ford, Sr., was ruining the company, his wife and daughter-in-law and Henry Ford II ousted Bennett and his cronies. Then Henry Ford II salvaged the dynasty, bringing in strong managers such as

Robert McNamara and Lee Iacocca. The company never regained its leadership of the auto industry, but he stopped the red ink. By 1950 the company turned a net profit of $265 million, and it went public in 1956. The $690 million stock sale was the largest up to that time.

Of course, the late Henry Ford II also made his mistakes, bringing out the Edsel in 1957 (a car that lost the company $250 million) and forcing out such executive stars as Lee Iacocca. The early 1980s were not only a time of industry-wide troubles, but a changing of the guard at Ford. Henry II retired as chairman in 1980. Although two younger Fords (Edsel II and William, Jr.) are being groomed for top management positions, the company was run by nonfamily members during the 1980s for the first time in its history.

Few would quarrel with the results. Ford's comeback was certainly as dramatic as that of Lee Iacocca's revamped Chrysler Corp. But in the early 1990s, the company faces a much tougher future. After spending $2.5 billion to buy Jaguar Plc. and $3.35 billion for Associates First Capital Corp, a consumer and commercial finance unit, top management will have to make these deals pay off. In 1989, it sold off its steel unit for a loss, and, in 1990 with a downturn in the defense industry, sold its aerospace unit.

A tougher car market has also hurt Ford's sales. Ford boosted its market share from 18% in 1986 to 22% in 1989, but lost 2 percentage points in 1990. One problem has been that Ford's older, more successful models, like Taurus and Sable, are showing signs of age, while its new models, such as the new Escort launched in the spring of 1990, haven't been extremely successful. Faced with a recession in the auto industry Ford lost $519 million in the fourth quarter of 1990 and analysts expect more red ink in 1991.

Chrysler Corporation

Chairman & CEO: Lee Iacocca	12000 Chrysler Drive
Employees: 124,000	Highland Park, Michigan 48288
Assets: $46.4 billion	313-956-5241

	1990	1989
Revenues (millions of dollars):	30,868	34,922
Net income (millions of dollars):	68	315
Share earnings (dollars):	0.30	1.36

What it does: Third-largest U.S. auto maker.

Everyone remembers 1979 and 1980, when Chrysler lost $2.7 billion. But that wasn't the first time the company had stumbled badly. Or, it seems, the last. After a remarkable turnaround in the early 1980s, Chrysler posted huge losses in the last half of 1990, and Lee Iacocca admitted that the company faced some difficult times ahead.

Chrysler was founded in the 1920s by Walter Chrysler, a tinkerer and mechanical wizard and former manufacturing vice president with GM. On his own he produced a car in 1924 that could go 50 miles an hour, an unheard-of speed for a low-priced auto. Consumers bought 32,000 of them. Chrysler became the third-largest auto maker in 1928 when it purchased Dodge.

After World War II, however, nothing went right at Chrysler. To cut costs, it simply upgraded the same model between 1942 and 1953, losing market shares. In the 1960s, when everyone wanted luxury cars, Chrysler came out with economy cars. Then, in the 1970s, when gas prices went through the roof, Chrysler built gas guzzlers few people wanted. Losses rose to over a billion dollars in 1979 and hit $1.7 billion in 1980.

But armed with guaranteed government loans and a new regime under Lee Iacocca, the company made a startling comeback. It dramatically cut costs, lowering its break-even point from 2.3 million cars to only 1.1 million, produced some new designs and best-selling cars, like its minivans, and streamlined production costs by using the same K car chassis it first used in 1981.

The question with Chrysler was simple: could it keep up the good work? It repaid $1.2 billion in government loans, reclaimed a big chunk of the market, and was careful not to create new overhead expenses. Like Ford and GM, it moved aggressively into financial services, with Chrysler Financial Corp. providing 11% of its revenues and fully 41% of its profits in 1989.

But new problems began to appear in 1987 with a $1.5 billion deal to acquire American Motors. Profits dropped from $1.4 billion in 1987 to $315 million in 1989. Morgan Stanley & Co. estimates that Chrysler could run a negative cash flow of $1 billion in 1991.

So what went wrong? Some of the problems can be blamed on the same management team which rescued Chrysler in the early 1980s. Iacocca and company spent a lot of time diversifying into aerospace and defense. But after buying Gulfsteam Aerospace in 1985, Chrysler decided to focus on its core auto and financial operations and in 1990, it sold the unit for $825 million.

Another problem was the development of new cars. By the start of 1991, Chrysler hadn't introduced a single new car whose development began after Iacocca arrived in 1978. Meanwhile its market share has dropped and rising costs have boosted the company's break-even point from 1.1 million before the AMC acquisition to about 1.9 million. To engineer comeback number two, Iacocca is spending more money on car development and working to cut costs. Iacocca, who turned 66 in October of 1990, vows to stay on until the job is completed.

AUTO RENTAL

THE MARKET

Americans rent cars by the day, week, or month about 40 million times a year and travel about 3 billion miles in rented cars, according to the American Car Rental Association. Only 25% of this travel involves vacation or leisure rentals, with the rest coming from commercial users, large and small businesses, and corporations. Most rentals (70% to 80%) are made at airports by passengers. Rental cars normally are disposed of after only 9 to 18 months, after having traveled 18,500 miles. In contrast, the average age of a typical American passenger car is 7.7 years.

THE MONEY

All of this travel adds up to a $11 billion industry in 1989, up from $936 million in 1974.

Table A-6   Five Largest Car Rental Companies

Rank	Company	Revenues (billions of dollars)
1.	Hertz	3.1
2.	Avis	2.8
3.	National	2.3
4.	Budget	2.0
5.	Dollar	0.6

Source: *Adweek*

TRENDS AND FORECAST

The industry was founded in 1916, about the time that the automobile was becoming a popular form of mass transportation. But it didn't really take off until the last two decades, largely because of the growing popularity of air travel. (Most customers rent their cars from airports.) As a result, the number of rental cars grew from 364,000 in 1973 to 756,000 in 1986.

In recent years, increased revenues and changes in the tax code have touched off an industry-wide restructuring. Several years ago, huge conglomerates found it highly profitable to own rental car companies because they could depreciate the value of the fleet. But with changes in the tax code limiting those write-offs, many of the largest car rental firms were put up for auction. UAL Corp., an airline, for example, bought Hertz in 1985 for $587.5 million and sold it in 1987 for about $1.3 billion to Ford and Hertz officials. Avis, the second largest car rental company, went private in 1987; Budget, the third largest, was sold in 1986 by Transamerica; and Chrysler bought Thrifty Rent-A-Car System for $263 million in 1989.

BANKING

THE MARKET

This may come as a shock, but the banking industry doesn't exist just to loan you money when you're a little short of cash.

Traditionally, banks are in the business of buying and selling money.

Banks buy money when they pay interest on bank accounts and when they borrow money from the Federal Reserve or the money markets. They must keep some of this money on deposit. But they do sell most of it by loaning it out at higher interest rates for mortgages, short-term business loans, consumer loans, auto loans, credit cards, and a bewildering array of other types of credit. In the process, banks are supposed to make money and keep the economy going, providing credit for business and consumers.

Today, however, banks sell more than money. As part of a trend toward deregulation in financial services, banks now sell investment banking services, real estate, insurance, mutual funds, and even their loans, which are packaged and sold as loan-backed securities. That has been good for most consumers, allowing them to get more services and high interest rates from their banks. But it also has put banks under increased pressure. As they struggled to fight off securities firms, insurance companies, and even retailers that have entered the financial services industry, profits tumbled, and the banking industry entered its worst crisis since the 1930s.

THE MONEY AND THE PLAYERS

Commercial Banks

In 1991, the nation's 12,338 commercial banks had over 57,000 branches and held $2.5 trillion in deposits. They had an estimated $2.5 trillion loans outstanding and employed 1,593,000 people.

Most commercial banks (92.4%) are small, with assets of under $300 million. They hold 21.1% of all bank assets. On the other end of the spectrum, the 99 largest banks hold 51.9% of all bank assets. The commercial banking industry had $16.6 billion in profits in 1990, down from $24.8 billion in 1988 and $17.8 billion in 1985.

Savings Institutions

The nation's savings and loan institutions hold $1.0 billion in deposits, have $1.3 billion worth of assets, and employ about 447,000 people at 25,443 branch offices. But billions in losses have reduced the number of thrifts from 3,517 in 1987 to 2,342 in 1991. Collectively the industry lost $2.4 billion in 1990, and another 563 S&Ls are expected to fail by the start of 1992. Since most deposits in the thrift industry are guaranteed by the federal government, it will cost taxpayers between $325 billion and $1.4 trillion to fix the mess—making the S&L bailout the largest financial disaster in the history of the world.

AMERICA'S BANKS: JUST WHAT KIND OF BUSINESS IS THIS?

Explaining the banking system used to be a lot like writing a dictionary. You could define each part of the banking industry, saying exactly what it did, whom it served, and what it could not do. Commercial banks, for example, specialized in serving businesses, making most of their money by giving businesses short-term loans. Savings institutions took in savings from small savers and used the money to make mortgage loans.

None of these institutions sold securities, acted as investment bankers by underwriting commercial paper, peddled insurance, or sold mutual funds. There were separate industries for all that stuff, thank you. And, since no state legislator ever got elected by championing the right of big New York City banks to take over local banks, interstate banking was verboten in most parts of the country. As a result, the U.S. banking industry had thousands of banks, many of which served only one city or state. In contrast, European countries usually adopted nationwide banking systems in which a few large banks dominated the market.

This nicely defined industry, with each part serving a specific market and customers, was largely the result of one factor—government regulation. The financial services and banking industry was and is one of the most heavily regulated industries in the U.S. Despite all the hue and cry over deregulation, 10 federal agencies plus at least one agency in every one of the 50 states and over 20 self-regulatory agencies still regulate financial markets and the banking industry. The Federal Reserve System, the Comptroller of the Currency, the Federal Deposit Insurance Corporation, the Office of Thrift Supervision, and the Resolution Trust Corporation all help regulate banks and thrifts on the federal level, making certain that a lot of paperwork must be shuffled through at least several bureaucracies before getting Uncle Sam's approval.

The Board of Governors of the Federal Reserve System supervises bank holding companies and state banks that are members of the Federal Reserve System. The Comptroller of the Currency regulates all national banks, chartering new ones and supervising the existing ones. The Federal Deposit Insurance Corporation (FDIC) supervises all state banks that are not members of the Federal Reserve System and that are covered by the federal insurance system. It insures deposits in about 98% of all commercial banks and regulates mutual savings banks. Fewer than 4% of all banks are state chartered and not subject to regulation by any federal agency. These banks, however, are regulated by state agencies. The Federal Home Loan Banking Board used to run the Federal Savings and Loan Insurance Corporation, which insured deposits at thrifts and regulated savings and loan institutions. But FSLIC went broke. In 1989, it was given a new name, the Federal Home Loan Bank System, and many of its old powers were transferred to new agencies. The Savings Associations Insurance Fund, which is run by FDIC, now insures deposits and regulates thrifts. The Resolution Trust Corporation was set up to manage bankrupt thrifts and sell their assets (it sold $138 billion worth of property in 1989 and 1990). The Office of Thrift Supervision, a separate office in the Treasury Department, also was set up to regulate thrifts, and the Federal Housing Finance Board, another new independent agency, runs the 12 regional banks that were operated by the Federal Home Loan Banking Board. These regional banks function as a kind of Federal Reserve for the thrift industry.

Confused? Well, you're in good company. Even most bankers don't understand the system. One thing is clear, however. During the 1970s and 1980s, rapid changes in the American and international financial systems forced government regulators to change many of the rules that had defined American banking for more than half a century. After 42 years of telling banks how much interest they could pay on savings accounts and other deposits, government regulators let banks set their own rates in 1986. New state laws and Supreme Court decisions broke down the barriers against interstate banking and sped the growth of large regional banks. With some significant restrictions, banks were permitted to sell insurance, offer customers discount brokerage services, provide investment banking services, and even underwrite municipal securities. In 1990, a Federal Reserve ruling gave the J.P. Morgan & Co. bank the right to act much like a Wall Street firm, with the power to buy and sell securities. This ended one of the most important regulatory features of American finance. For over half a century banks had been barred from selling stocks and Wall Street firms were not allowed to engage in banking. Ironically, that rule had forced the breakup of the J.P. Morgan financial empire into separate banking and securities firms during the 1930s.

The new rules had a number of far-reaching effects. One was increased competition between banks and other financial institutions. Savings and loan associations made loans to business and commercial real estate developers, traditionally the preserve of commercial banks. Large corporations, which once raised most of their short-term debt from commercial banks, found they could raise money at lower interest rates in foreign capital markets or by using the services of Wall Street firms. Securities firms such as Merrill Lynch offered certificates of deposit (CDs), gave customers checking accounts, and sold lines of credit, while finance companies, especially subsidiaries of large auto makers, moved into the auto loan market. Sears and other retailers, which were once content to sell power tools and lawn chairs, are peddling credit cards and stocks. Foreign banks, once a negligible factor in American finance, lured away many large corporate clients with discount loans, and Japanese banks grabbed 25% of the commercial banking market in California. Even a phone company, AT&T, is now hawking credit cards.

Meanwhile, large commercial banks aggressively expanded into markets that had once been dominated by other financial institutions. Competing with local banks around the country, they bought up out-of-state banks and set up large regional or national banking systems. Battling with Wall Street, they expanded their foreign operations, set up investment banking units, invested in leveraged buyouts, and even bought security firms in London and Tokyo. Going head-to-head with thrifts and finance companies in the business of providing financial services to the average American, they issued more credit cards and made more consumer loans than ever before. They also came up with new ways of maximizing their profits and capital. For example, by selling securities backed by mortgages, car loans, credit card receivables, and student loans, commercial banks could turn over their money much faster and produce higher returns on their capital.

Many of these changes were long overdue. But they also pushed bankers into a series of increasingly speculative loans, ranging from Third World debt in the 1970s to leveraged buyouts in the late 1980s. By the early 1990s,

American banking had entered its worst crisis since the 1930s, when over 10,000 banks went bust. As the nation's largest banks posted huge losses and the cost of the savings and loan bailout skyrocketed from about $17 billion in the early 1980s to at least $325 billion in 1990, government regulators scrambled to control the problems. Though virtually no one expects another Great Depression, it is clear the problems run very deep. Consider, for example, the rise and fall of the savings and loan industry.

THE SAVINGS AND LOAN CRISIS

The rise and fall of the savings and loan industry illustrates how the revolution in American finance has finally come to Main Street. The savings and loan industry was originally created in the 19th century to provide financial services, savings accounts, loans, and home mortgages to average Americans, who did not have enough money to open an account at commercial banks. During the Great Depression, Congress passed new laws giving the savings and loan industry a kind of a franchise over the home loan market. By the 1960s, industry executives liked to say they worked on the 3-6-3 system. You paid depositors 3% on their savings accounts, you loaned the money out at 6% to home buyers, and you were at the golf course by 3 P.M. It was a nice, safe, regulated industry with something to offer everyone. Working- and middle-class Americans bought houses with cheap home loans, the thrifts made money, and the economy prospered, thanks to a housing boom.

This all changed in the late 1960s and 1970s. Huge government deficits, the War on Poverty, the Vietnam War, and the oil crisis led to massive money creation and double-digit inflation. As banks and other financial institutions began offering NOW accounts, CDs and money market accounts that paid higher rates of interest than the thrifts were allowed to pay, consumers withdrew billions of dollars out of low-interest savings accounts at thrifts, putting many on the brink of insolvency. Worse, the thrifts also held billions of dollars worth of fixed-rate mortgages that paid low rates of return. Not surprisingly, when Ronald Reagan was elected president in 1980, nearly half the industry was losing money. A Federal Reserve study in the spring of 1980 estimated that two out of three thrifts were in danger of folding.

In 1978, 1980, and again in 1982, Congress passed legislation designed to solve the crisis. Unfortunately, nearly all these measures made the problem worse. To attract new depositors, thrifts were allowed to pay higher interest rates. Fine, except that many thrifts began offering above-market interest rates and accepting brokered deposits. (Typically, a broker like Merrill Lynch would take millions from an investor, break it into $100,000 lots so it was federally insured, and then put the money into CDs or accounts at thrifts that were paying the highest rates.) The brokered deposits allowed some thrifts to double or even triple in size each year. But high interest rates made it impossible to make money on old fixed-rate mortgages, the thrifts' traditional business.

Realizing that thrifts couldn't pay depositors 11% interest rates and then loan it out to home buyers at 9%, Congress and government regulators agreed that the thrifts should be allowed into new areas of business that might earn higher profits. The 1982 Garn-St Germain Depository Institutions Act and several subsequent regulatory decisions allowed thrifts, for the first time in their history, to make loans to businesses, invest in speculative commercial real estate, buy junk bonds, and even play the stock market. To help thrifts survive the difficult transition from regulation to deregulation, government regulators eased their accounting rules and lowered their capital requirements. To attract investors and raise capital, regulators allowed single investors to buy mutual savings banks, which had once been owned by many depositors. Government regulators also adopted a more lenient attitude. The number of bank examinations in the savings and loan industry dropped 55% between 1980 and 1983.

When signing the 1982 law, President Reagan noted that "it provides a long-term solution for troubled thrift institutions." Congress, the White House, and government regulators all believed that the thrift industry could grow out of its troubles. Unfortunately the problems in the thrift industry reflected deeper, more complex changes in the American and international financial system.

Over the past decade, rapid changes in the financial system have greatly increased competition among thrifts, larger commercial banks, Wall Street firms, insurance companies, and even foreign banks for deposits, consumer loans, and profitable investments. But many of the sleepy little thrifts lacked the capital and financial expertise to compete effectively with big money-center banks or Wall Street firms. Most thrift executives knew how to make home loans but had little understanding of the markets for commercial real estate or zero-coupon bonds. No matter. Many nearly insolvent thrifts began speculating in the stock market, junk bonds, or mortgage-backed securities as a last-ditch effort to save their institutions. "Heads I win, tails the FSLIC loses," became a common quip.

Policymakers also knew that the thrifts needed more capital and a larger deposit base to survive. But letting thrifts engage in dubious accounting practices and allowing them to reduce the amount of capital required to cover their loans was hardly the way to shore up the industry's finances. Government regulators could have carefully merged small thrifts with commercial banks or other financial institutions which were capable of providing long-term expertise and deep pockets. Instead, they allowed almost anyone into the industry. Real estate speculators and building contractors bought dozens of thrifts so they would have a private piggy bank to finance office buildings, condos, and resorts. Wall Street managed to raise over $3 billion for mutual savings banks, which eventually leveraged these public offerings into nearly $50 billion worth of bad loans. The SEC never complained, even though these banks had no real capital and virtually no hope of success.

Regulators also encouraged thrifts to take brokered deposits and pay above-market interest rates, believing that the practice would create larger, more competitive institutions. The thrifts would have more deposits that could be loaned out at higher rates. Accounting tricks would let them survive the difficult transition, and a few years down the line these sleepy little thrifts would be billion-dollar financial powerhouses. No one seemed to understand that big, unprofitable thrifts would only produce more costly bankruptcies.

As befits one of the biggest financial disasters in the history of the world, there is plenty of blame to go around. In fact, almost every sector of American politics and finance contributed to the disaster:

• Top Democratic leaders in Congress, such as former House Speaker Jim Wright, harassed government regulators and added tens of billions of dollars to the cost of the thrift bailout by blocking key legislation that would have let regulators close down insolvent thrifts.

• White House Chief of Staff Donald Regan, whose former employer Merrill Lynch was making millions by brokering deposits, stopped regulators when they tried to end the practice.

• The head of the House Banking Committee, Fernand St Germain (D–RI), who passed key legislation that exacerbated the S&L crisis, received more than $144,000 in contributions and was eventually voted out of office after press reports accused him of making more than $300,000 in profits from sweetheart deals with thrifts that wanted regulatory favors.

• A small army of lawyers, accountants, and appraisers made millions by issuing inflated appraisals and financial statements. Large accounting firms never complained about congressionally mandated accounting tricks that contributed tens of billions of dollars to the eventual cost of the bailout. For example, many thrifts had mortgages on their books that paid less interest than the average savings account. With the encouragement of government regulators, some thrifts sold off these loans at a loss, often getting only 60 or 70 cents on the dollar. But this didn't produce large losses, thanks to the new accounting rules. Thrifts could write off the losses over the life of the loan, say thirty years. Then they could take the money and immediately loan it out for speculative real estate ventures, charging huge fees. These fees could be booked as immediate profits. So, even though a thrift had just lost millions on its old mortgages and invested the money in speculative real estate ventures that probably wouldn't ever be paid back, its balance sheet looked great. The fees made it look like the thrift was making millions.

• Even with the help of government-sanctioned accounting tricks, thrift owners found it necessary to turn to a variety of illegal activities to make money. Government regulators estimate that fraud played a role in the collapse of at least 30% of all thrifts. Regulators have sent over 21,000 possible cases to prosecutors for criminal action, but federal agencies have the resources to investigate only a small percentage of the cases. Between 1988 and the start of 1991, the Justice Department had convicted 403 people of fraud in the S&L industry, with 79% of those resulting in prison terms. These convicted criminals were ordered to pay fines of $4.8 million and damages of $231 million, but most of this money has not been paid. (Defendants were ordered to pay $8.9 million in 1988 and 1989 but had paid only $23,700 by the summer of 1990.) At the start of 1991, the FBI was investigating 234 failed thrifts, and the Justice Department had 654 pending investigations. Thirty S&L executives had been sued for civil damages since October 1988, but the government had recovered only $12 million. Overall, the Justice Department believes that fraud in 507 S&Ls produced $6.4 billion in losses.

- The thrift fiasco provides an especially horrifying example of how special interest groups get their way in Congress. Thrift industry lobbyists, executives, and political action committees (PACs) gave over $11 million to congressional and presidential candidates during the 1980s in a successful effort to prevent effective government action against failing thrifts.

- Consultants, such as Alan Greenspan, used their prestige to tout the industry's virtues and promote deregulation. In 1984, Greenspan issued a report arguing that S&Ls should be allowed to make investments in commercial real estate financed by Charles Keating, the notorious real estate developer who had bought Lincoln Savings and Loan. Lincoln eventually collapsed under the weight of bad commercial real estate loans and junk bonds, costing taxpayers $2.5 billion, even though Greenspan once told federal regulators that Lincoln was a "vibrant and healthy" institution that "presents no foreseeable risk."

- State legislatures, flush with millions more in campaign contributions, gutted state regulatory agencies. This allowed some thrifts facing federal regulatory action to switch their federal charter to a state charter, thus avoiding even the nominal control that federal regulators exerted over the industry.

- The Federal Home Loan Bank Board, which was supposed to protect federally insured deposits from con artists and fraud, behaved more like a cheerleader than a regulator. Thrift industry executives sat on the board of directors of the FHLB's 12 regional banks, and, not surprisingly, the agency closely followed the dictates of top industry lobbyists. It made little attempt to regulate the rapidly changing industry, and when it became apparent that thrifts around the country were hemorrhaging red ink, the FHLB attempted to downplay the crisis by consistently underestimating the cost of a federal bailout. One FHLB head, M. Danny Wall, estimated the bailout cost to be $31 billion in 1988, even though the General Accounting Office (GAO) was insisting the cost would be at least $200 billion. The current head of the House Banking Committee, Henry Gonzalez, later described these figures as the worst cover-up since Watergate: "The bank board misrepresented facts . . . denied reality, and ultimately destroyed the credibility of the entire Federal Home Loan Bank system."

- Vice President Bush headed a deregulatory commission that recommended that many regulatory functions be transferred to state regulators, even though the state regulators were badly funded and woefully understaffed. Later, Bush received more than $600,000 in soft contributions for his 1988 presidential race, and federal regulators would file suit against his son Neil for regulatory violations that allegedly contributed to the $1 billion collapse of Silverado Banking, a Denver thrift. (Neil Bush, who served on Silverado's board of directors, eventually settled the charges.) Meanwhile, Michael Dukakis, Bush's Democratic opponent in 1988, decided not to make the S&L crisis an issue after being told how top Democrats obstructed regulators and had close ties to many thrift executives who were later indicted for fraud.

- The media, busy chronicling the lifestyles of the rich and famous, ignored the story until it was too late. Even now, little attention is paid to the underlying economic problems that caused the crisis in the first place.

All these mistakes proved to be very expensive. Each year through the 1980s, estimates of the cost of the bailout grew at an alarming rate: $17.5 billion in 1983, $59.7 billion in 1984, $69.2 billion in 1985, $91.7 billion in 1986, $130.2 billion in 1987, $170.4 billion in 1989. The decision by Democrats and Republicans to ignore the issue during the 1988 presidential campaign is believed to have added at least $50 billion to the cost.

In the early 1990s, the cost was still rising. In 1990, the GAO estimated that the cost would reach at least $325 billion over the next 30 years and could rise to at least $500 billion if interest rates rise and a recession exacerbates the thrifts' problems. Much of this cost is interest: at least $133 billion if the bailout costs $325 billion, $233 billion if costs rise to $500 billion. Others place the cost even higher. *The Stanford Law and Policy Review* estimated in 1990 that the bailout will cost $1.4 trillion over 40 years.

Whatever the final cost, the thrift crisis will have an important impact on the American economy during the 1990s. Financing the thrift bailout has already increased interest rates by 20 basis points, or one fifth of a percentage point. That doesn't sound like much, but over 30 years, an extra 20 basis points on $7.5 trillion worth of private sector debt would produce $300 billion in added interest costs. That will reduce the money business can spend on new investments and make America less competitive. Rising costs for the bailout in 1990 were an important factor in persuading Congress and the White House to raise taxes and many of the problems in the real estate industry can be traced to the thrift crisis. Tens of billions of dollars worth of loans from thrifts produced more offices, condos, and homes than anyone wanted to buy. In some states, real estate prices have already dropped 20% to 30% since 1986, and massive sales of real estate by government regulators should further depress prices. Worse, the problems in the thrifts have already spilled over into other sectors of the financial system, particularly commercial banking.

COMMERCIAL BANKS: ON THE BRINK OF DISASTER?

1990 was a year many commercial banks would like to forget. The General Accounting Office issued a report saying that the fund that insures commercial banks might be depleted in the next few years and that 35 large banks were likely to fail. Several major banks, such as Chase Manhattan, announced huge losses and massive layoffs, while many other banks, such as Citicorp, had their credit ratings cut. (Of the nation's fifty largest commercial banks, only one, Bank of America, had its debt rating upgraded in 1990.) Headlines in major newspapers asked if commercial banking was about to become the next savings and loan crisis.

A few numbers illustrate the seriousness of the problem: Commercial banks still have $40 billion worth of Third World debt that is not likely to be repaid at any time in the near future. Bad loans have jumped 50% in four years, from $43.7 billion in 1985 to $61.6 billion in 1989, as a depressed real estate market has produced over $20 billion worth of delinquent loans. Since 1987, commercial banks have been failing at a rate of 200 per year, compared with 10 in 1980 and just one in 1972. In the 1980s, 1,086 banks failed, more than double the number that crashed between 1934 and 1979. As a number of highly leveraged companies slip into bankruptcy, banks are sitting on $55 billion in loans that were used to finance leveraged buyouts and mergers. Credit cards, which produced huge profits in the 1980s, may produce huge losses in the 1990s if a recession makes it harder for consumers to make their payments. And delinquent real estate loans continue to increase, jumping 60% in 1990. Not surprisingly, bank stocks dropped 35% between April and November of 1990.

These problems have hurt the Federal Deposit Insurance Corporation, which insures bank deposits. The fund lost $5.1 billion in 1988 and 1989 and may have lost another $2 billion in 1990. The FDIC estimates that it had $13.2 billion in the summer of 1990, only 70 cents for each $100 of deposits, much less than $1.19 per $100 in 1985. The GAO, however, estimates that the fund is in even worse shape. Its 1990 report says that the $13.2 billion balance does not take into account $8 billion that might have to be spent to buy back assets of troubled Southwest banks. Moreover, 35 large banks with assets of $45.1 billion are expected to fail in the next few years, and the FDIC may have to spend $4.4 billion to $6.3 billion to pay off depositors. This means that the fund, while not technically insolvent, could be depleted within the next few years. Responding to these problems in the spring of 1991, the FDIC admitted the fund would be broke by the start of 1992. It announced plans to raise insurance fees and take other measures that would raise $64.4 billion by 1995.

Do these problems add up to an S&L-size bailout? Probably not. The number of problem banks actually decreased from 1,289 in 1989 to 1,046 in 1990, the lowest level since 1985. Using a worst-case scenario, where the nation slipped into a serious recession, *Fortune* and a leading bank consulting firm, Ferguson & Co., estimated that equity capital held by all banks would shrink by $86.3 billion and that taxpayers would be left with a $40 billion bill. Bad news, but hardly a 1930s-style disaster, when over 10,000 banks went bust.

More serious are long-term problems that are weakening the competitive position of American banks at home and abroad. Overseas, after three decades of expansion, financial problems have forced U.S. banks to sell businesses in Europe and Asia, and foreign banks are stealing their business at home. Foreign banks now control about 25% of U.S. banking assets. (The Japanese control 14% of all assets, up from only 3.8% in 1973.)

While rapid changes in the financial system have pushed banks into increasingly speculative loans, increased competition from other financial institutions has also eroded key profit centers. Banks must compete with finance companies owned by the Big Three auto makers in the auto-loan market. Banks also must battle companies like American Express, Sears, and AT&T in the credit card field. Securities firms and foreign capital markets continue to steal banks' corporate clients. And the thrifts that survive the shakeout in their industry will be larger and better able to compete in the lucrative consumer finance business.

Many top government regulators also argue that it's time for a change. Outgoing FDIC Chairman L. William Seidman notes that "the American banking and financial industry is in need of thorough reorganization if we are going to be competitive in the world." To address that problem, President Bush proposed landmark legislation in early 1991 that would radically reform America's banking and financial system. The package would: (1) Allow well-capitalized banks to have securities, mutual fund, and insurance affiliates; (2) Legalize nationwide banking; (3) Shore up the fund that insures bank deposits by charging higher premiums for undercapitalized banks, by increasing regulatory supervision of less well capitalized banks and by limiting insurance coverage to only one $100,000 checking or savings account per bank; (4) Restructure a byzantine system of bank regulation so that each bank had only one regulator, tie bank regulation more directly to a bank's capital, and impose fewer regulations on better capitalized banks; (5) Set up a streamlined regulatory system in which the Federal Reserve would regulate all state banks. A new department in the Treasury would regulate all national banks and thrift institutions, and the FDIC would insure bank deposits, thus losing a number of its current regulatory functions.

The proposals, which would create more competition between financial services firms, would improve the international competitiveness of American banks. But, its unlikely that Congress will pass any landmark legislation in the near future. Pointing to the record number of bank failures and the savings and loan bailout, critics argue for more, not less regulation. Meanwhile, the financial services sector is divided on which direction to go. The reform measures would probably trigger a period of consolidation and mergers within the American financial system that could hurt the profitability of Wall Street firms and smaller banks. Larger banks want to end the barriers that prevent them from setting up branches all around the country; smaller state banks will battle any law creating a nationwide banking system. Securities companies liked deregulation when it allowed them to take business away from commercial banks; they oppose it when banks say they should be allowed on Wall Street.

The changes are also likely to produce a difficult transition if adopted. In 1990 the Comptroller of the Currency estimated that existing competition among financial institutions will reduce the number of banks to about 11,000 by 1993, and other observers suggest that about 30% of all employees in the banking industry might lose their jobs during the next five years. Relaxed rules on interstate banking reduce the number even further by forcing many smaller banks out of business. But big banks are also likely to undergo some difficult times. Many analysts are forecasting a wave of mergers that may include some of the nation's largest banks. Still, doing nothing could create an even more serious problem affecting the international competitiveness of American banking. E. Gerald Corrigan, President of the Federal Reserve Bank of New York, noted in 1990: "While the data may suggest that U.S. firms are still quite capable of holding their own in an international context, there is no doubt in my mind that as a group their position has slipped . . . [in part because] . . . the U.S. banking system is simply out of step with the rest of the world, and more importantly, it is out of step with the reality of the marketplace."

BankAmerica Corporation
Chairman and President: Richard M. Rosenberg   Bank of America Center
Employees: 55,600   San Francisco, California 94104
Assets: $94.6 billion   415-622-2091
Deposits: $77.1 billion
Loans: $69.1 billion

	1990	1989	1985	1980
Net income (millions of dollars):	877	820	(337)	645
Share earnings (dollars):	3.85	3.79	—	4.33

In 1980, shortly before leaving to become the head of the World Bank, A. W. Clausen, the CEO of BankAmerica, announced earnings of $645 million, a record for any American financial institution. Seven years later he was back, trying to save a bank that had lost $1.9 billion between 1985 and 1987.

Ironically, in the 1970s Clausen sowed the seeds of disaster by boosting the bank's fixed-rate mortgages, agricultural lending, construction lending, and foreign loans. At the same time he rapidly expanded, creating a large, unwieldy bureaucracy that lacked central controls and scrimped on new technology.

These tactics quadrupled the company's assets and earnings during the 1970s but caused problems when all those real estate, farm, and foreign loans began to go sour. Earnings dropped steadily between 1981 and 1984. By 1985, BankAmerica was forced into the first layoff in its 81-year history and cut its dividend for the first time in 53 years. The year ended with a $337 million loss.

But that was only the beginning. Under Clausen's hand-picked successor, Armacost, the losses mounted. Armacost compounded the bank's problems by not moving decisively to slash costs. His decision to sell BankAmerica's headquarters and cut costs came too late to stem the company's $518 million loss for 1986.

By 1986, the company's financial troubles threatened not only its bottom line but its very existence. With raiders lurking in the wings, the board of directors ousted Armacost and made the surprise decision to rehire Clausen.

Clausen's tenure as head of the World Bank from 1981 to 1986, when the World Bank floundered and found itself unable to deal with the Third World debt crisis, did not bode well for BankAmerica's future or say much for Clausen's abilities as a crisis manager. But Clausen moved quickly to solve the bank's problems. He cut expenses, laying off 25,000 full-time employees, and sold assets to raise capital. The bank's offices in San Francisco and Los Angeles were put on the block, as well as FinanceAmerica, a finance company; Charles Schwab & Co., a discount brokerage, and several foreign companies. Clausen also emphasized the bank's traditional strengths. It had a massive branch-banking system in California, one of the strongest areas of consumer banking in the 1980s, and owned the Seattle First National Bank in Seattle, another booming city.

Soon earnings picked up. After a disastrous $955 million loss in 1987, the bank earned $820 million in 1988, and in 1989, the company restored its dividend.

Citicorp

Chairman and CEO: John S. Reed
Employees: 93,500
Assets: $230.6 billion
Deposits: $137.9 billion
Loans: $162.4 billion

399 Park Avenue
New York, New York 10043
212-559-1000

	1990	1989	1985	1980
Net income (millions of dollars):	318	498	998	499
Share earnings (dollars):	0.57	1.16	3.56	2.01

Hard times in the commercial banking industry have even hit Citicorp, the nation's largest bank. In 1990, Citibank had its credit rating downgraded and suffered as its stock continued to drop. After hitting $34 a share in 1987, Citicorp stock fell as low as $11 a share in 1990.

It was a bitter pill to swallow for an institution with a history of leading the American banking industry. Over the years the nation's largest bank, Citibank, has established a reputation for innovation and aggressive tactics. Since its creation in 1812, Citibank has battered down regulatory barriers, stormed into new markets, and ruffled more than a few feathers in Washington and on Wall Street.

Citibank's history could double as a history of banking innovations. In the 19th century it was one of the first banks to expand overseas. In the 1910s National City Bank of New York, as it was then called, lobbied to get the 1913 Federal Reserve Act to include provisions allowing U.S. banks to establish foreign branches, and in 1914 it became the first U.S. bank to open a foreign branch. In the 1920s it got into the business of selling foreign debt to U.S. investors, even though some of its Latin American bonds were from countries that had a long history of never repaying their debts. Some things, at least, never change.

Also in the 1920s, at a time when most commercial banks dealt only with businesses, the bank was one of the first to encourage individuals to open accounts, and in 1928 it was the first to offer loans to consumers.

Many of these innovations were very controversial, putting the bank on a collision course with Congress and government regulators. During the bull market of the 1920s, National City used securities subsidiaries to function as an investment bank, underwriting stocks, selling securities, and providing loans so investors could purchase stocks and bonds. But National City came under congressional fire in the early 1930s for touting some obviously bad stocks and bonds. Sensational Senate Banking Committee hearings into the company's fraudulent investment banking practices helped pass the Glass-Steagall Act, which separated commercial banking and investment banking.

That act placed strict limits on what kinds of businesses a commercial bank could undertake. But the bank never gave up its attempt to expand and diversify. In 1968, it created Citicorp as a bank holding corporation to explore a loophole in the Bank Holding Company Act of 1956. This law restricted what kinds of businesses a bank holding company could undertake but exempted one-bank holding companies so that small banks could provide accounting, real estate sale, and other services they needed to remain profitable. Citicorp wasn't small but it was legally only one bank, even though it had hundreds of branches. That allowed it to expand into other businesses, enabling it to acquire a mortgage banking firm and a management consultancy firm. Other banks quickly followed suit. By the end of 1969, a House Banking Committee study found that 27 conglomerates had acquired or established banks and that one-bank holding companies were engaged in 20 different financial activities and 99 nonfinancial activities. The total deposits of one-bank holding companies rose to $135 billion, or about 35% of total deposits. Congress closed some of the loopholes in 1970 but nonbanking subsidiaries of banks were given the right to expand across state lines and banks were given the right to expand into areas "closely related to banking." Over the next decade, that provision helped banks break down regulatory barriers that had prevented them from entering other businesses. In 1983, for example, the Federal Reserve ruled that discount brokerages were "closely related to banking."

More recently, Citicorp pioneered automatic teller machines in the New York City market; moved so aggressively into investment banking that almost overnight it became the second-largest publicly owned investment banker on Wall Street; moved into information services by snapping up Quotron; and bought up banks in Texas as part of its expanding national banking system.

Today, Citicorp is the nation's largest bank holding corporation and the world's second-largest bank. It does business with about 16.5 million customers, or about one in every five households in the United States, and has issued 27 million credit cards.

But the bank faces some difficult problems in the 1990s. Its attempt to compete with Wall Street has yet to pay off. After six years of losses, it was forced to sell its London brokerage firm, and its investment bankers got a black eye when they were unable to raise money to finance the UAL buyout in 1989. The bank still has $8.2 billion worth of Third World loans and has been badly hurt by a downturn in the real estate market. It is the nation's largest commercial real estate lender, with $13.2 billion in outstanding loans. But nonperforming real estate loans rose by $573 million in the third quarter of 1990 alone, to $2.2 billion. Bank analysts also complain that Citicorp's loan-loss reserves are thin. It has set aside enough reserves to cover only about 39% of its bad loans, way below the 70% many other large banks have. To help solve that problem, Citibank raised $1.19 billion in new capital in early 1991.

These problems come at a bad time. Citibank had hoped to expand into the California market when it opened up to out-of-state banks in 1990. But so far, Citibank has purchased only one small bank, with just $35 million in assets, and admits that it would be hard-pressed to finance a major purchase. For the moment, Citibank will have to use its tradition of innovation to solve short-term problems, not plot long-term expansion.

BEVERAGES: ALCOHOLIC AND NONALCOHOLIC

THE MARKET

Americans do a lot of heavy drinking. Every year the average American consumes some 23.7 gallons of beer and ale, 1.5 gallons of distilled spirits, 2.3 gallons of wine, about 45.7 gallons of soft drinks, 25 gallons a year of coffee, 25.9 gallons of milk, 5.5 gallons of fruit juices, and 5.2 gallons of bottled water. Some surveys indicate that soft drinks will soon replace tap water as the nation's most popular beverage for the first time in history.

THE MONEY

All of that hard drinking adds up to a tidal wave of revenues. Americans drink about $65.5 billion worth of alcoholic beverages each year. Consumers spend about $39.6 billion on booze at home; another $25.9 billion is spent at bars, restaurants, and other places outside the home.

Here's how U.S. beverage makers will do in 1991:

Soft drink makers will ship about $28.0 billion worth of canned and bottled drinks, up from $12 billion in 1980.

About $15.5 billion worth of beer will flow out of the nation's breweries, up from $9.4 billion in 1980.

U.S. wine and brandy makers will ferment a $4.3 billion river of wine, up from $2.3 billion in 1980.

And distillers will ship $3.9 billion worth of distilled liquor, up from $2.9 billion in 1980.

In 1989, $845 million worth of beer was imported (5.2% of the market), $1.0 billion worth of wine and brandy (24% of the market), and $1.3 billion worth of distilled liquor (25.5% of the market). Total imports hit $3.0 billion (12.0% of the market) in 1989, up from $2.1 billion in 1980 (12.3% of the market). Only $203 million worth of soft drinks were imported (0.19% of the market).

THE PLAYERS

The beverage industry remains highly competitive, at both the production and wholesale end, yet most of the industry is dominated by a few large producers. The beer industry has grown increasingly concentrated over the years, with the top five brewers capturing 91.5% of the market, up from only 38% in 1965. The same can be said for the soft drink industry, in which the top two producers, the Coca-Cola Company and PepsiCo, control 72.2% of the market, up from 58.8% in 1980. The top six soft-drink makers account for 90.6% of the market, up from 82.4% in 1980. The wine industry is less concentrated, with many small producers, but even so, the six largest American wineries control 60.2% of the market. In the liquor industry, the top five brands are Bacardi, Smirnoff, Seagram's 7 Crown, Popov, and Jim Beam, according to John C. Maxwell, Jr.

THE PEOPLE

There were about 52,600 people making alcoholic beverages in the U.S., down from 68,700 in 1980. Another 92,000 worked in the bottled and canned soft drink industry, down from 118,000 in 1980.

TRENDS AND FORECAST

An increasingly health-conscious public, tough drunk-driving laws, and increased taxes are expected to hold down consumption of alcoholic beverages for the next few years. Per-capita soft drink consumption, however, continues to grow. That should translate into increases of about 2% in revenues above inflation for the soft drink industry between 1991 and 1995. The combined value of alcoholic beverages should decline about 0.3% a year during the same period.

BEVERAGE TIME LINE

1855   The Miller Brewing Company is founded. A coin shortage during the Civil War sees the company mint its own Miller coins, which can be redeemed for a glass of beer.

1860   Eberhard Anheuser takes over a failing brewery. His son-in-law Adolphus Busch and Carl Conrad make the brew a success by producing a lighter beer than the beers that dominate the market. By 1901, Budweiser overtakes Pabst for the title of the best-selling beer.

1860s   Coffee becomes popular in the United States after it is issued with Army rations.

1869   Worried about teetotalers drinking wine at communion, Dr. Thomas Welch creates Welch's grape juice. His son Charles markets it as "Dr. Welch's Unfermented Wine."

1870s   To market his herb tea made from wild roots and berries to tough Pennsylvania coal miners, Charles Hires calls it "root beer"—hence, "Hires Root Beer."

1885   R. S. Lazenby invents the soft drink Dr Pepper, which he calls "Dr Pepper's Phos-Ferrates."

1885   The Borden's New York Condensed Food Company (today known as Borden, Inc.) introduces the first fresh milk in bottles. Company founder Gail Borden has already introduced the first condensed milk.

1886   Coca-Cola goes on sale at Jacob's Pharmacy in Atlanta, Georgia. The headache and hangover remedy is advertised as an "esteemed Brain Tonic and Intellectual Beverage" by its inventor, John S. Pemberton. In 1891 an Atlanta pharmacist, Asa G. Candler, buys rights to the product, and in 1892 he organizes the Coca-Cola Company. The company achieves rapid growth after Candler turns Coca-Cola into a five-cent soft drink. The drink is typically dispensed from soda fountains. Only in 1899 is it bottled for the first time by Benjamin F. Thomas and Joseph B. Whitehead. For one dollar they acquire the right to bottle the drink in every state of the union, buying the syrup from Candler and reselling it to local bottlers.

1898   Many colas appear around the country, hoping to cash in on the popularity of Coca-Cola. One, Pepsi-Cola, is introduced by a New Bern, North Carolina, pharmacist, Caleb Bradham.

1901   Satori Kato develops instant coffee. It doesn't become popular until Nestlé introduces it as Nescafé in 1938.

1909   The tea bag and Lipton tea are introduced to America. Sir Thomas Lipton does not invent the tea bag but he is the first to market name-brand tea bags.

1916   Coca-Cola introduces its distinctive bottle, developed by Chapman S. Root of the Root Glass Company. The bottle will be synonymous with the product for the next 58 years.

1920   Prohibition creates a boom for soft-drink, coffee, juice, and tea makers. Anheuser-Busch survives by selling yeast and sarsaparilla. There's also a booming market for bathtub gin. Nearly 1.4 billion gallons of hard liquor is sold illegally.

1923   Coca-Cola introduces the first "carry-home" soft drink carton, thus allowing grocers to sell larger quantities easily.

1928   Samuel and Allan Bronfman found Distiller's Company. In 1927, they bought Joseph E. Seagram & Sons. Even though it's Prohibition they ship large quantities of liquor that end up in the U.S. The family, which still owns the company, makes Seagram the world's largest producer of alcoholic beverages.

1929   C. I. Grigg invents a drink he calls "Bib-Label Lithianted Lemon-Lime Soda." In the 1930s, he comes up with a better name—7UP.

1933   The end of Prohibition hurts soft-drink makers. Coke sees sales drop from 27.7 billion gallons in 1930 to only 20 million in 1933.

1933   Ernest and Julio Gallo found E.&J. Gallo Winery with $5,900. It will become the largest U.S. wine producer. The same year Lewis Rosenstiel sets up Schenley Distillers Company.

1954   Instant dry milk is introduced by Carnation.

1962   Sugar-free soft drinks become widely available with the introduction of Tab (by the Coca-Cola Company) and Diet Pepsi. Some diet soft drinks were available on a limited basis in the 1950s.

SANKA

Dr. Ludwig Roselius spent years looking for a way to extract caffeine from coffee while leaving the taste intact. Finally, the head of the Cafe Haag firm in Bremen, Germany, succeeded. When Dr. Roselius brought his coffee to France, he called it Sanka, a contraction of the phrase *sans caféine,* "without caffeine."

Adolph Coors Company

Chairman and President: W. K. Coors   Golden, Colorado 80401
Employees: 10,700   303-279-6565
Assets: $1.7 billion

	1990	1989	1985	1980
Revenues (millions of dollars):	1,863	1,764	1,281	888
Net income (millions of dollars):	39	13.1	53	65.0
Share earnings (dollars):	1.05	0.36	1.52	1.86

What it does: America's fourth-largest brewer.

Most companies go out of their way to avoid political and social controversies. Boycotts, after all, are bad for business and worse for marketing strategies—facts that the Coors brewery has learned in a slow and costly fashion.

Back in the 1960s, Coors beer had a cult status and demand was so great the company couldn't produce enough of it. In only a few years, without almost any advertising, it jumped from being the 16th-largest-selling beer to being the 4th. A regional brewer that only produced 200,000 barrels a year in the early 1940s, it was spewing out 13.5 million barrels in 1976.

While the company was flying high, so were the political aspirations of the company's multimillionaire brothers, William and Joseph, who ran a family brewery founded in 1873. They put up the money to found the Heritage Foundation, battled unions tooth and nail, and backed the presidential campaign of their close friend, Ronald Reagan. Joseph Coors was considered a member of Reagan's kitchen cabinet.

Meanwhile, charges of discrimination and unfair labor practices set off a series of boycotts that since the mid-1960s have pitted the company against practically every liberal constituency in the United States—feminists, unions, Chicanos, blacks, and civil-rights leaders.

In several key states, boycotts by organized labor hurt sales in major cities. At the same time, the beer industry was undergoing a difficult restructuring, with regional brewers like Coors being forced either to go national or die. Coors's market share in California plummeted from 41% to only 14%.

Today, the next generation of Coors heirs, Jeffrey, Peter, and Joe Jr., are trying to repair the mistakes of their elders. They have hired public relations firms to improve the Coors image, funded minority projects, and pledged to increase minority employment. In 1987, they finally ended their feud with organized labor and the AFL-CIO agreed to call off its boycott.

But the brewery still has a long way to go to pick up the sales momentum it had in earlier years. Having bungled its opportunity to cash in on its cult status and become a major national brewery without having to spend much for advertising, the company had to do it the hard way, with expensive national ad campaigns. Coors has strengthened its position by introducing a number of new brands and expanded by buying Stroh Brewing Co. Its investments in aluminum and ceramics are also starting to help profits. The Coors family is now worth about $500 million.

Coca-Cola Company

Chairman and CEO: R. C. Goizueta   1 Coca-Cola Plaza, N.W.
Employees: 22,500   Atlanta, Georgia 30313
Assets: $9.3 billion   404-676-2121

	1990	1989	1985	1980
Revenues (millions of dollars):	10,236	8,966	7,904	5,913
Net income (millions of dollars):	1,382	1,193	678	422
Share earnings (dollars):	2.04	1.70	0.86	0.57

What it does: It is the world's leading soft drink company.

Coca-Cola has made some highly publicized marketing mistakes. First, Coke let its long-standing lead over Pepsi slip by failing to counter Pepsi's youth-oriented advertising. Then the company decided to change its age-old formula. What consumers wanted, some marketing genius decided, was a sweeter Coke—meaning something that tasted more like Pepsi. So in 1985, 99 years after Coke was invented, the company announced it was changing its famous formula.

Pepsi rejoiced, saying this proved it was winning the cola war, and consumers revolted. When the dust settled, Coke had to bring back the old Coke as "Coca-Cola Classic."

But a fight over Coke's top-secret soft drink formula hasn't been the only blunder the company has made recently. Columbia Pictures, which Coke bought for $752 million in 1983, has produced a bunch of canceled TV shows and box-office bombs, including the $17 million film *Fast Forward,* which earned only $500,000 at the box office and the 1987 flop *Ishtar,* which lost $25 million. Not surprisingly, the company was sold to Sony for $3.4 billion in 1989. Then, in 1990, Coca-Cola announced a fantastic new merchandising gimmick. Selected cans of Coke would contain something better than the real thing—real money. But after the company spent $100 million on the gimmick, in which paper bills would be pushed up out of the opened cans, consumers discovered the cans didn't work. Coke had to place advertisements in newspapers telling consumers not to drink from the cans, and eventually was forced to call off the whole mess.

Still, the company seems to have the same luck it did when Asa G. Candler bought the rights to the formula for only $2,000. The flap over whether the new or old Coke was the real thing was probably the best free advertising any company could ever hope for. Sales soared, and Coke's lead over Pepsi has steadily widened since 1985. It now holds 41% of the market, compared to only 31% for Pepsi.

Another bright spot is foreign sales. Coke gets 77% of its $8.9 billion in annual revenues from foreign sales. In Europe, it holds 43.6% of the soft drink market, and Coke does business in 155 countries—you can even buy Coke at the South Pole. To hold onto those foreign markets, Coke sunk more than $1 billion into foreign bottling operations in the last decade.

Since 1981, when Roberto Goizueta was appointed CEO, he has shaken up a company that looked like it was running out of steam. No longer are analysts saying it's only a matter of time before Coke slips behind Pepsi, and under Goizueta's direction the company has come up with a number of immensely profitable deals. For example, Coke announced in 1987 that it would merge its Columbia movie and TV divisions with Tri-Star in a stock swap to create a new entertainment giant. After 31% of the shares were redistributed to Coke shareholders, the soft-drink maker got back the $1.5 billion it invested in recent years to buy entertainment properties and still owns 49% of the company! As a result, the sale to Sony in 1989 was pure profit.

The Gallos   The story of Ernest and Julio Gallo is like a melodrama. Their company was founded on violent tragedy. They got embroiled in a lawsuit with a brother who accused them of cheating him out of his patrimony. Moreover, they were accused of using their company's enormous muscle in the wine industry to choke off competition and disdainfully undercut prices paid to the wine growers who depended on them for their livelihood.

Whatever their methods, they have made their E.&J. Gallo Winery in Modesto, California, the world's largest wine producer. One out of every four bottles of wine sold in the U.S. bears one of the company's brands, which include Chablis Blanc, Hearty Burgundy, Carlo Rossi, E.&J. brandy, and André champagne. The secretive Gallos don't divulge financial data, but in 1985 *Fortune* estimated that the company earned at least $50 million a year on sales of about $1 billion.

Ernest and Julio are the sons of an Italian immigrant, Joseph Gallo, who had a small vineyard. A stern taskmaster, Joseph worked his sons hard. Gallo survived Prohibition because of a government dispensation for making wine for religious and medicinal uses. In 1933, when the brothers were in their early 20s, Gallo shot his wife to death, tried to kill his sons, and then killed himself.

In the tragedy's aftermath, the brothers decided to get out of the vineyard business and make their own wine. They learned the process by reading instruction pamphlets at the public library and, when Prohibition ended, they sank $5,900 into a new winery. They divided their functions by having Julio oversee production while Ernest marketed the wine.

Over the years their operations grew, but their first major success didn't come until they introduced Thunderbird, a 60-cents-a-bottle, high-alcohol wine that became a favorite of skid row bums. Gallo made a fortune off the stuff but ever since has been trying to live down the sleazy image it gave the company. In the 1960s, it had another hit in another cheap wine, Ripple, apparently a favorite of a lot of teenagers.

The Gallos' image wasn't helped either when their younger brother, Joseph, who was 13 when their father died, charged that his brothers had cheated him. While researching their father's estate because of another feud involving the brothers, Joseph's lawyer found that his client had inherited an interest in their father's business. Joseph contended that E.&J. Gallo Winery was an outgrowth of that business, so he demanded a share.

As Gallo grew, it became the biggest grape purchaser in the region, which led to charges that the company exploited the vineyards it dealt with. The 1,500 vineyards that serviced Gallo were always on edge. The Gallos would reject a harvest out of hand or slash the price. With rare exception, the growers took it. In 1984, a grower complained to the California Department of Food and Agriculture that most of his harvest's price was cut to $275 a ton from $475. Gallo claimed the quality of the grapes wasn't high enough. Since the growers had no contract, the agency sided with the Gallos. Now the grape growers get a one-year contract from Gallo citing standards.

One reason for Gallo's success was an approach to marketing that left little to chance. Salesmen were told not only how to display merchandise, but what not to joke about (no dirty jokes) and how to cope with the various personalities of retailers.

Distributors knew that Gallo clearly didn't want them representing competitors. If a distributor didn't like it, he most likely lost Gallo's business. Because of its enormous market share, Gallo got its way. In 1976, the Federal Trade Commission said such a practice was unfair competition. For a while, Gallo had to abide by a consent order saying distributors wouldn't be punished for carrying competing brands. Then, in 1984, the FTC set aside the order, after Gallo argued that the market had become more competitive and now other wine makers had an edge.

In 1985, however, an Ohio distributor who had handled Gallo for 40 years sued the company for an alleged violation of antitrust laws after Gallo canceled him because he told them he couldn't afford the size of the sales force they required to push their products. Without Gallo products, he argued, he often couldn't get a foot in liquor stores to sell anything. Gallo won the case, saying the company wasn't in business to open doors so competing products could enter.

That bulldozer approach keeps working. For instance, when Gallo entered the wine cooler business there were 100 competing brands. With a heavy advertising campaign and cut-rate prices that squeezed most competitors when they tried to match them, Gallo's Bartles & Jaymes brand quickly bobbed to the top. Today, Gallo controls about 29% of the wine market, and the two brothers are worth over $600 million.

BOOK PUBLISHING

THE MARKET

Pundits have long predicted that book lovers are an endangered species who will lose out to a semiliterate generation weaned on television and music videos. Yet the average American buys about 6 books a year, up from only 2.75 per person in 1970. Not everyone reads books, however: only about 50% of the public has read a book in the last six months.

THE MONEY

Book publishing will be a $15.7 billion industry in 1991, up from $6.1 billion in 1980. A large share of the industry's sales is from trade books (37%), professional, scientific, and technical books (22%), and college, elementary, and high school texts (20%). Religious books account for about 7% of the market. In 1994, the publishing industry expects to sell about $27.3 billion worth of books.

THE PLAYERS

There are about 20,000 book publishing houses in the United States and they put out nearly 57,000 different titles a year that are sold in 22,926 bookstores. Ease of entry into the market has allowed many small publishers to go into business: over half of the publishers have fewer than five employees, 80% have fewer than 20 employees, 94% have fewer than 100 employees.

Most books are sold and produced by a few large houses. In 1958, according to author Maxwell Lillienstein, the 50 largest trade book publishers accounted for 65% of all trade book sales, none with an overwhelmingly dominant position. But as early as 1984, five publishers had 35% of all trade book sales. The largest company overall, including textbooks, is Simon & Schuster, the publishing division of Paramount Communications, which sold about 10% of all general-interest books.

Other studies indicate that in the 1980s, the four largest publishers in each of the following segments—mass-market paperbound books, book-club books, mail-order books, and general reference books—have controlled more than half of all sales. The top eight companies have accounted for over half the sales in textbooks, technical, scientific, and professional books, adult trade books, and juvenile books. The biggest eight religious publishers have about half of the market.

The same can be said of the bookstore business. There are 22,926 bookstores in the United States (up from 8,360 in 1957 and 1977 when there were 15,188). In recent years, chains have been rapidly expanding and, by 1990, their outlets numbered 8,489, according to the *American Book Trade Directory*.

Only about 36% of all books were sold in bookstores in 1990, up from 20% in 1975; another 20% were sold through book clubs or mail order, down from 26% in 1975; U.S. libraries and institutions accounted for 10% of all sales, up from 8% in 1975, when they bought 8%; college store sales increased to 18% from 15% in 1975, and falling enrollments dropped the share of purchases by high schools and elementary schools to 16%, down from 26% in 1975.

In recent years, a few large chains have increasingly dominated retail sales. By negotiating volume discounts from major publishers, chains such as Waldenbooks can heavily discount best-sellers and capture a larger share of the market. The top four companies (Waldenbooks, B. Dalton, Crown, and Barnes & Noble) now sell about 30% of all general interest books.

THE PEOPLE

There were 80,000 people employed by book publishers in 1991.

THE FORECAST

Book sales should continue to grow for several reasons. Libraries are committing more funds to book buying, and consumers are likely to buy more books, as they have in recent years. Consumer expenditures for books are expected to hit $27.3 billion in 1994, according to *Book Industry Trends,* and publishers' shipments should hit $21.1 billion, an 8.3% annual growth rate between 1990 and 1994. Sales of trade books should grow 12.2% per year to $6 billion; professional books are expected to increase from $3 billion in 1990 to $4 billion in 1994. Book clubs and direct-mail sales are expected to show more modest growth, with a 6.4% increase in book club sales and a 5% increase in mail order between 1990 and 1994. Paperback sales should grow 7.5% to 9.0% a year, and university press titles increase 8.2% through 1994.

Table B-1   15 Largest U.S. Book Publishers
(in millions)

Rank	Book operation/parent	1989 Revenues	1988 Revenues	% Change 1988–89
1	Simon & Schuster/Paramount	$1319	$1194	10.5%
2	Time Publishing Group/Time Warner	1148	1030	11.5
3	HarperCollins/News Corp.	1131	NA	NM
4	Reader's Digest Books/Reader's Digest Association	944	844	11.8
5	Random House/Advance Publications	850	760	10.6
6	Harcourt Brace Jovanovich Publishers/ HBJ Inc.	825	809	2.0
7	Bantam Doubleday Dell/Literary Guild Bertelsmann	775	745	4.0
8	Encyclopaedia Britannica	624	590	5.8
9	Maxwell-Macmillan/Maxwell Communications Corp.	530	NA	NM
10	McGraw-Hill Educational and Professional Publishing/McGraw-Hill	500	453	10.4
11	Times Mirror Book Group	500	425	17.6
12	The Thomson Corp.	496	NA	NM
13	Penguin USA-Addison-Wesley-Longman/ Pearson	477	405	17.8
14	Grolier/Hachette	447	417	7.2
15	Houghton Mifflin	404	368	9.8

Source: *BP Report*

PAUL SAMUELSON

Professor Paul Samuelson's famed *Economics* textbook, which taught a lot of people everything they think they know about that subject, is now in its 12th edition and has sold about 4 million copies. When first published in 1948, the book wasn't loved by one and all. A reviewer for *The Annals of the American Academy of Political and Social Science,* for instance, sniffed that "it drops wisecracks at times." The newest edition is the first of Samuelson's with a collaborator, Professor William Nordhaus of Yale University.

CHEMICALS

THE MARKET AND THE MONEY

In the past this industry brought us such things as nylons, Teflon, pesticides, and worries about environmental pollution. In the future, the chemical industry is moving into biotechnology, producing a new generation of drugs, food, and chemicals. (See the "Biotechnology" part of the "Technology" section.)

Over $297.1 billion worth of chemicals was shipped by U.S. companies in 1990, making the chemical industry not only one of the nation's largest but one of its most important. Petroleum refiners ship $131 billion worth of products that are not included in the above figure.

The chemical industry produces industrial chemicals that make modern manufacturing possible. It manufactures and develops pharmaceuticals that have revolutionized the health-care industry, supplies the fertilizers and pesticides that have made America the breadbasket of the world, and sells household products ranging from soaps to cosmetics.

The chemical industry is made up of several important sectors. Here's a glance at each:

Petrochemicals

Shipments of petrochemicals hit $124 billion in 1990 and should grow another 1% in 1991. This industry produces chemicals from petroleum products, which account for about 90% of all organic chemicals (i.e., chemicals made from organic materials such as petroleum). It is heavily dependent on the demand for such products as rubber, synthetic fibers, fertilizers, and other products, while its profit margins are closely tied to the price of oil.

Biotechnology

The market value of products in this area is growing rapidly as basic research moves toward practical applications. By 1995 sales should hit $5 billion, up from about $2 billion in 1990 and $350 million in 1986. There are about 1,150 U.S. companies in the biotechnology industry, and they spent $2.3 billion on research in 1990. (See the "Biotechnology" part of the "Technology" section.)

Industrial Chemicals

Shipments of industrial chemicals increased to $89.8 billion in 1990 from $68.0 billion in 1987. Most sales were for organic chemicals ($69.3 billion); shipments of inorganic chemicals such as alkalies, chlorine, and industrial gases totaled $20.5 billion, up from $17.2 billion in 1987. Industrial chemicals are used to produce plastics, synthetic fibers, solvents, and dyes. They play a role in steel production, the manufacture of other chemicals (about two thirds of all chlorine, for example, is used to produce organic chemicals), and dozens of other industries ranging from oil recovery to medical supplies and aerospace.

Agricultural Chemicals

Helped by a modest recovery in the sector, the market for agricultural chemicals hit $16.3 billion in 1991, up from $12.6 billion in 1987.

Rubber and Plastics

As plastics continue to replace metals, combined shipments of synthetic rubber and plastic materials increased to $37.8 billion in 1990 from $29.5 billion in 1987. Shipments of synthetic rubber, however, remained stagnant, largely because fewer autos and hence fewer tires were being manufactured.

Paints, Coatings, and Adhesives

Shipments of paints and related products hit $15.7 billion in 1990, up from $12.7 billion shipped in 1987.

Cleaning Preparations and Cosmetics

Shipments of soaps, cleaners, toilet goods, and cosmetics hit a total value of $38.7 billion in 1990, up from $32.4 billion in 1987. Sales of cosmetics, fragrances, and other toiletries accounted for over $16.7 billion of that total. Soaps and other detergents racked up $10.7 billion in sales.

The Pharmaceutical Industry

The value of shipments hit $49.6 billion in 1990, up dramatically from the $35.3 billion shipped in 1987. Between 1972 and 1985, shipments of pharmaceuticals grew 11% a year. (See the section "Health Care and Services.")

Petroleum Refining

The value of shipments from petroleum refiners increased 14.9% in 1990 to $131.1 billion. But that impressive gain was still below the $210 billion in shipments in 1981. The number of refineries also tumbled from 319 in 1980 to 205 in 1990 because more oil is being refined overseas. (See the section "Oil and Natural Gas.")

THE PLAYERS

The 100 largest chemical companies had sales of $186 billion in 1990, according to *Chemical and Engineering News*'s annual survey of the top 100 chemical producers, while the 50 largest companies had sales of $159 billion. The chemical industry employs 1.1 million people in 12,000 U.S. plants. Table C-1 (below) lists the 25 largest companies.

TRENDS AND FORECAST

The chemical industry faced tough times in the early and mid-1980s as declining markets for many traditional products and a strong dollar hurt sales. At the same time, the industry faced declining or stagnant markets for many products. High prices for oil caused many consumers to switch from petrochemicals, and a stagnant U.S. industrial economy reduced the demand for many chemicals used by auto makers, the construction industry, and farmers.

Environmental regulation further squeezed profits. Scandal over the EPA's lax enforcement of toxic waste dumps, the forced evacuation of several towns because of dioxins, and the leak of hazardous gases from a Union Carbide chemical plant in Bhopal, India, all increased the public's awareness of environmental hazards. Congress responded by tightening environmental laws and, in 1990, passed the Clean Air Act, which will add billions of dollars in costs.

All of these problems forced the industry into a painful restructuring during the 1980s, involving plant closings, layoffs, and major acquisitions. Nearly $39 billion worth of chemical companies were bought and sold during the 1980s. In 1989 alone, Sterling Drug was bought by Kodak for $5.1 billion, and Firestone was sold to Bridgestone for $2.6 billion. Many of the most active buyers have been foreign companies, which now own about 30% of the American chemical industry. The industry emerged from this turmoil stronger than ever before. Profits surged from $9.8 billion in 1985 to $24.8 billion in 1989. But a sluggish economy has reduced the demand for chemicals, and shipments are expected to grow only 1% in 1991.

Table C-1   25 Largest Chemical Producers

Company	Chemical sales In millions of $	% change from 1988	As a % of total sales	Chem. oper. profits (mil.$)	Oper- ating profit margin (%)	Oper. return on chem. assets (%)
1. Du Pont	15,249	3.6	42.9	2,769	18.2	22.1
2. Dow Chemical	14,179	4.0	80.6	3,543	25.0	29.0
3. Exxon	10,559	5.7	11.1	1,609	15.2	22.6
4. Union Carbide	7,962	4.7	91.1	1,225	15.4	19.8
5. Monsanto	5,782	4.5	66.6	929	16.1	20.7
6. Hoechst Celanese	5,658	5.4	94.0	576	10.2	NA
7. Occidental Petrol.	5,203	11.3	25.9	1,235	23.7	22.4
8. General Electric	4,929	39.0	9.0	1,057	21.0	13.0
9. BASF	4,461	6.0	82.3	NA	NA	NA
10. Amoco	4,274	(1.8)	17.8	744	17.4	23.6
11. Mobil	4,039	(5.6)	7.3	774	19.2	28.6
12. Shell Oil	3,833	(4.3)	16.2	941	24.5	24.6
13. Eastman Kodak	3,522	16.1	19.1	643	18.3	19.9
14. Chevron	3,328	3.9	10.4	532	16.0	21.5
15. W.R. Grace	3,256	4.0	53.2	406	12.5	16.7
16. Allied-Signal	2,993	(1.3)	25.1	355	11.9	18.9
17. Arco Chemical	2,663	(1.4)	100.0	580	21.8	21.8
18. Rohm & Haas	2,661	5.0	100.0	287	10.8	13.5
19. Air Products	2,481	10.9	93.9	425	17.1	15.0
20. Phillips Petroleum	2,449	(2.7)	19.8	652	26.6	47.3
21. Bayer USA	2,300	7.5	42.4	127	5.5	NA
22. American Cyanamid	2,241	3.4	46.4	236	10.5	13.2
23. Ashland Oil	2,230	6.7	26.3	98	4.4	13.2
24. Quantum Chemical	2,015	(9.2)	75.4	423	21.0	23.0
25. B.F. Goodrich	1,977	(4.7)	81.7	261	13.2	17.8

Source: *Chemical and Engineering News.*

E. I. du Pont de Nemours and Company

Chairman and CEO: E. S. Woolard, Jr.

Employees: 144,900

Assets: $38.1 billion

1007 Market Street

Wilmington, Delaware 19898

302-774-1000

	1990	1989	1985	1980
Revenues (millions of dollars):	39,709	35,099	29,403	13,652
Net income (millions of dollars):	2,310	2,480	1,118	716
Share earnings (dollars):	3.04	3.53	1.54	1.61

What it does: Du Pont runs about 90 major businesses in 50 countries and earns about one third of its revenues outside the United States. The nation's largest chemical producer, it gets about 40% of its revenues from chemicals. It also produces biomedical products, manufactures industrial and consumer products, and owns large reserves of oil, coal, and natural gas.

With a family fortune of over $8.6 billion, the du Ponts are the wealthiest and most powerful dynasty in the United States. Holding over 15% of E. I. du Pont de Nemours and Company, they are the only family to control one of the 10 largest industrial corporations. But since 1970, no family member has run the company.

Founder and French immigrant Irénée du Pont set up a gunpowder firm in the first decade of the 19th century. Thanks to government contracts and the War of 1812, business boomed. Later, the firm continued to grow because the French-trained owners made high-quality gunpowder. The du Ponts were also pioneers in setting up monopolies and controlling markets. After the Civil War they founded the Gunpowder Trade Association (later called the Gunpowder Trust) that dictated prices and kept profits high.

But with wars being scarce in the late 19th century, the family considered selling the business. But Alfred I. du Pont, T. Coleman du Pont, and Pierre S. du Pont of the family's Kentucky branch bought out the firm in 1902 for just over $12 million. By 1907, the company had already earned $47 million. But even though he kept the business in family hands, Alfred I. du Pont was forced out by T. Coleman and Pierre in 1915. Pierre, who bought out T. Coleman in 1914, then brought in his brothers, Irénée and Lammot, to run the company with him.

Early in the 20th century the company also absorbed the members of the Gunpowder Trust, becoming the nation's largest munitions manufacturer. During the First World War du Pont did a $1 billion business, producing 40% of the explosives fired by the Allies.

Armed with its wartime profits, the company made its first acquisitions outside munitions, buying a controlling interest in the ailing General Motors Corporation. With the Germans driven out of the chemical industry by the war, the du Ponts also moved into the chemical industry by buying up small, innovative companies. Since then such peacetime products as polyester, nylons, rayon, and cellophane have poured forth from du Pont almost nonstop.

Antitrust actions finally forced the family to sell its General Motors stock in the 1960s, and in 1971 the family tradition of running du Pont ended after 170 years. Of the 1,700 family members, only three were working for the company in the late 1970s even though the family controls 20% of the stock. One family member, Pete du Pont, a former Delaware governor, ran for president in 1988 as a Republican. Two others, Lammot du Pont Copeland, Jr., and Henry E. I. du Pont, managed to go bankrupt in the 1970s. However, the future of the family fortune remains brighter than that of many dynasties. The du Ponts have maintained control over their chemical company, a major feat considering the fact that many family members hardly know each other.

Meanwhile, the company has struggled with the difficulties of the chemical industry. Net income was only $1.1 billion in 1985, down from $1.4 billion in 1981. A weak market for chemical products and a strong dollar hurt its overseas sales, so du Pont trimmed its work force more than 20% to 141,000, streamlined operations, and improved productivity. The company also went on an acquisition binge, spending $6.8 billion to acquire Conoco, Inc., a major oil company. These measures paid off in the late 1980s, as net income hit a record $2.5 billion in 1989. Like other chemical companies, however, du Pont was hurt by a slowdown in the manufacturing sector in 1990. Faced with weakening demand, the company announced that it would reduce costs by $100 million.

W. R. Grace & Co.

CEO: J. Peter Grace
Employees: 116,900
Assets: $2.2 billion

1114 Avenue of the Americas
New York, New York 10036-7794
212-819-5500

	1990	1989	1985	1980
Revenues (millions of dollars):	6,754	6,115	5,193	6,101
Net income (millions of dollars):	202.8	257	128	284
Share earnings (dollars):	2.36	3.01	1.23	3.04

What it does: It is a leading producer of specialty chemicals, it distributes books, it makes specialty textiles, and it has interests in natural resources.

This is a company that turned bird droppings into a $6.7 billion business.

William Grace fled Ireland and built up the Grace shipping line from nothing by hauling guano, a fertilizer made chiefly of bird droppings. He also started a family tradition of using money to get political power. In 1880, he became New York's first Catholic mayor.

The company's current head, J. Peter Grace, is the third generation to run the business. When he took over the business, the company had huge holdings in agriculture, banking, and airlines in Latin America. But by 1977 the company was out of the shipping business. Believing Latin America was politically unstable, Grace sold off the company's operations there: in 1950 the company earned 66% of its sales from Latin America; by 1974, it was out of the continent.

Along the way, J. Peter Grace increased sales from $200 million to $6.1 billion in 1980 and created a huge, wobbling conglomerate. Grace has been driven by an urge to acquire, though there seems to be no rhyme or reason to his purchases. By the mid-1980s, the company operated restaurants in 35 states, owned 695 retail stores in 41 states, sold sporting goods through its Herman's Sporting Goods Retail Group, provided artificial insemination services for cows, and had holdings in oil and gas, laboratory equipment, and of course chemicals, which provide about 44% of its revenues.

Meanwhile, Grace continued the family tradition of being an expert on waste—government spending, not guano. As head of President Reagan's panel on government waste, Grace argued that there were exactly 2,478 things that could be done to save exactly $424.4 billion in government spending. Too bad all of politics isn't that precise. But no matter, Grace took his cause on the road, speaking around the country.

But while Grace claims his proposals will save the economy from being saddled with a huge government debt, Grace's critics complain that he should spend more time worrying about his company's profits. Earnings have been weak and in 1985 the largest Grace shareholder, the Flick Group of West Germany, decided to sell its 26% stake. Grace only owns 1% of the company's stock, and to fight off the prospect of an outside takeover he was forced to sell off the company's retail, restaurant, and agricultural chemicals divisions in the late 1980s.

That will leave the company back where it started—in the chemical business, where weak industry growth means cost cutting and streamlining. But profits have jumped from $128 million in 1985 to $202 million in 1990, and the company is now more focused on its core operations.

Then there's the problem of finding a successor to Grace. He has held the top job since 1945, longer than any other chief executive at a major company. Already he's outlasted one generation of successors. Only one of his children works for the company and is not considered likely to take over the business.

FORMICA

Formica is an example of how something takes on many uses. In 1913, Herbert A. Faber and Daniel J. O'Conor found a way to laminate insulation material for the electrical industry. They got an order to make commutator rings, replacing the mica with laminate—hence "for mica," or the Formica Company, as they called their Cincinnati-based firm.

In 1914, the young men decided to make sheet laminates. At first they had a tough time finding a supplier of resin, the key component, but eventually they did. Their first sheets of Formica laminate rolled off the press on July 4. Orders came for many uses: as parts for radios, refrigerators, and washers, and for use in the textile industry.

It wasn't until 24 years later, when a new melamine resin entered the process, that it became possible to make the tough, durable laminate in use today. Decorative laminate became the company's major product. One of the penalties of success was the company's fight in court in 1978 to retain registration of the Formica trademark against charges that the name was so popular it had become the generic name for all decorative plastic laminate.

VASELINE

When in his 50s, Robert A. Chesebrough, a chemist and entrepreneur, was gravely ill with pleurisy. He promptly ordered a nurse to rub him down with Vaseline and he lived another 40 years or so. Chesebrough's faith in the product had a lot to do with the fact that he was the first person to package and promote Vaseline as a healing balm. As a young chemist, he visited oil fields and was intrigued by the paraffinlike residue called rod wax found on oil pump rods. He was told the stuff was great for putting on cuts and burns. Chesebrough distilled it and found out it did have healing properties. By 1870, he was producing quantities of what he called Vaseline Petroleum Jelly. In 1881, Standard Oil, the source of his supplies, bought the company. When the Standard Oil Trust was dissolved in 1911, Chesebrough once again had an independent company. Only in 1955 did the company merge with Pond's, a maker of skin cream.

CLUBS

Private clubs may have an old-boy image as the exclusive preserves of the elite, but it was health, not snobbery, that brought more Americans—14 million—to clubs than ever before.

The nation's 10,000 private clubs currently employ nearly 1.5 million people, with an annual payroll of $4 billion. No exact figures for industry revenues are available, but the 4,000 clubs that belong to the Club Managers Association of America (CMAA) produce about $5.3 billion a year in revenues. Surprisingly, $2.76 billion in revenues from food and beverage sales outpaced the $2.57 billion the 4,000 CMAA members took in from dues.

The cost of maintaining a country club lifestyle is going up all the time. Managing a golf course alone costs an average of $20,000 a hole, up from under $4,000 a hole in 1965.

Soaring costs are changing the country club industry. Older, exclusive clubs are in a financial bind, forcing them to either raise their rates or cut back on services. That has produced a market characterized by very expensive clubs that offer a full range of sports (tennis, swimming, and golf); some country clubs that specialize in one sport, such as golf; and superclubs, which offer just about anything. One of the first superclubs was the $44 million Sweetwater Country Club, opened in 1983 outside Houston. For $15,000 a year, it offers 27 holes of golf, pools, locker rooms, weight rooms, a basketball court, tennis courts, sports shops, a spa, card rooms, racquetball courts, a ballroom, and a vast terrain of lakes, fairways, and oak trees. Since then other clubs have spent as much as $70 million on such amenities.

COAL

THE MARKET

When you hear about the energy crisis, nobody's talking about coal.

At the current rate of production (1,035 million tons in 1991), the U.S. has enough coal to last 250 years. And that's after 200 years of mining 50 billion tons of coal.

Coal accounts for about 23% of the energy Americans use. Primary consumers are the electric utilities (808.0 million tons in 1990), coke plants (39.0 million tons), other industrial and transportation companies (80.0 million tons).

Coal is also used in coke plants as part of the production of steel, and for combustion and as a feedstock in the chemical industry, in the stone, clay, and glass industry, and in the paper and allied products industry. Another $4.3 billion of coal was exported in 1990.

THE MONEY

OPEC, the oil embargoes of the 1970s, and the fall of the Shah of Iran were a boon for the coal industry. While consumers faced mounting energy bills, coal producers shipped $22.5 billion worth of coal in 1982, up from only $4.6 billion in 1972.

But slumping oil prices and a rusty market for steel have put a damper on coal shipments. Shipments hit only $21.7 billion in 1990. Part of the problem has been slumping coal prices. The cost of coal rose rapidly during the 1970s from $5 a ton in 1970 to $27 a ton in 1982, as oil prices skyrocketed. Since then the price of coal has followed oil back down, hitting $21 a ton in 1990.

Table C-2   The Largest Coal Producers
Top ten U.S. coal producers in 1989, in millions of tons.

Producer	Millions of tons
Peabody Holding	86.7
Consolidated Coal	53.5
AMAX Coal	38.4
ARCO Coal	31.1
Texas Utilities Mining	29.9
Exxon Coal and Minerals	28.1
Shell Mining	25.5
NERCO	24.5
Sun Coal	22.8
North American Coal	22.5

Source: National Coal Association.

THE PEOPLE

The growing demand for coal has not translated into increased employment. Technological advances and mechanization decreased the number of coal miners from 246,000 in 1978 to only 163,000 today.

TRENDS AND FORECAST

But prices for coal stagnated when oil prices slumped. Demand for coal has been growing 2% a year, faster than oil or gas, and domestic coal production should top 1 billion tons in 1990, a record. The Persian Gulf crisis briefly helped the coal industry, just as the energy crisis did during the 1970s and early 1980s. But oil prices soon fell, leaving coal producers with a number of problems. One key issue is environmental legislation aimed at cutting pollutants that cause acid rain. The U.S. government has committed $1.3 billion to 38 clean-coal projects designed to cut pollution from electric power plants that run on coal and should spend another $2.5 billion by 1992. But private coal users will still be forced to spend billions more, and many may decide to cut their consumption of coal. Moreover, the steel industry should continue to reduce its demand for coal, and a recession in 1991 will cut demand from utilities and the manufacturing sector.

Table C-3   Estimated International Recoverable Reserves of Coal
(billions of short tons)

United States/226	
U.S.S.R./172	
Germany/62	
S. Africa/58	
Aus./40	
Pol./33	
All Others/73	

25   50   75   100   125   150   175   200   225

Source: World Energy Conference, Survey of Energy Resources.

COMPUTERS

THE MARKET AND THE MONEY

In recent years, while computers got faster, computer sales slowed down. After double-digit growth in the early 1980s, sales of computer equipment first slowed in the mid-1980s. They recovered in 1988 with a 16% spurt, but slowed to 6% in 1989 and 4.2% in 1990. In 1991 sales will grow about 6.1% to $66.3 billion. Meanwhile, semiconductor manufacturers will have $23.7 billion in shipments in 1991, up from $22 billion in 1990.

The slowdown was particularly painful for an industry with such high expectations. Personal computers were going to remake the whole world. And there were numbers to support the hype: Retail sales of personal computers, for example, skyrocketed 60% to 70% between 1982 and 1984. Overall, factory shipments of U.S. computer equipment tripled from $6.1 billion to $20.4 billion in 1980 and then more than doubled again by 1984, hitting $49.2 billion. Along the way, manufacturers added a lot of infrastructure in hopes of duplicating growth rates that were only possible when the business was just starting out.

In many ways the slump was inevitable. Corporations were on a cost-cutting binge for several years and, by the mid-1980s, budgets for computers, data processing, and information were large enough to attract the attention of fat cutters. Many companies decided they could get along just fine with what they already had; other consumers sat on the sidelines, waiting for the dizzying advance of technology and the release of new models to slow down. A slowdown in defense orders also hurt. But not all sectors of the computer industry have fared so poorly. Worldwide shipments of software—the programs that allow computers to run—grew 20% to $29 billion in 1990 and will top $35 billion in 1991. Companies providing computer consulting and computer services also continued to boom. Their revenues hit $44.5 billion in 1990, up 18% from 1989. Here's how the computer market breaks down:

Supercomputers

These machines are the biggest and fastest on the market—capable of doing billions of operations per second. For that supercomputing speed, companies also pay a superprice, over $5 million per system The world market jumped 10% to $150.9 billion in 1990.

Mainframes

These huge systems got their name because the cabinet holding the processor and memory is the most expensive part of the system. In recent years mainframes, which sell for over $1 million, have faced increased competition from smaller, increasingly powerful computers. As a result, they only hold about 19% of the computer market, down from 36% five years ago. Sales, accordingly, have remained stagnant: $20.9 billion in 1989. Sales are expected to grow only 12% between 1990 and 1993, to about $23.5 billion. IBM remains the largest producer of mainframes, with 71% of the market. U.S. producers will sell about $13.4 billion worth of mainframes in 1991.

Medium-scale Computers or Minicomputers

These machines, which sell for $15,000 to $1 million, have in recent years become faster, smaller, and more powerful than ever before. Despite predictions that they would be squeezed out by increasingly less expensive and more powerful computers on the top end of the market and increasingly powerful personal computers (known as supermicrocomputers) on the low end of the market, about $17.4 billion worth of midrange computers were sold in 1987. Two big firms, IBM and Digital Equipment Corporation, account for about 40% of all sales.

Microsystems or Personal Computers

These small computers, which sell for as little as $100 and as much as $15,000, revolutionized the computer market. Thanks to PCs, computers are no longer huge machines that take up whole floors of specially designed, air-conditioned buildings. The total PC market in the U.S. topped $31.8 billion in 1990, up 14% from 1989, and should hit $50 billion by 1995. One rapidly growing segment of the small computer market is portable computers, sales of which hit $5.4 billion in 1990, up 30% from 1988. U.S. companies hold about 28% of the portable market and about 43% of the PC market. Sales should hit $8 billion in 1991.

Printers

The computer age hasn't done away with the need to produce paper. Americans bought $11 billion worth of printers in 1990, up 7% from 1989, and sales will hit $12 billion in 1991, according to BIS CAP International. BIS CAP estimates that $13.1 billion worth of printers will be sold in 1993.

Software

Software is the computer program, the language or instructions that tells the equipment (the hardware) what to do. Since many people still don't understand how to get the most out of their computer hardware, it's not surprising that software has been the fastest-growing part of the computer industry. U.S. sales jumped 20% to $29 billion in 1990, and the worldwide market hit $43 billion. That growth has produced one software billionaire, William Gates, the cofounder of Microsoft. (See the profile below.)

Semiconductors

A slump in computer equipment sales and tough foreign competition continue to hurt U.S. makers of computer chips. The Japanese now have 70% of the world market. But the value of factory shipments by U.S. manufacturers of semiconductors and related devices increased from $17.9 billion in 1987 to $22 billion in 1990. Sales are expected to grow to $23.7 billion in 1991.

Computer Professional Services

Considering the difficulty many people have with computers, it's no surprise that computer services are one of the fastest-growing sectors of the industry. Revenues for computer service companies jumped 19% to $37.8 billion in

1989, and rose another 17.6% in 1990 to $44.5 billion. Revenues are expected to grow 17% a year through 1993, when sales should hit $72.5 billion.

Workstations

Workstations are high-performance computers with advanced graphic capabilities that are used by scientists, engineers, graphic artists, and others. About 500,000 workstations were sold in 1990 for total sales of $8.5 billion, up 37% from 1989. Sales by U.S. manufacturers should grow another 30% in 1991 to $11 billion, and the world market should top $30 billion by 1995.

THE PLAYERS

Tables C-4 to C-6 (below) list some of the largest data processing companies, software producers, and personal computer makers.

Table C-4 The Largest Computer and Computer Equipment Companies

Rank	Company	Revenues	Net Income
1.	IBM	69,018	6,020
2.	Hewlett-Packard	13,233	739
3.	Digital Equipment	13,085	74
4.	Unisys	10,111	−437
5.	NCR	6,395	369
6.	Apple Computer	5,558	475
7.	Compaq Computer	3,626	455
8.	Pitney Bowes	3,267	213
9.	Wang Laboratories	2,635	−716
10.	Sun Microsystems	2,481	111

Source: Company reports.

Table C-5 The Most Popular Software Programs

	Brand	Co. Name Location	Total Sales (millions)
1	Windows/Word	Microsoft Corp. Redmond, Wash.	$803.5
2	Lotus 1-2-3	Lotus Corp. Cambridge, Mass.	$556
3	WordPerfect	WordPerfect Corp. Orem, Utah	$281
4	dBASE	Ashton-Tate Corp. Torrance, Calif.	$265.3
5	PageMaker	Aldus Corp. Seattle	$87.9

Source: *Adweek.*

Table C-6 The Largest Personal Computer Companies

Rank	Company	Sales in billions of dollars
1.	IBM	7.32
2.	Apple	3.03
3.	COMPAQ	2.64
4.	Zenith	1.60
5.	Hewlett-Packard	1.80
6.	Commodore	1.25
7.	Others, primarily clone makers	15.95

Source: International Data Corp.

Table C-7 Top 10 Worldwide Semiconductor Manufacturers

Rank	Company	Semiconductor sales (millions of dollars)		
		ICs	Discrete	Total
1.	NEC Corp.	4,165	660	4,825
2.	Toshiba	3,595	1,085	4,680
3.	Hitachi Ltd.	3,300	475	3,775
4.	Motorola Inc.	2,400	800	3,200
5.	Texas Instruments	2,860	40	2,900
6.	Mitsubishi	2,280	310	2,590
7.	Fujitsu	2,470	20	2,490
8.	Intel Corp.	2,400	0	2,400
9.	Matsushita	1,530	520	2,050
10.	Philips N.V.	1,205	475	1,680

Source: Integrated Circuit Engineering Corp.

THE PEOPLE

The computer revolution was supposed to do more than just put a computer in every home—it was also supposed to put food on the table, replacing jobs in declining smokestack industries. So far that promise has been largely unfulfilled. Total employment in the semiconductor industry dropped from 192,000 in 1984 to 166,000 in 1991. The number of people employed in the computer equipment industry tumbled from 374,000 in 1984 to only 270,000 in 1991.

Ironically, overseas production, one of the big reasons behind the slump in employment, is increasing sales and bringing the dream of a low-priced computer in every office closer to reality. Many of these clones are produced in Asia with cheaper labor. To compete, American manufacturers have moved manufacturing operations overseas, which has lowered costs and increased sales but also cut employment.

International Business Machines Corporation

Chairman and CEO: John F. Akers

Employees: 378,500

Assets: $87.6 billion

Old Orchard Road
Armonk, New York 10504
914-765-1900

	1990	1989	1985	1980
Revenues (millions of dollars):	69,018	62,710	50,056	26,213
Net income (millions of dollars):	6,020	3,758	6,555	3,562
Share earnings (dollars):	10.51	6.47	10.67	6.10

What it does: The 4th-largest industrial company in the United States, the largest electronics company in the United States, the world's largest computer maker. This company makes personal computers, telecommunications equipment, and mainframes, in which it holds about 70% of the market.

Unlike most creators of high-tech companies, the man behind the rise of International Business Machines (IBM) was a salesman, not a techie or an engineer. Thomas Watson was hired in 1914 to run the Computing-Tabulating-Recording Company, the producer of the electrical punch-card computing system developed for the 1890 census. Watson, who arrived with a reputation as a supersalesman, revamped the company (which changed its name to IBM in 1924) with daily pep talks to his salesmen, songs like "Hail to IBM," and a rigorous dress code—dark suits and white shirts.

The emphasis on sales set the pattern for IBM's growth. It dominated the market for time clocks and punch-card tabulators in the 1920s and the electric typewriter market in the 1930s and 1940s. Never known for its technical innovation, the company made its push into computers after others had already started, but it quickly bowled over the competition with an expert sales force that carefully tailored its products to consumer needs and with adept marketing. By the late 1960s the company held 80% of the world market.

The decade between 1975 and 1985 saw revenues more than triple; profits soared from $1.9 billion to $4.7 billion. Though competitors introduced the first minicomputer and personal computer, IBM came roaring back into the personal computer market as soon as it was apparent there was money to be made, capturing over half the market.

But problems loom. Smaller companies such as Digital Equipment Corporation cut into the market for large mainframes by convincing customers they could get along with minicomputers. Cheaper and often more sophisticated PCs, on the other end of the market, cut IBM's PC sales. And, as computer buyers increasingly wanted computer systems that would allow them to link together—network—their mainframes, midrange computers and even PC's into one system, IBM's various computers became less, not more compatible with each other.

These troubles hit home in a big way in the late 1980s. Profits slumped from $6.6 billion in 1984 to $3.8 billion in 1989. To compete with smaller, nimbler competitors, IBM has streamlined management and announced a raft of new products. It spent billions revamping its plants, cut product development time, and slashed costs. So far, however, management has not produced a dramatic turnaround. In the early 1990s, IBM was still dangerously dependent on the stagnant mainframe market, and a recession was hurting sales.

Digital Equipment Corporation

President and CEO: K. H. Olsen

Employees: 124,900

Assets: $11.6 billion

146 Main Street

Maynard, Massachusetts 01754-2571

617-897-5111

	1990	1989	1985	1980
Revenues (millions of dollars):	13,085	12,742	6,686	2,368
Net income (millions of dollars):	74	1,073	447	160
Share earnings (dollars):	0.59	8.45	3.71	2.73

What it does: A major designer and maker of computers, related equipment, and software supplies.

The news only three years ago at Digital Equipment Corporation (DEC) was phenomenal. Sales in 1987 grew 23% to over $9.3 billion. And that was just an average year: over the last 20 years, Ken Olsen's computer company has been growing at an annual rate of 20% to 30% a year. But no one was crying at DEC. Thanks to that success, DEC has emerged with the reputation as the only computer company to ever successfully challenge IBM.

The key to DEC's success is Olsen's emphasis on new products. While 40% of IBM's products are less than two years old, 85% of DEC's are. By creating the minicomputer, DEC played a major role in reducing the size of mainframes and laying the groundwork for the personal computer revolution.

Olsen grew up in a religious Connecticut family, whose fundamentalist values he keeps as a regular churchgoer and fund-raiser. In high school he acquired a reputation for technical wizardry by repairing radios. In the late 1940s at MIT, he worked on the university's first computer—which was nicknamed "the expensive typewriter."

When IBM won the contract to produce MIT's SAGE computer, Olsen was assigned to the liaison team. He hated Big Blue's regimented corporate bureaucracy, but it wasn't until 1957 that he carried out his vow that he could do better than IBM. He founded DEC with the idea of producing a minicomputer.

Reducing the size of computers and making them more accessible to many businesses was a profitable idea. Revenues hit $10 million by 1964 and $12.7 billion in 1989. But one of the great high-tech success stories of the 1970s and 1980s faces some difficult problems in the 1990s. DEC recorded its first-ever loss in 1990, and its stock slid from a high of $189 in September of 1987 to only $76 a share in July of 1990. The reason: sagging demand for mini-computers and a shift to cheaper hardware.

So the first company to battle IBM successfully now had something in common with its chief rival—slumping profits. To recapture its momentum, DEC has shaken up its management structure, creating 18 separate organizations, each responsible for marketing to a specific industry. Olsen brought in John and Peter Smith (who are not related) to shake up DEC's corporate bureaucracy, and the company announced plans to reduce employment by about 9,000. The Smiths pushed the company into new markets, introducing workstations and PCs, and trying to convince customers that its profitable VAX minicomputers can be used to connect workstations and PCs. Meanwhile, the company introduced its new minicomputer, VAX 9000, which should help profits in the short term.

But the basic problem still remains. As customers turn to workstations and PCs rather than minicomputers, which have always been DEC's bread and butter, the minicomputer market is expected to grow only about 3% a year, down from the double-digit growth of the mid-1980s.

Apple Computer, Inc.

Chairman and CEO: John Sculley   20525 Mariani Avenue
Employees: 14,500   Cupertino, California 95014
Assets: $3.2 billion   408-996-1010

	1990	1989	1985	1980
Revenues (millions of dollars):	5,558	5,284	1,918	117
Net income (millions of dollars):	475	454	61	12
Share earnings (dollars):	3.77	3.53	0.50	0.35

What it does: A leading maker of personal computers. Its Apple II's are sold mainly to schools and homes. Its Macintosh is aimed at the office market.

When John Sculley wrested control of Apple Computer, Inc., in 1985 from cofounder Steven P. Jobs, he must have thought he had just stuck his head in a blender. A slowdown in economic growth saw a slowdown in businesses buying big computers. There were 400 or so companies making or marketing personal computers, which seemed like 399 too many. Consumers were confused and starting to wonder whether they needed computers after all. The result was a slump that hit just about everyone and Apple worse than most.

Sculley put Apple through the wringer. He reorganized the company, including laying off about 20% of the work force and shutting down domestic and overseas operations. The Lisa computer, which never caught on, was abandoned. He beefed up the Macintosh for business use and succeeded in getting software companies to write better business software packages for the machine. He also effectively got rid of Apple cofounders Steve Jobs and Steve Wozniak.

What Sculley probably did best was sell the Mac door to door. The former president of PepsiCo had made his mark in marketing. Thus, when the company verged on introducing the new enhanced Macintosh computer, he marched into the headquarters of corporations such as General Electric and du Pont to huckster the machine personally. One of his selling points was that the PC was easy to use. The upshot was that Apple's profits shot up from $61 million in 1985 to $475 million in 1990. Apple was back in business in a big way.

Ironically, what Sculley did was prove that Jobs was on the right track. Jobs had marketed the Apple, the Apple II Plus, and the Macintosh as easy-to-use alternatives to IBM PCs and their clones. With his friend Wozniak, Jobs founded Apple in 1975 with the capital he got from selling his Volkswagen microbus. He managed to turn that into a $300 million fortune.

Jobs was one of the first people to realize the microprocessor's potential for putting low-cost computing power into the hands of individuals. Unlike other computer pioneers, Jobs thought consumers would find personal computers more appealing if sold in a "user-friendly" consumer package instead of an industrial-style steel box.

Thus, he humanized his computers. The packaging plus the name Apple set Jobs's first computer apart from the cold, impersonal world usually associated with the computer industry. The strategy worked. Besides selling his Apple to a much wider audience than techies, Jobs kept coming up with add-ons for the Apple. Soon hosts of people adapted his PC to thousands of different uses.

Stories about Jobs's own interests also set him apart from the mainstream of corporate America. He dabbled with such esoterica as meditation, vegetarianism, and communal and primal therapy. But Jobs wasn't either much of a businessman or much of an administrator. Production schedules ran way behind and a couple of major products flopped, such as the Lisa and the Apple III, which were designed to attract business users. Eventually, he brought Sculley into the operation. In time, the top officers were at each others' throats over what the company needed. Cofounder Wozniak left the company in disgust and Jobs was kicked upstairs and then left. The most obvious reason for Sculley's winning the day was that, in 1985, Apple posted its first loss.

Jobs, however, hasn't left the computer business. He got a group of investors, including H. Ross Perot, to finance a new computer company, Next, Inc., and its innovative computer hit the stores in 1989. Sculley, meanwhile, faces new challenges at Apple. The good news is that Apple finally introduced some badly needed lower-priced computers in 1990. The bad news is that Apple will have to learn how to make money on lower-priced machines, which have tight margins. Making the corporate change from its successful, higher-priced, high-margin Macintosh should keep Sculley very busy.

Microsoft Corporation

Chairman and CEO: William H. Gates   One Microsoft Way
Employees: 2,000   Redmond, Washington 98052-6399
Assets: NA   206-882-8080

	1990	1989	1985	1982
Revenues (millions of dollars):	1,183	804	140	24
Net income (millions of dollars):	279	171	24	3
Share earnings (dollars):	2.34	3.03	0.26	0.05

What it does: Develops and markets systems and applications for microsoftware. Its MS-DOS operating system is used by IBM and IBM-compatible microprocessors. A new operating system, OS/2, is for IBM's newest PCs.

When the computer industry shook out the technical wizards who lacked the savvy to run the companies they founded, William H. Gates III stood apart. The chairman of Microsoft Corporation, one of the biggest software companies in the business, not only remained in control but took the company to ever-new heights. In 1990, only 34, he headed the nation's most successful software company and had built up a personal fortune of over $2.5 billion.

One of Gates's biggest successes came in 1987 when he convinced a reluctant International Business Machines, already a star customer, to use a newly developed piece of software called Windows in its personal computers. With IBM as a customer, Windows became the nation's most popular software in the early 1990s.

With his big glasses and messy, mousy hair, the boyish-looking Gates was a stereotype of the computer nerd who launched a company when he was only 19 years old. In 1975, he dropped out of Harvard and teamed up with another computer junkie, Paul Allen, whose stake in the company was worth about $1.2 billion in 1990. They cofounded Microsoft to sell a version of the BASIC computer language they had written while in high school in Seattle.

The third person involved in Microsoft's rise, Kazuhiko Nishi, was another young computer junkie. Fast-talking, excitable, and flamboyant, he learned everything he could about computers and started a newsletter about them after dropping out of Tokyo's prestigious Waseda University. In 1978, Nishi flew to the U.S. to talk to Gates about becoming Microsoft's Far East agent. They struck a partnership arrangement. At the time, Microsoft sold software that let people write programs for personal computers. Both Nishi and Gates wanted to help companies design PCs and supply their software.

When he returned to Japan, the brash Nishi persuaded a manager at the big NEC Corporation to meet Gates and Allen. The result was NEC's gambling on letting Nishi and his American friends play a major role in the design of a new PC. The resultant P8100 was a success and helped make PCs hot in Japan. Also, Gates and Nishi soon became famous in Japan by giving dozens of press interviews on the future of technology. Microsoft benefited by Japanese companies' buying software and design services.

The deals Nishi struck grew bigger. For instance, an accidental meeting with the president of Kyocera Corporation, a major industrial ceramics firm, resulted in the company's backing a laptop computer, which Nishi had thought up. Gates and Nishi made the machine and lined up distributors on three continents. Their biggest coup came in 1980 when IBM chose Microsoft MS-DOS operating system software for a prototype PC. The IBM contract was worth gold, immediately making Microsoft one of the most important companies in the software business.

As Microsoft became more successful, relations between Gates and Nishi deteriorated. Gates put more organizational structures in place, including the use of seasoned managers. Those managers couldn't stand Nishi's cowboy way of doing business. His unorthodox approach was what was needed for a little company out to make its mark, but it proved expensive and wasteful for a big company. Eventually, Gates and Nishi's partnership dissolved.

CONSTRUCTION

THE MARKET AND THE MONEY

The real estate market is in a depression, taking a number of banks with it. But $445 billion worth of new construction was put up in 1990 and the International Trade Administration says the industry should grow 1% a year through 1994. That would appear to be a dramatic improvement over 1982 when $247 billion was spent and 1977 when $188 billion was spent on new construction.

Unfortunately, a lot of that growth can be accounted for by inflation. If we adjust for inflation and express the value of new construction in constant 1987 dollars, about $383 billion was spent on new construction in 1991, down from $394 billion in 1990 and $411.6 billion in 1986, the peak year of the real estate boom.

Overall, new construction in 1990 equaled 8.1% of the GNP, up from 7.7% in 1982 but well below the postwar peak of 11.9% in 1966.

Table C-8 (below) shows how, adjusted for inflation and expressed in 1987 dollars, the country spends its construction dollars.

THE PLAYERS

The construction industry remains one of the few major industries that is dominated by small businesses. Only about 5% of all construction firms have receipts of more than $2.5 million a year and there are more than 1.4 million self-employed workers in the construction industry, indicating that there were many small proprietors or working partners. The typical U.S. construction firm has only nine employees and annual receipts of $688,077.

In contrast, the nation's largest construction firms, such as Bechtel, are multinationals that do a large proportion of their business overseas. Overall, the top 250 international contractors did $94 billion worth of business outside the U.S. in 1989, with U.S. contractors capturing about 28%. That represents a big drop from 1980 when the 250 largest firms did $108.9 billion worth of business and U.S. companies captured 41% of those revenues.

Table C-8   Value of New Construction Put in Place, 1986–1991
(in billions of 1987 dollars except as noted)

Type of construction	1986	1987	1988	1989	1990[1]	1991[2]
Total New Construction	411.6	410.2	405.2	399.9	394.8	383.3
Residential	195.4	194.6	190.3	182.0	172.9	167.7
Single-family	106.6	114.4	112.0	108.3	99.6	94.7
Multifamily	32.4	25.5	21.4	20.7	18.0	16.2
Home Improvement	56.3	54.7	56.8	53.1	55.2	569
Private Nonresidential	130.5	124.9	124.1	126.7	124.9	118.5
Manufacturing facilities	14.3	13.7	14.4	17.2	18.9	19.3
Office	29.7	26.9	27.0	26.6	23.4	19.9
Hotels & motels	7.7	7.4	6.5	7.1	7.5	6.0
Other commercial	29.3	29.0	28.9	28.6	27.2	24.5
Religious	2.8	2.8	2.7	2.8	2.8	2.9
Educational	2.4	3.4	2.8	3.1	3.3	3.4
Hospital & institutional	5.6	6.0	7.0	7.0	7.4	7.7
Misc. buildings	2.9	3.2	4.2	3.7	3.6	3.6
Telecommunications	9.2	9.2	9.7	8.2	8.5	8.5
Railroads	2.9	2.5	2.7	2.5	2.4	2.2
Electric utilities	15.6	12.7	10.2	10.6	10.6	10.8
Gas utilities	3.4	3.2	3.4	4.1	4.2	4.4
Petroleum pipelines	0.3	0.4	0.4	0.3	0.3	0.3
Farm structures	2.1	2.5	2.2	2.2	2.3	2.3
Misc. structures	2.3	2.6	2.1	2.7	2.7	2.7
Public Works	85.7	90.7	90.8	91.4	97.0	97.3
Housing & redevelopment	3.2	3.3	3.2	3.6	3.6	3.6
Federal industrial	1.7	1.5	1.4	1.2	1.3	1.3
Educational	11.4	11.5	13.7	15.5	17.7	18.6
Hospital	2.4	2.6	2.6	2.3	2.5	2.7
Other public buildings	13.7	14.2	13.9	13.8	15.2	15.6
Highways	24.9	27.0	28.4	27.4	27.7	27.1
Military facilities	3.9	4.3	3.4	3.3	3.6	3.3
Conservation & development	5.0	5.5	4.6	4.6	4.7	4.9
Sewer systems	7.8	9.0	8.3	8.5	8.9	8.5
Water supplies	3.2	3.7	3.8	3.7	4.1	4.2
Misc. public structures	8.5	8.1	7.5	7.6	7.7	7.7

[1]Estimate.
[2]Forecast.
Sources: U.S. Department of Commerce; Bureau of the Census and International Trade Administration (ITA). Estimates and forecasts by ITA.

THE PEOPLE

There were some 5.3 million people employed in the construction industry in 1990. About 1.4 million self-employed people worked in the construction industry as proprietors or working partners.

Unions now represent only 17% of all construction workers, down from at least 75% 15 years ago.

HOUSING

There are now about 103 million places to live in the United States. If you want to buy all of them, it will cost you about $6.7 trillion dollars. Or, if you have more modest ambitions, the value of the average single-family house is now $89,300. That's good news if you bought a house in the Great Depression, when the average price was $2,938, and watched the market go up, but bad news if you want to buy one today. The average new American house now sells for $112,500, up from $64,600 in 1980.

Rising prices have made buying that dream house a nightmare for many people. The percentage of housing units that are owner-occupied rose from 44.9% in 1910 to 64.4% in 1980 but is now around 64%. As a result, about 36% of all residences are rented.

The vast majority of Americans (67%) live in what the government describes in unhomey language as "single-unit housing"—meaning homes where only one family lives. Another 12.4% live in housing complexes of two to four units and 16.2% live in apartment buildings of five or more units. Mobile homes house 4.4% of the population.

Table C-9   The Biggest Home Builders Aren't So Big

In the housing industry, big isn't so big. The average U.S. home is built by a contractor that builds fewer than 25 a year, and the nation's largest home builder, Trammell Crow Company, produced only 9,451 housing units in 1990, less than 1% of the 1.81 million housing starts that year. There are more than 93,000 home builders and the 100 largest home builders provided only 15% of the market. Here's how *Builder* magazine ranks the builders:

Rank	Company	1990 Housing Starts	Revenues (millions of dollars)
1.	Trammel Crow Residential	9,451	976
2.	Centex Corp.	7,548	2,289
3.	Ryland Group Inc.	7,506	1,313
4.	William Lyon Companies	6,021	1,185
5.	Boston Capital Partners	6,000	400

Source: *Builder*.

CONSTRUCTION TRIVIA

Cement dates back to the Roman period, when builders mixed ash from volcanoes with lime. The mixture would harden when mixed with water. An Englishman, Joseph Aspdin, invented a better-quality cement in 1824 known as "portland cement" because it looked like rocks from the Isle of Portland when it hardened. Reinforced cement, which revolutionized modern building, dates from 1845, when the Frenchman J. L. Lambot built boats out of it.

The world's tallest office building is the Sears Tower in Chicago. Its 110 stories rise 1,454 feet into the air. Nearly 16,700 people work in the building, which was completed in 1974 and has 16,000 windows. But the Tower's total area is only 4.4 million square feet, only a little more than half the area of the twin towers of the World Trade Center in New York City. The taller of the two World Trade Center towers rises 1,362 feet; both towers together have 8,740,000 square feet, making them *the world's largest office buildings* in terms of rentable space.

The invention of the elevator can be traced to the construction industry. In the 1850s, contractor Elisha Graves Otis, building a bedstead factory in Yonkers, New York, developed a plan for hoisting platforms to move materials and therefore speed construction. He called his invention (later the basis of the Otis Elevator Company) an "elevator."

The largest U.S. hotel is the Hilton Hotel in Las Vegas with 3,174 bedrooms, 125,000 square feet of convention space, and a 10-acre rooftop recreation deck.

The contractor that built most of the largest projects over the years is undoubtedly the Army Corps of Engineers. In 1776, troops under George Washington built two forts on Dorchester Heights, Boston, giving them a commanding position above Boston Harbor. Realizing that similar construction projects might be needed in the future, Washington created the Army Corps of Engineers. Since then it has undertaken some of the world's largest construction jobs, such as flood control projects in the Mississippi River Valley.

The largest private house in the world is the 250-room Biltmore House that was constructed for the Vanderbilts in the 1880s on 119,000 acres of land. The house and 12,000-acre estate, currently owned by Vanderbilt heirs George and William, is valued at $55 million.

The biggest building to be demolished, a kind of reverse construction record, was the 21-story, 600-room Traymore Hotel in Atlantic City in 1972.

COSMETICS, SOAPS, AND CLEANING PREPARATIONS

THE MARKET AND THE MONEY

Keeping America clean and beautiful, at home and at the factory, put about $38.7 billion into the coffers of American companies in 1990, up from $32.2 billion in 1987. More than 20,000 cosmetics and personal hygiene products now crowd the nation's stores.

Soaps and detergent manufacturers, for example, cleaned up with $10.7 billion worth of factory shipments.

The so-called polish and sanitation goods industry—makers of polishes, household bleaches, toilet bowl cleaners, scouring powders, and stuff like Windex—wiped up about $5.8 billion in factory shipments.

Even prettier factory sales come from the cosmetics, fragrance, and toiletries industry: American manufacturers ship about $18.6 billion worth of cosmetics, fragrances, and toiletries. Retail sales were much higher, at least $28 billion.

Unlike most industries, this industry has cleaned up foreign competitors. Imports control only about 2% of the market. Even in the cosmetics and toiletries sector, in which French perfumes have had a long-standing romance with American consumers, only $685 million worth of imports hit the market in 1990.

THE PEOPLE

About 126,000 people are employed in this industry, about the same as in 1984.

The Procter & Gamble Company

Chairman and CEO: E. L. Artzt   1 Procter & Gamble Plaza
Employees: 73,200   Cincinnati, OH 45202
Assets: $20.6 billion   513-983-1100

	1990	1989	1985	1980
Revenues (millions of dollars):	24,081	21,398	13,552	10,772
Net income (millions of dollars):	1,602	1,206	635	640
Share earnings (dollars):	4.49	3.56	3.80	3.87

What it does: Sell a wide variety of soaps, foods, over-the-counter drugs, and toiletries, including Tide, Crest, Ivory soap, peanut butter, mouthwash, Spic and Span cleaner, Crisco shortening, Pampers disposable diapers, Charmin toilet paper, Folger's coffee, Pringle's potato chips, Pepto-Bismol, Vicks, acne products, Head and Shoulders shampoo, drugs, vitamins, Duncan Hines cake mixes, Citrus Hill fruit juices, and Noxzema.

It all started with lard. William Procter and James Gamble used lard to make soap and candles in 1837. They got a big boost from contracts to supply

soap and candles to the Union Army during the Civil War. Another boost
came in 1878 when the company introduced a new kind of white soap called
Ivory. (Later a mistake in its factory produced a batch of soap that floated,
which was an immediate hit with consumers. Soon all Ivory soap was made
according to the new formula.) Crisco shortening, Tide, Duncan Hines,
Charmin, Pampers, and thousands of other products eventually followed.

Massive advertising expenditures ($1.8 billion in 1989), a reputation for
quality backed by years of research (the company's top-selling Tide took 20
years to develop), and a willingness to buy into a market with timely acquisitions made the company the nation's largest supplier of household products.

But in the late 1970s P&G stumbled. Its share of the lucrative disposable
diapers market slipped from 69% in 1978 to only 47% in 1985. The toothpaste wars cut P&G's lead from 19 percentage points in 1979 to only 1.5
points in 1985. The company seemed to have neglected its primary money-
makers, and when it flexed its marketing muscle to fight back, the costs were
astronomical. About $1 billion was spent advertising its two new versions of
Pampers alone. But the costly campaigns helped the company return to the
top of the heap, regaining its lead in toothpaste and disposable diapers.

At the same time, the company made some important acquisitions. It
bought Richardson-Vicks, Inc., for $2 billion, to become almost overnight
one of the nation's largest over-the-counter drug makers, and in 1989 moved
into cosmetics with the acquisition of Noxell Corp. The move into cosmetics
and pharmaceuticals, which are growing faster than P&G's other mature,
slow-growth markets, has helped the company's bottom line. Net income
jumped from $635 million in 1985 to $1.6 billion in 1990.

Revlon, Charles Revson, and Ronald Perelman   Charles Revson founded
Revlon in 1932 with $300 and over the years built it up with a nearly infal-
lible eye for marketing, packaging, and advertising. He even managed to
stand out in an industry known for strong, autocratic entrepreneurs. A
megalomaniac who did everything by instinct rather than research, Revson terrorized his employees, phoning executives at two in the morning
about insignificant details of a new advertising campaign. He lavishly
endowed charities and hospitals and probably spent more on underwear
than most of his employees earned in a year, yet he was known to throw a
fit if he caught an employee discarding pencil stubs. But no matter—for
years the company battled Avon for the top of the cosmetics market.

Things turned ugly after Revson's death in 1975. The new CEO, Michel
Bergerac, gave the company some needed financial controls, but earnings
slid as competitors raced ahead. Estée Lauder took over the top end of
the cosmetics market while low-priced brands such as Maybelline and
Cover Girl took over the lower end of the market. Bergerac's diversification into drugs, medical equipment, and other products never quite
worked out. By 1985 Revlon was number three in the cosmetic industry
and slipping.

That's when, an upstart, Ronald Perelman, entered the scene. Perelman
grew up rich but determined. Armed with an M.B.A. from Wharton and

experience in running his family's metal fabricating business, he started with a $2 million investment in Cohen-Hatfield Industries, a small jewelry distributor, bought MacAndrews & Forbes Group, licorice extract and chocolate maker, and used it as a vehicle for ever larger takeovers: Technicolor, and then Pantry Pride in 1985. Using the profits from selling off Pantry Pride's assets and $700 million in junk bonds, he financed his $1.8 billion takeover of Revlon in late 1985.

Perelman created his empire with a simple strategy: buy undervalued assets with cash and junk bonds, sell off assets to reduce debts, and keep the core businesses as cash cows, producing more income for even larger takeovers. Even when he didn't capture his price, Perelman made money. In 1986, for example, he made a $4.1 billion bid for Gillette, but the deal fell through when the Ivan Boesky insider-trading scandal made it difficult to obtain financing—so Perelman had to settle for a $43 million profit. By 1990, such methods had made Perelman the third-richest man in America with a net worth of over $2.5 billion. But heavy debts forced him to sell some of Revlon's brands in 1991.

Max Factor   Max Factor brought a little bit of Hollywood to the average American woman. His cosmetics were originally created for motion picture stars, and his success led other women to want to look like them. Factor was more than willing to oblige.

Quite literally, Max Factor worked with makeup most of his life. At 13, he dropped out of school and became a makeup apprentice with a traveling opera company in Eastern Europe. He displayed an early aptitude for working with the creams and rouges and other secrets of the trade and in time was appointed a makeup man with Russia's Royal Ballet.

In 1904, he emigrated to the U.S. with his wife and three children, setting up a wig-and-makeup concession at the St. Louis World's Fair. Eventually, he opened a cosmetics shop in Los Angeles, where he and his children made the products that were sold. As the film industry established itself in L.A., business picked up. In 1914, when Henry B. Walthall became the first actor in filmdom to wear makeup, Max Factor was the man who had done the job on him and his reputation, if not Walthall's, was assured.

He made a fortune doing the faces of Hollywood stars and was working for every studio. The demands of film with its harsh lights and screen magnification led Factor to create a new greasepaint that didn't leave actors and actresses with a caked look the way traditional makeup did. His makeup looked realistic on film. Factor also developed several other cosmetics, including a pancake makeup that could be used when films were made in color.

Factor got caught up in the glitter of Tinsel Town. He opened a huge, white, neoclassical cosmetics factory, which was as gaudily glorious as anything a movie mogul could have created. Colored floodlights bathed the entrance on opening day, and legions of film stars, such as Claudette Colbert and Jean Harlow, dedicated various rooms. The glitz naturally helped Factor. By 1930, his products were sold in more than 80 countries. After he died in 1938, his sons ran the company until they sold it for $480 million to Norton Simon. The brand is now owned by Revlon.

ELIZABETH ARDEN

Florence Nightingale Graham moved to New York from Toronto in 1908 and didn't become a nurse but a cosmetician. Two years later, she changed her name to Elizabeth Arden and opened her own business. She appropriated Elizabeth from a friend and Arden from a poem. By 1914, she was on her way to becoming a multimillionaire. The key to her success was two products she and a chemist, A. F. Swanson, developed: Ardena Skin Tonic and Amoretta. In all, she developed more than 300 cosmetics. When she died in 1966 at age 75, she was a successful thoroughbred horse breeder.

CREDIT CARDS

THE MARKET AND THE MONEY

For millions of Americans, plastic credit is a way of life—so much so that they don't just have just one card, but an average of 6.9 each. That's 1.3 billion credit cards held by American consumers.

All those cards let consumers rack up $260 billion worth of charges each year, up from a mere $83.2 billion in 1982. Visa cards alone are used for about 5,340 charges every minute during the busy Christmas buying season. Thanks largely to plastic, consumer installment credit stands at a record 19.4% of disposable income. And, it seems, the better educated you are, the more you love going into debt: college graduates put an average of $391 on their credit cards every month, people with some college education charge $159, high school graduates rack up $83, and those with some high school charge $51 a month, according to the Federal Reserve and *American Demographics* magazine. About 35% of all consumers pay off their credit-card balance each month but the average outstanding balance is now over $1,200.

THE PLAYERS

Nearly 2,500 companies issue credit cards, but the top three easily outdistance their rivals. There are about 250 million Visa, MasterCard, and American Express cards in the wallets and purses of American consumers. Consumers charge $134 billion a year on their Visa cards, $83.4 billion on

MasterCards, $65 billion on American Express cards, and $14.5 billion a year on their Discover cards. Citibank is the nation's largest bank issuer of credit cards, with about 16% of the bank card market, or about $25 billion in credit-card balances. A new entry, AT&T, introduced a Visa card in 1990 that already has the largest companies worried. Typically, about 2% of all accounts are delinquent, and banks write off about $3.3 billion a year in bad credit-card debts.

American Express Company

Chairman and CEO: James D. Robinson III   American Express Tower
Employees: 107,200   World Financial Center
Assets: $137.7 billion   New York, New York 10285-4805
212-640-2000

	1990	1989	1985	1980
Revenues (millions of dollars):	24,332	58,164	46,803	5,504
Net income (millions of dollars):	338	1,157	810	356
Share earnings (dollars):	0.69	2.70	1.78	1.32

What it does: Second-largest financial services company in America. Best known for traveler's checks and credit cards, this diversified financial services company is also an investment banker, and retail stockbroker.

In 1986 American Express acquired the distinction of being the first service company—financial or otherwise—to earn more than $1 billion in profits. But by the start of the 1990s, the most successful financial services firm of the 1980s was in deep trouble.

Many companies had been busy creating diversified financial services by putting banking, consumer lending, credit, brokerage, insurance, real estate sale, mortgages, and other financial services under one roof. The idea was great but in practice few companies figured out how to integrate all of these new businesses into one profitable company. Real estate brokers didn't sell enough mortgages, executives used to running a securities firm or a retail outlet didn't know how to handle insurance salespeople or real estate brokers. The result for many companies was predictable: poor profits.

American Express seemed to be an outstanding exception. After paying $915 million in 1981 for the nation's most profitable national retail brokerage, Shearson Loeb Rhodes, it bought the major Swiss bank, Trade Development Bank, for $520 million in 1983, Investors Diversified Services now (IDS Financial Services), for $727 million in 1983, and the investment bankers Lehman Brothers Kuhn Loeb for $380 million in 1984. Then in 1987 it snapped up the problem ridden E. F. Hutton Group for $961 million. The result was record profits of $1.1 billion in 1986, on sales of $14.65 billion, making American Express the largest service company in the U.S.

The architect behind those numbers is James D. Robinson III, CEO of American Express. Scion of a well-connected Atlanta banking family, Robinson was only 40 when he took over American Express in 1977. Today, he is known for his clout and his salesmanship on Capitol Hill.

Wall Street is also impressed with Robinson and how American Express became one of the few companies to thrive under financial deregulation. But part of that success could be traced into the company's history. American Express actually got its start pushing for another kind of deregulation. Founder Henry Wells fought the government's postal monopoly successfully in 1845 when he started delivering mail between New York and Buffalo for only 6 cents a letter, compared to 25 cents for the government. The U.S. Post Office soon dropped its rates, however, and regained its lost customers.

Wells, though, stayed in the express mail business, forming American Express with his two main competitors in 1850. Its traveler's checks appeared in 1891. Later, American Express capitalized on its traveler's check experience and reputation to become the largest credit-card company.

Robinson's plan in the 1980s was to capitalize on the company's fantastic success with the little green card. He wanted to create a huge financial services conglomerate that could offer one-stop shopping for virtually every type of financial services. But even in the 1980s, when Robinson was viewed as something of a legend by investors, the company's expansion didn't always go smoothly. A foray into insurance with Fireman's Fund produced not only lots of red ink but an SEC investigation. When the cable boom didn't turn out to be as profitable as expected, the company sold off its share of the Warner Amex Company, a joint venture with Warner Communications. In 1987 the company wrote off $870 million to boost loss reserves for bad Latin American debt.

These problems grew worse in the late 1980s, particularly at Shearson Lehman Hutton. The acquisition of E. F. Hutton proved disastrous, adding over $1 billion in overhead. Shearson's deals also caused problems. It got stuck with a $500 million bridge loan to Prime Computer after the junk bond market crashed, and its reputation was hurt when it came out on the wrong side of the battle for RJR Nabisco. Meanwhile, Shearson's Balcor real estate unit racked up $114 million worth of bad real estate loans.

Amex desperately looked around for a partner to inject more money into Shearson, but was unable to find an outside investor or stir up interest in a public offering of stock. So Amex finally had to buy the 39% stake it didn't own in the spring of 1990. Since 1989, it has injected about $1.2 billion into the firm.

Robinson now says he wants to get the firm back to basics and admits it tried to do too many things at once. In 1990, he sold the Geneva-based Trade Development Bank, which was Amex's attempt to enter the lucrative business of private banking for wealthy clients. Despite its troubles, Amex remains financially sound, thanks to its control over one of the great franchises in American business, those little green, gold, and platinum cards. Membership does have its privileges.

DEFENSE AND AEROSPACE

THE MARKET AND THE MONEY

Sometimes success can be bad for business. Only a decade ago, the defense industry was happily fighting communism with the biggest military buildup in the history of the world. As defense spending jumped from $137 billion in 1980 to $298.9 billion in 1991, Washington pumped nearly $3 trillion into the business of war. But then, something went wrong: America won the Cold War.

Today, the fall of the Berlin Wall, reform in the Soviet Union, the collapse of Communist rule in Eastern Europe, and the ongoing budget crisis in Washington have overrun the defense industry with budget cutters, red ink, and lay-offs. So far, coping with a world where the peace dividend is more important than the Red menace has been difficult. Many of the nation's largest defense contractors took huge write-offs in 1989 and 1990, and in 1989, the 12 largest companies in the aerospace/defense sector saw profits plunge 25%.

Of course, not all the news is bad: The Persian Gulf crisis illustrates that governments around the world still need weapons more powerful than a slingshot, and the commercial side of the aerospace/defense industry is stronger than ever. The bad news, however, is very bad. Adjusted for inflation, defense budgets have declined 15.9% since fiscal 1985, and the budget for new weapons dropped from $96.8 billion in 1985 to $64.1 billion in 1991. Despite the spectacular success of many high-tech weapons during the Iraq invasion, many big-ticket items that began development during the booming Reagan years, such as Star Wars and the Stealth bomber, have little support in Congress. Iraq's invasion of Kuwait helped industry lobbyists fight back attempts to cut the defense budget even more but it also hurt the industry's one bright spot—sales of commercial aircraft.

Even so, the aerospace industry shipped $121.2 billion worth of new airplanes in 1990, up 7.7% despite a drop in orders for military aircraft. Sales of guided missiles, space equipment, and space vehicles will hit $19.6 billion in 1991, up from $16.0 billion in 1987. A $234.9 billion backlog of orders for aircraft bodes well for the future of commercial aircraft even if the airline industry does fly into trouble.

Table D-1 Shipments of U.S. Aircraft, 1971–1991
(values in millions of dollars)

Year	Aircraft total		Total		Civil						Military	
					Large Transports		General Aviation[1]		Rotorcraft			
	Units	Value	Units	Value	Units	Value	Units	Value	Units	Value	Units	Value
1971	11,161	6,593	8,142	2,971	223	2,580	7,466	322	453	69	3,019	3,622
1972	13,072	6,220	10,542	3,417	199	2,787	9,774	558	569	72	2,530	2,803
1973	16,539	8,176	14,688	4,814	274	3,873	13,646	828	768	113	1,851	3,362
1974	17,192	8,595	15,292	5,270	317	4,207	14,166	909	809	154	1,900	3,325
1975	16,918	9,355	15,179	5,305	285	4,006	14,056	1,033	838	266	1,739	4,050
1976	17,865	9,001	16,489	4,705	217	3,155	15,451	1,226	821	324	1,376	4,296
1977	19,392	9,092	18,047	4,512	159	2,672	16,904	1,488	984	352	1,345	4,580
1978	19,881	10,179	18,885	6,460	241	4,308	17,811	1,781	833	371	996	3,719
1979	19,302	15,028	18,465	10,598	376	8,030	17,048	2,165	1,041	403	837	4,430
1980	14,660	18,845	13,613	12,953	383	9,793	11,877	2,486	1,353	674	1,047	5,892
1981	11,860	20,157	10,798	13,287	388	9,731	9,457	2,920	953	636	1,062	6,870
1982	6,248	19,266	5,089	8,619	236	6,254	4,266	2,000	587	365	1,159	10,647
1983	4,409	23,012	3,356	10,266	262	8,493	2,691	1,470	403	303	1,053	12,746
1984	3,931	22,570	2,995	8,354	188	6,343	2,431	1,681	376	330	936	14,216
1985	3,597	28,988	2,678	10,987	273	9,051	2,029	1,431	376	505	919	18,001
1986	3,261	35,145	2,154	12,193	329	10,643	1,495	1,262	330	288	1,107	22,952
1987	3,003	36,008	1,804	12,226	361	10,585	1,085	1,364	358	277	1,199	23,777
1988	3,202	33,683	2,017	15,845	422	13,588	1,212	1,923	383	334	1,185	17,838
1989	3,471	30,902	2,448	17,129	398	15,074	1,535	1,804	515	251	1,023	13,773
1990[2]	3,215	39,794	2,232	25,321	524	23,200	1,118	1,921	590	200	983	14,473
1991[3]	3,211	43,455	2,410	29,834	610	27,555	1,200	2,075	600	204	801	13,621

[1] Excludes off-the-shelf military aircraft.

[2] Estimate.

[3] Forecast.

Source: U.S. Department of Commerce, International Trade Administration (ITA); general aviation (through 1989), General Aviation Manufacturers Association; rotorcraft (through 1989), Aerospace Industries Association. Estimates and Forecasts by ITA.

GUNS, BUTTER, AND THE ECONOMY

Remember the 1960s, when President Johnson decided we could afford guns and butter—a war on poverty and a war on communism in Southeast Asia? For a while, fueled by huge federal spending, the economy went into over-drive. But in the end the public got neither guns nor butter. Soon we were stuck with the economic counterpart to the famous domino theory: massive government spending soon produced inflation and reallocated money from the private sector to the public. That worked against productivity and invest-ment. The economy had a hangover from all the free-flowing government money that lasted through most of the 1970s and early 1980s.

Up to then, few people had doubted the economic benefits of military spending. After all, the U.S. spent 11% of its GNP on defense in 1955, far more than it did at the height of the Reagan defense buildup in 1984, when defense ate up only 6.4% of the GNP, or even at the height of the Vietnam War, when 9.6% of GNP went for guns. And in the 1950s and 1960s, the economy seemed to be doing just fine. Government expenditures for defense created jobs and produced all sorts of great spin-offs—like Tang, high-powered computer chips, jet engines, and graphite tennis rackets—that vastly improved life on the home front.

Headaches produced by lavish spending for guns and butter in the 1960s and early 1970s, however, produced a more skeptical view of military spend-ing. Already, some economists returned to the traditional view—once expressed by 18th-century economist Adam Smith—that military spending diverts money from the private sector and more productive uses.

Noting that about one-third to one-half of all the nation's scientific talent since the beginning of the Cold War has gone into military-related research, critics of defense spending argue that government support for defense research and development channels money away from the private sector and research that would improve productivity and produce profitable consumer products. While Americans build tanks and missiles, the Japanese and Ger-mans build Sonys and cameras. We get higher taxes. They get a bigger share of the world market for consumer goods.

Of course, declining productivity and the inability of American companies to compete on the world market aren't just the fault of military spending. But in recent years it has become more apparent that guns don't always pro-duce butter. The President's Commission on Industrial Competitiveness, for example, found in 1985 that the Pentagon's research is now so exotic that it has few commercial applications. According to government estimates, mili-tary research eats up 27% of all research and development (R&D) in the U.S., in contrast to only 4% in Germany and 1% in Japan. (Private esti-mates put the figure at 35% to 40% of all R&D.) The result, according to economists Mary Kaldor, Margaret Sharp, and William Walker, is that coun-tries with low military budgets have done well on the world market, while countries such as the U.S. and the United Kingdom, with higher expendi-tures as a percentage of GNP, do poorly.

Such arguments have taken on a new urgency in the 1990s, as Congress debates how much to cut defense spending in its effort to balance the budget.

A longtime critic of defense spending, Seymour Melman, argues that defense spending has been "a major factor in America's decline to the status of a second-class industrial power." He complains that each year since 1951, the Defense Department has controlled a pool of capital larger than the annual profits of all American corporations. Between 1947 and 1989, defense spending ate up resources equal to all the equipment, factories, and buildings in the United States. To pay for this buildup, he argues, the government went deeply into debt. That caused interest rates to rise, thus making it harder for private companies to invest in factories, and increased the money future generations will have to spend paying off the national debt. Worse, in his view, a large share of the nation's research and development budget went to weapons, not civilian applications that could improve productivity or make American goods more competitive on the international market.

The Pentagon counters that the nation needs a certain level of defense spending to maintain an infrastructure—factories and skills—in case of a war or national emergency. Otherwise it is impossible to mobilize quickly and efficiently for war, as the U.S. learned at the beginning of World War II. Also, there is a great deal of evidence to suggest that defense spending has helped certain sectors of the economy. Many of the fastest-growing regions in the U.S.—California and the South—have received the largest shares of defense spending.

At any rate, shifting economic gears from military spending to peacetime spending won't be easy. Four and a half decades of what Melman calls the permanent war economy have left their mark. The so-called military-industrial complex employs 6.5 million people and military personnel. Everyone likes the idea of a peace dividend, but few political leaders are apt to want a peace dividend if it means creating massive layoffs or an economic recession.

Moreover, most defense contractors, used to cost-plus contracts and customized production methods that are right out of the Middle Ages, are ill-equipped to convert their war machines to peacetime production. Remember, for example, the buses that New York defense contractor Grumman sold to New York City in the 1970s. Like many defense contractors who were trying to survive the end of the Vietnam War, Grumman decided to start making buses. The buses had lots of high-tech features but also a nasty habit of losing their wheels or developing cracks in the frames. Eventually Grumman admitted defeat in battle against New York City potholes and scrapped its bus-making operation.

Similar problems are likely to create a strange fusion of war and peace during the 1990s. The Pentagon has increased its funding of high-tech projects that have more civilian applications, such as high-definition television, and a number of government agencies are looking for new wars to fight. Already the military is angling for a bigger role in the war against drugs, and the highly secretive National Security Agency is using its high-tech spy satellites to supply Washington with economic intelligence for the war against foreign competition. Meanwhile, the end of the Cold War hasn't meant the end of hot spots in the Third World. The Bush administration has been looking to increase arms sales to Third World countries, and the Persian Gulf crisis is likely to force the Pentagon to buy more conventional weapons, an area that was slighted during the Reagan buildup.

COSTS, CORRUPTION, AND NATIONAL DEFENSE

The Cold War may be over, but the battle against graft and corruption in the Pentagon goes on.

Besides the usual scandals about billion-dollar defense systems that don't work and $4 computer chips that anyone but the Pentagon could buy for 40 cents, the 1980s and early 1990s saw a raft of corruption and cost-overrun cases. Consider:

• In 1990, congressional investigators uncovered the newest versions of the $400 toilet seat: The Air Force grudgingly admitted that it paid $120 apiece for 207 paper-cup dispensers. Not to be outdone, the Pentagon then spent $3,000 on a pair of pliers. How else would you install a $120 paper-cup dispenser?

• A four-year investigation into defense-procurement fraud, called Ill-Wind, forced William Graves, a top defense consultant, to plead guilty in 1990 to charges that he bribed former Navy acquisitions chief and consultant Melvyn Paisley and senior Air Force official Victor D. Cohen. (Both Paisley and Cohen—who has not been charged—denied any wrongdoing.) This investigation into illegal trafficking in secret Defense Department documents that would help contractors win bids has already netted 32 guilty pleas and $14.9 million in fines against a number of top Defense Department contractors, including Raytheon, Hazeltine, Teledyne, Whittaker, Boeing, Loral, RCA, Hughes Aircraft, and Grumman.

• Also, in 1990, Northrop agreed to pay $17 million for falsifying test data on the Cruise missile and Harrier jet, the second-highest fine ever levied, and General Electric agreed to pay $16.1 million, the third-highest fine. The largest fine ever levied came in 1988, when Sundstrand Corp. paid $115 million to settle charges that it had overbilled for military hardware.

• A *New York Times* survey of government audits of NASA and the space shuttle found that at least $3.5 billion was wasted through abuses and mismanagement. The shuttle, which blew up in 1986 because of design flaws, was projected to cost $675 million when first proposed but it ended up costing $1.47 billion and was nowhere near as productive as NASA planners had first envisioned. Instead of a 65,000-pound payload, it could only carry 53,000 pounds; instead of the 60 planned fights a year, it could only manage 22. As a result, the cost per launch soared from a planned $28 million to $279 million. The cost per payload pound soared from $270 to $5,264.

• Government investigators found that kickbacks from subcontractors—which do $50 billion worth of Defense Department business—were widespread. Employees from such major companies as Hughes Aircraft Company, the Northrop Corporation, Hughes Helicopters, the Raytheon Company, and Teledyne were convicted of taking kickbacks from subcontractors.

• But despite a decade of investigations, many contractors convicted of fraud do not face any permanent damage to their business. In 1990 *The Wall*

Street Journal reported that fewer than 20% of all large defense firms convicted of corrupt activities were cut off from getting large contracts in the
future. In fact, the Pentagon often needs parts from the contractor so badly,
it is unable to impose tough sanctions. During the height of the Persian Gulf
crisis, in September of 1990, the Pentagon had to lift its suspension of
Northrop because the firm was the only supplier of key parts for the AV-8B
Harrier fighter bomber.

The problems go beyond a few abuses. What's at fault is the way the military does business.

Many of the worst problems can be traced to the Pentagon. Government
regulations and red tape, for example, add billions to Defense Department
bills. Remember those $4 computer chips that should cost 40 cents? The
problem wasn't a greedy defense contractor but the Pentagon's demand for
extra testing and paperwork.

Every year, the military signs over 200,000 contracts. Unfortunately, most
of those contracts are wrapped up in miles of red tape. Military procurement
remains one of the most complex systems known to man—which may explain
why a lot of expensive weapons systems never work. Defense firms typically
face over 44,000 specifications for a weapons system. The instructions on procurement run 32 volumes and take up six feet of shelf space. One Pentagon
study found that regulations accounted for one-third of procurement costs.

An example of how Pentagon red tape costs money is a simple comparison
between how the private and public sectors carry out a contract. McDonnell
Douglas, for example, found that specifications for a military aircraft were set
out in over 24,000 documents, insuring that the project was quickly snarled in
lots of red tape and costly paperwork. In contrast, a $2 billion McDonnell
Douglas contract to supply Delta Air Lines with passenger aircraft produced
only 10 documents. Freeing defense contractors from costly red tape might
do more than just cut costs. It could improve the quality of weapons.

Also, military planners encourage waste by adding lots of whistles and giz-
mos to design specs. As a result, weapons systems get so complicated they
can only be operated and serviced by highly trained personnel. And contractors are constantly forced into costly delays by military planners who suddenly decide a weapon system suddenly needs to do something it was never
intended to do.

Even worse is the cozy relationship between the military and private sector that has grown up over the years. As late as the early 1980s, most military contracts were still awarded without competitive bidding on a cost-plus
basis—meaning that the contractor was assured of making a profit no matter
how high costs rose. Pentagon bureaucrats also had little incentive to rock
the boat. Many officers and officials counted on retiring from their military
jobs to cushy, high-paying jobs with defense contractors.

Since then, the Pentagon has tried to improve the way it does business.
Under strict new procurement policies, about 75% of all contracts and 63%
of the money spent by the Pentagon in 1989 fixed the price so that the manufacturer would have to absorb cost overruns. But strict fixed-price con-

tracts haven't proved to be a miracle solution to the problem of cost over-runs. The defense industry is believed to have suffered over $1 billion in overruns on fixed price in the late 1980s. By the early 1990s, many large con-tractors refused to bid on fixed-price contracts, complaining that changes in military specifications had forced them to absorb huge losses. As a result, the use of fixed-price contracts has declined.

Congressional critics say a more promising method of controlling costs is to reduce cumbersome regulations and simplify weapons systems. Simpler weapons systems would also need less maintenance and be more reliable in the jungles and deserts where most regional conflicts are likely to be fought in the 1990s.

THE BUSINESS OF FLYING BUSINESS

Corporate airplanes are often a symbol of management waste, a perennial target of shareholder discontent. Yet according to the annual survey of busi-ness aviation by Aviation Data Service, 328 of the 500 largest industrial cor-porations own their own plane.

Actually, many of the complaints about corporate jets are misplaced. Most of the large business fleets of aircraft and helicopters are owned by oil, aerospace, and defense companies. They use these planes to demonstrate the planes they sell or to reach far-flung oil fields. Helicopters are often used to reach oil rigs at sea.

But even if many large companies need planes for business, not enough of them have been buying new planes. In the 1980s the industry was in its worst recession ever. General aviation manufacturers, which produce small fixed-wing aircraft for business, regional airlines services, and recreation, shipped 17,811 planes in 1978 valued at $1.78 billion, but in 1987, only 1,160 planes valued at only $1.32 billion were delivered.

Obviously, that has hurt the companies that make most of the planes American businesses and corporations use. Some of the largest—Beech Air-craft, a subsidiary of Raytheon Company; Cessna, bought by General Dynamics in 1985; and Piper Aircraft, a subsidiary of Lear Siegler—have all seen huge drops in sales.

One important factor behind the decline of sales of business aircraft is the ruined oil economy. Many oil companies sold off their planes, glutting the market and cutting demands for new aircraft.

General Dynamics Corporation

Chairman and CEO: Stanley C. Pace
Employees: 102,000
Assets: $6.6 billion

Pierre Laclede Center
St. Louis, Missouri 63105
314-889-8200

	1990	1989	1985	1980
Revenues (millions of dollars):	10,173	10,043	8,164	4,743
Net income (millions of dollars):	(577.9)	293	373	195
Share earnings (dollars):	—	7.01	8.80	3.58

What it does: The nation's largest defense contractor.

General Dynamics, which gets nearly 90% of its revenues from government contracts, provides the Defense Department with such major weapons systems such as the F-16 fighter, the M-1 tank, the Tomahawk cruise missile, and the Trident submarine, as well as some bad publicity for the Pentagon.

The head of its Electric Boat Division had to flee the country to avoid federal prosecution on kickback charges. The company was suspended twice in 1985 from bidding on government contracts. Four current and former executives were indicted for overcharges connected with the Sergeant York anti-aircraft gun. Some of the more notorious charges included allegations that the company got the Pentagon to pay for its corporate barbershop, dog-kennel fees, and country-club dues.

None of the allegations were proven and the Justice Department eventually dropped all charges. That confirmed the company's contention that the indictments shouldn't have been filed to begin with. But by that time the damage to the company's reputation had been done.

To clean up its image, General Dynamics hired Stanley Pace—an executive known for his honesty and integrity. Pace brought in an ad agency to clean up the firm's image and put through tough new management rules. The scandals haven't ruined the company's defense business, but profits have fallen since 1987, when the company earned $437 million. Even worse, easing Cold War tensions battered the company's stock, which lost 75% of its value between 1986 and October 1990. More bad news came in 1990 when the company took a $500 million writeoff for cost overruns on its contracts. But General Dynamics got a $3 billion tank contract with Saudi Arabia in the summer of 1990, and Iraq's invasion of Kuwait has rescued some of the company's weapons that had been under heavy fire from budget cutters. Some analysts expect General Dynamics to rebound from its losses in 1990 with $10 billion of sales and profits of about $250 million in 1991.

Lockheed Corporation

CEO: Daniel Tellep
Employees: 77,800
Assets: $6.9 billion

4500 Park Granada Boulevard
Calabasas, California 91399
818-712-2000

	1990	1989	1985	1980
Revenues (millions of dollars):	9,958	9,891	9,535	5,396
Net income (millions of dollars):	335	6	401	28
Share earnings (dollars):	5.30	0.10	6.10	0.51

What it does: Primarily engaged in the research, design, and production of military aircraft, missiles, space systems, and electronic systems.

Here is a company with a knack for getting into trouble and surviving. Lockheed was founded in 1916 by Allan and Malcolm Loughead, who later changed their names to Lockheed, and Jack Northrop, who later founded another famous defense contractor that bears his name. The company went bankrupt in 1931 but under new owners began producing military planes. In the 1960s Lockheed became the nation's number-one defense contractor.

At this point, the company lost some key defense contracts and fell behind in the production of new planes. In 1971, Lockheed escaped bankruptcy by only one vote, when Congress approved a $250 million bailout. Such a narrow escape from disaster would have prompted most companies to behave themselves for a while. Instead, Lockheed used some of its new cash to bribe foreign officials, including a former prime minister of Japan and Prince Bernhard of the Netherlands.

More recently, profits returned, but the controversies haven't gone away. A few years ago, the company got into hot water by somehow managing to lose 1,400 top-secret documents relating to the Stealth program, a research project intended to produce planes that cannot be detected by radar. Then, the company got its usual bad publicity when Representative John Dingell cited internal Air Force findings that Lockheed's 50-plane contract for C-5B transport planes was overpriced by about $1 billion. After negotiations, the company agreed in 1987 to give up $350 billion on the Air Force's option to buy 21 planes. More bad news came in 1989, when a huge write-off on fixed-cost contacts pushed profits down to only $6 million.

McDonnell Douglas Corporation

CEO: Sanford N. McDonnell   P.O. Box 516
Employees: 109,164   St. Louis, Missouri 63166
Assets: $8.3 billion   314-232-0232

	1990	1989	1985	1980
Revenues (millions of dollars):	16,255	14,581	11,618	6,125
Net income (millions of dollars):	306	(37)	346	145
Share earnings (dollars):	7.99	—	8.60	3.65

What it does: The leading manufacturer in fighter aircraft for the military and commercial aircraft.

In the early 1980s, James Worsham, the president of the Douglas division of McDonnell Douglas Corporation, literally bet the company on a deal. He signed a contract with American Airlines that would allow American to return $400 million worth of narrow-body MD-80s within 30 days if it didn't like them.

The gamble was particularly risky, for in the 1970s and early 1980s, McDonnell Douglas Corporation's commercial airline manufacturing business had lost money, reflecting the aerospace giant's lost dominance in the jet airplane business. Sales of commercial jets dropped from 300 in 1968 to only 50 in 1982.

American decided to keep the planes and, in 1986, McDonnell Douglas's jet operations actually made money. It shipped an estimated 95 jets, nearly twice as many as it had four years earlier.

The company got its name in 1967 when two large family-owned companies, McDonnell and Douglas, merged. Douglas had been created by Donald Wills Douglas in 1920 and got off the ground with its famous DC series in the 1930s. But the company lost control of the new jet plane market to

Boeing in the late 1950s and was losing money by the time it was taken over by James S. McDonnell. He created McDonnell in 1939 and built it up with fighter sales. McDonnell's nephew Sanford played a major role in convincing the company's board to put up the money for the risk MD-80s.

But more problems developed in the late 1980s. Serious production problems on the MD-80 and the firm's newest commercial aircraft, the MD-11, plus write-offs on defense contracts, produced a loss in 1989. Nonetheless, the firm does have a backlog of $36.53 billion orders, up 27.6% from 1989. It has launched a program to cut $700 million in costs and plans to lay off 17,000 people. Analysts expect this bitter medicine to keep the company back in the black in 1990 and 1991.

Boeing

Chairman and CEO: Frank A. Shrontz   7755 East Marginal Way South
Employees: 161,700   Seattle, WA 98108
Assets: $14.5 billion   206-655-2121

	1990	1989	1985	1980
Revenues (millions of dollars):	27,595	20,276	13,636	9,426
Net income (millions of dollars):	1,385	675	566	601
Share earnings (dollars):	4.01	1.96	1.67	1.85

What it does: Leading manufacturer of commercial and military aircraft.

Boeing is one of the few American airplane makers constantly able to make money selling commercial aircraft. Since introducing the 707, the first commercially successful jetliner, Boeing has set the industry standard for jetliners. More than half of the jetliners outside the Soviet Union were made by Boeing. And its military aircraft are no less famous: the company built the famous flying fortress, the B-17, as well as the famous B-52 and the Minuteman missile.

It all started in 1916 when pilot William Edward Boeing got tired of waiting six months to get spare parts for his aircraft. So he set up a factory near downtown Seattle. Today the company is the city's largest employer.

Despite Boeing's successes in pioneering commercial jetliners, the company hasn't always flown smoothly. In the late 1960s, the airline industry didn't go for Boeing's 747 jumbo jet, and in the 1970s when Congress cut funding for the SST (supersonic transport) plane, the company was forced to cut its work force from 105,000 to only 38,000.

Boeing's strength in the commercial aircraft business, however, helped it profit handsomely from the boom in air travel during the 1980s. Between 1985 and 1990, it sold record numbers of commercial aircraft and by mid-1990 had a backlog of $84.1 billion in orders, up 41.8% from 1989. Most of these orders, $77.5 billion, were for commercial aircraft.

Nonetheless, Boeing's attempt to expand its defense operations has not gone smoothly. It lost $559 million in 1989 producing military aircraft, and its stock was hammered in 1990 by the Persian Gulf crisis. Analysts feared that rising jet-fuel prices would hurt air travel and reduce orders for commercial planes. True, but aircraft fleets are older than ever before and orders for new planes keep coming in, producing a record profit of $1.4 billion in 1990.

THE ARMS TRADE

Coups d'état, invasions, guerrilla wars, buying communist arms and selling them to anticommunist guerrillas, shoring up an embattled despot—it's all part of the arms trade, a risky but lucrative profession. Self-styled "merchants of death" do $30 billion a year in legitimate business and billions more in the black market arms trade.

Arms dealers aren't too particular about ideology, only the ability to pay. Many arms dealers have no qualms about arming dictators on the right, religious fanatics like Khomeini, or guerrilla armies on the left. Sometimes arms dealers work on their own, subverting the foreign policy of their own country by selling stolen parts and arms to enemy nations. Sometimes they act as proxies for the CIA or the KGB.

Since sales often take place in a shadowy world of offshore dummy corporations and Swiss bank accounts, most arms dealers don't have to worry about adverse publicity. Disclosure of secret U.S. arms sales to Iran was a rarity that put several arms dealers on the cover of *Time* magazine and in the witness stand at 1987 congressional hearings.

But even before the Iran arms scandal brought the industry a lot of unwanted publicity, all was not right in the international arms trade. Around the world the war business is booming. Worldwide military expenditures now top $1 trillion and have been growing 3.5% a year faster than inflation. But restrictions on sales of certain high-tech weapons and the cash-strapped third world have also cost arms traders billions in sales. As a result, the international arms trade rose only slightly from $52.6 billion in 1982 to $56.0 billion in 1987, the most recent figures available from the U.S. Arms Control and Disarmament Agency.

No comparable international statistics are available for the early 1990s, but U.S. arms sales abroad seem to have recovered. Ironically, the end of Cold War tensions has shifted the market for arms back to the Third World. U.S. officials approved $7 billion worth of sales in 1986, $12 billion in 1988, and were considering $30 billion in 1990. Though many debt-strapped Third World countries can't afford new arms purchases, the major powers are happy to sell whatever they can. Weapons contractors, hurt by defense budget cuts at home and in the Soviet Union, which badly needs cash to modernize its economy, believe arms sales will increase in the aftermath of the Persian Gulf crisis. Already, the Bush administration has accelerated plans to sell 36 F-15s, manufactured by McDonnell Douglas, to Saudi Arabia.

Between 1983 and 1987, the Soviet Union was the world's largest arms dealer, supplying 40.5% of the $237.8 billion in arms sold during that period. The U.S. was a distant second with 23% of the market, followed by non–U.S. NATO (18.4%). The tables below show where the guns went and who supplied them.

Table D-2   The Arms Trade

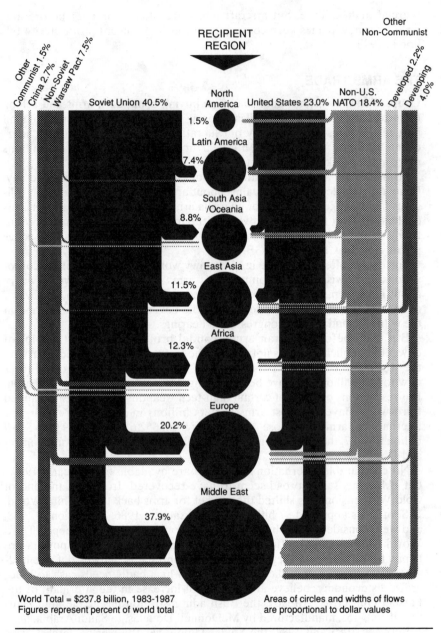

RECIPIENT REGION

Other Non-Communist

Other Communist 1.5%
China 2.7%
Non-Soviet Warsaw Pact 7.5%
Soviet Union 40.5%
United States 23.0%
Non-U.S. NATO 18.4%
Developed 2.2%
Developing 4.0%

North America 1.5%

Latin America 7.4%

South Asia/Oceania 8.8%

East Asia 11.5%

Africa 12.3%

Europe 20.2%

Middle East 37.9%

World Total = $237.8 billion, 1983-1987
Figures represent percent of world total

Areas of circles and widths of flows
are proportional to dollar values

Source: U.S. Arms Control & Disarmament Agency.

424

Table D-3 Top 10 Defense Contractors
(Fiscal Year 1990)

Rank	Companies	Thousands of Dollars	Percent of Total	Cumulative Percent of Total
	Total	130,758,093	100.00	100.00
	Total, 100 Companies/Subsidiaries	86,670,694	66.28	66.28
1	McDonnell Douglas Corporation	6,631,362		
	McDonnell Douglas Astronautics	57,453		
	McDonnell Douglas Hlcptr Co	1,433,102		
	McDonnell Douglas Inco Inc	3,153		
	McDonnell Douglas Info Sys Co	13,489		
	McDonnell Douglas Trning Sys	72,214		
	Vitek Systems Inc	654		
	Total	8,211,427	6.27	6.27
2	General Dynamics Corporation	6,045,889		
	Braintree Maritime Corporation	236,308		
	Cessna Aircraft Company Inc	23,896		
	Total	6,306,093	4.82	11.10
3	General Electric Company	5,566,452		
	Canadian General Electric Co	5,282		
	Elano Corporation	576		
	Gelco Corporation	1,198		
	General Electric Base Support	83		
	General Electric Cgr	288		
	Managment Technical Svcs Cmpany	13,692		
	National Broadcasting Co Inc	105		
	Reuter Stokes Canada Limited	66		
	Reuter Stokes Inc Del	97		
	Transport Intl Pool Inc	1,125		
	Total	5,588,964	4.27	15.37
4	General Motors Corporation	415,799		
	Adam Opel Aktiengesellschaft	429		
	Ami Instruments Inc	55		
	Delco Electronics Corporation	5,751		
	Electronic Data Systems Corp	259,336		
	G M Hughes Electronics Corp	6,244		
	Hughes Aircraft Company	3,275,012		
	Hughes Danbury Optical Systems	43,675		
	Hughes Electro Optical Opns In	77,830		
	Hughes Training Sys Inc	22,407		
	Kalvar Corporation	32		
	Total	4,106,570	3.14	18.51
5	Raytheon Company	3,730,675		
	Beech Aerospace Services Inc	120,073		
	Beech Aircraft Corporation	42,913		
	Raytheon Service Company	51,717		
	Raytheon Support Services Co	9,728		
	Raytheon Tech Asst Co Inc	39-		
	Raythn Mdtrrn Sstms Cmpny	356		
	Speed Queen Company	86		
	Switchcraft Inc	311		
	United Beechcraft Inc	36		
	United Engineers & Constrs	115,099		
	Total	4,070,955	3.11	21.63

Table D-3 Top 10 Defense Contractors (continued)
(Fiscal Year 1990)

Rank	Companies	Thousands of Dollars	Percent of Total	Cumulative Percent of Total
6	Lockheed Corporation	1,495,836		
	Analytyx Electronic Systems	8,197		
	Lockheed Aeromod Center Inc	10,115		
	Lockheed Aeroparts Inc	1,183		
	Lockheed Engineering & Science	3,700		
	Lockheed Missile & Space Co	1,741,832		
	Lockheed Sanders Inc	192,799		
	Lockheed Space Operations Co	24,559		
	Lockheed Support Systems Inc	73,076		
	Lockheed Western Export Co	825		
	Murdock Engineering Company	506		
	Total	3,552,628	2.71	24.34
7	Martin Marietta Corporation	3,490,973		
	International Light Metals	1,019		
	Total	3,491,992	2.67	27.01
8	United Technologies Corp	2,756,718		
	Adaptive Optics Associates	560		
	Carrier Corporation	2,111		
	Hamilton Standard Electronics	825		
	International Fuel Cells Corp	450		
	Norden Systems Inc	78,611		
	Otis Elevator Company	41-		
	Sikorsky Intnl Products	15,411		
	United Tchnologies Opt Systems	541		
	United Tech Auto Group Oprtns	469		
	Usbi Co	111		
	Total	2,855,766	2.18	29.20
9	Grumman Corporation	0		
	Grumman Aerospace Corporation	2,489,272		
	Grumman Data Systems Corp	179,428		
	Grumman Technical Services Inc	28,266		
	Total	2,696,966	2.06	31.26
10	Tenneco Inc	0		
	Case J I Company	19,094		
	Newport News Industrial Corp	609		
	Newport News Shpblding Drydock	2,367,576		
	Packaging Corporation Of Amer	27		
	Sperry Marine Inc	22,593		
	Tennessee Gas Pipeline Co	36		
	Total	2,409,935	1.84	33.10

Table D-4   The Burden of Military Spending Around the World

This chart shows the relative burden of military spending around the world. The far left column shows military expenditures (ME) as a percentage of gross national product (GNP). The chart also breaks down countries by GNP per capita. The breakdown shows that Ethiopia, for example, spends between 5% and 9.99% of its GNP on its military even though it is very poor, with a GNP of under $200 per capita. It is safe to assume that Ethiopian military spending is a greater burden on its people than military spending in the U.S. and other more affluent countries.

ME/GNP* (%)	GNP per capita (1987 dollars)					
	Under $200	$200–499	$500–999	$1,000–2,999	$3,000–9,999	$10,000 and over
10% and over	Vietnam Cambodia† Laos†	Yemen (Aden)† Afghanistan† Guyana†	Cape Verde† Yemen (Sanaa) Morocco Albania	North Korea Jordan Syria Angola† Mongolia†	Oman Iraq† Israel Saudi Arabia Soviet Union Libya Nicaragua† Bulgaria	Qatar†
5–9.99%	Ethiopia Mozambique	Zambia† Pakistan	Zimbabwe El Salvador Thailand Honduras Bolivia Ecuador Botswana Senegal	Egypt Lebanon† Cuba† Gabon†	Iran Poland Czechoslovakia Greece Romania Hungary Singapore†	East Germany Un. Arab Emir.† United States Kuwait
2–4.99%	Tanzania† Guinea-Bissau Burkina Faso Somalia† Madagascar	China Mauritania India Liberia Chad Togo Sri Lanka Burundi Burma Sudan Mali Kenya Equat. Guinea† Lesotho Benin† Indonesia Cen. Afr. Rep.† Rwanda	Ivory Coast Guatemala Papua N. Guin.† Dominican Rep. Swaziland Philippines Jamaica	Peru South Korea Congo Turkey South Africa Chile Venezuela Malaysia Tunisia Algeria Suriname Yugoslavia Panama	Taiwan Bahrain Portugal Trinidad & Tob.† Spain	United Kingdom France Norway Netherlands West Germany Belgium Sweden Australia Italy New Zealand Canada Denmark Switzerland
1–1.99%	Zaire† Bangladesh Malawi The Gambia† Nepal	Haiti Guinea† Uganda†		Cameroon Uruguay† Argentina Fiji† Colombia Paraguay	Ireland† Malta	Finland† Austria Japan
Under 1%		Ghana Sao Tome&Prin. Niger† Nigeria Sierra Leone†		Brazil Costa Rica Mexico Mauritius	Cyprus Barbados†	Luxembourg Iceland

*Countries are listed within blocks in descending order of ME/GNP.
†Ranking is based on a rough approximation of one or more variables for which 1987 data or reliable estimates are not available.
  Source: U.S. Arms Control & Disarmament Agency.

EDUCATION

THE MARKET AND THE MONEY

Knowledge may be power, but getting it costs money. About $377.8 billion was spent for education in America's schools during the 1990–1991 school year, up from $288.4 billion in 1986–1987 and $247.2 billion in 1984–1985. That money goes to educate some 58 million students in American schools and colleges. Each year, students receive nearly 1 million bachelor's degrees, 289,000 master's degrees, 72,000 first professional degrees, and 34,000 doctorates.

Thanks in part to all that money, today's Americans are better educated than ever before.

Almost one fifth of the population (20.3%) has graduated from college, up from only 11.0% in 1970. Only 23.8% of the population has not graduated from high school, compared to 76.5% in 1940. And the median education of Americans is 12.7 years, up from 8.6 in 1940.

Education, of course, doesn't end with graduation. The American Society for Training and Development estimates companies spend a hefty $45.5 billion a year on formal courses and training programs for 39.5 million employees, about one third of the workforce. Another $180 billion; they estimate, is spent annually for unstructured on-the-job training and supervision.

BUYING AN EDUCATION

In recent years, the costs of higher education have gone through the roof. During the 1980s, the cost of educating a student in a public school increased 105.6%, or 40% faster than inflation, while the cost of attending a private college increased 133.9%, 59.5% faster than inflation. Today, it cost $9,391 to send a student to a four-year university and the cost of sending a son or daughter to a more prestigious private university was even higher, hitting $17,990 at Bennington, the nation's most expensive school; $17,100 at Harvard; $17,020 at Yale; and $16,835 at Stanford. Tuition between 1970 and 1987 increased about 7.8% a year, and about 9.8% between 1980 and 1987, twice as fast as the 4.9% annual inflation rate for the 1980s.

A lot of these increases were forced on college officials to make up for expenses that were deferred during the 1970s. With double-digit inflation, faculty salaries lost 20% of their purchasing power and new construction and debt service were deferred. Now the bills are coming due. Faculty costs are once again going up, and colleges are forced to pay for long-overdue construction and maintenance.

These rising costs have hit families and students hard. Students unable to pay the $90,000 it now costs to get an Ivy League education have turned away from private schools. But while the cost of an education has skyrocketed, student aid increased only 42% during the 1980s. Adjusted for inflation, that means the amount of aid available actually declined by 3%, to $28 billion.

Yet many parents continue to pay the price. With a tight marketplace, many parents and students are working harder than ever for the prestigious sheepskin from one of the nation's top schools. The number of students borrowing money to pay for college has more than quadrupled from 991,000 borrowing an average of $1,311 in 1975 to 1990, when 4.6 million borrowed an average of $2,694. Thus, a generation graduates from school with heavy debts. In 1985, the median debt for college graduates of public schools was $8,000; by 1990, the average debt was about $14,000. No wonder $8.5 billion in student loans are in default.

THE M.B.A. BUSINESS

A tighter job market and increasing skepticism about the value of a liberal arts degree have combined to produce an explosion in business education, especially M.B.A.'s.

As recently as 1960, only 4,643 M.B.A.'s (Masters of Business Administration degrees) were granted. But by 1970, the number of M.B.A.'s jumped to 21,599, then to 54,000 in 1981, and hit over 67,000 at 700 schools in 1991. And more are on the way, with another 200,000 students studying for M.B.A.'s.

Students are fighting for places in the country's top B-schools. And why not? Average starting salaries at Harvard Graduate School of Business Administration, where only 12% of the applicants are accepted, is $78,930. Salaries at Stanford University Graduate School of Business, where only 10% of the applicants are accepted, are slightly more, at $79,135. And in many cases an M.B.A. is a ticket to advancement. Harvard boasts that its graduates make up about one fifth of the top three officers of *Fortune* 500 companies and that over 3,500 Harvard alumni head U.S. corporations.

ACADEMIA AND CORPORATE AMERICA

University research and the prospects of improving American technology are going hand and hand as corporations increasingly fund academic research. Corporate donations to colleges and universities are up dramatically in recent years, hitting $1.8 billion a year or about 23% of the $8.2 billion given each year.

If the past is any yardstick, corporate gifts to universities are a good investment. At Stanford, for example, a close working relationship between academia and business in the 1930s helped produce the legendary Silicon Valley. (See the profile of the area in the "Electronics" section.) More recently, cash-strapped universities and businesses needing new technology have entered into new partnerships, breaking down the anti-business climate that infected many universities during the 1960s. In the 1980s, Harvard Medical School, for instance, teamed up with du Pont for genetic research; Carnegie-Mellon University is cooperating with Westinghouse in robotics;

the Massachusetts Institute of Technology is working with Exxon on combustion research and with such firms as ITT and General Motors at its Poly-
mer Processing Laboratory. Stanford continues to work with corporate
sponsors in microelectronics and biotechnology. Monsanto has a 10-year,
$52 million pact with Washington University.

Despite fears among some critics that universities are sacrificing their
independence, the alliance between industry and academia could work wonders for both. Faced with declining government spending for research, universities have watched their laboratories age and deteriorate. Corporate
spending allows them to improve their facilities and hire new researchers. At
the same time, business, faced with foreign competition, needs new technology to increase productivity and profits.

Funding for research and development at universities is now $13 billion a
year, way up from $6 billion in 1980 or the $2.3 billion spent in 1970. Nationwide funding has also grown to over $136 billion today, up from around $60
billion in the early 1970s. Industry and government each spend about half.
But these outlays don't match what was spent in the early 1960s, when the
economy was much healthier. After adjusting for inflation, funding for
research and development remained virtually stagnant between 1967 and
1977. And, as a percentage of the GNP, it actually declined between 1964,
when it was 3%, and today, now fallen to 2.6%. Total research and development spending has increased since 1975, when it was 2.2% of GNP. But
much of this money went into the military buildup of the 1980s. Nondefense
research and development as a percentage of GNP actually declined from
1.9% in 1982 to 1.7% in 1988. That leaves the U.S. far behind its main international competitors in nondefense research and development. Germany
spends 2.6% and Japan spends 2.8% on nondefense research.

Business Week estimates that the largest American corporations spent
about $65 billion in 1989, up 10% from 1988. But when you adjust for infla-
tion, the increase was only 5.6%. On the surface that may seem impressive,
but it is actually a much smaller growth rate than the 1970s, when R&D was
growing 8 percentage points faster than inflation. Worse, the slowdown in
American R&D is letting foreign companies catch up. *Business Week* estimates that the 200 largest foreign companies around the globe spend $63.4
billion on R&D, almost as much as the 894 U.S. companies *Business Week*
surveyed.

EDUCATION ON THE JOB

In the 1990s employee training on the job is now a $45.5 billion industry.
According to a 1990 survey by *Training* magazine 39.5 million employees
received 1.3 billion hours of formal employer-sponsored training at a total
cost of $29 billion in 1990. What American business gets for this money will
probably make the difference between improved productivity in the workplace and declining competitiveness in the international market.

American employers have discovered that they need better-educated
employees to run highly automated factories or high-tech offices, yet many

employees enter the job market unable to adapt to an increasingly complex workplace. A 1986 study by the U.S. Department of Commerce found that some 17 million Americans, or about 13% of adults, were illiterate. Earlier studies found that 14% of the population can't fill out a check properly and nearly 33% can't do simple math. Jonathan Kozol, author of *Illiterate America,* estimates that illiteracy costs the economy $20 billion a year.

For many businesses, the costs of poorly educated employees are easy to see. In auto companies, supervisors quickly discovered that employees could not understand and operate some of the new robots and automated machinery. To remedy the problem, GM had to spend $200 million in basic skills programs; Ford is spending another $120 million.

But in many cases, the costs of illiteracy and poor education are more difficult to detect. No one knows how many employees work slowly or are unable to get the most out of their office machinery because of educational handicaps. But one visible sign of the problem is the fact that the service economy has seen virtually no improvement in productivity even though companies have spent tens of billions of dollars on new computers and telecommunications equipment in the past decade.

In other cases, the problem of improving productivity isn't so much teaching people basic educational skills as teaching them how to adapt to new markets and technology. Training systems will have to teach managers how to administer high-tech workplaces, how to use more cost-efficient management techniques, and how to get employees to improve the quality of their products. Education and training aimed at getting the most out of America's human resources will, in the long run, probably improve productivity more than new technology.

Table E-1   Who Gets Training on the Job

Job category	Organizations providing training (%)	Mean number of individuals trained	Number of individuals trained (in millions)	Mean number of hours delivered	Total hours of training delivered (in millions)
Salespeople	40.4	65.1	4.02	40.7	163.61
Professionals	59.6	68.1	6.21	35.5	220.46
First-Line Supervisors	73.3	38.4	4.31	35.4	152.57
Middle Managers	75.9	25.4	2.94	35.1	103.19
Customer-Service People	45.0	91.6	6.31	33.0	208.23
Executives	67.3	7.9	0.81	32.9	26.65
Senior Managers	58.5	13.0	1.16	31.2	36.19
Production Workers	33.3	195.4	9.95	30.7	305.47
Office/Administrative Workers	66.7	36.6	3.74	19.0	71.06
Total			39.45		1,287.42

Source: *Training:* October, 1990, *The Magazine of Human Resources Development.* Copyright 1990 Lakewood Publications Inc.

Table E-2   Spending on Education Around the World

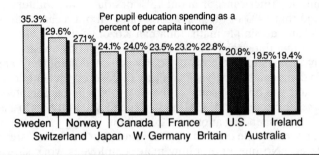

Per pupil education spending as a percent of per capita income

35.3%	29.6%	27.1%	24.1%	24.0%	23.5%	23.2%	22.8%	20.8%	19.5%	19.4%

Sweden | Norway | Canada | France | U.S. | Ireland
Switzerland Japan W. Germany Britain Australia

Source: Economic Policy Institute.

Table E-3   Business Support of Education

In recent years voluntary corporate support for education has grown dramatically, exceeding support from foundations, religious organizations, and all other groups. In 1985, for the first time ever, contributions from business slightly exceeded the $1.46 billion in contributions given by alumni.

(millions of dollars)

	1970	1975	1980	1985	1986	1987	1988
Estimated voluntary contributions for colleges and universities, total	1,780	2,160	3,800	6,315	7,400	8,500	8,200
Business contributions	269	357	696	1,574	1,702	1,819	1,853
Percentage of total	15.1%	16.5%	18.3%	25%	22.9%	21.4%	22.6%

Source: Council for Financial Aid to Education, *Voluntary Support of Education,* annual.

ELECTRONICS

THE MARKET

What steel and heavy industry were to the 19th-century American economy, electronics is to the 21st century. Auto companies, appliance manufacturers, machine tool makers, and companies in a host of other mature manufacturing industries are all hoping that high-tech electronics will allow them to improve designs and survive a tough battle with foreign competitors.

But it would be wrong to see the market for electronics products only in terms of the distant future. Despite the industry's futuristic image, companies involved in the design, development, manufacture, assembly, application, or servicing of electronic equipment, systems, or components already form one of the nation's largest industries. By producing products as varied as industrial robots for the factory, miniature electronic circuits for silicon chips, electronic mail for business, lasers for Star Wars, and television sets for the living room, the industry is now the largest manufacturing employer in the U.S. One out of every nine manufacturing jobs is in electronics, the American Electronics Association reports. Overall, 4% of all jobs are in electronics or in an industry that would not exist without electronics. Employment in the electronics industry is three times that of automotive manufacturing and nine times that of the basic steel industry.

THE MONEY

The ever-expanding range of electronics products has translated into one of the world's fastest-growing industries. The U.S. electronics industry has grown from a $200 million industry in 1927 to $266 billion in 1990. Sales of electronics products grew 50% faster than the rest of the economy during the 1980s and the U.S. electronics industry now rivals the chemical, auto, and steel industries in size. *Electronic Business* estimates that the U.S. electronics industry will grow from $268 billion in 1990 to $580 billion in 2000. This is the industry breakdown it found:

- Sales of computers and office equipment totaled $69.7 billion, about 26% of the $268 billion in electronic sales in 1990 and should grow to $185.6 billion (32%) in the year 2000.
- Communications equipment accounted for 29% of the market ($77.7 billion). By 2000, their sales will hit $179.8 billion (31%).
- Instruments and controls made up 19% ($50.9 billion) of all sales in 1990 and will hit 18% ($104.4 billion) by the end of the century.
- Components were 21% ($56.2 billion) of all sales in 1990 and will be 16% ($92.8 billion) by the year 2000.
- Consumer electronics sales topped $13.4 billion (5%), and should hit $29 billion (5%) in 1990.

Worldwide, sales now top $505 billion. The U.S. still has the highest volume of shipments, followed by Japan ($106 billion), and Europe ($98 billion).

THE PLAYERS AND THE PEOPLE

About 1.9 million people are employed in the electronics industry. Although many parts of this highly competitive industry are dominated by small firms, a few large firms capture a large part of the sales. Table E-4 (below) lists the country's 25 largest electronics companies.

TRENDS AND FORECAST

There's little doubt that the demand for electronics will grow dramatically over the next few years, as it has in the past. But it is questionable how much of this growth will benefit U.S. companies. In the last decade, the U.S., long the leader in electronics and high technology, has faced increasing competition from foreign producers. The U.S. now exports $55.5 billion worth of electronic equipment but imports $68.6 billion.

Table E-4   Top 25 Electronics Companies

Company	1990 Electronic sales in latest available 4 quarters	Percent of Gross
1. IBM	$52,358,000,000	80.0
2. General Electric	18,546,000,000	33.0
3. General Motors	16,912,000,000	13.6
4. Hewlett-Packard	13,030,000,000	100.0
5. Digital Equipment	12,943,000,000	100.0
6. Xerox	12,522,000,000	70.0
7. AT&T	11,195,000,000	31.0
8. Unisys	10,063,000,000	100.0
9. Motorola	10,010,000,000	100.0
10. Texas Instruments	6,289,000,000	97.0
11. Apple Computer	5,588,000,000	100.0
12. NCR	5,564,000,000	92.0
13. Raytheon	5,426,000,000	60.2
14. Rockwell International	4,888,000,000	39.8
15. Honeywell	4,638,000,000	75.0
16. Tandy	4,400,000,000	100.0
17. Westinghouse Electric	4,229,000,000	33.0
18. Lockheed	4,173,000,000	43.0
19. Compaq Computer	3,805,000,000	100.0
20. Intel	3,517,000,000	100.0
21. TRW	3,266,000,000	43.0
22. GTE	3,107,000,000	17.3
23. Harris	3,100,000,000	100.0
24. McDonnell Douglas	2,996,000,000	10.8
25. Litton Industries	2,979,000,000	59.0

Source: *Electronic Business.*

Behind the wave of imports are several factors. A strong dollar and lower overseas labor costs allowed foreign competitors to undercut U.S. rivals in the mid-1980s. As a result, many U.S. companies closed or sold off their operations. In 1979, six American companies made television sets; today Zenith is the only one left. Similarly, U.S. manufacturers supply less than 10% of all the VCRs sold in America. Unlike some U.S. high-tech companies that made important technological breakthroughs and then stumbled when it came to bringing their products to the market, Japanese and other foreign producers have proved to be remarkably adept at adapting basic U.S. technology, cutting production costs, and, most importantly, finding consumer applications for high-tech breakthroughs. Moreover, at least in the 1970s, Japan and West Germany spent more of their GNP on nondefense research and development than the U.S. With 65% of U.S. research and development money going to defense, both Japan and Germany far outstrip the U.S. in civilian applications of high technology and electronics. As a result, U.S. companies face the dismal prospect that, unless this trend is reversed, they may fall behind in basic research and technological development.

Increased foreign competition has prompted American companies to change the way they do business. To cut costs, many manufacturers have moved their operations overseas, allowing foreign producers to make the products and then putting their names on the goods. Critics say "out-sourcing" leaves U.S. companies without the technological and production skills they need to compete in the future and a strong dollar should slow the movement of electronics jobs overseas. But it's also clear that out-sourcing lets U.S. companies cut costs and concentrate on marketing and product development. The trend also allows the U.S. to respond more quickly to changes in the market (an important factor in a highly volatile industry like electronics) than they would if they manufactured all of their own parts and products.

SILICON VALLEY

In Palo Alto, California, there's a garage known as "the birthplace of modern electronics." There, Lee De Forest perfected the vacuum tube, which was the basis of radio transmission and the beginnings of modern media. But that's not the only famous garage near Silicon Valley and the Bay Area of San Francisco. For some reason, this area has been to modern electronics what the Tigris-Euphrates Valley was to early civilization.

Consider: In the early 1900s, amateur radio hams in the Bay region began experimenting with ham radios, much like the Silicon Valley computer whizzes who built the first personal computers and video games in the 1970s. One, Ralph Heintz, established the first wireless communication from an airplane to the ground and went on to found Heintz & Kaufman, a pioneer in the field of aircraft radio. Another was Charles Litton, who eventually founded Litton Industries. An Oakland company named Magnavox produced the first public address system. Sigurd and Russell Varian and William Hansens invented the klystron that was the basis of modern radar systems and William Hewlett and David Packard founded their company in another Palo Alto garage.

A key factor in the development of Silicon Valley as a high-tech paradise was the presence of Stanford University, just as MIT brought early computer wizards such as Ken Olsen of Digital Equipment Corporation and An Wang of Wang Laboratories to the Boston area.

In 1925, Fred Terman, son of the man who developed the IQ test, took charge of a radio communications laboratory in Stanford. Like many early Silicon Valley companies, it started in less than perfect quarters—an attic. But Terman's influence was to shape the direction of the area's technology for the next 40 years. Many of his students, such as William Hewlett and

David Packard, founded major electronics companies, and he talked Stanford University into giving the Varians use of the physics lab during the final stages of their research into radar. In the next 30 years, that minor investment brought the university $2 million in royalties.

But Terman did more than inspire a generation of talented researchers. Noticing that many firms moved out of the region and that many of his most talented students were forced to move east to find jobs, Terman worked with the University to create the Stanford Industrial Park on land left to it by Leland Stanford, the railroad tycoon. Stanford's bequest prohibited the university from selling the land, so developing the fields as an industrial park was about the only way the university could make money on it. Early tenants were Varian Associates and Hewlett-Packard.

At this point, in the early 1950s, a critical mass began to form between the university's research facilities and Silicon Valley's new high-tech entrepreneurs. As the region's reputation grew, national companies, such as Lockheed, Sylvania, Admiral, Kaiser, and General Precision moved into the area. And as the first generation of companies grew into industrial giants, young scientists left them to form new, innovative companies.

Success, of course, has its price. Picturesque orchards gave way to suburban sprawl and traffic jams. Many of the older, once-entrepreneurial companies have developed the hierarchical formal management culture of eastern companies they once ridiculed.

Hewlett-Packard Company

President and CEO: J. A. Young   3000 Hanover Street
Employees: 93,500   Palo Alto, California 94304
Assets: $11.1 billion   415-857-1501

	1990	1989	1985	1980
Revenues (millions of dollars):	13,538	11,898	6,505	3,099
Net income (millions of dollars):	771.0	829	489	269
Share earnings (dollars):	3.06	3.52	1.91	1.12

What it does: It is the largest maker of electronic test and measurement equipment and a leading maker of minicomputers.

David Packard and William Hewlett founded this electronics and computer giant in a Palo Alto garage with an investment of $538 each. Their Stanford University professor, Fred Terman, remembers he could always tell how business was going by where their car was parked. If it was parked in their garage, orders were down; if the car was parked in the driveway, business was booming.

And boom it did, after they invented the audio oscillator to measure sound waves. Walt Disney put in their first big order because he needed the equipment to create the elaborate sound system for the film *Fantasia.*

Since then, the founders and the company have prospered as the country's largest manufacturer of electronic test and measurement instruments, a leading minicomputer maker, the nation's ninth-largest electronics manufacturer, and a leading manufacturer of computer peripherals. David Packard, who provided the business savvy, has become one of the most visible prophets of Silicon Valley and a Republican party power broker. He was appointed Deputy Secretary of Defense under President Nixon, was chairman of the United States–Japan Advisory Commission under President Reagan, and subsequently headed the President's Blue Ribbon Commission on Defense Management. His stake in the company is worth about $1.4 billion, while William Hewlett's stake is worth about $665 million.

CONSUMER ELECTRONICS

The Market

The typical American home is becoming a sophisticated media center, thanks to consumer electronics. Currently there are 485 million radios in the U.S. and 201 million televisions reaching 98% of all households. VCRs can be found in 65% of all homes (up from 20% in 1984), color TVs in 95%, home computers in 21%, audio systems in 88%, telephone answering machines in 24%, cordless telephones in 22%, and projection TVs in 4%. Each year, Americans buy 41.1 million radios, 4.7 million audio systems, 296 million blank videocassettes, 382 million blank audio cassettes, 12.8 million VCRs, 36.4 million units of portable audio tape equipment, 21.1 million color TVs, 8.0 million telephone answering machines, 2.3 million black-and-white TVs and 4.4 million personal computers, 12.4 million microwave ovens, 6.3 million cordless phones and 20.0 million phones with cords, according to the Electronic Industries Association.

THE MONEY

Retail sales of consumer electronics top $43 billion a year, and factory shipments (from domestic and foreign producers) total $22.7 billion, up from $9.4 billion in 1979.

The Players

Imports dominate the markets. TVs, audio cassette recorders, VCRs, portable and table radios, and automobile tape players are a few of the products that are mostly or exclusively imported. Imports now supply 65% of the consumer electronics market. U.S. manufacturers sold about $7.0 billion worth of consumer electronics goods in 1990, compared with $13.1 billion worth of imports. The U.S. currently runs a trade deficit of about $11.3 billion in consumer electronics, up from $6.2 billion in 1981, but a slight improvement over the 1989 deficit ($12.0 billion).

FOOD

THE MARKET

Americans eat up an estimated $383.7 billion worth of food and beverages each year. Table F-1 (below) shows how they spent those food dollars.

TRENDS AND FORECAST

America's food business, from agriculture to processing plants to the super-market, was once the most successful in the world. Thanks to its efficiency, Americans only spend about 12% of their income on food, less than any-

Table F-1 The Food Industry
(factory shipments by U.S. producers in millions of dollars)

Industry	1988	1989[1]	1990[1]
MEAT PRODUCTS	74,385	80,099	88,628
Meat packing plants	43,108	45,739	49,831
Sausage & other prepared meats	15,291	15,786	18,514
Poultry slaughtering/processing	15,985	18,574	20,284
DAIRY PRODUCTS	41,289	43,370	48,471
Creamery butter	1,741	1,766	1,455
Cheese, natural & processed	10,849	11,785	14,009
Dry, condensed, evaporated	6,176	6,439	7,228
Ice cream & frozen desserts	4,574	4,602	4,948
Fluid milk	17,949	18,778	20,831
PRESERVED FRUITS AND VEGETABLES	37,011	40,400	42,806
Canned specialties	4,834	4,967	5,276
Canned fruits & vegetables	12,837	14,465	15,554
Dried fruits/vegetables & soups	2,106	2,607	2,490
Pickles, sauces & salad dressings	4,825	5,207	5,531
Frozen fruits & vegetables	6,872	7,170	7,490
Frozen specialties	5,538	5,985	6,465
GRAIN MILL PRODUCTS			
Cereal breakfast foods	5,667	6,415	6,876
BAKERY PRODUCTS	20,956	22,733	24,256
Bread, cake & the like	13,470	14,470	15,372
Cookies & crackers	6,075	6,820	7,431
Frozen bakery products, except bread	1,412	1,443	1,453
SUGAR AND CONFECTIONS			
Candy products	7,474	7,825	8,240
BEVERAGES			
Malt beverages	13,742	14,319	14,835
Wine, brandy, & brandy spirits	3,523	3,830	4,127
Distilled & blended liquors	3,194	3,361	3,611
Soft drinks & carbonated water	20,809	21,990	23,320
SUBTOTAL	228,049	244,342	264,170
Processed fishery products	5,501	6,645	6,800
TOTAL FOR 25 SECTORS	233,550	250,987	270,970
ESTIMATED TOTAL FOR ENTIRE FOOD & BEVERAGE INDUSTRY	328,875	353,506	383,652

[1]Estimate.
Source: U.S. Department of Commerce, Bureau of Census and International Trade Administration.

where in the world. In third-world countries, families spend as much as 62% of their budgets on food. (See also the "Agriculture," "Beverages," and "Restaurants" sections.)

But in recent years, the food business has been undergoing a tumultuous reorganization. During the 1980s, 1,154 mergers took place, producing some of the biggest deals of the 1980s. R. J. Reynolds, for example, paid $4.9 billion for Nabisco, while Philip Morris paid $5.6 billion for General Foods in 1985. And 1986 saw Beatrice Companies arrange for a $6.2 billion leveraged buyout. In 1989, Kohlberg Kravis Roberts & Co. cooked up a $24.7 billion leveraged buyout of RJR Nabisco Inc. By the end of the 1980s, more than $120 billion worth of deals were completed in the food and tobacco industries.

These megadeals reflected the interest tobacco companies have in diversifying out of their core businesses and the fact that it's simpler to increase your market share in a mature market, such as food, by buying a new company. At the same time, domestic producers are continuing to fight to cut costs by selling off unprofitable operations so they can finance the expensive advertising campaigns needed to promote new products.

One new problem facing the American food industry has been fighting off increased foreign competition. Already overseas farmers are undercutting the prices of many American farmers, and foreign investors have spent nearly $20.1 billion buying U.S. food companies or setting up their own U.S. subsidiaries. So far, however, American producers are holding their own. Farm exports rebounded in the late 1980s, and U.S. food companies have also been buying up foreign food companies. Direct investment overseas by American food processors is now more than $15.5 billion, up from $9.6 billion in 1984.

POPCORN POPPING PROFITS

If you're an average American, you will eat about 46 quarts of popcorn this year, according to the Popcorn Institute. And if you wonder why anyone would start a trade association to represent popcorn makers, remember, this is a big business. The Popcorn Institute represents popcorn makers that produce 685 million pounds of popcorn a year—about 85% of the total U.S. production. Annual sales of popcorn easily top $1 billion.

Popcorn has always been big at the movies, where theater owners count on getting an extra buck worth of profit at the concession stand from every ticket buyer. But it wasn't until the 1970s that popcorn sales really took off at the retail level. Pillsbury played a major role by introducing popcorn that could be popped in a microwave oven, and heavy advertising by other companies got consumers thinking of popcorn. The result: sales of unpopped popcorn rose as much as 16% a year and the amount of unpopped popcorn sold at retail stores rose from 171 million pounds in 1979 to over 271 million recently, according to Selling Areas-Marketing, Inc.

THE BAGEL WARS

In recent years, Lender's, the nation's largest bagel baker, and Sara Lee have squared off over the $400-million- to $500-million-a-year bagel market. Americans already eat about 8 million bagels a day, but about four out of every five Americans have not yet tried one. Lender's and Sara Lee want to change all that and make bagels a national food, as popular in Peoria as they are in New York.

The first shot in the bagel wars was fired in August of 1985, when Sara Lee introduced its frozen bagel line, challenging Lender's, which holds about 34% of the market. Sara Lee soon had 6% of the market.

Lender's responded by opening the world's largest bagel plant in the middle of Illinois, calling its plant the "Bagel Capital of the World." The Mattoon, Illinois, plant can turn out 1 million bagels a day thanks to automated bagel lines, an 80-foot-tall, 250-foot-long bagel freezer, and a 70-yard-long bagel oven.

While Sara Lee and Lender's battle for control of the bagel market, no one agrees on how bagels originated. One story has it that a Polish baker gave one to the King of Poland in 1683 after he defeated Turkish invaders. Another version says they were invented around 1610 by poor Polish Jews who considered the white roll a delicacy. The name comes from the German word *boug* meaning "ring."

PIZZA FACTS

Pizza now has a major share of the U.S. food market. Consider a few facts about this $15-billion-a-year industry:

- Americans eat about 75 acres of pizza every day—and that's a big pizza pie.
- The average American eats seven pizzas a year.
- All of this is produced by the 45,000 pizzerias in the U.S. They represent about 10.8% of all restaurants, more than the 8.5% of restaurants specializing in hamburgers.
- Pizza chains have captured about 55% to 60% of the $15 billion national pizza market.

FIRSTS IN FOOD

1808 The first canned food is developed for Napoleon's army.

1819 Ezra Daggett and Thomas Kensett set up the first canning operation in the U.S. William Underwood founds one of the nation's oldest canning companies in 1822, the William Underwood Company. His

CANNED FOOD

Canned food was first developed for Napoleon's army. (See "Firsts in Food" below.) Today it is one of the country's most popular ways of preserving foods. There are about 1,700 canning plants in the U.S., Puerto Rico, and the Virgin Islands, producing some 1,400 different canned food items. Each year, more than 1 billion cases of canned food are packed in 37 billion metal and glass containers. The average American eats about 150 pounds of canned food a year, about 11% of the food we eat each year.

GRILLING FOR DOLLARS

You may think that barbecues are fun but, for the Barbecue Industry Association, this is serious business. An estimated 180 million Americans enjoy barbecued foods every year, generating $6 billion in sales of briquets, grills, charcoal, lighter products, tools, and groceries.

The competition is heating up. As sales of barbecue sauce have grown 33% over the last three years, major food companies, Kraft, General Foods, and others, have beefed up their ad campaigns. Kraft, for example, spends about $10 million a year to capture a larger share of the $350 million market for barbecue sauce.

grandson pioneers the use of heat sterilization and the scientific use of bacteriology to make food canning safer.

1892   Henry Heinz gets the idea of making his company's slogan "57 Varieties" when he sees an advertisement for "21 Shoe Styles." The Heinz company already has more than 60 varieties—Henry just likes the sound of the number 57.

1894   Milton Hershey markets his Hershey's Milk Chocolate bar.

1897   Dr. John Dorrance develops a way of taking the water out of soup without hurting the flavor. Dorrance is a nephew of Joseph Campbell's partner and Campbell's Condensed Soup markets the product. Unlike earlier soups, which had been sold in bulky cans, Campbell's Soup is much lighter and more convenient for grocers and consumers.

1904   An ice cream stand runs out of dishes so a nearby Syrian-American pastry maker, Ernest Hamwi, makes pastries in the shape of cornucopias. It is the origin of the ice cream cone.

1914   Morton Salt adds magnesium carbonate to its salt, which allows the salt to pour in wet weather—hence the famous slogan, "When It Rains It Pours."

1912   The National Biscuit Company (now Nabisco) markets Oreo cookies. Since then it's sold more than 100 billion Oreos, enough to stretch to the moon and back twice.

1913   Stuck with a lot of extra peanuts, Philip Lance starts roasting them and making peanut butter, which had been invented in 1890. To demonstrate how good his product is, he smears it on bread and gives it to customers—hence the first commercial peanut butter sandwich.

1914   Eskimos, the experts on all things frozen, play a role in the development of frozen food. Clarence Birdseye, while visiting Labrador, notices that the Eskimos frozen food resists spoilage. He develops the first quick freezing technique in 1924 and in 1930 his Bird's Eye Frosted Foods hit the market.

1923   A peanut butter sandwich and a chocolate bar get mushed together in H. B. Reese's lunch bag. The Reese's Peanut Butter Cup is born.

1925   The Jolly Green Giant is introduced on vegetable cans, but at this time he is portrayed as a dwarf. A decade later a new variety of peas called "green giants" is introduced, so the dwarf becomes both a giant and "jolly."

1927   Mrs. Daniel Gerber tells her husband she's tired of straining vegetables by hand for their young daughter. Dan Gerber and his father, who are already in the canning business, solve the problem by introducing the first nationally distributed strained baby food, Gerber.

1930   The Continental Baking Company introduces the first sliced bread under its Wonder Bread label. The same year, the company introduces Hostess Twinkies.

1936   Robert Hunsicker manufactures dog food by hand in his basement. It is the beginning of Alpo.

1937   Sylvan Goldman of Oklahoma City invents the shopping cart so his customers can buy more.

1949   Charles Lubin develops Sara Lee Original Cheese Cake. He is the first to market bakery products in supermarkets. In the 1950s he sells his goods in the aluminum foil that they were baked in, thus creating a popular marketing technique.

1954   C. A. Swanson & Sons introduces the TV dinner. Today sales of complete frozen dinners top $1 billion a year.

POTATO CHIPS

A disgruntled diner and a disgusted Indian inadvertently teamed up in 1853 to create what have become America's top snack food—potato chips. The setting was the gracious Moon's Lake Hotel in Saratoga Springs, New York. The Indian was a chef, George Crum. The diner's name was lost and is probably best forgotten. Anyway, the patron ordered french fries but kept snottily sending them back to the kitchen, saying they were too thick. The peeved Crum finally sliced them wafer-thin and fried them to a crisp. The diner was finally delighted, and so were a lot of other folks who tried what became a specialty at the hotel and then spread far and wide.

FOREST AND PAPER PRODUCTS

THE MARKET

Trees are some of man's best friends. Just look at the industries that depend on them: logging, paper, sawmills, construction, publishing, furniture, and the container industry are some of the primary consumers. As a result, the forest and paper products industry is heavily dependent on the state of the economy and consumer spending. (The joke in Oregon, a state that is heavily dependent on lumber, is, "When the economy gets the sniffles, Oregon gets pneumonia.") A weak economy and lower consumer spending, for instance, cut housing starts, which lowers the demand for wood; cut advertising dollars, which lowers the publishing demand for paper; and hurt the demand for consumer goods, which cuts demand for paper used to package various products.

THE MONEY

The first American business was a sawmill, established in Jamestown in 1608, and one of the first American exports, shipped to England that same year, was lumber. In 1990, the wood products industry cut down $57.9 billion worth of wood products. The industry's revenues included $18.8 billion from saw mills, and $13.4 billion from logging camps and log contractors.

Paper and allied products added another $130 billion, up from $98 billion in 1985. There are 820,000 people employed in the wood products, lumber, and paper industries.

Table F-2   The Wood Products and Paper Industry

	1990 Shipments in Billions of Dollars	1990 Employment
Total wood products	57.9[1]	470,700
Logging	13.4	86,500
Sawmills and planing mills	18.8	148,000
Hardwood dimension and flooring	1.7	28,300
Millwork	9.4	88,800
Wood pallets and skids	2.1	28,700
Hardwood plywood	2.2	20,200
Softwood plywood	4.9	36,100
Reconstructed wood products	2.9	22,800
Wood preserving	2.4	11,300
Total paper and allied products	132	625,900
Pulp mills	5.5	13,900
Paper and paperboard mills	52.1	185,000
Corrugated and solid fiber boxes	18.1	106,000
Folding paperboard boxes	6.9	51,000
Setup paperboard boxes		
Sanitary paper products	14.1	37,500
Flexible packaging materials	11.7	70,100
Paper coated and laminated NEC	7.9	33,000
Envelopes	3.2	28,400
Other paper and paperboard products	12.9	101,000

[1]Subtotals may not equal totals for industry due to rounding.
Source: International Trade Administration.

Weyerhaeuser Company

Chairman and CEO:
  G. H. Weyerhaeuser
Employees: 42,900
Assets: $16.4 billion

Corporate Headquarters Building
Tacoma, Washington 98477
206-924-2345

	1990	1989	1985	1980
Revenues (millions of dollars):	9,024	10,106	5,206	4,536
Net income (millions of dollars):	393.7	341	200	321
Share earnings (dollars):	1.87	1.56	0.88	1.65

What it does: The biggest company in wood products in terms of net sales. A major producer of pulp, paperboard, and corrugated containers.

Frederick Weyerhaeuser arrived in America in 1852 from Germany. By the time he died in 1914, his Weyerhaeuser Timber Company owned about 2 million acres of forest. Today, the company's far-flung operations involve just about every aspect of the wood products industry: its sawmills produce lumber, paper mills produce wood pulp and papers, packaging operations produce containers and packages. Its real estate and financial services operations could even sell some of the company's millions of acres of timberland.

But hard times have forced the family-controlled giant to change its ways. An industry-wide slump caused earnings to drop. The Canadians dumped lumber on the U.S. market at cheaper prices. Other companies slashed labor costs by obtaining hefty givebacks from unions or, when that failed, shutting unionized plants and opening nonunion ones. In response, under CEO George Weyerhaeuser—the third generation of the family to run the company—the company cut labor costs, sold off nonessential operations, and slashed its payroll from 42,800 in 1981 to 35,000 in 1987.

Already the bitter medicine is paying dividends for the sick company. Earnings jumped from $140 million in 1982 to $584 million in 1988. Weyerhaeuser will, however, be hurt by an economic slowdown in 1991, which has cut construction demand for wood, and advertising demand for paper. Even so, increased capital spending and more efficient operations mean Weyerhaeuser will remain one of the most competitive players in the industry during the 1990s.

CHRISTMAS TREES

Christmas trees first appeared about 400 years ago in Germany and by the 19th century the custom had spread through most of northern Europe. In America, it's safe to say that today's Christmas tree business was an outgrowth of the American Revolution: Hessian mercenaries fighting on the side of the British brought the German custom to the U.S. By 1851, demand was so great that Mark Carr hauled two ox sleds of Christmas trees from upstate New York to the streets of New York City, where he set up the first Christmas tree retail lot. Today, Americans buy over 32 million natural Christmas trees, according to the National Christmas Tree Association. About 100,000 people are employed full- or part-time in the Christmas tree industry. Sales top $600 million a year.

FRANCHISES

THE MARKET

If the American commercial landscape looks redundant, it is. Since 1960, franchises have become one of the most popular ways of marketing goods and services. Already one third of all retail dollars are spent at franchise operations. Nine out of 10 people over the age of 12 eat regularly in fast-food franchises. Every night of the year more than 300,000 people stay in Holiday Inns, a franchise operation.

THE MONEY

Franchise sales hit $716.7 billion in 1990, up from about $143 billion in 1972. Franchises owned by large chains account for 12% of sales while independent franchises get the largest share (88%). Sales can also be broken down another way. About 71% of these sales came from product and trade name franchisers, such as gas stations, soft drink bottlers, and auto dealerships, which have independent sales relationships with the suppliers. The rest were earned by franchise operations known as *business format franchisers*. In those operations, which include McDonald's, the franchise operators not only use a product, trade name, or service, but also use the company's marketing strategy, its business format, its manuals for quality control and operations, and, at times, even its architectural design for the outlet.

Retail franchise sales, which include the $50-billion-a-year fast-food franchise business, dominate the franchise business, accounting for 87% of all franchise sales and 33% of all retail sales in the U.S.

THE PLAYERS

There are over 533,000 franchise establishments in the U.S.

THE PEOPLE

About 7.3 million people earn a living from franchises.

TRENDS AND FORECAST

The first franchise operations were started by the I. M. Singer Company in 1851 to sell sewing machines. In 1898, General Motors used franchises to enhance its marketing, and, soon afterward, the idea spread to other auto makers, soft drink producers, gasoline service stations, and a variety of other businesses. Franchising really took off when Ray Kroc turned McDonald's into the largest fast-food restaurant. (See the profile of McDonald's in the "Restaurant" section.) Franchise operations often offer owners a competitive advantage with nationwide and local advertising that increases product identification, direction and management help in daily operations, and a well-established reputation for reliability and quality. As a result, franchise sales now equal about 20% of the GNP and may grow to as much as half of all retail sales by the year 2000.

FUNERALS

Americans now spend $10 billion to $12 billion a year on funerals and about $2,750 for the average funeral at the country's 22,000 funeral homes. About 14% of all Americans who die are cremated. Industry analysts expect that figure to grow to as much as 30% by 2000.

Most funeral home companies continue to be small, family-run operations. Service Corporation International (SCI) of Houston, Texas, is, however, a notable exception. Aided by a public offering in 1969, SCI began buying funeral homes from retiring owners and today is the country's largest owner and operator of funeral homes. It has 551 funeral homes in 33 states, 126 cemeteries in 26 states, florists, and even a casket company for the closest thing to full service in the funeral industry. Its $518 million in annual sales produce $41.3 million in profits.

GAMBLING

THE MARKET AND THE MONEY

All of the talk about speculation on Wall Street and merger mania pales in comparison to a much older form of speculation—gambling. Americans now bet over $250 billion a year, according to *Gaming and Wagering Business* magazine. Overall, gamblers lose about $30.2 billion a year on their legal and illegal bets.

As always, the big winners are the people taking the bets. *Gaming and Wagering Business* breaks down the $290 billion gambling industry as follows: About $196 billion was bet at casinos; $19.5 billion on lotteries; $13.9 billion was legally bet on horses; $3.2 billion on greyhounds; $3.8 billion on bingo; $3.8 billion at card rooms; $4.0 billion at charitable games; $1.8 billion at legal bookmakers; and $0.4 billion on Indian reservations. That adds up to about $246.4 billion in legal gambling. In addition, Americans bet about $43.1 billion illegally. Most illegal gambling involved sports ($29.5 billion), horses ($8.1 billion), and numbers rackets ($5.6 billion).

Gaming and Wagering Business also reports that gamblers did the best at casinos, where they lost $7.8 billion, about 4.0% of the total amount they bet. Bettors faced the worst odds at government-run lotteries, where they lost $9.6 billion, nearly half (49.4%) of what they bet.

THE PLAYERS

In legal gambling, the most successful players are state and local governments. They pull in $19.5 billion a year in revenues and $9.6 billion in profits from lotteries. Each year some 56 million people walk into a casino, betting over $196 billion. For their trouble, they collectively lose $7.8 billion.

Gamblers who visit all 50 states, Puerto Rico, Washington D.C., and the Virgin Islands, will find that they can bet on a horse race in 31 jurisdictions, a greyhound race in 15, state-run lotteries in 33, card rooms in 9, and bingo in 47.

TRENDS AND FORECAST

There was a time when gambling was the closest thing to a no-risk business. That is, of course, if you were the one taking the bets.

Take slot machines. Operators pay about $5,000 for each machine. You don't need someone to operate a slot machine. You just line the machines up against a wall and bettors pump money into them. At popular casinos, a $5,000 machine will earn over $100,000 a year. Each year bettors lose over $3 billion at the slots, more money than they drop at the tables.

The odds are also very good if you run the tables. Typically the odds are rigged in favor of the house by a small margin. In roulette the odds are about 5.3% in the house's favor, 1.5% in baccarat, and 1.4% in craps. For slots, the house advantage is a hefty 11%. But odds are even worse than they seem. These odds are for each bet and very few bettors go all the way to Atlantic City or Las Vegas to place one bet. If the house advantage is 5.3% at roulette and if you bet five times in a row, you'll lose on the average, 5.3% on each bet, or 23.8% of your original investment after five bets. As a result, bettors at most Atlantic City casinos post heavy losses, dropping about 16% of their money in craps and blackjack, 25% in roulette, and 15% in baccarat.

But in recent years, the money-making machine has not produced the same old profits. The big problem is increased competition and ever-growing costs. At the Las Vegas gambling tables, success lured other operators into the market. Legalized gambling in Atlantic City cut into the profits in Vegas and overbuilding in Atlantic City has reduced profits there. New federal rules that require casinos to report all cash transactions over $10,000 are also cutting into the betting of high rollers, who want to keep their cash flow hidden from the IRS.

The biggest disaster has come, however, from the casino economy. In 1988, Donald Trump battled Merv Griffin, the producer of such well-known T.V. game shows as "Wheel of Fortune," for control of Resorts International in Atlantic City. Griffin ended up with Resorts International, but Trump got to keep its Taj Mahal casino, which Resorts had never finished. Griffin soon realized he'd paid too much to enter the softening Atlantic City gaming market, and Resorts went into bankruptcy in 1989, leaving junk bond investors with 78% of Resorts' stock and Griffin with 22%. Trump, who was already hurt by a depression in the real estate industry, bragged about how he'd beaten Griffin in the art of the deal. He claimed Griffin got the older Resorts property while he made money on his raid and got the Taj Mahal, which would be the largest, gaudiest gaming palace ever built. The only problem was that the Taj Mahal was so big, Trump's four casinos and hotels in Atlantic City would have had to capture more than half the gaming revenues in Atlantic City just to make the payments on the $1.2 billion in junk bonds he used to buy his casinos. After it opened, the Taj Mahal did a record amount of business, $125 million in revenues in 1990, but 20% of it had to go to pay interest on junk bonds. In its first three months, the casino lost $14 million, thanks to $24 million in interest, and by the summer of 1990, the end of the junk bond, the casino economy of the 1980s finally caught up with Donald Trump. He missed several bond payments, *Forbes* dropped him from its list of the 400 wealthiest Americans, and Trump's bankers put him on a tight budget. (He could spend no more than $2.0 million a month.)

Many of the same problems hang over the gaming industry in the early 1990s. Thanks to overbuilding, 1989 was the first year when gaming revenues did not keep up with the nation's overall economic growth. New casinos opening in 1990 boosted total revenues but won't do much for the industry's bottom line, since they took business away from many of the older casinos. Then, war in the Middle East put the kibosh on the travel industry and further hurt casino revenues. With tight economic conditions in 1991, the odds are that the gaming industry faces another year of sluggish growth.

GREETING CARDS

THE MARKET

Americans buy 7 billion greeting cards a year, sending 2.2 billion on Christmas and another 850 million on Valentine's Day, according to the Greeting Card Association. And don't forget the 1.6 billion birthday cards sent each year.

THE MONEY

All of those cards added up to about $3.7 billion worth of factory shipments in 1991, up from $2.9 billion in 1987.

THE PLAYERS

Three major companies hold about 80% of the greeting card market. But in recent years many smaller card makers have appeared, producing innovative, offbeat cards. The public loves the new designs and these so-called "alternative" card makers now number about 500 (up from 200 in 1982). Their segment of the market (about 15% of total sales) is growing three times faster than the industry as a whole.

The two largest card makers remain Hallmark Cards and American Greetings Corporation.

THE FORECAST

Industry receipts are expected to grow 2% to 3% a year faster than inflation over the next few years. Alternative card makers can expect more competition from the major producers, which are fighting back to regain their share of the market.

Table G-1   Sending a Card: The Most Popular Holidays for Card Makers

Holiday	Number of cards sent
Christmas	2.2 billion
Valentine's Day	850 million
Easter	185 million
Mother's Day	145 million

Source: Greeting Card Association.

HALLMARK

More than 20 million copies of Hallmark's "Thinking of You" card have been sold.

HEALTH CARE AND SERVICES

THE MARKET AND THE MONEY

Health care costs continue to hit feverish levels. Total costs of health care and services will hit $756.3 billion in 1991, up from $496.5 billion in 1987. Way back there in 1972, they were only $93.9 billion.

Such bills might put the economy and corporate profits in intensive care. U.S. companies now spend about $91 billion providing health insurance to 130 million workers and family members. Health care services have been growing 12.5% over the past 20 years and are expected to jump 11% to 13% between now and 1993. By the year 2000, health care could cost Americans as much as $1.5 trillion.

Table H-1   The Cost of Health Care

Here's how the country spends its health care dollars:

(billions of dollars)

Item	1987	1988	1989[1]	1990[2]	1991[3]	Percent change			
						1987–88	1988–89	1989–90	1990–91
TOTAL EXPENDITURES	492.5	544.0	604.1	675.7	756.3	10.5	11.0	11.9	11.9
Health services and supplies	475.2	524.1	583.5	653.0	731.3	10.3	11.3	11.9	12.0
Personal health care	436.7	480.0	530.7	589.4	657.1	9.9	10.6	11.1	11.5
Hospital care	193.8	211.7	232.8	257.2	285.7	9.2	10.0	10.5	11.1
Physicians' services	93.0	105.1	117.6	131.9	148.3	13.0	11.9	12.2	12.4
Dentists' services	27.1	29.4	31.4	33.8	36.5	8.5	6.8	7.6	8.0
Other professional services	21.2	23.8	27.0	30.7	35.0	12.3	13.4	13.7	14.0
Home health care	4.1	4.5	5.4	6.5	7.5	9.8	20.0	20.4	15.4
Drugs and other medical nondurables	38.7	41.5	44.6	48.0	51.7	7.2	7.5	7.6	7.7
Vision products and other medical durables	10.7	12.0	13.5	15.3	17.4	12.1	12.5	13.3	13.7
Nursing home care	39.8	42.8	47.9	54.1	61.4	7.5	11.9	12.9	13.5
Other personal health care	8.3	9.3	10.5	11.9	13.5	12.0	12.9	13.3	13.4
Program administration and net cost of private health insurance	23.9	27.9	35.3	44.6	53.5	16.7	26.5	26.3	20.0
Government public health activities	14.7	16.2	17.5	19.0	20.7	10.2	8.0	8.6	8.9
Research and construction	17.3	19.8	20.6	22.7	25.0	14.5	4.0	10.2	10.1
Research[4]	9.0	10.3	11.0	12.2	13.5	14.4	6.8	10.9	10.7
Construction	8.2	9.5	9.6	10.5	11.4	15.9	1.5	9.4	8.6

[1]Preliminary.
[2]Estimate.
[3]Forecast.
[4]Research and development expenditures of drug companies and other manufacturers and providers of medical equipment and supplies are excluded from "research expenditures," but they are included in the expenditure class in which the product falls.
Note: Numbers may not add to totals because of rounding.
Source: Health Care Financing Administration, Office of the Actuary Estimates and forecasts by U.S. Department of Commerce, International Trade Administration.

In the 1950s, patients picked up about two thirds of their medical bills. But by 1990, federal, state, and local governments paid 42% of all personal health care expenditures; private health insurance picked up 31%, and patients paid only 24%.

Worse, health care costs are eating up an even bigger share of the GNP. About 5.9% of the GNP went to health care in 1965; by 1980 it was 9.1%, according to the Department of Health and Human Services. In 1988, a record 11.5% of the GNP was leeched off by the health care industry. By 2000, health care will consume 15% of the GNP.

THE PLAYERS

There are some 585,600 doctors in the country. They average $210,500 in revenues and receive about $116,400 after paying such expenses as nurses' wages, rents, and malpractice insurance. About 19,600 new doctors graduate from the nation's medical schools each year. Money spent on physicians' services topped $100 billion for the first time in 1987, and hit $148.3 billion in 1991. Another $36.5 billion was spent on dental care.

TRENDS AND FORECAST

The health care industry is undergoing a major transformation in the way it spends money and provides services. Here are the winners and losers:

HMOs

Capitalizing on a cost-conscious market, HMOs (health maintenance organizations) have grown dramatically. There are now 575 HMOs that provide health care to over 37.4 million Americans, up from 1984, when 337 plans served 16.7 million. HMOs typically provide all a patient's health care for a fixed fee. That has given them an incentive to cut costs but many doctors have attacked the HMOs for skimping on services. But despite their popularity, HMOs have faced financial problems in recent years. One of the largest, Maxicare Health Systems, went bankrupt in 1989 after spending $446 million to buy two other HMOs.

Hospitals

Hospitals are the hardest hit by cost cutting. At the high-water mark of health care inflation in 1982, hospitals racked up 42% of the nation's health care bill. Today, the nation's 6,800 hospitals face a sicker financial climate. Hospitals are stuck with 1.3 million beds, many more than they need. Occupancy rates fell from 75% in 1980 to around 65% in 1989. Many hospitals closed, and in 1989 publicly owned hospitals reported $1 billion in losses on $4.4 billion in revenues. Altogether there are about 2,054 hospitals in the U.S. with 390,180 beds. Of these, 824 hospitals with 122,523 beds are investor owned.

Medical and Dental Equipment

For manufacturers of medical and dental equipment and supplies, a cost-cutting environment was a mixed blessing. The U.S. market for medical and dental equipment and supplies rose from $14.1 billion in 1982 to an estimated $21.1 billion in 1987 and hit $29.9 billion in 1991. To reduce costs, hospitals and doctors have pushed for better deals. Also, companies face more price competition in many traditional products. At the same time, however, cost-saving products, which allow patients to avoid spending additional time in hospitals, show strong sales.

Pharmaceuticals

A brighter spot in the health care industry is pharmaceuticals. Helped by a weaker dollar, pharmaceutical shipments rose from nearly $26.8 billion in 1984 to $39 billion in 1987 and $49.6 billion in 1990, and profits for the industry jumped 15%–18%.

FAT PROFITS FOR THE DIET INDUSTRY

When Americans set out to lose weight, their wallets usually get lighter faster than they do. Each year, Americans chow down about $346 billion of food and beverages. Then they go out and spend another $10 billion trying to win the battle of the bulge with such things as diet food, health club memberships, diet drugs, fat farms, and weight loss classes. Diet pills and diet powders bring in at least $3 billion from 950 clinics offering weight control programs. Routinely, strange diet books based on eating all the watermelon or pizza you want become best-sellers. Market research shows that 60% of all American women are on a diet at some point during the year.

What comes of all this? Certainly not thinner people. About the only things hotter at the food counter than dietary products is high-calorie food. The average American eats 150 pounds of caloric sweeteners (such as corn syrup and sugar) every year, up 20 pounds in only a decade. Makers of high-calorie ice creams such as Häagen-Dazs and Frusen Glädjé have increased their sales, as have cookie makers. The average American is six pounds heavier than he or she was in the 1960s, and nearly 34 million Americans need to lose 35 pounds or more. Makers of large-size clothing are now doing an $8 billion business.

No matter. Obviously, it's the thought that counts in the diet industry. And thoughts of a new thinner self have pushed some companies into large profits.

Take Weight Watchers. It was founded in 1963 by a 214-pound housewife named Jean Nidetch. By organizing weekly meetings at which people talked about their food binges the way alcoholics discuss uncontrollable drinking binges, she discovered a way to shed pounds and add heft to her pocketbook. Today, more than 25 million Americans have attended Weight Watchers meetings. About 4 million people currently attend seminars or buy its products. Taken over by H. J. Heinz Company in 1978, the $1.3 billion diet empire now includes a magazine, diet books, seminars, and diet frozen dinners.

Table H-2   The Largest Investor-Owned Nursing Homes

As the country gets older and older, privately owned nursing home companies become increasingly attractive investments. Here are the five largest:

Rank	Company	Beds	Units
1.	Beverly Enterprises	96,268	885
2.	ARA Living Centers	26,180	240
3.	Manor Care	21,637	160
4.	Health Care & Retirement Corp.	16,799	132
5.	United Health	16,018	141

Source: *Modern Healthcare.*

PSYCHIC INCOME

A few numbers tell a lot about the nation's state of mind: About 5 million people now visit psychiatrists, up from only a half-million 30 years ago. One in five Americans has had some type of mental health treatment, compared to about one in eight in 1960. And the stigma of seeing a psychiatrist is vanishing. Years ago, visiting a psychiatrist could damage a person's reputation or, as it did with Senator Thomas Eagleton in 1972, cost him a vice-presidential nomination.

But as psychotherapy has become more acceptable, business, insurers, and governments face mounting psychiatric bills. Seeing a shrink can cost $50 to $125 a session and many patients spend over $3,000 a year. Total cost is $23 billion a year and growing 10% to 20% a year, much faster than any other part of the nation's health care costs.

Take phobias for example, the nation's number-two mental health problem after alcoholism. An estimated 13 million Americans have phobias such as a fear of flying, fear of heights, or one of the most common phobias, the fear of leaving the house—agoraphobia. Fear of flying alone is believed to cost the airlines about $1.5 billion a year. Not surprisingly, some 50 centers now treat phobias.

BUSINESS AND AIDS

AIDS is already a major epidemic. By the start of 1990 some 78,312 cases of AIDS had been reported in the U.S., with 44,071 of those victims already dead. As many as 50,000 to 125,000 people show signs of infection and another 1,500,000 people may carry the disease but show no symptoms, according to the Centers for Disease Control. Worldwide over 150,000 cases are reported and 5 to 10 million people carry the virus.

AIDS poses major economic and ethical problems for American business. Insurance companies face rising claims for medical care, while businesses wonder where they will find the money to treat employees with AIDS. The disease has already infected the blood supply and a misplaced fear of catching AIDS while donating blood has hurt efforts to replenish it. Before a 1987 ruling by the Supreme Court prohibiting discrimination against persons with AIDS, widespread public hysteria about the disease often led employers simply to dismiss AIDS patients, provoking an ethical and legal crisis for many companies.

With some drugs showing promise for prolonging the life of AIDS patients but no cure in sight, treating and caring for AIDS patients promises to be a billion-dollar industry. Direct medical costs for treating AIDS patients hit $11.1 billion in 1991, and indirect costs totaled $55.6 billion, way up from the $7 billion spent in 1986. The average lifetime medical expenses from diagnosis to death per AIDS patient range from $80,000 to

$150,000. New drugs, which offer the promise of prolonging the lives of some patients, are also expensive.

Insurance officials now believe the disease may cost them as much as $10 billion a year. Already, the U.S. Commerce Department reports that the AIDS virus reports could cause "huge underwriting losses for health and life insurance companies" and that "the stability and solvency of the industry could be affected by the impact of the AIDS virus." To cut those losses, many life insurance companies now screen for the AIDS virus. But some states have prohibited AIDS testing by insurance companies, and the policy faces a number of court challenges.

ASPIRIN

When the U.S. government sold off properties after the First World War that had been seized from enemy aliens, it created a bonanza for some companies. For instance, the booty included stock in the Friedrich Bayer & Co., of New York, which had a plant that made a lot of drugs and a little-known product called Aspirin. Sterling Drug, Inc., seeing Aspirin as an analgesic it needed for its own product line, bid $5.3 million for the Bayer Company. Bringing its own marketing expertise to bear, Sterling turned *aspirin* into a household word.

GILLETTE

Young King Gillette was always casting around to invent a disposable something so that people would have to keep buying the thing. In 1895, annoyed one day that his straight razor was so dull it was unusable, he had a eureka—a razor with disposable blades.

But one person's good idea hits another's crazy bone. For years his pals joshed him about the silly thing he was trying to invent. Worse, toolmakers smirked and told him to forget it when asked for help in solving problems to get a blade holder to work. Finally, he badgered an MIT instructor, William E. Nickerson, into collaborating with him.

In 1903, the first year the Gillette safety razor hit the market, a grand total of 51 were sold at $5 apiece. But by 1906, production soared to 300,000 razors and 500,000 blades. Business really took off during the First World War when the U.S. military, concerned about battlefield sanitary conditions, ordered 3.5 million razors and 36 million blades. When the soldiers returned home, Gillette's business continued to boom thanks to a generation of young men who had gotten used to the razors.

Table H-3   Disabilities in America

About 37.4 million Americans, about 24% of everyone over the age of 15, have difficulty performing one or more basic physical activities. About 13.5 million people (7.5%) have a severe disability. A partial breakdown:

19.2 million people have difficulty walking a quarter mile.
 7.9 million are unable to walk a quarter mile.
18.2 million have difficulty lifting a weight equivalent to a full bag of groceries.
 7.8 million are unable to lift the same weight.
18.2 million people have trouble climbing a flight of stairs without stopping to rest.
 5 million can't climb a flight of stairs.
12.3 million people have trouble reading newsprint even with glasses or contact lenses.
 7.7 million have hearing troubles.
481,000 can't hear a normal conversation.
 2.5 million have a problem making their speech understood.

Source: U.S. Census Bureau.

HOTELS AND LODGING

THE MARKET

Sometimes it's a wonder that you can catch anyone at home. Sixty-three percent of all U.S. residents take one or more trips for business or pleasure at least 100 miles from home every year. Each day about 11 million Americans travel at least 100 miles from home on a trip requiring an overnight stay. Each year Americans take more than 330 million vacation trips and spend 1.8 billion nights away from home. Another 34 million foreigners visit the U.S. each year, staying an average of 8 nights.

Typically, lodgers break down like this: 36% are business travelers, 45% are on vacation, and 16% are visiting friends or relatives. The average hotel stay is 3.5 days for pleasure and 1.3 days for business.

THE MONEY

The lodging industry generated some $61.9 billion in revenue in 1990 (up from $17.7 billion in 1977 and $38.9 billion in 1984); it pays over $12.2 billion a year in wages and salaries and $4.1 billion in federal taxes. The average room rate for a hotel or motel alone is $59.47.

In recent years, dramatic growth in the number of rooms available, however, cut into the industry's profits. The industry's occupancy rate fell to 58% in 1989, and although it has recovered to 59% in 1990, there is still an oversupply of rooms. Laventhol & Horwath estimated that the industry's per-room profit fell from $481 in 1984 to a *loss* of $748 in 1987 and $429 in 1988.

THE PLAYERS

There are 45,000 lodging establishments in the U.S., with some 2.6 million rooms, according to the American Hotel and Motel Association. About 59% of the rooms were occupied each night in 1990, versus 67.9% in 1984. The nation's 25 largest chains control over 50% of all hotel rooms in America. Worldwide there are about 10.5 million rooms. After the hotel building boom of the early 1980s, construction declined from $7.2 billion in 1987 to $5.9 billion in 1989.

THE PEOPLE

The lodging industry employs 1.7 million people, and pays over $12.2 billion a year in wages and salaries. The lodging industry created over 250,000 jobs since 1987.

TRENDS AND FORECAST

The outlook for the lodging industry in the near future is mixed. On the plus side, rapid growth in number of middle-aged and retired Americans augurs well for the industry since these age groups have more money and time to spend on travel. And a weakened dollar should also help spur domestic travel.

Overbuilding, as noted above, has cut into profits, and high vacancy rates continue to cause problems for hotel owners. At the same time, stagnant corporate profits are forcing many companies to look for ways to cut their travel and entertainment budgets. Rising gas prices, if they hold up in the summer of 1991, more expensive air fares, and a slumping economy add up to more bad news. The industry's recovery from the overbuilding of the 1980s will probably have to wait at least until 1992.

LAW

THE MARKET AND THE MONEY

The U.S. is one of the most litigious nations ever created, spending more money (an estimated $940 billion in 1991) on legal bills and employing more lawyers (about 800,000) than any other major country. About half of these legal fees are spent by business, with individuals picking up the rest of the tab. The legal services industry employs about 900,000 people.

Going to court was never cheap, but since the early 1970s the bill for legal services has exploded. Americans spent only $10.9 billion on legal services in 1972, but in 1991 they should spend $100 billion.

The number of cases and suits brought by American lawyers is also skyrocketing. There are no detailed statistics on the number of cases filed in all of the nation's courts, but in U.S. district courts the number of tort cases filed grew to 43,759 in 1990 from 41,593 in 1985, while the number of personal injury cases caused by product liability increased to 18,679 from 12,507. The number of cases cases involving contract disputes increased to 61,975 from 46,039, and civil rights cases, including employment cases, decreased to 18,793 from 19,553 in the same period, according to the annual report of the Administrative Office of the U.S. Courts. Overall, the number of civil cases filed in U.S. district courts totaled 217,879 in 1990.

With more cases than ever before filed in U.S. courts, it's not surprising that the number of jury awards in liability and malpractice cases has skyrocketed. The number of tort cases filed in federal court increased 62% in the last decade while product liability cases increased 370%. At the same time the number of jury awards in liability and malpractice cases tripled and the number of million-dollar verdicts in medical malpractice cases rose from 20 in 1980 to 71 in 1984. The growth in mergers and acquisitions and personal bankruptcies has also helped hike legal fees.

About $38 billion was spent in 1990 to litigate or settle claims made in personal injury cases, a study by the C. V. Starr Center for Applied Economics at New York University says.

Another growth sector of the legal industry has been prepaid legal plans. Currently some 15 million Americans are covered by prepaid plans, which charge annual fees for providing such services as telephone consultation, letter writing, documents review, and general legal advice.

On an individual level, the legal services business provides some hefty salaries. The average lawyer's household makes $121,913 a year, an American Bar Association study says, and has a net worth of $500,000. One in nine lawyers is a millionaire.

THE PLAYERS

There are some 800,000 lawyers in the U.S. and about 900,000 people are employed in legal services. About 20% of all attorneys are women but with women accounting for nearly half of all new law school graduates, women will be making a larger impact on the industry. By 1992, there are expected to be one million lawyers in the U.S.

Table L-1   The Top 10 U.S. Legal Services Firms by Revenues

Rank	Law firm	Gross revenues (in millions of dollars)	Size Lawyers/partners
1.	Skadden, Arps	517.5	948/197
2.	Baker & McKenzie	341.5	1,339/432
3.	Jones, Day	320.0	1,052/369
4.	Shearman & Sterling	281.0	487/123
5.	Gibson, Dunn & Crutcher	280.0	611/194
6.	Davis Polk & Wardwell	240.5	380/96
7.	Sullivan & Cromwell	230.0	345/95
8.	Latham & Watkins	223.5	475/170
9.	Cravath, Swaine & Moore	213.0	288/64
10.	Fried, Frank	213.0	368/104

Source: *The American Lawyer,* July/August 1990.

Table L-2   Where the Lawyers Are: States with the Most and Least Lawyers per Capita

Rank	State	Number of lawyers per 1,000 residents
1.	Washington, D.C.	40
2.	New York	3.57
3.	Alaska	3.37
7.	Illinois	2.84
8.	California	2.74
22.	Texas	2.12
33.	Pennsylvania	1.92
49.	South Carolina	1.34
50.	West Virginia	1.32
51.	North Carolina	1.27

Source: *Legal Times,* September 23, 1985.

According to the American Bar Foundation there is about one lawyer for every 310 Americans. Most of these lawyers (64%) practice in small firms with 2 to 3 lawyers, 29% practice in 4-to-10-lawyer firms, and 7% are employed in large firms with 10 or more lawyers. The median age of a lawyer is only 38, down from 45 to 46 in 1970.

An Altman & Weil survey of law-firm economics breaks down how lawyers spend the money they receive for legal services: about 15.2% of all receipts is spent on support staff, 13.3% on miscellaneous expenses, 7.3% on occupancy, 3.3% on paralegals, 3.2% on equipment, and 1.6% on reference materials. The rest, 56.1% of all receipts, becomes lawyers' incomes.

TRENDS AND FORECAST

The number of students in law school increased dramatically in the late 1970s and early 1980s, peaking in 1991, when a record 127,261 students were enrolled. The number of law students declined, to 117,813 in 1987, largely because an oversupply of young lawyers cut salaries and job opportunities. There is little doubt that the legal services field will continue to grow as it has in the past. Clinics and government programs serve many poor people who were once unable to afford legal services. And with the price for many simple legal services falling or remaining stable, more people will turn to lawyers. Coupled with the fact that more businesses require high-priced legal services to navigate their way through complex government regulations, product liability suits, mergers, financing, and overseas trade, the industry should continue to see rapid growth.

NOTHING'S SACRED

More and more members of the clergy and religious groups are getting sued these days. Some 2,000 or so cases are pending nationwide and some $100 million was awarded in a recent 18-month period to those suing the religious, according to one estimate. The most serious cases involve child abuse, paternity, and embezzlement. "At one time, churches were protected by charitable immunity, but that's not the case anymore," the Reverend Dean Kelley of the National Council of Churches told *The New York Times*.

LEASING

"Don't buy—lease" is becoming the motto of American business. About 8 out of every 10 companies lease equipment. In 1991, American businesses are expected to lease more than $140 billion worth of equipment. That's a dramatic change from 1978, when Americans leased $22.3 billion worth of equipment.

Leasing plays a major role in a company's decision to acquire new equipment. It finances 45% of all capital expenditure for aircraft, 35% for railway equipment, 31% for motor vehicles, 23% for ships and boats, and 15% for computers, and plays a major role in the acquisition of agricultural and production machinery and medical equipment.

In 1985, about 26% of the money spent on leasing went for computers, 11.8% for telecommunications equipment, 10.5% for aircraft, 6.9% for trucks and trailers, 6.2% for industrial equipment, 5% for manufacturing equipment, 4.2% for project equipment, 2.8% for medical equipment, 2.4% for construction equipment, 1.7% for agricultural equipment, and 1.7% for railroad equipment, according to a survey by the American Association of Equipment Lessors.

Why lease? Executives give the following reasons, according to a poll by Lieberman Research, Inc.: 38% because it improves their cash flow, 28% because of tax benefits, 17% for better asset management, 17% because it is convenient, and 7% for accounting or balance-sheet reasons. Others add that leasing allows a company to acquire equipment without having to make major cash outlays and gives a company more flexibility, allowing it to trade in computers and other high-tech equipment as more advanced models hit the market. Many companies like the fact that leasing allows them to finance 100% of the cost of new equipment.

But while leasing continues to be attractive to many companies, the changed tax code dampened the kind of growth the industry saw in the early 1980s. While the industry grew at an annual rate of 19.7% between 1978 and 1985, it grew only 8% between 1985 and 1986 and grew about 6.9% in 1990.

MACHINE TOOLS

THE MARKET

The machine tool industry is small, accounting for only about 10 cents of every $100 in goods and services produced in the U.S., according to the National Machine Tool Builders' Association. But its products play a key role in the economy. Machine tools are used in factories around the world to cut, form, or shape the metal used in a variety of products, ranging from power plants to household appliances. The major consumers of machine tools are companies in such metalworking industries as aerospace, the auto industry, weapons manufacturing, machinery production, and toolmaking, to name a few.

Table M-1 Trends: Machine Tools
(in millions of dollars except as noted)

Item	1987	1988	1989	1990	Percent change 1987–88	1988–89	1989–90
Industry data							
Value of shipments	4,658	4,993	6,691	7,026	7.2	34.0	5.0
Value of shipments (1987$)	4,658	4,812	6,186	6,262	3.3	28.6	1.2
Total employment (000)	46.4	48.0	49.0	49.0	3.4	2.1	0.0
Production workers (000)	27.5	28.5	29.2	29.2	3.6	2.5	0.0
Average hourly earnings ($)	13.05	—	—	—	—	—	—
Product data							
Value of shipments	4,042	4,354	5,835	6,126	7.7	34.0	5.0
Value of shipments (1987$)	4,042	4,199	5,398	5,464	3.9	28.6	1.2
Trade data							
Value of imports	2,397	2,476	2,915	—	3.3	17.7	—
Import/new supply ratio	0.372	0.363	0.333	—	–2.4	–8.3	—
Value of exports	1,011	1,226	1,513	—	21.3	23.4	—
Export/shipments ratio	0.250	0.282	0.259	—	12.8	–8.2	—

Source: U.S. Department of Commerce: Bureau of the Census; International Trade Administration (ITA).

TRENDS AND FORECAST

No immediate turnaround is seen for the machine tool industry. The industry is threatened by a shift to plastic and the decline of several big customers of machine tools, such as the steel industry. Although several hundred small companies have already gone out of business, more mergers or bankruptcies are expected. Still, a weaker dollar will keep imports from grabbing a larger market share, and some U.S. producers are more efficient. The survivors, Daniel R. D. Senso of Standard & Poor's believes, will be companies offering sophisticated machine tool systems that include integrated software.

MAGAZINES

THE MARKET AND THE MONEY

The periodicals industry had revenues of over $22.1 billion in 1990, about half of which came from advertising. Consumer magazines received $6.7 billion in advertising, and business publications took in $2.8 billion.

There are more than 11,556 different magazines in the U.S. in 1990, most of which have very small circulations. The nation's 1,859 consumer magazines sell 324 million copies per month and produce about 65% of the industry's revenues. Business and professional magazines produce 34%; farm periodicals earn 1%. Comic books are a $125-million- to $150-million-a-year business, with companies such as Marvel selling 7.2 million a month. Another $431 million worth of magazines were exported in 1989.

THE PLAYERS

There are some 3,200 magazine companies in the U.S., but only 4 account for 22% of the money earned by the magazine industry. The largest magazines are listed in Table M-2 (below).

Table M-2   20 Largest Magazine Publishers, 1990

Rank	Magazine	Average paid circulation per issue (in thousands)
1.	Modern Maturity	22,443
2.	NRTA/AARP News Bulletin	22,105
3.	Readers Digest	16,396
4.	TV Guide	15,837
5.	National Geographic	10,182
6.	Better Homes and Gardens	8,002
7.	Family Circle	5,159
8.	Good Housekeeping	5,105
9.	Ladies Home Journal	5,022
10.	McCall's	5,011
11.	Woman's Day	4,512
12.	Time	4,258
13.	Guidepost*	4,131
14.	National Enquirer	4,019
15.	Redbook	3,947
16.	Star	3,615
17.	Sports Illustrated	3,507
18.	Playboy	3,436
19.	Newsweek	3,227
20.	People	3,176

*No advertising
Source: Magazine Publishers Association.

Table M-3   Top Magazine Advertising Industries, 1990

Rank	Industry	Expenditures (millions of dollars)
1.	Automotive	$899.5
2.	Toiletries and cosmetics	679.3
3.	Direct response	530.8
4.	Business and consumer services	516.3
5.	Food and food products	444.3

Source: Magazine Publishers Association.

The Annenbergs and Triangle Publications   The founder of the Annenberg media dynasty was Moses Annenberg, a German-Jewish immigrant who got into the newspaper business during the bloody circulation wars in Chicago. (At that time, rival newspapers hired armed thugs to make certain their papers got distributed and their competitors' didn't.) Annenberg thrived. In 1920, he founded the *Daily Racing Form* and later he founded the Nationwide News Service, a telephone and telegraph wire service with a monopoly on horse racing information. It served bookies in 39 states and was a veritable gold mine, giving Annenberg America's highest income in the 1930s, about $6 million a year. By the late 1930s the Annenberg empire also included newspapers in Philadelphia and Miami.

But in the late 1930s President Roosevelt, angry with Annenberg-owned newspapers' attacks on the New Deal, unleashed a massive IRS investigation. Moses was convicted of $9.6 million in income tax evasion, the largest conviction until the 1980s, and sent to prison.

When Moses died in 1942, his only son, Walter, was suddenly forced to take over the family business at age 32. His problem was trying to salvage the family finances and at the same time clear its reputation, tarnished by his father's income tax evasion conviction and published reports linking his father to organized crime.

Walter solved the family's financial problems once and for all in 1952, when he brought out *TV Guide,* which in 1974 became the first magazine ever to sell more than 1 billion copies in a year. The family's reputation also improved, thanks to beefed-up editorial quality at *The Philadelphia Inquirer,* lavish political contributions to the Republican party, and huge charitable contributions, including the creation of the Annenberg School of Communications at the University of Pennsylvania.

Today, Walter is a close friend and confidant of former President Reagan, and he served as ambassador to England under President Nixon. The family has sold off its 19 TV and radio stations and such newspapers as *The Philadelphia Inquirer* to Knight-Ridder. Then Annenberg sold off his Triangle holdings to Rupert Murdoch's News Corp. for over $3 billion.

S. I. Newhouse, Jr.   After S. I. Newhouse, Jr., bought *The New Yorker* in 1985, the talk of the town was that he would shake things up at the prestigious magazine. Well, that wasn't idle gossip. Newhouse first installed Steven T. Florio as publisher, and Florio promptly and unceremoniously dumped most of the circulation and ad salespeople. And, after a delicate waiting period, Newhouse replaced legendary editor William Shawn with Robert A. Gottlieb, former editor-in-chief of Alfred A. Knopf, Inc.

Such behavior struck a lot of people as high-handed when it came to the venerable magazine, which in its 60 years had become a benchmark for literary excellence. But what a lot of people didn't realize—and Newhouse very much did—was that *The New Yorker* had been showing its age. There were even people audacious enough to wonder whether *The New Yorker* hadn't simply run its course. Circulation was static. Ad pages had plummeted. The magazine was only holding its revenue growth by driving up ad prices, which made advertisers mad.

That Newhouse moved quickly to solve the problems wasn't unusual. Close attention to the bottom line has always been his company's successful guiding principle.

Newhouse's Advance Publications, Inc., is the largest privately held communications conglomerate in the nation. As chairman, he oversees all the magazine and book operations, which include Condé Nast Publications and Random House. Some 25 newspapers and several cable TV systems are under the direction of Newhouse's brother, Donald, who is president of Advance.

When people describe S. I., they inevitably use terms such as "a workaholic" and "a modest man who is private to the point of self-effacement" and say that "in business, he's a highly intelligent professional who hires good people and delegates to them."

Actually, those phrases echo the descriptions of his father, who started the Newhouse empire in 1922 by buying a Staten Island newspaper when he was only 16 years old. Like his father, Newhouse is at his desk by 5 A.M., but he is, if anything, even more active than his father was.

Newhouse began making his mark in 1960 when he begged his father to buy Condé Nast. His father did and told him to "go in and learn what makes it work." Joining as a member of *Glamour*'s merchandise and promotion department, he swiftly learned as much as he could and wound up beefing up circulation.

After that, he ran from one success to another. For instance, he launched the health and fitness magazine *Self* in 1979 before anybody else in the business recognized the potential for such a publication. Also in 1979, he acquired *GQ—Gentleman's Quarterly.* The magazine's circulation has since topped 700,000, up from 180,000, and ad pages have jumped above 2,000 from 800. Four years later, Advance gobbled up *Gourmet,* and ad pages went up there too.

Newhouse showed his ingenuity again in 1983 when the 80-year-old *House & Garden* underwent a metamorphosis from a home improvement magazine to an architectural magazine that competes with *Architectural Digest.* Ad revenues doubled just between 1983 and 1985.

Newhouse's only flop to date has been his attempt at reviving the high-society magazine *Vanity Fair.* When he acquired *The New Yorker,* pundits said it was a graceful way to distract everyone while Newhouse killed off the expensive loser. But hold on. In its first two years, Advance dumped an estimated $30 million into *Vanity Fair* and went through several editors, but in 1985 ad pages began going up and in 1986 circulation almost doubled from the 1984 level, to 400,000. Newhouse hasn't shown any signs of pulling the plug, and some analysts have said even *Vanity Fair* might become a winner.

"Si's philosophy is get it done," notes one of his employees. "That's what happens."

MINING

THE MARKET

"Without minerals, modern society wouldn't exist," notes Simon D. Strauss, one of the nation's leading mining and metals authorities. Indeed, one only has to glance around and see that derivatives of minerals are used just about everywhere: food and clothing, highways and housing, office complexes and computers. Raw materials production accounts for only 1% of the GNP, but materials derived from minerals make up 9% of the GNP.

Smelters, refiners, and other processers of intermediate goods such as aluminum, cinder blocks, fertilizers, and steel consume minerals directly. Some 90 metals and nonmetallic minerals are produced, including such high-value metals as gold and silver and nonmetallics such as gravel and sand, which are only profitable when produced in vast quantities.

THE MONEY

Mining has been in the doldrums for years. Nonfuel mineral production in 1990 was estimated to be about $32.2 billion, up from the $23.3 billion it had been each year since 1984. Indeed, since 1974, after 30 years of rapid growth, the market has slowed for most minerals and, in a few cases, actually declined. On a constant-dollar basis, the value of mineral production has declined annually by about 4.4% since 1979. In current dollars, production value increased in 1978–1979 and peaked in 1981. There was greater price volatility in metals than in nonmetals: the value of metals increased 16% in 1987 after dropping 6% in 1985, while the value of nonmetals increased only 2% in 1983 and dropped only 3% in 1984. However, following about four flat years, metals increased 24%, 25%, and 19% in 1987, 1988, and 1989 respectively. Higher prices that started in late 1987 continued into 1990.

U.S. production was little affected by the 1986 runup in prices of precious metals caused by turmoil in South Africa. The value of nonmetallic mineral production, however, has risen every year but three since 1961. One exception was a 14% decline in 1982. In 1985 and 1986, it rose 2% and 4%, respectively.

THE PLAYERS

Six U.S. companies ranked among the world's 20 largest mining companies in 1985: Fluor Corporation, Irvine, California; Aluminum Company of America (Alcoa), Pittsburgh, Pennsylvania; Kaiser Aluminum and Chemical Corporation, Oakland, California; Rosario Resources Corporation, Greenwich, Connecticut; AMAX, Inc., Greenwich, Connecticut; and ASARCO, Inc., Jersey City, N.J.

Table M-4 Trends: Metals and Industrial Minerals Mining
(in millions of dollars except as noted)

Item	1987	1988	1989	1990	Percent change 1987–88	1988–89	1989–90
Industry Data							
Value of shipments	26,346	29,200	30,590	32,333	10.8	4.8	—
Value of shipments (1987$)	26,346	28,339	28,485	28,361	7.6	0.5	–0.4
Total employment (000)	154	164	172	—	6.5	4.9	—
Production workers (000)	118	126	132	—	6.8	4.8	—
Average hourly earnings ($)	11.25	11.68	12.03	—	3.8	3.0	—
Trade Data							
Value of imports (BuM)	3,336	4,181	4,125	—	25.3	–1.3	—
Import/new supply ratio	0.112	0.125	0.119	—	11.6	–4.8	—
Value of exports (BuM)	2,648	3,244	2,248	—	22.5	–30.7	—
Export/shipments ratio	0.101	0.111	0.073	—	9.9	–34.2	—

Source: U.S. Department of the Interior: Bureau of Mines (BuM); U.S. Department of Commerce: Bureau of the Census; U.S. Department of Labor, Bureau of Labor Statistics.

THE DIAMOND CARTEL

Why does the diamond market seldom get soft? The answer is the Central Selling Organization, which is an amazing marketing system. CSO is controlled by the prominent South African diamond mining firm De Beers, which, with its affiliates, accounts for about 50% of the world's gem and industrial diamond production.

Competitive selling would undercut the price of diamonds, wrecking gems' lure as a long-term investment. To make sure that doesn't happen, CSO buys 50% of the diamonds that De Beers and its affiliates don't produce and thus acts as a cartel.

Even so, recessions occasionally hit diamonds too. The price of a top-quality one-carat flawless polished diamond rose to about $65,000 in 1980 and then plummeted to about $19,000 in 1982. The U.S. Justice Department takes a dim view of the monopolistic CSO practices, but so far the U.S. hasn't been successful with any of the legal proceedings it has brought to bear, since neither CSO nor De Beers has offices in the U.S.

GOLD

The U.S. surpassed Canada in 1986 to become the world's third-largest gold producer, after South Africa and the Soviet Union, according to the Gold Institute.

The institute's annual report, *World Mine Production of Gold,* 1985–1989, estimates that production by South Africa and the Soviet Union will be 54.5% by 1989, down from 58.4% in 1986 and 66.3% in 1984. Total world production in 1986 was 50.8 million ounces, up from 48.6 million ounces in 1985 and 46.2 million ounces in 1984.

Meanwhile, the U.S. produced about 3.5 million ounces in 1986, up considerably from 2.4 million ounces a year earlier. One reason for the increase: The U.S. Mint sold about 1.8 million ounces of gold for the minting of eagle coins.

TWO BITS

Ever wonder why *two bits* means a quarter? Since there were no American coins in colonial days, Spanish milled dollars or "pieces of eight" were popular coins in circulation. They were often cut into pieces, or "bits," to make change. *Two bits* referred to a quarter's worth of silver.

GOLD COINS

The U.S. stopped issuing gold coins when the nation went off the gold standard in 1933 during the Great Depression. Up to then, the government had issued 75 million eagle pieces ($10), 88 million double eagles ($20), 20 million quarter eagles ($2 1/2), and 19 1/2 million $1 pieces. Also, there were only a few $4 ("Stella") gold pieces minted in 1879 and 1880, and they are the rarest U.S. coins today.

There were also commemorative coins issued to celebrate the Louisiana Purchase Exposition (1903), the Lewis and Clark Expedition (1904–1905), the Panama-Pacific Exposition (1915), the McKinley Memorial (1916–1917), the Grant Memorial (1922), and the Philadelphia Sesquicentennial (1926). Today, a set of the Panama-Pacific coins, consisting of two $50 gold coins, a $2 1/2 gold coin, a $1 gold coin, and a 50-cent silver coin, all in uncirculated condition, is worth about $25,000.

A high-relief double eagle $20 gold piece designed by Augustus Saint-Gaudens and dated 1907 was considered the most beautiful gold coin ever made. President Theodore Roosevelt approved the design because he wanted U.S. coins to be art objects, but only 20 of the coins were struck because pragmatic bankers were afraid they wouldn't stack neatly. One of these coins sold in 1975 for $225,000—a world record for a single coin.

INDUSTRIAL DIAMONDS

Until the middle of the 19th century, diamonds weren't much good for anything but admiring, lusting after, hoarding, and putting in jewelry. Unsuitable diamonds were thrown away.

Then in 1862, the not-so-hot diamonds became industrial diamonds when the first diamond drill was built to bore into rock cores. Today, diamonds are used as grit in cutting and polishing, in glass cutters, in saw blades for cutting stone, and in dies for high-speed drawing of fine wire.

In 1955, General Electric produced synthetic diamonds that became fierce rivals of natural diamonds. Today, synthetics account for about 80% of all industrial diamonds by weight.

THE ONLY DIAMOND MINE IN THE U.S.

Apparently, the only active diamond mine in the U.S. is located near Murfreesboro, Arkansas. It is a tourist attraction.

BIRTHSTONES

Month	Stone
January	Garnet
February	Amethyst
March	Aquamarine or bloodstone
April	Diamond
May	Emerald
June	Pearl or alexandrite
July	Ruby or star ruby
August	Peridot or sardonyx
September	Sapphire or star sapphire
October	Opal or tourmaline
November	Topaz
December	Turquoise or zircon

GOLD DISCOVERED

Gold was discovered in California on January 24, 1848, by James W. Marshall at Sutter's Mill, starting the famed Gold Rush. By 1849, 80,000 prospectors had moved there. The Alaskan Gold Rush of 1898 brought more than 30,000 people to the territory.

Cecil Rhodes   In 1870, when he was 17 years old, Cecil John Rhodes, the British imperialist and diamond magnate, went to Africa from England to join his brother Herbert on a cotton plantation. The next year, the brothers staked a claim in the newly opened Kimberley diamond fields, where Cecil was to make most of his fortune.

He returned to England in 1873 to attend Oxford, but Africa was in his blood, and his repeated trips there delayed his taking a degree until 1881. One of those trips inspired him to dream of British domination of Africa, "from the Cape to Cairo," as he spoke of it.

Meanwhile, his power within the diamond industry grew ever greater and, in 1880, he started the De Beers Mining Company, which at the time was the second-largest diamond producer. The next year, the year he received his Oxford degree, he entered the Parliament of Cape Colony, a seat he was to hold until his death in 1902.

Largely at his instigation, Great Britain, in 1885, established a protectorate over Bechuanaland. Three years later, the conniving Rhodes had the Matabele ruler give him mining concessions in Matabeleland and Mashonaland. Through the British South Africa Company, he soon established complete control over the region. He also established a monopoly of Kimberley diamond production by the creation of De Beers Consolidated Mines.

In 1890, Rhodes became prime minister of Cape Colony and actually attempted to become a dictator. He limited African voting by disenfranchising illiterate people. He also became involved in an aborted plot to overthrow the government and he was forced to resign as prime minister in 1896. The following year, the British House of Commons found him guilty of grave breaches of duty as prime minister and administrator of the British South Africa Company.

After that, he spent his time primarily developing the country that was named Rhodesia in his honor. When he died, he left most of his huge fortune to public service, including the establishment of Rhodes scholarships at Oxford for students from British colonies, the U.S., and Germany.

MOTORCYCLES

THE MARKET

Motorcycles, once a mode of transportation associated with Hell's Angels and California state troopers, are now a big and quite respectable business. More than 7.7 million motorcycles, scooters, and ATVs (all-terrain vehicles) are in use in America, according to the Motorcycle Industry Council. About 6 million Americans own motorcycles, another 38.9 million people ride them, and motorcycles are ridden about 15.57 billion miles a year.

THE MONEY

The industry generated an estimated $7.2 billion in consumer sales, service, and state taxes and licensing in the U.S. in 1985, according to the Motorcycle Industry Council. About $2.79 billion of that total, 38.7%, came from retail sales of new motorcycles, scooters, and ATVs. Those retail sales were down from 1984, when $2.83 billion worth of motorcycles were sold, but up from 1981 ($2.16 billion) and 1970 ($1.03 billion).

THE PLAYERS

Over the past few decades, imports have captured most of the U.S. market in motorcycles. The four leading imports, Honda (28.9% of the market), Yamaha (27.7%), Kawasaki (15.6%), and Suzuki (14.2%), hold 94.6% of the market. Harley-Davidson, the fifth-largest manufacturer with a 13.9% share of the market, is the only large U.S. producer remaining. There are some 12,845 retail outlets selling motorcycles and related products.

THE PEOPLE

With most motorcycles produced overseas, few Americans are employed in the manufacture of this product. Retail outlets employ 62,555 people with an estimated payroll of $777 million.

THE FORECAST

The boom the industry saw in the 1960s and 1970s is over, and sales slumped 13% in 1990. An agreement by several major Japanese producers to stop production of all-terrain vehicles because of safety concerns will further hurt the industry. A number of dealers went out of business or diversified into new areas of business. Harley-Davidson, America's only major producer, was once on the verge of bankruptcy, but it has made major progress in cutting costs, improving quality, and attracting new customers. The company is profitable and growing. Still, foreign producers such as Honda will continue to expand their market shares, and there is little chance that Harley or any other American producer will regain a major share of the U.S. motorcycle market.

HONDA MOTORCYCLES

It took a Japanese to make motorcycles socially acceptable in America. Until the 1960s, the popular image of a guy on a motorcycle was a thug who was out to terrorize nice little towns. (We didn't know Malcolm Forbes was a motorcyclist then.) Aware of the problem, Soichiro Honda, head of Honda Motor Company, softened up Americans with a clever ad campaign when he introduced his motorcycles to the U.S. market in 1962. The national ad campaign, designed by Grey Advertising of Los Angeles, centered on the slogan, "You Meet the Nicest People on a Honda." The models in the ads looked more like Pat Boone than Hell's Angels. Within six years, the company sold a million motorcycles in the U.S. By the early 1970s, the company had run most U.S. competitors off the road, capturing almost half of the U.S. market. (And in 1975, Honda introduced its first family car, the Civic, and has been a major thorn in U.S. car makers' sides ever since.)

MOVIES, VIDEOCASSETTES, AND MOVIE THEATERS

THE MARKET

The 1980s saw Hollywood ride off into the sunset with record profits and revenues. In 1990, box-office receipts broke the $5 billion mark for the second time as domestic theaters sold 1.06 billion tickets. The average ticket cost moviegoers $4.75.

Since the 1950s, increased competition from television has hurt movie ticket sales, which are now no higher than in the 1960s and still way below the 4 billion sold before television. But despite predictions to the contrary, the rise of new sources of entertainment such as cable and home video during the 1980s did not hurt Hollywood. In fact, media fragmentation, which hurt the networks by draining off viewers, helped Hollywood because it supplied the laughs, drama, and entertainment for all the media, from ABC to HBO.

In the early 1990s, more changes were in the offing. Early in the home video craze, increased demand for any kind of films boosted film production to 578 films in 1987, way up from the 173 to 240 films made each year between 1973 and 1983. Many of these films were never released into theaters before being sold to home video or the foreign market. But as the decade wore on, the novelty of renting movies faded, and viewers became more choosy. They tended to rent, and increasingly buy, only the big box-office hits. Once again, film production dropped, to only 438 English-language films in 1990. Today, over two-thirds of all American homes have a VCR, and Americans rent or buy 220 million prerecorded cassettes and buy another 325 blank cassettes, up from 5.5 million prerecorded and 22.5 million blank cassettes in 1981.

THE MONEY

New markets and new media added up to blockbuster sales for the largest movie studios. Home video, cable, television, and, increasingly, foreign sales have become even more important than money made from U.S. movie theaters. Paul Kagan estimates that movies generated $13.1 billion for U.S. movie distributors in 1990, way up from $5.4 billion in 1984. In 1989, when the industry had $11.7 billion in revenues, only $2.21 billion (19%) came from domestic theaters. The rest came from home video ($5.3 billion), foreign movie theaters ($1.55), pay cable ($750 million), syndication to broadcast stations ($458 million), syndication to broadcast networks ($198 million), cable networks ($198 million), and pay-per-view networks ($113 million). All these figures illustrate the growing importance of foreign markets, which provided Hollywood with 40% of its revenues. Foreign revenues for home video totaled $1.98 billion; foreign television hit $759 million; and foreign theaters hit $1.55 billion. Kagan expects revenues for movie distributors to hit $19.2 billion by 1994.

Finally, these revenues do not include the business of producing television programming, which is now a much larger business than film production at nearly all the major studios. Veronis Suhler & Associates estimate that television producers and distributors had $7.9 billion in sales in 1989. They believe the television production business will grow to $10.4 billion in 1991 and $11.7 billion in 1994, an annual growth rate of 15.1%. Meanwhile domestic box-office receipts will inch up from $5.0 billion in 1989 to $6.5 billion in 1994, an 8.2% annual increase.

The average film now costs $23.5 million ($14.3 million for production and $7.1 million for marketing), up from $18.5 million in 1988 and $9.3 million in 1980. But the rising cost of moviemaking isn't simply a matter of better special effects or inflation. In recent years, studios have discovered the strange fact that spending more on a movie is less risky than spending less. Paul Kagan reports that over the last five years, films with a budget of $5 million to $15 million had a lower rate of return than those whose budget was higher than $30 million.

Why? A well-known star can attract moviegoers to the theaters during the critical first weekend of the film's opening. But star quality is also important in the long run. High-profile stars make it easier to sell home videos, and they boost foreign revenues, which are increasingly critical to a film's success. Also, the growth of many different markets helps producers and distributors cover costs from a big-budget film. Fifteen years ago, a high-budget film that bombed at U.S. movie theaters had little chance of ever earning the studio any money. Today, when U.S. box-office receipts bring only about one-fifth of a film's revenues, distributors can still make money overseas or with sales to other media. *Rambo III,* for example, was a real weakling at

U.S. theaters. It pulled in only $54 million, not even enough to cover its production costs of $63 million and far less than the tens of millions of dollars spent to distribute and promote the film. But overseas it racked up more than $200 million.

The blockbuster mentality has also produced a bidding war for top-name actors, directors, and script writers. Actors like Arnold Schwarzenegger and Bruce Willis can command $7 million to $15 million a film, while top directors can get over $6 million. Even star writers are receiving $1 million to $4.5 million for a script.

THE PLAYERS

Even though it costs American producers millions to produce the average film, 438 pictures were made in 1990, including 112 that were released by the major studios. These films are shown on 23,132 screens (2,148 of which are drive-ins) in the U.S. and Canada. About 10% of those films released each year will produce 45% of all box-office revenues. Each of the four largest movie theater chains—United Artists Theater Circuit, Cineplex Odeon, American Multi-Cinema, and General Cinema—has over 1,400 screens in North America.

Despite all that's been said about the rise of independent film production, the major studios still capture most of the market. Table M-5 (below) lists the top film studios and what shares they have held of the film exhibition market.

Table M-5   Shares of the Film Exhibition Market, 1970 to 1990

Year	Columbia	Twentieth Century Fox	MGM/UA	Paramount	Universal	Warner Bros.	Disney	Orion	Tri-Star
1970	14%	19%	9%	12%	12%	5%	9%	3%	—
1975	13	14	11	11	25	9	6	5	—
1980	14	16	7	16	20	14	4	2	—
1981	13	13	9	15	14	18	3	1	—
1982	10	14	11	14	30	10	4	3	—
1983	14	21	10	14	13	17	3	4	—
1984	16	10	7	21	8	19	4	5	5%
1985	10	11	9	10	16	18	3	5	10
1986	9	8	4	22	9	12	10	7	7
1987	4	9	4	20	8	13	14	10	5
1988	4	12	10	15	10	11	20	7	6
1989	8	7	6	14	17	17	14	4	7
1990	5	13	3	15	13	13	16	6	9

Source: *Variety.*

Recently, major film studios or their parent companies have been buying up theaters. MCA, Cannon, Paramount, and Tri-Star have all bought shares in theater chains. These purchases broke down the long-standing legal barrier between movie producers and theater owners that had been established to increase competition in the 1940s.

Increased concentration and the growing importance of foreign markets have also changed the landscape of the American film industry. At home, foreign media giants, which need foreign sales just as much as Hollywood, have been on a shopping spree for U.S. film producers and studios.

Columbia Pictures was sold to Sony in 1989, MGM was bought up by Pathé in 1990, and in the fall of 1990 MCA and its Universal Studios were sold to Matsushita for a record $6.1 billion. All this prompted a wave of editorials, and lots and lots of material for satirists. One cartoon showed the typical Hollywood producer, sitting at his pool, smoking a cigar as he called up his new Japanese bosses at Columbia Pictures: "I've got a great new package deal," he explained. "It's a war film with a new slant on Pearl Harbor."

In fact, American film companies are not losing their competitive edge, and unlike firms in many other industries, seem to be increasing their market share. A 1989 Booz Allen report estimates that the international demand for television programming will grow from 250,000 weekly hours to over 450,000 by 1995. But a large share of the growth has been captured by U.S. producers, primarily the Hollywood studios, which can sell reruns of American television for far less than it costs local producers to make their own series.

Similarly, the rising production costs have put the kibosh on local movie production. Unlike the U.S., where there are 250 million potential customers, few foreign countries are large enough to support a film industry that can make money on a film costing $30 million or $50 million, and very few independent film companies can afford to spend the millions of dollars an American studio might spend to advertise its films abroad. As a result, the British film industry, for example, is now much smaller than it was in the 1960s, and U.S. movies capture a large share of the box office in most countries, including Japan, where U.S. films regularly outgross Japanese films. Japan alone imports more than $201 million worth of American films each year.

As a result, the growing global market for films is not likely to mean more French or Japanese films hitting the American screen. Quite the opposite. The importance of foreign markets has pushed American producers into producing more of the classic Hollywood male-oriented action films. Films with stars like Mel Gibson, Tom Cruise, Sean Connery, and Arnold Schwarzenegger are big box-office attractions all around the world, while comedies and films starring women seem to have a much harder time crossing the border into big foreign sales.

THE PEOPLE

About 107,600 people are employed in movie theaters, down from 114,800 in 1982 and 126,700 in 1972.

Table M-6   Most Successful Movies of All Time
(U.S. and Canada)

Rank	Film (initial release year, distributor)	Rentals (millions of dollars)
1.	*E.T., The Extra-Terrestrial* (1982, Universal)	228.6
2.	*Star Wars* (1977, Fox)	193.5
3.	*Return of the Jedi* (1983, Fox)	168.0
4.	*Batman* (1989, Warner)	150.5
5.	*The Empire Strikes Back* (1980, Fox)	141.6
6.	*Ghostbusters* (1984, Columbia)	132.7
7.	*Jaws* (1975, Universal)	129.5
8.	*Raiders of the Lost Ark* (1981, Paramount)	115.6
9.	*Indiana Jones and the Last Crusade* (1989, Paramount)	115.5
10.	*Indiana Jones and the Temple of Doom* (1984, Paramount)	109.0

Note: Movie rentals are the share of the box office proceeds that go to distributors; the remainder is kept by the theaters. Rentals are those earned through December 1990.
Source: *Variety*.

MUSIC

THE MARKET

For years sales of records were stuck in the same old groove, producing a stagnant market for prerecorded music. Critics blamed everything from the aging of America to the lack of interesting new popular music. Whatever, the industry shipped 726.2 million records and tapes in 1978 but, by 1982, that number had dropped to 577.7 million. Even by 1987, when sales recovered to an estimated 663.3 million records, tapes, and compact discs, sales were below the 1978 peak. In 1986, the last year for which a detailed breakdown of sales is available, 22% fewer singles were sold than in 1985 and the number of long-playing (LP) and extended-play (EP) records dropped from 167 million in 1985 to 125.2 million. In 1990, shipments reached some 976.5 million units, up from 848.1 million in 1989. Increases in sales of cassettes and compact discs made up the difference. At the same time, the industry has become more dependent on a few big hits. In recent years only megahits by artists such as Michael Jackson and Bruce Springsteen produced the sales and profits the industry needed to stay above water.

THE MONEY

Rising album prices and increased revenues from cassettes and compact discs have propped up the industry's revenues, but only barely. Industry revenues more than doubled between 1973 and 1978, when they hit $4.1 billion. But then weak sales dropped revenues to only $3.6 billion in 1982. Since then sales have recovered, hitting $4.5 billion in 1986 and $4.67 billion in 1987. But record manufacturers shipped some $8 billion worth of cassettes, discs, and records in 1990.

Thirty years ago, everyone was saying rock was just another fad. Well, rock music now holds 33% of the market, followed by pop/easy listening (20%), country (10%), black dance music (9%), shows/soundtracks (4%), gospel (4%), classical (4%), jazz (3%), children's music (3%), and other recordings (10%), according to the Recording Industry Association of America.

TRENDS AND FORECAST

Demographics and technology are both ganging up on this industry. An older public means there are fewer young people to buy records. And, in the last decade, technological changes have hurt sales. Cassette machines let consumers tape albums at home, hurting sales of records. Record and tape piracy, counterfeiting, and bootlegging have also been made easy by these newer technologies. Consumers tape enough music to fill up 564 million albums a year, costing the record industry as much as $1.5 billion in sales. To recoup some of those losses, the industry has been pushing, unsuccessfully, to add a tax to blank cassette tapes. But not everyone shares this dim view of home taping. Many critics say home taping increases the public's interest in music and, in the long run, does not harm sales.

Another problem is music that follows the same old formulas. The industry is stumbling in the area of developing new talent. With sales falling, the recording industry is not taking any chances with new talent. Since 1978, the number of new-album releases has dropped almost 50% and seems likely to stay low. Skimping on long-term investments always bodes badly for the future of any industry.

Table M-7 Manufacturers' Unit Shipments
(millions net after returns)

	'78	'79	'80	'81	'82	'83	'84	% Chg. '83–'84	'85	% Chg. '84–'85	'86	% Chg. '85–'86	'87	% Chg. '86–'87	'88	% Chg. '87–'88
Disc Singles	190.0	195.5	164.3	154.7	137.2	124.8	131.5	+5%	120.7	–8%	93.9	–22%	82.0	–13%	65.6	–20%
LP's/EP's	341.3	318.3	322.8	295.2	243.9	209.6	204.6	–2%	167.0	–18%	125.2	–25%	107.0	–15%	72.4	–32%
CD's						.8	5.8	+625%	22.6	+291%	53.0	+134%	102.1	+93%	149.7	+47%
Cassettes	61.3	82.8	110.2	137.0	182.3	236.8	332.0	+40%	339.1	+2%	344.5	+2%	410.0	+19%	450.1	+10%
CD Singles															1.6	NA
Cassette Singles													5.1*	NA	22.5	+341%
TOTALS	726.2	701.1	683.7	635.4	577.7	578.0	679.8	+18%	653.0	–4%	618.3	–5%	706.8	+14.3%	761.9	+8%

Manufacturers' Dollar Value
(millions of dollars at suggested list price)

	'78	'79	'80	'81	'82	'83	'84	% Chg. '83–'84	'85	% Chg. '84–'85	'86	% Chg. '85–'86	'87	% Chg. '86–'87	'88	% Chg. '87–'88
Disc Singles	260.3	275.4	269.3	256.4	283.0	269.3	298.7	11%	281.0	–6%	228.1	–19%	203.3	–11%	180.4	–11%
LP's/EP's	2473.3	2136.0	2290.3	2341.7	1925.1	1689.0	1548.8	–8%	1280.5	–17%	983.0	–23%	793.1	–19%	532.3	–33%
CD's						17.2	103.3	+500%	389.5	+277%	930.1	+139%	1593.6	+71.3%	2089.9	+31%
Cassettes	449.8	604.6	776.4	1062.8	1384.5	1810.9	2383.9	+32%	2411.5	+1.2%	2499.5	+4%	2959.7	+18.4%	3385.1	+14%
CD Singles															9.8	NA
Cassette Singles													14.3*	NA	57.3	+301%
TOTALS	4131.4	3685.4	3862.4	3969.9	3641.6	3814.3	4370.4	+15%	4387.8	+.4%	4651.1	+6%	5567.5	+19.7%	6254.8	+12%

*1987 figures represent six month sales only.
Source: RIAA Market Research Committee.

477

Table M-8 World Sales of Records, Tapes, and CD's 1988

(figures in millions)

Region	Singles & EP's[2] Maxi-singles	LP's	Tapes[1]	CD's	Retain value[3]	Local currency	US dollar value*
Argentina†	0.002	2.3	12.2	—	ARA	121,447.4	56.61
Australia	5.6	7.5	17.0	5.7	AUD	488.0(e)	384,348.8
Austria	3.3	3.8	2.2	2.2	ATS	1,661.7(e)	128.28
Belgium	6.3	3.0	1.9	4.5	BEF	5,078.7	130.87
Brazil	0.3	42.8	12.6	0.7	USD	497.0	82.80
Canada	5.2	8.1	34.4	8.9	CAD	661.1	565.17
China†	—	—	110.0	—	CNY	—	550.0
Colombia†	2.0	4.2	2.0	0.01	COP	N/A	22.0
Czechoslovakia	2.0	10.4	2.3	0.3	CSK	645.0	64.5
Denmark+#	1.0	5.4	1.7	2.3	DKK	N/A	N/A
Finland	0.8	5.4	5.3	1.5	FIM(e)	557.3	131.80
France	42.1	19.4	31.0	25.9	FRF	6,456.0	1,032.96
Germany	31.6	58.1	59.9	39.2	DEM	2,910.0	1,581.00
Greece	—	4.8	3.3	0.2	GRD	6,248.0	37.98
Hong Kong	—	1.672	4.878	1.227	HKG	.275	.35
Hungary	0.9	3.8	4.3	0.04	HUG	1,385.0	22.33
India	—	0.5	130.0	—	INR	2,600.0	154.20
Indonesia†	—	—	410	—	IDR	N/A	59.0
Ireland	0.6	0.8	2.1	0.2	IEP	22.6(e)	32.62
Italy	4.9	15.5	22.7	7.1	ITL	408,000.0	301.33
Japan	22.8	8.7	61.2	92.4	JPY	380,514	2,655.98
Korea	—	7.0	36.5	0.2	KRW	94,800.0	115.4
Malaysia†	—	0.1	2.7	0.5	MYR	22.2	8.8
Netherlands	8.4	8.4	4.8	17.8	NLG	805.0	387.84
New Zealand	0.7	1.2	5.2	1.2	NZD	95.2	56.12
Norway	0.8	2.3	4.0	1.9	NOK	725.0	105.70
Peru	0.6	0.5	1.2	—	PEI	N/A	N/A
Philippines	.900	.475	3.8	.161	PNP	294.5	13.84
Portugal	0.9	2.6	3.2	0.4	PTE	10,107.1	5,155.62
Singapore	—	.165	4.875	.816	SGD	63.057	32.19
Spain	1.6	17.8	23.3	2.5	ESP	38,288.3	328.51
Sweden	4.3	10.4	4.8	3.2	SEK	1,600.00	250.72
Switzerland	3.2	4.5	5.0	7.3	CHF	305.0	188.06
Taiwan	—	.650	24.5	1.4	USD	150.480	5.82
Thailand	—	.13	40.9	.62	TNB	127.997	4.96
United Kingdom	60.1	50.2	80.9	29.2	GBP	1,107.8	1,762.50
United States	89.7	72.4	450.1	149.7	USD	6,254.8	6,254.8
	300.60	384.99	1,626.75	409.274			406,629.46

[1]Tapes means cassettes and 8-track cartridges; 95% of tapes now sold in the world are cassettes.
[2]Singles also include maxi singles; EP's have become insignificant in most countries.
[3]Retail value includes taxes.
*Based on a rate of exchange as of 11/21/89
†Figures from 1987.
+IFPI members only.
(e) estimated
—nil or insignificant
#Includes 62,825 CD singles (3" × 5")
Source: Inside the Recording Industry, 1989 Statistical Overview, the Recording Industry Association of America and IFPI National Groups and affiliated organizations.

Table M-9   Top-paid Entertainers

Forbes estimates entertainment's biggest earners. Perspective: median compensation of 800 leading corporate executives in 1986 was $706,000.

Rank	Star/occupation	Gross income in millions		
		1989	1988	Two-year total
1.	Bill Cosby, comedian	$55	$60	$115
2.	Michael Jackson, singer	35	65	100
3.	The Rolling Stones, rock group	44	44	88
4.	Steven Spielberg, director	23	64	87
5.	New Kids on the Block, rock group	61	17	78
6.	Oprah Winfrey, TV talk show hostess	38	30	68
7.	Sylvester Stallone, actor/writer	25	38	63
8.	Madonna (Louise Ciccone), singer	39	23	62
9.	Arnold Schwarzenegger, actor	20	35	55
10.	Charles M. Schulz, cartoonist	26	28	54
11.	Johnny Carson, TV talk show host	25	25	50
12.	Jack Nicholson, actor	16	34	50
13.	Eddie Murphy, comedian	26	22	48
14.	Paul McCartney, singer	34	11	45
15.	Julio Iglesias, singer	22	22	44
16.	Bruce Willis, actor	28	8	36
17.	The Who, rock group	5	30	35
18.	Sean Connery, actor	27	8	35
19.	Bon Jovi, rock group	10	25	35
20.	Prince (Roger Nelson), singer	15	20	35

Source: *Forbes,* October 1, 1990 (c)

479

NEWSPAPERS

THE MARKET

Besides having an important political and social role by conveying news about domestic and international issues, newspapers constitute one of the largest advertising markets in the U.S. About 63 million daily newspapers are circulated in the U.S. each day and more than 108 million American adults read a daily paper at least once a week. Weekly papers reach another 50 million people.

THE MONEY

Newspapers continue to lead all other media in advertising volume. Retail and classified advertising revenues were about $30 billion in 1990. That was $5 billion more than was spent on their nearest competitor, television. Ads account for 80% of all newspaper revenues. Total newspaper revenues were down nearly 3% in 1990 in constant dollars.

THE PLAYERS

There are 1,657 daily newspapers in the U.S., which reach about 63 million people. Sunday newspapers now number 809, reaching 63 million people, and weekly newspapers total 7,600, reaching 52.9 million people.

Control of the news continues to be held in a very small number of hands. The top 25 companies own 565 newspapers reaching 37.9 million people every day, or about 58.6% of all the people who read newspapers. Only 143 companies own more than one newspaper but these chains own 1,247 newspapers, about 76% of all daily newspapers, and control 83% of daily newspaper circulation.

THE PEOPLE

There were about 458,000 people employed in the newspaper industry in 1989, up from 419,900 in 1980 and 248,500 in 1947.

TRENDS AND FORECAST

Total newspaper circulation grew rapidly between 1904 and 1954, from 50.5 million to 136.4 million. But faced with increasing competition from television and other media, daily newspaper circulation stagnated and has remained virtually constant since 1970.

Table N-1 Daily Newspapers in the U.S.

| Year | Morning and evening | | Sunday | |
	Number	Circulation (thousands)	Number	Circulation (thousands)
1946	1,763	50,927	497	43,665
1960	1,763	58,882	563	47,699
1970	1,748	62,108	586	49,216
1980	1,745	62,201	735	54,672
1985	1,674	62,723	797	58,817
1986	1,657	62,489	809	61,515
1987	1,645	62,826	820	60,111
1988	1,642	62,694	840	61,474
1989	1,626	62,649	847	62,008

Source: American Newspaper Publishers Association, *Facts About Newspapers: 1990. Editor & Publisher.*

Stagnant circulation and increased competition from TV produced an industry-wide shakeout in the 1960s and 1970s. In many cities, many papers closed or merged with other papers, often leaving one paper, such as *The Washington Post,* holding a near-monopoly over the newspaper market of a major city. Even the survivors struggled to attract new readers with special lifestyle or suburban sections. To reduce costs, publishers went on the offensive with unions, demanding changes in work rules and less expensive union contracts while spending millions to install electronic printing and production technology. Capital expenditures rose to $1 billion for the first time ever in 1985, from $805 million in 1982, according to *Presstime.* That dramatically lowered labor costs from 37% of total expenditures in 1975 to only 30% by 1983.

But after decades of struggle, lowered costs and rising advertising expenditures have made newspapers increasingly profitable—a fact that outside investors soon noticed. The value of newspaper properties has skyrocketed in recent years. Newspaper chains continue to buy more newspapers and the number of papers owned by chains increased by 17% in 1985 alone. Lured by record prices for newspapers and media properties, several independent newspaper families sold their holdings.

By 1987, a slowdown in advertising revenues lowered the value of many media properties, especially independent TV stations. But high-tech production, cost cutting, and innovative marketing during the last decade have put newspapers in a better position to weather the slowdown in ad revenues than many of the free-spending media companies, such as CBS, which are struggling to adapt to a new age of austerity. Though the industry continues to face strong competition from television, cable, and other media, profit margins are remaining high.

Table N-2   The 20 Largest Newspaper Companies

Rank	Company	Daily circulation	Number of dailies
1.	Gannett Co. Inc.	6,022,929	82
2.	Knight-Ridder Inc.	3,794,809	28
3.	Newhouse Newspapers	2,997,699	26
4.	Times Mirror Co.	2,626,259	8
5.	Tribune Co.	2,608,222	9
6.	Dow Jones & Co. Inc.	2,409,955	23
7.	Thomson Newspapers Inc.	2,127,123	122
8.	The New York Times Co.	1,919,094	27
9.	Scripps Howard	1,570,957	21
10.	Cox Enterprises Inc.	1,280,040	18
11.	Hearst Newspapers	1,207,089	13
12.	Media News	1,123,552	19
13.	Freedom Newspapers Inc.	938,862	27
14.	Capital Cities/ABC Inc.	898,927	9
15.	The Washington Post Co.	826,871	2
16.	Central Newspapers Inc.	824,782	7
17.	Donrey Media Group	790,982	57
18.	Copley Newspapers	767,955	12
19.	McClatchy Newspapers	753,558	11
20.	The Chronicle Publishing Co.	742,410	6

Source: American Newspaper Publishers Association.

Table N-3   The 10 Largest Daily Newspapers

Rank	Newspaper	Average daily circulation
1.	The Wall Street Journal	1,935,866
2.	USA Today	1,387,233
3.	Los Angeles Times	1,210,077
4.	New York Daily News	1,180,139
5.	The New York Times	1,149,683
6.	The Washington Post	824,282
7.	Chicago Tribune	740,713
8.	Newsday	711,264
9.	Detroit Free Press	639,767
10.	San Francisco Chronicle	569,257

Source: American Newspaper Publishers Association.

The Washington Post Company

CEO: Katharine Graham
Employees: NA
Assets: $1.5 billion

1150 15th Street, N.W.
Washington, D.C. 20071
202-334-6600

	1990	1987	1985	1980
Revenues (millions of dollars):	1,438	1,315	1,079	660
Net income (millions of dollars):	175	186	114	34
Share earnings (dollars):	14.45	14.52	8.66	2.44

What it does: Publisher of *The Washington Post* and *Newsweek* magazine. Operates television stations and is a major cable TV operator.

In the late 1960s and 1970s *The Washington Post* was alternately lambasted and heralded for its hard-hitting coverage of the Vietnam War, U.S. foreign policy, and of course the Watergate scandal. But controversy is nothing new at *The Washington Post*. Founded in 1877, it prospered as a sensationalist daily but declined in the 1920s. Copper magnate and financier Eugene Meyer purchased the paper in 1933 and began its rehabilitation by improving editorial quality. When Meyer became president of the World Bank in 1946, he handed the paper over to his daughter, Katharine, and her husband, Philip Graham.

During the next 15 years, Philip built up the paper and the family's media holdings, acquiring *Newsweek* and television stations. He also used the paper to become a well-known liberal Washington insider, pushing the political career of Lyndon Johnson and acting as a close political confidant of the Kennedys. After his suicide in 1963 many people mistakenly thought his shy and retiring wife, Katharine, would be unable to manage the paper. As publisher of the *Post,* she hired the Washington bureau chief of *Newsweek,* Ben Bradlee, as editor, kept the paper well managed, and continued to expand the family's media holdings. Bradlee, for his part, expanded the paper's coverage, introduced more critical reporting of the Washington scene, and gained a national reputation.

Since breaking the Watergate story, the *Post* has battled *The New York Times* for the title of the nation's best, or at least most influential, newspaper. The *Post* is now the nation's 8th-largest daily and The Washington Post Company is the 16th-largest newspaper company in the U.S.

Since 1979, Katharine Graham's son, Donald E. Graham, has served as publisher. Under Donald's management, the paper has emphasized local news and become more sedate, a fact that itself has produced a controversy over whether the paper is as hard-hitting as it should be.

The company, which also owns *Newsweek,* four TV stations, and a cable network, saw profits drop 12% in 1986 to $100 million on revenues of $1.2 billion, largely because of financial problems at *Newsweek*. In 1987, profits rose to $186 million, through the sale of assets. But with the *Post* enjoying a virtual monopoly in Washington, D.C.—reaching 76% of the households in the nation's capital—the paper can easily finance an ever-expanding Graham media empire. Katharine Graham controls a majority of the voting stock and the Graham family holdings were worth $662 million in the summer of 1987.

News Ltd.

CEO: K. Rupert Murdoch   2 Holt Street
Employees: NA   Sydney, Australia 2010
Assets: NA   011-612-288-3000

	1989	1985	1984	1980
Revenues (millions of dollars):	5,955	1,640	1,610	NA
Net income (millions of dollars):	375	64	83	
Share earnings (dollars):	2.39	.48	.61	

What it does: This Australian company with major operations in the U.S. and the United Kingdom primarily produces newspapers, magazines, theatrical films, and TV programming.

Rupert Murdoch has undoubtedly replaced William Randolph Hearst as the media mogul everyone loves to hate. Liberals fume at his habit of injecting a right-wing slant in the editorials and news of his papers. Wall Street wonders about his habit of borrowing every cent he can get his hands on. And, with banner headlines, innuendo, and half-naked girls, he has singlehandedly revived the fine art of yellow journalism. No one, right, left, or center, has ever accused him of good taste.

As with Hearst, Murdoch equated size with power and dreamed of a vast media empire. However, his grasp exceeded his ability to pay for it. By 1990, News Corp. had the largest restructuring talks with more than 100 financial institutions worldwide.

At one point, Murdoch owned 49% of his Australian News Ltd., giving him control of Twentieth Century Fox Film Corporation; Fox Broadcasting Company (which owns 6 television stations and reaches 22% of U.S. television homes); one of Australia's most popular commercial networks, the 41-station 10 Network; the Sky Channel, an English-language television program service seen by 5 million households in 14 Western European countries; 21 U.S. trade and consumer magazines, including *New York* magazine; about 30% of the newspaper circulation in Britain; 4 daily newspapers, and 8 weeklies that reach 1.95 million readers every day; the book publisher HarperCollins; and, of course, his Australian newspaper empire of 8 dailies and 26 nondailies that reaches 1.14 million readers a day, including *The Sunday Mail,* his first paper. That list doesn't include his airline, oil, or real estate holdings. Overall, the Murdoch empire reaches one quarter of all English-speaking people in the world.

Murdoch has set his sights on ever bigger fish. In 1985, Murdoch announced plans to start a fourth television network, the Fox Broadcasting Company. The idea was hardly new. Over the years, several other billionaires and media powers, such as former Metromedia owner John W. Kluge and Paramount, have dreamed of capturing a share of the lucrative network TV market. But so far, the idea of a fourth network has remained the business equivalent of the Holy Grail—a romantic dream promising great riches and offering almost certain failure.

For a fourth TV network, Murdoch bought half of Twentieth Century Fox from Marvin Davis and six Metromedia stations from John Kluge, who had dreamed of starting a fourth network for nearly 20 years. That $2.6 billion investment created the Fox Broadcasting Company, which overnight could reach 22% of all households. Building from that base, Murdoch planned to offer some original programming, such as *The Late Show Starring Joan Rivers.* But, as in most of his operations, he planned a cut-rate network and kept costs low by avoiding the temptation to offer complete prime-time programming. Later, as the network produced more revenues, it added more programming.

The huge debt Murdoch piled up has undermined his megamedia dreams. The company had to defer repayments of loans, $2.4 billion of which were due before June 30, 1991. The effect of restructuring was to raise interest on the debt and to sell more than $1 billion in assets over the next several years. To raise cash, News Corp. had already sold off such assets as the health care publisher J. B. Lippincott Co., *New York Magazine,* the tabloid *Star,* and a 49 percent interest in its Hong Kong newspaper business. How well Murdoch can get his business back in harness is a question better answered by his bankers.

The Hearsts   The Hearst empire began in silver and ended up in newsprint, where it mined even greater riches.

George Hearst founded the family fortune with gold and silver mines. Though he suffered a few serious financial setbacks, he was remarkably successful in finding new mining properties, including three of the West's most profitable mines, the Ontario Mine of Utah, the Homestake in South Dakota, and the Anaconda in Montana.

Later, to fulfill his political ambitions, he purchased the San Francisco *Examiner* and served in the U.S. Senate. It was his son, William Randolph, however, who created the Hearst media dynasty. William got his first editorial experience running the *Harvard Lampoon.* When he was tossed out of Harvard, he went to work at Joseph Pulitzer's *New York World.* There he learned yellow journalism, which was Pulitzer's specialty, not the kind of investigative or thoughtful efforts that now win Pulitzer Prizes.

The lesson that sex, violence, and sensationalism sell papers was one that Hearst soon applied to his father's *Examiner.* Circulation took off and Hearst rapidly expanded his empire, using a formula that became his trademark—a mixture of crusading journalism, sensationalism, and, at times, outright lies. His papers, for instance, fabricated some of the stories that helped lead to the Spanish-American War and gained a reputation that has tarnished the Hearst papers ever since.

But it would be wrong to view the Hearst legacy as simply one of sensationalism. Hearst was one of the first publishers to understand the importance of creating a media conglomerate to cut costs and increase circulation. He profited from the fact that new printing and telecommunications technologies made it possible to create mass-market newspapers. And he boosted salaries and editorial spending as a way of increasing circulation. By 1935 he had 90 newspapers, as well as such magazines as *Good Housekeeping, Cosmopolitan,* and *Harper's Bazaar.*

Like his father, Hearst had political ambitions, and his newspaper empire helped him win two terms in the House of Representatives. But he failed in presidential campaigns and after 1917, when he began his love affair with actress Marion Davies, he passed his time spending money. He spent millions buying art and millions more on promoting Davies's acting career, with little success. By the mid-1930s his free-spending ways had brought his empire to the brink of financial ruin and he was forced to give up daily control of his papers. Though the empire survived, many of his papers continued to lose money. By the late 1970s, the Hearst empire only published 10 papers.

Today the family runs a far-flung and highly profitable media conglomerate. It is a powerhouse in book publishing with Arbor House, Avon, William Morrow & Co., and various trade publications. It is the 24th-largest electronic media company, with 6 VHF TV stations, interests in cable networks, 4 AM radio stations, and 3 FM radio stations. It is the 12th-largest newspaper publishing empire, with 15 dailies including the San Francisco *Examiner*, the *Los Angeles Herald Examiner*, and the *Houston Chronicle*. It has 13 magazines including *Cosmopolitan, Good Housekeeping, Popular Mechanics, Town & Country, Redbook, Sports Afield*, and *Esquire*, which it bought for $40 million, just to name a few. A hundred years after William Randolph Hearst took over his father's San Francisco *Examiner* in 1887, the company had somewhere between $2 billion and $3 billion in estimated revenues. (It doesn't put out financial statements.)

In the 1980s, the Hearst empire has been growing at a breathtaking pace. Since 1979, Frank A. Bennack, the company president, has spent $1.5 billion on acquisitions. That growth has helped the family trust grow to an estimated $2 billion.

Yet while the empire is growing, the family is taking a smaller role in its affairs. Although about 15 Hearst family members work at the privately owned company or serve on its board of directors, only one is responsible for line operations—William Randolph Hearst III, the publisher of the San Francisco *Examiner*.

The Times Mirror Company

CEO: Robert F. Erburu   Times Mirror Square
Employees: 30,600   Los Angeles, California 90053
Assets: $2.9 billion   213-972-3700

	1990	1987	1985	1980
Revenues (millions of dollars):	3,633	3,154	2,947	1,857
Net income (millions of dollars):	180	266	237	139
Share earnings (dollars):	1.40	2.06	3.49	2.04

What it does: Major newspaper publisher with cable TV, broadcast TV, book publishing, information services, and magazine holdings. (n) adjusted for stocksplit.

The Chandlers   The crown jewel of the Chandler media empire is the *Los Angeles Times*, the fourth-largest newspaper in the U.S., which produces about 30% of the company's revenues. The Chandler family media empire also includes the nation's eighth-largest cable television business with some 825,000 subscribers, four network television stations, 272,000 acres of timberland, and such popular magazines as *Outdoor Life, Popular Science,* and *Golf.*

Since World War II, heavy spending on editorial has made the *Los Angeles Times* and other Times Mirror newspapers some of the best in the country. But quality and an evenhanded editorial stance are relatively new phenomena. In earlier years, the *Los Angeles Times* had a reputation as an unabashed apologist for California's elite, a paper that hewed to one political line and ignored or ridiculed all others.

General Harrison Gray Otis bought the paper in the 1880s and ran it with Harry Chandler, who married his daughter. They refused to let unions into the paper (only for a brief period in the late 1960s was the *Los Angeles Times* a union paper) and spent decades attacking such ideas as the eight-hour day. In politics, the paper either ridiculed or refused to cover liberal politicians it didn't like, gaining a reputation for censoring ideas of which it disapproved. Its unabashed editorial support for Richard Nixon virtually created his career.

But the idea that a paper's news stories ought to support the publisher's voting habits changed dramatically under the stewardship of Otis Chandler. He took over the paper in 1960, beefed up editorial, and gave its writers new independence.

Over the years, the Chandlers and the current outside managers have followed one consistent strategy: invest for the long haul. Currently the company is pushing hard to enter the New York market with the prize winning Long Island paper, *Newsday.* The paper is losing $10 million a year, but has already dramatically improved circulation. If successful, the expansion could position the company in one of the nation's largest markets. But as in many of its previous expansion plans, the company's heavy spending has crimped profits and hurt the price of its stock.

OIL AND NATURAL GAS

THE MARKET

The U.S. is the largest market for energy products in the world. Even though we have less than 5% of the world's population we use 25% of the energy produced each year.

Nearly two-thirds (65.1%) of the energy we use each year comes from oil and natural gas, down from 77% in 1973. Oil is our most popular energy source (41.3% of the energy consumed), followed by natural gas (23.8%), coal (23.4%), nuclear power (7.6%), and hydroelectric power (4.7%).

Nearly all of our natural gas consumption comes from domestic producers, which supply 17.2 trillion cubic feet of gas a year compared to about 1.5

trillion cubic feet of imports. However, the news is not so good for oil. In 1990, when the Persian Gulf crisis once again focused attention on foreign oil, imports supplied nearly half (47.3%) of America's consumption. Americans now consume 16.9 million barrels a day, up from 11.6 in 1972, shortly before the first energy crisis. But since domestic producers pumped only 8.9 million barrels (down from 9.4 million in 1972), the country has to import about 8.0 million barrels of oil each day (up from only 2.2 million in 1972). The U.S. now consumes 6.21 billion barrels of oil a year but has only 25.9 billion barrels of oil reserves.

Just as cheap oil during the 1950s and 1960s left America vulnerable to the OPEC boycott in 1973, cheap oil during the 1980s forced oil companies to cut domestic production and encouraged consumers to use more energy. The biggest users of oil are transportation (66%), industrial (26%), residential and commercial (8.3%), and electric utilities (4.8%). But for natural gas, the picture is quite different. The largest users are industrial (49%), residential and commercial (47%), electric utilities (17%), and transportation (3.5%).

THE MONEY

All the energy used by American consumers adds up to a lot of dollars. Each year Americans spend $393 billion on energy, most of which, $186.5 billion, is spent on petroleum products. Another $57.5 billion is spent by consumers on natural gas.

Because of its importance as an energy source, the petroleum industry sends an enormous amount of money cascading through the economy. Revenues can be broken down into various sectors:

U.S. producers ship $75.1 billion worth of natural gas and petroleum. About $36.8 billion worth of oil and natural gas is imported.

U.S. petroleum refiners ship $131.1 billion worth of refined petroleum, and the country imports another $11.8 billion.

On the retail level, nearly 115,000 gas stations sell $102 billion worth of gas, auto products, and services.

Before the Persian Gulf crisis, cheap oil hurt the manufacturers of oil equipment. Shipments of oil-producing equipment dropped to only $2.2 billion in 1987, down from $10.1 billion in 1981, before recovering to $3.5 billion in 1991.

Gas utilities have some $45.5 billion worth of annual revenue.

THE PLAYERS

During the oil boom of the early 1980s there were nearly 29,000 independent oil companies. Since then, well over a third of them have gone out of business. Not surprisingly, the top oil companies play a major role in U.S. production, with the largest 6 accounting for about one third of U.S. oil production and the largest 20 oil companies controlling about three fifths of all U.S. oil production. (See Table O-1, the chart of largest oil and gas companies, below.)

The power of imported oil declined during the first half of the 1980s, when fresh memories of the oil embargo cut consumption and increased domestic production. Imported oil dropped from a peak of 46.5% in 1977 to 27.8% in 1985. OPEC accounted for 67% of the world's market in 1973 but saw its share decline steadily thereafter, to 48% in 1979 and only 35% in the mid-1980s. Steadily falling oil prices also cut OPEC's revenues from a peak of $430 billion in 1980 to only $110 billion in 1989. By 1990, lower prices had allowed OPEC to improve its market share to 45%, but the Iraq war cast a long shadow over OPEC's future, making it less likely that it will dominate the oil market of the 1990s.

Table O-1   10 Largest American Oil Companies

Rank	Company	Revenues	Net Income
1.	Exxon	105,885	5,010
2.	Mobil	58,770	1,929
3.	Texaco	41,235	1,450
4.	Chevron	39,262	2,157
5.	Amoco	28,277	1,913
6.	Shell Oil	24,423	1,036
7.	Atlantic Richfield	18,819	2,011
8.	Phillips Petroleum	14,032	779
9.	Sun	11,909	229
10.	Unocal	10,740	401

Source: Company reports.

THE PEOPLE

About 204,000 people were employed in the petroleum and natural gas industry, according to the U.S. Department of Labor.

TRENDS AND FORECAST

The invasion of Kuwait by Iraq in August 1990 once again touched off a national debate about oil. Seventeen years after the first Arab oil embargo taught Americans the danger of being dependent on foreign oil, consumers and economists were once again worried that rising oil prices would send the economy skidding into a recession (or worse).

That the oil and natural gas industry plays such a major role in the health of the economy comes as no surprise to anyone who lived through the oil crisis of the 1970s. Following the first oil embargo, from mid-October 1973 to mid-March 1974, nearly 20,000 gas service stations, about 10% of the total, were shut down. In just one year, a jump in world oil prices cost the U.S. economy about $60 billion in lost production. Rising oil prices also helped fuel the inflationary fires of the 1970s, which eventually forced the Federal Reserve to adopt a tight-money policy that sent the economy spinning into the worst recession since the 1930s. And rising imports of oil hurt the U.S. trade balance. The U.S. had a negative trade balance in petroleum of $4.6 billion in 1972 before the embargo and a trade deficit of $79.3 billion in 1980.

The energy crisis forced a major reevaluation of U.S. energy policy.

Congress deregulated large parts of the nation's natural gas reserves. The federal government tightened fuel standards for cars in an attempt to reduce gas consumption, and funding was provided for alternative energy sources such as synthetic fuels and solar energy. And a separate cabinet-level agency was created, the U.S. Department of Energy. Under the Reagan administration, the federal government also moved to open up government-owned lands for oil and natural gas production.

A more important factor in changing consumption and production was the role of private markets. As long as oil was cheap, industry and consumers bought petroleum-based products. While the GNP, adjusted for inflation, grew only 8.9% between 1929 and 1940 and total energy consumption actually declined 0.7%, the use of petroleum grew 39.8%. Between 1929 and 1973, petroleum use grew 6.58 times, outracing the GNP, which grew 3.98 times, and overall energy consumption, which grew 3.13 times, according to the U.S. Department of Energy.

In the 1970s and early 1980s this picture changed. Between 1970 and 1984, use of petroleum as energy grew only 14.6%, while the GNP, adjusted for inflation, grew 52.6% and total energy use grew 9.4%, according to the U.S. Department of Energy.

U.S. production also responded to market pressures. A barrel of Saudi light went for $1.35 in 1970, rose to $2.10 in 1973, and then, under pressure from the Arab oil embargo, skyrocketed to $9.60 in 1974. The same scenario was repeated a few years later, when the Iranian embargo sent the price of Saudi light up from $13.34 in 1979 to $26.00 in 1980 and $34.00 in 1982. That meant the price of Saudi light grew 1,974.1% between 1970 and 1984, while the price of a barrel of U.S. oil at wellhead rose 713.8%, according to the Energy Information Administration. These price hikes meant U.S. reserves that had been unprofitable in pre–oil embargo days were once again good investments.

The total number of oil and gas wells drilled grew from 37,602 in 1973 to 82,101 in 1982, a record. Crude oil production grew slowly from 2.9 billion barrels in 1976 to 3.17 billion in 1983, while imports fell more than half from 2.41 billion in 1977 to only 1.17 billion in 1985. These were the boom years for the oil and natural gas industry—the value of production at wellhead grew from $17.7 billion in 1973 to $138.2 billion in 1981.

But once again the market broke. Prices for a barrel of oil dropped to $28 in 1984, as low as $10 in 1986, and then stabilized at $17 to $19 in the beginning of 1987. That sent the oil industry into turmoil. Wells drilled with the expectation that oil would sell for $30 and $40 a barrel now were unprofitable. Domestic oil and natural gas exploration dropped dramatically. The number of wells dropped to an estimated 39,423 in 1986 and only 37,508 in 1987, half the level in 1984 and the lowest since 1974. In contrast, 88,101 wells were completed in 1981, a record. There were only 920 active rigs in 1987, compared to 3,970 in 1981, according to Hughes Tool Company. Only 3,957 wildcat wells were expected to be drilled in 1987, a 48% drop in only a year, according to *Oil and Gas Journal*.

Oil companies cut their drilling and exploration expenses dramatically, as much as one-third to two-thirds in 1986 alone. That has wreaked havoc on the oil equipment and oil services industry. Expenditures for drilling and equipping wells fell from $43.2 billion in 1981 to only $11.8 billion in 1986 and only $10.9 billion in 1987, according to *Oil and Gas Journal.* Twelve major U.S.-based equipment and oil service companies posted losses of $1 billion in 1985. By 1986 the Hunt brothers' Penrol Drilling Corporation, the largest owner of offshore rigs worldwide, went into bankruptcy.

The oil price drop caused a number of observers to warn that the U.S. was going to become dangerously dependent on foreign oil. In some ways, they were right. Cheap oil did cut domestic production, and imports rose from about one-third of the American market to about 47%. But it would be very wrong to assume that the Persian Gulf crisis was about to produce a replay of the 1970s, when the economy sank into a nasty mix of inflation, rising unemployment, and sluggish economic growth.

First, the Persian Gulf crisis made it clear that OPEC will continue to have a hard time propping up the price of oil. During the 1980s, the cartel had found it harder and harder to maintain even a facade of unity. Iran and Iraq blasted each other's oil fields for 8 years, and in 1982 and 1983 the Saudis refused to agree on oil quotas. An even more worrisome split developed in the late 1980s. Some countries, like Kuwait, wanted to increase production to recapture the market share OPEC had lost. Kuwait and others did not want to increase the price of oil, since that would hurt Western countries where Kuwait had invested billions of petrodollars. But other countries, like Iraq and Iran, which were heavily dependent on their oil revenues to revive their war-battered economies, wanted to increase prices. The debate, which was further polarized by religious and political differences, came to a head in 1990, when Iraq invaded Kuwait.

Prices rose dramatically after the invasion of Kuwait but soon dropped. Even though the war badly damaged the oil fields in Kuwait and Iraq, the price of oil has remained low, and several factors are likely to moderate oil prices for years to come. Despite the destruction, there is still a fundamental oversupply on the market. The dramatic price rises in the fall of 1990 were based on the notion that war would disrupt supplies or cut production, at least for several months. When this didn't occur and other producers, notably Saudi Arabia, were able to take up the slack, prices fell. Moreover, the Saudis need oil revenues to pay for the cost of the war, and Kuwait and Iraq need to keep pumping oil to rebuild their economies, making it unlikely that OPEC will be able to enforce strict production quotas to push up oil prices. For American consumers, the new world order is likely to mean cheap oil for years to come.

Over the long term, however, a different picture emerges. Annual oil discoveries are only 40% of what they were in the 1950s and 1960s, when 35 million barrels of oil was found each year. By the first decade of the 21st century, and maybe sooner, oil prices are likely to began rising unless the Western economies take measures to cut consumption. Today's cheap oil will make it hard to prepare for the next energy crisis.

Table O-2   Value of U.S. Fossil Fuel Production, 1949 to 1989
(billions of dollars)

Year	Crude oil		Natural gas (Marketed production)		Bituminous coal, Subbituminous coal, and lignite		Anthracite		Total	
	Nominal	Real	Nominal	Real	Nominal	Real	Nominal	Real	Nominal	Real
1949	4.68	19.91	0.33	1.40	2.14	9.11	0.38	1.62	7.53	32.04
1950	4.95	20.71	0.44	1.84	2.50	10.46	0.41	1.72	8.30	34.73
1951	5.69	22.67	0.52	2.07	2.63	10.48	0.42	1.67	9.26	36.89
1952	5.79	22.71	0.64	2.51	2.29	8.98	0.39	1.53	9.11	35.73
1953	6.32	24.40	0.76	2.93	2.25	8.69	0.31	1.20	9.64	37.22
1954	6.44	24.49	0.87	3.31	1.77	6.73	0.25	0.95	9.33	35.48
1955	6.88	25.29	0.94	3.46	2.09	7.68	0.21	0.77	10.12	37.20
1956	7.30	25.98	1.11	3.95	2.41	8.58	0.24	0.85	11.06	39.36
1957	8.09	27.80	1.17	4.02	2.50	8.59	0.23	0.79	11.99	41.20
1958	7.37	24.81	1.32	4.44	1.99	6.70	0.19	0.64	10.87	36.59
1959	7.47	24.57	1.57	5.16	1.97	6.48	0.18	0.59	11.19	36.80
1960	7.42	24.01	1.79	5.79	1.95	6.31	0.15	0.49	11.31	36.60
1961	7.58	24.29	1.99	6.38	1.85	5.93	0.14	0.45	11.56	37.05
1962	7.76	24.33	2.22	6.96	1.89	5.92	0.13	0.41	12.00	37.62
1963	7.96	24.57	2.36	7.28	2.01	6.20	0.16	0.49	12.49	38.54
1964	8.03	24.41	2.33	7.08	2.17	6.60	0.15	0.46	12.68	38.55
1965	8.15	24.11	2.57	7.60	2.27	6.72	0.13	0.38	13.12	38.81
1966	8.72	24.91	2.75	7.86	2.42	6.91	0.10	0.29	13.99	39.97
1967	9.39	26.16	2.91	8.11	2.55	7.10	0.10	0.28	14.95	41.65
1968	9.79	25.97	3.09	8.20	2.55	6.76	0.10	0.27	15.53	41.20

Year										
1969	10.42	26.18	3.52	8.84	2.80	7.04	0.10	0.25	16.84	42.31
1970	11.19	26.64	3.73	8.88	3.77	8.98	0.11	0.26	18.80	44.76
1971	11.71	26.37	4.05	9.12	3.90	8.78	0.11	0.25	19.77	44.52
1972	11.71	25.18	4.28	9.20	4.56	9.81	0.09	0.19	20.64	44.38
1973	13.07	26.40	4.98	10.06	5.05	10.20	0.09	0.18	23.19	46.84
1974	22.00	40.74	6.48	12.00	9.50	17.59	0.15	0.28	38.13	70.61
1975	23.45	39.54	8.85	14.92	12.47	21.03	0.20	0.34	44.97	75.83
1976	24.37	38.62	11.57	18.34	13.19	20.90	0.21	0.33	49.34	78.19
1977	25.79	38.32	15.82	23.51	13.70	20.36	0.20	0.30	55.51	82.49
1978	28.60	39.61	18.18	25.18	14.49	20.07	0.18	0.25	61.45	85.11
1979	39.45	50.19	24.16	30.74	18.36	23.36	0.20	0.25	82.17	104.54
1980	67.93	79.26	32.09	37.44	20.20	23.57	0.26	0.30	120.48	140.57
1981	99.40	105.74	39.51	42.03	21.51	22.88	0.24	0.26	160.66	170.91
1982	90.03	90.03	45.56	45.56	22.62	22.62	0.23	0.23	158.44	158.44
1983	83.05	79.93	43.57	41.93	20.11	19.36	0.21	0.20	146.94	141.42
1984	84.10	78.09	48.49	45.02	22.75	21.12	0.20	0.19	155.54	144.42
1985	78.88	71.13	43.17	38.93	22.06	19.89	0.22	0.20	144.33	130.15
1986	39.63	34.79	32.57	28.60	21.00	18.44	0.19	0.17	93.39	82.00
1987	46.93	39.97	28.97	24.68	21.05	17.93	0.16	0.14	97.11	82.72
1988	37.48	30.90	30.10	24.81	20.83	17.17	0.16	0.13	88.57	73.01
1989	44.15	34.96	30.56	24.20	20.40	16.15	0.15	0.12	95.26	75.43

Source: Energy Information Administration.

493

Table O-3 International Consumption of Petroleum Products, 1960–1988

(millions of barrels per day)

Organization for Economic Co-operation and Development (OECD)[1]

Year	Australia	Canada	France	West Germany	Italy	Japan	Spain	United Kingdom	United States	Other OECD	Total	Brazil	China	Mexico	U.S.S.R.	Total world	Noncommunist world
1960	0.22	0.84	0.56	0.63	0.44	0.66	0.10	0.94	9.80	1.28	15.47	0.27	0.17	0.30	2.38	21.34	18.32
1961	0.23	0.87	0.63	0.79	0.54	0.82	0.12	1.04	9.98	1.45	16.46	0.28	0.17	0.29	2.57	23.00	19.57
1962	0.25	0.92	0.73	1.00	0.67	0.93	0.12	1.12	10.40	1.62	17.74	0.31	0.14	0.30	2.87	24.89	21.20
1963	0.29	0.99	0.86	1.17	0.77	1.21	0.12	1.27	10.74	1.85	19.26	0.34	0.17	0.31	3.15	26.92	22.90
1964	0.32	1.05	0.98	1.36	0.90	1.48	0.20	1.36	11.02	2.03	20.70	0.35	0.20	0.33	3.58	29.08	24.76
1965	0.35	1.14	1.09	1.61	0.98	1.74	0.23	1.49	11.51	2.30	22.44	0.33	0.23	0.34	3.61	31.14	26.45
1966	0.37	1.21	1.19	1.80	1.08	1.98	0.31	1.58	12.08	2.61	24.20	0.38	0.30	0.36	3.87	33.56	28.53
1967	0.41	1.25	1.34	1.86	1.19	2.14	0.36	1.64	12.56	2.72	25.48	0.38	0.28	0.39	4.22	35.59	30.08
1968	0.45	1.34	1.46	1.99	1.40	2.66	0.46	1.82	13.39	3.08	28.05	0.46	0.31	0.41	4.48	38.96	32.96
1969	0.49	1.42	1.66	2.33	1.69	3.25	0.49	1.98	14.14	3.49	30.94	0.48	0.44	0.45	4.87	42.89	36.37
1970	0.51	1.49	1.89	2.43	1.84	3.85	0.56	2.09	14.70	3.88	33.23	0.51	0.62	0.50	5.30	46.38	39.08
1971	0.54	1.53	2.05	2.61	1.93	4.18	0.60	2.09	15.21	3.95	34.71	0.56	0.79	0.52	6.65	50.00	41.05
1972	0.54	1.62	2.24	2.76	2.07	4.36	0.67	2.24	16.37	4.29	37.15	0.65	0.91	0.56	6.10	52.42	43.80
1973	0.59	1.71	2.42	2.92	2.15	5.07	0.74	2.30	17.31	4.38	39.58	0.77	1.12	0.61	6.57	56.39	46.92
1974	0.62	1.74	2.26	2.61	2.09	4.96	0.78	2.14	16.65	4.23	38.08	0.83	1.38	0.67	7.01	55.91	45.69
1975	0.60	1.69	2.14	2.52	1.94	4.50	0.84	1.87	16.32	4.11	36.53	0.87	1.58	0.74	7.47	55.48	44.47
1976	0.62	1.74	2.28	2.71	1.99	4.77	0.98	1.86	17.46	4.40	38.81	0.97	1.68	0.80	7.65	58.74	47.32
1977	0.66	1.75	2.24	2.84	1.91	5.23	0.93	1.88	18.43	4.43	40.29	1.01	1.83	0.84	8.18	61.63	49.36
1978	0.61	1.74	2.17	3.05	1.95	5.14	0.95	1.85	18.85	4.47	40.76	1.06	1.81	0.99	8.47	63.30	50.52
1979	0.61	1.86	2.39	3.07	2.01	5.48	0.98	1.93	18.51	4.72	41.57	1.18	1.85	1.10	8.58	65.17	51.99
1980	0.59	1.87	2.26	2.71	1.93	4.96	0.99	1.73	17.06	4.50	38.60	1.16	1.77	1.27	9.00	63.14	49.66
1981	0.58	1.77	2.02	2.45	1.87	4.85	0.94	1.59	16.06	4.14	36.27	1.10	1.71	1.40	8.94	60.93	47.73
1982	0.62	1.58	1.88	2.37	1.78	4.58	1.00	1.59	15.30	3.82	34.52	1.08	1.66	1.48	9.08	59.54	46.29
1983	0.59	1.45	1.84	2.32	1.75	4.40	1.01	1.53	15.73	3.67	33.79	1.01	1.73	1.43	8.95	58.86	45.72
1984	0.61	1.47	1.75	2.32	1.65	4.58	0.91	1.85	15.73	3.63	34.50	1.07	1.74	1.48	8.91	59.92	46.73
1985	0.63	1.50	1.78	2.34	1.72	4.38	0.85	1.63	15.73	3.72	34.27	1.13	1.78	1.53	8.95	59.94	46.68
1986	0.63	1.51	1.77	2.50	1.74	4.44	0.88	1.65	16.28	3.90	35.28	1.30	1.92	1.47	8.98	61.46	48.07
1987	0.64	1.55	1.79	2.42	1.86	4.48	0.90	1.60	16.67	4.00	35.91	1.32	2.08	1.52	9.00	62.73	49.15
1988	0.67	1.60	1.80	2.42	1.81	4.73	0.96	1.68	17.28	3.99	36.94	1.35	2.13	1.53	8.86	64.23	50.74

[1]"Other OECD" includes the United States territories of Puerto Rico, Virgin Islands, and Guam.

Note: Sum of components may not equal total due to independent rounding.

Sources: United States: 1960 through 1976—Bureau of Mines, Mineral Industry Surveys, *Petroleum Statement, Annual,* 1977 through 1980—Energy Information Administration, Energy Data Reports, *Petroleum Statement, Annual,* 1981 and forward—Energy Information Administration, *Petroleum Supply Annual.* U.S.S.R.: 1960 through 1976—U.S.S.R. Central Statistical Office, *Narodnoye Khozyaystvo SSSR (National Economy U.S.S.R.)* and *Vneshnyaya Torgivlya SSSR (Foreign Trade of the U.S.S.R.),* annual issues. 1977 through 1979—U.S.S.R. Central Statistical Office, *Narodnoye Khozyaystvo SSSR (National Economy U.S.S.R.),* annual issues; U.S.S.R. trade as imports reported by their trading partners in official trades statistics of the respective countries. 1980 and forward—Energy Information Administration, *International Energy Annual.* China: 1960 through 1979—Central Intelligence Agency, unpublished data. 1980 and forward—Energy Information Administration, *International Energy Annual.* All other countries: 1960 through 1969—Bureau of Mines, *International Petroleum Annual,* 1969. 1970 through 1978—Energy Information Administration, *International Petroleum Annual, 1978.* 1979 and forward—Energy Information Administration, *International Energy Annual.*

494

Table O-4   Worldwide Oil Reserves
(1,000 billions of barrels)

	1978	1980	1985	1990	Change 1990–1980	% change 1990/1980
Australia	2,000,000	2,130,000	1,430,900	1,676,500	−453,500	−21.3
Brunei	1,550,000	1,800,000	1,400,000	1,375,000	−425,000	−23.6
India	3,000,000	2,600,000	3,500,000	7,516,400	+4,916,400	+189.1
Indonesia	10,000,000	9,600,000	8,650,000	8,200,000	−1,400,000	−14.6
Malaysia	2,500,000	2,800,000	3,000,000	2,950,000	+150,000	+5.4
Others	699,270	425,200	549,000	827,451	+402,251	+94.6
Total Asia-Pacific	19,479,270	19,355,200	18,529,900	22,545,351	+3,190,151	+16.5
Norway	6,000,000	5,750,000	8,300,000	11,546,204	+5,796,204	+100.8
United Kingdom	19,000,000	15,400,000	13,590,000	4,255,620	−11,144,380	−72.4
Others	1,862,500	2,626,400	2,535,500	3,020,273	+393,873	+15.0
Total Western Europe	26,862,500	23,776,400	24,425,500	18,822,097	−4,954,303	−20.8
Abu Dhabi	31,000,000	28,000,000	30,500,000	92,205,000	+64,205,000	+229.3
Divided Zone	6,200,000	6,260,000	5,420,000	5,200,000	−1,060,000	−16.9
Dubai	1,400,000	1,400,000	1,440,000	4,000,000	+2,600,000	+185.7
Iran	62,000,000	58,000,000	48,500,000	92,860,000	+34,860,000	+60.1
Iraq	34,500,000	31,000,000	44,500,000	100,000,000	+69,000,000	+222.6
Kuwait	67,000,000	65,400,000	90,000,000	94,525,000	+29,125,000	+44.5
Oman	5,650,000	2,400,000	3,500,000	4,250,000	+1,850,000	+77.1
Qatar	5,600,000	3,760,000	3,350,000	4,500,000	+740,000	+19.7
Saudi Arabia	150,000,000	163,350,000	169,000,000	254,959,000	+91,609,000	+56.1
Syria	2,150,000	2,000,000	1,450,000	1,730,000	−270,000	−13.5
Others	666,000	377,300	720,750	6,108,191	+5,640,891	+1,495.1
Total Middle East	366,166,000	361,947,300	398,380,750	660,247,191	+298,299,891	+82.4
Algeria	6,600,000	8,440,000	9,000,000	9,200,000	+760,000	+9.0
Angola-Cabinda	1,160,000	1,200,000	1,800,000	2,024,000	+824,000	+68.7
Congo Republic	360,000	400,000	480,000	830,000	+430,000	+107.5
Egypt	2,450,000	3,100,000	3,200,000	4,500,000	+1,400,000	+45.2
Libya	25,000,000	23,500,000	21,100,000	22,800,000	−700,000	−3.0
Nigeria	18,700,000	17,400,000	16,650,000	16,000,000	−1,400,000	−8.0
Tunisia	2,670,000	2,250,000	1,514,000	1,750,000	−500,000	−22.2
Others	2,260,150	782,100	1,796,550	1,732,620	+950,520	+121.5
Total Africa	59,200,150	57,072,100	55,540,550	58,836,620	+1,764,520	+3.1
Argentina	2,503,000	2,400,000	2,266,000	2,279,900	−120,000	−5.0
Brazil	880,000	1,220,000	1,976,000	2,816,000	+1,596,000	+130.8
Ecuador	1,640,000	1,100,000	1,400,000	1,514,000	+414,000	+37.6
Mexico	14,000,000	31,250,000	48,600,000	56,365,000	+25,115,000	+80.4
Venezuela	18,200,000	17,870,000	25,845,000	58,504,000	+40,634,000	+227.4
United States	29,500,000	26,500,000	27,300,000	25,860,000	−640,000	−2.4
Canada	6,000,000	6,800,000	7,075,000	6,133,495	−666,505	−9.8
Others	3,147,000	2,632,500	3,228,700	3,547,969	+915,469	+34.8
Total Western Hemisphere	75,870,000	89,772,500	117,690,700	157,020,364	+67,247,864	+74.9
Total Non-Communist	547,847,920	551,923,500	614,567,400	917,471,623	+365,548,123	+66.2
China	20,000,000	20,000,000	19,100,000	24,000,000	+4,000,000	+20.0
U.S.S.R.	75,000,000	67,000,000	63,000,000	58,400,000	−8,600,000	−12.8
Others	3,000,000	3,000,000	2,000,000	1,700,000	−1,300,000	−43.3
Total Communist	98,000,000	90,000,000	84,100,000	84,100,000	−5,900,000	−6.6
Total World	645,847,920	641,623,500	698,667,400	1,001,571,623	+359,648,123	+56.0
Total OPEC	440,185,000	435,831,300	476,415,000	767,100,000	+331,268,700	+76.0
OPEC as % of world	68.2%	68.0%	68.2%	76.6	—	—

Source: *Oil & Gas Journal.*

Table O-5　Where We Get Our Energy
(in quadrillion Btu)

Year	Petroleum	Percentage of total	Natural gas	Percentage of total	Coal	Percentage of total	Nuclear	Percentage of total	Hydroelectric	Percentage of total	Total*
1973	34,840	46.9	22,512	30.3	12.970	17.5	910	1.2	3,056	4.1	74,288
1980	34,202	45.0	20,390	26.8	15,420	20.3	2.739	3.6	3,120	4.2	75,955
1984	31,004	42.1	18,510	24.5	17,070	23.3	3.546	4.8	3,720	5.3	74,060
1986	31,890	43.1	16,530	22.4	17,320	23.4	4,480	6.1	3,500	4.7	73,930
1990	33,644	41.3	19,414	23.8	19,060	23.4	6,185	7.6	2,942	3.6	81,453

*Total includes other sources not listed separately.
Source: Energy Information Administration.

ENERGY TIME LINE: THE OIL, GAS, COAL, AND NUCLEAR POWER INDUSTRIES

400,000 to 360,000 B.C.   *Homo erectus,* the first erect hominid, uses fire to cook meat.

A.D. 347   The Chinese bore 800 feet into the ground in search of oil and gas.

615   The Japanese drill wells for natural gas.

700s   Windmills can be found in the Arab world.

900   The Chinese pipe gas through bamboo and use it for lighting.

Middle Ages   Sicilians gather oil off the coast for use as fuel. Other Europeans use oil as medicine and fuel but its use is limited by their crude methods of producing oil. Typically, medieval Europeans gather oil by skimming it off ponds.

1577   Origin of the word *gas* can be traced back to the laboratory of Baptist Van Helmont of Brussels. While this alchemist is heating some unidentified material, a small explosion occurs. He calls it *gas.*

1700   Around this time, several steam engines are invented. In 1707 a Frenchman, Denis Papin, describes a steam engine he's created and builds the first steamboat. Thomas Savery patents a steam engine in 1698, and in 1705 Thomas Newcomen and Savery invent the Newcomen steam engine. The Newcomen engine plays an important role in the Industrial Revolution.

1700s   But through most of the early Industrial Revolution water and the waterwheel provide most of the power. Overshot waterwheels, similar to those used in 18th-century Europe, date from the 4th or 5th century A.D. in the Roman Empire.

1783   James Watt invents a steam engine that dramatically improves the efficiency and power of the Newcomen steam engine. In 1881 his name, "Watt," became an international unit of power.

1792   William Murdock of Scotland lights his house with gas produced from coal.

1800   The first modern electric battery is invented by an Italian, Alessandro Volta. His name was the source of the word *volt,* a measurement of electricity.

1812   The first gas company is created in London.

1816   The first gas company in the U.S. is created in Baltimore after Rembrandt Peale gives a public demonstration of gas lighting. The first street lamps are lit in 1817. By 1852 gas lights outnumber oil lamps in New York City and by 1859 over 300 U.S. cities are lit by gas.

1818   F. De Larderel builds the world's first geothermal plant in Tuscany, Italy, when he uses heat rising out of the ground to process boric acid.

1820   Natural gas is discovered near Pittsburgh, Pennsylvania, during drilling for salt water. The gas is accidentally ignited and the saltworks plant burns down.

1838   The first practical electric motor is invented by an American, Thomas Davenport, who uses it to power a drill.

1840   Gas meters appear, allowing companies to charge customers based on the amount of gas they use. Before this invention gas companies charged a flat fee.

1850   Oil and natural gas producers still obtain these products from coal or by skimming them off ponds and streams. The meager production became inadequate as whale oil used to light homes became less abundant.

1859   The first oil well is dug in Titusville, Pennsylvania, by Edwin Drake. He is hired by a Yale professor, Benjamin Silliman, and a group of businessmen who have created the Pennsylvania Rock Oil Company. At a depth of 69$^1/_2$ feet Drake hits oil, touching off an oil boom in Pennsylvania. Silliman's company eventually becomes Seneca Oil Company. In contrast to the 69$^1/_2$ feet Drake drills to hit oil, the average well in 1987 is 4,711 feet deep.

1860   There are 206 gas companies. They produce 4 billion cubic feet of gas which is sold for $11 million, according to the 1862 U.S. census report.

1861   The first oil refinery is set up in the oil region of Pennsylvania.

1865   The first railroad tank car is invented.

1878   A Frenchman, Mouchot, produces a small solar power plant that is strong enough to operate a steam engine.

1878   Pennsylvania passes a law to preserve petroleum production, perhaps the first conservation legislation ever.

1878   Thomas Edison patents his electric lamp.

1879   The first oil pipeline is created, running 110 miles through the Allegheny Mountains to Williamsport, Pennsylvania. A shorter, 5-mile pipeline had been laid in 1865 between Pithole City and the Oil Creek Railroad. Today, there are some 227,000 million miles of pipelines for oil and refined production.

1881   The first electric power station is built in England. It is powered by natural gas and most of its electricity is used to light lamps in Godalming, Surrey.

1884   The first steam turbine is built by an Englishman, Sir Charles Algernon Parsons.

1886   The German ship *Gluckauf* is the first tanker designed to transport oil.

1887   The first electric heating system is patented in the U.S. by Dr. W. Leigh.

1900   Natural gas has been found in 17 states, with Pennsylvania ranking as the leading producer. But the value of total production is only $23.7 million.

1900s   At the beginning of the century, kerosene is the main product of U.S. oil refiners and gas is considered a waste product. As the auto creates more demand for gas, refiners search for a way of producing more gas during the refining process. This problem is solved in 1913 by the development of the thermal cracking process by Dr. William Burton and Dr. Robert Humphreys.

1911   The Supreme Court dissolves Standard Oil, the world's largest oil monopoly, into 34 competing companies.

1912   One century after the first gas company is founded, there are 2,090 natural gas companies.

1914   Thomas Edison invents the first alkaline storage battery.

1918   Natural gas is discovered in Potter County, Texas. This is part of the world's largest producing gas reserve, the Panhandle Field, which covers 1.6 million acres.

1920   The production of cheap cars by Henry Ford dramatically increases the number of cars on the road to 9 million from only a half-million in 1910 and fuels the demand for gas that is key to the development of the oil industry. But powering cars isn't the only way that the auto industry creates demand for oil: eventually petroleum asphalt is used to pave roads.

1921   The gas industry serves 49 million people and supplies gas to 7 million gas stoves and 1.5 million gas water heaters.

1930s The creation of the Tennessee Valley Authority and other electrification programs during the Roosevelt administration increases the use of electricity and energy.

1938   The Natural Gas Act is passed, beginning federal regulation of the gas industry. The law gives the Federal Power Commission authority to regulate transportation and sale of natural gas.

1946   Demand for oil and natural gas continues to skyrocket. For the first time, petroleum supplies more of the nation's energy than coal.

1953   The world's first nuclear power plant goes into operation in the U.S.

1960   The Organization of Petroleum Exporting Countries (OPEC) is formed. Iran, Iraq, Saudi Arabia, Kuwait, and Qatar, the original members, are later joined by Venezuela, Indonesia, Libya, Abu Dhabi, Algeria, Nigeria, Ecuador, and Gabon. With oil selling for $1.80 a barrel, the organization has little power. But four years later the organization begins the first of many moves that will increase its power: in November of 1964, OPEC negotiates a larger share of oil-company profits. However, in 1967, an OPEC boycott following the Six-Day War fails to catch on and the price of oil remains at $1.80, and in 1969 the discovery of oil in Alaska and the North Sea seems to indicate that OPEC's power will wane. In fact, the opposite occurs. After threatening to nationalize their oil fields, OPEC nations negotiate an ever-larger share of profits from the major oil companies, and in 1971, for the first time, the organization agrees on a price increase. Following the Yom Kippur War in 1973, OPEC doubles its price to $5.12 a barrel, and by 1981 the price hits $35.00 a barrel. But a growing worldwide oil glut forces price cuts and OPEC has lost its market share in recent years.

1963   The first breeder reactor starts working in the U.S.

1965   An electrical blackout in the northeast leaves 30 million Americans in seven states over an 80,000-square-mile area without power.

1972   Cheap oil and gas has created an economy heavily dependent on oil and gas as energy sources. About 75% of all energy needs are taken care of by oil and natural gas, up from 57.8% in 1950.

1973–1974   America's dangerous dependence on foreign oil becomes apparent when OPEC embargoes shipments of oil to the U.S.

1977   The Department of Energy Organization Act creates the Federal Energy Regulatory Commission, which replaces the Federal Power Commission. This independent regulatory commission has power over the transmission of natural gas, sales of natural gas drilled before 1977, interstate pipelines, interstate sale of electricity, interconnection rates and charges among electric utilities, stock issues of electric utilities, and oil pipelines.

1979   The Iran oil embargo touches off a new wave of shortages and price hikes. Spot market prices rise from less than $3 a barrel in 1973 to more than $40 in 1980. This causes many oil and natural gas companies to make plans as if oil prices will continue rising. When oil prices begin to fall in 1981, a wave of bankruptcies and heavy losses follows.

1980   When oil prices hit the skids, the prices for stocks of oil companies drop to absurdly low levels—making the companies attractive to takeover attempts. These companies' assets are worth two and sometimes three times as much as the stock. Since many believe that oil prices will eventually recover, buying these low-priced stocks is much like buying oil at $5 a barrel. In 1981, the sale of Conoco to du Pont touches off a major industry-wide restructuring. Several large companies, such as Marathon Oil, Gulf Oil, and Getty Oil, are also sold. Other companies, such as Atlantic Richfield and Phillips Petroleum, leverage their balance sheets or make other moves to fend off raiders. The trend puts more money in individual stockholders' pockets but reduces money available for exploration and development, making the U.S. potentially more dependent on OPEC in the 1990s.

1983   The first sun-powered industrial complex is put into operation in Lyons, France.

1985   OPEC sees its share of U.S. consumption of oil fall to only 11.6%, down from 33.6% in 1977.

1986   As oil prices drop momentarily below $10 a barrel, oil rig counts fall to the lowest level since 1940. Bad loans made to energy producers during the boom period of 1979 to 1981 cause major banks in Texas and the southwest to post record losses. By the end of the year, an OPEC production agreement stabilizes prices at around $18 a barrel.

1990   The invasion of Kuwait by Iraq sends the price of oil up from $13.75 in July to over $40 in October. U.S. troops are sent to the Persian Gulf to protect the oil fields.

1991   The oil industry faces an uncertain future. After a quick war, oil prices fell even though oil fields in Kuwait and Iraq are badly damaged.

Exxon Corporation

Chairman and CEO: Lawrence G. Rawl   225 E. John Carpenter Freeway
Employees: 104,000   Irving, Texas 75062-2298
Assets: $87.7 billion   214-444-1000

	1990	1989	1985	1980
Revenues (millions of dollars):	105,519	86,656	86,675	103,143
Net income (millions of dollars):	5,010	2,975	4,870	5,650
Share earnings (dollars):	1.86	2.32	3.23	3.25

What it does: The world's biggest petroleum company.

Talk about a mess. On March 24, 1989, the *Exxon Valdez* tanker ran aground in Prince William Sound in Alaska, spilling about 11 million gallons of oil on some of the most pristine coastline in America. In 1989, the company spent over $1.7 billion cleaning up the mess, but that wasn't enough for state and federal authorities. In 1990, the company was indicted on criminal charges of violating various environmental and marine safety laws.

But when one digs beneath the oil spill mess, Exxon's prospects look much better, thanks to a massive restructuring during the 1980s.

Long described as a jumbo elephant, Exxon is now a trimmer elephant. Faced with a 50% drop in crude oil prices, the behemoth cut its work force to 102,000 from 182,000. Capital and exploration spending was down 40% in 1986 from 1985. The oil refining operation was cut 1.5 million barrels a day.

Moreover, the company shed its nuclear and Reliance Electric Company subsidiaries to an investment group that included Prudential-Bache Securities and Citicorp Capital Investors. And the company in 1986 also sold the Exxon headquarters in midtown Manhattan for $610 million; the building, which will continue to serve as the company's headquarters, was jointly owned by Exxon and the Rockefeller Group.

The company also slowed down its acquisition strategy. The last big acquisition was in 1985, when Exxon picked up 49% of Hunt Oil Company's interest in a production-sharing deal with the Yemen Arab Republic, including the huge Alif oil field.

But don't feel sorry for the giant just because oil hit a downturn. The slimming down was applauded on Wall Street as necessary for a highly profitable company to stay that way. The nation's second-largest corporation (after General Motors) still managed to have enormous profits in 1987, $4.84 billion on revenues of $84.12 billion, not bad by any measure.

Today, Exxon and its divisions and affiliated companies operate in the U.S. and more than 80 countries. The main business remains energy, involving exploration for and production of crude oil and natural gas, manufacturing of petroleum products, and sale and transportation of crude oil, natural gas, and petroleum products. The company also explores for mines and sells coal.

Exxon Chemical Company is a major maker and marketer of petrochemicals. Exxon also explores for and mines minerals other than coal.

Moreover, the company conducts extensive research programs supporting its businesses and provides capital to new innovative ventures, some of which aren't related to its lines of business.

Historically, Exxon is an offshoot of the Standard Oil Company. The company was incorporated in New Jersey in 1892 as the Standard Oil Company of New Jersey as a result of a court order to dissolve John D. Rockefeller's monopolistic Standard Oil Trust. (See the profile of the Rockefellers on page 117.) Before long, however, the trust was back in business under a different name, Standard Oil Company. In 1911, the Supreme Court, operating under the Sherman Antitrust Law, then broke Standard Oil into 34 oil companies.

On its own, Standard Oil of New Jersey set itself up as a holding company and grew through a dizzying series of mergers and acquisitions involving U.S. companies and companies all over the world. In 1928, for instance, the company acquired shares in Creole Petroleum Company of Venezuela. In 1932, the company bought stock in Standard Oil of Indiana. By the mid-1940s, the company had acquired ownership of oceangoing tankers, and soon it had pipeline activities and interests in synthetic rubber, chemicals, coal, minerals, and power generation—all of which made it very big indeed.

Marvin Davis   By the time Marvin Davis graduated from Syracuse University in 1947, his father, Jack, was interested in oil. An English immigrant and former boxer, the elder Davis packed his beefy, six-foot-four-inch son off to set up an office in Denver to look for black gold.

Look he did. Davis the younger traipsed around the Rocky Mountains, drilling one dry hole after another. A wildcatter, he went after highly speculative wells in uncharted regions, figuring if you drill enough you've got to make a strike sooner or later. He also proved good at raising other people's money for his explorations. By the 1960s, he was head of Davis Oil Company and had made several discoveries in Wyoming.

When oil prices skyrocketed in the late 1970s, Davis found himself courted by legions of celebrities, including Gerald R. Ford and Henry A. Kissinger, who wanted to invest in his wells. Davis's business boomed and he turned his little oil company into TCF Holdings, with interests in real estate, banking, and energy worth $1 billion or so.

Along the way, Davis earned himself a reputation as a tough, demanding deal maker and proved himself a master at timing. For instance, he stoked up a bidding for his oil properties and then sold about a third of them to Hiram Walker Resources Ltd. for $630 million. Then he sold 80% of his real estate company's interests in four new office buildings in Denver to Prudential Insurance Company for $500 million. A short while later, the price of oil sank and the office building market nosedived.

That was about the time Davis got interested in show biz. He said he wanted "fun investments" and decided to take over Twentieth Century Fox Film Corporation. What could be more fun than running a movie studio?

For help with the takeover, he turned to the commodities trader Marc Rich, with whom he had been involved in some big gas and oil deals.

(Rich subsequently became a fugitive from justice and Davis got into hot water himself over some of the deals he had made with Rich.) They didn't have much trouble with Fox, which was a mess. Senior managers were at each other's throats, and an attempted leveraged buyout had just flopped. Davis actually managed to look like a white knight. He bid $720 million for the company (but he only put up $55 million). And he promised to keep the management in place.

So much for promises. Within weeks, Fox chairman Dennis C. Stanfill resigned, charging that Davis interfered with his running of the company, and he filed a $40 million breach-of-contract suit against Davis. Other executives quit or were fired. Davis then began shifting Fox's assets to his holding company. To pay his huge debt, he sold off Fox's music publishing, the Coca-Cola bottling operation, and various real estate holdings, as well as theaters in Australia and New Zealand. All told, he took some $500 million from Fox. Nonstudio revenue disappeared.

In the interim, Davis was bitten by the show biz bug. He hit the celebrity circuit, making a mad round of parties and gatherings. He paid $22 million for Kenny Rogers's Beverly Hills mansion and had his own star-studded parties.

Unfortunately, there's more to making movies than playing like a movie mogul. Davis waded into Fox's business, hiring his 26-year-old son, John, as a producer and giving him a seat on the board. And he applied his oil well theory to movie-making: If you make enough, you're bound to have a hit.

He didn't hit any celluloid gushers but managed to make a lot of losers. Fox was bathed in red ink and, by 1985, Davis sold his Fox interests (except for some real estate) to media mogul Rupert Murdoch for $575 million. But Davis still did OK. Even after paying off his whopping debt, he was believed to have made at least $350 million from the Fox deal.

Since then, Davis seems to have kept his touch. He bought the Beverly Hills Hotel in 1986 from another corporate raider, Ivan Boesky, and sold it a year later for a $65 million profit. In 1989, he was one of the last to profit from takeover speculation. After making a bid for Northwest Airlines and UAL, he sold his stakes for over $125 million. By the summer of 1990, *Forbes* estimated that he was worth at least $1.65 billion, and *Financial World* ranked him as the highest-paid investor on Wall Street.

PACKAGING AND CONTAINERS

THE MARKET

Providing the containers and packaging for most of the products consumed in the U.S. is a monumental task. Each year, Americans buy some 109 billion metal cans (including 37 billion beer cans, 41 billion soft drink cans, and 27 billion food cans), 42 billion glass containers, 18.7 billion plastic bottles, 2.4 billion pounds of plastic used as refuse bags and film, 2.4 billion aerosol containers, 2.1 billion plastic food containers, and 81.1 billion metal and plastic tops and closures for containers. No wonder the garbage can fills so quickly.

THE MONEY

Producing a wide variety of packaging and containers adds tens of billions of dollars to the economy. American manufacturers produced $12.1 billion worth of metal cans in 1990, $4.7 billion worth of glass containers, $3.4 billion worth of plastic bottles, $9.1 billion worth of all types of bags, except for textile bags, $6.9 billion worth of folding paperboard boxes, $19.5 million worth of corrugated and solid fiber boxes, paperboard boxes, and $2.6 billion worth of sanitary food containers.

PACKAGING FIRSTS

1795   Nicolas Appert discovers a method of preserving food in airtight glass jars covered with five layers of cork. The process, which is still used, is called appertization.

1810   Peter Durand takes out a patent on a process using tin cans to preserve food. Bryan Donkin and John Hall produce the first food in tin cans in 1813.

1830s   While working at his father's store, Francis Wolle is faced with the tedium of making handmade paper bags. So he invents a machine that can manufacture paper bags, which he patents in 1852. In 1883, Charles Stillwell invents a machine to make grocery bags with a flat bottom.

1840   No one has yet invented the can opener so labels commonly instruct consumers to "cut round on the top near to the outer edge with a chisel and hammer." When the first can opener makes its appearance is something of a mystery, one of those subjects that seems to have eluded academic study. The first wall-mounted can opener does not appear until 1927. It is marketed by the Central States Manufacturing Company of St. Louis.

1896   Colgate Company, founded as a soap shop 90 years earlier by William Colgate, introduces the first toothpaste in a tube.

1908   Small paper cups, later called Dixie cups, appear.

1947   R. J. Reynolds markets Reynolds Wrap. The rolls of aluminum foil radically change household food storage and cooking.

1952   Dow Chemical markets a plastic film, Saran Wrap.

1960   The aluminum can for soft drinks is introduced, replacing glass containers, which have dominated the market.

1963   The flip-top for aluminum cans is introduced by Alcoa, doing away with the need to use a can opener or "the church key."

1971   Dow Chemical introduces its Ziploc plastic bags.

PETS

THE MARKET

About 52.8% of all American households have a pet, with 38.7% of all households owning a dog and 29.4% owning a cat. About 25% to 30% of the 51.6 million dogs owned by pet lovers in America are purebred but only 7% of the 56.2 million cats have pedigrees. There are some 340 million to 500 million tropical fish around and 27 million caged birds are owned by Americans. Pet owners buy 9.4 billion pounds worth of pet food and pay 115 million visits to veterinarians every year.

THE MONEY

Americans spend about $4 billion a year on veterinarian care ($2.6 billion for dog care and $1.3 billion for cat care) and another $6 billion on pet food ($3.6 billion for dog food and $2.4 billion worth of cat food). Pet store sales of fish total about $219 million a year.

The average dog owner spends about 6% of his or her grocery bill on dog food and the average cat owner spends about $1,100 a year on the pet.

One of the fastest growing areas is gourmet pet food. About $1.5 billion worth of gourmet dog food and $207 million worth of gourmet cat food were sold in 1986.

THE PLAYERS

Some 20,959 veterinarians get most of their business from treating small pets (as opposed to farm animals). About 10,000 pet shops dot the land, along with 11,000 pet grooming shops, 7,000 kennels, 300 pet cemeteries, and 19,000 dog food vendors. The pet food business, like the human food business, is highly concentrated, with the largest seven companies controlling over 76% of the market. Many of the top pet food companies, such as Nestlé and H. J. Heinz, are also among the top food companies.

TRENDS AND FORECAST

Although Americans spend four times more feeding pets than babies, the pet food industry has only been growing 2% to 3% a year. As dog ownership has declined, from 41% of all households in 1981 to 38% in 1990, consumption of dog food has also declined, from 7.2 billion pounds in 1985 to 7 billion in 1990. But because more and more households own cats, the market for cat food has been growing at an annual rate of 8% a year, according to Business Trend Analysts. Since pet ownership is peaking and perhaps reaching a saturation point, sales of dog food should grow only about 2% a year and annual growth of cat food should grow 5% a year through 1991.

PHOTOGRAPHY

THE MARKET AND THE MONEY

There are so many shutterbugs around it sometimes seems as if every man, woman, and child has two cameras. Indeed, saturation is a problem in the photography business.

The big picture reveals an industry that sold some $19.7 billion worth of equipment and supplies in 1990. But a closer look reveals that American companies saw their factory shipments drop $16 billion in 1984 while sales of imports grew from 2.9 billion in 1984 to $6 billion in 1990. That decline can be blamed on a saturated consumer market for traditional photographic equipment and supplies, increased foreign competition, and other types of leisure activities, such as use of VCRs, that have cut into sales of photographic equipment.

To improve profits, photography companies are pushing new products, such as photocopiers, micrographics equipment, and laser printers.

THE PLAYERS

Kodak, which virtually created the consumer photography industry, dominates the industry. With $19.1 billion in sales and $703 million in profits in 1990, it sold a whopping four fifths of all color film in the U.S. (See the profile below.) Far behind is number two, Polaroid, with $2.0 billion in sales and $151 million in profits. Imports, however, have captured a major share of the market, 20% of the market for photographic equipment supplies and a higher percentage in certain parts of the industry, such as 35-millimeter cameras, in which they have a virtual monopoly.

THE PEOPLE

About 98,000 American workers find employment in the photographic equipment or supply industry. That is a dramatic cutback from the 119,000 employees working in the industry as recently as 1982. With companies continuing to cut costs and fighting to maintain profits in a stagnant market, further cutbacks are expected.

TRENDS AND FORECAST

This is a mature industry with few prospects for growth in its traditional products. Even with a weaker dollar, U.S. producers will lose business and the overall market will remain flat.

Eastman Kodak Company
CEO: Colby H. Chandler
Employees: 121,450
Assets: $24.1 billion

343 State Street
Rochester, New York 14650
716-724-4000

	1990	1989	1987	1980
Revenues (millions of dollars):	19,075	18,398	13,305	9,734
Net income (millions of dollars):	703	529	1,178	1,153
Share earnings (dollars):	2.17	1.63	3.52	4.77

What it does: World's largest producer of photographic supplies. Also manufactures chemical products.

For years now, Kodak has been trying to get in touch with its innovative past. Kodak staked its future on the disc camera, while the Japanese came out with improved, low-priced 35-millimeter cameras that took much better pictures. So consumers bought Japanese. Kodak's film monopolized the market until Japanese film makers brought out faster-speed film. Again consumers bought Japanese. Kodak's market share fell from nearly 100% to 82% in only 15 years. And consumers were complaining about the quality of Kodak's photo finishing. Many customers stopped paying 20% more to get Kodak to develop their pictures. Photo finishing sales fell to only $60 million in 1986 from $200 million five years earlier.

Turning things around hasn't been easy. The company abandoned its guaranteed lifetime employment policy, cutting 25,000 jobs and thinning management ranks by 25%. It fought off Fuji Photo Film Company in the film market and beat back competition from one-hour minilabs that cut into the demand for its photographic paper. But there still is a long way to go.

But competition seems to be revitalizing the company. Increased emphasis on product development led to the introduction of 100 new products in 1986, the most ever. The company is also hard at work on systems to produce instant photographic images electronically, a process that one day might replace conventional photography. In early 1985, Kodak spent $5.1 billion in cash to buy Sterling Drug Inc., making it a big player in the $110 billion a year worldwide pharmaceutical market.

Kodak is also aggressively expanding into new areas. With its plastics and chemical business bringing in $2 billion a year, the company started a drug company from scratch and moved into the batteries industry with a lithium battery that lasts twice as long as most batteries. It became one of the three top U.S. makers of floppy magnetic disks for computers.

Those new products would continue the company's tradition of technological innovation, started by its founder, George Eastman. Irritated by the size and weight of early photography equipment, he worked to make photography simpler, cheaper, and more accessible to the average American. In 1884, he introduced the world to a new product—film on rolls. In 1888, he followed up that success with the world's first light portable camera. The $25 camera came with 100 exposures' worth of film. After the pictures were taken, the customer mailed in $10 and the camera to Kodak.

By 1900, Kodak brought out the Brownie camera, which cost only a dollar, and the first 15-cent rolls of film. These created a mass consumer photography market and Kodak's fortune. Today, Kodak will have to show the same creativity George did.

PRINTING

THE MARKET AND THE MONEY

The printing and publishing industry in the U.S. produces most of the books, magazines, greeting cards, advertising flyers, and business forms we use, all of which adds up to a $168.5 billion industry. Businesses that specialize in printing books do a $4.1 billion business; commercial printers (including letterpress, lithographic, and gravure printers) add $56.5 billion; typesetters do a $2.2 billion business; platemakers $2.9 billion; and shipments of business forms add $7.8 billion. (See the "Newspapers," "Book Publishing," "Magazines," and "Greeting Cards" sections.)

Table P-1   Trends: Commercial Printing
(in millions of dollars except as noted)

Item	1987[1]	1988[2]	1989[3]	1990[4]	Percent Change		
					1987–88	1988–89	1989–90
Industry Data							
Value of shipments[5]	44,670	48,665	52,335	56,525	8.9	7.5	8.0
Value of shipments (1987$)	44,670	46,793	47,926	49,410	4.8	2.4	3.1
Total employment (000)	552	575	575	590	4.2	0.0	2.6
Production workers (000)	400	420	420	430	5.0	0.0	2.4
Average hourly earnings ($)	9.90	10.10	10.30	—	2.0	2.0	—
Product Data							
Value of shipments[6]	43,827	47,750	51,350	55,460	9.0	7.5	8.0
Value of shipments (1987$)	43,827	45,913	47,024	48,479	4.8	2.4	3.1
Trade Data							
Value of imports (ITA)	414	421	400	425	1.7	–5.0	6.3
Value of exports (ITA)	289	388	370	380	34.3	–4.6	2.7

[1]Industry and product data are preliminary. Trade data are adjusted to conform to the 1987 SIC.
[2]Estimated, except for exports and imports.
[3]Estimated.
[4]Forecast.
[5]Value of all products and services sold by establishments in the commercial printing industry.
[6]Value of products classified in the commercial printing industry produced by all industries.
Sources: U.S. Department of Commerce: Bureau of the Census; International Trade Administration (ITA). Estimates and forecasts by ITA.

RADIO

THE MARKET

Radio reaches 99% of all households and there are some 541 million radios in use, according to the Radio Advertising Bureau, including 127 million car radios. Every day radio reaches 80% of all Americans, and during the course of a week 96% of the population listens to radio. The average American over the age of 12 spends about one eighth of his or her day, or 3 hours and

19 minutes, listening to the radio. In the average hour, listeners hear 12.7 commercials lasting a total of 10 minutes and 6 seconds on AM radio and 11.9 commercials totaling 9 minutes and 17 seconds on FM.

THE MONEY

Radio advertising topped $8.4 billion in 1989, from $7.3 billion in 1987, which was more than double the $3.55 billion of revenues in 1980.

THE PLAYERS

There are 8,807 commercial radio stations in the U.S., of which 4,863 operate on the AM band and 3,944 are commercial FM stations. In addition, there are 1,263 noncommercial FM stations, bringing the total number of radio stations, commercial and noncommercial, to 10,070.

THE PEOPLE

There are currently 116,400 people employed in radio, up from 94,427 in 1980 and 64,939 in 1970.

Table R-1   Most Popular Types of Programming on Radio, 1987–1988

How AM and FM stations program by format. There are 4,975 commercial AM stations and 4,269 commercial FM stations licensed by the Federal Communications Commission operating in the United States (as of 12/31/89); 1,422 non-commercial stations can also be found, primarily on the FM dial.

A programming format usually defines the kind of audience attracted to a particular radio station.

(percent of AM, FM stations programming each format)

Format	AM	FM	Total AM/FM
Adult contemporary	15.6%	28.5%	24.0%
Country	23.6	22.7	22.4
Religion/Gospel	11.9	3.8	8.1
CHR/Top 40	2.7	15.8	8.0
Oldies	8.4	4.5	6.5
Middle of the road	7.7	2.2	5.2
Talk	6.8	0.2	3.9
AOR	1.0	6.2	3.1
Easy listening	1.5	5.4	3.1
News	5.4	0.2	3.1
Spanish	3.2	1.0	2.2
Big band/nostalgia	3.4	0.7	2.2
Urban contemporary	1.4	2.2	1.7
Diversified	2.3	0.8	1.6
Classic rock	0.6	2.5	1.4
Black	1.9	0.7	1.4
Agricultural	1.6	0.8	1.2
Jazz	0.5	0.9	0.6
Classical	0.4	0.8	0.6

Source: *Radio Facts 1990,* Radio Advertising Bureau.

Table R-2   Radio Advertising Revenues

Year	Network	(in millions of dollars) National spot	Local/retail	Total
1989	427	1,530	6,463	8,420
1988	382	1,402	6,109	7,893
1987	371	1,315	5,605	7,291
1986	380.0	1,332.6	5,313.1	7,025.7
1985	328.7	1,319.4	4,915.0	6,563.1
1984	288.0	1,184.4	4,412.0	5,884.4
1983	253.5	1,022.8	3,739.0	5,015.3
1982	217.5	909.4	3,365.0	4,491.9
1981	195.9	854.3	3,007.0	4,057.2
1980	157.9	746.2	2,642.9	3,547.0
1979	138.5	637.3	2,396.6	3,172.4
1978	126.4	589.7	2,179.2	2,895.3
1977	118.1	521.3	1,873.1	2,512.5
1976	92.2	494.6	1,639.3	2,226.1
1975	72.7	416.3	1,403.3	1,892.3
1974	60.3	386.8	1,308.8	1,755.9
1973	59.4	382.3	1,205.4	1,647.1
1972	65.0	384.3	1,098.4	1,547.7
1971	55.1	378.0	954.6	1,387.7
1970	48.8	355.3	852.7	1,256.8
1969	50.9	349.6	799.9	1,200.4
1968	54.7	342.2	733.4	1,130.4
1967	58.2	298.3	641.2	997.6
1966	57.4	292.6	607.6	957.7
1965	54.3	261.3	553.0	868.7
1960	44.9	208.0	401.6	654.5
1955	64.1	120.4	272.0	456.5
1950	131.5	118.8	203.2	453.4
1945	134.0	76.7	99.8	310.5
1940	73.8	37.1	44.8	155.7
1935	39.7	13.8	26.1	79.6

All expenditures in actual dollars for that year.

Sources: Federal Communications Commission 1935 through 1980. Radio Advertising Bureau compilations 1981 to present from: Ernst & Whinney—network; Radio Expenditure Reports—national spot, projected to estimated total from previous trends of RER's share of total FCC billings 1978–1980; Radio Advertising Bureau's Local Business Barometer—local/retail.

RAILROADS

THE MARKET

Railroads are, at the same time, the nation's most popular way of moving freight and one of America's least popular ways to travel.

Americans ride 12 billion passenger miles on railroads each year. That's only about 0.66% of the 1.812 billion passenger miles American travelers rack up each year. That makes railroads the least common way of taking a trip, behind private autos, domestic airways, and even buses. The nation's largest passenger railroad, Amtrak, carries 20.9 million passengers and takes in $1.2 billion in revenues.

But railroads are still the largest mover of freight in the U.S., handling 37.2% of all freight tonnage (see Table R-3, below). In 1987, railroads are expected to have moved 930 billion ton-miles worth of freight—a common measure of freight referring to the movement of one ton of goods (2,000 pounds) for one mile. Put in another way, America's largest railroad lines (Class 1 carriers with revenues of over $92 million, which account for over 90% of the freight handled by the industry) shipped 19.3 million carloads in 1985, or about 1.3 billion tons worth of goods over the nation's 161,000 miles of track. Coal (536.7 million tons), farm products (124.6 million tons), non-metallic minerals (not including fuels, 107.2 million tons), and chemicals and allied products (106.1 million tons) accounted for the most freight tonnage. Coal (5,669 million carloads), farm products (1,467 million carloads), chemical and allied products (1,288 million carloads), and food and kindred products (1,201 million carloads) filled up the most train cars among Class 1 carriers.

Table R-3   Trends: Class 1 Railroads
(in millions of dollars except as noted)

Item	1987	1988	1989	1990[1]	1991[2]	1987–88	1988–89	1989–90	1990–91
						Percent Change			
Operating revenue (billion $)	26.6	27.9	28.0	28.3	28.6	4.9	0.4	1.1	1.1
Revenue ton-miles (billions)	944	996	1,014	1,035	1,045	5.5	1.8	2.1	1.0
Average employment (000)	271	259	252	239	232	−4.4	−2.7	−5.2	−2.9
Average hourly earnings ($)[3]	14.29	15.00[4]	15.68[4]	16.30[4]	—	5.0[4]	4.5[4]	4.0[4]	—

[1]Estimate.
[2]Forecast.
[3]Nonsupervisory employees only, including overtime.
[4]Nationwide rail labor contracts expired on July 1, 1988, and are still being renegotiated. This figure does not include projections of wage levels under new contract covering the period beyond that date.
Source: Association of American Railroads; U.S. Department of Labor; Bureau of Labor Statistics; Railroad Retirement Board; and Federal Railroad Administration estimates developed from forecasts of numerous individuals and agencies.

TRENDS

A few figures show the decline of American railroads:

- Railroads operate about 161,000 miles of track today. In 1960, they operated 217,552 miles, down from a peak of 254,251 in 1916.
- Class 1 railroads carried 1,312.1 million tons of goods in 1985, down from 1970 (1,484 million tons), 1951 (1,477 million tons), and 1943 (1,421 million tons). But during this same period, railroad companies' share of total freight shipped fell from 72.5% of all freight in 1943 to 56.8% in 1951, 39.8% in 1970, and 37% today.
- Amtrak carries about 20.9 million passengers a year, far fewer than the 706.5 million passengers who rode the rails in 1947 and the 1.2 billion passengers who took a train trip in 1920.

Still, it would be wrong to see the future of railroads as a simple reflection of the past, with the industry continuing to decline. Railroads have held their share of transportation revenues since deregulation in 1980 and are working hard to improve long-term profitability.

Several major mergers, successful efforts to cut labor costs, and deregulation have all helped the railroads. The Railroad Revitalization and Regulatory Reform Act of 1976 was the first piece of transportation deregulation. It allowed railroads some limited rate-setting authority. Following deregulation of the airlines in 1978 and the trucking industry in 1980, Congress passed and President Carter signed into law more substantial legislation, the Staggers Rail Act of 1980. This act introduced price competition and limited the Interstate Commerce Commission's jurisdiction over rates to those rates where a railroad dominated a market.

The act was a major shot in the arm for the ailing industry. After it eased the rules on mergers, several major mergers took place and the industry-wide restructuring helped reduce costs and increase efficiency. Letting railroads have more freedom over rates helped them compete more effectively with trucking, and in 1983 the Interstate Commerce Commission ended a half-century-long ban that prevented airlines from acquiring trucking companies.

Productivity has also soared, up 380% since 1955, and unit labor costs have fallen 36% in the last decade. Even so, labor costs still eat up nearly half of operating revenues. And the average cost of a railroad worker is about $45,000, far higher than the $26,799 earned by the average trucker in wages and benefits, according to the Association of American Railroads.

All of this adds up to modest growth, reviving an industry that was once thought to be dying. Freight tonnage is supposed to grow only slightly, at an annual rate of 1.8% through 1992, according to the U.S. Commerce Department. But lower fuel costs, mergers that improve the utilization of equipment, and cheaper labor costs will all help the industry reduce costs and hold its share of the country's transportation dollars. The big uncertainty is the economy, since railroad revenues are closely tied to the health of construction, agriculture, steel, autos, chemicals, and especially coal, which accounts for about 40% of its tonnage, according to Commerce Department estimates. (See the section "Mining.")

RESTAURANTS

THE MARKET

As one wit once put it, "eating out" is America's favorite cuisine. Americans eat out 3.7 times a week, for a total of 45 billion meals in restaurants and school and work cafeterias each year. About 42% of our food dollar goes to restaurants, up from 1955, when the average American spent about 25.4 cents of every food dollar eating out, and 1980, when 36 cents of every food dollar was spent away from home.

During a two-week period, about 8 out of 10 adults will eat out at least once. The average check is $3.64.

The most popular meal for eating out may surprise you. It is dinner, which accounts for 39% of the meals eaten away from home. Lunch is a close second with 38%, breakfast 9%, and snacks 15%, according to a survey commissioned by the National Restaurant Association.

THE MONEY

The food service industry grossed about $241.3 billion in 1990, up from $199.8 billion in 1987. That included, in part, $156.4 billion in full service and fast food restaurants; $9 billion in bars and taverns; $15.1 billion in hotels and motels; $26.2 billion in businesses, schools, hospitals, and nursing homes; and $1.1 billion in the military, according to the National Restaurant Association. Despite the sales figures, however, by 1990 the business was saturated, and the number of food service establishment closings exceeded the number of openings.

THE PLAYERS

There are about 464,000 restaurants in the U.S. Most of the money (51%) is earned by the 400 largest food service companies, which account for $94.3 billion, according to *Restaurants & Institutions*. The top 100 food service companies capture 26.9% of all revenues. Leading the pack is McDonald's, which opened its 9,000th unit in Sydney, Australia, in February of 1986, and since then has been opening a new restaurant every 17 hours. The second-largest company in the restaurant business is Pillsbury, which owns Burger King, a chain that opens a new restaurant every day.

Despite Burger King's and McDonald's heroic efforts to put a fast-food restaurant on every block, the number of restaurants has dropped since 1972, when there were 274,000 eateries.

THE PEOPLE

Some 8 million people are employed in the food service industry, earning $52 billion in wages and benefits, according to the National Restaurant

Association. About 57% of these workers are women; one quarter are teenagers.

TRENDS AND FORECAST

After years of rapid expansion, growth in the food service industry has slowed down since 1984. In 1990 sales were expected to have increased 1.8%, to $241.3 billion, according to National Restaurant Association estimates.

Over the next decade, several demographic trends favor the restaurant business: More working parents and single-parent households, for example, mean more people will be eating out. An increasingly older population is cause for some concern since older people spend less of their food budget eating out (only 28% for those 55 to 64 compared to 58% for those under 25 and 39% for those 25 to 34 years old). But older Americans are eating out more than ever before, so an increasingly healthy and mobile older population may not hurt the industry's long-term outlook. The Tax Reform Act of 1986, which reduced to 80% the deductions for entertainment and business meals, hasn't yet done any significant damage to the industry.

Industry problems include tougher drunk-driving laws that will continue to hurt liquor sales and a decline in the teenage population that will drive up wages and costs. The industry also remains heavily dependent on the growth of discretionary income among consumers. With consumer debt at record levels, consumer spending is not likely to grow as fast as it did during the 1960s or 1970s. Still, the long-term outlook remains bright as Americans spend more and more of their food budget away from home. Look at some of the findings of the *Restaurants and Institutions* Annual Report:

RESTAURANT TRIVIA

- The fast-food industry is facing new attitudes toward diet. Hamburgers, which took a 51% bite out of fast-food sales in 1979, have slipped to 49%. Steaks account for 19% of fast-food sales, compared to 21% in 1979. The winners were chicken, which grew from 9% to 10%, and health food and pizza, which grew from 8% in 1979 to 12% today.
- Steakhouses do an $8.8-billion-a-year business.
- Cafeterias do a $3-billion-a-year business.
- Americans eat $7.2 billion worth of pizza a year outside their homes.
- Mexican fast food adds up to a lot of pesos—$2.4 billion in annual sales.
- Chicken consumption is 279 million pounds. Restaurants specializing in chicken do a $7.6 billion business annually.
- The Super Bowl is also a lucrative food market. Interstate United sold $1.2 million worth of food and beverages during the 1984 Super Bowl.
- The average cost of an airline meal hit $5 in 1985 as airlines spent $1.4 billion on food. In 1975 the average meal cost $2.41. Still, food accounted for only 3.1% of the airlines' operating cost, down from 1975, when it accounted for 3.4% of costs.

McDonald's Corporation
CEO: F. L. Turner
Employees: 127,000
Assets: $7.5 billion

McDonald's Plaza
Oak Brook, Illinois 60521
708-575-3000

	1989	1987	1986	1980
Revenues (millions of dollars):	6,065	4,893	4,144	2,184
Net income (millions of dollars):	727	596	480	221
Share earnings (dollars):	1.95	3.14	3.73	1.63

What it does: The major force in the fast-food industry. At the beginning of 1989, there were some 8,270 units in the U.S. and 2,892 in other nations.

Seeing the exploding growth of suburbia and the growing interest in fast food, a 52-year-old entrepreneur named Ray Kroc struck a deal in 1954 with the two McDonald brothers to franchise their San Bernardino, California, burger stand. Kroc's first McDonald's opened in 1955 in Des Plaines, Illinois. By 1958, a sign appeared over its golden arches: "100 million hamburgers served." Kroc bought out the McDonalds in 1961 for a paltry $2.7 million and achieved systemwide sales of $1 billion by 1972. Shortly after his death in 1984, the company celebrated its 30th anniversary by selling its 50 billionth burger. The company was the first food service company to become part of the prestigious Dow Jones Industrial Average.

In recent years, McDonald's has worked overtime to keep the 20 million customers who visit the chain every day all around the world. When Americans lost some of their ardor for beef, the company started selling Chicken McNuggets and started testing McPizza and salads. The company relies on a $550 million advertising budget to beat Burger King, Wendy's and other competitors in the burger wars. As the country has become saturated with fast-food chains, McDonald's has aggressively expanded overseas, mostly in Japan, Canada, Germany, the United Kingdom, and Australia. Revenues topped $6 billion in 1989, up 12% from 1988, and net income of $727 million soared up 22% from a year earlier. The figures are whoppers, especially in 1990 when more restaurants closed than opened.

RETAIL

THE MARKET AND THE MONEY

Retail sales hit $1.81 trillion in 1990, up from $1.71 trillion in 1989. Department store sales are projected to total $161 billion in 1988 while apparel and accessory stores will rack up $93 billion in sales. Eating and drinking establishments should ring up sales of $172 billion according to the U.S. Dept. of Commerce.

About one third of all retail establishments are small, with no paid employees; about 43% have fewer than 10 employees. Larger stores, with more than $500,000 in annual sales, earn more than three quarters of all retail sales. The largest 50 retailers control about one fifth of the market and stores with 10 or more branches account for 95% of all department store sales, 56% of all drug store sales, half of all shoe sales, one quarter of the revenues of eating places, and 57% of all grocery store sales.

THE PEOPLE

The retail trade employed about 19.3 million people in 1989, up from 11.8 million in 1972. About 18% of all nonagricultural workers earn their paychecks in the retail industry.

Wal-Mart Stores, Inc.

CEO: David S. Glass   P.O. Box 116
Employees: 185,000   Bentonville, Arkansas 72712
Assets: $6.4 billion   501-273-4000

	1989	1987	1985	1980
Revenues (millions of dollars):	20,649	11,909	6,401	1,643
Net income (millions of dollars):	837	450	271	55
Share earnings (dollars):	.95	.80	.48	.11

What it does: A discount retailer, operating some 860 department stores in 22 states.

When seen rattling around the dirt roads of Bentonville, Arkansas, in his old Ford pickup truck with his hunting dog, it's kinda hard to believe that unassuming Sam Moore Walton can scrape together more than a few bucks to buy shotgun shells down at Wal-Mart, the big discount store on the other side of town.

But, heck, "Mr. Sam," as he's known to folks around Bentonville, could buy out the whole darn store if he wanted. Fortunately for him, he doesn't have to. He is the major stockholder in the company which owns that Wal-Mart and 860 or so others in 22 states in the midwest and the Sunbelt. According to *Forbes* magazine that makes him the richest man in the country, with, oh, say, about $6 billion in stock.

Table R-4 How the Country Spent Its Retail Dollars
(billions of dollars)

Kind of Business	Establish- ments[3] (1,000) 1982	1987	Sales (mil. dol.) 1982	1987	Annual Payroll (mil. dol.) 1982	1987	Paid Employees[3] (1,000) 1982	1987
Retail trade, total	1,425	1,506	1,039,029	1,494,112	123,619	177,706	14,468	17,793
Building materials and garden supplies stores	70	74	49,939	81,487	6,221	9,760	504	668
Building materials, supply stores	36	38	34,827	60,525	4,179	6,929	307	432
Hardware stores	21	20	8,335	10,535	1,250	1,564	127	138
Retail nurseries, lawn and garden supply stores	8	11	2,873	5,411	456	822	47	71
Mobile home dealers	5	5	3,904	5,015	336	445	24	27
General merchandise stores	36	35	124,066	181,147	15,163	19,586	1,876	2,003
Department stores (incl. leased depts.)[4,5]	10	11	107,163	156,922	(NA)	(NA)	(NA)	(NA)
Department stores (excl. leased depts.)[4,5]	10	11	103,289	147,181	12,836	16,688	1,552	1,688
Variety stores	12	10	8,090	6,762	1,085	926	161	121
Misc. general merchandise stores	14	14	12,687	27,204	1,241	1,971	163	194
Food stores[6]	190	191	240,520	301,847	23,530	29,819	2,348	2,855
Grocery stores	138	138	226,609	285,481	21,364	27,084	2,031	2,502
Meat and fish (seafood) markets	12	11	5,274	5,616	563	606	62	59
Retail bakeries	19	22	3,543	4,871	979	1,353	159	185
Fruit and vegetable markets	3	3	1,330	1,802	135	186	17	20
Candy, nut, confectionery stores	5	6	801	1,182	129	199	23	31
Dairy products stores	5	3	1,375	880	163	106	27	17
Automotive dealers[6]	94	103	189,677	333,420	16,731	28,688	1,035	1,373
New and used car dealers	28	28	154,726	280,529	12,309	22,205	699	940
Used car dealers	12	15	6,273	10,849	450	809	36	55
Auto and home supply stores	41	46	19,638	25,460	3,072	4,152	229	286
Boat dealers	4	5	2,870	6,824	304	620	23	35
Recreational and utility trailer dealers	3	3	2,767	5,687	231	453	16	26
Motorcycle dealers	5	4	2,877	3,475	308	382	27	27
Gasoline service stations	127	115	94,719	101,997	4,768	6,414	604	702
Apparel and accessory stores[6]	141	149	54,622	77,391	7,455	9,725	967	1,121
Men's and boys' clothing stores	19	17	7,735	8,869	1,224	1,361	123	115
Women's clothing and specialty stores	52	60	19,743	28,531	2,649	3,519	385	455
Women's clothing stores	45	52	18,002	25,868	2,383	3,150	351	419
Family clothing stores	19	18	13,451	21,117	1,671	2,362	219	268
Shoe stores	39	39	11,275	14,411	1,571	1,880	189	205
Children's and infants' wear stores	6	6	1,356	2,101	172	245	28	37
Furniture and homefurnishings stores	100	110	45,314	74,783	6,287	9,904	543	703
Furniture stores	32	33	17,223	25,997	2,608	3,828	214	247
Homefurnishings stores	27	32	8,848	16,374	1,320	2,389	124	176
Household appliance stores	12	11	5,697	8,332	697	953	59	65
Radio, television, computer, and music stores	30	34	13,545	24,080	1,662	2,734	146	215
Computer and software stores	(NA)	4	(NA)	2,651	(NA)	325	(NA)	22

Table R-4 How the Country Spent Its Retail Dollars (continued)
(billions of dollars)

Kind of Business	Establish-ments[3] (1,000)		Sales (mil. dol.)		Annual Payroll (mil. dol.)		Paid Employees[3] (1,000)	
	1982	1987	1982	1987	1982	1987	1982	1987
Eating and drinking places	352	391	101,723	148,776	25,708	38,582	4,666	6,100
Eating places[6]	284	333	93,158	139,282	23,987	36,633	4,341	5,787
Restaurants and lunchrooms	135	155	47,136	66,364	12,935	18,796	2,291	2,822
Refreshment places	120	138	35,678	56,870	8,185	13,269	1,610	2,352
Drinking places	68	59	8,565	9,495	1,721	1,950	325	313
Drug and proprietary stores	52	52	36,242	53,824	4,605	6,476	496	574
Miscellaneous retail stores	264	286	102,207	139,440	13,150	18,754	1,430	1,694
Liquor stores	37	35	17,340	18,597	1,310	1,454	167	157
Used merchandise stores	19	18	3,798	4,305	730	823	80	81
Misc. shopping goods stores	108	123	32,524	49,460	4,623	6,481	566	706
Sporting goods stores and bicycle shops	20	22	6,718	10,077	844	1,218	96	121
Book stores	10	11	3,133	5,116	401	581	58	72
Stationery stores	5	5	1,495	1,814	257	287	28	27
Jewelry stores	24	28	8,352	11,994	1,433	1,921	132	163
Hobby, toy, and game shops	8	10	3,238	7,031	325	614	46	76
Camera, photographic supply stores	4	4	1,884	2,294	225	276	21	21
Gift, novelty, souvenir shops	24	32	4,620	7,459	694	1,055	110	151
Luggage, leather goods stores	2	2	589	839	94	122	11	11
Sewing, needlework, and piece goods stores	10	10	2,495	2,836	350	406	62	65
Nonstore retailers	23	23	20,155	33,894	2,942	4,523	274	318
Catalog and mail-order houses	8	7	11,254	20,347	1,194	1,932	103	123
Merchandising machine operators	6	5	4,727	5,692	935	1,090	84	74
Direct selling establishments	9	11	4,175	7,855	813	1,501	88	121
Fuel and ice dealers	13	13	16,818	14,250	1,405	1,834	95	100
Florists	24	27	3,416	4,810	711	1,019	104	125
Tobacco stores and stands	2	2	576	518	68	57	9	7
News dealers and newsstands	2	2	500	703	60	90	9	10
Miscellaneous retail stores, n.e.c.[6][7]	35	44	7,078	12,902	1,301	2,472	127	191
Optical goods stores	11	14	1,729	3,415	404	811	34	54

NA Not available.
[1]Based on 1972 Standard Industrial Classification; see text, section 13.
[2]Represents the number of establishments in business at any time during year.
[3]For pay period including March 12.
[4]Includes sales from catalog order desks.
[5]Establishments defined as department stores with 25 employees or more.
[6]Includes other kinds of businesses, not shown separately.
[7]N.e.c. means not elsewhere classified.
Source: U.S. Bureau of the Census, *1987 Census of Retail Trade*, RC87-A-52.

518

Ever since *Forbes* came out with Mr. Sam's little secret in 1985, life has gotten more complicated for him. He used to sneak off and do some bird hunting whenever the mood struck. Now, he sneaks around whenever he gets wind that yet another reporter is in this town of 9,900 or so citizens to bird-dog him until he answers questions such as, "What's it like to be filthy rich?" and "How did you make so much money?"

The answer to the first question is easy. Though a lot of folks might find it hard to believe, money doesn't mean a heck of a lot to Mr. Sam. A folksy guy, he always lived modestly. He doesn't know what all the fuss is about, because, as he says, "It's only paper money." (His shrunk by $2 billion in the market meltdown of October 1987.)

As for the second question: Mr. Sam is the personification of the American work ethic. He spotted an opportunity, worked hard, was a square shooter with his employees and customers, and kept plowing his profits back into the business to make it better and bigger.

After graduating from the University of Missouri in 1940, he got a job with J. C. Penney at $85 a month. When war broke out, he spent three years as an Army intelligence officer. When he left the service in 1945, he borrowed $25,000 and opened a five-and-dime in Newport, Arkansas. When the landlord refused to renew his lease several years later, he packed up and moved to Bentonville. (One reason he picked the little town was because of the good hunting around there.)

In 1962, he got the notion that small-town people would appreciate a discount general store with friendly folks selling quality merchandise. He liked people so much that he believed his salespeople—"associates," as he called his employees—should like people a lot too and treat customers real well. He opened his first store and his instincts paid off. He opened another and then another and then . . .

In 1970, Wal-Mart went public. The company joined the Big Board two years later when sales were $72 million and there were 41 stores. Employees got stock options after working a year for the company, and Mr. Sam always encouraged his associates to put whatever money they could into the company. As a result, there are an awful lot of millionaires walking around Bentonville today thanks to a landlord who once made Mr. Sam go to another town.

TUPPERWARE

In 1950, Earl Tupper had a problem. Five years earlier, Earl had developed the first airtight plastic containers, which he called Tupperware. But sales weren't so hot. Then he had an idea. Maybe Tupperware could be sold at parties women gave in their homes in exchange for a little gift. Four years later, sales hit $9 million as an army of 9,000 women held Tupperware parties. Rexall Drugs bought his company in 1958.

TIFFANY

Charles Tiffany came to New York in 1837 with the idea of opening a store that was a far cry from his dad's general store in Plainfield, Connecticut. He opened a jewelry store. Soon, he and a partner had a growing reputation for the quality of the English and Italian jewelry they sold. When the European diamond market became depressed in 1848, they began making their own jewelry. Their designs, such as the Tiffany ring setting—a diamond mounted in raised prongs—became much sought after, making Tiffany & Co. the biggest jewelry firm in the U.S. After Charles's death in 1902, his son Louis Comfort Tiffany, who died in 1933, began making the iridescent glass used in jewelry and vases, among other things that bear his name.

LENOX CHINA

That the U.S. makes fine china owes a lot to Walter Lenox. Until 1894, when he started making porcelain dinnerware modeled after that made by the Irish company Belleek Pottery, all fine china was imported. His company came to prominence when Tiffany's placed a large order about 10 years later. But not everybody's happy for everybody who gets Lenox. When Nancy Reagan gave the company a $209,508 order for White House dinnerware, she was widely criticized for her extravagance.

FULLER BRUSH

The work world didn't start out promising for the young Canadian Alf Fuller. By the time he was 18, he had been fired as a ticket taker after taking a break by joyriding in a car and crashing, fired as a stable hand for forgetting to take care of a horse, and fired as a messenger—a job his brother gave him—after losing a package. In 1905, figuring the only way he couldn't get fired was working for himself, he started selling brushes door to door. Surprising everybody, he was successful. The next year, he began making the brushes he sold. By 1910, he had 25 salesmen pounding on people's doors to sell Fuller brushes. In 1943, the year Alf retired, his company's sales were $10 million.

PARKER PEN

When George S. Parker was teaching telegraphy in Janesville, Wisconsin, he sold pens to his students. As the salesman, he felt an obligation to fix the pens when they went on the fritz, which they constantly did. While tinkering, he concluded he could make a better pen. By 1890, he had patented his first pen and, with a partner, W. F. Palmer, launched the Parker Pen Company.

During the First World War, Parker's Trench Pen was the favorite of American soldiers on the front; they could make their own ink by dissolving a pill of black pigment in water in the pen's cap. Sales rose after the war, declined for a bit during the Depression, and then rose again when the company introduced the Parker Vacuumatic, which more than doubled the capacity of similar-sized pens. Parker toured the world, creating an international network of distributors. In 1939, the Parker 51 fountain pen with its classic design was introduced and became a best-seller and the model for fountain pens ever since.

FOOD

The Market and the Money

In 1990 Americans spent about $380 billion on food at all types of retail outlets and about $359 billion of the total sold in the country's 154,000 grocery stores and supermarkets. But most of those sales took place in the country's 30,505 supermarkets, according to *Progressive Grocer*. Large chains with 11 or more supermarkets or grocery stores also controlled a large part of the market. These chains rang up $214.6 billion worth of total $380 billion in retail food sales. The average customer spent $16.33 every time he or she visited a supermarket, up from $14.33 in 1981, according to the Food Marketing Institute.

Consumers are finding more items on supermarket shelves and buying more nonfood items in supermarkets and groceries. The average supermarket carries 26,000 different items, up from 12,000 in 1983. About 5,100 new products make their way onto supermarket shelves each year. And nonfood items account for 25% of all supermarket sales, up from 6% to 8% in the 1960s. Americans now buy nearly half of their magazines and one third of their nonprescription drugs in supermarkets.

The Players

The average supermarket has $206,543 in sales per week, or about $8.43 of sales per week for every square foot in the store. Profits in this business are still determined by volume, with the average supermarket earning 1.19 cents of profit for every dollar of sales.

Just as supermarkets (stores with more than $2 million in average sales) capture a large proportion of industry sales (71.8%), large chain operators (those companies with 11 or more establishments) also hold a large share of the market, about 55%.

The People

The food retailing industry employs about 3.2 million people, up from 2.48 million in 1982.

Trends and Forecast

The outlook continues to be favorable for food retailers. Increased use of computers, less expensive labor contracts, and a trend toward large superstores or superwarehouses have also reduced costs for many operators. However, a slow growing population and a trend toward eating out will slow the industry's growth and hurt profits.

COUPONS

U.S. manufacturers issue about 270 billion coupons a year. But only a relatively small proportion, about 2.7%, are actually redeemed, for an approximate value of $7.29 billion, according to the Food Marketing Institute.

A.1. SAUCE

The story goes that a chef at the court of England's King George IV was always looking for new ways to pamper his sovereign's palate. One day, after being particularly delighted by a sauce, the king summoned the chef, whose name was Brand, and complimented him. "This is A1," George burped. The sauce caught on and Brand left His Majesty's service to sell the condiment. The product came to America when Heublein struck an arrangement with the Brand people around the end of the First World War. Now A.1. sauce is the leading bottled steak sauce in the U.S.

ANIMAL CRACKERS

A couple of bakeries tried selling animal cookies, but what they lacked was National Biscuit Company's clever marketing when it launched Barnum Animals in 1902. Kids loved the little packages decorated with circus animals and they thought the little string on top of the box was a great handle. (Actually, the handle was just a piece of luck for the company, which had put the string there so the boxes could be hung on Christmas trees.)

OREO COOKIES

Nobody's sure how Oreo cookies got their name. And National Biscuit Company, which introduced them in 1912, isn't sure how they became the runaway best-selling cookie in the world. They came to market with two other cookies, Mother Goose Biscuits and Veronese Biscuits, from which the company apparently expected great things. But people were really waiting for Oreos. Today, about 5 billion Oreos are eaten each year by Americans alone.

HERSHEY

In 1884, Milton Hershey talked a banker into giving him a $700 loan to launch his candy business in Lancaster, Pennsylvania. When the note fell due, Hershey not only couldn't pay, but he wanted to borrow $1,000 more to buy equipment. To press his case, he invited the banker to his "factory," which turned out to be a shabby little place where his "employees"—his mom and his Aunt Mattie—sat wrapping caramels. In defiance of his profession, the banker gave him the loan. A little while later, Hershey received enough money for candy he had shipped to England to pay off his debts and his business expanded like mad.

Hershey started making chocolate after he saw a demonstration by German chocolate makers at the Chicago Exposition in 1893. When the exposition ended, he bought the demonstration equipment, hired some professional chocolate makers, and, convinced that chocolate was the way to go, sold off his caramel business in 1900 for $1 million. His strategy was to concentrate on one product, mass-produce it, and price it so everyone could afford it. Needless to say, it worked.

SHOPPING MALLS

The Market

There are approximately 24,700 shopping centers in the U.S., covering nearly 3.4 billion square feet of leasable space, up from only 100 shopping centers in 1950. In 1985 alone, construction on over 2,171 shopping centers was started, a record. Half of all retail sales are made in shopping centers, up from 42% in 1982 and 25% in 1974, according to the Urban Land Institute.

Table R-5   The Largest Shopping Malls in the U.S.

Rank	Center Location	Owner	Total gross leasable space (thousands of square feet)
1.	Del Amo Fashion Center Torrance, California	Carson-Madrona Company The Torrance Company	2,650
2.	Lakewood Center Mall Lakewood, California	Macerich Company	2,400
3.	Woodfield Shaumburg, Illinois	Woodfield-Taubman Company The Homart Development Company	2,300
4.	Randal Park Mall North Randall, Ohio	The Edward J. DeBartolo Corporation	2,097
5.	South Coast Plaza and Town Center Costa Mesa, California	C. J. Segerstrom and Sons	1,800

Source: *Shopping Center Development Handbook, 2nd Edition,* Executive Group of the Commercial and Retail Development Council of the Urban Land Institute.

The Money

Retail sales at American shopping centers have climbed to over $500 billion, according to the International Council of Shopping Centers, up from $273 billion in 1978. Since few owners or managing companies of shopping centers are publicly held, there are no figures on profitability.

The People

Nearly 7 million people are employed in shopping centers.

Table R-6   The Largest Shopping Center Developer-Owners

Rank	Company	Square feet
1.	The Edward J. DeBartolo Corp.	69,107,396
2.	JMB Properties	68,838,357
3.	Melvin Simon & Associates, Inc.	60,997,145
4.	Equitable Real Estate	60,560,072
5.	The Rouse Co.	45,000,000
6.	Jacobs, Visconsi & Jacobs Co.	35,762,911
7.	The Hahn Co.	35,303,000
8.	Crown American Corp.	33,075,730
9.	The Cafaro Co.	31,795,406
10.	Leo Eisenberg Co.	26,885,235

Source: *Shopping Center World,* March 1990.

THE WORLD'S LARGEST SHOPPING MALL

The title of the world's largest shopping mall belongs to the West Edmonton Mall, located in the unlikely setting of Edmonton, Canada. The 110-acre mall has over 800 shops, several dozen restaurants, 34 theaters, an 18-hole miniature golf course, a 10-acre water park for swimming and sunning, two dozen amusement rides, and a 360-room hotel. And if that isn't enough to attract visitors, there are also monkeys, tigers, and four submarines that prowl a 438-foot-long lake infested with real sharks. Believe it or not, it's all indoors under one roof.

The developers, the four Ghermezian brothers—Raphael, Eskandar, Nader, and Bahman—have spent over $650 million to build the mall, even though they admit Edmonton's 500,000 population is too small to support the project. So why did they build it?

The project was conceived in the late 1970s during the oil boom when Edmonton's economy and population were booming. After coming to Canada in the 1950s from Iran, the Ghermezians had bought some 15,000 acres of underdeveloped Edmonton land for under $200 an acre. By the early 1980s that same land was selling for $40,000 an acre. But as the mall was being built, the oil economy went bust and now it's an open question whether the mall can survive. Normally, a mall this size would need to be in a city five times Edmonton's population. The Ghermezians scoff at that criticism, arguing that they had always meant the tourist trade to support the mall. The mall's amusement park will attract tourists, but how many of them will be willing to brave the 40-degree-below temperatures of Edmonton in the winter for a vacation shopping spree remains to be seen.

STEEL

THE MARKET

Once the mighty symbol of American manufacturing, steel is now the symbol of its decline. As manufacturers replace steel with products such as plastic, consumption of steel continues to fall. After a modest rebound in 1988 and 1989, the U.S. economy consumed only 78 million tons of steel, down from the 98.9 million consumed in 1984 and far less than the average of 107 million tons of steel consumed in the U.S. during the 1970s. With imports cutting into the market, U.S. steel makers' production is way down from 127 million tons in 1977. (See also the "Mining" section for information on closely related markets.)

Table S-1 Steel Mill Product Trends
(in millions of tons except as noted)

Item	1980	1986	1987	1988	1989	1990[1]	1991[2]	Compound annual rate of growth 1980–90	Percent change 1990–91
Raw Steel Production	111.8	81.6	89.1	99.9	97.9	96.5	92.0	–1.5	–4.7
Continuous casting (percent)	20.3	55.2	59.8	61.3	64.8	67.0	69.0	12.7	3.0
Steel mill product shipments	83.8	70.3	76.7	83.8	84.1	84.0	80.0	0.0	–4.8
Exports	4.1	0.9	1.1	2.1	4.6	4.1	3.5	0.0	–14.6
Imports	15.5	20.7	20.4	20.9	17.3	16.8	16.9	0.8	0.6
Apparent domestic consumption	95.2	90.0	95.9	102.7	96.9	96.7	93.4	0.2	–3.4
Exports as a % of shipments	4.9	1.3	1.4	2.5	5.5	4.9	4.4	0.0	–10.4
Imports as a percent of apparent consumption	16.3	23.0	21.3	20.4	17.9	17.9	18.1	0.6	4.1

[1]Estimate.
[2]Forecast.
Source: U.S. Department of Commerce: Bureau of the Census, International Trade Administration; industry sources.

TRENDS AND FORECAST

In case you haven't heard, the steel industry was in bad shape for most of the 1980s. Consider a few facts:

- Many U.S. steel companies are producing more red ink than steel. Between 1982 and 1986, the six largest steel makers lost $12 billion. In April 1985, Wheeling-Pittsburgh went into bankruptcy, and in 1986, LTV, the second-largest steel maker, followed.
- Since 1972, some 700 steel plants and related facilities have been closed, cutting total capacity by 22%. Most cuts came between 1982 and 1984, when steel capacity was reduced by 20 million tons, or about 14%, the U.S. Commerce Department says.
- The steel industry had the capacity to turn out 127.9 million tons at the start of 1986 but operated at only two thirds capacity. In 1987, after closing 450 plants since 1980, the industry was operating at only 80% capacity.
- Competing with high-tech foreign producers, the domestic steel industry badly needed to modernize its plants. But in 1986 the steel industry spent only 780 million on capital, down from 1984's $1.2 billion and way less

than the $2.4 billion spent in 1981 before a recession hit the steel market. After the bankruptcy of Wheeling-Pittsburgh Steel Corporation in 1985 and LTV's bankruptcy in 1986, investors may not be willing to cough up the capital needed to save the industry.

- Demand for steel in certain key sectors of the economy, such as the auto industry, will continue to drop. Domestic auto makers continue to lose ground to foreign producers and the cars they do make use less steel.
- It cost steel makers an estimated $3.2 billion to shut plants between 1983 and 1988, or about $75,000 per laid-off worker. That severely limits the amount of capital they can spend on modernizing existing plants.
- Steel operations that haven't slipped into bankruptcy face tough competition from companies that are operating out of Chapter 11. Analysts estimate that the companies in bankruptcy (24% of the market) have negotiated savings in labor, energy, and raw materials that save them as much as $50 a ton. Those cost advantages will hurt companies such as Bethlehem that face heavy debt loads.

Yet the steel industry managed to forge some profits. After losing $12 billion between 1982 and 1986, the six largest producers made money in 1987, and 1988 profits grew about 20% to $1.2 billion. Capacity has been cut by 27% since 1982, according to the U.S. Commerce Department, and the industry has spent $8 billion to upgrade its plants. Productivity grew 15% a year between 1982 and 1985, and a weaker dollar has increased the industry's competitiveness. In 1987 it cost U.S. steel makers 29% less to make a ton of steel than it did in 1982. As a result, U.S. steel was actually cheaper to produce than Japanese steel. While Japanese production costs soared 24% to $508 a ton, U.S. steel makers could forge a ton of steel for only $431. U.S. companies hope that this advantage will allow them to recapture 4 million tons of production from foreign producers.

But long-term problems remain; with consumption still dropping, U.S. producers will have to shut down more plants and reduce their capacity. Low cost mini mills have done the best, increasing their share of the market from 5% in 1970 to 20% in 1985. Profits, then, continue to depend on how well the industry can reduce excess capacity, cut costs and modernize its plants.

USX Pittsburgh

CEO: David M. Roderick
Employees: 69,424
Assets: $17.2 billion

600 Grant Street
Pittsburgh, Pennsylvania 15230
412-433-1121

	1990	1989	1987	1980
Revenues (millions of dollars):	19,462	17,533	14,836	12,492
Net income (millions of dollars):	818	965	206	504
Share earnings (dollars):	3.14	3.53	.54	5.77

What it does: Still the nation's largest steel maker, the company now has extensive holdings in energy, oil, chemicals, real estate, and transportation. Steel now provides less than one third of its revenues and energy provides over half.

After it lost $1.5 billion in 1982 and 1983, some analysts said 1986 was supposed to be the year when things finally got better at USX Corporation, once known as U.S. Steel Corporation. The company had earned a $598 million profit in 1985 and analysts said the steel industry was out of the intensive care ward. Instead, the country's largest steel maker was hit with new problems. A $3 billion deal for Texas Oil was completed in February of 1986, just as oil prices took a plunge. A July reorganization of the company dropped *Steel* from the company's name. In August, the United Steelworkers of America went on strike. In the fall, with no settlement in sight, corporate raider and Australian financier Robert Holmes à Court and later Carl Icahn bought up large chunks of the company's stock. Icahn made an $8 billion bid to take control of the company in October, but his bid failed. By the end of 1986, thanks to non-recurring charges, losses totaled a whopping $1.833 billion on revenues of only $14.9 billion—down 29% in only a year. In 1987, revenues declined to $14.8 billion, but the company managed to eke out a $206 million profit.

The problems facing USX today were unthinkable in the 1960s. The company was set up by J. P. Morgan in 1901 but traces its lineage back to steel and coke operations created after the Civil War by Andrew Carnegie. This frugal Scotsman trounced his competitors with a simple strategy of massive capital spending to improve productivity, a tough stance at the bargaining table that produced some of the bloodiest strikes in the nation's history, and a penchant for expanding production during depressions, thus lowering prices and forcing competitors out of business. Carnegie finally sold his steel company for nearly $500 million to J. P. Morgan in 1901. Morgan added several other companies and created U.S. Steel, a company that controlled 65% of the steel market in 1902.

Although the company's share of the market had dropped to 40% by 1930, U.S. Steel remained a powerhouse until the late 1970s. By then, the company had forgotten Carnegie's tradition of spending money to improve plant productivity; the newest plant was built in 1953. Absurd as it seems, many of its other mills dated back to the 19th century. No wonder the company was hard hit by the drastic downturn in the steel industry and increased foreign competition.

Chairman David M. Roderick has spent most of the 1980s pushing the company through a painful period of retrenchment. Roderick closed more than 150 plants and facilities, cut steel-making capacity by 24%, sold $3 billion in assets, and laid off more than 50,000 employees, two thirds of the company's white- and blue-collar workers. Even so, steel operations took a $978 million loss between 1980 and 1985.

At the same time, the company has moved in new directions, struggling to find new products and industries that can help it survive into the 21st century as one of the nation's largest corporations. The company shelled out $5.9 billion in 1982 for Marathon Oil Company and $3 billion for Texas Oil and Gas Corporation in 1986. Its aptly named U.S. Diversified Group unit, which was up for sale in early 1988, is involved in such businesses as real estate and transportation. As early as 1985, steel provided only about one third of the company's revenues, down from 73% in 1976. USX had only 11.2% of the market in the second quarter of 1987, a shadow of its glory days, when it held well over half of the market.

With its energy businesses accounting a large share of revenues, it was hardly any surprise when the company changed its name in 1986 to USX Corporation, replacing the word *Steel* in its name with an *X*. The insider-trading scandal on Wall Street may have saved USX from Carl Icahn and the raiders. With all the problems facing the company, management may wish it was so lucky. But in 1987, there were hints that the company was finally making its long-awaited revival. For the year, USX earned a $206 million profit, and despite losses in the fourth quarter, its profits per ton of steel doubled from $18 in the third quarter to $36 in the fourth. Quotas on foreign steel, a weaker dollar, and increased spending for capital goods also allowed the company to increase prices and profits. Rising energy prices are expected to help the bottom line as well. By 1990, the company had profits of $818 million on revenues of $19.4 billion.

Table S-2   Big Steel

Rank	Company	1990 Corporate sales (thousands of dollars)	1990 Net income (thousands of dollars)
1.	USX	19,462,000	818,000
2.	LTV	6,138,000	70,900
3.	Bethlehem Steel Corporation	4,929,000	—
4.	Inland Steel Industries, Inc.	3,870,000	—
5.	National Steel Corp.	2,507,000	—
6.	Armco, Inc.	1,788,000	—

Source: Annual Reports.

TECHNOLOGY

BIOTECHNOLOGY

Biotechnology offers the possibility of altering and manipulating the building blocks of life through molecular and cellular manipulation, enzyme technology, microbial technology, genetic engineering, and bioprocess engineering. Potential applications range from pesticides and more productive plants and animals in agriculture to new drugs in the health field, biodegradable plastics in the chemical industry, metal-leaching organisms that would aid in the metal recovery industry, biosensors in the factory, and vitamin supplements in the food industry, just to name a few. No doubt biotechnology will eventually touch off a revolution in the farm, factory, and health-care fields, just as the development of the chemical industry did in the earlier decades of the 20th century.

Some 500 firms are now involved in the field, providing goods and services, including more than 200 large firms that have expanded into the field with in-house operations or through joint ventures. So far these firms derive a significant share of their revenues from research and development contracts. The U.S. Department of Commerce believes that shipments of products based on technologies using monoclonal antibodies or recombinant DNA hit $1.3 billion in 1989, way up from $60 million in 1984. AIDS testing using monoclonal antibodies produced $75 million to $100 million in revenues in 1987. Another $4.5 billion has been invested in this field.

Market value of biotechnology rose to about $1.5 billion by 1990, according to U.S. Commerce Department analysts. Yet, as with most emerging technologies, many new companies may not survive the transition from research to the actual development and marketing of products. And many research investments may not pay off in the near future. As a result, investments in this industry remain risky, holding a potential for high returns and big losses.

INFORMATION

The Market

Imagine pressing a button and having instant access to some of the nation's largest libraries. Press another button and you have news that hasn't even hit the newsstand. If the idea interests you then you'll probably understand all the hype about computer databases and the videotext industry. In recent years, database companies promised companies and consumers that they could obtain information easily and quickly through their computers, accessing breaking news on mergers as well as databases on industry performances and old newspaper articles on Hollywood stars. In 1990, there were several million suscribers to databases.

The Money

Revenues for electronic information services were expected to reach some $10.8 billion in 1991, a 20% increase over 1990's $9 billion. Financial information companies, such as consumer and credit reporting services and money market reporters, accounted for the biggest chunk of the industry. Next came major airlines' transport information services. About 80% of the revenues come from on-line services, those delivered over telephones and broadcast systems to subscribers, personal computers or terminals. The U.S. produces 56% of the world's 4,000 databases.

The Players

In terms of the number of subscribers to an electronic information service, Prodigy Services has 900,000 and CompuServe has 795,000. Both are systems operators. They are service bureaus connecting users to data sources.

Four major companies today dominate the electronic financial information service industry. They are: Dow Jones, whose News Retrieval has some 335,000 subscribers and revenues of $125.3 million and whose Teletrate stock quotes have 85,000 subscribers and $481.7 million in revenues; Reuters (U.S.), with 203,000 subscribers and $1.2 billion in revenues; Quotron, with 85,000 subscribers and $282 million in revenues, and ADP, with 70,000 subscribers and $166.4 million in revenues.

Table T-1   Top 10 American and European Electronic Information Companies
(worldwide revenues, 1989)

Rank	Company	Millions of dollars
1.	Dun and Bradstreet	1,670
2.	Reuters Holdings TPLC	1,590
3.	American Airlines SABRE	864
4.	Dow Jones Inc.	755
5.	Covia's Apollo	693
6.	Automatic Data Processing Inc.	615
7.	Worldspan (Delta Airlines, Northwest Airlines, and TWA)	584
8.	System One (Continental, General Motors Electronic Data Systems)	461
9.	Mead Corp. (Mead Data Central)	391
10.	TRW	345

Source: Link Resources Corp.

Trends and Forecast

No doubt the computer database and electronic information industry will one day take its place with book publishing as a major industry. Already computerized information services have been a boon to Wall Street and companies that need ready information on the market, credit ratings, etc. Database companies positioned to capitalize on that part of the industry will continue to do well: business subscribers to videotext services have been growing at a rate of 50% per year.

But all the hype about future sales and a new age of information has not impressed the general public. Many full-text databases for newspapers charge well over $100 an hour for time spent on-line. Since most databases have only a limited history, tracking information back only to 1980 or 1979, many researchers find that a computer has not replaced a good librarian. Similarly, the average consumer has found little reason to pay $100 an hour or more to access newspaper articles.

Such problems have also hurt companies in the field. New companies face the startup costs of putting large amounts of information on-line. Some media companies such as CBS and The New York Times Company entered the field but found it was difficult to recoup their huge investments. When profits did not live up to their expectations, they dropped out. The remaining companies have settled into profitable niches, with the largest ones catering to businesses and brokerage houses that need instant information and are willing to pay heavily for it.

LASERS

The Market

Once considered a high-tech curiosity, the stuff of a Buck Rogers serial rather than a business with practical applications, lasers are transforming dozens of industries. Current applications of lasers range from shooting down missiles to scanning prices in supermarkets, from the shaping of corneas to repairing detached retinas. Lasers can be used on credit cards to produce holograms that may dramatically cut credit-card fraud, in laser light shows, in laser printing and desktop publishing, in missile guidance, in neurosurgery to remove brain tumors, in satellite communications, in satellite tracking, in sighting military targets, in the treatment of skin ailments, and in videodisc and compact audio disc players.

The Money

Only three decades after the first laser was developed in 1960, scores of practical applications for laser technology added up to about a $828 million worldwide commercial market for lasers in 1991, up from $474 million in 1985. In 1991, the most popular industrial use of lasers was to process materials ($207 million), followed by research and development ($176 million), medicine ($124 million), and optical data storage (107 million), according to *Lasers and Optromics* magazine.

The Players

Some 100 companies make lasers but only a handful of these companies earn more than $10 million a year. The largest is Spectra-Physics, Inc.

Trends and Forecast

With some of the industry's sales and technological development tied to military spending, the future of Star Wars and the U.S. defense buildup will play an important role in the industry's future. Another major uncertainty is how well companies manage to find practical applications for technological breakthroughs. Sales grew only 6% in 1986 after growing 20% to 30% a year between 1980 and 1985. The Commerce Department sees the market growing at 8% annually through 1995.

ROBOTS AND OFFICE AUTOMATION

The Market

Faced with tough competition, American manufacturing and service companies are rushing to automate their workplaces. By adding robots in factories and high-tech phone systems, professional workstations, microcomputers, and word processors to the office, managers hope to cut costs and dramatically improve productivity, allowing them to compete with cheaper offshore labor.

The Money

The office automation market (which includes such products as word processors, office telephone equipment, key systems, dictation equipment, electronic typewriters, computers, copiers, and calculators for the office) hit $17.9 billion in 1984 and increased to about $500 billion in 1991. In industry, the U.S. automation market (which includes robotics and computer-based and programmable controllers of industrial equipment) is now worth about $30 billion by some estimates. (Not included in those figures is the tiny but growing market for home robots, which may be cute but, as yet, can't replace a maid. Some 10,000 to 12,000 of these robots were sold for $20 million in 1984. Manufacturers of home robots predict this industry will hit $1 billion to $2 billion in sales by the end of this decade.)

The largest portion of the industrial automation market is the $7 billion industry of producing control and processing equipment. Much smaller is the robotics industry. Robots worth $392 million were shipped in 1989 by American producers; foreign producers sold another $400 million worth in 1989 to American business. But sales dropped in 1986, with U.S. suppliers selling only 5,713 units worth $363.8, and industry projections indicate that sales may have fallen another 30% in 1987. Currently, there are 16,000 robots in American factories, about one third as many robots as in Japanese factories. The Robotic Industries Association estimates that nearly a quarter of a million industrial robots will be in use in the U.S. by 1995. Another important area of growth is the computer-aided design, manufacture, and engineering (CAD/CAM, CAE) industry, which hit $4 billion in 1986, up from $765 million in 1981. CAD/CAM involves technology that uses computers to design and manufacture products; CAE involves tools that design and simulate the performance of integrated circuits and systems.

Trends and Forecast

Most analysts and U.S. government statisticians see a bright future for the office and industrial automation industry, as illustrated by some of the projections cited above. But, as with all high-tech industries, a bit of skepticism is in order. The history of technology is filled with optimistic projections followed by disappointing results. Despite the need to automate the workplace, actual sales remain heavily dependent on the ability of American companies to finance new equipment. For example, faced with sluggish auto sales, General Motors decided in 1986 to cancel $80 million worth of contracts for robots, forcing GMF Robotics Corporation (owned equally by General Motors and Japan's Fanuc Ltd.) to lay off 200 employees (about 28% of its work force) and delay plans for an automated factory where robots would produce robots. As a result, sales plummeted in 1986 and 1987, illustrating how rosy predictions are heavily dependent upon the state of the economy and American industry. During 1989, the industry added about $100 million to its backlog in spite of a substantial increase in shipments. Shipments rose about 10% in 1990 and were expected to grow 6% in 1991.

TELECOMMUNICATIONS

THE MARKET

Judging by the numbers, a lot of people never get off the phone. There are about 250 million phones in the U.S. and about 100 million individual customers who use over 139 million access lines. Some 93.3% of all homes have a telephone, with each customer paying an average of $727 per year for each access line. For their money, Americans make about 48.5 billion long-distance calls a year. Businesses make about 20% of all long-distance calls within the U.S. and about 63% of all calls are made during regular business hours. To provide those services, phone companies have $207.3 billion worth of equipment and spend $20 billion a year on new construction and equipment, creating a large market for telecommunications equipment. Phone companies have invested about $252 billion worth of plant and equipment.

THE PLAYERS

There are 1,354 telephone companies in the U.S. but only a few dominate the market. Sixteen of the 24 former Bell System companies made into independent companies by the AT&T divestiture rank among the 20 biggest phone companies, according to the United States Telephone Association. The market dominance can also be found in the long-distance market, where, despite tough competition from U.S. Sprint and MCI, AT&T has kept about four fifths of the market. Only two other companies, MCI and U.S. Sprint, have more than 1% of the long-distance market.

TRENDS AND FORECAST

Like several other industries—most notably power utilities and railroads—phone companies traditionally operated in markets characterized by very little competition and a great deal of government regulation. The theory behind this state of affairs was simple: Phone companies were considered a kind of natural monopoly that should be regulated rather than dismantled. Since the cost of setting up a phone company was so high and the benefits of having two competing phone companies so small, government trustbusters made little effort to dismantle the powerful Bell System. Instead, large phone companies were heavily regulated.

The result was AT&T, not only the largest company in the world but one of the best phone systems in the world. But in the 1960s and 1970s technological and political changes touched off a sweeping restructuring of the phone industry. New technology made it economically feasible for companies to set up their own telecommunications systems outside AT&T, making the idea of a "natural monopoly" in the telecommunications industry less attractive. Prodded by court rulings, a sluggish FCC began allowing private long-distance systems in the late 1960s.

At that time, AT&T was coming under increasing attack from antitrust lawyers at the Justice Department. In 1956, AT&T settled a 1949 Justice Department antitrust suit by agreeing to limit its business to common-carrier communications services and to government contracts. The company also agreed to manufacture only those products needed by the Bell System and to make its rich store of patents available to anyone without charge.

But the 1956 settlement didn't end AT&T's antitrust problems. In 1974, the Justice Department filed a new antitrust suit charging AT&T, Western Electric, and Bell Laboratories with a conspiracy to monopolize the industry. The suit languished during the mid-1970s, but in 1982 the Justice Department and AT&T announced a new consent decree. Under its terms AT&T divested itself in 1984 of 22 local operating companies. These companies are broken into seven holding companies, the so-called Baby Bells. AT&T was also released from the 1956 decree that restricted the businesses it could enter.

For several years after the AT&T breakup, the Baby Bells thrived while their former parent company struggled. The Baby Bells jacked up local rates an average of 40% a year and used their cash to enter new businesses. Southwestern Bell, for example, spent $1.2 billion to buy Metromedia's cellular telephone operations, and others have even expanded overseas.

But the Baby Bells suffered a setback in their fight for further deregulation when the courts held in September 1987 that they could not move into long distance or phone manufacturing. Then in December the FCC ordered the Baby Bells to cut $1 billion off the access fees they charge to let long distance companies complete their calls to local customers. Long distance companies such as AT&T pay half their $50 billion in revenues to the Baby Bells in access charges, but the Baby Bells had wanted to cut access charges by only $210 million.

As a result, the Baby Bells face a tougher financial climate. State regulators are less likely to let them jack up local phone rates while the courts and congress are unlikely to let them enter a number of new businesses. Nonetheless, the lobbying fight goes on, as Baby Bells argue they should be given more freedom to set up data bases over phone lines and even enter the cable TV industry.

The FCC issued a number of decisions that dramatically changed the nature of the industry. Between 1968 and 1982, the FCC helped break the phone monopoly by allowing other companies to sell devices that connect with AT&T networks and by permitting consumers to buy their own telephones. In 1980 it increased competition by allowing independent companies to resell AT&T services, and in 1982 it allowed smaller, nonmonopoly companies to change services or rates without regulatory approval. It has reduced the regulatory burden of entering new markets, such as cellular mobile phones, by holding lotteries instead of lengthy hearings. By shifting costs from long distance to local usage, the commission moved toward market pricing of long-distance services, which had traditionally been set higher than necessary in order to subsidize local service. (That subsidy amounted to about $11 billion in higher long-distance rates a year, or about 40% of long-distance revenues, before divestiture.)

But not all of those decisions increased competition. Many new companies entered the industry when FCC mandated discounts on local network connection fees, allowing companies to buy access from local companies at lower prices than AT&T and retail it at a profit. But these discounts are ending, putting some companies out of business and limiting the price edge of surviving companies, such as MCI. Both U.S. Sprint and MCI posted large losses in the final quarters of 1986, and some analysts look for an industry shakeout. According to this line of thinking, a few large companies will survive—such as MCI with its backing from IBM—while smaller companies will be forced to consolidate or find a profitable niche.

Yet despite an industry-wide restructuring that is expected to cut jobs and force many smaller long-distance companies out of business, the outlook is generally bright for industry revenues. U.S. Commerce Department analysts expect revenues of the telephone and telegraph service industries to grow at an annual rate of 3 to 5% through 1992.

American Telephone and Telegraph Company

CEO: Robert E. Allen
Employees: 278,600
Assets: 43,775

550 Madison Avenue
New York, New York 10022
212-605-5500

	1990	1989	1987	1985
Revenues (millions of dollars):	37,285	36,112	33,598	34,417
Net income (millions of dollars):	2,735	2,697	2,044	1,557
Share earnings (dollars):	2.51	2.50	1.88	1.37

What it does: It provides long-distance services and sells and manufactures telecommunications equipment.

In the decades after Alexander Graham Bell patented the phone in 1876, his company wrote the book on how to be a successful monopoly.

Graham took little interest in managing the Bell Telephone Company and the bankers who financed the company soon took control. One of their first problems was fighting off the hundreds of legal challenges to Bell's patents. Western Union, for example, had bought rights to another phone created by Elisha Gray (Gray had the misfortune of filing his patent for a phone only two hours after Bell did) and hired Thomas Edison to build a better phone system. But it agreed to stay out of the phone business in exchange for 20% of Bell's phone rental receipts.

Winning those legal battles gave the company time to grow larger and stronger under the protection of Bell's patents. By the time the company's patents expired in 1893, the company was large enough to quash the independent phone companies by cutting rates and refusing to connect them to the Bell System. In 1899 the company was reorganized as American Telephone and Telegraph, with AT&T running the long-distance business and acting as a holding company for local phone companies. The company merged with Western Union in 1910 but, under growing attack for its power, AT&T was forced to get out of the telegraph business and submit to increased government regulation.

The company's economic clout was also aided by its leadership in technology. AT&T bought up a large interest in Western Electric in 1881, and in the 20th century Western Electric and Bell labs were to develop such products as television transmission, the silicon solar cell, the transistor lasers, and satellite communications. That technological innovation made the company a power in the defense and space industry, supplying equipment for the Pentagon and NASA.

By 1979 the company had $113 billion in assets, was the nation's largest employer with over a million workers, and churned out some $45.3 billion in sales. Its monopoly on phone service had grown from 50% in 1910 to 80%. But in the early 1980s it was becoming apparent that the days of the world's largest monopoly were numbered. Support for various proposals to deregulate the phone industry was growing in Congress. The company was in court with the Justice Department and William McGowan's MCI over antitrust violations.

Finally, in 1982, as a 1974 Justice Department antitrust suit was finally moving toward trial, AT&T cut a deal that allowed it to retain the competitive business of long-distance service and equipment manufacturing while spinning off its 22 operating phone companies that are now grouped into seven regional holding companies of about equal size.

Analysts claimed that the company—with its reputation as a lumbering, slow-footed giant—would lose sales in the telecommunications equipment market and as much as 40% of its long-distance service by 1990 to upstarts like MCI. The bright spot was that AT&T could enter the growing computer and office automation field, expand international sales, and enlarge its base in the telecommunications equipment field, while shedding local phone service (some three quarters of its assets), which might be less profitable in a deregulated environment.

Things didn't work out that way. With an advertising budget 8 to 10 times larger than rivals such as Sprint and MCI, AT&T held onto most of the long-distance market it was supposed to lose.

By 1989, AT&T still held about 75% of the market. But its share of interstate switched minutes fell to about 67% in 1989, from more than 80% in 1984.

And competing in a deregulated environment has not been easy. The company has ordered massive layoffs of employees, who had once considered their jobs lifetime sinecures. Deregulation of the phone industry has also given foreign companies, especially Japanese companies, a growing share of the U.S. market. Local phone companies, which were once required to do business with AT&T, can now shop for the best price.

By 1987, there were promising signs that Chairman James E. Olson's management had led the company through the trauma of divestitures. Losses were slashed in the computer operations by 70%, $1 billion was cut out of back-office expenses and the company held its status as the world's largest supplier of telecommunications equipment, with 30% of the world market. The results boosted earnings to over $2 billion.

MCI Communications MCI started in 1968 with just three employees, at a time when AT&T served the telecommunications needs of most of the country. But by breaking Ma Bell's monopoly on long-distance service in a landmark antitrust case, William G. McGowan, chairman and chief executive officer of MCI Communications Corporation, forever changed the industry. He won a $17 billion settlement with AT&T (later reduced to a paltry $133 million) and helped create political support for a plan to deregulate the telecommunications industry.

That victory translated into tremendous growth for his fledgling empire. MCI also entered into a partnership with IBM (which gave Big Blue 16% of MCI stock) that could give it $400 million in reserves to draw upon. But for McGowan and his new backer IBM the tough part may very well be competing and surviving in a deregulated marketplace. AT&T is 12 times larger and has been able to outspend MCI eight to one in long-distance advertising. Through rate cuts AT&T countered MCI's price advantage and confounded early predictions that AT&T would lose much of the long-distance market. Going head to head with a colossus like Ma Bell has also forced MCI to cut costs, sell its paging and cellular phone unit, and cut back on marketing its electronic mail system. Losses totaled $431.5 million in 1986 on revenues of $3,592 million. MCI's charismatic chairman gave up control of day-to-day operations following a heart transplant, but has since returned to direct long-term strategy.

ITT Corporation

CEO: Rand V. Araskog
Employees: 116,500
Assets: 49,043

320 Park Avenue
New York, New York 10022
212-752-6000

	1990	1989	1986	1985
Revenues (millions of dollars):	20,604	20,054	17,437	14,663
Net income (millions of dollars):	958	922	540	294
Share earnings (dollars):	7.28	6.52	3.23	1.89

What it does: The diversified conglomerate has automotive, electrical, hotel, and insurance components. In December 1986, the company combined its telecommunications operations with those of Compagnie Générale d'Electricité, forming a joint venture, Alcatel N.V., based in the Netherlands. ITT holds 37%.

ITT was founded in 1920 by sugar broker Sosthenes Behn and took off in 1925 when an antitrust suit forced AT&T to sell off its overseas manufacturing operations. After buying that business, the company succeeded in becoming for the whole world what AT&T was to the U.S. ITT controlled major phone systems in Europe and Latin America and produced much of the phone equipment used around the world.

But in the 1960s, fearing takeovers and regulation by foreign governments, ITT under Harold Geneen expanded out of its core telecommunications business. Geneen wanted to make the company a diversified conglomerate and, by the late 1970s, it was the largest baking company in the U.S., the second-largest hotel chain, a book publisher, and an insurance company, as well as a power in the telecommunications industry overseas.

The company had also added to its reputation for intrigue, which started when ITT had helped rearm Nazi Germany. More recently, ITT channeled secret funds to overthrow Chile's President Allende, who had pledged to nationalize the company's phone operation in the 1970s, and made illegal contributions to President Nixon.

But Geneen's conglomerate was never very profitable. What was lacking was a way of melding all the different businesses into a profitable company. Profits were a paltry $382 million on sales of $22 billion in 1979.

So, under CEO Rand V. Araskog, the company began a campaign to trim down and shape up its balance sheet. Araskog sold off $4 billion worth of companies like C&C Cola and Continental Baking. But ITT was still in such different businesses as financial services, defense electronics, semiconductors, insurance, automotive supplies, pump making, and telecommunications. Sales in 1985 dropped to $20 billion but profits were only $294 million.

The company also stumbled badly in its attempt to revitalize its core telecommunications operation. Araskog had dreamed of making the company a technological powerhouse, but ITT had ignored the U.S. telecommunications and information market for too long. Its personal computer never made a dent in the U.S. market, and after spending $1 billion to develop its System 12 switching technology, problems forced the company to give up trying to adapt it to the American market. Realizing the company couldn't capitalize on the promise of a growing telecommunications market, ITT decided to sell a major stake in its European telecommunications and equipment operation to Compagnie Générale d'Electricité of France, ending its reign as Europe's largest supplier of equipment. In 1989, the company's long-distance telephone business was sold.

Today, ITT's largest business is insurance. ITT Financial Corporation produces only 7% of sales but 30% of earnings. The company may find its future as a financial powerhouse.

Table T-2 Top 20 Telephone Companies

Rank	in Order of Access Lines as of December 31, 1989	Access Lines	Operating Revenues
1.	Bell Atlantic Corp.* Philadelphia, Pennsylvania	17,056,802	10,226,894,000
2.	BellSouth Corp.* Atlanta, Georgia	16,720,367	11,995,872,345
3.	Ameritech Corp.* Chicago, Illinois	15,899,000	9,353,339,000
4.	NYNEX* New York, New York	14,960,953	11,086,660,000
5.	Pacific Telesis Group* San Francisco, California	14,202,949	7,998,678,086
6.	US West Communications* Englewood, Colorado	12,306,536	8,128,848,000
7.	GTE Corp. (US Only)* Irving, Texas	12,300,000	9,558,000,000
8.	Southwestern Bell Corp.* St. Louis, Missouri	11,444,061	7,408,690,000
9.	United Telecommunications, Inc.* Overland Park, Kansas	3,811,980	2,365,400,000
10.	Contel Service Corp.* Atlanta, Georgia	2,591,090	2,120,605,610
11.	Southern New England Telephone Co.* New Haven, Connecticut	1,875,000	1,419,414,000
12.	Centel Corp.* Chicago, Illinois	1,590,716	886,051,000
13.	ALLTEL Corp.* Hudson, Ohio	1,123,590	801,575,000
14.	Puerto Rico Telephone Co. San Juan, Puerto Rico	803,713	591,586,958
15.	Cincinnati Bell Telephone Co.* Cincinnati, Ohio	781,064	489,119,931
16.	Rochester Telephone Corp.* Rochester, New York	610,338	359,880,000
17.	Century Telephone Enterprises, Inc.* Monroe, Louisiana	296,034	190,538,000
18.	Telephone & Data Systems, Inc. Chicago, Illinois	263,914	168,046,000
19.	Pacific Telecom, Inc. Vancouver, Washington	252,732	211,967,000
20.	Lincoln Telephone & Telegraph Co. Lincoln, Nebraska	219,417	128,220,545

*Formerly part of AT&T.
Source: *Phone Facts 1990,* United States Telephone Association.

Table T-3   Average Daily Calls and Toll Messages
(Bells and independents)

Local calls	1,161,352,890
Toll messages	102,183,979
Local calls per average access line	9.89
Toll messages per average access line	0.871

Source: *Telephone Statistics:* United States Telephone Association.

TELEVISION AND CABLE

THE MARKET

There are now 92.1 million households with television sets and 53.7 million homes with cable. The average American home has a television set on 6 hours and 55 minutes a day, a decline from 1986, when the set was on 7 hours and ten minutes a day.

THE MONEY

Television advertising hit $28.3 billion in 1990 and is expected to rise to $34.1 billion in 1992. In 1989, network advertising, which has been hurt by slumping audience shares, dropped 0.7% to $9.1 billion and is expected to remain soft in the early 1990s. National spot advertising, which increased 2.9% to $7.4 billion, and local spot, which grew 4.7% to $7.6 billion, have also been weak, barely keeping up with inflation. But barter syndication advertising jumped a hefty 42% to $1.3 billion, national cable increased 27% to $1.2 billion, and local cable increased 30% to $330 million.

Cable operators, who get their money from both advertising and subscription fees, racked up $21.4 billion in revenues in 1989, up from $16.1 in 1987.

All the new competition has been good for one part of the industry—television production. Veronis Suhler & Associates estimate that television producers and distributors had $7.9 billion in revenues in 1989, up from 5.0 billion in 1984. They expect the television production industry to grow to $10.4 billion in 1991 and $11.7 billion in 1994, an annual growth rate of 15.1%.

TRENDS AND FORECAST

The 1980s saw major changes in the television business. An advertising slump cut network revenues already hurt by increased competition from cable, independent television, and the threat of a fourth network. The government did not stop outside buyers from taking over networks, allowing Laurence Tisch to take over CBS, Capital Cities to take over ABC, and General Electric to take over NBC's parent, RCA. By the end of the decade, 11 of the 20 top broadcasting companies merged or were acquired by a new owner, and over $35 billion worth of radio and television stations had been sold.

Most of the turmoil in the television industry can be traced to the fact that this is a mature industry undergoing a technological revolution. While the number of potential viewers is growing very slowly, more companies are fighting for a share of the pie. Back in the 1970s, the 3 major networks had over 91% of the viewing audience, but by 1990, their share had shrunk to under two thirds. Besides CBS, NBC, and ABC, viewers and advertisers can choose between Rupert Murdoch's fourth network (Fox Broadcasting), first-run syndication (television producers who sell shows like "Wheel of Fortune" directly to local stations), superstations (such as Turner Broadcasting System), independent television stations (local stations that are not affiliated with one of the 3 major networks), barter syndicators (to lower the cost of buying a program, a local station will give the television producer air time that can be sold to advertisers), local cable systems (which have set up large regional networks to sell advertising time on their systems), dozens of cable-channel networks (CNN, the Discovery Channel, Black Entertainment Network, etc., which offer advertisers a great way to reach a niche audience), regional sports networks (a cheaper way to sell products during sporting events), or even taped movies for VCRs (advertisers bet the viewers won't fast forward through the sales pitch at the start of the tape).

These changes in the business of television are altering the kinds of programming viewers can expect to see, the ways advertisers hawk their product, and the ways television producers fund their programing in the 1990s.

On the programming side, cable television has opened up an opportunity for more niche programing. There are now cable channels designed to attract young kids (Nickelodeon), women (Lifetime), sports fanatics (ESPN and many new regional sports networks), and comedy buffs (HA! and The Comedy Channel). At the same time, the networks have had to move away from the traditional high-budget, mass-market fare that dominated the airwaves of the 1970s. Smaller audiences mean that a trendy show like "thirtysomething" can survive with ratings that would have gotten it axed in the early 1980s, if it attracts the right kind of viewers (particularly younger affluent women). Programmers are also airing shows like "Twin Peaks" which would have never even been commissioned as pilots ten years ago, hoping that they will lure young affluent cable viewers back to network television. Both "Twin Peaks" and "thirtysomething" were axed in 1991, but the strategy of taking big risks with programing has worked quite well at Fox, where shows like "The Simpsons," the first animated show on prime time since the 1960s, were big hits.

Changing economics also made comedy king during the 1980s and early 1990s, when sit-coms dominated the network schedules. Media critics like to point out that audiences always turn on the laughs when faced with adversity, hence the popularity of lavish musical comedies during the 1930s and sit-coms during the 1980s that had little to do with the real-life dramas of trade deficits, factory layoffs, and stagnant incomes.

Maybe so. But during a decade when networks were cutting programing costs, comedy had economic advantages as well. Today, the 3 major networks pay a television producer only part of the cost of producing the show. The producer can make his money back only by selling the reruns and by reducing the cost of the show. Comedies let producers reduce production costs because such programs are cheaper to make than hour-long action shows. Even better, comedies are easier to sell to local stations, which have also realized that there is money to be made in laughs. The young kids and families who tend to watch television between 6 and 8 P.M. are unlikely to watch an hour-long police drama but will tune in to a show like "Cheers" or "The Cosby Show." The producer and distributor, who could make as much as $500 million selling reruns of a show like "Cosby," can laugh all the way to the bank with a hit comedy.

Foreign markets have also become increasingly important, financing the cost of many high-budget action series and miniseries. Producers of many programs are signing co-production deals with the BBC or even Japanese television networks. Such a deal gives the foreign stations a high-budget American television program for very little money, while the producer can cover some of his or her costs and reduce the risks. Even the network news divisions, which have been under fire from network bean counters, have been looking overseas for dollars. They hoped to increase their revenues by selling their news to cable and foreign networks while cutting costs by using more satellite material from foreign stations.

Media fragmentation has also changed the ways advertisers use television. Cable and local television stations have become increasingly attractive buys for advertisers looking to reach smaller targeted audiences, a fact that explains the rapid growth of cable advertising and the more modest but still healthy increases in local spot advertising. But these changes have also created headaches for mass marketers trying to sell Big Macs and soap to tens of millions of people. Faced with slumping audiences, the networks no longer want to guarantee advertisers that a show will receive a specified rating, and want to end the traditional practice of giving advertisers free airtime when a show is less popular than expected. Naturally, the advertisers are fighting this idea.

The networks are also trying to move into other media. ABC already owns several cable channels, including ESPN, and NBC jointly owns several cable channels, including CNBC, with Cablevision. All three networks hope the FCC will end rules limiting their right to own and produce television programing. If FCC rules preventing the networks from producing prime-time network programing are ended, expect the networks to buy Hollywood studios.

In 1991, an economic slowdown is expected to hurt advertising growth for the whole television industry, and over the next few years, the outlook for the networks isn't much brighter. They will probably continue to lose audiences and face stagnant advertising revenues. Cable will continue to see large increases in advertising revenues, but could face a profit crunch if Congress reregulates the industry, as many expect it will.

Table T-4   Television Advertising Trends and Projections

(in millions of dollars)

		1981	1982	1983	1984	1985	1986	1987	1988	1989	1990
Total	Television	12,650	14,329	16,786	19,670	20,772	22,881	23,904	25,686	26,561	28,330
	Cable	N.A.	N.A.	350	572	769	855	963	1,196	1,197	1,375
	Network	5,575	6,210	7,017	8,526	8,285	8,342	8,500	9,172	9,110	9,565
	Spot	3,730	4,360	4,796	5,488	6,004	6,570	6,846	7,147	7,354	7,905
	Local	3,345	3,759	4,323	5,084	5,714	6,514	6,833	7,270	7,612	7,875
	Nat'l syndication	N.A.	N.A.	N.A.	N.A.	N.A.	600	762	901	1,288	1,610

Source: McCann Erickson.

Table T-5   The Cable Industry at a Glance
(System operators, in millions of dollars)

Item	E1989	E1990	E1991	E1992
[1] Basic cable subscriptions	51.5	53.7	56.1	58.6
[1] Pay cable subscriptions	43.8	45.6	46.0	48.0
Basic cable revenues	9,300	10,575	11,530	12,730
Pay cable revenues	4,751	4,828	5,080	5,240
[2] Other revenues	4,830	5,990	6,650	7,300
Total cable revenues	18,881	21,393	23,260	25,270
Net income	2,344	2,680		
[3] Operating cash flow	7,890	9,410		
Average monthly basic rate ($)	$15.50	$16.75	$17.50	$18.50
Average monthly pay rate ($)	$9.25	$9.00	$9.25	$9.50

[1]At year end.
[2]Includes advertising, installation, converter rentals, pay-per-view, expanded basis service, and other revenues.
[3]Includes operating income before depreciation and amortization, interest or taxes.
E—Estimated.
Source: Cable Advertising Bureau; *CableVision* magazine; estimates by Standard & Poor's.

NBC   When Robert C. Wright took over NBC, late-night talk-show host David Letterman joked that the former head of GE's plastics division and small appliance operations would push for a miniseries about the development of the toaster oven.

The joke says a lot about what's happening at the networks. Since GE took over RCA, and with it NBC, Wright is the first manager from the appliance and financial services company to take over NBC. Wright did head a cable company for several years but, unlike his predecessor Grant Tinker, Wright has little in his background to prepare him for the difficulties of running a major network. How Wright handles the company will be a test case of network management in an age when all three networks have fallen under the control of outside corporations.

Already, Wright's hands-on style indicates that he is using traditional management techniques to improve company profits. Even though NBC was on top of ratings, Wright started his tenure in 1986 by cutting 150 jobs and circulating memos asking department heads to cut 5% of their budgets. Then he had the temerity to suggest that all employees contribute to a political action committee, angering the news division and producing a flap that was played out on the front pages of *The New York Times*.

So far, however, Wright has gotten high marks from analysts for pursuing an innovative vision of the industry's future. He has put together a couple of innovative cable deals, including a joint venture with Cablevision that give NBC half ownership of several cable channels. NBC hopes that it can lay part of its costs off onto the cable operations and profit in the longterm from the faster-growing cable industry. NBC has also become a leader in expanding its international operations by buying foreign production companies and a stake in a New Zealand television station. But Wright's attempt to make NBC News profitable produced only several highly publicized flaps over its poor coverage of breaking news. Even worse, many of NBC's old hits are showing signs of wear. By the fall of 1991, NBC's audience had fallen and it was locked in a tight ratings battle with CBS and ABC.

TOBACCO

THE MARKET

Increased concerns about health, rising prices, and fewer younger smokers have caused consumption of tobacco products to fall dramatically in the last decade. The percentage of adults who smoke has dropped from 55% to below 30%. The number of cigarettes smoked per capita dropped to below 3,200 in 1990, down from 4,092 in 1976, while per-capita cigar consumption fell from 75 in 1976 to 42 in 1984 and per-capita consumption of smoking tobacco dropped from .75 pounds to only .36 pounds. Analysts expect consumption to drop as much as 5% a year for the next five years. Remaining smokers are also expressing a growing fondness for stronger cigarettes. Brands with over 15 milligrams of tar or more capture 48% of the market, up from 40% in 1980. Americans smoked about 563 billion cigarettes in 1988. That same year, cigar consumption fell under 3 billion for the first time in recent history, only one third of the peak reached in 1964. Americans in 1987 smoked 22.6 million pounds of smoking tobacco, only one third of the 1970 peak. About 70% of all smoking tobacco was used by pipe smokers; the other 30% was used by people who roll their own cigarettes.

THE MONEY

The tobacco industry shipped about $20.4 billion worth of cigarettes in 1989, up from $14.3 billion in 1984 and $4.2 billion in 1972. Most of those revenues came from cigarettes, which accounted for $16.6 billion. Cigar makers continued their decline, getting only $184 million, while makers of chewing and smoking tobacco sold $1.1 billion worth of products, up from $875 million in 1984.

THE PLAYERS

Many small farmers depend on the tobacco industry for their livelihood, but most of the industry sales are captured by the largest cigarette producers. The largest, Philip Morris, holds about 37% of the market, followed by R. J. Reynolds (32%), Brown & Williamson (11.5%), Loew's (8.1%), and American Brands (7.2%).

THE PEOPLE

About 44,000 people find employment in the cigarettes, cigar, chewing tobacco, and smoking tobacco industry, down from 49,700 in 1982 and 54,900 in 1972.

TRENDS AND FORECAST

Faced with declining per-capita consumption and slow growth in industry sales, many larger producers have diversified into new fields. R. J. Reynolds, which now gets about three fifths of its revenues from nontobacco sources, spent $5 billion to acquire Nabisco in 1985, while Philip Morris paid $5.6 billion for General Foods. To grab a bigger share of a shrinking pie, tobacco companies have also experimented with pricing and marketing gimmicks to attract new customers.

Overall, the threat of liability suits and declining consumption continues to hang over the industry. Cigar makers will undoubtedly continue their decline, while growing health concern about snuff could derail growth in that industry. Faced with these prospects, it's likely that tobacco companies will continue to view their operations as a way of raising money to expand into other industries, as the leading firms have already done. The only bright spot has been exports, which hit nearly $4 billion in 1990, up from nearly $1.1 billion in 1980.

TOYS

THE MARKET

Toys are for kids and, of course, the adults who buy them. Currently, prospective buyers are parents, relatives, and grandparents of the 51.3 million children under 15 in the U.S. About 30% of all households have one child under the age of 12.

THE MONEY

Shipments of dolls, toys, and games were $4.2 billion in 1990, the same as in 1988. Part of the problem was that no particular toy was a hit. Kids spending their disposable income on video games also took a toll. In fact, electronic video games were the topselling toy, continuing a rebound that started in mid-1986. One in four of the 90 million households in the U.S. owns video-game systems. Retail sales alone for this market were $3.5 billion.

Big money in this industry comes in the form of a hit, such as Monopoly (over 100 million sold in the last 50 years) or the Cabbage Patch Kids, which earned Coleco $600 million in 1985 alone and helped the company earn a record $82.6 million in profits. In contrast, Coleco took a $118.6 million charge against earnings in 1984 because of poor sales from its Adam computer, and without a hit in 1986, the toy company lost money. But in recent years, the industry has faced problems. Factory shipments of U.S. toy makers were only $2.8 billion in 1987, down from $3.8 billion in 1984.

THE PLAYERS

Americans buy their toys at discount stores (35%), toy stores (16%), variety stores (8%), department stores (6%), Sears, Ward's, or Penney's (5%), and catalog showrooms (3%). About 32% of these stores are located in shopping centers; 16% are downtown stores and 26% are neighborhood stores. In 1984, the top three toy store chains were Toys "R" Us ($1.65 billion in sales), Child World ($450 million in sales), and Kay Bee ($325 million in sales), according to *Discount Store News*.

THE PEOPLE

Employment in the toy, doll, and game industry declined to 37,300 in 1990, down from 39,900 in 1984 and 71,700 in 1972. Wages also remain low, about $8 an hour, compared to $10.45 for all manufacturing workers.

POOL TABLES

When he moved from Switzerland to Cincinnati, John Brunswick was sorely disappointed by the quality of the town's bumpy billiard tables. A professional cabinetmaker, he set about making a professional pool table. In 1845, he showed his flawless table to pool hall owners, who immediately placed orders for ones just like it. Brunswick cranked them out for the next 20 years and then merged with two rivals to form the Brunswick Corporation. The company got into the bowling business in the 1880s when big pool halls began putting in bowling alleys. Brunswick started making bowling balls and pins.

MONOPOLY

If George Parker's parents had had it their way, Monopoly would still only be a market most companies dream about. Young George had a flair for making up board games. When only 16, he created a game called Banking and managed to make and sell 500 of them around Christmastime. His parents apparently found such a pursuit trivial and, for some reason, steered him toward journalism. A respiratory illness, however, forced him to give up his job reporting for a Boston newspaper. He fell back on his old passion for making games. With his brother Charles, he formed Parker Brothers (brother Edward joined two years later) and went on to make such games as Monopoly and Clue.

Lionel Trains For a while, Joshua Lionel Cowen was stuck. Around the turn of the century, he had invented a tiny electric motor and got it to rotate a fan. The electric fan had worked like a charm, but it didn't give a breeze. Then he recalled carving toy locomotives as a child. His tiny battery-powered motor, he thought, could power little trains.

He was right, of course, which he learned after designing a little railroad car and a 30-foot circle of brass track. Initially, he saw the train as a way to attract attention to other merchandise in store windows. But the first store he sold it to asked for six more the next day. A customer had bought the first. Taking a hint, Lionel took his invention to novelty shops, where it sold right away.

As more and more homes got electricity, more people bought the little trains. Business really picked up in 1903 when he issued a catalog of items, such as different kinds of cars and a little suspension bridge, which set a lot of boys and men salivating. Lionel patented a track design, the Lionel Standard, which became the standard for rival companies as well.

During the First World War, Lionel had to get out of the toy business temporarily in order to make equipment for the armed forces. When peace returned, Lionel smoothly went back to trains. The Depression hit the company hard, and luckily salvation came with the introduction of the Mickey Mouse handcar, the hottest-selling toy in 1934. A miniature Mickey and Minnie Mouse stood on a little car on either side of a handbar. Their rubber legs moved up and down as the handbar seesawed between them.

The Second World War saw the company once again making military equipment. Inadvertently, Lionel wound up one of the biggest chicken and egg producers in the nation. This came about because Lionel researchers determined that day-old egg whites bound paint to the bowls of compasses the company was making better than anything else. Eggs were in short supply, so the company set up its own chicken and egg operation.

Back in the train business after the war, Lionel grudgingly shifted the style of trains the company made to diesel from steam. His belief in authenticity overruled his preference for steam engines. The first Lionel diesel, the Santa Fe F-3, turned out to be the best-selling engine ever. And more than kids and hobbyists turned to the little trains. The trains were put to work carrying radioactive material in military and cancer research laboratories. They even hauled hamburgers from kitchen to customer in some luncheonettes.

In the late 1950s, the company ran into trouble because of a marketing decision. Big discount retail stores were opening, driving Lionel's longtime customers, the small hobby shops, out of business. Instead of capitalizing on the greater volume of business the discounters offered, Lionel remained loyal to the little guys. Competitors capitalized by going with the big discounters and Lionel lost market share. The company also failed to recognize competition from model planes and slot cars that were siphoning off sales. Also, when television began consuming so much consumer time, interest in hobbies fell off. From a peak of $32.9 million in 1953, sales plunged to $14.4 million in 1958. Cowen sold his holdings and retired.

Things went from bad to worse. The company tried to diversify into everything from fishing tackle to cameras and microwave equipment. Rising costs saw the company move manufacturing operations to Japan and quality deteriorated. The once-hefty catalog shrank to a puny eight pages. Finally, Lionel went belly-up.

In 1969, General Mills bought the remaining equipment and designs for trains from the Lionel Corporation and began paying Lionel royalties for the use of the name. In 1970, under General Mills, a new Lionel catalog was issued and advertising was pitched at young fathers who had grown up with the trains in the 1940s. The tactic worked. Every year, little girls as well as little boys are introduced to the joys of Lionel trains.

TRAVEL

THE MARKET

Americans like to get around. Each year, they make a mind-boggling 1.3 billion trips longer than 100 miles and spend over 5.2 billion nights away from home. That makes the travel industry (which includes 30 interrelated businesses from lodging establishments to airlines, restaurants to cruise lines, as well as car-rental firms, travel agents, and tour operators) the third-largest retail service industry in America. (Many of these subcategories of the travel business are discussed in separate sections. See the "Airlines," "Amusement Parks," "Auto Rental," "Hotels and Lodging," "Restaurants," and "Railroads" sections.)

THE MONEY

Americans spent about $374.3 billion on travel in 1990, up from $322.9 billion in 1988, or 5.7% of the GNP.

In 1985, when $257 billion was spent while traveling, Americans spent $50 billion on public transportation (which grew at an annual rate of 9.9% between 1980 and 1985), $40 billion on auto transportation (a 1.9% annual rate of growth), $46 billion on lodging (a 12.1% annual rate of growth), $76 billion on food (a 9.5% annual rate of growth), $26 billion on amusement and recreation (an 11.5% annual rate of growth), and $19 billion on incidentals (a 7.9% annual rate of growth). The tourism and travel industry also generated $25 billion in federal, state, and local taxes.

Americans spent $140 billion on vacations in 1986 and spent about another $125 billion on business travel.

Each year, about one fifth of all Americans take a business trip or visit a convention. That totals 185 million business trips in 1985, up 14% from 1984. Business spends 41% of its travel and entertainment budget on air travel, 22% on lodging, 17% on meals, 14% on entertainment, and 6% on auto rentals, according to the American Express Travel Management Services.

A weaker dollar also put more money into the coffers of the travel industry. The number of overseas visitors to the U.S. hit 38.5 million in 1989. In 1989 overseas visitors spent $43.3 billion. In contrast, Americans spent $43.1 billion abroad, producing a travel trade surplus of $1.2 billion, according to the U.S. Commerce Department.

THE PLAYERS

The travel service industry includes U.S. airlines, intercity bus companies, Amtrak, automobile services, commercial lodging places, campgrounds and trailer parks, eating and drinking places, amusement and recreation facilities, automobile rental, taxicab companies, travel agents, and general merchandise and miscellaneous retail stores that provide services for people away from home.

THE PEOPLE

Nearly 6 million people are directly employed in the industry, which pays some $55 billion in wages and salaries and is the top employer in 13 states. It is the first-, second-, or third-largest employer in 41 states. Directly or indirectly, the travel industry employs about 1 of every 15 working Americans.

Table T-6   Trends: Travel Services for U.S. Citizens Traveling in the U.S.

| | | | | | | Percent Change | | | | |
| | | | | | | Compound Annual | | Annual | | |
Item	1987	1988[1]	1989[1]	1990[2]	1991[2]	1982–91	1987–91	1988–89	1989–90	1990–91
Expenditures ($ billions)	299.9	322.9	350.0	377.3	403.7	9.0	7.7	8.4	7.8	7.0
Employment (millions)	5.49	5.65	5.83	5.90	5.95	4.6	2.0	3.2	1.2	0.8
Travel Price Index (1982–1984 = 100)	114.9	119.5	125.8	134.0	142.0	4.5	5.4	5.3	6.5	6.0

[1]Estimate.
[2]Forecast.
Source: National Travel Survey of U.S. Travelers in the U.S., U.S. Travel Data Center.

TRAVEL TRIVIA

- When planning vacations, Americans in 1986 chose to go to cities rather than the beach for the first time in history. About 31% planned to visit a city, 30% were going to the shore, 18% visited a small town or rural area, 8% headed for the mountains, 7% went to the lake, and 7% visited a state or national park.
- Forty-one foreign visitors arrive in the U.S. every minute. Foreign visitors spend $22,000 a minute and generate $291 worth of local taxes, $851 in state taxes, and $1,392 in federal taxes every minute. Fifty-five foreign tourists arriving in the U.S. create one job.
- Foreign tourists are keen on sampling American cuisine. Collectively they consume 4,400 pounds of hamburger every hour.
- About 11% of all jobs created in 1984 were in the travel and tourism industry.
- Twelve cents of every dollar spent on tourism goes to taxes.
- Back to nature is now a big business. There are 13,000 campgrounds in the U.S. The 8,000 private campgrounds in the U.S. took in about $2 billion in 1985 and retailers sold about $775 million worth of camping equipment, excluding clothing and footwear.
- If foreign tourism dropped 1%, 28,000 jobs and $95 million worth of taxes would be lost.
- California has over 512,000 people employed in the travel and tourism industry, more than any other state.
- State governments go all out to attract tourists. States spent $189 million on tourist promotion in the 1984–1985 fiscal year, with Illinois heading the list at $14.4 million. California spends $5.8 million a year to advertise its sights, up from nothing in 1984. Even Iowa, with the lowest advertising budget of any state, spends $1.4 million. Illinois says its campaign to attract tourists created 2,200 jobs and $30.8 billion in tax revenues.
- Travelers annually spend the most money in these states: California ($29 billion), Florida ($17.6 billion), New York ($15.6 billion), Texas ($14.9 billion), and New Jersey ($11.4 billion), according to the Travel Industry Association of America.
- About 228 million visitors annually travel to U.S. Forest Service recreational sites. The Forest Service offers 114,664 developed family camp and picnic sites, 320 swimming developments, 1,106 boating sites, and 307 winter-sports sites. All of these facilities could accommodate 1.67 million people. About 15.2 million hunters use Forest Service lands, as do 15.6 million fishermen.

TRUCKING

THE MARKET

In the transportation industry, trucks haul less freight than railroads but make far more money than any form of transportation.

Trucks haul 77% of the dollar value of all freight carried in America and 40% of the total freight tonnage, according to the American Trucking Associations. The industry's 5.3 million trucks log over 1.1 trillion ton miles, carrying 2.4 billion tons of freight.

Without the trucking industry, a lot of products would have a tough time reaching factories and retail outlets. About 85% of all furniture, fixtures, and appliances are carried to market by trucks. Nearly 80% of all the food, rubber products, and plastic goods are moved by trucks, as well as 70% of all lumber, wood products, steel, sheet metal, cable, wire pipes, rods, and other semifinished metal products. Moreover, about two thirds of all U.S. communities rely on trucks exclusively for freight transportation.

THE MONEY

The revenues in this growing market added up to an estimated $276.3 billion in 1990, up from $205.3 billion in 1985. Revenues were $254.4 billion in 1990.

Profit margins for the whole industry are not available, but truckers regulated by the Interstate Commerce Commission earned $1.4 billion in profits on $50.7 billion in revenues in 1986. Two UPS companies were the two largest trucking companies, with $7.4 billion in combined revenues. The third largest, Yellow Freight Systems, had $1.6 billion in revenues.

THE PLAYERS

There are some 160,000 trucking firms in the U.S., as well as many other firms operating trucks as part of their business. Deregulation made it easier for smaller firms to enter the industry but the increased competition has put a crimp on profits. Profit margins for trucking companies regulated by the ICC dropped from 2.92% in 1978, before deregulation, to only 0.77% in 1982. In 1986, profit margins only hit 2.78%. Meanwhile 3,467 trucking companies went bankrupt between 1980 and mid-1987.

THE PEOPLE

The trucking industry employs or contributes to the employment of some 7.4 million people as drivers, deliverymen, managers, warehouse workers, office support staff, truck dealers, highway construction personnel, and workers in truck manufacturing plants, according to the American Trucking Associations.

TRENDS AND FORECAST

In the 1970s, like the rest of the transportation industry, trucking was heavily regulated. Under the 1935 Motor Carrier Act, which was passed at the urging of the railroad companies, trucks were brought under the jurisdiction of the Interstate Commerce Commission. By the mid 1970s the ICC had the power to certify truckers and regulate the services they provided, their rates, and mergers and acquisitions.

The Motor Carrier Act of 1980 removed many of these regulations, allowing truckers increased freedom to set rates and making it easier to enter the trucking business. More than 19,000 new firms entered the industry in the first two years alone after the act became effective. Many new firms were low-cost, nonunion companies that helped lower freight rates, giving consumers a break but causing hard times for many firms with expensive Teamster contracts. As in most other segments of the transportation industry, deregulation led to mergers and a few larger companies getting a larger market share in some parts of the freight business. For example, the 10 largest companies in what is called the less-than-truckload segment of the industry now have 60% of the market, up from under 40% in 1978.

The effects of deregulation and increased competition are likely to continue for some time, with new bankruptcies and pressure on unionized firms likely to continue.

The Teamsters   The dubious distinction of being the most corrupt union falls to the Teamsters. Though one of the nation's most politically powerful unions with 1.7 million members, the union has been crippled by the fact that every one of its presidents between 1951 and 1981 was indicted and convicted for crimes committed while in office. Past president of the Teamsters, Jackie Presser was indicted for bilking the union out of more than $700,000 by putting organized crime figures on the union payroll for no-show jobs.

The union traces its origins back to the Team Drivers International Union, founded in 1898, and the Teamsters National Union, founded in 1902 when some Chicago members of the Team Drivers rebelled against union leadership. Samuel Gompers patched up their differences and the International Brotherhood of Teamsters was born in 1903. The first president, Cornelius Shea, was indicted and acquitted for extorting money from company owners, creating a climate of scandal that has dogged the union ever since.

The union's biggest advances occurred in the 1930s, when it engaged in a long and bloody organizing campaign. During that drive Jimmy Hoffa, a tough-talking charismatic son of a coal miner, rose in the ranks by organizing several successful strikes. Hoffa, a Trotskyite in the 1930s, combined an infectious enthusiasm for unions with a penchant for violence. Truck owners were not shy about using violence either. Hoffa's first contact with organized crime was with local mobsters who were hired by management to stop the union. After several meetings with Hoffa the mob agreed to remain neutral in future union-management disputes.

The union's real strength, however, was not violence but its ability to deliver higher wages and benefits. Industry working conditions and wages were abominable as late as the 1940s and the Teamster leadership held the respect of most members simply because of its ability to deliver the bacon, which largely remains true today.

But by the 1950s it was apparent that the union had strong connections with organized crime. Investigations of union corruption by the Kefauver Committee, the Kennedys, and later investigators uncovered a number of alarming problems. Union racketeers, for example, bilked the pension fund out of hundreds of millions of dollars, making it difficult for many former truckers to collect their pensions. The Teamster pension fund was so misused it became known as "the bank for the mob" because of its long-standing practice of loaning money to mob-backed enterprises. It has been said that Teamster money built Las Vegas as well as poured millions into nearly bankrupt businesses whose only qualification for a loan was making a kickback to trustees of the pension fund. The Teamster Pension Fund for the Central States was so badly run that the Labor Department imposed a trusteeship over it in the late 1970s.

Equally profitable was providing insurance for the teamsters. Allen Dorfman, a former schoolteacher with no experience in insurance, used his organized crime ties to set up an insurance company that earned $10 million a year in premiums by providing the Teamsters with insurance. Others set up businesses that charged exorbitant fees for managing health and welfare insurance funds. In one case, a mobster, Louis Ostrer, managed to eat up 75% of the $5.1 million in insurance premiums Teamsters union locals collected. One Teamsters local in New Jersey is currently under federal receivership to prevent a mob-dominated leadership from running the union's finances. Hoffa himself was sent to prison and was eventually assassinated by organized crime figures when he attempted to return to union leadership.

Still, corruption doesn't seem to hurt the union's political power. Because of Hoffa's feud with the Kennedys, the Teamsters became the only union to embrace the Republican Party. That won them favors from President Nixon and later President Reagan. President Reagan, who appointed Presser to his transition team in 1980 and the inauguration committee in 1984, came under strong attack from his own President's Commission on Organized Crime for associating with a union leader with reported organized crime ties.

The leadership's preoccupation with scams has, however, weakened the Teamsters' economic clout. The union has been losing members since deregulation. Tainted by charges of corruption, it has been unable to win new members. At the same time, deregulation forced many union trucking companies out of business because of competition from lowcost nonunion haulers. That has forced the union to temper its wage demands and makes the leadership more vulnerable to union dissidents who would like to clean house. Until that happens there is little chance the union will attract new members and unionize an increasingly nonunion industry.

UTILITIES: ELECTRICAL

THE MARKET

Although only 8% of U.S. homes had electricity in 1907 and less than half as late as 1924, 98.8% of U.S. homes had electricity by 1956. Today, utilities serve about 106 million customers, virtually the whole population. The average customer pays $1,532 a year for electricity, with the average residential customer paying $708 and the average commercial customer paying $4,239 in 1988.

The nation's 93.6 million residential customers consume 34.4% of the nation's electricity. The 11.6 million commercial customers eat up 26.3% and the 708,000 industrial customers consume 36%. Electrical utilities produce most of their electricity (57.4%) from coal. Nuclear power (17.7%), hydroelectric power (9.7%), natural gas (10.6%), and oil (4.6%) produce the rest of our electricity.

THE MONEY

Electrical utilities had revenues of $162.5 billion in 1988, most of which was generated by investor-owned electrical utilities. These companies had $125.5 billion in operating revenues in 1985, up 4.5% from 1984.

THE PLAYERS

Privately owned utilities produce about three quarters of our electricity. There are 2,009 privately owned electric power plants with a capacity to produce 514.9 million kilowatts, compared to 1,466 publicly owned plants that have the ability to produce 157.6 million kilowatts.

TRENDS AND FORECAST

The outlook for electrical utilities is bright. Several factors should boost earnings. First, the industry should have more cash now that construction expenditures are slowing down. The industry spent heavily in the late 1970s and early 1980s on new plants. Dramatic cost overruns for nuclear plants hurt earnings in many cases and forced at least one system to default on bonds issued to finance construction costs, but by 1990 most of those plants were completed or written off. Generally speaking, electrical utilities should have more cash and better earning prospects in the early 1990s than they did through much of the 1980s. At the same time the cost of fuels, such as coal, used to produce electricity is expected to continue to fall.

But some problems remain. Some utilities with new nuclear plants may not be allowed rate increases that will allow them to recover the costs of these plants. As the nuclear plants of the 1960s grow old and need to be replaced, utilities could face astronomical shutdown costs because of the cost of entombing nuclear wastes. And new regulations to control acid rain could force many utilities using coal-fired generating plants to make costly capital improvements.

Table U-1   Utilities at a Glance

This chart summarizes the state of the electrical utility industry, showing generating capacity, fuel used, sales, customers, revenues, balance sheets, and other basic data.

Item	Unit	1970	1975	1980	1982	1983	1984	1985	1986	1987	1988
Net generation											
Total	Bil. kWh	1,532	1,918	2,286	2,241	2,310	2,416	2,470	2,487	2,572	2,702
Average annual change[1]	Percent	7.3	4.6	3.6	–2.3	3.1	4.6	2.2	.7	3.4	5.0
Net generation, kWh per kW of net summer capability[2]	Rate	4,554	3,903	3,952	3,652	3,720	3,805	3,771	3,734	3,809	
Investor owned	Bil. kWh	1,183	1,487	1,783	1,712	1,764	1,849	1,918	1,928	2,022	
Percent of total utilities	Percent	77.2	77.5	78.0	76.4	76.4	76.5	77.7	77.5	78.6	(NA)
Publicly owned	Bil. kWh	349	431	503	530	546	567	552	559	550	
Municipal	Bil. kWh	71	82	87	77	73	75	74	79	86	
Federal	Bil. kWh	186	221	235	241	258	254	233	225	205	
Cooperatives and other	Bil. kWh	91	128	182	212	215	239	245	255	258	
Source of energy:											
Coal[3]	Percent	46.0	44.6	51.0	53.4	54.8	55.9	57.2	56.2	57.4	56.9
Nuclear	Percent	1.4	9.0	11.0	12.6	12.7	13.6	15.5	16.6	17.7	19.5
Oil	Percent	12.0	15.1	10.8	6.5	6.3	5.0	4.1	5.5	4.6	5.5
Gas	Percent	24.3	15.6	15.1	13.6	11.9	12.3	11.8	10.0	10.6	9.4
Hydro	Percent	16.2	15.6	12.1	13.8	14.4	13.3	11.4	11.7	9.7	8.3
Type of prime mover:[4]											
Hydro	Bil. kWh	248	300	276	309	332	321	281	291	250	
Steam conventional[5]	Bil. kWh	1,240	1,414	1,726	1,628	1,661	1,742	1,778	1,756	1,837	
Gas turbine	Bil. kWh	16	22	24	14	14	15	14	14	16	
Steam nuclear	Bil. kWh	22	173	251	283	294	328	384	414	455	
Internal combustion	Bil. kWh	6	6	4	2	2	2	2	2	2	
Net summer capability											
Total[6]	Mil. kW	336	491	579	614	621	635	655	665	675	
Average annual change[1]	Percent	7.2	7.9	3.4	2.6	1.2	2.3	3.2	1.5	1.6	
Hydro	Mil. kW	64	78	82	83	84	85	89	89	90	
Steam conventional[7]	Mil. kW	248	333	397	421	425	431	437	441	442	
Gas turbine	Mil. kW	13	37	43	44	43	44	44	43	43	
Steam nuclear	Mil. kW	7	37	52	60	63	70	79	85	94	
Internal combustion	Mil. kW	4	5	5	5	5	5	5	5	5	
Number of prime movers											
Prime movers, total[8]	Number	9,717		11,084					10,611	10,406	(NA)
Hydro	Number	3,108		3,275					3,489	3,488	
Steam conventional	Number	2,813	(NA)	2,862	(NA)	(NA)	(NA)	(NA)	2,536	2,437	
Gas turbine	Number	658		1,447					1,439	1,408	
Steam nuclear	Number	16		74					99	109	
Internal combustion	Number	3,118		3,410					2,998	2,917	
Consumption of fuels											
Net generation by fuel[9]	Bil. kWh	1,284	1,618	2,010	1,932	1,978	2,095	2,189	2,196	2,322	
Average annual change[1]	Percent	7.7	3.3	2.2	–5.0	2.4	5.9	4.5	.4	5.7	
Coal	Bil. kWh	704	853	1,162	1,192	1,259	1,342	1,402	1,386	1,464	
Percent of total	Percent	54.9	52.7	57.8	61.7	63.7	64.0	64.1	63.1	63.0	
Petroleum	Bil. kWh	184	289	246	147	144	120	100	137	118	
Gas	Bil. kWh	373	300	346	305	274	297	292	249	273	
Nuclear	Bil. kWh	22	173	251	283	294	328	384	414	455	
Fuel consumed:											
Total energy equivalent	Quad. Btu	13.40	15.19	18.57	17.49	17.75	18.53	18.79	18.59	19.39	
Coal	Mil. sh. tons	320	406	569	594	625	664	694	685	718	758
Oil	Mil. bbl.	339	506	421	251	247	206	174	232	199	248
Gas	Bil cu. ft	3,932	3,158	3,682	3,226	2,911	3,111	3,044	2,602	2,844	2,635

NA Not available.
[1]Change from immediate prior year except for 1970, change from 1960.
[2]Net summer capability is the steady hourly output that generating equipment is expected to supply to system load, exclusive of auxiliary power as demonstrated by test at the time of summer peak demand.
[3]Includes small percentage (.5%) from wood and waste, geothermal, and petroleum coke.
[4]A prime mover is the engine, turbine, water wheel, or similar machine which drives an electric generator.
[5]Fossil fuels only.
[6]Includes wind, solar thermal, and photovoltaic, not shown separately.
[7]Includes fossil steam, wood, and waste.
[8]Each prime mover type in combination plants counted separately. Includes geothermal, wind, and solar, not shown separately.
[9]Includes small amounts of wood, waste, wind, geothermal, solar thermal, and photovoltaic.
Source: 1970, U.S. Federal Power Commission, *Electric Power Statistics*, and press releases; thereafter, U.S. Energy Information Administration, 1975 and 1980, *Power Production, Fuel Consumption, and Installed Capacity Data—Annual,* and unpublished data; thereafter, *Electric Power Annual, Annual Energy Review,* and unpublished data.

557

Table U-2   Top 5 Nations in Nuclear Energy

Country	Number of plants	Capacity (megawatts)
U.S.	126	116,939
France	63	63,068
Soviet Union	73	61,938
Japan	51	40,484
West Germany	26	27,580

Source: *Nuclear World News*, August 1987.

VIDEO GAMES, JUKEBOXES, AND PINBALL MACHINES

THE MARKET

Imagine an industry where people put money in a slot and you collect it. That's the coin-operated amusement industry, a world of video games, arcades, pinball machines, jukeboxes, and pool tables.

THE MONEY

Coin-operated games take quarters, nickels, and dimes, but the coin-operated game and music industry isn't small change. Total revenues stood at $7 billion, and that was a $1.9 billion drop from 1982, the height of the video game fad, when Americans pumped $8.9 billion worth of change into games, according to a survey by *Play Meter*.

THE PLAYERS

The coin-operated game industry is made up of 4,500 operators who had an average of 129 videogames, 39 pinball machines, 10 coin-operated jukeboxes, and 13 crane and rotaries at a total of 413,000 locations. That may confirm your suspicions that video games are everywhere, but actually the number of coin-operated games and outlets has declined. In 1983, there were 11,000 operators who had 1,876,389 coin-operated games at 417,267 locations. While the number of operators and games has declined, however, the average revenues have increased from $546,000 to about $900,000 in 1989, according to *Play Meter*.

TRENDS AND FORECAST

The industry faced a few hard years in 1983, 1984, and 1985, when revenues dropped by more than half. In 1987, the industry had its first year since 1982 when the number of operators or revenues didn't decline. But even though the remaining operators are healthier than ever, the survivors are looking into expanding into other areas such as coin-operated food and beverage machines, pay phones, or cigarette machines as a way of hedging their bets. And although the worst is over, tough drinking laws are hurting revenues at taverns, and coin-operated games are still a favorite scapegoat of local governments, which have long viewed pinball machines and video games as a breeding ground for juvenile delinquents. That has translated into high taxes that threaten profit margins. Video games, it seems, have grown from a youthful fad into a mature industry with stagnant revenues.

WHOLESALE TRADE

THE MARKET

"I can get it for you wholesale" is no meaningless refrain. There are over 440,000 wholesaling firms acting as middlemen and -women between suppliers and a variety of government agencies, professionals, and retail outlets that buy their products. Few consumers ever see these wholesale merchants, but they perform a vital economic function by grading and sorting products into smaller lots, by extending credit to retailers, by providing marketing and promotional help, by establishing markets for manufactured products, and by distributing a wide variety of goods, from motor vehicles and auto parts to wheat, groceries, chemicals, paper, beer, and gasoline.

THE MONEY

Wholesale merchants racked up an estimated $1.05 trillion in sales in 1990, with durable goods contributing $533.4 billion in sales and nondurable goods hitting $522.3 billion. In 1989, the total was $999.8 billion, with $511.5 billion in nondurable goods and $488.6 in durable goods.

THE PLAYERS

Though the wholesale industry is composed mostly of small, highly competitive firms, a few larger firms garner most of the sales. In the *1982 Census of Wholesale Trade,* which contains the most recent available figures, only 1.6% of all wholesale establishments had annual sales of $25 million or more. But these large firms accounted for nearly half (46%) of all wholesale sales. On the other end of the scale, 88.7% of all wholesalers had less than $5 million in annual sales; collectively, these smaller firms racked up only 26.7% of all wholesale sales.

THE PEOPLE

Employment in this industry hit 4.6 million, up from 3.9 million in 1980 and 2.7 million in 1970.

PART VII

The Biggest Companies in the World and the United States

Table 1   100 Biggest Companies in the World

1989		Sales $ Millions	Profits $ Millions	Assets $ Millions	Stock-holders' Equity $ Millions	Employees Number
1	GENERAL MOTORS	U.S.	126,974.3	4,224.3	173,297.1	34,982.5	775,100
2	FORD MOTOR	U.S.	96,932.6	3,835.0	160,893.3	22,727.8	366,641
3	EXXON	U.S.	86,656.0	3,510.0	83,219.0	30,244.0	104,000
4	ROYAL DUTCH/SHELL GROUP	BRITAIN/NETHERLANDS	85,527.9	6,482.7	91,011.0	48,307.5	135,000
5	INT'L BUSINESS MACHINES	U.S.	63,438.0	3,758.0	77,734.0	38,509.0	383,220
6	TOYOTA MOTOR	JAPAN	60,443.6	2,631.1	49,672.8	25,761.0	91,790
7	GENERAL ELECTRIC	U.S.	55,264.0	3,939.0	128,344.0	20,890.0	292,000
8	MOBIL	U.S.	50,976.0	1,809.0	39,080.0	16,274.0	67,900
9	HITACHI	JAPAN	50,894.0	1,446.7	52,253.2	17,184.3	274,508
10	BRITISH PETROLEUM	BRITAIN	49,484.4	3,498.8	51,042.4	17,412.4	119,850
11	IRI	ITALY	49,077.2	1,177.7	N.A.	N.A.	416,200
12	MATSUSHITA ELECTRIC INDUSTRIAL	JAPAN	43,086.0	1,664.0	48,217.9	21,590.1	193,088
13	DAIMLER-BENZ	W. GERMANY	40,616.0	3,584.6	37,133.5	9,710.6	368,226
14	PHILIP MORRIS	U.S.	39,069.0	2,946.0	38,528.0	9,571.0	157,000
15	FIAT	ITALY	36,740.8	2,410.8	46,355.2	12,597.5	286,294
16	CHRYSLER	U.S.	36,156.0	359.0	51,038.0	7,233.0	121,947
17	NISSAN MOTOR	JAPAN	36,078.4	889.7	35,713.4	12,423.3	117,330
18	UNILEVER	BRITAIN/NETHERLANDS	35,284.4	1,729.7	20,804.4	4,441.5	300,00
19	E.I. DU PONT DE NEMOURS	U.S.	35,209.0	2,480.0	34,715.0	15,798.0	145,787
20	SAMSUNG	SOUTH KOREA	35,189.1	515.1	28,415.6	3,561.8	176,947
21	VOLKSWAGEN	W. GERMANY	34,746.4	523.2	33,661.7	6,810.2	250,616
22	SIEMENS	W. GERMANY	32,659.6	786.8	34,390.5	9,531.9	365,000
23	TEXACO	U.S.	32,416.0	2,413.0	25,636.0	9,180.0	37,067
24	TOSHIBA	JAPAN	29,469.3	930.8	31,676.8	6,630.7	125,000
25	CHEVRON	U.S.	29,443.0	251.0	33,884.0	13,980.0	54,826
26	NESTLÉ	SWITZERLAND	29,364.8	1,474.5	22,976.0	8,565.2	196,940
27	RENAULT	FRANCE	27,456.9	1,457.3	21,143.1	3,890.9	174,573
28	ENI	ITALY	27,119.3	1,125.9	41,479.1	10,363.1	82,748
29	PHILIPS' GLOEILAMPENFABRIEKEN	NETHERLANDS	26,992.5	648.1	28,807.4	8,848.8	304,800
30	HONDA MOTOR	JAPAN	26,484.3	758.5	17,206.1	6,789.6	71,200
31	BASF	W. GERMANY	25,317.0	1,071.3	20,791.1	8,190.1	136,900
32	NEC	JAPAN	24,594.8	502.6	25,204.6	5,192.1	104,022
33	HOECHST	W. GERMANY	24,403.0	1,025.6	19,737.8	6,678.9	169,295
34	AMOCO	U.S.	24,214.0	1,610.0	30,430.0	13,684.0	53,648
35	PEUGEOT	FRANCE	24,090.5	1,616.1	18,584.2	6,673.0	159,100
36	BAT INDUSTRIES	BRITAIN	23,528.9	2,123.2	18,655.5	7,560.7	311,917
37	ELF AQUITAINE	FRANCE	23,501.4	1,132.4	33,261.9	10,885.0	78,179
38	BAYER	W. GERMANY	23,021.2	1,107.5	21,388.6	9,154.2	170,200
39	CGE (CIE GÉNÉRALE D'ÉLECTRICITÉ)	FRANCE	22,575.0	774.5	31,018.2	4,723.6	210,300
40	IMPERIAL CHEMICAL INDUSTRIES	BRITAIN	21,889.4	1,733.0	18,197.0	8,095.1	133,800
41	PROCTER & GAMBLE	U.S.	21,689.0	1,206.0	16,351.0	6,215.0	79,300
42	MITSUBISHI ELECTRIC	JAPAN	21,213.3	415.0	20,380.6	4,812.8	85,723
43	ASEA BROWN BOVERI	SWITZERLAND	21,209.0	589.0	24,156.0	3,907.0	189,493
44	NIPPON STEEL	JAPAN	20,767.0	607.9	26,143.7	5,486.2	64,504
45	BOEING	U.S.	20,276.0	973.0	13,278.0	6,131.0	159,200
46	OCCIDENTAL PETROLEUM	U.S.	20,068.0	285.0	20,741.0	5,899.0	53,500
47	DAEWOO	SOUTH KOREA	19,981.4	114.5	28,986.2	4,645.3	91,056
48	UNITED TECHNOLOGIES	U.S.	19,765.5	702.1	14,598.2	4,740.3	201,400
49	FUJITSU	JAPAN	18,734.1	541.1	19,770.5	7,239.4	104,503
50	EASTMAN KODAK	U.S.	18,546.0	529.0	23,652.0	6,642.0	137,750

562

Table 1   100 Biggest Companies in the World (continued)

1989			Sales $ Millions	Profits $ Millions	Assets $ Millions	Stock-holders' Equity $ Millions	Employees Number
51	THYSSEN	W. GERMANY	18,298.9	408.0	11,154.3	2,430.5	133,824
52	USX	U.S.	17,755.0	965.0	17,500.0	5,737.0	53,610
53	DOW CHEMICAL	U.S.	17,730.0	2,487.0	22,166.0	7,957.0	62,111
54	XEROX	U.S.	17,635.0	704.0	30,088.0	5,035.0	111,400
55	TOTAL	FRANCE	16,926.8	346.1	15,313.0	3,736.6	41,200
56	MITSUBISHI MOTORS	JAPAN	16,839.9	147.4	11,276.0	1,740.8	37,908
57	SONY	JAPAN	16,680.2	563.8	17,811.1	6,867.6	78,900
58	PETROBRAS	BRAZIL	16,359.9	512.6	16,065.5	8,320.9	67,676
59	ROBERT BOSCH	W. GERMANY	16,263.0	332.8	13,142.9	3,946.7	174,742
60	ATLANTIC RICHFIELD	U.S.	15,905.0	1,953.0	22,261.0	6,562.0	26,600
61	USINOR	FRANCE	15,630.1	1,061.0	17,121.8	3,358.7	96,933
62	MAZDA MOTOR	JAPAN	15,572.5	99.1	9,906.2	2,599.2	28,382
63	PEPSICO	U.S.	15,419.6	901.4	15,126.7	3,891.1	266,000
64	INI	SPAIN	15,277.4	702.6	31,245.4	6,121.7	151,423
65	PEMEX (PETRÓLEOS MEXICANOS)	MEXICO	15,257.8	320.1	42,314.4	24,200.2	164,744
66	RJR NABISCO HOLDINGS	U.S.	15,224.0	(1,149.0)	36,412.0	1,237.0	48,000
67	MITSUBISHI HEAVY INDUSTRIES	JAPAN	15,007.1	482.3	23,527.1	5,815.4	55,500
68	MCDONNELL DOUGLAS	U.S.	14,995.0	219.0	13,397.0	3,287.0	127,926
69	BRITISH AEROSPACE	BRITAIN	14,895.2	382.0	14,814.7	3,842.5	125,600
70	VOLVO	SWEDEN	14,637.7	836.9	16,245.1	5,249.3	75,340
71	NIPPON OIL	JAPAN	14,562.7	216.3	13,388.2	3,626.6	9,669
72	TENNECO	U.S.	14,439.0	584.0	17,381.0	3,277.0	90,000
73	GRAND METROPOLITAN	BRITAIN	14,274.6	1,805.9	15,450.8	4,536.7	152,175
74	BMW (BAYERISCHE MOTOREN WERKE)	W. GERMANY	14,097.7	296.2	12,245.5	3,152.6	66,267
75	PECHINEY	FRANCE	13,986.8	523.5	13,416.5	2,486.7	70,000
76	PETRÓLEOS DE VENEZUELA	VENEZUELA	13,677.3	2,718.0	8,907.0	6,551.7	46,940
77	ELECTROLUX	SWEDEN	13,299.8	355.1	10,591.5	2,360.1	152,913
78	DIGITAL EQUIPMENT	U.S.	12,866.0	1,072.6	10,667.8	8,035.7	125,800
79	WESTINGHOUSE ELECTRIC	U.S.	12,844.0	922.0	20,314.0	4,384.0	121,963
80	ROCKWELL INTERNATIONAL	U.S.	12,633.1	734.9	8,938.8	3,977.6	108,715
81	CIBA-GEIGY	SWITZERLAND	12,597.9	951.8	16,926.0	10,536.7	92,553
82	PHILLIPS PETROLEUM	U.S.	12,492.0	219.0	11,256.0	2,132.0	21,800
83	RUHRKOHLE	W. GERMANY	12,422.1	30.0	13,686.7	757.9	124,838
84	BRIDGESTONE	JAPAN	12,379.1	68.2	11,408.3	3,056.4	93,193
85	FERRUZZI FINANZIARIA	ITALY	12,046.9	226.8	24,922.7	2,513.0	44,546
86	THOMSON	FRANCE	12,027.1	78.0	16,863.5	1,535.5	100,000
87	ALLIED-SIGNAL	U.S.	12,021.0	528.0	10,132.0	3,412.0	107,100
88	MINNESOTA MINING & MFG.	U.S.	11,990.0	1,244.0	9,776.0	5,378.0	87,600
89	HEWLETT-PACKARD	U.S.	11,899.0	829.0	10,075.0	5,446.0	95,000
90	MANNESMANN	W. GERMANY	11,872.5	246.2	9,600.4	2,721.7	125,785
91	HANSON	BRITAIN	11,833.0	1,861.7	17,477.0	1,753.3	89,000
92	KUWAIT PETROLEUM	KUWAIT	11,796.5	735.2	22,725.9	14,655.4	15,372
93	SARA LEE	U.S.	11,738.3	410.5	6,522.7	1,914.9	100,000
94	BTR	BRITAIN	11,544.0	1,082.1	9,759.7	2,578.4	109,501
95	RHÔNE-POULENC	FRANCE	11,463.1	642.0	14,406.3	3,684.1	86,100
96	INTERNATIONAL PAPER	U.S.	11,378.0	864.0	11,582.0	5,147.0	63,500
97	CONAGRA	U.S.	11,340.4	197.9	4,278.2	949.5	48,131
98	PETROFINA	BELGIUM	11,269.7	554.2	10,349.3	4,029.9	23,600
99	IDEMITSU KOSAN	JAPAN	11,249.3	13.1	9,844.5	327.4	5,292
100	ENIMONT	ITALY	11,191.5	522.1	14,192.6	4,194.9	52,656

Source: *Fortune* ©1990 Time Inc. Magazine Company. All rights reserved.

563

Table 2   100 Biggest Industrial Companies in the United States

Rank 1990	1989		Sales $ millions	% change from 1989	Profits $ millions	% change from 1989	Assets $ millions	Market value 3/8/91 $ millions	Earnings per share 1990/$
1	1	GENERAL MOTORS Detroit	126,017.0	(0.8)	(1,985.7)	(147.0)	180,236.5	23,898.3	(4.09)
2	3	EXXON Irving, Tex.	105,885.0	22.2	5,010.0	42.7	87,707.0	68,941.9	3.96
3	2	FORD MOTOR Dearborn, Mich.	98,274.7	1.4	860.1	(77.6)	173,662.7	16,013.3	1.86
4	4	INT'L BUSINESS MACHINES Armonk, N.Y.	69,018.0	8.8	6,020.0	60.2	87,568.0	74,995.1	10.51
5	6	MOBIL Fairfax, Va.	58,770.0	15.3	1,929.0	6.6	41,665.0	25,869.6	4.60
6	5	GENERAL ELECTRIC Fairfield, Conn.	58,414.0	5.7	4,303.0	9.2	153,884.0	58,140.8	4.85
7	7	PHILIP MORRIS New York	44,323.0	13.4	3,540.0	20.2	46,569.0	62,157.8	3.83
8	10	TEXACO White Plains, N.Y.	41,235.0	27.2	1,450.0	(39.9)	25,975.0	16,737.8	5.18
9	9	E.I. DU PONT DE NEMOURS Wilmington, Del.	39,839.0	13.2	2,310.0	(6.9)	38,128.0	25,454.2	3.40
10	11	CHEVRON San Francisco	39,262.0	33.3	2,157.0	759.4	35,089.0	26,397.7	6.10
11	8	CHRYSLER Highland Park, Mich.	30,868.0	(14.6)	68.0	(81.1)	46,374.0	3,253.2	0.30
12	12	AMOCO Chicago	28,277.0	16.8	1,913.0	18.8	32,209.0	26,770.3	3.77
13	15	BOEING Seattle	27,595.0	36.1	1,385.0	42.3	14,591.0	17,010.3	4.01
14	13	SHELL OIL Houston	24,423.0	12.5	1,036.0	(26.3)	28,496.0	N.A.	N.A.
15	14	PROCTER & GAMBLE Cincinnati	24,376.0	12.4	1,602.0	32.8	18,487.0	30,170.0	4.49
16	16	OCCIDENTAL PETROLEUM Los Angeles	21,947.0	9.4	(1,695.0)	(694.7)	19,743.0	5,816.1	(5.82)
17	17	UNITED TECHNOLOGIES Hartford	21,783.2	10.2	750.6	6.9	15,918.3	6,105.4	5.91
18	20	DOW CHEMICAL Midland, Mich.	20,005.0	12.8	1,384.0	(44.4)	23,953.0	14,309.5	5.10
19	19	USX Pittsburgh	19,462.0	9.6	818.0	(15.2)	17,268.0	7,826.2	3.14
20	18	EASTMAN KODAK Rochester, N.Y.	19,075.0	2.9	703.0	32.9	24,125.0	14,809.9	2.17
21	22	ATLANTIC RICHFIELD Los Angeles	18,819.0	18.3	2,011.0	3.0	23,864.0	20,599.1	12.15
22	21	XEROX Stamford, Conn.	18,382.0	4.2	243.0	(65.5)	31,495.0	5,384.0	1.66
23	23	PEPSICO Purchase, N.Y.	17,802.7	15.5	1,076.9	19.5	17,143.4	25,623.0	1.35
24	25	MCDONNELL DOUGLAS St. Louis	16,351.0	9.0	306.0	39.7	14,965.0	1,552.0	7.99
25	36	CONAGRA Omaha	15,517.7	36.8	231.7	17.1	4,804.2	5,801.5	1.87
26	26	TENNECO Houston	14,893.0	3.1	561.0	(3.9)	19,034.0	6,099.3	4.37
27	30	PHILLIPS PETROLEUM Bartlesville, Okla.	14,032.0	12.3	779.0	255.7	12,130.0	7,308.8	2.18
28	24	RJR NABISCO HOLDINGS New York	13,879.0	(8.8)	(429.0)	—	32,915.0	N.A.	N.A.
29	33	HEWLETT-PACKARD Palo Alto, Calif.	13,233.0	11.2	739.0	(10.9)	11,395.0	12,072.1	3.06
30	27	DIGITAL EQUIPMENT Maynard, Mass.	13,084.5	1.7	74.4	(93.1)	11,654.8	9,916.0	0.59
31	32	MINNESOTA MINING & MFG. St. Paul	13,021.0	8.6	1,308.0	5.1	11,079.0	20,059.8	5.91
32	35	INTERNATIONAL PAPER Purchase, N.Y.	12,960.0	13.9	569.0	(34.1)	13,669.0	6,828.9	5.21
33	28	WESTINGHOUSE ELECTRIC Pittsburgh	12,915.0	0.6	268.0	(70.9)	22,033.0	8,449.4	0.91
34	41	GEORGIA-PACIFIC Atlanta	12,665.0	24.5	365.0	(44.8)	12,060.0	3,815.0	4.28
35	29	ROCKWELL INTERNATIONAL El Segundo, Calif.	12,442.5	(1.5)	624.3	(15.0)	9,738.1	6,733.5	2.56
36	31	ALLIED-SIGNAL Morristown, N.J.	12,396.0	3.1	462.0	(12.5)	10,456.0	4,040.6	3.35
37	46	SUN Radnor, Pa.	11,909.0	20.0	229.0	133.7	9,000.0	3,636.9	2.14
38	34	SARA LEE Chicago	11,652.0	(0.7)	470.3	14.6	7,636.4	8,549.8	1.87
39	38	CATERPILLAR Peoria, Ill.	11,540.0	3.7	210.0	(57.7)	11,951.0	5,524.6	2.07
40	39	GOODYEAR TIRE & RUBBER Akron	11,453.1	3.7	(38.3)	(118.5)	8,963.6	1,410.8	(0.66)
41	47	JOHNSON & JOHNSON New Brunswick, N.J.	11,232.0	14.1	1,143.0	5.6	9,506.0	29,895.7	3.43
42	48	MOTOROLA Schaumburg, Ill.	10,885.0	13.1	499.0	0.2	8,742.0	8,478.2	3.80
43	37	ALUMINUM CO. OF AMERICA Pittsburgh	10,865.1	(2.7)	295.2	(68.8)	11,413.2	5,729.0	3.40
44	49	ANHEUSER-BUSCH St. Louis	10,750.6	13.4	842.4	9.8	9,634.3	13,374.0	2.96
45	40	UNOCAL Los Angeles	10,740.0	3.1	401.0	54.2	9,762.0	6,715.1	1.71
46	50	BRISTOL-MYERS SQUIBB New York	10,509.0	11.5	1,748.0	134.0	9,215.0	40,332.6	3.33
47	51	COCA-COLA Atlanta	10,406.3	13.5	1,381.9	(19.8)	9,278.2	34,915.5	2.04
48	44	GENERAL DYNAMICS St. Louis	10,182.0	1.3	(578.0)	(297.2)	6,573.0	984.5	(13.86)
49	43	UNISYS Blue Bell, Pa.	10,111.3	0.1	(436.7)	—	10,288.6	1,011.1	(3.45)
50	45	LOCKHEED Calabasas, Calif.	9,977.0	0.5	335.0	16,650.0	6,860.0	2,622.7	5.30

Table 2   100 Biggest Industrial Companies in the United States (continued)

Rank 1990	1989		Sales $ millions	Sales % change from 1989	Profits $ millions	Profits % change from 1989	Assets $ millions	Market value 3/8/91 $ millions	Earnings per share 1990/$
51	55	COASTAL Houston	9,593.1	11.5	225.6	32.6	9,229.6	3,353.6	2.15
52	52	RAYTHEON Lexington, Mass.	9,362.3	6.4	557.3	5.4	6,119.4	5,081.4	8.53
53	54	MONSANTO St. Louis	9,047.0	4.2	546.0	(19.6)	9,236.0	7,738.9	4.23
54	42	WEYERHAEUSER Tacoma	9,024.3	(10.7)	393.7	15.4	16,355.8	4,952.4	1.87
55	56	UNILEVER U.S. New York	8,680.0	7.0	N.A.	—	N.A.	N.A.	N.A.
56	58	ASHLAND OIL Russell, Ky.	8,554.4	6.7	182.1	111.2	5,117.9	1,910.5	3.27
57	64	AMERICAN BRANDS Old Greenwich, Conn.	8,270.3	13.8	596.0	(5.5)	13,835.2	9,266.5	2.99
58	62	TRW Cleveland	8,169.0	10.3	208.0	(20.9)	5,555.0	2,508.0	3.39
59	63	BAXTER INTERNATIONAL Deerfield, Ill.	8,148.0	10.1	40.0	(91.0)	8,517.0	9,245.4	(0.05)
60	57	ARCHER-DANIELS-MIDLAND Decatur, Ill.	7,925.3	(1.6)	483.5	13.9	5,450.0	6,825.9	1.63
61	61	TEXTRON Providence	7,917.6	6.4	283.0	9.2	14,891.5	2,596.3	3.18
62	66	DEERE Moline, Ill.	7,881.0	9.1	411.1	8.1	10,664.3	3,948.1	5.42
63	70	MERCK Rahway, N.J.	7,824.1	16.8	1,781.2	19.1	8,029.8	40,875.9	4.56
64	60	BORDEN New York	7,632.8	0.5	363.6	—	5,284.3	5,050.9	2.46
65	53	UNION CARBIDE Danbury, Conn.	7,621.0	(12.8)	308.0	(46.2)	8,733.0	2,535.6	2.10
66	67	EMERSON ELECTRIC St. Louis	7,573.4	7.1	613.2	4.3	6,376.4	9,545.6	2.75
67	69	RALSTON PURINA St. Louis	7,133.2	6.3	396.3	(6.2)	4,394.5	6,073.9	6.46
68	89	AMERADA HESS New York	7,081.1	26.7	482.7	1.3	9,056.6	4,030.7	5.96
69	65	HONEYWELL Minneapolis	6,985.2	(3.5)	381.9	(36.8)	4,746.2	4,317.6	5.03
70	68	AMERICAN HOME PRODUCTS New York	6,917.2	2.5	1,230.6	11.7	5,637.1	17,998.2	3.92
71	73	W.R. GRACE New York	6,774.7	7.0	202.8	(19.9)	6,226.5	2,646.1	2.36
72	74	WHIRLPOOL Benton Harbor, Mich.	6,647.0	5.2	72.0	(61.5)	5,614.0	1,910.3	1.04
73	80	PFIZER New York	6,599.7	11.8	801.2	17.6	9,052.0	17,750.6	4.77
74	71	TEXAS INSTRUMENTS Dallas	6,567.0	(0.4)	(39.0)	(113.4)	5,048.0	3,628.9	(0.92)
75	79	HANSON INDUSTRIES NA New York	6,558.3	10.5	456.4	(40.0)	12,027.3	N.A.	N.A.
76	93	LYONDELL PETROCHEMICAL Houston	6,508.0	21.1	356.0	(4.8)	1,372.0	1,870.0	4.45
77	85	GENERAL MILLS Minneapolis	6,486.7	11.9	381.4	(7.9)	3,289.5	8,961.0	4.64
78	86	KIMBERLY-CLARK Dallas	6,447.9	11.6	432.1	2.0	5,283.9	6,971.3	5.40
79	78	NCR Dayton	6,395.0	7.4	369.0	(10.4)	4,547.0	6,335.2	5.43
80	88	CAMPBELL SOUP Camden, N.J.	6,223.4	9.0	4.4	(66.4)	4,115.6	9,087.6	0.03
81	101	COOPER INDUSTRIES Houston	6,222.2	21.3	361.4	34.9	7,167.5	5,485.4	2.81
82	90	ABBOTT LABORATORIES Abbott Park, Ill.	6,210.3	13.9	965.8	12.3	5,563.2	20,317.4	2.22
83	84	MARTIN MARIETTA Bethesda, Md.	6,142.7	5.6	327.6	6.7	3,610.5	2,400.5	6.52
84	72	LTV Dallas	6,138.3	(3.5)	70.9	(73.2)	6,511.2	229.0	0.38
85	75	NORTH AMERICAN PHILIPS New York	6,119.0	(1.3)	(645.7)	—	3,377.3	N.A.	N.A.
86	83	PPG INDUSTRIES Pittsburgh	6,118.4	5.6	474.8	2.1	6,108.2	5,504.7	4.43
87	82	H.J. HEINZ Pittsburgh	6,112.4	4.8	504.5	14.6	4,487.5	9,666.2	1.90
88	76	REYNOLDS METALS Richmond	6,075.7	(2.0)	296.6	(44.3)	6,527.1	3,748.1	5.01
89	91	BAYER USA Pittsburgh	5,903.7	8.8	149.2	(3.1)	5,035.7	N.A.	N.A.
90	77	HOECHST CELANESE Bridgewater, N.J.	5,881.0	(2.2)	201.0	(24.7)	6,082.0	N.A.	N.A.
91	102	CPC INTERNATIONAL Englewood Cliffs, N.J.	5,800.4	13.1	373.9	14.2	4,490.3	6,204.1	4.83
92	94	STONE CONTAINER Chicago	5,770.4	7.6	95.4	(66.6)	6,690.0	885.0	1.59
93	87	QUAKER OATS Chicago	5,744.2	0.3	169.0	(16.7)	3,326.1	4,303.7	2.15
94	103	COLGATE-PALMOLIVE New York	5,740.2	12.3	321.0	14.6	4,157.9	4,995.3	4.56
95	96	APPLE COMPUTER Cupertino, Calif.	5,558.4	5.2	474.9	4.6	2,975.7	7,483.5	3.77
96	98	NORTHROP Los Angeles	5,502.6	5.8	210.4	—	3,094.2	1,230.3	4.48
97	81	JAMES RIVER CORP. OF VIRGINIA Richmond	5,422.7	(8.1)	78.2	(69.3)	5,741.4	2,195.8	2.45
98	104	SCOTT PAPER Philadelphia	5,390.9	6.4	148.0	(60.6)	6,900.5	3,295.3	2.01
99	92	BASF Parsippany, N.J.	5,381.2	(0.7)	N.A.	—	3,643.0	N.A.	N.A.
100	100	LITTON INDUSTRIES Beverly Hills	5,273.0	2.8	178.8	0.3	5,196.2	1,777.9	7.26

ACKNOWLEDGMENTS

Foremost, we wish to thank Fred Hills, our editor who from the outset understood why there should be this book and whose advice and editing were invaluable. We also wish to thank Alex Kamaroff of the Irene Goodman Literary Agency, who first believed in the *Business Almanac.*

Putting together a book of this magnitude requires the help of a great many people. We would like to thank James Winslow and Frank D'Angelo for their painstaking research and fact checking. We also owe a debt of gratitude to Steve Messina for his extremely thorough copy editing of the first edition, which paved the way for the team who worked on this revised edition, and Daphne Bien for her editorial work.

Others we should thank right away include Ivan Boesky, who showed that arbitrageurs can lead lives as exciting and shady as Mississippi riverboat gamblers; T. Boone Pickens, who managed to scare half of corporate America to death with his takeover raids on companies, and USX Corporation for coming up with one of the dumbest and least imaginative corporate names ever, replacing "Steel" with an "X," as it tried to weasel out of the fact that it bore a lot of responsibility for how lousy America's steel industry has become.

In addition, there were hundreds of people at companies, government agencies, trade associations, and elsewhere who assisted us by providing facts and figures. We are indebted to them all and we appreciate their generosity. We also wish to thank the Standard & Poor's analysts, financial experts, *Wall Street Journal* writers and editors, and others who were kind enough to read sections of the book to determine whether our work contained any glaring omissions or blunders.

In particular, we would like to thank the following people:

James L. Loper, Academy of Television Arts and Sciences
AFL-CIO
Andrew J. Sobel, Airport Operators Council International
David Cohen, American Bankers Association
Charles Antin, American Booksellers Association

American Business Women's Association
M. Jane Moss, American Car Rental Association
William E. Kingsley, American Council of Life Insurance
John Hatch, American Electronics Association
Douglas G. Pinkham, American Gas Association
Steven E. Trombetti, American Hotel and Motel Association
Samuel C. Hoyt, American Institute of Certified Public Accountants
James Hughes, American Iron and Steel Institute
Thomas R. Horton, American Management Association
Wayne A. Lemburg, American Marketing Association
Cyndee Miller, American Marketing Association
Jens Knutson, American Meat Institute
John A. Knebel, American Mining Congress
Joseph J. Lorfano, American Newspaper Publishers Association
Linda Rogers, American Petroleum Institute
Charlotte Scroggins, American Productivity Center
C. A. Siegfried, Jr., American Rental Association
Catherine D. Bower, American Society for Personnel Administration
Helen Frank Bensimon, American Society for Training and Development
Bob Schabazian, American Stock Exchange
James A. Morrissey, American Textile Manufacturers Institute
Linda Rothbart, American Trucking Associations
William W. Carpenter, Amusement and Music Operators Association
Associated General Contractors of America
Association of Bank Holding Companies
Marsha D. Lewin, Association of Management Consultants
J. Christopher Svare, Bank Administration Institute
Philip C. Katz, Beer Institute
Charles L. Smith III, *Black Enterprise* magazine
Barbara A. Schwartz, Chicago Board of Trade
Ann Richardson, Club Managers Association of America
J. Dudley Waldner, Comic Magazine Association of America Inc.
George N. Christie, Credit Research Foundation
Jim Williams, Credit Union National Association
Bill Daniels, Daniels & Associates
Colette M. Urban, Data Processing Management Association
Karen Wysocki, Direct Marketing Association
Mark V. Rosenker, Electronic Industries Association
Frank B. McArdle, Employee Benefit Research Institute
Lance A. Selfa, Farm and Industrial Equipment Institute
Fertilizer Institute
Robert Van Riper, Financial Accounting Foundation
Byron Klapper, Managing Director, Fitch Investor Services, Inc.
Barbara L. McBride, Food Marketing Institute
Annette Green, Fragrance Foundation
Vincent L. Turzo, Gulfstream Financial Associates Inc.
George W. Wells, Health Insurance Association of America

Matthew D. Ubben, Helicopter Association International
Raymond C. Ellis, Jr., The Hospitality, Lodging & Travel Research
    Foundation Inc.
Independent Bankers Association of America
Cathryn E. Kittell, The Institute of Chartered Financial Analysts
Carol Fraser, Insurance Information Institute
Hubert L. Harris, International Association for Financial Planning
International Association of Amusement Parks and Attractions
John Chapman, International Council of Shopping Centers
Scott F. Gray, International Exhibitors Association
William B. Cherkasky, International Franchise Association
Marvin Gropp, Magazine Publishers Association
Bruce Butterfield, Manufactured Housing Institute
Joyce Healy, Manufacturers Hanover Trust
Susan Boucher, Manufacturing Jewelers & Silversmiths of America
Jeffrey R. Waddle, Meeting Planners International
Warren Lasko, Mortgage Bankers Association of America
Teri Brouwer, Motorcycle Industry Council
National Association of Accountants
Walter W. Wurfel, National Association of Broadcasters
Enno Hobbing, National Association of Securities Dealers
Louise Gates, National Association of Temporary Services
National Association of Wholesaler-Distributors
Richard Lampl, National Business Aircraft Association
Lynn E. McReynolds, National Cable Television Association
Corey Rosen, National Center for Employee Ownership
Laura M. Oatney, National Futures Association
James A. Gray, National Machine Tool Builders' Association
Ann Walker Smalley, National Restaurant Association
Julie P. McCahill, National Soft Drink Association
James Dunaway, Newspaper Advertising Bureau, Inc.
Profit Sharing Council of America
P. Robert Farley, Publishers Information Bureau
Daniel S. Flamberg, Radio Advertising Bureau
Mary Walker Fleischmann, Real Estate Securities and Syndication
    Institute
Alan Gottesman, L. F. Rothschild & Co.
Linda Rohr Weber, Salomon Brothers
Evan Cooper, Securities Industry Association
H. Ted Olson, Specialty Advertising Association, International
Adele Archer, Standard & Poor's
Mark Bachmann, Standard & Poor's
Michael Crehan, Standard & Poor's
Daniel DiSenso, Standard & Poor's
Denise Gleason, Standard & Poor's
Heather Goodchild, Standard & Poor's
John Hardy, Standard & Poor's

Gerald Hirschberg, Standard & Poor's
Andrew Hornick, Standard & Poor's
Thomas Hyland, Standard & Poor's
Joseph Hynes, Standard & Poor's
Michael Kaplan, Standard & Poor's
Thomas Mockler, Standard & Poor's
Robert Nelson, Standard & Poor's
Norman Schindler, Standard & Poor's
Richard Siderman, Standard & Poor's
Scott Sprinzen, Standard & Poor's
Edward Tyburczy, Standard & Poor's
Angela Uttaro, Standard & Poor's
William Wetreich, Standard & Poor's
William Wong, Standard & Poor's
Marci Shapiro, Standard & Poor's
Mauri Edwards, The Sunglass Association of America
Robert M. Grebe, Television Bureau of Advertising
James B. Poteat, Television Information Office
Douglas Thomson, Toy Manufacturers of America
William W. Mee, Trade Show Bureau
Kathy Baumann, United States Telephone Association
Douglas Frechtling, U.S. Travel Data Center
William Carley, *The Wall Street Journal*
Sandy Jacobs, *The Wall Street Journal*
Dan Machalaba, *The Wall Street Journal*
Alfred L. Malabre, Jr., *The Wall Street Journal*
Tim Metz, *The Wall Street Journal*
Stanley Penn, *The Wall Street Journal*
Roger Ricklefs, *The Wall Street Journal*
Jeff Tannenbaum, *The Wall Street Journal*
Hank Gilman, *The Boston Globe*

INDEX